MW00815173

SHOCK CITIES

HAROLD L. PLATT

Shock Cities

The Environmental Transformation
and Reform of Manchester and Chicago

The University of Chicago Press
Chicago & London

HAROLD L. PLATT is professor of history at Loyola University
Chicago. He is the author of *City Building in the New South: The Growth of
Public Services in Houston, Texas, 1830–1920* and *The Electric City: Energy and
the Growth of the Chicago Area, 1880–1930.*

The University of Chicago Press, Chicago 60637
The University of Chicago Press, Ltd., London
© 2005 by The University of Chicago
All rights reserved. Published 2005
Printed in the United States of America

14 13 12 11 10 09 08 07 06 05   1 2 3 4 5

ISBN: 0-226-67076-7 (cloth)

This project was supported by a grant from the Graham Foundation
for Advanced Studies in the Fine Arts.

Library of Congress Cataloging-in-Publication Data

Platt, Harold L.
   Shock cities : the environmental transformation and reform of
Manchester and Chicago / Harold L. Platt.
      p.   cm.
   Includes bibliographical references and index.
   ISBN 0-226-67076-7 (cloth : alk. paper)
      1. Urban ecology—Illinois—Chicago—History.   2. Industries—
Environmental aspects—Illinois—Chicago—History.   3. Urban
ecology—England—Manchester—History.   4. Industries—
Environmental aspects—England—Manchester—History.   I. Title.

   HT243.U62C486   2005
   307.76′09773′11—dc22

                                        2004012103

♾ The paper used in this publication meets the minimum
requirements of the American National Standard for Information
Sciences—Permanence of Paper for Printed Library Materials,
ANSI Z39.48-1992.

For Abbey and Dylan

CONTENTS

List of Illustrations :: ix
Preface :: xiii

PART ONE   CREATING INDUSTRIAL ECOLOGIES

1   Introduction: The Industrial City and the Paradox of Progress :: 3

LAND

2   "They Are All Little Manchesters" :: 24

3   Mudhole in the Prairie :: 78

WATER

4   "A Fountain Inexhaustible": Chicago and Environmental
Profligacy :: 135

5   "The Hardest Worked River": Manchester and Environmental
Catastrophe :: 196

AIR

6   The Technological Construction of Industrial Ecologies :: 232

7   The Social Construction of Industrial Technology :: 273

PART TWO   REFORMING INDUSTRIAL CITIES

8   Introduction: Public Health and the Politics of Environmental
Reform :: 301

LAND

9   The Environmental Justice Movement in Manchester :: 313

10   The Environmental Justice Movement in Chicago :: 333

WATER

11   "Monstrous Waste": Water Supply in Chicago and Manchester :: 362

12   "Clever Microbes": Sanitation Science in Manchester and
Chicago :: 408

AIR

13   "Invisible Evil": Pollution and Class Politics in Manchester :: 442

14   Visible Smoke: Pollution and Gender Politics in Chicago :: 468

15   Conclusion: Machine Age Cites :: 493

Notes :: 499
Index :: 611

ILLUSTRATIONS

FIGURES

2.1 Topographical map of Lancashire :: 32

2.2 Profile map of Irwell River :: 33

2.3 Population of Manchester area, 1801–1881 :: 37

2.4 Mersey-Irwell and Ribble basins :: 42

2.5 Manchester-Liverpool canals, c. 1800 :: 43

2.6 Manchester area townships :: 50

2.7 Kay map of police districts, 1832 :: 66

3.1 Chicago harbor, 1849 :: 79

3.2 Topographical map of Chicago area, c. 1830 :: 81

3.3 Great Lakes basin :: 82

3.4 Chicago wards, 1847 :: 83

3.5 Chicago wards, 1863 :: 84

3.6 Thompson plat of Chicago, 1830 :: 88

3.7 Kinzie addition plat of Chicago, 1834 :: 89

3.8 Illustration of lake levels :: 91

3.9 Profile map of Chicago and Illinois River valleys :: 94

3.10 Population of Chicago, 1830–1860 :: 96

3.11 Natural timber of Chicago, 1830 :: 100

3.12 Chicago's original municipal water-supply system :: 112

4.1 Medical map of Chicago, 1863–1870 :: 143

4.2 Chicago mortality, 1843–1920 :: 144

4.3 Chicago harbor, 1870 :: 147

4.4 Calumet Plan :: 150

4.5 Bushnell medical map of Hyde Park and Stockyards districts, 1898 :: 165

4.6 Postfire working-class residential construction :: 170

4.7 Cumulative surplus in Chicago waterworks fund, 1855–1893 :: 179

4.8 Average daily per capita water consumption in Chicago, 1855–1920 :: 181

4.9 Daily water consumption in Chicago, 1855–1920 :: 181

4.10 Number of persons per tap in Chicago, 1855–1920 :: 182

4.11 Capacity of waterworks in Chicago, 1855–1920 :: 185

4.12 Fuel efficiency of waterworks in Chicago, 1855–1920 :: 186

6.1 U.S. annual per capita alcohol consumption, 1790–1920 :: 238

6.2 Manchester and Chicago barley malt consumption, 1855–1900 :: 243

6.3 Coal consumption in Chicago, 1850–1920 :: 246

6.4 Eastern coal region :: 249

6.5 Street improvements in Chicago, 1876–1900 :: 255

6.6 Street paving types in Chicago, 1876–1900 :: 256

6.7 New brewery locations in Chicago, 1890–1900 :: 269

8.1 Population of Manchester and Chicago, 1870–1930 :: 305

9.1 Manchester annexations :: 315

9.2 Charles Rowley :: 317

10.1 Unsanitary districts in Chicago, 1906 :: 337

10.2 Workshop districts in Chicago, 1906 :: 338

10.3 Spot map of typhoid fever deaths, August 1902 :: 345

10.4 Detail map of typhoid fever epidemic, 1902 :: 346

11.1 Comparative canal dimensions :: 375

11.2 Chicago waterworks, 1892 :: 379

11.3 Infant mortality in Chicago's wards, 1890 :: 382

11.4 Conversions of midden privies and pail closets to water closets in Manchester, 1891–1917 :: 401

12.1 SDC water withdrawals :: 423

12.2 Sewer outfalls in Lake Michigan :: 425

12.3 Sanitary district channels, 1917 :: 426

14.1 Per capita coal consumption in Chicago, 1880–1930 :: 474

14.2 Coal use by district in Chicago, 1912 :: 476

14.3 Coal steam plants in Chicago central business district :: 477

TABLES

2.1 Manchester incorporation referendum, 1838 :: 63

2.2 Kay sanitation report, 1832 :: 67

3.1 Bituminous coal trade in Chicago, 1856 :: 115

4.1 Mayors of Chicago, 1865–1887 :: 172

5.1 Manchester sanitary census, 1868 :: 218

6.1 Chicago North Side horse infrastructure, 1892 :: 254

6.2 Chicago brewery firm size, 1866–1886 :: 264

10.1 Sanitary Bureau nuisance abatement activity, 1902–1903 :: 354

11.1 Typhoid fever in Chicago, 1885–1914 :: 377

11.2 Chicago waterworks revenues, 1893–1913 :: 380

11.3 Manchester pail closet conversions, 1873–1888 :: 396

13.1 Comparison of mortality rates in Ancoats and suburban districts, 1891–1892 :: 461

13.2 Comparison of sunlight levels in Ancoats and Didsbury, 1891–1892 :: 461

PREFACE

Like my previous work, this book is about the city. More than in my previous work, people, rather than their technological systems and institutional structures, are at the center of the story. This shift in emphasis is the result of my recasting the history of the city within an environmental context. My first book, on Houston, is told from inside the council chambers and boardrooms where decision makers worked out plans for building a modern infrastructure. My second book, on Chicago, traces the development of electricity out into the streets, examining the impact of technology on how and where people lived. Marking a departure from those studies, this book plugs the networked city into its larger ecological setting of land, water, and air. At the same time, the environmental point of view focuses prime attention on the city's most precious natural resource, human beings. Their health and well-being and their efforts to improve the quality of daily life constitute the pivot point around which revolve all the stories I've chosen to tell in the pages that follow.

Although cities in general are very old, places like Manchester and Chicago were fundamentally new. They became shock cities, the horror and wonder of contemporary society on both sides of the Atlantic. They were different from the great centers of trade and the capitals of empires of the past. Instead, they became industrial cities: Cottonopolis and Porkopolis. Innovative technologies of production and energy as well as novel ways of organizing those technologies into what was called the factory system engendered a new form of built environment whose patterns of land use, shapes on the ground, and social geography made it an original creation of the nineteenth century.

From an environmental perspective, industrial cities were also unique in generating unprecedented amounts of pollution that endangered the lives of their inhabitants. Urban centers, of course, have always had environmental impacts, especially as marketplaces with voracious appetites for the natural resources of their hinterlands. Plato could look out his window and watch the erosion of the hillsides caused by deforestation. But the scale and scope of the changes in the land, water, and air caused by the factories' machines and their coal-fired steam engines were different. The amount of pollution was so great that it enveloped the industrial cities in their own microenvironments. A classic Darwinian case of this phenomenon was the genetic shift in the coloration of a species of moths to adapt to Manchester's smoke-filled atmosphere, which had turned the bark of the city's trees from light to dark.

I use the term *industrial ecologies* here in a commonsense way to describe these changes and their feedback effects on the health and well-being of the people living within them. Manchester in the 1840s and Chicago a half-century later became shock cities because their terrible pollution problems made them paradoxical portents of the technological future and throwbacks to social barbarism. Their residents produced a cornucopia of material wealth but at the cost of destroying the quality of life within which to enjoy it. Although located in very different environmental settings, both cities suffered from dreadful slums, frightening epidemics, and appalling infant mortality rates. The chapters that follow tell the story of how Manchester and Chicago responded to this paradox of progress.

In my more than ten years of work on this project, I have accumulated an enormous debt of gratitude to institutions, colleagues, friends, and family. The acknowledgments here are a pale reflection of the deep feelings of appreciation I have for all of their help. A failing memory also prompts me to apologize at the outset to everyone I've forgotten to mention by name, especially the legions of research assistants. Their invaluable help in combing through newspapers on microfilm was one of the ways that my home institution, Loyola University Chicago, provided support. Loyola also supported me by providing research sabbaticals, a fellowship at the Center for Ethics and Social Justice, travel aid, and a book subvention award. Equally important, the congenial atmosphere within the Department of History helped make the long years of research and writing a pleasant and rewarding period of my life.

A second institution, Manchester University, also deserves credit for making this book possible. My election as its Simon Senior Research Fellow in 1995–1996 gave me a year to collect primary sources and to follow Lewis Mumford's maxim of urban studies: walk the city. My attachment to the Centre for the History of Science, Technology, and Medicine and the Wellcome Unit for the History of Medicine brought me in contact with a bright and diverse group of scholars, including John Pickstone, Jon Harwood, Roger Cooter, Penelope Gouk, Jeff Hughes, and Lyn Schumaker. I am especially grateful to another Mancunian, Bill Luckin, who encouraged me to apply for the fellowship and who became a close friend during my stay in his city. His gentle but critical commentary has guided this project along virtually from start to finish. Along the way I spent many enjoyable evenings with him and Roger at their favorite pub, The Beach. Sharing a pint inside this munchkin-sized eighteenth-century inn somehow best captured the spirit of Manchester and English life.

Collectively libraries and librarians are crucial to the researcher. I want to single out the staff of the municipal reference section of the Harold Washington Library Center for special praise. They were always willing to go the extra mile to find the public records I needed, often searching through obscure reports within reports when the original source was no longer available. I was frequently amazed at the hidden places where they located the requested documents. Other librarians also offered help with a sense of professionalism and dedication, including those at the Cudahy Library of Loyola University, the Chicago Historical Society, the Newberry Library, the University of Manchester, the British Library, and the local history section of the Manchester Central Library.

Parts of chapter 1 were published as "'Shock City Revisited': Comparative Perspectives on the Environmental History of Manchester and Chicago," *OASIS*, no. 43 (February 2000): 1–19. A version of chapter 5 appears as "'The Hardest Worked River': The Manchester Floods and the Industrialization of Nature, 1850–1880," in *Cities and Catastrophes: Coping with Emergency in European History*, edited by Geneviève Massard-Guilbaud, Harold L. Platt, and Dieter Schott (Frankfurt: Peter Lang, 2002). Parts of chapter 10 were published as "Jane Addams and the Ward Boss Revisited: Class, Politics, and Public Health in Chicago, 1890–1930," *Environmental History* 5 (April 2000): 194–222. Parts of chapters 11 and 12 were published as "Chicago, the Great Lakes, and the Origins of Federal Urban Environmental Policy," *Journal of the Gilded Age and Progressive Era* 1, no. 2 (April 2002): 122–53. A version of chapter 12 appears as "'Clever Microbes': Bacteriology and Sanitary Technology in Manchester and Chicago during the Progressive Age," *Osiris* 19 (2004): 149–66 (copyright 2004 by the History of Science Society). A version of chapter 13 appears as "The Invisible Evil: Noxious Vapour and Public Health in Manchester during the Age of Industry," in *Smoke and Mirrors: The Politics and Culture of Air Pollution*, edited by E. Melanie DuPuis (New York: New York University Press, 2004). A version of chapter 14 appears as "'Invisible Gases': Smoke, Gender, and the Redefinition of Environmental Policy in Chicago, 1900–1920," *Planning Perspectives* 10 (January 1995): 67–97; www.tandf.co.uk/journals/titles/02665433.html.

Joining the European community of scholars was one of the most worthwhile aspects of the project. A previous contact with one colleague, Dieter Schott, blossomed into full friendship. He has been an inspiration of hard work and critical thinking. I was fortunate enough to be introduced by him to Genevieve Massard-Guilbaud, another tireless worker for the highest standards of scholarship. I am very grateful as well for the support of Paul Laxton, David Dunster, Martin Simes, Michael Worboys, Anthony Sutcliffe, Richard Rogers, Derek Keene, Marjatta Hietala, Urszula Sowina, and Bernt Ostendorf.

Closer to home, I am indebted to many friends and colleagues for their generous support. I want to thank Delores Greenberg, Jo Hays, Joel Tarr, Martin Melosi, Christopher Hamlin, Angela Gugliotta, Sarah Elkind, Sally Metzler, John Cumbler, Christoper Sellers, Wendy Plotkin, Michael Ebner, Ann Keating, John Jentz, Christine Rosen, Paul Barrett, Melanie DuPuis, Georg Leidenberger, Clay McShane, Tom Misa, and David Stradling. Louis Erenberg and Susan Hirsch provide a home away from home, a place where I can always count on some tea and sympathy. Maureen Flanagan provides a continuous stream of enlightenment on urban politics as well as on the politics of the profession. Suellen Hoy and Walter Nugent provide encouragement and good cheer in settings of fine food and good wine. I appreciate the help and support of Douglas Mitchell, Timothy McGovern, Christine Schwab, and Meg Cox from the University of Chicago Press.

This book is dedicated to my children, Abbey Platt Baugh and Dylan Plattwood. They have helped keep scholarship within the bounds of the larger flow of life. They have helped me balance the life of the mind with the deeper and more important affairs of the heart. I owe them more than words can express for their love and support.

PART ONE

Creating Industrial Ecologies

CHAPTER ONE

Introduction

The Industrial City and the Paradox
of Progress

Of all the foreign visitors to the United States, none has been more extensively or frequently quoted than Alexis de Tocqueville. In 1831–1832, the twenty-six-year-old French aristocrat toured the country for nine months, collecting materials for what would become a two-volume classic, *Democracy in America*. He seems to have captured something elemental about the "first new nation" at an extraordinary moment of promise in its brief history. Like the young republic itself, the generation following that of the founding fathers was part of a coming of age, a blossoming of a distinctly American character. To be sure, self-conscious elites were actively engaged in contriving a cultural identity. Yet Ralph Waldo Emerson's philosophical essays, Thomas Cole's landscape paintings, and Noah Webster's original dictionary were emblematic of a deeper social need to give definition to the national experience.

The timing of Tocqueville's visit combined fruitfully with his own probing search for the meaning of liberal society to produce an account filled with insight on virtually every aspect of American life and politics. Whether on race relations, domestic manners, or partisan strategies, his observations illuminated essential qualities of the national spirit. Scholars and critics have drawn upon his commentary ever since as prophecy to help explain the subsequent unfolding of history.[1]

Little appreciated, however, is the fact that the traveler also toured England during a critical period between writing the first and second volumes of his work about Jacksonian America. After nurturing volume 1 to publication in 1835, he decided to take a well-deserved holiday across the Channel to where the Parliamentary Reform Act of 1832 had wrought a liberal revolution without resort to violent upheaval. The Frenchman's second trip to London was a tremendous success because high society now welcomed him as an international celebrity. After a triumphal reception, he ventured beyond the capital city for the first time, heading northwest toward the port of Liverpool, from which he would depart for Ireland on the next leg of his trip. Along the way he stopped at Birmingham, where the independent shopkeepers and artisans reminded him of what he had perceived in the United States, a country driven by individual enterprise, self-reliance, and moral uplift. As he insinuated, "They are generally very intelligent people but intelligent in the American way."[2]

But Manchester painted a very different, disturbing picture of an industrial city that appeared to throw progress into reverse. According to the Tocqueville scholar Seymour Drescher, his diary entries for the three days in July that he spent in the cotton textile center represent "the most powerful description of his journey." Rather than ushering in a more egalitarian era, Manchester seemed to demonstrate that the engines of modernity could bring about a return to an age of feudalism. In the industrial version of feudalism, factory owners replaced landlords as the aristocracy of wealth and power.

His walking tours in "this new Hades" conjured up nightmare images of social division and bloody conflict between the privileged few and the disfranchised many. Such a prospect clearly frightened Tocqueville, who remained faithfully rooted to the conservative core of his elite heritage. "Cottonopolis" stimulated thoughts of an explosive dystopia because it was a community being torn apart by stark contrasts, "a combination of the advantages of a rich country and of a poor country; of an ignorant and an enlightened people; of civilization and barbarism. So it is not surprising," he concluded with a revealing touch of sarcastic alarm, "that Manchester already has 300,000 inhabitants and is growing at a prodigious rate."[3]

While Tocqueville's visit to Manchester was certainly not the only new influence affecting the making of volume 2 over the next five years, his impressions of this industrial city contributed significantly to a complete shift in style, tone, and mood from volume 1. "One might argue that there are two books here, not one," the scholar Max Lerner opines. "In one of them the atmosphere is open and the predestined circle makes a wide sweep, while in the other there is a constricted atmosphere and a cramped circle rather than one of vast limits. A critic might even complain that the two books, while they coexist, do not fuse." What was it about his visit to Manchester that cast such a dark cloud of doubt and foreboding over his earlier enthusiasm about the future course of American democracy?

The portrait he painted in his diary of a city of extremes suggests that he was witnessing an unprecedented transformation of urban space and society into separate spheres segregated by class and ethnicity/religion. On the one hand, any analysis based on polar opposites is prone to distortion and hyperbole. A good example of this kind of exaggeration is Tocqueville's judgment that "Here humanity attains its most complete development and its most brutish; here civilisation works its miracles, and civilised man is turned back almost into a savage." While these superlatives are overstated, they accurately reflect his impression of a society in the midst of splitting apart into mutually antagonistic camps.[4]

On the other hand, the particular dichotomies that concerned him help identify important dimensions or vectors of this process of reconstructing the city into landscapes of inequality and exclusion. Consider that Manchester represented a new urban form that seemed to obliterate all connection between the built environment and the natural world. The traveler had entered an alien world, and this provoked uncomfortable feelings of vertigo and disorientation. As he wandered through a bewildering maze of city streets, all of his senses came under attack from a barrage of strange sights, smells, and sounds:

> A thousand noises disturb this damp, dark labyrinth, but they are not at all the ordinary sounds one hears in great cities. The footsteps of a busy crowd, the crunching wheels of machinery, the shriek of steam from boilers, the regular beat of the looms, the heavy rumble of carts, those are the noises from which you can never escape in the sombre half-light of these streets. You will never hear the clatter of the hoofs as the rich man drives back home. . . . Never the gay shouts of people amusing themselves, or music heralding a holiday. . . . Crowds are ever hurrying this way and that in the Manchester streets, but their footsteps are brisk, their looks preoccupied, and their appearance sombre and harsh. Day and night the city echoes with street noises.

The land, too, seemed stripped of every familiar vestige of nature. "The soil has been taken away," he lamented, "scratched and torn up in a thousand places, but it is not yet covered with the habitations of men. The land is given over to industry's use." The cotton mills had turned the rivers from attractive amenities offering solace and renewal into repulsive sewers "stained with a thousand colours by the factories." Even the air contributed to an aura of unreality because a "sort of black smoke covers the city. The sun seen through it is a disc without rays."[5]

In sharp contrast, Tocqueville stood on more solid ground when he placed Manchester in its larger environmental context. He spoke with confident authority, for example, about the economic benefits accruing from its advantageous geographic setting. The city is located at the base of a crescent-shaped range of coal-laden hills called the Pennines, which funnel rain-fed streams down the valley and through it before they join the Mersey River on its final short passage past the great port of Liverpool. An abundant supply of soft rainwater and a humid climate combine to make the area a perfect site for spinning, weaving, and dying cotton fibers. Manchester's success as a textile manufacturing center had been assured, Tocqueville reported, by the construction of a commercial infrastructure that included three strategic canals and one of the earliest railroads.

But what struck him most about this urban metamorphosis was the way in which the factory system was driving a sharp wedge of social and physical segregation between the classes. "On this watery land, which nature and art have contributed to keep damp," Tocqueville commented, "are scattered palaces and hovels." Manchester was sorting itself out into novel patterns of land use marked by a growing division between work and home, commerce and manufacturing, slum and suburb. He felt overwhelmed by the sheer size of the cotton mills lining the waterways that snake through the city.

Each of these massive six-to-eight-story buildings employed hundreds and hundred of workers. Forced by low wages to walk to work, they lived in the shadow of the mills along the riverbanks in filthy, ramshackle neighborhoods. "Look up," Tocqueville exclaimed in horror, "and all around this place you will see the huge palaces of industry. You will hear the noise of furnaces, the whistle of steam. These vast structures keep air and light out of the human habitations which they dominate; they envelop them in perpetual fog; here is the slave, there the master; there the wealth of some, here the poverty of most; . . . here the effects, there the causes." A similar passage outlining the deepening chasm between workers and manufacturers shows up in volume 2 of *Democracy in America*, where Tocqueville asks rhetorically, "What is this, if not an aristocracy?" His answer was strongly colored by the sharp, gendered perspectives and class dimensions of factory life in Cottonopolis.[6]

The giant textile mills were ruled by men and served mostly by women and children. This represented yet another paradoxical source of disorientation for the tourist from France. Tocqueville could envision these industrial empires as both throwbacks to an age of feudalism and forerunners of a new hierarchy of social control. One spinning mill he visited employed 1,500 people who toiled twelve hours a day, six days a week. Three quarters of its workers were women and children, creating conditions of authority and dependency in modern industry that harkened back to that earlier agrarian regime of lord and peasant, master and servant.

While the concentration of production appeared regressive, it could also be viewed as the inevitable and ultimately progressive application of the laws of the market. Tocqueville acknowledged that the highly mechanized textile factory represented the epitome of the modern principles of division of labor and economies of scale. Moreover, with technological ingenuity designers had created machines that took advantage of discriminatory practices that forced women and children to accept lower rates of pay than their male counterparts. Tocqueville remained troubled in spite of the economic logic of the cotton mill. Its tendency to divide society into two mutually exclusive and antagonistic camps haunted him. In effect, the manufacturers were climbing the ladder of success on the backs of their workers, pushing them down to suffer marginal existences and endangered lives.[7]

Together the physical and social transformations under way in Manchester forced Tocqueville to confront the fundamental dilemmas of the industrial city during the age of progress. As perhaps only he could put it, "From this foul drain, the greatest stream of human industry flows out to fertilise the whole world. From this filthy sewer, pure gold flows." For the Frenchman the tension was too great between the cornucopia of material goods produced by the city and the city's toxic zones of human misery, sickness, and death. He declared the factory system and the class conflict that it engendered to be just a passing "monstrosity."

Although he criticized the "business aristocracy" for creating one of the harshest regimes in history, he resolved the paradox of progress with weak assurances that it did not pose an immediate danger. By pushing the problem into the distant future, he found a safe way to relieve his anxiety that this rootless class of urban capitalists would mount the single greatest challenge to the spirit of democracy. Ultimately, the traveler concluded, Manchester was the result not of the laws of economic and technological progress, but of an unbridled form of individualism. "Everything in the exterior appearance of the city attests the individual powers of man," he explained, "nothing the directing power of society. At every turn human liberty shows its capricious creative force."[8]

The Industrial City in Perspective

Unfortunately, Tocqueville was wrong. Manchester as a template of the modern city proved more the rule than the exception as the forces of industrial capitalism swept across the world during the remainder of the nineteenth and the early twentieth centuries. He blamed the "evident lack of government" for the "disorder, dirtiness, improvidence" that made the city so perplexing, a "noisome labyrinth" of extremes. What was missing, he believed, was the strong and tireless hand of the State to constrain the excesses of this civic anarchy. But in the end he dismissed the possibility of a new type of class struggle between factory owners and workers as a temporary delay in the irreversible march of civilization toward liberty and equality.[9]

Tocqueville's commentary reveals how the built and the natural environments are shaped by human agency rather than some inner logic of the machine. One of the most effective research strategies for exposing the ways in which social and cultural forces play a configurative role in the formation of environmental policy is the adoption of a comparative approach, especially a cross-national one. Such an approach is especially useful for putting in sharp relief differences in national political cultures and institutional arrangements, including the jurisdictions of various governmental units over neighborhood, metropolis, and region. Cross-national comparisons are also critical in giving the urban environment a voice of its own. Since the location of each place is unique, the contrasts between the locations root the study of the city in a framework of its ecological setting.

If the Frenchman had come to Chicago during his travels in the United States, he would have arrived in a small frontier village on the banks of the Great Lakes. In less than forty years, however, he could have returned to find a thriving industrial city that resembled Manchester to a remarkable extent. Like it, Chicago became a place of contrasts between distinct functional and residential districts. The social geography of the city was also marked by well-defined boundaries of class and ethnicity/religion. Both cities, moreover, developed industrial ecologies, their natural environments transformed into an alien world of surreal landscapes, toxic waterways, and polluted skies.

Although the built environments of the two cities grew along parallel paths of development, Tocqueville would not have had any trouble distinguishing between them. Their natural settings set them apart from one another. One was located in a river valley while the other bordered a gigantic lake. The differences this produced were vividly reinforced by shapes on the ground. Manchester was essentially a pile of bricks, built in a land where trees had become a scarce resource. Having become the world's largest lumber market, Chicago was a horizontal city of wood outside of its central business district. Only in the central business district might the traveler have had some difficulty telling where he was because of the trans-Atlantic conformity to historical styles of commercial architecture. But just beyond he would immediately notice that whereas English workers lived in back-to-back row houses, these Americans resided in detached cottages and two- or three-story apartment buildings. If he kept going toward the periphery, he would also see that whereas Manchester began to overlap other aged communities, Chicago eventually petered out somewhere on the prairie.

Despite these superficial differences, there were deeper and more historically significant similarities among industrial cities. But to simply say the reason for these similarities is capitalism does not shed much light on the subject. Certainly, an educated observer like Tocqueville was acutely aware that he was witnessing the emergence of a novel form of urban topography. Manchester had long roots stretching back to the Roman Empire, but a new city was rapidly growing over the old by the time of the Frenchman's visit. It was more like Chicago than it was like other ancient cities such as London, Paris, and Rome. Each of them had an extensive core of historic and monumental buildings, including luxury dwellings. In these capital cities, heavy manufacturing would be grafted onto the fringes of this built-up district. In contrast, in the second cities of the Age of Steam the new forces of production would play the more influential role in shaping land use and settlement patterns.

The ways in which society made use of technology go a long way in accounting for the close resemblance among industrial cities. But technology drives history only to a limited extent. Beliefs and values are equally important because they determine how technology is used and for what ends. Attention must be focused on the interactions of culture and technology to highlight the similarities in both the physical and social contours of places like Manchester and Chicago.[10]

In the nineteenth century, the streetcar and the railroad expanded the boundaries of the city, and the integrated "walking city" underwent a metamorphosis into a disjointed patchwork of separate spheres: central business district, industrial slum zones, respectable residential neighborhoods, and detached suburban enclaves. The new scale of manufacturing, the advent of railroads, and the related increases in pollution had major impacts on this process of sorting out where businesses and residences were located within enlarging perimeters of settlement. Cities like Manchester and Chicago sustained a healthy commercial sector, but the factories provided the jobs that nurtured their growth to extraordinary size. As they became bigger, more intensive uses and rising values of land overran the suburban fringe; a new fringe would develop, but its upscale district of elegant mansions might later become a seedy area of ramshackle boardinghouses. The transformation happened time and time again.[11]

The emergence of a new type of physical topography went hand in hand with an equally historic metamorphosis of social structure. The process of class formation among the factory workers took place simultaneously with the creation of an urban middle class. Each group defined itself as the polar opposite of the other. In the industrial city class struggle extended from categories of economic standing and ethnicity/religion to identities of place. In Manchester, for example, certain pubs became the preserve of the spinners, while others catered exclusively to the merchants. Social status became embodied in locational identities that went beyond individual buildings to embrace whole streets and neighborhoods. Although the boundary lines between the various districts of the city were rarely marked on a map, residents knew where they were as clearly as if they were national borders.

Environmental factors strongly reinforced these social patterns of spatial segregation by class and ethnicity/religion. The new levels of pollution generated by the factories were sufficient reason to get as far away from the factories as practicable within the commuting limits of transportation technology. Recurring public health crises caused by frightening epidemics added another very good reason to move away from the crowded slums of the industrial *quartiers*. Medical authorities confirmed that disease sprang from dirt and disorder, and members of the upper classes, fascinated with quantification, conducted studies that further linked mortality rates to substandard conditions. In short, the industrial city represented a new type of landscape that was degraded not only by unhealthy surroundings but also by the dangerous masses of people living within it.

Searching for respectability, members of the middle classes adopted a moral environmentalism to explain the city's bifurcated social geography of inequality and exclusion. Moral behavior was the causal factor; physical conditions were the effect. In other words, immorality bred the stunted existence of the slums while decency resulted in the good life of the suburbs. The urban elites proclaimed that the poor had only themselves to blame for their misery, suffering, and early deaths, and many believed that the hardship they suffered was divine retribution for a life of sin. At the same time, the elites justified their own social and spatial distance from the slums in self-righteous terms.

Urban reform meant changing the moral environment by converting individuals to virtuous behavior. According to this approach, upgrading the physical conditions of city life was a futile waste of money and good intentions. Any such effort would soon be undone by the lower orders of the unrepentant and intemperate masses. Thus, during the Victorian Era, a broad consensus of belief in moral environmentalism among the respectable classes in the United Kingdom and the United States helped to produce a convergence of conditions in the industrial city.[12]

The two countries also shared a cultural view of nature that sheds light on the reasons that places like Manchester and Chicago developed along parallel lines in spite of diverse environmental settings. Christian theology had long asserted divine sanction to human domination of the earth. More recently the Enlightenment had added to the alienation of Western society from the natural world. Scientific rationalism depended on the segmentation of things, obscuring the holism and interdependency inherent in the organic. In related ways, market economics was based on the quantification of things into common units of monetary value. Science and capitalism represented two very powerful forces of modernization that reduced nature to a mere set of commodities. A forest of trees was seen as so many board-feet of lumber; a herd of buffalo was envisioned as a certain number of tongues, tails, and hides.[13]

Adherence to this viewpoint was especially strong in the new-style industrial cities, which gobbled up natural resources at a voracious rate. More was considered better. This ethos of production meant that the rewards of wealth, power, and status went to the makers of useful things, and the costs of the harmful by-products of production were paid by society at large—but not in equal measures. The burdens of pollution from the factories, for example, fell disproportionately on residents in the inner city as opposed to those living in the garden suburbs. The democratic promise of a rising standard of living as measured by a rise in per capita wealth became the shibboleth of the industrialists and their defenders. In the meantime, the degradation of the natural environment and of the quality of urban life was written off as the price of progress toward this goal.

The Paradox of Progress

Tocqueville had an uncanny ability to anticipate the central questions that would arise during the age of industry. In Manchester he witnessed the early stages of a historic process that was beginning to create a society of affluence and leisure but seemed to be destroying the very thing it was ultimately seeking to enhance, the quality of daily life. "One point appears to be prominent," a physician would reiterate a generation later to the Literary and Philosophical Society of Manchester. "The necessary employment to earn a livelihood in towns has carried with it the seeds of disease and death."[14] In other words, cities' role as places to work seemed incompatible with their role as places to live. It was not so much a question of their size or density: London had been a big city of over half a million people for more than a century. Instead, new energy systems based on coal and steam technologies were causing profound environmental damage to the land, water, and air. Equally important, coal-fueled steam engines for mining, transportation, and power were allowing the workplace for manufacturing goods to be relocated to economically strategic centers of labor and trade. People moving in to fill the increasing number of jobs in the factories and mills, in turn, were bursting through the previous demographic and spatial boundaries of the metropolis, a process that gave rise to yet more ecological and health problems on a regional scale.

To examine Tocqueville's paradox of progress, then, we need to apply not only comparative methods but also the holistic perspectives of environmental studies to the study of the industrial city as an energy system. Such an inclusive model of research suggests that we study energy in the context of an ecological cycle, starting with the extraction of fuels in the countryside and extending to their various uses in the city and their eventual return to the surrounding hinterland as waste by-products. This approach requires an understanding of medicine and the physical sciences as well the humanities and the social sciences. The resulting complexity of environmental history is both its single greatest burden and its single greatest opportunity. Cutting across the boundaries of so many academic disciplines helps to reverse the unfortunate fragmentation of social history and the tendency to know more and more about less and less. The goal is to broaden the conceptual boundaries of the field of urban history to embrace environmental perspectives, but without losing sight of the central drama played by the city's people, politics, and patterns of settlement.[15]

The new sources of energy flowing into factories filled with machinery had profound effects on people's relationship to nature. The movement from a traditional reliance on hand tools and organic woods for fuel and material to an age of mechanization, coal, and iron strongly reinforced trends in Western civilization toward the commodification of nature. For many contemporaries, this revolution in energy and production promised to liberate society from toil and want. Others, however, lamented the degradation of the environment. To them, the industrial city was to blame for society's alienation from nature. The resulting debate between the so-called utilitarians and Romantics over the paradox of progress formed one of the central dimensions of Victorian culture.[16]

A useful way to organize this study of energy and environment in the industrial city is to divide the city's physical and social geography into three overlapping, concentric circles: neighborhood, metropolis, and region. These spatial divisions correspond roughly to discrete levels of environmental concerns and politics. All of these environmental elements and geographic zones not only share common space, they interact together to create infinitely complicated ecologies of feedback loops and evolutionary changes. The very nature of this problematical relationship between humans and the environment demands such a conceptual framework of historical analysis in order to focus attention with any meaningful precision.

In the neighborhoods, for example, the quality of the land as embodied in such immediate surroundings as dwellings, yards, streets, and workplaces often assumed first importance to the well-being of their inhabitants. Here pollution problems centered on removing the tons of organic and industrial waste, ashes, and other garbage that were generated or dumped in close proximity to where people lived and worked. For the most part local communities looked to City Hall to provide environmental services and utilities such as street paving and cleaning. Moreover, municipal authorities traditionally wielded police powers to protect the public health and welfare by abating specific nuisances, regulating offensive behaviors, and setting minimum standards of human decency for conditions of housing and employment.

While the delivery of public services to the neighborhoods often rested in the hands of local aldermen, the quality and availability of water usually became a primary responsibility of the city as a whole. Building a technological infrastructure of drinking-water supplies and sanitary drains required systematic planning and ecological approaches that took account of the area's hydraulic topography and climate. Although most waterworks and sewerage schemes originated from perceptions of local needs, extralocal units of government and business often became involved in their financing and engineering and in the resolution of land and water rights disputes.

In a similar way, problems of air quality often had local origins but regional impacts. Like contaminated water, gases and smoke belching out of one chimney easily mixed with other toxic emissions nearby, and eventually dispersed over a relatively large area defined by major geographic features and weather patterns. In the battle for clean air, local government again formed the first line of defense. Yet metropolitan, if not national, solutions would have to be imposed before any permanent victories were won in reducing air pollution. We can begin to appreciate why Tocqueville considered problematic the notion of improving the environmental quality of daily life in a society that was using methods of production and consumption that were more and more energy intensive.

The structural components of the city's industrial ecology—spatial growth, energy networks, and manufacturing activity—will be better understood with a tighter focus on selected sites, which will help shed light on the complex interplay between the built and natural environments. Adoption of this type of historical viewpoint, historian Bill Luckin proposes, will situate "the experience of the individual within the flux of social and technological change [while] laying bare the dialectic between technology and dominant ideology."[17] With my choice of sites I strive to achieve these objectives by presenting an argument that encompasses both the environmental impacts of modern technology and the corresponding formation of public policy.

Moreover, each case study—the city streets, the waterworks, the brewery—represents an aspect of the urban experience common enough to facilitate comparative studies across national boundaries. For example, the city streets in many respects represent the quintessential urban experience. Equally important, according to social scientists, transportation technology put to use on those streets is perhaps the single most powerful influence giving shape and direction to the city's spatial patterns of growth. Water management systems with their related infrastructure of supply service and sanitary sewerage are basic to the public health of the city and allowed it to grow to unprecedented size during the nineteenth century. Consider the pumping station, the engineer's ultimate test of steam-engine efficiency. Its simple equation—coal in, water out—established industry standards for fuel consumption. More important, the formation of water management policies for the city's various neighborhoods set society's moral benchmarks of environmental justice.

The final site, the brewery, was selected because it consumed such large amounts of energy in the form of heat, power, and refrigeration. Its voracious appetite for coal makes it the perfect candidate for a case study of industrial air pollution. Beer making also involved organic reactions that became subject to scientific investigation. In the 1870s Louis Pasteur's studies of yeast germs helped turn the brewery into one of the earliest examples of a completely self-contained, continuous manufacturing process, including automated assembly lines in the bottling plant. The scientist's experiments had even greater subsequent affects on microbiology and medicine. In addition, the gender, ethnic, and class implications of the production of alcoholic beverages put the brewers in the middle of one of the era's hotly contested cultural and political battlefields.

Close attention to the three selected sites will go a long way toward exposing the main contours of the multifaceted linkages among science, technology, and medicine that inspired a new generation of urban environmentalism. The high profiles of the subjects of the three case studies in campaigns for municipal reform from the 1880s to the 1900s will illuminate important questions about gender politics, scientific theories of disease, the social construction of public health, and the authority of experts. Contemporaries appropriately called the high-energy culture of consumption born in the early twentieth century the Machine Age.

The ambiguity inherent in this moniker accurately reveals that modern society emerged without resolving its paradoxical relationship to the industrial city. Still acting as a powerful magnet for people seeking jobs, the city seemed more unlivable than ever. Many of our current environmental dilemmas followed in the wake of that age's new waves of suburbanization, which now rode on a high-energy crest created by automobiles and electricity. The political formation of urban space that continues to fuel metropolitan sprawl has also left unanswered deeper, more troubling moral issues of social and environmental justice.[18]

Shock City Revisited

Despite the limits of Tocqueville's vision, his insights on Manchester offer a useful point of departure. The Frenchman, of course, was not the only tourist abroad who recorded his impressions. On the contrary, he was part of a small army of intrepid explorers who created an entire literary genre of travel accounts. While some went to remote or exotic places, others were attracted to the great centers of world civilization. And like him, they were drawn to the urban frontiers of the future, where they had similar surrealistic experiences of disorientation and amazement. "Every age has its shock city," British historian Asa Briggs explains, "It was a centre of problems, particularly ethnic and social problems, and it provoked sharply differing reactions from visitors." In fact, these very impressions of "horror and fascination" are what attracted an international parade of observers to the shock cities and gave them their special importance.

Underscoring of contemporary perceptions and representations allows the scholar to make a critical distinction between the idea of the city and more objective measures of its demographic and physical conditions. Briggs suggests that Manchester became the first shock city of industrialization during the 1840s and that Chicago played an equivalent role a half-century later at the close of the Victorian Era. Each place seemed to present a look into the future, "a new phenomenon, a portent, a place which the 'clear-minded' had to visit if they wished to understand the world."[19]

In important respects, travelers' accounts of shock cities were remarkably similar despite great differences in time and location. True enough, the very nature of short stays in foreign places limited the travelers' observations to the most obvious characteristics of the cities' physical appearance and public spaces. Cities that appeared to be on the edge of tomorrow evoked ambiguous reactions as thrilling vanguards of progress and frightening throwbacks to barbarism. Beginning with Dr. James P. Kay's report on Manchester's 1832 outbreak of cholera, *The Moral and Physical Condition of the Working Classes Employed in the Cotton Manufacture in Manchester*, the industrial city was portrayed time and time again as a living hell. Consider the Frenchman Léon Faucher's mixed review, written about a decade later, of what he sarcastically called the "Utopia of Bentham." "Manchester [is] the most interesting, and in some respects, the most monstrous ["industrial agglomeration"] which the progress of society has presented. The first impression is far from favourable. Clouds of smoke vomited forth from the numberless chimneys, labour presents a mysterious activity, something akin to the subterraneous action of a volcano."[20]

This bewildering sense of disorder in the midst of what appeared normalcy to the inhabitants often unsettled visitors, which helps to account for their confused impressions of horror and wonder. In the case of Manchester and Chicago, the tourists were struck by the stench and filth of the streets, the divisions between the residential quarters of the social classes, and the acceleration of movement in the city centers. Friedrich Engels, for example, provided a classical portrait of the slums of Manchester. Following Kay's model, the German exclaimed, "And as for the dirt! Everywhere one sees heaps of refuse, garbage, and filth. There are stagnant pools instead of gutters and the stench alone is so overpowering that no human being, even partially civilized, would find it bearable to live in such a district."

When Jane Addams moved into a working-class neighborhood just west of Chicago's central business district a half-century later in 1889, she found the same conditions. "The streets are inexpressibly dirty," the social reformer wrote, "sanitary legislation unenforced, the street lighting bad, the paving miserable and altogether lacking in the alleys and smaller streets, and the stables foul beyond description." The British journalist William T. Stead concurred that "the first impression which a stranger receives on arriving in Chicago is that of the dirt, the danger, and the inconvenience of the streets." Complementary depictions of suffocating palls of black smoke polluting the air, deadly rivers of sewage, and industrial wastes poisoning the water completed the picture of these human-created disaster areas.[21]

Although visitor accounts of shock cities are significant as environmental narratives, their deeper and more important meaning lies in their analysis of the impacts of industrialization on the city's social geography. Kay, for example, easily perceived how the growth of factories along the textile center's three rivers went hand in hand with specialized land use and spatial segregation by class. Starting in the 1790s, the city had experienced steady growth, the population increasing over a fifty-year period from less than fifty to three hundred thousand inhabitants, with a total of nearly a million people living in the surrounding conurbation.

The urge to get away from the pollution and disorder at the center of Cottonopolis had triggered a suburban exodus by the well-to-do, which contributed to a profound transformation of the urban landscape. Epidemics of deadly diseases and immigration of Irish-Catholic peasants during the 1830s convinced the middle classes to follow in a virtual stampede to get away from the inner city. "The township of Manchester chiefly consists of dense masses of houses," Kay wrote. "Some of the central divisions are occupied by warehouses and shops, and a few streets by the dwellings of some of the more wealthy inhabitants; but the opulent merchants chiefly reside in the country, and even the superior servants of their establishments inhabit the suburban townships. Manchester, properly so called, is chiefly inhabited by shopkeepers and the labouring classes." During the interval between the doctor's investigation in 1832 and the travelers' accounts of the mid-1840s, the lines demarking the separate spheres of slum and suburb hardened into sharply drawn neighborhood boundaries. "In a single decade—1835–1845," scholar Robert Fishman observes, "Manchester achieved a higher degree of suburbanization than London did in the whole century from 1770 to 1870."[22]

By the time Engels arrived in 1842, the process of segregation by class and ethnicity/religion was virtually complete. Significantly, he depicted the bifurcation of urban space in terms not only of physical separation but of social distance as well. Picturing land-use patterns as a series of rings or belts, Engels drew a direct correlation between class and distance from the inner core of businesses and warehouses. The poor were forced to live within walking distance of their jobs, and the middle classes resided "in regularly laid out streets near working class districts [while] the villas of the upper classes enjoy healthy country air and live in luxurious and comfortable dwellings which are linked to the centre of Manchester by omnibuses which run every fifteen or thirty minutes."

Engels boldly accused the better classes of Manchester, charging them with purposely condemning the working poor to lives of misery and death in the industrial slums. What struck the German after his extended stay of twenty-two months in the city was the conscious manipulation of the built environment by the ruling elite to insulate themselves from the working classes. "These plutocrats," he railed, "can travel from their houses to their places of business in the centre of the town by the shortest routes, without even realizing how close they are to the misery and filth which lie on both sides of the road." They commuted along "metropolitan corridors" lined on both sides by an unbroken façade of retail shops. Engels admitted that similar commercial strips were found in most big cities and that the economics of land rents largely accounted for them. "But in my opinion," he asserted, "Manchester is unique in the systematic way in which the working classes have been barred from the main streets."[23]

The Political Formation of Urban Space

Engels's indictment poses one of central challenges of the age of industry, the question of social and environmental justice. "We can and should criticize the appalling living conditions in Victorian cities," Briggs declares, "the absence of amenities, the brutal degradation of natural environment and the inability to plan and often even to conceive of the city as a whole."[24] Calling for multidisciplinary and comparative methods, the historian tapped Britain's rich academic traditions to make "human geography" the centerpiece of his model of research. A focus on the city-building process allowed him to give considerable attention to questions of social justice, shedding light on the industrial city's class conflict and ethnocultural strife.

Since the term *environmental justice* did not exist during the century and a half covered by this book, definitions are required in order to give it meaning for that period. In spite of the absence of the term, each generation of city dwellers has had a more or less explicit definition of the minimum standards of human decency, which include elements of basic survival such as housing, fuel, clothing, nutrition, and sanitation. At times these standards were embodied in municipal regulations establishing police power over the health, safety, and welfare of the public. Local building codes that set rules for the types of building materials, the sizes of rooms, the dimensions of windows, and so on are a good example. At other times these standards were reflected in public regulation of the price of basic commodities such as bread and coal. Analogous information is available for determining what contemporaries believed were basic levels of clothing, fuel, and food needed to survive. In other words, historical evidence can help recreate what each generation believed to be a set of physical, measurable goods and services necessary to maintain a minimally decent quality of life in the city.

If such general standards could be used to hold those contemporaries to account, then what do I mean by the term *environmental justice*? First of all, it is a special kind or subset of social justice that has a spatial dimension. It is social equity or fairness in the geographic distribution of both the city's positive amenities and its negative burdens of pollution and disease. Those who were topographically positioned in advantageous central and suburban locations enjoyed urban benefits such as street paving and lighting, sewerage and garbage pickup, and public parks and boulevards in a natural setting.

Those whose dwellings were located in flood plains or marshlands or in the shadow of smoke-belching mills bore the burdens of overcrowded, jerry-built slums, disease-spreading backyard privies, water-supply shortages, and the lack of green space in an industrial landscape.

To be sure, the impersonal equation of ground rents was the single most powerful influence in sorting out the social geography of the city. But the extent to which the public sector played a role in legitimizing and reinforcing these patterns—what I term *the political formation of urban space*—can be weighed by contemporary scales of social equity. It can also be assessed against current categories of class, race, gender, and ethnicity/religion in order to make possible a better understanding of contemporary attitudes toward society and nature.

Beyond collective measurements of distributive justice in spatial terms, the question of environmental justice also raises the issue of basic human rights. Does each individual have a claim on society to meet contemporary standards of minimum decency? Does society have an obligation to provide every person an adequate place to live, enough food to eat, and affordable access to medical services? These kinds of rights questions are heavily loaded with ideology and morality, which make them difficult to answer. While the effort to answer them poses a worthwhile pursuit for the historian, they are too big and complicated to take on as a whole in this work.

Here the discussion of human rights will be limited to issues raised within the public sectors of law and politics that involve an environmental dimension. For example, if a municipal government finances the construction of a waterworks by levying taxes on every household, then do all households have a right, in return, to enjoy the benefits of the improved supply in their homes and neighborhoods? Moreover, how should we judge a city council that purposefully discriminates against certain geographic districts and social classes by setting policies that effectively deny them access to the new supplies?

The effort to come to grips with these kinds of questions unavoidably infuses historical narrative with a personal moral voice. My goal is not to impose a particular understanding of environmental justice as some kind of higher law or to argue that it is better than others. Instead, my purpose is simply to challenge us to acknowledge more openly the moral dimensions of environmental policy making. Admittedly, there are few tasks of research more difficult than that of drawing causal links between the industrialization and the spatial segregation of the city. Just sorting out the relationship between environmental politics and public health is a formidable exercise. Here we can learn from the sanitarians of the Victorian Era because some of them took a broad, inclusive view of matters ranging from housing and nutritional standards to morality and lifestyles.[25]

An integral part of this exercise, moreover, must be the decoding, or unpacking, of contemporary representations of science, technology, and medicine. Even a radical like Engels recognized that appearances in shock cities were often deceiving. "When the middle classes zealously proclaim that all is well with the working classes," he contended, "I cannot help feeling that the politically 'progressive' industrialists, the Manchester 'bigwigs,' are not quite so innocent of this shameful piece of town planning as they pretend."[26]

To gain an appreciation of the politics of social and geographic exclusion we need to understand in much greater detail exactly how the urban environment affected the health and quality of life of its inhabitants. This effort will require not only precise mapping of the health and welfare of the city's neighborhoods, but also careful evaluation of the conditions inside its workplaces. Such an approach will give this field of study an equivalent to the new social history's "history from the bottom up."[27]

An investigation along these lines will help us draw distinctions between individual impulses to escape from the pollution, disease, and disorder of the industrial city and orchestrated efforts to keep these problems away from the protected enclaves of the affluent. As Engels and other travelers to shock cities noted, the better classes took steps not only to remove themselves from the factory districts but also to lock the working classes into those districts. One anthropologist suggests that "the human landscape can be read as a landscape of exclusion. . . . Because power is expressed in the monopolization of space and relegation of weaker groups in society to less desirable environments, any text on the social geography of advanced capitalism should be concerned with the question of exclusion."

Spatial segregation reflects not only these negative motives, but also society's positive efforts to organize the environment. Pollution ideas are tied to notions of purity, cleanliness, and moral order, according to Mary Douglas. "In chasing dirt," she contends, "we are not governed [alone] by anxiety to escape disease, but are positively re-ordering our environment, making it conform to an idea" of social order.[28] In this sense, then, spatial segregation by class and ethnicity/religion was driven by both fears of infection by the lower strata of society and hopes of creating a suburban environment of health, safety, and beauty.

In both Manchester and Chicago, the lower classes were confined to the toxic wastelands of the rivers' industrial corridors. Dumping in these neighborhoods did not necessarily seem unjust or discriminatory. Indeed, polite society and its representatives in local government blamed the moral failings of the poor for their high rates of sickness and death. Kay blamed the Irish Catholics for the Manchester's problems. In Chicago similar depictions of the depraved, bestial nature of the immigrant were common. In 1891, for instance, Health Commissioner John D. Ware placed responsibility for a typhoid epidemic on the victims themselves. "In almost every case where death had occurred," he righteously proclaimed, "the plumbing was notoriously bad, the drainage worse, and in many instances not the slightest effort had been made to keep house and surroundings in sanitary condition."[29]

Although the psychological roots of geographic exclusion in the industrial city may be hard to locate with precision, their institutional manifestations are plainly visible in the form of public health and environmental policy. Briggs claims that "constant interest . . . in the 'Sanitary Idea' characterized the Victorian city, which was the locus and focus of all theories and policies of environmental control." The main focus of this reform movement was the water management system of drinking supply and indoor plumbing. He considers the "hidden network of pipes and drains and sewers one of the biggest technical and social achievements of the age."

It is just this research into the construction of the networked city that is producing some of the most exciting and significant contributions to the field of urban environmental history, not the least of which is the introduction of gender perspectives. A much tighter integration of the histories of science, technology, and medicine is also shedding new light on the provision of urban infrastructure and public health services. What has been missing in this otherwise commendable recent outpouring of scholarship is sufficient attention to the question of environmental justice in the city.[30]

We need to take up the challenge posed by Engels by putting power relationships and public policy center stage. Scholars have long complained about the failure of the new social history to incorporate politics as a causal factor in its mode of analysis. Terrence J. McDonald offers not only the most comprehensive indictment regarding this problem, but also the most compelling recent appeal "to bring the state back in." The burden of urban history, he proposes, is to restore agency to government and ideology in the making of urban society.[31] Our conceptualization of politics must undergo a transformation analogous to E. P. Thompson's reformulation of class from a static category into a dynamic process.

If postwar scholarship tended to restrict the study of urban politics to tight channels, the adoption of environmental perspectives can go a long way toward opening up broad areas of the public sector for historical investigation. However, historians have asked few questions about the role of City Hall and partisan politics in the making of the city's separate spheres of social segregation and exclusion. To what extent was the public sector responsible for horrible slums like the one Jane Addams moved into on the near West Side of Chicago? What part did public policy play in degrading the quality of life in these places to a point below accepted standards of human health and decency? And what was the complicity of local regimes in helping to maintain these intolerable conditions in the face of their unfortunate victims' demands for improvements?[32]

To address issues of environmental justice in the city, we must extend the scope of inquiry far beyond electoral contests to embrace a wide variety of governmental and political activities. In the case of the land and its uses, for instance, the public sector was actively involved in creating the built environment in many ways, including the provision of public works and utility services; the enactment of building, plumbing, and health codes; and the enforcement of these regulations. Collectively these activities cut across every level of city government from that of the lowest street sweepers to that of the highest elected officials and jurists.

Such an environmental approach, moreover, exposes the true foundation underlying political activity at the local level. From the origins of municipal government right down to the present, the roots of urban politics have always grown out of the economic concerns of property owners, real estate developers, and manufacturing interests. Graft from gamblers, pimps, and saloon keepers, the focus of many classic urban history texts, may have helped grease the money machines of the political parties, but contributions from landowners have supplied the fuel to keep them running. And property taxes, of course, form the fiscal base of city government, giving landlord and tenant alike a stake in the distributive justice of the administration of public policy. Finally, environmental perspectives on urban politics can help situate ethnicity, patronage, and political machines within broader, more inclusive frameworks of analysis.[33]

A model of research designed along these lines should begin to supply some answers to explain why Tocqueville was wrong in predicting that the industrial city would be only a transitory setback in the inexorable march of progress toward liberty and equality. A close look at the political formation of urban space offers a way to start unpacking his thesis that "the clear lack of government one sees in Manchester" largely accounted for its landscapes of exclusion. "The roads . . . show, like the rest, every sign of hurried and unfinished work," he argued, "incidental activity of a population bent on gain, which seeks to amass gold so as to have everything else all at once, and in the interval, mistrusts the niceties of life."[34] Upon this basic proposition he would construct a series of assumptions to arrive at the reassuring conclusion that the democratic hands of the liberal state would soon respond by tying checkreins on the "monstrosity" of unbridled capitalism. But if we uncover a more conscious, organized strategy to institutionalize public policies of spatial segregation by class and ethnicity/religion then his entire conceptual framework collapses like a house of cards. In place of Tocqueville's prediction, a mode of analysis grounded in environmental studies can build a more solid case for the agency of government and ideology in the creation of the slums and the suburbs. Urban political regimes played a significant part in making these sharp divisions in land-use patterns the most persistent, characteristic urban form in Great Britain and the United States.

Of course, the impacts of increasingly energy intensive methods of consumption may be causing a metamorphosis of the industrial city into the more blurred phenomenon of postmodern sprawl. Nonetheless, these changes are only widening the gaps in the quality of daily life in various neighborhoods while reinforcing the barriers between those neighborhoods. This study is devoted to gaining a better understanding of the cultural and political origins of the division of the metropolis, which generates many of our most intractable problems. By taking up the challenge thrown down first by Engels and later by Briggs and others, I hope to put questions of social and environmental justice on center stage of the drama of urban life during the age of industry.

CHAPTER TWO

"They Are All Little Manchesters"

Introduction: The Creation of an Industrial Ecology

In the autumn of 1849, a young writer for London's *Morning Chronicle* was sent to Manchester to make yet another report on the social conditions of the industrial slum. Coming near the end of a long train of urban investigations stretching back eighteen years to Dr. James P. Kay's *Moral and Physical Condition of the Working Classes*, the dispatches of Angus B. Reach broke little new ground, but his mission adds to our understanding of energy and environment in the age of industry in three important ways.

First, the purpose of Reach's assignment underscored that Manchester's moment as a shock city was drawing to a close. A terrifying outbreak of cholera in London, not some novel catastrophe or upheaval in Cottonopolis, was the original focus of the story. Coverage of the story in London drew fresh attention to the tragic plight of the urban poor, confronting an alarmed public with the paradox of progress and its inescapable moral dilemmas of social and environmental justice. "No man of feeling or reflection," the journalist exclaimed in the midst of the epidemic, "can look abroad without being shocked and startled by the sight of enormous wealth and unbounded luxury, placed in direct juxtaposition with the lowest extremes of indigence and privation. Is this contrast a necessary result of the unalterable laws of nature, or simply the sure indication of an effete social system?"

Reach's errand in the Northwest was to establish a baseline of the unhealthiest places in the kingdom against which to measure the capital's working-class districts. The shift of public interest away from Manchester helps explain why the reporter traveled along the same well-trodden paths that had already been surveyed by Kay, Tocqueville, Engels, and many others. Depicting what had now become ordinary, the reporter briefly sketched the metropolitan corridor leading to the "queen of the cotton cities." A pall of smoke gradually obscured the sun, and, like other writers before him, the train traveler felt like he was plunging headlong from the natural world into a monstrous inferno, descending from civilization to hell.[1]

The normalization of the industrial slum into the commonplace is evident in a second way that gives special significance to Reach's dispatches. Whereas his predecessors had only covered the central city, he extended his investigation to the city's far-reaching hinterland of mill towns, coal mines, and weaver villages. He assumed that by mid-century business travel to and repeated accounts of shock city had made "most Englishmen . . . familiar" with the manufacturing centers of the region. Just after penetrating the farthest ring of the city's outstretching web of roads, rails, and canals, however, Reach noted that its industrial ecology of polluted air and poisoned rivers seemed to be suffocating the earth even far from the central city:

> Presently the tall chimneys begin to figure conspicuously in the landscape. The country loses its fresh rurality of appearance; grass looks brown and dry, and foliage stunted and smutty. The roads, and even the footpaths across the fields are black with coal dust. Factories and mills raise their dingy masses everywhere around. Ponderous wagons, heavily laden with bales or casks, go clashing along. You shoot by town after town—the outlying satellites of the great cotton metropolis. They have all similar features—they are all little Manchesters.[2]

By one count there were 280 cotton towns within a twelve-mile radius of Manchester's Royal Exchange, the financial heart of this great conurbation. Reach compared and contrasted conditions in a select sample of these satellites, placing emphasis on familiar features of everyday life and work. By broadening the compass of the investigation, he helped illuminate some of the crucial changes that created industrial ecologies, giving them their distinctive physical form and social geography.[3]

Third, this account of the textile districts is valuable because Reach was such a masterful writer, blending together the literary genres inspired by shock city to create vivid pictures. No less an authority than British historian E. P. Thompson considered the reporter's observations "the most impressive survey of labour and poverty at mid-century which exits." The twenty-nine-year-old journalist seems to have absorbed the works of Kay and Engels as well as Dickens and Disraeli, distilling them into his own brilliant style of urban realism. Moreover, a detailed knowledge of everyday life in London's streets helped turn his extended stay in Manchester into a unique opportunity to write intimate and revealing portraits of its working-class districts. Reach was one of the few visitors to shock city to make personal contact with the mill hands on the shop floors and in the neighborhoods. His firsthand accounts not only contribute to an assessment of the quality of everyday life in the slums, but also demonstrate the agency of the people who lived there.[4]

Reach can serve, then, as a guide to the industrial city at a historic watershed in the formation of environmental policy. During the previous twenty years, public perceptions had been shifting from looking at Manchester as an isolated phenomenon to seeing it as a generic template of a widespread problem that had profound national, if not imperial, implications. Kay's local report had grown and matured into Edwin Chadwick's moral crusade. A year before Reach embarked on his mission, Chadwick's "Sanitary Idea" had reached culmination in Parliament's enactment of Great Britain's first urban-centered public health act. The act represented the crest of a wave of sweeping national and local reforms undertaken by policy makers seeking desperately to restore social order during a tumultuous period of rapid urbanization. Because of their pivotal timing, the reporter's dispatches supply a unique vantage point from which to search both backward for the ecological roots of the industrial city and forward for the future directions of its environmental engineering and planning.[5]

This exploration of the paradox of progress logically begins at the cornerstone of Reach's conceptualization of the textile district, which he envisioned in broad geographic terms as an integrated metropolitan complex on a regional scale. At the time of Kay's 1832 pamphlet, for example, the local township boundaries of Manchester contained a population of 142,000 people while the metropolitan area embraced 271,000 inhabitants, and the county over 1,336,000.[6]

Our first set of questions seeks to uncover the origins of these settlement patterns. Why did the critically important cotton trade become increasingly concentrated in Lancashire? And what part, if any, did particular elements of the regional ecology play in this process? How did market-driven forces of production spawned by the revolution in textiles cause basic changes in people's relationship to nature? When did these transformations begin, and can distinct stages be identified in the rise of the country's first great industrial conurbation?

A closely related set of questions aims to expose the linkages between energy and environment as both gave shape to the spatial and demographic patterns of this network of cities. How did technological change affect the amounts and types of energy resources people sought to extract from nature? And what role, if any, did the resulting energy transitions play in demarking turning points or stages in the development of a regional landscape of mill towns? Only after we examine these market forces can we raise the next set of questions about intentionality in the political formation of urban space.

Finally, this exploration of the origins of an industrial ecology will return to Reach's report for guidance in sorting out the human and the environmental costs of this transformation at mid-century.

"Coals at the Heels of It"

A grand party on an open meadow just outside of Manchester on 17 July 1761 provides a convenient point of departure. For on that historic day, Duke Francis Egerton gathered Lord Stamford and other local aristocrats at Barton Moss to witness the inauguration of an energy transition. They were among the first to see fifty-ton barges effortlessly floating high overhead on an aqueduct that spanned one hundred feet across the River Irwell. About five miles downstream from town, the amazing sight, touted as "the greatest artificial curiosity in the world," became an instant tourist attraction. A quarter-century later this achievement of Egerton, now called the Duke of Bridgewater, would become legendary. One of the pilgrims to this shrine of progress wrote breathlessly:

> The spectator was, therefore, here gratified with the extraordinary sight, never before beheld in this country, of one vessel falling over the top of another; and those who at first ridiculed the attempt, as equivalent to building a castle in the air, were obliged to join in admiration of the wonderful abilities of the engineer, from whose creative genius there was scarcely any thing within the reach of possibility which might not be expected.[7]

True enough, neither the party's host nor his guests would have used modern terminology like *energy transition* to describe the meaning of the demonstration they watched and toasted, with glasses raised high, on that glorious summer afternoon. As the quotation implies, their immediate attention was focused on the achievement's obvious significance as a triumph of transportation, not energy. Egerton had proved that engineers could build improved shipping lanes anywhere, and the fast-spreading news of the Barton aqueduct heralded a new era of canal building in England.[8]

Nonetheless, the duke's vision for the project was, to a remarkable extent, to revolutionize the use of energy in the city by slashing fuel prices. For him the barge's heavy load was more valuable than the tolls he anticipated receiving once he opened the privately owned and operated waterway to commercial traffic. His well-known axiom that a canal enterprise had to have "coals at the heels of it" to generate profits expressed a belief that the fuel would become an increasingly important necessity of urban life.[9]

The heavy cargo being towed across the water bridge that summer day had begun its journey about two and a half miles upstream, deep inside his Worsley mine. By digging a tunnel, called a sough, of unprecedented size into the side of the coal-laden hill, he had cleverly solved two key problems in slashing the cost of delivering the bulky commodity to the forty to fifty thousand inhabitants of the Manchester/Salford area. The underground channel both drained the otherwise submerged veins of black gold and was the source of an uncontested supply of water to keep the canal barges afloat. The packhorses that used to trudge loads of 280 pounds down the unpaved turnpike from the mine to the city were taught a new route to follow on the towpath. By reducing production and transport costs, Egerton was able to save small consumers more than half of their fuel bills. Although his dramatic price cut failed to trigger an overnight transformation in energy use, he lived to see his dream come true by the end of the century.[10]

The duke's project deserves close examination as a model of the region's energy system on the eve of momentous, albeit separate, technological breakthroughs in the use of steam to spin cotton fibers and drive machines. And like the factory system of production that emerged over the next forty years, his coal canal embodied a symbiotic interaction of flowing water, draft animals (and human bodies), and fossil fuels. The Industrial Revolution that followed occupies a vast terrain of historiography that I must circumnavigate for the most part in order to avoid getting lost in a thicket of academic debate. Instead, I follow a line of inquiry focused more narrowly on the roles played by energy and environment in the creation of a manufacturing district, stopping to examine bits and pieces of scholarship on this great transformation as needed along the way.[11]

In Lancashire the duke's heavy reliance on flowing water as opposed to the other available forces of nature that could be harnessed to perform work perfectly mirrored more general patterns of energy use during the earliest stages of textile mechanization. Between 1761 and 1801, the urban market for coal was limited almost entirely to meeting demands for heat, not power. Britain's first energy crisis, resulting from the stripping bare of its forests to acquire fuel, long antedated Bridgewater's plans to reengineer the regional economy and environment into an industrial ecology. "In the 17th century," according to one estimate, "England was alone in living beyond any possible income of renewable fuels.... In 1700, the woodland equivalent of the coal burned would have needed to cover well over a fifth of the kingdom." Having reached the limits of one natural resource as early as the thirteenth century in London, the island had begun a gradual conversion to another it had in abundance. By the mid-eighteenth century, coal was used not only for warming hearths, but also for firing the ovens of a growing number of businesses, such as bakeries, breweries, and soap and candle making establishments. Moreover, the use of bricks as the preferred building material in the fire-prone cities revived as improved transportation and mining techniques drove down the price of the fuel needed to make the bricks. In 1780 Manchester consumed about 400 tons of the duke's coal a week, or 20,800 tons in a year at a time when his cheap rates briefly allowed him to enjoy a virtual local monopoly.[12]

Until the following decade, coal was used as an energy fuel to power steam engines almost exclusively to pump water out of coal and metallurgical mines. The first practical steam engine had been designed by Thomas Newcomen in 1712 to meet just this need, and it raised 60–120 hogsheads (3,900–7,800 U.S. gallons) of water an hour. Except for this one special purpose, however, steam engines were simply too feeble and expensive to compete against either draft animals and humans or waterpower. Most crippling of all, perhaps, steam engines went only up and down while most machines were driven by rotary motion.

The cities' growing demand for coal was forcing miners to dig deeper and deeper underground, where problems of drainage and ventilation increased proportionately. The horse wheels that had previously been relied on to lift much smaller volumes of water not far from the surface had begun to reach a limit, not so much of the animals' strength as of their endurance. Although teams of horses could be rotated with greater frequency, the weak but steady oscillations of Newcomen-type engines offered some mine operators a better solution to the problem of constant seepage of surface rainwater. By the time of the inauguration of the Barton Aqueduct in 1761, according to recent estimates, the number of engines that had been built in Great Britain was between 320–350, and about 200–250 of them were still in service.[13]

If the duke's management of the Worsley mine is indicative of general practice, however, waterpower remained the preferred means of driving machines whenever possible until well after the turn of the century. Even at the very source of the energy fuel, the duke installed three different types of water-driven machines to help the miners get the coal out of the ground. To provide ventilation to the miners deep inside the pit, he channeled a stream of water from above the mine to fall through a funnel connected to a spinning bellows that shot a stream of cool air and water into the tunnels. When the digging began to go lower than the underground waterways, pumps were brought in and connected to piston-type water engines. In a third ingenious innovation, the force of gravity was employed to lift coal in areas inaccessible to the expanding network of subterranean canals. When drums of water were filled as a counterweight, baskets full of coal could be hauled up with little effort. Returning the empty coal bins to the bottom of the pit required only opening a plug in the bottom of the water drums.[14]

The very makeshift nature of these devices reflects a long and comfortable familiarity with waterpower technologies that harnessed the eternal force of gravity. The steam engine suffered in comparison from the very novelty of its mysterious alchemy, which transmuted two of the most basic forces of nature—fire and water—into work. Early Newcomen devices were not only strange, but also weak and inefficient compared to waterwheels, which could be set in triple tandem to generate the equivalent of twenty-five horsepower. A stable of eighty real horses would have been required to keep the pumps running at the same pace.

The concentration of the new steam-powered pumping machines in England's most highly developed coal mining region, the Tyne River basin in the Northeast, adds further evidence of the primacy of waterpower over steam during the formative period of the Industrial Revolution. A careful investigation by industrial archeologist Eric Clavering shows that the limits of water-driven machines were neither technological nor environmental. Instead, the turn to steam power by some of the larger mine operators in the eighteenth century stemmed from strategic decisions to avoid costly legal conflicts with surrounding property owners over the collection and diversion of rainwater from their lands. As Clavering points out, a rash of protracted court cases underscored the fact that there is no such thing as a "free" natural resource; even the rain belonged to someone. Ultimately, disputes over land and water rights were settled by Parliament, which often passed private laws containing grants to these resources. Between 1758 and 1803, for example, the legislature passed 165 canal acts on behalf of private developers like Francis Egerton.[15]

The reliance of the canal duke and his contemporaries on flowing water to drive their machines significantly reinforced the natural advantages of the region around Manchester as one of the best places to make cotton and woolen goods. More than any other single causal factor, ecological conditions shaped the location of textile production during both the long preceding period of hand methods and the emerging era of inanimate power and factory mechanization. As early as the thirteenth century, the area had attracted spinners and weavers from both home and abroad because its site, topography, and climate combined to supply them with rain, and plenty of it.

The systematic measurement of rainfall, however, awaited the pioneering experiments of Manchester's preeminent scientist, John Dalton, at the end of the century.[16] But the people of the region did not need a weatherman to tell them that they could count on getting wet an average of every other day throughout the Mersey-Irwell Rivers Basin (MIRB) (see figs. 2.1 and 2.2). Moreover, the textile makers took advantage of the common knowledge that the amount of precipitation climbed in rough proportion with the elevation of the hills by planting weaver villages all around the market centers in the valley. Upland weavers could build their loomshops in the attic, while those in Manchester, Salford, and Stockport had to put theirs in the cellar, where floors were left unfinished to enhance humidity levels. The origins of these cities' notorious underground dwellings—Alexis de Tocqueville's "damp, dark labyrinth"—created the very conditions that were needed to keep the brittle fibers and threads from constantly breaking.

The rain also provided the textile makers with abundant supplies of clean, soft running water for finishing work such as washing, bleaching, dyeing, and printing the cloth. The growth of these tasks into specialized trades helped give birth to strings of town sites stretching up the valleys along the riverbanks. By the sixteenth century, the term *Manchester cottons*[17] appropriately expressed contemporary perceptions of a close association between product and locale. It also meant that many of the nation's best and most creative spinners and weavers were clustered around the city. "The people in and about the town," J. Aiken commented in 1795, "are said to be in general the most industrious in their calling of any in the northern parts of the kingdom."[18]

From the headwaters of the MIRB, rainwater flows approximately seventy miles down to the sea, and it was this rainwater that fueled the growth in the production of cotton goods during the second half of the eighteenth century. Comprising 587,000 acres, the region is formed by a chain of the Pennines hills shaped like a colossal amphitheater facing south and west toward the stormy Atlantic Ocean. Modern records set the range of average annual precipitation from thirty-five inches at Manchester (125 feet above sea level) to double that amount amid the 1,500–2,000-foot peaks behind it. With an average of fifty inches of rain a year, the district around the city was twice as wet as the London area. The only place in England with more rainfall than

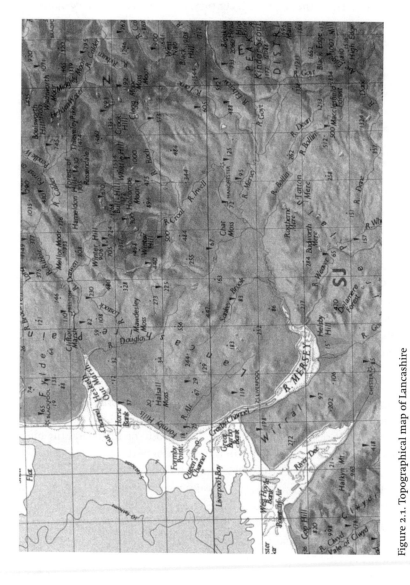

Figure 2.1. Topographical map of Lancashire

Source: *Atlas of Britain and Northern Ireland* (Oxford: Clarendon, 1963), 60–61.

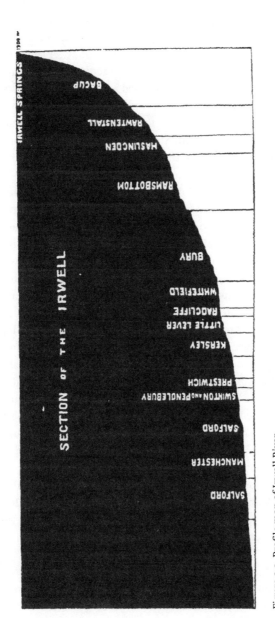

Figure 2.2. Profile map of Irwell River

Source: Charles A. Burghardt, "The Pollution of the River Irwell and Its Tributaries," *Literary and Philosophical Society of Manchester, Proceedings* 25 (1886): 198.

the MIRB is the comparatively mountainous and inaccessible Lake District a hundred miles farther to the north along the Atlantic coastline.

Two-thirds of the precipitation coming down around Manchester becomes runoff. This amounts to about 22,750 gallons per acre for each inch of rain, giving the MIRB a yearly flow of 650 billion gallons of water that finds its way to the estuary above the port of Liverpool. This incredibly large and relatively accessible source of power must have seemed a great natural blessing to Lancashire's textile makers as they began to compete in world markets during the second half of the eighteenth century. Even a hundred years later, according to one close observer, the rivers and streams of Lancashire and Cheshire "are still amongst the great sources of the manufacturing, as well as the pastoral and agricultural wealth of the two counties."[19]

But the rains that fill these fountains of prosperity also produce the region's most costly environmental hazard, flash floods. As early mill owners learned to their chagrin, particularly heavy downpours could send a wall of water careening down the valley with so much force that their entire works, not just the waterwheels, were swept away. At the same time, two features built into the natural ecology significantly reduced the potential for this kind of damage. First, the hilltops were covered with peat moss that acted like a sponge, soaking up water during storms and slowly releasing it afterward. Second, the steep and tapered shape of the riverbanks in the valleys helped to contain flood surges and dissipate their force. As the volume of water rose higher, the space between the embankments became wider, slowing the speed of the swelling currents. To be sure, monster storms pushed across the North Atlantic by gale-force winds occasional overcame these natural regulators of the region's hydraulic ecology. For example, one of Manchester's local historians found two notable floods of the Irwell recorded in the seventeenth century and three during the next. In contrast, the ten serious inundations between 1800 and 1870 evoked childhood memories of "that rugged ascent" up Hunt's Bank "before the road levelers (how mercilessly they did level hereabout!) came to clear away ... the waterside between the two bridges." These city builders were by no means the only ones making changes in the land in hopes of reaping rich rewards in return.[20]

Hands and Feet, Hooves and Yokes

The shotgun-like burst of innovation that took place in the Manchester watershed between 1765 and 1800 should come as no surprise given the dispersed settlement of its impressive pool of talent. Although the architects of the first industrial revolution lived in relative isolation from each other, the close timing of their breakthroughs in textile, power, and transportation technologies is more than a coincidence. The common thread tying these inventors and dreamers like the canal duke together was rising demand for cotton goods in domestic, foreign, and colonial markets. Joseph E. Inikori used modern "import substitution industrialization theory" to posit that by mid-century, the common cloths of Lancashire had largely completed a long struggle at home to replace textiles of comparable quality imported from India. The driving force of change in the following period, he contends, was the effort of Manchester's merchants to stave off stagnation by taking away business from this formidable competitor in the highly lucrative Atlantic slave trade. All-cotton fabrics represented an important currency of exchange not only in the purchase of enchained captives in Africa but in the clothing of those captives in the Americas as well. The importation of raw cotton from the British colonies completed this circle of mercantilism, generating what could easily be construed as a general gain in the wealth of the nation.[21]

In order for England to penetrate and compete successfully in these promising export markets, its textile industry had to boost volume and quality while sharply cutting unit costs. The most obvious roadblock to the attainment of both these goals came at the very beginning of the process. By the 1750s, the farmer-weavers of Lancashire faced a yarn famine because the hands and feet of the spinners simply could not move fast enough to keep up with the demand. The best contemporary observer, Aikin, confirms that "no exertion of the masters or workman could have answered the demands of trade without the introduction of spinning machines."

Since most of the work in this family endeavor was devoted to getting the raw material ready for spinning, some adapted barnyard horse wheels to help with the tedious job of carding the fibers. Nonetheless, preparing a pound of cotton and spinning it into yarn throttled output because it required at least five hundred hours of work. One contemporary account estimated that it took three spinners to keep one weaver supplied in cotton weft. Moreover, with hand methods one generally could not twist and stretch the fibers tightly enough for them to compete against India's all-cotton checks, muslins, and calicos. For example, a pound of spun cotton at the top end of quality (100 count) would stretch 47.7 miles as opposed to only 9.5 miles for the thicker, weaker threads at the low end (20 count). Compared to the labor available for making even this inferior product, a virtually inexhaustible supply of feet and hands, young and old, seemed available among these industrious families to operate the weaving looms.[22]

The story of the invention of cotton spinning technology has been told many times and does not bear repeating here except in summary form. For our purposes, attention must focus instead on the ways in which these machines changed the patterns of settlement and energy use in the Manchester region and their role in its resulting transformation into a manufacturing district.

The first breakthrough came in 1764, three years after the duke's party at Barton Moss, when the frustrated Lancashire weaver James Hargreaves created the spinning jenny. It multiplied the hands of spinners sixteen to thirty times, and it spread quickly through the region. Five years later, Richard Arkwright patented the water-frame spinning machine, and it was followed in 1779 by the spinning mule of Bolton's Samuel Crompton. An early adopter of Hargreaves's invention, Crompton had worked in secret for six years blending its best features with those of Arkwright's machine into his own version, which was soon competing against both of them. Mechanization began to take command in spite of the destructive outbursts of the Luddites. Carding and roving machines sped up these time-consuming steps of preparation; devices called scutchers mechanized hand beating, or willowing, to remove impurities from the raw cotton; and so on.

Crompton's mule spindle proved to be the key technology because it doubled the quality of the best yarns from 40 to 80 count, a seemingly impossible feat in England at the time. Although initially the spinning mule was designed for human power, the number of hands embodied by each machine multiplied rapidly to 150–300 spindles by the 1790s. When preparation machines were also used, the time required to make a pound of cotton yarn dropped dramatically to only one to two hours. Now cotton could be used not only for the woof but also for the warp in place of more expensive wool and linen. In economic terms, this revolution in the means of production translated into a fantastic average annual reduction of 15 percent in the cost of making fine yarns for a thirty-year period between 1770 and 1800. Manchester's merchants profited handsomely by capturing the demand for cotton goods at home and by boosting sales abroad fivefold. By 1803 cotton goods had become Britain's single most valuable export.[23]

The need for more energy grew commensurately in symbiotic patterns among people and animals, land and water. The machine-breaking Luddites were wrong; the new technology fueled a revolutionary pace of expansion in the demand for work and workers. Old and new methods reinforced each other. For example, Aikin could juxtapose horses, which ran the carding and other preparation machines, with children, perhaps fifty thousand of them by the late 1780s, who were put to work tending the new spinning machines. Their smaller bodies and fingers seemed perfected suited to the complicated technology of the multispindle jennies and mules. In addition, our intrepid observer reported that farmers were breeding and raising more horses

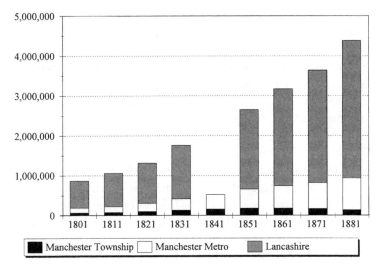

Figure 2.3. Population of Manchester area, 1801–1881
Source: Data from Henry Baker, "On the Growth of the Commercial Centre of
Manchester, Movement of Population, and Pressure on Habitation—Census Decenniad
1861–1871," *Manchester Statistical Society, Transactions* (1871–1872): 87–106; and Henry
Baker, "On the Growth of the Manchester Population, Extension of the Commercial
Centre of the City and Provision for Habitation—Census Period 1871–1881," *Manchester
Statistical Society, Transactions* (November 1881): 1–27.
Note: Figures for Lancashire are not available for 1841.

because environmental conditions in the MIRB seemed perfectly suited for
these purposes. "The wetness of the climate is unfortunate to the growth of
corn and the ripening of fruit," he noted, "but is serviceable to pasturage, and
produces an almost perpetual verdure in the fields." Forty-four percent of the
farmland was tilled, but an even larger 56 percent was given over to grazing.[24]

The most immediate result of the rapid shift from yarn famines to yarn
surpluses to be underscored here is the equally fast buildup of the number
of hands and feet employed at weaving looms. The population boom in Lancashire in the second half of the eighteenth century represented, according
to Aikin, "an increase almost unparalleled!" His figures for 1788, for instance,
show 350,000 textile workers, including 100,000 children (see fig. 2.3). At the
heart of this growth, Manchester flourished as its merchants directed and
coordinated the far-flung operations of the putting-out system.

Climatic conditions gave this region an initial advantage over other cotton
textile districts, but the city's extraordinary group of enterprising businessmen deserves credit for mastering the organizational skills to exploit those

advantages over such a far-flung territory. Recent studies of the built environment of Manchester confirm that warehouses and showrooms were of equal importance to factory buildings in the construction of the prototypical landscape of the industrial city. Offering the place with the most immediate communications among buyers, sellers, and producers, the urban market center became a new home for hand loom weavers as well as factory operatives and machine builders. The number of workers in city and country grew in tandem during the first stages of the revolution in production technology and energy use, and they drew upon every available source of power.[25]

The use of horses for transportation and to power machines also rose steeply during the initial stages of textile mechanization. The wagon trains of the chapmen had to carry more raw cotton longer distances as the spinners and weavers spread up the river valleys and as more yarn and finished goods had to be brought back to the storerooms in the city below. More animals were also put to work driving the ever-lengthening list of ingenious inventions that multiplied the work that one machine tender, or "operative," could accomplish when no longer using hand methods of making cotton yarn. Horses supplied a familiar, organic source of power, but what they added in ready availability, they took away in quick exhaustion and lagging pace of work. Although several teams could be rotated to keep the spinning machines running at the steady speeds needed for the making of fine yarns, the harnessed energy of gravity offered a more advantageous, albeit capital-intensive, alternative source of natural power.[26]

Arkwright deserves credit for envisioning a factory system built upon the power of flowing water. Waterwheels figured into the design of the scale and the power requirements of his spinning machines from the beginning. In 1771, his first cotton mill on the Derwent River in Derbyshire started with a thousand spindles. He quickly mechanized the preparatory steps, and his plans soon called for a more complete integration of energy and production under a single roof, embedded in the millwork that transmitted power from the prime mover to the machines. In 1782, he erected the first large-scale unified cotton mill in Manchester, a five-story factory driven by a waterwheel with a nine-meter diameter. It came with a built-in power assist from a steam engine constructed by a local inventor. In spite of its rotary motion, this Newcomen-like machine was still used in the traditional manner as a pump to raise water. In this case, the heat machine lifted water from a holding tank below the building at Shude Hill to a reservoir above it, to help keep the waterwheel turning during dry spells.

The race was on to exploit the force of gravity. Cotton mills sprang up like mushrooms along the lengths of the basin's rivers and streams. By 1787, the MIRB had over two hundred spinning factories. Communities that were clustered around existing mills grew larger at the same time that new villages were planted farther and farther upstream in previously inaccessible locations. As the best place in the valley for waterpower, Stockport briefly emerged as the leading contender for the largest urban center of the region. Attracting some of the region's most creative talents, the town became renowned for model mills and innovative leadership in power technology. Nonetheless, the need to bring the factory to the waterpower site meant that decentralization remained the dominant overall pattern of industrialization. In addition, cleaner water higher up the valley attracted a new generation of power-driven textile plants engaged in finishing processes, such as machine printing works in the Accrington District east of Blackburn and bleachworks in the area around Bolton.[27]

By the late 1780s, the pathways of rainwater down the Pennines had begun to define the outlines of a manufacturing district. An interdependent network of urban places was taking shape that resembled several loose strings of pearls stretching up and out from a central intersection at or near Manchester. If the search for waterpower tended to point new settlement toward higher elevations, the coming of steam engines that could drive machines instead of only pumps restored the industrial primacy of the valley towns.

The cotton trade's seemingly insatiable demand for power had not escaped the attention of the machine builders. Here again we run into a tale told many times over: that of James Watt and his solution in the 1780s to the problem of how to turn the up-and-down strokes of the steam engine into rotary motion. In 1789, Peter Drinkwater was the first to install one of Watt's machines in a Manchester cotton factory. The Piccadilly Mill combined human muscles to drive the spinning-mule machines of 144 spindles each and a steam engine to turn the roving machines. Other local mechanics soon took the next step of linking the steam-powered prime mover directly to the spinning machines.[28]

Once this idea was proven to be a big step forward, it spread quickly throughout the region. "More steam engines of every kind were built between 1790 and 1800," Asa Briggs points out, "than the rest of the 18th century put together." Lancashire gained fifty Boulton and Watt models alone during the decade, three times more than any other county in Britain. One of the model's chief selling points was fuel efficiency: it multiplied the amount of work that could be generated with a pound of coal by a factor of two or three over Newcomen-type engines. Watt also claimed that factory owners could double the output of their prime movers by attaching them directly to the millwork rather than using them as pumps to feed the waterwheels.

In the end, however, Watt adopted the measure called horsepower (hp) to equate the strength of his machines with the work performed by hooves and yokes, in accordance with the most commonly understood notion of power. Custom building each engine during this period, Watt and his Birmingham partner, Matthew Boulton, would most frequently be called upon to fashion the engine in proportion to the size of the horse wheel and the number of animals the machine was going to replace. They could also supply cotton manufacturers with rough equations indicating the number of spindles an engine with a particular level of horsepower could keep spinning. These rule of thumb methods, for example, matched a ten-horse engine with a thousand-spindle mill of Arkwright water frames. Although still tied to rivers and streams for boiler water and fuel supplies, the steam engine freed factories from the need to be located at a falls. Location at one of those sites now represented an obstacle to the flow of coal and cotton to the mills.[29]

As the region entered a historic energy transition to supplement traditional sources of power with fossil fuels, then, locational advantage shifted back toward the urban centers in the valley, which had the better access to the marketplace. The next formidable barrier to the expansion of the cotton trade was transportation. The cost of each pound of freight mounted quickly when the product had to be moved inland by horses and their drivers.

Beginning in 1721, a private navigation company had undertaken the job of providing improved movement on the Mersey-Irwell Rivers route, but transporting the raw cotton from the docks of Liverpool to scattered work sites throughout the Manchester watershed and then returning the finished goods to the great port remained a tedious and uncertain journey marked by numerous layovers caused by low water, dangerous obstructions, and bad weather. With a light load and perfect conditions, the struggling navigation company could make the fifty-seven-mile journey in one of its sail-equipped, thirty-five-ton barges in a week. The more usual time freight spent in transit was twice that—after it had already spent two to three weeks sitting on the wharf awaiting pickup. Service was so slow that chapmen and teamsters could compete against the navigation company. At the time of the canal duke's triumph in 1761, a survey of the traffic passing over the Warrington Bridge on a busy Saturday counted 3 wagons, 127 carts, and 385 packhorses.[30]

The spectacular success of the duke's Worsley-to-Manchester waterway triggered a national canal-building mania, one that the duke had every intention of exploiting to the fullest. Riding a wave of admiration, Egerton launched an even more audacious plan, to completely bypass the Mersey-Irwell navigation route by digging a canal thirty-four miles from his downtown docks at Castle Field to the Liverpool estuary at Runcorn. Once he opened the entire length of the artificial river in 1776, travel times and costs dropped spectacularly. Passengers on one of the new luxury packet boats could be transported not only more safely and smoothly than by overland coach, but also more quickly, at 12 miles per hour, when pulled by a succession of teams of three horses each, while a horn-blowing, liveried rider warned pedestrians to get out of the way. First-class travelers leaving Manchester at 8:00 a.m. could now reach Liverpool by 4:30 p.m. The growth of traffic on the canal is reflected in the duke's account books, which reported an increase from £12,500 in revenue in the first year to £80,000 sixteen years later. More important, the Bridgewater Canal represented a link between regional and national networks that took shape during the final quarter of the eighteenth century.[31]

In the midst of fighting wars against foreign rivals and its thirteen rebellious colonies, Britain constructed an elaborate system of highways for waterborne traffic that crisscrossed the country and opened up its interior. In Lancashire several artificial rivers were built alongside the natural ones to improve the flow of traffic between the upland towns and the center of trade below (see figs. 2.4 and 2.5). Canals to Manchester came on line at the very time that the steam engine was being adapted to industry's need for more power. Most of these transportation companies could take advantage of the county's widespread bounty of black gold, which allowed them to heed the duke's injunction to have "coals at the heels of it." Pit heads and fuel yards became as ubiquitous as cotton mills and smokestacks. The coming of peace at the turn of the century and the resumption of commercial intercourse with the continent set the stage for a rapid buildup and consolidation of Manchester as the hub of an emerging textile district. But rising levels of pollution of land, water, and air showed all the telltale signs of turning this thriving regional conurbation into a health-threatening industrial ecology.[32]

The Twin Birth of the Industrial Slum and the Garden Suburb

Between 1790 and 1815, ongoing revolutions in manufacturing, power, and transportation converged in Manchester, catapulting it over Liverpool and other urban rivals so that it captured the crown as the "queen of the cotton cities." The 1798 opening of A. and G. Murray's eight-story factory on the partially completed Rochdale Canal set a new standard for large-scale integration of steam engines and textile mechanization. It also triggered a boom that would double the number of factories in the city to 111 in just four years.

The scale of production also soared. The number of spindles in the average mill multiplied more than sixfold over the course of the period. In

Mersey and Ribble Basins

0 ————— 5 miles

Figure 2.4. Mersey-Irwell and Ribble basins
Source: L. E. Breeze, *The British Experience with River Pollution, 1865–1876* (New York: Lang, 1993). Reprinted with permission.

1814, for example, the two largest spinning-mule factories—the Murrays' and McConnel and Kennedy's—housed 170,000 spindles, or more spindles than the entire country of Switzerland. A census of the Manchester area conducted by Samuel Crompton counted nearly 4.2 million mule spindles, which, he estimated, kept busy 50,000 hand weavers and 250,000 workers in related jobs,

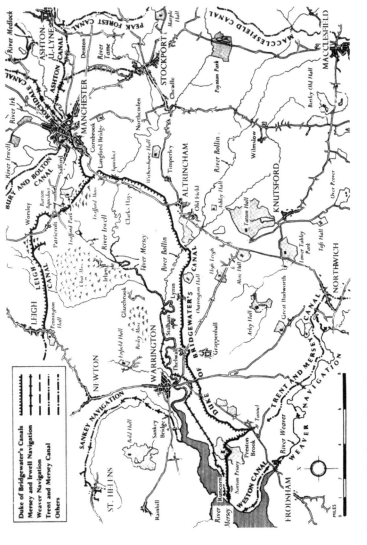

Figure 2.5. Manchester-Liverpool canals, c. 1800

Source: Duke of Bridgewater, map c. 1800, as reprinted in Hugh Malet, *Bridgewater: The Canal Duke, 1736–1803*, rev. ed. (Manchester: Manchester University Press, 1977).

from machinists to merchants. A visionary, the Duke of Bridgewater could literally see his dreams coming true. Standing on his wharf at Castle Field, he could watch an endless stream of goods, people, and, of course, coal flowing up and down the valleys before rejoining the larger currents of the Atlantic cotton and slave trade. The father of Britain's canal system must have taken great satisfaction in the fulfillment of his prophecy.[33]

But the aging aristocrat might also have been concerned about the unintended consequence of this good fortune: the inescapable deterioration of the urban environment. The conclusion that air quality was rapidly declining was unavoidable. In 1800, local authorities complained "that the increase of . . . steam engines, as well as the smoak issuing from chimnies used over Stoves, Foundaries, Dressers, Dyehouses, and Bakehouses, are become a great Nuisance to the town." From his vantage point at the confluence of the city's waterways, the duke could not have avoided noticing their murky discoloration and the putrid smell from swelling loads of human and industrial wastes. In a similar way, the successful buildup of his shipping yard appeared to go hand in hand with a spreading blight on either side of it. Makeshift hovels and pigsties clung desperately to the steep banks of the poisoned rivers, creating village-like shantytowns that housed the city's wretchedly poor and criminally dangerous. Budding pockets of human squalor were just one of many distressing signs that the urban landscape was undergoing a complete makeover. The duke died in 1803 at the age of sixty-seven, well before this environmental and social metamorphosis would turn into a full-blown public health catastrophe a quarter-century later.[34]

The simultaneous transformation of Manchester's spatial relationships in its larger regional and national contexts can best be understood in terms of economic synergies. Geographers argue that a dynamic process of "accumulative and circular growth" sets in to boost one place inexorably ahead of the others once it gains an initial advantage by specializing in some kind of economic activity. Moreover, the strengthening magnetic appeal of the insurgent city for additional and related activities acts to retard the growth of those activities in nearby places. To be sure, however, all things are not equal, and geographers' theories must be fitted to the unique ecological contours of each region.[35]

In the case of Lancashire, these concepts help explain why the energy demands of textile mechanization triggered Manchester's irreversible burst into first place in the race for the urban crown of the MIRB, but they don't tell the whole story. As we have seen, this region's climate and topography gave it some initial advantages, although other counties, such as Nottingham and Derbyshire, also contained sizable colonies of spinners and weavers. The early cotton machines multiplied not only the work performed by each body, but also the absolute number of workers and animals. The effort to harness the power of flowing water to supply the need for more power to drive the machines further enhanced the locational advantages of the Manchester district. The construction of cotton mills up the river valleys reinforced previous patterns of dispersed settlement until the 1790s, when the demands of manufacturers for more power led to the coupling of rotary-motion steam engines to factory millworks. Then the valley towns enjoyed the best access to cheap coal and other supplies. However, the completion of the turnpike and canal systems during the decade went a long way toward equalizing transportation costs among the towns in the watershed.

To account fully for Manchester's ascendancy over the Northwest requires stories of human agency in addition to geographic pictures of environmental, economic, and technological change. The city's enterprising merchants continued to play the starring roles in this rich drama involving tens of thousands of people caught up in the revolution in spinning yarn, making textiles, and trading goods. They seized the opportunity opened by the steam-powered spinning mill to turn their far-flung putting-out system into an urban-based business structure. At the same time, firm size and specialization remained remarkably fluid. Appropriately termed the *warehouse system* by historians Robin Lloyd-Jones and M. J. Lewis, the structure was the architectural representation of an industry reorganized along more physically concentrated forms of production.

Once a supply of cotton yarn became readily available within Manchester, the city's merchants were able to gain greater control over the hand weavers by giving preference to those living near the mills. Better communications and management resulting from tighter spatial proximity, in addition to savings in freight bills, also encouraged the cotton barons to underwrite schemes to build related businesses, such as finishing works, chemical plants, and machine shops, close to the city. In 1815, for example, the areas just outside of a burgeoning inner zone of warehouses and showrooms contained 77 machinery-making plants and 240 chemical or finishing firms. By the time the full impacts of the transportation improvements put upstream and valley towns on more equal terms with one another in the 1810s, Manchester's entrepreneurs had already cemented their home base as the center of this great conurbation.[36]

Under the direction of these merchants, the truly unique feature of Lancashire's urban hierarchy became its highly integrated network of upland satellite cities orbiting around the metropolis in the river basin below. Business historians are undoubtedly correct that the steam-driven spinning mule attracted to Manchester not only factory operatives, but also weavers and finishers, machine makers and tenders, porters and teamsters, and broken-down drunks and cotton-textile lords. In fact, Crompton's estimate of the number of local jobs created by his invention alone is a good example in support of the geographers' economic model of accumulative and circular growth.

The entire interrelated web of mill towns grew in tandem, with shifting leads and lags among them that reflected the rise and fall of various specialized technologies and processes. Rich in coal as well as flowing water, the MIRB became pockmarked with collieries in or near the established cotton towns to meet their demands for more energy. Steam boiler plants with their imposing chimneys and belching smoke also dotted the watershed's increasingly polluted landscape. Functioning like a highly integrated economic unit, Angus Reach's manufacturing district was, in a true sense, an industrial ecology. In a larger national context its accelerating economic development stood in marked contrast to what seemed like atrophy in the textile towns of the other regions. Their loss may have been Lancashire's gain, but Lancashire's cities would pay a heavy social and environmental price for cramming so many industrial workers and polluting factories into the same small space.[37]

In the 1790s, the rapid concentration of the textile trade within Manchester created explosive pressures, bursting apart a traditional urban form that had dated back to the Middle Ages. The rising success of the warehouse system produced insatiable demands for more room and better transportation. According to Aikin, "Manchester may bear comparison with the metropolis itself in the rapidity with which whole new streets have been raised, and in its extension on every side towards the surrounding country." He estimated that the new, albeit unpaved, highways of commerce doubled the size of the settlement area of the city. He noted that most of the highways "are wide and spacious, with excellent and large houses, principally made of brick on the spot." But for a vast majority of the newcomers, they were all one-way streets leading toward the town center.[38]

Increasing densities throughout the enlarging periphery added to the streams of pedestrians, carts, and wagons trying to get into the urban core. Between 1773 and 1801, the central area defined by the township absorbed a population boost of 241 percent, from 22,500 to 76,800 inhabitants. Over the course of the next decade, housing had to be created or found for another fourteen thousand people, and densities within the city quadrupled to 114 people per acre. By 1809, street traffic had become bad enough to prompt an irate citizen to write a pamphlet entitled "Directions for Walking the Streets of Manchester and the Conduct of Carriages." The proponent of this hopeless cause protested that "in walking down Market-street-lane to the

Exchange, it is likely that a person will be pushed all ways, at least twenty times, sometimes against the houses, others off the flags [that is, flagstones], notwithstanding his endeavour to walk regular; the fact is, without rule you are forced in and out, running against one another, to the annoyance of all, and the hindrance of those upon business, who being anxious to get forward, push along irregularly and increase the confusion."[39]

The unpleasant noise and inconvenience of heavy traffic began intruding on and eventually breached one after another of the previously protected central city preserves of the social elite. In 1792, even the venerable Exchange Building was demolished to make way for a larger replacement that would accommodate the increased activity. The mounting demands of business for more space as close as possible to this new temple of trade sent land values soaring within a quarter-mile radius, encompassing most of the old town. This gave even stubborn holdouts among the home owners plenty of positive incentive to sell out and move away. At the tail end of this succession from residential to commercial land use in the early 1830s, the merchant Richard Cobden wrote a tongue-in-cheek letter to his brother, Frederic, describing his anticipated real estate coup. The financial community would be so impressed, he boasted,

> that all the world will be at my heels soon. My next door neighbour, Brookes, of the firm of Cunliffe and Brookes, bankers, has sold his house to be converted into a warehouse. The owner of the house on the other side has given his tenants notice for the same purpose. The architect assures me if I were to put up my house tomorrow, I might have 6,000 guineas for it. So as I gave but 3,000 and ... there being but one criterion of a man's ability—the making of money—I am already thought a clever fellow.[40]

Unlike in London and other big cities, however, commercial expansion of Manchester's core had to compete for priority of land use with vigorous industrial construction. The emerging business district sat on the high land wedged between the Irwell and Medlock rivers, with the Irk River slashing across at the top. As the business district pushed outward, it did not take long before the warehouses ran into the cotton mills, finishing plants, and machine shops being built along the rivers and canals. This area represented a donut ring from one-quarter mile to a mile out from the Exchange.

For the first time trade and manufacturing made equally legitimate claims to needing access to central waterfront locations. In the 1790s, the Bolton and Rochdale canals were cut through the area, both exacerbating and relieving the overcrowding. On the one hand, intense competition ensued for choice sites along these transportation arteries within the core. On the other hand, these artificial rivers extended beyond the core, creating long ribbons of new factory sites through districts previously inaccessible to cheap freight rates and abundant water supplies for steam boilers and textile processing. While the canals and their multiple local branches helped open up more land to industrial development, they also added to the congestion of traffic trying to move into and out of the center of town.

Adding to the din and confusion of the streets, air pollution spewing from rows of factories virtually surrounding the core area caused further deterioration in the quality of the urban environment. After the overnight doubling of the number of new, mammoth-sized mills at the turn of the century, the atmosphere must have become heavily laden with smoke and smut. One indication of the dimming of natural illumination was the introduction of gas lighting in Manchester. The inventive designers of the fireproof Salford Twist Mill included a gas making plant in the plans they developed from 1803 to 1805. Coal was placed inside a closed container, or retort, and baked until it released gases that had illuminating properties when ignited in Bunsen-burner type fixtures. Besides significantly reducing the high risk of fire in the cotton mills that had used oil lamps or candles, the new fixtures allowed higher levels of lighting at a great saving in cost. This innovation was quickly incorporated into the plans of other large factories.

But gas lighting added to the demand for more energy, and it had its own negative impacts on the urban environment. Two of its main by-products were highly toxic coal tars, which were mostly dumped into the nearest waterway, and giant clouds of black smoke, which paradoxically contributed to the blotting out of the sun. A traveler from Holland in 1808 found conditions to be simply intolerable. Preshadowing the shock city writers, he exclaimed, "The town is abominably filthy, the Steam Engines pestiferous, the Dyehouses noisesome and offensive, and the Water of the River as black as Ink."[41] It did not take long for others to come to the similar conclusion that commercial and residential land uses were incompatible with adjacent clusters of industrial structures, like cotton mills, that burned mountains of coal and spewed out oceans of toxic wastes.

In Manchester, the squeezing together of the warehouse system and the factory system in such close proximity engendered the Siamese twins of the industrial slum and the garden suburb. In a dialectical way they created each other as environmental degradation of the central city gave rise to the creation of outlying subdivisions of rustic, park-like residential retreats. Next to gigantic commercial buildings and cotton mills, human-scale structures like houses and shops seemed to shrink to insignificance. In sharp contrast to the patterns of urban growth in London and other great capital cities, those in the textile district of Manchester made living in the inner zones less and less desirable. Although exclusive bourgeois enclaves had appeared previously in London, preindustrial patterns of residency among traditional elites in that city's center made the move to the suburbs only one option for new members of the well-to-do classes. Mancunians, however, would construct a new urban topography, a social geography that presented a stark picture of spatial segregation by class and ethnicity/religion. More than anywhere else, Robert Fishman agrees, they "established the pattern of middle-class suburbanization in the industrial city."[42]

In the 1800s, the protosuburban harbingers of a complete exodus by all who could afford it began to take shape along major highways about a mile out of town. Two prominent examples of protosuburbs were Grosvenor Square on Oxford Road and Ardwick Green on London Road. Their designs suggest origins in the merchants' displacement from central city homes rather than their attraction to some kind of suburban ethos. The estates' open public spaces bordered by detached houses and accessed by major thoroughfares expressed urban planning ideals. The indefatigable Aikin took notice of the substantial "country residences" around Ardwick Green. "Some years ago it was regarded as a rural situation," he remarked, "but the buildings of Manchester have extended in that direction so far as completely to connect it with the town; and this quarter is principally inhabited by the more opulent classes, so as to resemble, though on a small scale, the west end of the city of London." Moreover, the two residential projects were still within easy walking distance of the core zone. After 1808, regular hackney cab service also became available. Significantly, both of these portents of bourgeois utopia were located upwind of the factory smoke, setting the direction of future suburban growth to the south and southwest.[43]

For those who could least afford to move to the outskirts of town, living as close as possible to the mill gates was critical to getting and holding a job. Throughout the nineteenth century, low wages forced the vast majority of the labor force to walk to work rather than pay for transportation, severely limiting their choice of housing stock and neighborhood location. Every extra step became a hardship for Manchester operatives who had to trudge back and forth to and from exhausting twelve-to-fourteen-hour shifts. The seasonal ups and downs of employment added further pressure on the workers to stay near the gates, whence news about jobs and hiring spread outward through the community by word of mouth. Tighter lines of communication also helped fuel the growth of preexisting urban colonies of hand

Figure 2.6. Manchester area townships
Source: City of Manchester, Medical Officer of Health, *Annual Report* (1893).

loom weavers. In fact, textile historian Geoffrey Timmins argues that these communities strongly influenced the locational decisions of the early mill builders. The concentration of high-count mule spinning in the city during the 1790s, in turn, set into motion a self-reinforcing pattern of settlement that packed poorly paid textile workers in the shadows of the factories and warehouses.[44]

Perhaps the first and certainly the most notorious industrial slum in Manchester was an area known as Ancoats (see fig. 2.6). Its history as a distinct place stretches back to the twelfth century, when it was only a hamlet. A square-shaped area, it was contained almost entirely within the donut ring between one half and one mile from the Exchange, on the northeast side of the city. Timmins calculates that at the advent of steam-powered fine spinning, its weaver village had at least 145 cottages with 600 looms. Yet the favorite image that contemporaries remembered about Ancoats into the 1820s was that of a vista in which nature predominates, not machines. One witness lamented fifty years later:

> The Broad Green has disappeared. The orchards of the Hopwoods and, the granges of the Traffords, the green lanes, the bright woodlands have been covered over by the habitations of man. The little hamlet is now a mighty hive of industry. . . . Whilst we glory in the progress and prosperity of the present we may regret the disappearance of the clear stream, the green lanes, the merry songbirds, the smokeless sky that made fair and beautiful the old Ancoats that has for ever passed away.[45]

This sea change from rural to urban had begun in earnest during the 1790s with the announcement that the Rochdale Canal was coming right through the middle of the district.

A closer look at the transformation of Ancoats helps expose the intimate spatial relationship between the factory and the slum that shaped the creation of a new urban form, the industrial city. In this case, change grew out of the seedbed of the fabulous success story of four migrants from Scotland, the Murray brothers and McConnel and Kennedy. Arriving in the 1780s, these entrepreneurs became machine makers and mill designers. They also engaged in spinning cotton on a small scale by following the common practice of renting space and power in mills owned by others. Their contacts back home opened rewarding markets among hand weavers for the relatively cheap, fine yarns produced by the factory system. At the turn of the century, the two partnerships were ready to put their accumulating expertise and profits into the construction of adjacent spinning-mule mills on the canal.

The new enterprises set records not only for their economies of scale but also for their quality of goods. The factories attained maximum counts in the 170s—and in the 250s by the 1810s. Each mill became a complex of buildings as the Scotsmen expanded their businesses, figuring out along the way what would become the standard guidelines for organizing work within the modern mill. By the 1810s, the two factories were employing 2,235 workers and producing almost 20 percent of the city's total output of yarn. With the sheer magnitude of both the mills and the number of homes required for so many workers and their families, a new kind of community completely overran the colony of hand loom weavers.[46]

To meet demands for more shelter, the fields of Ancoats were subdivided and crammed with as many dwellings as possible. Making matters worse, much of the new housing for the factory operatives was built below standards necessary for human decency, creating an instant slum at the mouth of the mill gates. From 1790 to 1830, about eight hundred homes were built for five to seven thousand people in a thirty-five-block area sandwiched in between the factories and warehouses that gradually became solid walls lining the embankments of the waterways. The flimsy hovels were, as reformers would say, jerry-built: they were thrown together with the cheapest labor and materials. "At the time they were erected sanitary science was in its infancy," a medical examiner observed almost a hundred years later, in 1889, "and one is tempted to think the houses originally were only intended to furnish the minimum amount of shelter and comfort necessary for existence. Subsoil drainage, damp-proof courses, ventilation under the floors, ventilation of the rooms, etc. were things unthought of in connection with the houses of the poor, and in this district are conspicuous by their entire absence."[47]

With Manchester's sustained rate of growth, the building patterns established in Ancoats became a template for mixed industrial areas composed of substandard dwellings, public houses, polluting factories, and busy warehouses. As later investigators noted, most of the houses built in this area were purposely planned to maximize land use while minimizing costs. These economic imperatives were expressed in streets designed as narrow lanes and dead-end courts and in row after monotonous row of tiny "back-to-backs," attached houses with shared walls in the rear as well as on the sides.

This neighborhood of shoddy construction did not escape Aikin's attention when he conducted his comprehensive survey of the city. He was alarmed by what he saw and concluded that the neighborhood "unfortunately vies with, or exceeds, the metropolis, in the closeness with which the poor are crowded in offensive, dark, damp, and incommodious habitations, a too fertile source of disease!"[48] But his cry went unheeded because the pattern was

soon repeated in other areas lying just beyond the commercial core and forming an irregular collar around it. Only after his worst fears came true during
a deadly cholera epidemic in 1832 were those in authority finally shocked
into confronting the new type of urban space, the industrial slum, and the
desperate plight of the working people forced to live in it.

As Manchester entered the nineteenth century, its spatial and environmental transformation into the archetype of the industrial city was nearly
complete. The appearance of Ancoats and other instant slums in the inner city
added another powerful incentive for members of the middle classes to move
as far away as commuter services would allow. The more these filthy warrens
of the working poor, along with the riverbank shantytowns of the wholly
destitute, became integral parts of the core zone, the less desirable that zone
became as a place to live. Thus the slums helped feed the growth of the suburbs, and the suburbs, in turn, reinforced land-use patterns of segregation
by economic function and by social categories of class and ethnicity/religion.

The emerging urban form of Manchester was increasingly marked by physical and social boundaries that divided it into mutually exclusive separate
spheres. A central business district of a quarter-mile radius gave way to a ring
of teeming industrial neighborhoods and then, at a safe distance, a different
world of bucolic garden estates. Various industrial and commercial corridors
strung this fragmented topography together. Soon an escalating series of
frightening health crises and mass uprisings would galvanize the elites into
beginning to enact public programs that significantly widened the gap in
the quality of daily life between the slums and the suburbs. Before turning
to political questions of intentionality, however, I focus on the relationship
between spatial segregation and class formation at the street level to uncover some final insights into the origins of the industrial city's landscape of
inequality.

In Manchester the public house, or pub, is the site that best illuminates
how specific places and groups became identified in class terms. In the case of
the public house, this complex interaction of structure and agency resulted in
separate spheres of gender as well as socioeconomic status. Without denying
that the workplace is the primary location of class struggle, urban scholar
Clive Behagg shows that the semiprivate space of the pub became an important extension of shop-floor culture and its group solidarity: often, for
example, a pub became closely associated with a particular cotton mill or
artisan trade. Here then was an arena or theater outside the control of the
bosses where workers could act out folk rituals of collective strength and
enforce their sense of justice, sometimes by using violence and intimidation.
Equally important, the workers took possession of their pubs, making them

off-limits to those outside the neighborhood or trade. To members of the middle classes especially, they became forbidding places cloaked in secrecy and danger. "When the workplace was reinforced by an active relationship with the public house," the cultural historian points out, "working-class culture appeared at its most impenetrable."[49]

In a parallel way, the merchants appropriated the taverns and pubs in the central business district as their own exclusive preserves. They turned them into extensions of the workplace, and conducted many of their face-to-face negotiations in these convivial settings. Lloyd-Jones and Lewis state, for example, that "public houses were extensively used by outside manufacturers as meeting places for the purchase and sale of goods and were an important part of Manchester's marketing/economic structure." Each tradesperson became a known regular at a particular establishment. Sometimes a tradesperson would have the name and location of a favored spot printed on business cards and would set up an informal office there and merely rent warehouse space.[50]

The merchant pubs in the business center and their counterparts in the surrounding workers' neighborhoods illustrate a much larger process by which group identities became attached to particular places. The physical transformation of Manchester into distinct districts fostered among its inhabitants a highly dynamic and contested series of mental maps of its fractured topography. These contrasting visions of the community, in turn, played a configurative role in guiding class conflict in new directions. Whether in the form of violent protest in the streets or polite debate in the chambers of government, the struggle for power in the industrial city would become centered on the question of who exercised control over the environment.[51]

The restoration of international peace in 1815 guaranteed the uninterrupted economic ascendancy of Manchester and its regional conurbation as the end of war against the United States and France ushered in a sustained period of rising prosperity throughout the Atlantic world. King Cotton became not only the engine of U.S. economic growth, but a big part of Great Britain's as well, climbing to a peak of one-half the total value of the latter's exports over the next fifteen years. During this period of voracious demand, coal-fueled steam plants pushed past waterwheels in supplying energy to the mills. The 1820s also proved the pivotal decade in the shift from hand to power looms in the city, although the weavers of Lancashire would continue to hang on as specialists for another two decades before going into absolute decline. The tremendous expansion of the textile industry continued to boost Manchester's locational advantages, feeding its growth into the center of a conurbation of metropolitan proportions. As figure 2.3 shows, the population of the area doubled between 1801 and 1831, and then doubled again in just twenty years. The patterns of land use that defined the industrial slum, which had appeared initially in Ancoats, spread from patchy spots hugging the waterways into a more or less solid ring around an emerging business district in the middle.

At first the merchants of Manchester adopted a business strategy of urban concentration to promote the power loom. The mill was redesigned to integrate spinning and weaving machines under one roof. After 1830, however, improved transportation and communications facilitated a reversal of locational priorities in favor of more dispersed patterns of new construction. In that year, the railroad was declared a success when George Stephenson's *Rocket* passed its test trials on the Manchester-to-Liverpool run. The postal mail and the electronic telegraph followed on the heels of this historic achievement, giving the merchants faster ways to send orders to distant points. Taken together, these technological advances provided merchants with a set of powerful new tools to forge tighter lines of managerial control over much wider geographic fields of operation. As the world headquarters of the textile industry, Manchester increasingly became a city of warehouses. One survey of land use in the early 1850s counted 1,683 warehouses, ten times the number of mills. Although Manchester retained its lead as the single largest textile manufacturing city, its share of the total output of cotton goods began to shrink. Bolton, for example, surpassed Manchester in yarn-spinning production.[52]

The gradual deconcentration and specialization of manufacturing in the MIRB spread ever-higher levels of pollution throughout the larger conurbation, creating an industrial ecology. As in the central city, more and more of the additional demand for industrial power was being supplied by fossil fuels in spite of steady technological gains in harnessing the energy of flowing water. Roads, rails, and wires wove a regional network of cities together in solid bonds of interdependency. Shrinking both time and space, these technologies facilitated businesspeople's ability to transplant the factory system throughout the district.[53] The new technologies also helped engineers to design mills in the satellite cities whose scale and scope were on a par with that of the mills in Manchester.

Sometime between 1835 and 1840, Manchester reached a significant plateau in its energy consumption. Not only did its steam engines cross the threshold of generating a combined total of ten thousand horsepower, but they also helped set the record of more than a million tons of coal being burned in a year. Industry accounted for about half of this fuel usage, and the other half went to the heating and lighting of other buildings. Analogous growth in the number of human and animal inhabitants added commensurate amounts of organic wastes to an urban environment that was becoming increasingly overcrowded and overloaded. The risk of a public health disaster loomed ever larger because the neighborhoods of the working classes had become filthy: they had been provided with virtually no infrastructure of sanitation or even an adequate and dependable supply of clean water.[54]

Class Formation and the Origins of Urban Politics

The war's end in 1815 intensified not only the pace of economic growth in Manchester but also the political struggle of the social classes for control of the urban environment. This long-simmering local contest broke into open warfare almost immediately after the lifting of the heavy repression of the national patriotic campaign of Church and King, which had stifled civic life. As E. P. Thompson notes, "Almost every radical phenomenon of the 1790s can be found reproduced tenfold after 1815."[55]

However, this battle of the classes does not fit neatly into a simple Marxian labor-versus-capital mold. On the contrary, the defining characteristics of the new politics of the industrial city are the diversity of special interest groups and those groups' mobilization in the public arena through organizational vehicles and coalition building. The urban concentration fostered by the factory/warehouse system created an ever more complex and tangled web of distinct social and spatial group identities. Even the term *working class* is a misnomer because labor historians have identified several distinct groups within this category. To be sure, Manchester was the scene of several classic violent confrontations between the merchants, manufacturers, and militia on one side of the barricades and the artisans, operatives, and weavers on the other. A widening gulf between the swelling number of city dwellers and the shrinking proportion of eligible voters was a virtual guarantee that disfranchised groups would be forced into the streets in order to bridge the gap by using extralegal forms of expression. Yet these contentious gatherings represented just one pole of a broad spectrum of political activity aimed at shifting the balance of power in the formation of public policy. Questions of legitimacy, of who rules, were deeply enmeshed in debates over the best ways to cope with the rapid change and degradation of the urban environment.[56]

In Manchester, traditions of elite rule and exclusive privilege played an important configurative role in framing the parameters of local political culture. Between the 1790s and the 1840s, the battle for the reins of local government had three phases, each marked by a crisis of legitimacy. Snapshots of these stages help reconstruct the emergence of a modern, middle-class version of a politics of exclusion. The structure of power remained antidemocratic, barely changing in location from a closed circle of Anglican Tory aristocrats related to the lord of the manor, Sir Oswald Mosley, to a slightly larger, more permeable sphere of Dissenter Liberal plutocrats belonging to the congregation of the Unitarian Cross Street Chapel. The city was unique in the intimate bonds of family, faith, and ideology that completely polarized these two groups and made their political struggles so personal and venomous. Indeed, highly dramatic scenes in each round of the fight between them seem to have so captured the attention of some historians that those scholars have lost sight of the working classes entirely. Derek Fraser, for example, states that "the evidence appears to point overwhelmingly to a contest for power within the urban middle class itself and between that urban elite and the landed gentry."

It is true that very few workers were rich enough to qualify to vote in local elections. However, their ability to mobilize a collective presence in the streets repeatedly demonstrated that they represented more than just a passive audience of public life and policy formation. Broader perspectives on the shift of power in Manchester reveal that the urban masses played a pivotal role during each crisis of legitimacy. The results, however, did little to change the political culture of privilege and hierarchy. Instead, the final outcome of these three public convulsions was a shift in power from one elite to another that reinforced social and spatial barriers between the classes. Together the case studies illustrate dramatic moments in a much longer, day-to-day process of class formation and the development of political identity.[57]

The culmination of local tensions leading up to the dawn of the new politics was the St. Ann's Square riots of 1792, which resulted in the creation of the police commission. In this snapshot, the ancient oligarchy is pitted against the insurgency of the new masters of industry. After the city began to grow rapidly in the 1760s, its medieval forms of manorial government seemed increasingly anarchistic as well as antagonistic to the needs of the cotton trade. The lord of the manor, for example, still controlled the main administrative institution of local government, the court leet. The merchants were particularly galled by the tolls they had to pay for goods passing through the city or merely stopping briefly in transit at their warehouses. The new economic issues of access to markets and transportation deepened social fissures between the self-perpetuating oligarchy of Oswald's high-church Tory relatives and a rising generation of wealth. These new businessmen tended to find community within dissenting religious sects with a strong emphasis on rationalism and education. Only the richest need apply to the Cross Street Chapel—manufacturers like McConnel and Kennedy and the Murray brothers, and their counterparts in banking and commerce.

As a tightening web of partnerships, intermarriages, and associations wove them together in bonds of social solidarity, the new businessmen felt strong enough by 1786 to mount an assault on the market tolls. A town meeting was called to repeal the tolls, but the oligarchy soon restored its manorial rights through litigation in the court leet. Striking back, the oligarchs turned the external threat posed by the French Revolution into a powerful club to beat down their domestic opposition. Rallying a mob behind patriotic banners in the public square next to the Exchange, they instigated frightening attacks against the allegedly traitorous businessmen and their churches. "The tumultuous riots of 1792 were not merely tolerated," the semi-official history of the city admits, "but even encouraged, by the police officers of the Court Leet and by some of the local magistrates."[58]

To the extent that the rival elites appealed to the working class for support, they empowered it and lent legitimacy to its claim of a right to participate in the government of the city. But this is not to say that the factory workers and hand weavers needed leaders outside of their own ranks to organize them behind demands for political representation and social justice. The hardships suffered by the disruptions of war after 1789 brought twenty years of class struggle: bread riots, Luddite uprisings, and work stoppages to protest intolerable conditions verging on starvation.

Every open meeting of a sizable number of people in the streets, a tactic of the disfranchised, can be considered a "contention for power." The scene that played out in the shadow of the Exchange in 1792 was different, however, because for the first time those in charge of the public authority turned the angry mob on members of their own class rather than protecting their peers from the mob's wrath. The subsequent period of religious and political repression would forge among the Nonconformists a remarkable sense of unity and a determination to overturn the manorial aristocracy. In a political culture heavily weighted in favor of the status quo, this was no easy task. In the wake of the attacks, for example, the Tory high churchmen rammed legislation through Parliament aimed at strengthening both their control over the urban environment and their hold on the reins of power.[59]

The 1792 law establishing the police commission launched the first stage of urban politics in Manchester, which lasted until the peace of 1815 lifted the veil of state censorship from the public sphere. Redrawing the social boundaries of the urban polity, the reform act is embodied in a snapshot of St. Ann's Square at the moment when the ruling elite exposed its willingness to use any means necessary—fair or foul—to preserve its local hegemony. The oligarchy sought to bolster the legitimacy of this power in three ways.

First, it acknowledged the need to address the deterioration of the urban environment by creating broad new authority to regulate the use of land within the city; to undertake infrastructure improvements; and to levy taxes to pay for these public works projects as well as urban services such as the provision of night watchmen, street scavengers, and lamplighters. The oligarchy also broadened the political base by extending voting rights to a handful of the richest landowners, those with a minimum annual rental value of thirty pounds. The police commission was composed of the officers of the manorial institutions plus representatives chosen by an electorate numbering in the low hundreds in spite of the fact that the population had swelled to over seventy-five thousand people.

These two provisions went into the making of a third feature of the law to ensure that this small minority of insiders would enjoy the benefits of these reforms while the vast majority of outsiders would bear the costs. The law was contrived to exempt the biggest property holders and to shift the effective tax burden to the working classes and small shopkeepers in the form of higher rents. In fact, so much of the existing property value was taken off the rate books that it took several years before the growth of the city generated enough revenue to get the new administration off the ground. Only with the emergence of a virtual autocrat, Thomas Fleming, did the police commission finally, in 1810, become an effective instrument of environmental control. The judgment of local historians that "for some time he was almost the 'uncrowned king' of Manchester" personifies the formative image of the city's political culture.[60]

The second snapshot is of the infamous "Peterloo Massacre." In this tragic tableau, the traditional aristocracy is pitted against the working classes. Deep class divisions are evident in sharp relief in what came to be considered "a major event in British history and arguably the single most important day in Manchester's history." On 16 August 1819, between sixty and one hundred thousand workers gathered in neat ranks and files on St. Peter's Field in the interzone between the business center and the industrial slums. For Fleming and the ruling oligarchy, the unprecedented display of dignity in the workers' orderly procession through the streets might have been the most unnerving circumstance of all. The local cavalry charged into the defenseless crowd, causing at least eleven deaths and hundreds of injuries.

The Peterloo Massacre is emblematic of a period of open class warfare that raged at every level of urban society for more than a decade. The vicious ferocity of the cavalry charge ultimately exposed the underlying weakness of the old regime, whose resort to brute force contributed to the further erosion of its claim to legitimacy while bolstering sympathy for the working classes among Liberal Dissenters, many of whom joined the labor unions' constitutional reform campaign for freedom of speech, press, and assembly. This new alliance between the middle and the working classes appears to have emboldened the city's insurgent Dissenters to mount their own frontal assault on the bastions of the entrenched establishment.[61]

The formation of distinct sociospatial identities among these groups matured into the creation of political organizations during the across-the-board, hand-to-hand combat to gain control of the local government. By combining forces, they took only four months to topple the autocratic regime of Thomas Fleming, which collapsed under a barrage of corruption charges. Then they set siege to the bastions of manorial authority. The battles of the churchwardens and the police commissioners serve to illustrate how political conflict helped to define rather vague and fluid boundaries of class consciousness.

Beginning in 1820, the Nonconformists politicized the annual process of setting rates for mandatory contributions to the official, Anglican Church. A year earlier, the ruling oligarchy had anticipated this protest movement by having Parliament pass a law giving the largest landowners disproportionate voting power. Each of the approximately one hundred top property owners could cast up to six votes to every vote cast by each of the five hundred or so Nonconformist householders who were allowed to cast ballots. Yet the insurgents doggedly disputed successive proposals to equip the churches, pay their choirs, and buy "extravagant" silver plates. This ongoing acrimony led to complete victory for the Dissenters early in the next decade when the rates were dropped altogether in favor of voluntary contributions.

In the case of the police commission, the battle pitted the captains of the cotton industry against the small businesspeople and shopkeepers. After members of the working classes made breaking the streetlamps a symbolic act of political defiance, the police commissioners retaliated by installing a system of gaslights in the central business district. This urban technology became a political instrument for the commissioners to reassert their authority over the public spaces of the city. Started as an icon of law and order in 1817, the gasworks soon proved a highly lucrative commercial venture as shops, pubs, and hotels in the smoke-ridden central city became customers.

The polarizing controversy during the 1820s revolved around whether the profits from the gaslights should be used to subsidize street improvements or returned to consumers in the form of rate cuts. The police commission appointed a governing board of the gasworks, which was dominated by the big merchants and manufacturers. The board was happy to finance road projects at the expense of the mostly disfranchised tradesmen. A loophole in the 1792 law, however, allowed anyone contributing £10 to the highway subscription fund to become a voting member of the commission.

By 1826, the gas consumers had qualified between six hundred and eight hundred members, enough to throw the meetings into deadlock and the oligarchy into another crisis of legitimacy. Attempting to restore its dominion, the ruling elite resorted to a politics of exclusion. In 1829, the oligarchy used its clout in Parliament to retighten the boundaries of class privilege. The new law squeezed out ratepayers under £16 and made only minor concessions by opening access to office holding to property owners with rates between £28 and £30.

Not content with restricting the franchise to 2.8 percent of the adult male population, the inner circle of Manchester aristocrats also redrew the lines between political districts to more closely reflect the existing class segregation and thus ensure their control over the political formation of urban space. This gerrymandering meant that in the richest districts each commissioner represented 270 people, while in the poorest districts, where a mere 0.5 percent of the adult male population could pass the test of wealth, a single commissioner was supposed to stand for nearly 2,400 residents. A similar politics of class segregation was being enacted on the national stage with the passage of a major reconstruction of the body politic that brought in the bourgeoisie but shut out the proletariat. "No other statute," the historian V. A. C. Gatrell reasons, "asserted so unequivocally the ancient association of property with power than the Reform Act [of 1832]; no other act so categorically sorted men into two distinct groups, one privileged, the other not, or so clearly defined the areas of political action each could legitimately inhabit. In Manchester, as elsewhere, economic inequality was thus endowed with a political correlative." The groundwork laid on the national level cleared the way for Britain's middle classes to launch a final assault on the ancien régime at the local level. Their triumph was short-lived, however, because suddenly a hidden enemy of biblical proportions, a cholera epidemic, besieged their communities.[62]

The third snapshot of human catastrophe in the industrial slums of Manchester depicts the dilemmas of environmental justice embedded in the emergence of a new urban politics. In this picture, a frightened and outraged mob of slum-dwellers is pitted against the upper classes and their official institutions. The 1832 epidemic caused terror verging on panic, and it eventually took almost nine hundred lives in the metropolitan area. The painful intestinal disease took its first victim on 17 May; it then spread rapidly through the riverbank shantytowns and mill-gate neighborhoods crowded with substandard housing, despite efforts to isolate the sick in special hospitals set up by the police commission.

The deadly scourge put severe strain on the process of organizing special-interest-group identity around categories of social class and spatial location. By September, social tensions had reached a snapping point. Upon hearing rumors that doctors were killing helpless patients, an enraged mob stormed and wrecked one of the special hospitals. Well-justified fears of infection grew into paranoid fantasies of apocalypse because the medical people had to fight blindly against an invisible adversary they could not identify, let alone cure. Moreover, the fact that this was the first great epidemic to sweep through urban Europe (and America) in the nineteenth century made it all the more shocking. "It is hardly surprising, therefore, that cholera became enshrined as the 'ultimate' fever of Victorian Britain," according to urban scholar Bill Luckin, "and in that sense the Victorian obsession with the infection and its causation was central to the full emergence of pollution as a major social problem in the newly industrialising society; and integral, also to that mode of thought which would, by the end of the century, come to be recognised as distinctively 'environmental.'" [63]

The ultimate crisis of legitimacy posed by the epidemic of 1832 gave new urgency to the movement in Manchester for a more representative form of city government. Still, it took a decade of unrelenting political and legal skirmishing before the Dissenting Liberals overturned the manorial oligarchy with a town council and declared victory. The main characteristic of this period was a maturing of social identities of class and place in institutional organizations such as denominational/ethnic church parishes, partisan ward clubs, and trade union locals. In the case of Manchester's middle-class elite, Richard Cobden led the drive to get a municipal charter of incorporation that would supersede the old system. Rallying supporters behind the manifesto "Organize Your Borough," the textile trader convinced what he called the shopocracy to join his core group of supporters from the Cross Street Chapel. But labor leaders believed his reform cause was a smokescreen to hide a conspiracy of the factory bosses to gain even greater control over the lives of their workers. They joined in alliance with grateful Tories in a last ditch defense of the status quo.

The final showdown came in 1838, when a special referendum on the new municipal charter of incorporation fanned the political flames of class bitterness into a white heat. "Early nineteenth-century petitioning campaigns were notorious for fraud," a British historian has observed, "but the Manchester incorporation petition battle belongs in a class by itself."

Table 2.1 Manchester incorporation referendum, 1838

	For incorporation	Against incorporation
Signatures submitted	11,783	31,947
Signatures validated	7,984	8,694
Assessment of signers submitted	£215,201	£320,777
Assessment of signers validated	£188,076	£165,841

Source: Nicholas C. Edsall, "Varieties of Radicalism: Attwood, Cobden, and the Local Politics of Municipal Incorporation," *Historical Journal* 16 (1973): n. 26.

Cobden's skills of organization proved superior to those of the Tory/Radical coalition. Perhaps it is fitting that the climax of this long-running dispute hinged on a count of property values, not qualified voters (see table 2.1). Although rearguard tactics kept the Liberals at bay for another four years, their assumption of the reigns of power was ensured after Parliament created the town council of the Corporation.

The town council became the institutional vehicle for legitimizing the social authority of the new ruling class in the quasi-aristocratic trappings of public office. Soon after the town council took full control of local government, Fraser notes, "royal visits reinforced the ceremonial tendency of chain, mace, and robes, and Cobden ... [became] highly critical of the snobbery and mummery to which the Manchester corporation had become addicted." The insiders found their own version of the Fleming-style autocrat in town clerk Joseph Heron. Unique among British municipal administrators in longevity and influence, Heron personified the regime of absolute Liberal hegemony that went uncontested by the Tories for the next fifty years.

Only the disfranchised masses of urban workers continued to protest, and even the achievement of new levels of organizational strength was not enough to force significant change in the city's political culture of elite rule and exclusive privilege. The Plug Riots of 1842, usually considered the first general strike in labor history, brought industry to a standstill when workers shrewdly removed the stoppers from the steam boilers. This massive demonstration, however, made no headway against the thick walls of exclusion that barred the great majority of Mancunians from participating in decisions crucial to their health, safety, and quality of daily life.[64]

The Political Formation of Spatial Segregation

More than any other single event, the cholera epidemic of 1832 had a profound influence in shaping the direction of public policy and city planning.

The deep-seated fears of social disorder this kind of human disaster aroused among middle-class Liberals were reflected in the appearance of several new literary genres about city life. An examination of these impressions of Manchester's social and spatial transformation is essential to an understanding of the public and private decisions that were responsible for determining the quality of the urban environment for the next half-century.

Narrative themes about class conflict became the most popular literary response to the sudden attraction to Manchester as a horror and a wonder, the first shock city of the age of industry. Elizabeth Gaskell's *Mary Barton*, Charles Dickens's *Hard Times*, and Disraeli's *Sybil* are perhaps the best known of this type. A new realism made them pregnant with meaning about the anxieties of the middle classes, revealing their uneasy awareness of their growing distance from the mass of working people. But the novels' romantic moralism made the new literature equally barren of ideas about political reform, exposing an acquiescence to an emerging social geography of separate spheres.[65]

In contrast, a second genre appeared that purposely sought to mobilize public opinion behind an urban agenda of practical improvements. To achieve its goals, this mode of expression came wrapped in a new literary guise, that of the neutral scientific report. The single most influential example of this type of work was the first, James P. Kay's 1832 pamphlet, *The Moral and Physical Condition of the Working Classes Employed in the Cotton Manufacture in Manchester*, which became the prototype of what historian Paul Boyer calls "moral environmentalism." Containing a strong dose of religious fervor, the doctor's pioneering study represented a paradoxical alchemy of impartial statistics, social ethics, and blatant prejudice.[66]

Close scrutiny of the making of this classic account of the industrial slum sheds light on the parameters of environmental reform among Manchester's ascendant middle-class elite. Kay was the son of a Rochdale cotton merchant and had received medical training from the University of Edinburgh's William Alison, the leading spokesperson of what Christopher Hamlin calls "political medicine." After graduating in 1827, the twenty-three-year-old physician returned to Lancashire to become senior physician of the Ardwick and Ancoats Dispensary. He also joined the Cross Street Chapel. The importance of membership in this Unitarian congregation cannot be overstated: as the fountainhead of Manchester Liberalism it exerted tremendous influence on the city and the nation for a generation.

In 1832, Kay naturally looked to his congregation for support in organizing a response to the cholera epidemic. They set up not only a traditional charity to aid the needy, but also the innovative Manchester Statistical Society, one of the earliest of these organizations that perfectly reflected middle-class fascination with numbers. Devoted to quantitative social analysis, the Statistical Society helped Kay hire agents to conduct a door-to-door survey of the city's working-class districts. His compilation of the data in his benchmark report had the effect of cloaking virulent racial and class prejudice with the mantle of scientific objectivity. An examination of these attitudes helps explain the resulting public and private decisions that collectively would create a segregated city of slums and suburbs.[67]

At base, Kay's investigation represents a defense of the class interests of his fellow merchants, manufacturers, and professionals. Against charges that they were responsible for the horrid living conditions that were producing so much sickness, death, and misery among the working class, the doctor asserted that these evils "result from *foreign and accidental causes*. A system, which promotes the advance of civilization and ... promises to maintain the peace of nations ... cannot be inconsistent with the happiness of the *great mass of people*."[68] To support these views, Kay adopted organic metaphors to imagine the city as both a natural system and a social body. The former allowed him to cast current medical belief in miasma and filth theories of disease causation in familiar terms for his middle-class readership. He used his intimate knowledge of central-city neighborhoods to advantage, painting a graphic picture of the horrors of the industrial slum. What made his narrative style so powerful was its mood of dark foreboding about these forbidden zones. He almost always portrayed them as breeding grounds of not only fatal infections but also violent convulsions.

In this sense, Kay's pamphlet sounded the alarm, arousing Mancunians to undertake the sanitary reforms necessary to cleanse the city and save the community. Only by the restoration of the city's proper circulation of clean water and pure air could the spread of disease from the poor to the rich—or worse, the spark of revolution—be prevented. Kay pointed to the condition of Ancoats as a good example of the worst environmental effects of the factory system on its workers. He appealed to the local authorities to cure the city by paving the streets, installing sewers, removing garbage, and enacting a building code with minimum standards for new houses.

At the same time, however, the metaphor of the social body gave Kay a way to shift blame from physical to moral causes and from the city builders to the victims themselves. The bottom line for Kay was their immoral behavior. He was especially vicious toward the Irish Catholics, whom he considered a degenerate race that acted like a malignant cancer corrupting the larger body of solid Lancashire stock. "The contagious example which the Irish have exhibited of barbarous habits and savage want of economy, united with the

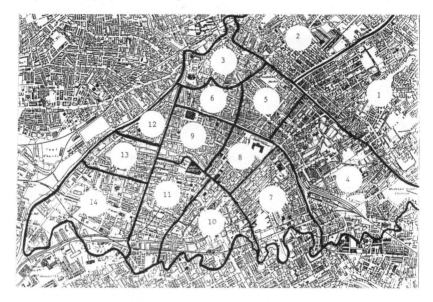

Figure 2.7. Kay map of police districts, 1832
Source: J[ames] P[hillips] Kay[-Shuttleworth], M.D., *The Moral and Physical Condition of the Working Classes Employed in the Cotton Manufacture in Manchester* (1831; reprint, Shannon: Irish University Press, 1971).

necessarily debasing consequences of uninterrupted toil, have demoralized the people," he claimed.

In effect, Kay condemned the immigrants for being forced by abject poverty and discrimination to live in the most awful possible locations. These shantytowns clung to the sloping banks of the Irwell River on the fringes of the area that was becoming the central business district. This notorious neighborhood of human misery and violent crime had been given the name Little Ireland. The report leaves little doubt that Kay ultimately believed that his designs for engineering the urban environment took a distant place behind more pressing demands for educational reform and moral uplift (see fig. 2.7 and table 2.2).[69]

Kay intended his report to enlist affluent Mancunians in the cause of reform, but it may have had just the opposite effect. His expert testimony on the horrors of the slums may have reinforced the impulse to escape from the city and its problems. In any case, a complete and extremely rapid suburban exodus began soon after the cholera epidemic. To be sure, impetus behind decisions to move, even by members of a relatively small, homogenous group, cannot be reduced to a single factor; on the contrary, those decisions involve

Table 2.2 Kay sanitation report, 1832

District number	Number of streets inspected	% Unpaved	% Uncleaned	Number of houses inspected	% Without privies
1 (Ancoats)	114	55.3	56.1	850	38.4
2	180	51.7	51.1	2,489	30.3
3	49	4.1	57.1	213	44.2
4	66	56.1	78.8	650	38.5
5 (CBD)	30	6.7	40.0	413	16.0
6 (CBD)	2	50.0	100.0	12	41.7
7	53	24.5	32.1	343	23.0
8 (CBD)	16	12.5	43.8	132	15.2
9 (CBD)	48	0.0	41.7	128	19.5
10	29	65.5	79.3	370	62.7
11 (rich residential)					
12	12	0.0	33.3	113	46.0
13	55	5.4	41.8	757	23.4
14	33	39.4	24.2	481	28.7
Totals	687			6,951	
Average		28.6	52.2		32.9

Source: J[ames] P[hillips] Kay[-Shuttleworth], M.D., *The Moral and Physical Condition of the Working Classes Employed in the Cotton Manufacture in Manchester* (1831; reprint, Shannon: Irish University Press, 1971), 30.

a complex mix of push and pull calculations. For example, the traditional sites of elite homes in the city center were becoming crowded out by inexorable pressures for more commercial space. Fashion too played a role as the "out-of-town villa" and the Georgian terrace styles of residential architecture came into vogue. Moreover, the continuing cotton boom meant steady environmental degradation of the urban core by the surrounding industrial zones of polluting factories and unhealthy slums. When all these factors are taken together, the flight of the well-to-do to the outskirts of town became irresistible—it bordered on a stampede.[70]

The social pinnacle of this reordered urban space was Victoria Park. In 1836, the development's prospectus announced its advantages, including ready access to the business district and "total freedom from manufacturers and from their disagreeable effects." An architect laid out the streets and grounds of the 180-acre site and supervised the construction of a complete system of waterlines, sewers, and drains. He and later residents insisted on macadam roads to sustain an illusion of rustic country charm, even though it was more costly to maintain them than to maintain stone pavement. In Victoria Park, located two miles south of the city's center, land use was restricted to detached housing that would be surrounded by walls and gates guarded by private police officers.

The original home owners formed an exclusive circle; the list of the home owners was a virtual who's who of Manchester Liberalism. These were the new men of the age of industry, the merchants, manufacturers, and professionals who were making fortunes in the cotton trade. Paradoxically, they were also outsiders in terms of religion and politics, which helped give them an extraordinary social cohesion as embodied in such institutions as the Cross Street Chapel and the Manchester Statistical Society. The most outspoken member of this group remained Richard Cobden, who used the incorporation campaign as an organizational stepping stone in mounting a national reform movement, the Anti–Corn Law League. With the triumph in 1838 of his parliamentary battle for municipal incorporation, several residents of Victoria Park would assume positions of official authority as councilors, aldermen, and mayors.[71]

Kay's report illuminates the downside of middle-class perceptions of the industrial city, but it sheds little light on the positive aspects of the project to foster a suburban ethos. To hold the well-to-do blameworthy for removing their families from the smoke, dirt, and miasma of the central city is misguided. Fishman castigates the residents of Victoria Park for building a "world of class privilege [in which] access to clean air and water must be bought and is available only to a few." In contrast, Mary Douglas underscores the constructive efforts of society to reorganize urban space in ways that embody its notions of purity, cleanliness, and moral order. The move to more pleasant, healthy habitations in the midst of pastoral settings, then, was motivated by both pressure to escape a dreadful environment and a desire to create an ideal one.[72]

An answer to the question of who was responsible for the city's landscapes of inequality requires an evaluation of the private and public decisions that produced and maintained residential districts whose conditions were below contemporary standards of human decency. In the case of Manchester, evidence of such policies based on class discrimination is not difficult to uncover. During the interval between Kay's investigation in 1832 and the publication of the travelers' accounts of the mid-1840s, the lines demarking slum and suburb hardened into sharply drawn neighborhood boundaries. A visitor from France, Léon Faucher, wrote:

> The town, strictly speaking ... is only inhabited by shopkeepers and operatives; the merchants and manufacturers have detached villas, situated in the midst of gardens and parks in the country. This mode of existence within the somewhat contracted horizon of the family circle, excludes social intercourse, and leads to a local absenteeism. And thus at the very moment when the engines are stopped, and the counting-houses are closed, everything which was the thought—the authority—the impulsive force—the moral order of this immense industrial combination, flies from the town, and disappears in an instant. The rich man spreads his couch amidst the beauties of the surrounding country, and abandons the town to the operatives, publicans, mendicants, thieves, and prostitutes, merely taking the precaution to leave behind him a police force, whose duty is to preserve some little of material order in this pell-mell of society.[73]

Engels went beyond merely accusing Manchester's Liberals of social and environmental injustice. He attempted to identify specific private practices and public policies that created and sustained the industrial slum. In the case of the housing market, he drew on personal experiences in the Ancoats District, where he watched house-building activity. Moreover, he exploited the insights he acquired because of his foreign observer's sensitivity to another country's peculiar institutional traditions. In England, he pointed out, ancient rules of land tenure had led to an urban system of leases that limited a developer's use of a property to twenty to thirty years, after which time the developer's improvements would be transferred to the property's owner.

He believed the cross purposes of landlords and rental agents were the original reason for the construction of jerry-built dwellings. He watched some of these being thrown up on the few remaining empty lots in the neighborhood. "Here the cottages have a clean and tidy appearance," he remarked, but it "is only a pretence, because after ten years it will have vanished." Engels projected that these superficial structures would have a maximum life span of forty years. He indicated support for his estimate by pointing to the buildings erected during the first factory boom at the turn of the century. "There are already many old and dilapidated houses in Ancoats, many of which will shortly be quite uninhabitable," he observed. "I cannot think of any more scandalous and demoralizing system of housing the workers than this."[74]

Discriminatory legislation reinforced patterns of spatial segregation to widen and deepen the divide between the slums and the suburbs. Inspired by Kay's report, the nation embarked on a public health crusade. In the 1840s, England started building systems of water management that would create technological networks for the cities equivalent to the human body's natural systems for circulation and cleansing. Promoted by Edwin Chadwick, the "Sanitary Idea" quickly became a shibboleth of middle-class urban reform during the Victorian Era. Chadwick's plans were comprehensive: from access to a water closet for every city dweller to the recycling of the resulting liquid waste as fertilizer on sewage farms. Manchester, however, stubbornly held out against mounting pressure from the national government to require indoor plumbing in new residential construction.

Like Kay, local authorities would continue to assert that the moral failings of the poor were the primary cause of the city's chronically high death rates. Until the 1890s, they would insist that some alternative form of dry conservancy—privies, pails, and scavengers—was better suited to the dissolute habits of the working classes. Chadwick's infrastructure of modern sanitation would produce only marginal improvements in public health, according to Dr. Richard Baron Howard, Kay's successor at the Ardwick and Ancoats Dispensary. In rebuttal to the Sanitary Idea, the physician confounded the behavioral with the environmental to propose that "The chief of the causes [of infectious disease] here alluded to are, all the depressing passions of the mind, imperfect nutrition, exposure to cold and moisture, arising from deficiency of clothing and fuel, or from the damp and dilapidated state of dwellings, the state of exhaustion and fatigue arising from too long continued toil, without adequate repose, neglect of personal cleanliness, and the languor and exhaustion consequent on intoxication."[75]

Manchester's Liberals would institutionalize moral environmentalism into a politics of exclusion and inequality. Town Hall set the pattern in the mid-1840s by offering modern urban services to the suburbs while denying them to residents living in Manchester's own industrial districts. Manchester swam against the political currents of the first great wave of Parliamentary enthusiasm for public health reform. "It became the central plank of Manchester's sanitary policy," a careful study by A. Wilson concludes, "that different forms of sanitation would be implemented in different parts of the city; the determining factor was the ruling elite's perception of the social stratification of the resident population." In the decade following the successful insurgency of the Nonconformists in 1838, the local government took full responsibility for water, sewerage, and solid waste services, giving local authorities virtually complete control of the environmental infrastructure of the city. Relatively early public investment in these utilities as well as gas lighting gave Manchester the reputation of a pioneer of municipal socialism.[76]

Closer inspection, however, reveals that municipal capitalism is a more fitting description of Town Hall's management of public services. Running the local government like a private business, the town council applied calculations of profitability as the litmus test in determining the scope and the quality of the sanitary technology supplied to the various districts of the central city and the surrounding suburbs. Manchester's dissenting insurgents had become rhetorical champions of democratic ideology in their battle for a municipal charter, but once admitted into the inner sanctum of the ruling elite, they quickly slammed the door behind them. Fewer than 20 percent of adult males met the minimum standards of wealth to qualify to vote, and this figure was much higher than the actual turnout for the noncontested, self-perpetuating elections.

Even within the city council, a political culture of hierarchy, authority, and privilege prevailed. Each of its all-powerful committees was ruled by a strong chairman; each operated as an autonomous business and did its work in virtual secrecy from the others. At the same time, an overarching, if unspoken, consensus among city officials directed policy making along a narrow path toward the goal of enhancing the power and wealth of the municipal corporation. Even the provision of services essential to public health, such as water supply and sewerage, were considered primarily in terms of their ability to make money for the Corporation and thereby reduce the tax bills of the property owners.[77]

A series of decisions to deny the working classes access to indoor plumbing in their homes represented the first steps in the institutionalization of a policy of environmental inequality under the reign of the Liberals. In 1842, the new municipal council was confronted with the daunting task of responding to the national sanitary commissioners who observed that environmental conditions in Manchester had deteriorated significantly since Kay's investigation. Dr. Howard confessed that his report had "created a very strong sensation at the time amongst the more wealthy portion of the inhabitants" but that "no very great permanent advantages resulted." For example, the public sector had added fewer than thirty-five miles of new sewers, leaving about half of the city's streets unimproved.

In a similar way, the Corporation had also ignored Kay's recommendations for better design and construction standards for residential districts. Howard admitted that "the practice of building houses at the backs of those fronting the streets, with only an extremely narrow passage intervening, and the doors of the former opening directly opposite the privies and uncovered cesspools of the latter, is still shamefully common." In the face of this local indifference, an outside enterprise headed by Chadwick, the Town Improvement Company, made an official proposal to take charge of the entire business of creating a sanitary city, from laying water lines to sweeping the streets. But having fought so long to gain power, Manchester Liberals had no intention of giving any of it away.[78]

Forced into action, the local authorities moved to capture the potential profits of public health reform for the Corporation. In 1845, the council began taking charge of scavenger services from the various individuals who had been privately contracting with the landlords for the removal of ashes and human wastes, or night soil. Statistics gathered from the tollgates leading out of the city showed that 42,000 cartloads of waste a year were being carried to the countryside, where they were sold to farmers for three shillings each. The councilors believed they could turn the total annual receipts of £6,300 into a rewarding financial asset. To help ensure the success of this business enterprise, they sponsored legislation in Parliament empowering the city to order building owners to supply privies and ash pits not only for new homes but for older ones as well. Field surveys by the city showed that one-third of the population of approximately 350,000 inhabitants had such limited access to privies that among this portion of the population an average of seventy people were forced to use each one. Over the next three years, the city issued 4,361 orders for improvements in facilities used by over 25,000 people living in existing houses and cellars.

Yet enforcement of the building code and even an upgrading of the department's services failed to make the venture profitable. In 1848–1849, for instance, the scavenger department's receipts amounted to £4,500, or just half of its expenses. Persistent losses suffered in the operation of the waste removal service only seemed to stiffen the resolve of the council members to make it pay, even at the tragic cost of excessively high infant mortality rates. Their single-minded determination to achieve the goal of profitability would also have tremendous repercussions on their parallel plan to take over the city waterworks.[79]

The council's 1852 decision to withhold access to indoor plumbing from the central city while extending it to the suburbs marked an irreversible turning point in the political formation of urban space. For the next thirty-five years, Manchester Liberals would enforce a policy of spatial segregation. But the local government's hand was forced on the issue of a woefully inadequate water supply when a challenge to the prerogatives of the Corporation came in the form of several private bills for franchise rights to bring more water to Manchester. To city officers, these offers posed a threat to an important potential source of both political power and revenue. In 1847, the officers launched a successful counteroffensive in the national legislature by proposing to buy out the existing utility company and to underwrite the construction of a large-scale reservoir project. The grand ambition of the engineering scheme to capture the rainfall of an eighteen-thousand-acre area of the Pennines was matched only by the enormous risks the scheme posed to the fiscal integrity of the municipal government.[80]

Fearing financial disaster, Manchester's Liberals gave higher priority to increasing the income of the Corporation than to fulfilling the Corporation's duty to protect the public health. In the early 1850s, local officials faced the alarming prospect that both of its new business ventures, the scavenger service and the waterworks, might turn into long-term liabilities instead of money-making assets. The reservoir project continued to absorb huge amounts of capital while delivering far less water than promised. The council believed it had found a face-saving remedy when it cleverly linked the financial futures of the two urban utilities together. They reasoned that the capital costs of the waterworks could be minimized if the dependence of the working classes on the outdoor privy could be maximized. A plan incorporating these trade-offs would produce additional benefits for the municipal treasury by causing major reductions in the need for costly sewers and drains, as well as for the sewage treatment facilities that might be required if the Corporation began discharging large volumes of pollution into the rivers.

To achieve their objectives, the councilors purposely set residential rates for the use of water closets and bathtubs at levels that most families living in the industrial districts simply could not afford. Although the service charges represented luxuries beyond the reach of the vast majority of these Mancunians, they were relatively minor burdens that fit comfortably within the domestic budgets of members of the middle classes. In 1855, the city began implementing its sanitation policy by extending water mains to Victoria Park and other affluent suburban enclaves on the south side of the city. The availability of an abundant supply of pure, soft rainwater to the homes of the elite facilitated the installation of a growing array of household technologies, modern conveniences that significantly widened the gap in the quality of daily life between the slums and the suburbs.[81]

In the end, the mass of working-class residents paid a disproportionate share for the million-pound public works project that they were mostly barred from using. A dual system of property taxes and user fees may have been ideally suited to securing underwriting at a reasonable rate of interest, but it meant that residents were forced to pay for services whether or not they received them. And both public officials and private landlords conspired to make access to indoor plumbing all but impossible to the vast majority of tenants who lived in modest rental units. While being forced to haul water from standpipes in the streets, they were subsidizing the cost of supplying the factories and mills approximately three-quarters of the total water supply.

In spite of mounting political pressure at home and in Parliament, Town Hall held steadfast to the fundamental proposition that the poor had only themselves to blame for their wretched condition. Its testimony on the causes of the slums recited the same script without deviation. In 1868, for example, the council explained that "the state of such districts arises, no doubt to a considerable extent, from the nature and character of the population, and from their filthy and dissolute habits, and also from the overcrowding of their dwellings. St. George's district is occupied almost exclusively by an Irish population; the houses are much overcrowded, and generally in a very dirty condition. Deansgate district is largely occupied by the criminal and vicious classes." Feeling secure behind the walls of their suburban sanctuaries, the business elite could afford to turn a deaf ear to the voices of protest, listening only to the shopocracy's never ending refrain calling for lower taxes.[82]

Conclusion: The Victorian City of Separate Spheres

In the fall of 1849, when Angus Reach arrived at the tail end of Manchester's time as an international attraction, he landed in the midst of its first open policy debate on the future of the urban environment. His intimate portraits of the industrial slum supply an important counterweight to the cold statistics on its physical and social conditions. These rich tableaux of life in the neighborhoods infuse their residents with agency, turning them from faceless victims into ordinary individuals with familiar concerns about family, work, and community. A review of his reports helps to make possible a preliminary assessment of the human costs involved in the metamorphosis of the industrial city into a landscape divided into segregated and unequal zones. Combining quantitative data and personal observations, Reach found not only reason for despair in the recent mortality rates, but also reason for optimism in the current experimental models of environmental improvement that held promise of slashing these ghastly figures.

The more the reporter observed, the more he came to appreciate that diversity of experience was the most distinctive trait of modern city life. He was struck in particular by the wide range of access to urban amenities and the ways in which these differences in the quality of daily life affected the residents' willingness to invest their individual and collective identities with a sense of place. Like other observers, he used a planetary metaphor to describe the outlines of the city's new spatial form as three concentric circles, with the inhabitants of each spinning in their own separate orbit. The inner core was a depopulated business district, and the suburban fringe was "a sort of universally-stretching West-end." What interested him most, however, was the rich mosaic of neighborhoods in the ring of industrial slums in between, which contained "the great mass of smoky, dingy, sweltering, and toiling Manchester."

Searching for a baseline of urban poverty, Reach discovered that some of the more recently built worker *quartiers* were decidedly better than the older ones. But he found none of Manchester's back streets any worse than those he had investigated in London and Glasgow. Moreover, each of the satellite mill towns he visited had their own aging districts like Ancoats, where "are situated some of the most squalid-looking streets, inhabited by swarms of the most squalid-looking people."[83]

If the working-class slum had become an all too common part of the Victorian city, Reach collected convincing evidence of the near heroic efforts of its inhabitants to overcome the shortcomings of their immediate surroundings. "Certainly the setting of the picture is ugly and grim enough," he explained. A "black, mean looking street, with a black unadorned mill rising over the houses, and a black chimney pouring out volumes of black smoke upon all—these do not form very picturesque accessories to the scene, but still you are glad to see that, amid all the grime and dinginess of the place, there is no lack of homely comforts, good health, and good spirits." On Saturday afternoons, for example, the workers set about cleaning their houses and neighborhoods after the factories stopped and the bosses fled in packed omnibuses to "the snug and airy dwellings of the suburbs." Children hauled water, women scoured, and the men helped with the heavy work, sometimes. Each house Reach visited displayed those little personal touches and beloved knickknacks that said "This is our home, our family."

People tried to make the best of it by forging community. They gathered in the streets and the pubs, watched their children play in front of the houses, and felt free to move about within local boundaries. The building of institutions, including churches, schools, libraries, and even botany clubs, also played a prominent part in this process. At the same time, Reach could not help noticing differences in people's attachment to place depending on the quality of the housing stock and the environmental amenities of the neighborhood. He compared Ancoats with Hulme, one of the newer working-class districts that had just been absorbed as a result of the municipal incorporation act (see fig. 2.6). Although residents of both received the same wages, the homes in Hulme were better furnished and maintained. "The secret," he believed, "is that they live in better built houses, and consequently take more pleasure and pride in their dwellings."[84]

For Reach, the medical mapping of mortality strongly reinforced impressionistic evidence of direct links between environmental surroundings, sense of identity, and attachment to place. He drew upon the surprisingly sophisticated study of Hulme that H. P. Holland had conducted in response to the 1842 national inquiry on the sanitary conditions of the cities. The township health inspector of Chorlton-upon-Medlock had created a statistical survey of this working-class estate with nine categories of environmental quality relating to housing stock and street improvements. Mortality rates were twice as high on the worst residential streets as on the best. After accounting for private-sector factors relating wealth to health, Holland still calculated a 25–30 percent gap in the death rate that could be attributed to the comparative lack of public infrastructure and services on the streets where poor people lived. Current researchers confirm that there was a six-to-seven-year difference in average life expectancy between the suburbs of Manchester and the city itself, which in 1841 had a depressingly low average life span of 25.3 years. "It is the . . . sharp deterioration and prolonged period of excessive mortality, 1830–1860," they reason, "which seems the most remarkable epidemiological feature." Encountering this chronic disease and misery, Reach had little choice except to echo the well-known refrain about Manchester's unenviable reputation of "pre-eminence in the statistics of death."[85]

The journalist ended his commentary on a note of cautious optimism. He was encouraged by various civic efforts to make practical demonstrations of urban environmental improvements. He had been impressed by a model lodging house in Ancoats, a decent housing estate in Hulme, and a mill-gate neighborhood in Hyde supplied with indoor water that was becoming a cleaner, more cheerful place to live. He was also hopeful about factory operatives striving against difficult odds to better their condition. However, while the future growth of the industrial city was full of possibilities, he could foresee no quick or easy solutions for the great majority of families who lived in areas "built upon a bad plan, or rather upon no plan at all, save perhaps, that promising a yearly return of shillings in the pound."[86]

For Reach, ultimate responsibility for the conditions of the working classes lay with the captains of industry who helped create the slums in the shadows of their cotton mills and warehouses. Only if they accepted a moral duty to reform the city could the paradox of progress be resolved with a favorable outcome of social and environmental justice. At mid-century the journalist considered himself less a chronicler of a dark age of urban anarchy than a witness of a dawning era of civic progress.

Across the Atlantic, Chicagoans shared similar hopes for their city's bright future as a beacon of progress and prosperity. A comparison of its origins to those of Manchester highlights the importance of the natural setting of a city in shaping both its economic prospects and its environmental problems. In Chicago as in Manchester, the regional ecology and its energy resources interacted with demography, technology, and social organization to create a new type of settlement pattern, the industrial city.

In contrast with the case of Manchester, the template of land use in Chicago was set during a period when the local economy was driven overwhelmingly by commercial activity: Chicago was the gateway between the two halves of a vast continent. And unlike the inheritors of the ancient site of Roman Mamucium, the town planners of the American Midwest enjoyed the advantage of virgin soil. These boosters believed they could stamp their ambition of erecting a profitable city on a landscape of natural abundance. The speculators who chose the swampy ground at the southern end of Lake Michigan as the up-and-coming place perfectly expressed this bold optimism in the official seal of their local government: "*Urbs in Horto*," the Garden City. To make their dream real, Chicagoans would have to find a way to lift their budding metropolis out of the mud.

CHAPTER THREE

Mudhole in the Prairie

Introduction: "The Garden City"

On the morning of Tuesday, 12 March 1849, Chicago seemed to be under surprise attack. Between nine and ten o'clock, the twenty thousand people of this frontier community were suddenly startled by a thundering noise that sounded like salvos of cannon fire coming from the southwest. The barrage of explosions signaled the beginning of a truly frightening assault on the town, but the enemy was a wall of water, not an army of invaders.

Only the boatmen on the Chicago River knew that the crackling blasts meant the ice was breaking up and heading their way. Big snowstorms giving way to a rapid warm-up and three days of heavy rain had already alerted them of potential peril, and the shallow waterway was already rising rapidly under the wharves. Still, even experienced sailors could not have anticipated the size and fury of the ice jam being pushed relentlessly forward by the force of the floodwaters behind. They were soon abandoning their boats and running for their lives as a wave of water and ship debris two stories high pushed all before it, smashing bridges, crushing canal boats, snapping hawsers, and lifting some of the biggest vessels completely out of the river.

By now the entire population was drawn to the riverfront by the terrible commotion. "The cries and shouts of the people," a reporter wrote, "the crash of the timber, the toppling over of vessel masts, the terror-stricken crowds of people assembled in the adjoining streets, were sights and sounds never to

Figure 3.1. Chicago harbor, 1849
Source: A. T. Andreas, *History of Chicago*, 3 vols. (1884–1886; reprint, New York: Arno, 1975), 1:200.

be forgotten by those who witnessed them." One boy was swept away with the Madison Street bridge as he watched the approaching ice jam, which crushed another child who also got too close. After demolishing the final bridge across Clark Street with a tremendous boom, the floating mass of ice and debris again became dangerously snarled at the elbow in the Main Branch at State Street. Seeing the unfrozen mouth of the river just beyond, several heroes emerged from a cheering crowd to axe free some of the largest ships, ending the immediate threat of further destruction. A bridge of smashed boats remained tangled together, forming the only means of getting back and forth across the river in the days that followed (see fig. 3.1).[1]

The story of this natural catastrophe and its multifaceted repercussions helps illustrate the environmental dilemmas confronting Chicagoans at a historic crossroads in their endeavor to become the central place, the gateway to the West. The strategic, albeit waterlogged, location of the would-be metropolis was both its greatest asset and worst liability. A year earlier, as the historian William Cronon has shown, city builders had completed the construction of the basic components of an external infrastructure for commercial trade and transportation. The achievement of this milestone announced that Chicago was open for business as a major transfer point, or entrepôt, between the two pieces of a vast continental empire. The inrush of Yankees and immigrants alike to the urban frontier would soon create a boomtown.

The flood, however, highlighted the glaring lack of an internal infrastructure of urban utilities and services. The promoters of this unlikely town site had made no public plans for draining excess surface water, removing human and animal wastes, or protecting drinking supplies from contamination. The costs of this neglect became painfully evident in the wake of the disaster. Two people had been killed and several had suffered serious injury. Property losses were put at $108,000, with damages to ships accounting for about 80 percent of the cost.[2]

More important, the much feared cholera epidemic that had swept across Europe in 1848 reached Chicago five weeks after the flood. It stayed on to become a permanent and undesirable immigrant that extracted ever-larger death tolls. In 1849, Chicago lost 678 souls to the ghastly intestinal disease that can kill within hours of the appearance of the first symptoms. About one out of every ten people contracted the infection that year, and a third of those succumbed to it. By 1854, the scourge was taking an average of fifteen lives a week. It accumulated a record 1,549 victims for that year, to say nothing of those lost to concurrent plagues of smallpox, scarlet fever, typhus, and typhoid. The death rate soared to astronomical levels, making the town the unhealthiest place in the United States. Chicago faced a crisis that threatened what had appeared to be a highly promising future.[3]

The original cause of the flood gave contemporaries an excellent opportunity to accurately assess the geographic scope of the environmental problems facing the city. They already knew from trudging through the mud a good part of the year that the center of the settlement was a peninsula of marshland only a couple feet higher than the surface of Lake Michigan on the east and of the Chicago River on the north and west. They also knew that spring thaws and thunderstorms often produced freshets, or sudden surges in the flow of the normally sluggish stream. In the past they had welcomed these seasonal events as a costless and natural way that the river was cleansed and its accumulation of filth purged into the lake. But what they could not have predicted was the freak conjunction in March 1849 of fast-melting snow and record rainfall that would cause a monumental ice jam on the Des Plaines River, ten miles southwest of the city (see figs. 3.2 and 3.3). Acting like a dam, the ice forced the floodwaters to spill eastward across a low-lying area called Mud Lake and into the western end of the South Branch of the Chicago River rather than following its normal course downstream in the other direction. The enormous wave of diverted water sharply raised the level of the stream and its top sheet of ice, which accounted for the artillery-like retorts as the ice was breaking up. The disaster taught the elementary lesson that any feasible plan for drainage and flood protection of the city would have to encompass a much larger area defined by the city's hydrology.[4]

Equally important, the tragic loss of life and property in the wake of the deluge confronted contemporaries with the disparity between the thriving

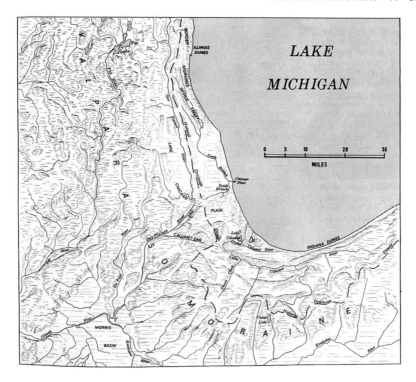

Figure 3.2. Topographical map of Chicago area, c. 1830
Source: Harold M. Mayer and Richard C. Wade, with the assistance of Glen E. Holt,
Chicago: Growth of a Metropolis (Chicago: University of Chicago Press, 1969), 7.

prosperity of the business realm and the abject poverty of the public sector.
Only two years earlier, Chicago's "triumph of privatism" had been institutionalized in a new municipal charter that divided the land into what Robin
Einhorn calls a "segmented system" of wards, elongated strips that handed
the property owners almost complete control over the timing, extent, and
cost of street and other infrastructure improvements (see figs. 3.4 and 3.5).
Local government was given few duties beyond acting as the property owners'
administrative agent.[5]

While it precluded the waste of taxpayers' dollars by corrupt politicians,
the segmented system left the public sector virtually without financial means
to respond to needs related to the common welfare, health, and safety of
the city. Delivering his inaugural address a few days after the flood, Mayor
James Woodward laid out an urgent agenda of public works projects: rebuild
the bridges, construct a "general system of sewers," preserve the lakefront,
equip the fire department, establish a professional police force, appoint a city

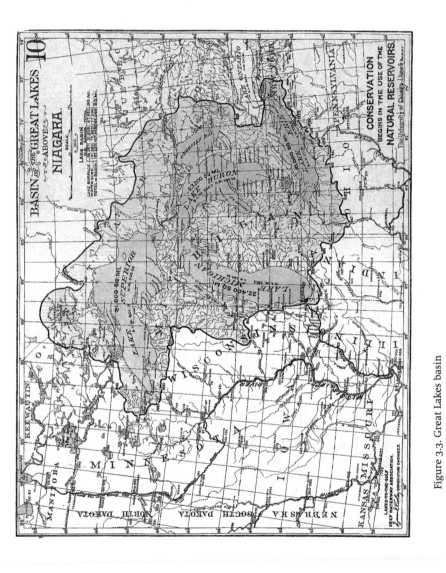

Figure 3.3. Great Lakes basin

Source: Lakes-to-the-Gulf Deep Waterway Association, *The Deep Waterway between the Great Lakes and the Gulf of Mexico, Development of the Deep Waterway in Relation to Conservation* (St. Louis, MO: Lakes-to-the-Gulf Deep Waterway Association, 1911).

Note: The basin is the shaded area in the figure.

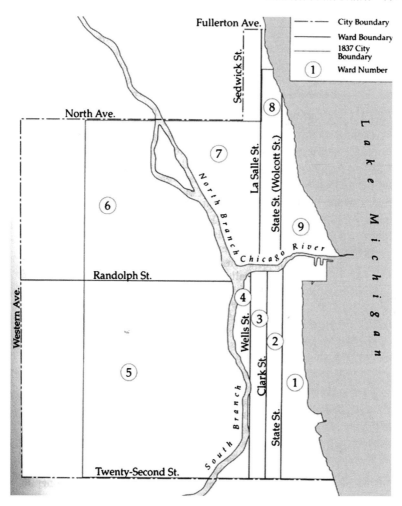

Figure 3.4. Chicago wards, 1847
Source: Robin Einhorn, *Property Rules: Political Economy in Chicago, 1833–1872* (Chicago: University of Chicago Press, 1991), 81.

physician, and organize a citywide cleanup in preparation for the anticipated arrival of cholera. Yet he confessed that few if any of these objectives could be achieved because of the "empty state of the Treasury." As his prescient testimony came to be translated into longer and longer lists of the sick and dying, the immediate emergency of public health triggered what became a permanent crisis of legitimacy.[6]

An examination of the environmental origins and political resolution of this formative era of Chicago history provides a useful case for comparison to

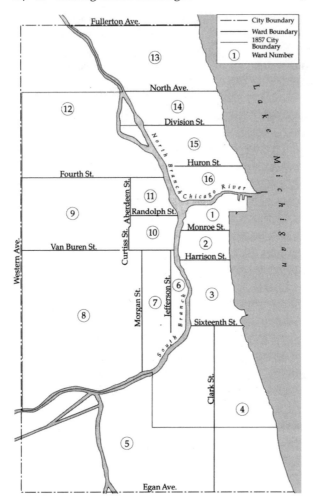

Figure 3.5. Chicago wards, 1863
Source: Robin Einhorn, *Property Rules: Political Economy in Chicago, 1833–1872* (Chicago: University of Chicago Press, 1991), 184.

Manchester. Between the plating of its first street grid in 1830 to the redrawing of its ward borders in 1863 along ethnic and class lines, Chicago followed traditional patterns of growth as a commercial city.

Public and private efforts to lift the settlement out of the mud occupy the first part of this chapter.[7] The second part then explores how conflicts over these city building projects contributed to the emergence of a distinctly urban political culture during the Civil War. With the triumph of the new partisan system of wards, a politics of growth would begin to widen the bifurcation of the boomtown into a riverfront corridor of working-class slums for immigrants and a lakefront preserve of middle-class suburbs for the native-born. As Chicago took on a more industrial cast, its land-use patterns began increasingly to resemble those produced by the exclusionary zoning in Manchester.

"Half Dry and Half Wet"

For the founders of Chicago, managing the land turned into the arduous task of gaining control of its watery ecology. In contrast to Lancashire's hilly terrain, the stark flatness of the countryside was the most striking characteristic of the midcontinent extending from central Ohio across the Mississippi Valley to the Rocky Mountains. As a German traveler remarked, Chicago's town site was located "in a country even more level than that around Berlin." While creating it was an incredibly fertile plain for agriculture, poor drainage on such flat surfaces kept a good portion of the Midwest's prairies partially submerged as wetlands. The region's other outstanding feature was the Great Lakes, appropriately named since they hold one fifth of the planet's supply of fresh surface water.

These two elements of nature came together at the mouth of the Chicago River to create one of the most advantageous sites for a commercial entrepôt in this vast expanse of space. The site had long been inhabited by Native Americans, who in 1673 showed the first Europeans in the area, Jacques Marquette and Louis Joliet, the canoe portage across Mud Lake. It was as close as the voyageurs would ever come to finding the fabled Northwest Passage: the water route down the Des Plaines, Illinois, and Mississippi rivers led ultimately to the Gulf of Mexico, not the Pacific Ocean. Yet the rise of the Atlantic slave and cotton trade during the following century would make the plantation South a much more lucrative market than Asia for the farm products of the Midwest. In the early 1800s, the ascendancy of St. Louis as the first urban center of the region reflected the key importance of the river highways in shaping the Midwest's initial settlement patterns, but with the 1825 opening of the Erie Canal linking New York City to Buffalo and the Great Lakes, the stage was set to turn an army outpost at the other end of this inland sea into a serious rival for the crown of great marketplace.[8]

The ways that Chicago's boosters achieved this strategic goal by the time of the outbreak of the Civil War is the subject of Cronon's masterful reinterpretation of nineteenth-century American history from an environmental perspective. Perhaps the most profound insight of *Nature's Metropolis* is that town and country were joined in dynamic bonds of interdependence; each created the other. Between the two stood the market, both as an abstract concept of production, consumption, and exchange and as a physical location where these transactions took place. For Cronon's purposes, the city can be viewed as a disembodied node in the flow of trade and Chicago can be treated as a case study of larger national processes. Acknowledging the limits of this approach, Cronon disclaims having much "to say about most of the classic topics of urban history: the growth of neighborhoods within the city, social conflicts among classes and ethnic groups, the actions of municipal authorities, even the environmental history of public services like sewage disposal or water supply."[9] These are the very topics that are taken up here to shed light on the city as an industrial ecology. In addition, I take into account pure water, clean air, and uncontaminated land as limited natural resources in spite of the difficulties in assigning comparable market values to them in terms of commodity prices.

In spite of its shortcomings, Cronon's seminal work establishes a useful chronology, delineating a series of stages in Chicago's ascent over St. Louis, Milwaukee, and other rivals as the capital of the midcontinent. He agrees with previous historians that the opening of the Erie Canal–Great Lakes route and the treaties removing the Indians from the area eight years later in 1833 signaled the end of the frontier phase of the community. A "city booster" stage came next, with the construction of the publicly financed Illinois and Michigan Canal acting as an economic pump primer to launch the settlement as an entrepôt city. Local entrepreneurs, led by William B. Ogden, funneled their money into similar projects to create a commercial infrastructure.

The consensus among historians is that 1848 marked the completion of the assembly of this essential technology of capitalism. Cronon's list of firsts that occurred in that year in the Chicago area include the belated start of traffic on the canal; the use of the telegraph, railroad, and locomotive; the completion of a toll road made of wood planks; the arrival of an oceangoing steamship; the establishment of the Chicago Board of Trade, the federal district court, and the stockyards; and the operation of a steam-powered grain elevator. During the 1860s, Cronon suggests, the city supplanted St. Louis as the central city of the region. The pivotal difference between the two places was that eastern investors had designated Chicago as the crossroads where all transportation lines from the East would terminate and all routes to the West would begin.[10]

Building upon the solid foundations of Cronon's study, then, my first goal is to flesh out the interplay between external markets and local developments, paying particular attention to the effects of the energy demands of a commercial economy on urban land-use patterns. Given the almost complete reliance on waterborne vessels instead of horse-drawn vehicles, it should come as no surprise that Chicago's riverfront largely defined the original layout of the would-be entrepôt. The advent of the steamboat and the completion of the Erie Canal radically changed the site's economic promise from that of a fur-trapping colony of fewer than one hundred civilians to that of an investment frontier. Five years later, in 1830, the needs of shipping merchants and land speculators went hand in hand in the production of the first plat of streets and subdivisions.

Actually, city planners had two maps drawn, both with the purpose of gaining public funding to transform the shallow, twisting stream into a su-perhighway of trade connecting the Atlantic Ocean to the Gulf of Mexico. The first was drawn to persuade the federal government to cut a channel through the sandbar blocking direct access to the safe haven of the river harbor. The second, which depicted an area covering about three hundred acres, was drawn to aid in the selling of town lots. The sales would underwrite the costs of a state-sponsored canal between Lake Michigan and the Illinois River (see fig. 3.6). In 1832, the U.S. Congress responded by appropriating twenty-five thousand dollars for the sandbar project, and the state canal commissioners followed four years later by starting work on the ninety-seven-mile-long water-way from Chicago to Ottawa/LaSalle. But frustration replaced hope only three years later. Neither project brought the expected quick payback of rising land values and trade receipts. Instead, a national depression drove the state of Illinois to the verge of bankruptcy, while the bubble of real estate speculation burst, plunging many investors over the brink into financial ruin.[11]

Both maps embodied planning ideals for a great emporium that com-pletely ignored the topography of the land as well as the haphazard siting of the existing buildings, and the boosters soon began expanding this rigid template of city lots to stretch over larger and larger pieces of the prairie (see fig. 3.7). "None of this resembled the real Chicago!" local historian Perry Duis exclaims. In the case of the street grid, commercial needs for uniform property lines and straight transportation routes meant overlooking the idiosyncrasies of a swampy terrain. After the inauguration of local govern-ment in 1833, township authorities required that the original homesteads be moved out of the way or torn down. They also blithely designated virtually bottomless quagmires as major thoroughfares. More serious problems arose when planners simply drew a direct line through the sandbar at the mouth of the river without first taking into consideration the ecological relation-ship between the lake and the river. Members of the Army Corps of Engineers who were in charge of the project were slow to learn the lesson that they had about as much chance of success in pursing such an approach as the child who tries to build a sand castle at the water's edge on the beach.[12]

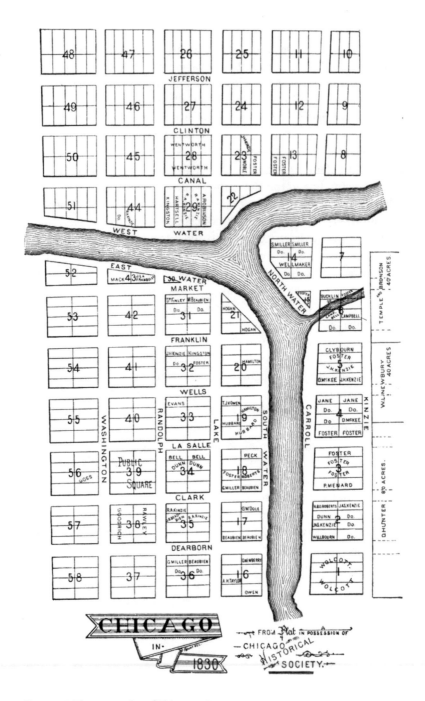

Figure 3.6. Thompson plat of Chicago, 1830
Source: A. T. Andreas, *History of Chicago*, 3 vols. (1884–1886; reprint, New York: Arno, 1975), 1:112.

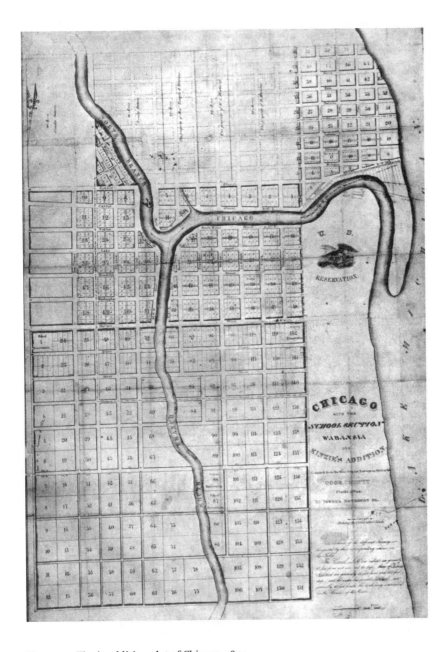

Figure 3.7. Kinzie addition plat of Chicago, 1834
Source: Kinzie addition plat, 1834, as reprinted in Harold M. Mayer and Richard C. Wade, with the assistance of Glen E. Holt, *Chicago: Growth of a Metropolis* (Chicago: University of Chicago Press, 1969), 21.

Closer examination of what the engineers thought would be a simple job of digging a ditch through the sandbar exposes the intricate complexities of the environmental dynamics of land, water, and climate coming together at the site of Chicago. The final sharp bend of the river to the south made the ship captain's job of navigating into the harbor a difficult, time-consuming maneuver. In the winter of 1821–1822, the soldiers from Fort Dearborn had been put to work cutting a channel about 450 feet long through the sandbar and reinforcing the channel with wooden piers. Spring freshets had helped carve a new mouth for the river, but by the end of the year, that mouth had clogged up and the waters again flowed southward into the lake.

Armed with funds for the construction project a decade later, the engineers of the corps followed the same plan and got the same results. In July 1834, a hundred-ton schooner, the *Illinois*, successfully navigated the channel to become the first lake vessel to gain entrance to the harbor. Silting, however, again closed the harbor by the end of the season. The pattern of deposits indicated that the prevailing shoreline currents ran from north to south. Consequently, sedimentation formed first at the north tip of the pier and eventually recreated the shape of the sandbar itself. These currents seemed especially powerful during the winter months, when defensive countermeasures such as dredging were out of the question. As the sandbar choked off the direct passage, ship captains still had to come around from the south to avoid foundering on new underwater obstructions.

These setbacks did not seem to deter the army officers in charge of the public works project in the least. Still vainly hoping that the river's natural currents would be strong enough to keep the new mouth open, they simply extended the artificial channel deeper and deeper into the lake. By the end of the 1830s, slightly over two hundred thousand dollars had been spent, and there was precious little to show for it except a rotting set of piers that now protruded 1,260 feet into the lake. Some of the engineers attempted to adapt to the lake currents by offering alternative plans: perhaps piers could be angled to the northeast or the river could be forced into a narrow channel in order to speed up its lethargic currents. Policy makers in Washington, however, would support little more than the holding action of dredging, which again proved a largely futile exercise of spending good money after bad.[13]

The civil engineer's interactions with the river and the lake and with the climatic conditions at the entrance to the harbor underscored three lessons crucial to the future prospects of Chicago as the location for a regional center of trade. First, the relentless currents of Lake Michigan along the shoreline laid to rest the fallacy that the lake was simply a huge container of still, fresh water. Covering over twenty-two thousand square miles and with an average depth of 280 feet, it was big enough to produce an internal thermodynamics of stratification between warm and cold, and between shallow and deep layers of water. Also, seasonal heating and cooling contributed to the stirring of the oblong-shaped body of water in a counterclockwise direction. Second, the unintended consequences of constructing the pier extensions focused the attention of city boosters on the serious costs to be paid for ignoring the environmental context of a project. An accretion of land would build up on the north side of the pier, but the structure failed to stop new sandbars from forming at the opening to the river. On the south side of this barrier to the lake's currents, eddies ate away at the shoreline, including federal land ceded to the city as a public park. The problem only grew worse with each extension of the artificial channel farther into the lake. By 1850, twenty of the park's thirty-five acres had already disappeared under the water, along with pieces of the beachfront promenade Michigan Avenue.

And third, the rapid clogging of the new mouth of the Chicago River made clear that it had no substantial source of supply other than surface runoff. The tidal-like oscillations of the lake's water level accounted for most of the observed flow of the river. The force of the wind and the fluctuation of barometric pressure could push the lake's water level up on one side as much as two feet while lowering it a similar amount on the other. Long-term and seasonal cycles also played roles in lifting and lowering lake levels (see fig. 3.8). When they went up at the Chicago end, the water in the river appeared to reverse course and move upstream. In a like manner, the river's water emptied back into Lake Michigan when the levels went down.

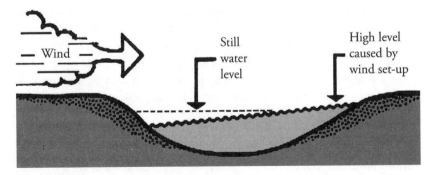

Figure 3.8. Illustration of lake levels
Source: U.S. Environmental Protection Agency, Great Lakes National Program Office, *Great Lakes Atlas*, 3rd ed. (Washington, DC: U.S. Environmental Protection Agency, Great Lakes National Program Office, 1999).

By watching the harbor entrance, would-be city builders learned that any plans for establishing an urban settlement along the banks of the Chicago River would need to take into account its environmental interactions with the lake beyond. In the case of the erosion of the lakefront, property owners and common people alike paid a high price for not heeding the warning signals that this balance of nature had been upset. For over a decade, attempts to build a breakwater ended in costly disappointment. As in the case of the harbor project, engineering and financial constraints hamstrung efforts during the 1840s to meet the challenges presented by the lake's complicated dynamics.

Property owners along the shoreline demanded protection but refused to pay for it. After years of wrangling with them in the courts, in 1852 City Hall accepted the offer of the Illinois Central Railroad Company to complete the breakwater project at its own expense. In exchange, the city council granted the railroad a highly advantageous right-of-way on submerged land all the way up to the old fort and sandbar, which became the location of its terminal. The affected landowners as well as anyone using the public parks now would have to look across railroad tracks erected on ugly pilings to see the beautiful, albeit no longer peaceful, vistas of the lake. Chicagoans paid a heavy price in the environmental degradation of the quality of life.[14]

The rivers had their own secrets to tell that were equally essential to the success of the site not only as an investment frontier but also as a place to make a home for the shiploads of newcomers arriving from the East. The almost numbing monotony of the prairie left surveyors with few visual cues to identify the topography of the terrain. The difficulty of figuring out how to drain soggy land without knowing the angle and pitch of its slope was underscored by one of the most astute travelers to the city, John Lewis Peyton. Coming the year before the great flood of 1849, this son of a prominent Virginia family still envisioned the Chicago River as the centerpiece of the settlement. "The city," he explained, "is situated on both sides of the Chicago River, a sluggish, slimy stream, too lazy to clean itself, and on both sides of its north and south branches, upon a level piece of ground, half dry and half wet, resembling a salt marsh."

The leading citizen, William Ogden, invited Peyton to dine with him and other members of the social elite, including U.S. Senator Stephen Douglas. Peyton recounted that the men's conversation turned to the related subjects of land values and drainage problems. The very next morning, he joined an excursion to look over some potentially lucrative property. Douglas was particularly eager to get his opinion about a large parcel of wetland about twelve miles south of town in the vicinity of Lake Calumet. The prairie vertigo of a featureless landscape made the parcel's future worth problematic. The visitor recalled:

Here we are upon a frozen lake or swamp, with alternative ridges of sand, this was the section to which he referred. It was not supposed possible to drain this swamp, and consequently the land was considered valueless. We spent the residue of the day making our *reconnaissance*, and ascertained that while, apparently, a dead level and a hopeless swamp, it was in reality an inclined plain, with its lower section, on the sandy bluffs of Lake Michigan, susceptible, at an inconsiderable cost comparatively, of being thoroughly drained.... The next morning Judge Douglas informed me of his purpose to purchase a large portion of this apparent waste.[15]

Like the seeming paradox that a ridge of sand dunes could be a low point, the hydraulics of the area's system of rivers offered important evidence about the lay of the land.

The dynamics of the city's watercourses revealed insights about Chicago's location that were a final key to unlock environmental knowledge essential to erecting upon this improbable topography a city that was not only profitable, but also livable. Among the first facts nonindigenous explorers learned was that less than twelve miles west of the lake the normal direction of the flow of water was toward the Mississippi River. Although the conclusion was counterintuitive, the traditional canoe route suggested that Lake Michigan was the high point, contained by a narrow lip of sand dunes and soil before the land fell away toward the southwest. In the late 1820s, the surveyors of the canal route established that after crossing the bowl-like depression of Mud Lake, the land rose to a second summit only twelve feet above the level of the lake, forming a midcontinental hydraulic divide. The land sloped so gently to the west of the divide that water flowed downstream for thirty miles to Lockport before again matching the elevation of Chicago. Then more dramatic drops in the watercourse began: it descended 77 feet to Joliet and a total of 147 feet at Ottawa/LaSalle before again leveling off for the final 225-mile journey and 30-foot decline to the mouth of the Illinois River (see fig. 3.9).

This regional setting told the planners of the great emporium of trade at Chicago that developing the use of the land would mean for the most part managing the flow of the water. The flood of 1849, then, was less a surprise

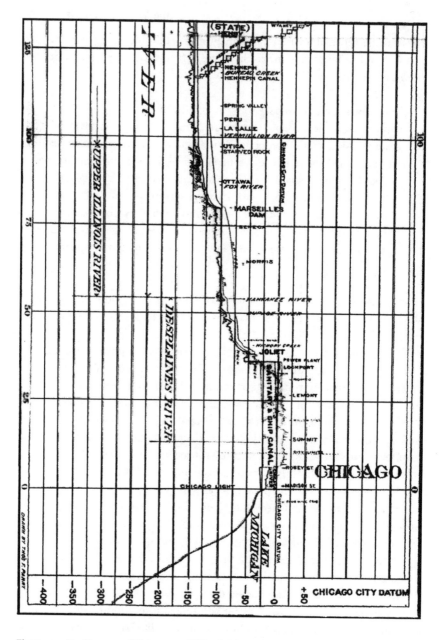

Figure 3.9. Profile map of Chicago and Illinois River valleys

Source: Lakes-to-the-Gulf Deep Waterway Association, *The Deep Waterway between the Great Lakes and the Gulf of Mexico, Development of the Deep Waterway in Relation to Conservation* (St. Louis, MO: Lakes-to-the-Gulf Deep Waterway Association, 1911).

than it was yet another reminder of the high cost of paying inadequate attention to the community's collective need for environmental control.[16]

A City upon a Marsh

In the first years of the colonies that became the United States, John Winthrop dreamed and prophesied about a holy "city upon a hill." Two centuries later, the plans of the American boosters of Chicago were literally and figurative more down-to-earth. If they had little appreciation of the water flowing around them, they were all too aware that the ground beneath their feet kept giving way. Apocryphal stories of whole rigs—wagons, teams, and drivers—vanishing in bottomless pits of mud became a stock part of local lore that historians have faithfully repeated ever since. By the late 1830s, however, such frontier bravado was wearing thin; it was becoming subject to its own satire. "Our streets are becoming respectable," a newspaper writer taunted during the annual spring rains, "no instances of horses and oxen being lost entirely during the past day or two." For businesspeople envisioning the city as the major transfer point between the East and the West, its marshy topography was no laughing matter.[17]

On the contrary, easing overland movement posed a challenge of equal importance and difficulty to that which the planners faced when trying to facilitate maritime shipping. The necessity of transporting heavily laden wagons across wetlands had always restricted trade to the seasons when the unpaved roads were hard enough for the draft animals to get in and out of town. After the onrush of people in search of opportunity began in 1833, the formidable problems of imposing a Cartesian grid on the site of Chicago became impossible to ignore. Lifting the city out of the mud became essential for residents living within its borders as well for customers coming from beyond them. As the population soared into the thousands, the demand for paved streets and sidewalks became universal (see fig. 3.10).

The question of who would pay for these improvements was almost as vexing as that of how to build them. During the ensuing public debate, the two problems soon became joined as leaders struggled to keep costs to a minimum while enhancing the amenities of urban life to the maximum. In 1848, the answers endorsed by the community were institutionalized in the segmented system of municipal government. But only a year later, the flood and the plagues that followed would start a new round of strident controversy about a solution that privatized the public sector while deadly diseases ravaged the community.

The first significant battle, over wharfing privileges on the river, was emblematic of the political tensions embedded in the effort to reshape the land

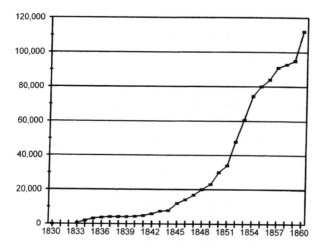

Figure 3.10. Population of Chicago, 1830–1860
Source: Data from U.S. Bureau of the Census.

to the needs of a commercial entrepôt. For the canoes of the fur trappers, the soft, sloping embankments of the waterway were perfect, but for the ever-larger lake vessels, the embankments were a barrier to trade. Moving passengers and cargo was almost as costly inside the harbor as offshore, where they had to be shuttled back and forth on flat-bottomed rafts. The deep hulls of the lake schooners and steamships forced town planners to abandon their original scheme of an open river levee in favor of new designs for a harbor resembling a seaport.

The river had to be dredged to a depth of at least ten feet and piers built to permit direct, efficient transfers between land and water. Anglo-American law had long regarded the use of shipping docks and marketplaces as special privileges subject to public regulation and taxation. In 1835, this traditional understanding found expression in a town charter that empowered the trustees to collect fees for the use of the wharves or for the leasing of them at auction, giving preference to adjoining landowners. Led by John Kinzie and other insiders, the trustees offered these property holders the rights to the "water lots" for a maximum of 999 years in exchange for a one-time payment set at minimum rates on a front-footage basis. They further sweetened the deal by pledging the resources of the local government to pay for the dredging, virtually guaranteeing a windfall for the leaseholders.

Supporters claimed that the plan would open up the harbor for development while critics complained that it would choke off opportunity for everyone except the privileged few. Naming the insiders, one of the daily newspapers identified pioneers Kinzie, Gurdon Hubbard, and others who held land in the Kinzie Addition fronting the north side of the river closest to the lake. Sounding the antimonopoly alarm, the local opposition soon found downstate allies who helped pass new legislation, taking jurisdiction away from the town trustees and giving it to the canal commissioners. This policy reversal predictably generated a tangle of lawsuits.

As long as the contest remained deadlocked in the courts, few investors were willing to come forward to bid on the large number of unsold and disputed leases. Moreover, the depression of 1837 halted both private payments and public works to improve the river. In the meantime, the insiders gained a head start in establishing their docks and warehouses. After the return of prosperity in the mid-1840s, pressure to settle the matter finally led the state legislature to surrender to the prior rights vested in the city and its leaseholders, including Kinzie. This fiasco of public policy had long-term negative effects on the commercial development of the waterfront. As late as 1854, for example, dockage facilities remained restricted to less than one-sixth of the forty-two miles of river frontage within municipal boundaries.[18]

Like the harbor plan, the impetus for the construction of better streets and sidewalks came from the canal project, which accounted not only for the initial wave of real estate speculators and job seekers, but also for the early patterns of land use. In sharp contrast to the site of Manchester, that of Chicago belonged first to the national government, which in turn gave it to the State of Illinois, which would finance the construction of the water highway. In drawing a template of urban space, the canal commissioners followed the federal practice of laying out a checkerboard pattern of alternating public and private blocks. In addition, they set aside generous tracts for civic amenities such as schools, churches, parks, and squares. Wide streets and narrow alleys complemented the division of the land into public and private space. In 1833, the time came to begin making these planning ideals real as planners anticipated that the state agency would soon call for construction contracts and workers to fulfill them.

The public works project opened the floodgates of emigration to the Midwest, and people poured into the city and the surrounding area of prime farmland. "The cry is still they come," a local daily proclaimed in June 1835, "Strangers to the amount of some hundreds fill our public houses and streets; our wharves are covered with men, women, and children, just landed from vessels. . . . Some build tents upon the spot where they are landed from the boat in the middle of our streets, then raise them and move on. Cook County, which two years ago exhibited a few scattered dwellings along the groves or by the streams, is now rife with thriving settlements; and some smart villages have arisen, too, as by enchantment." The once-empty town lots with a few hundred pioneers became crowded with twenty thousand inhabitants by the time the canal finally opened in April 1848, and the steady deterioration of environmental quality made Chicago anything but a place of enchantment.[19]

What had served well enough for a small colony around a fort quickly became a place with too many feet and hooves, carts and wagons. The marshland at Chicago was unusually wet because a floor of impermeable clay lay just underneath its thin layer of sandy soils. Such a delicate ecosystem had very little capacity to act as a natural sponge. It soon became saturated and even submerged when it rained. The absence of trees on the peninsula south of the fork of the Main Branch of the river was an unmistakable indicator of especially low-lying wet land. In comparison, tree coverage was fairly widespread on the north side of the fork, while substantial groves of oak, poplar, and ash still bordered the river on the west. The clustering of the pioneer dwellings in the north and west was another sign that the south division was particularly prone to flooding.[20]

Nonetheless, the least environmentally suitable location became the most commercially desirable one because most overland trade initially entered this part of town. The entire flow of traffic from the east had to go around the bottom of the lake and come up the shoreline to reach Chicago. Before 1833, moreover, the peopling of Illinois and Indiana from the south meant that most farms with surpluses to sell had been established below the river in an arc stretching to the southwest. Like the voyageurs, the travelers and teamsters followed trails marked out long before by the Indians, and once they arrived at the settlement, the river acted as a barrier to the northern and western divisions of the city. A census taken in conjunction with the incorporation of Chicago as a city in 1837 shows that nearly 60 percent of the 4,135 residents now lived in the division with the lowest land. That many people, to say nothing of their horses and farm animals, soon churned the fragile ground into a foul-smelling quagmire of mud, urine, manure, and trash. The legendary posters stuck in this muck by merchants warning customers to avoid "The Shortest Road to China" and cautioning "No Bottom Here" reflected a frustrated sense of urban sarcasm more than an easygoing spirit of frontier humor.[21]

The first strategy for erecting a city upon a marsh involved a simultaneous effort to raise buildings, sidewalks, and streets just above its flood-prone surface. The basic building materials readily available in the immediate vicinity—clay bricks, limestone, and lumber—were commonly employed in all three types of projects. Bricks were preferred for substantial residential and commercial buildings in cold northern climates, but they were more expensive than wood. On Chicago's soft ground, construction costs for brick buildings soared to luxury levels because solid foundations were required to support the great weight of the bricks. Some builders began using fill to raise the grade before laying the foundation, though flooding still made basements and cellars impractical. The small, heavy bricks were useless for roadways because they would sink and eventually disappear under the soggy soil. After digging through the soft layers of clay, Chicagoans often found limestone, which was also relatively easy to excavate and shape. It furnished architects with strong as well as beautiful building blocks with which to distinguish especially large and impressive edifices, such as grand hotels, church towers, halls of government, and chambers of commerce. Limestone was not useful for building roadways, however. Like brick, it would sink and disappear into the soggy ground.[22]

What wood lacked in strength and durability it more than made up for in low cost, so it became the most frequently used construction material. Some of the first houses were built on spiles, or large stakes that lifted floors off the ground. In 1832, carpenters adapted these stand-alone foundations to invent a new way of using lumber studs to build the walls, creating what became known as the balloon frame. Up the buildings went, fast and cheap. These comparatively lightweight structures had another key advantage in an investment frontier where property titles frequently changed hands and values fluctuated wildly. The buildings could be jacked up, put on wheels, and rolled to an entirely different location, creating a minor industry and giving new meaning to the concept of house moving.

In the next year alone, workers hammered together more than 150 houses and twenty shops using the new balloon-frame technique. Typical was the store put up by Eli B. Williams, who arrived that spring with his family from Connecticut. Trees cut down along the banks of the North Branch of the Chicago River furnished the framing boards, the flooring came from a new sawmill in suburban Naperville, and the outside sheathing of poplar shingles had been shipped across the lake from St. Joseph, Michigan. Soon local supplies were exhausted, but Lake Michigan's coastline, hundreds of miles long, and its broader watersheds to the north opened access to a cornucopia of timber, turning Chicago into the greatest lumber market in the world.[23] (See fig. 3.11.)

Getting people's feet out of the muck served the interests of merchants as well as pedestrians. Tradespeople depended on the space in front of shop doors to display their goods and to post advertisements for all who happened to pass by. Wooden planks were a cheap material with which to build sidewalks, but they proved of dubious value as street paving when laid like

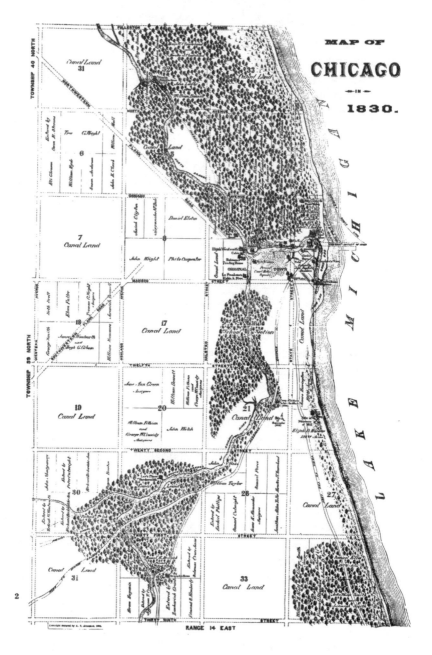

Figure 3.11. Natural timber of Chicago, 1830

Source: A. T. Andreas, *History of Chicago*, 3 vols. (1884–1886; reprint, New York: Arno, 1975), 1:112–13.

floorboards on top of muddy ground. The simple frame design of wooden spiles, studs, and planks was more than adequate to support foot traffic, but it could not be simply copied to the needs of roadways that had to bear the much heavier loads of wagons and their teams. In 1834, a year after his arrival, Williams spearheaded the first street improvement project, digging drainage ditches on each side of Clark Street, the main route to the south. Elected president of the town trustees, he had to borrow sixty dollars on his own credit to make a loan to an empty public treasury.[24]

Over the next several years, wooden pavements evolved from single boards laid across treacherous puddles to toll roads made of sidewalk-like planking that stretched across the prairie. In the year before the transportation revolution of 1848, about seventy thousand farm wagons made the trip into the city, spurring investment in the privately operated highways. To accommodate this influx of trade, the city council approved the petition of the shopkeepers along the main commercial strip, Lake Street, to pave it using the same construction methods.

Between 1847 and 1851, merchants spent at least $31,000 putting down several miles of planking in the town center. They didn't get much for their money because the heavy traffic soon dislodged some of the boards, which were becoming waterlogged and buried under new accretions of mud and manure in any case. "The streets of Chicago," an observer wrote, "were covered with planks, beneath which lay an untold depth of black mud, jets of which were thrown up as wagons passed." The failure of these experiments with low-cost, wooden streets a few inches above a soft, wet surface pointed Chicagoans back to the drawing board for a better strategy of building a city upon a marsh. The great flood hammered home the point that they would have to design a more effective way of draining such a low-lying piece of land.[25]

The destruction of the bridges by the natural disaster of 1849 also helped the boosters to accept that systematic plans would have to replace makeshift approaches to environmental control. Efforts to link the three divisions of the city together highlighted the tensions inherent in the thriving boomtown between a frontier spirit of volunteerism and more commercial calculation of self-interest. The dilemmas of equity contained in the question of who should pay for the bridges were exacerbated all the more in Chicago by the conflicts that were bound to arise between the people trying to get across the river and the boat pilots determined to keep their vessels moving along it.

In terms of costs and benefits, there was little dispute that landowners profited most from street and sidewalk improvements in front of their properties, although everyone else also obviously enjoyed a gain in comfort and ease of travel. Payment for this kind of linear urban infrastructure could be accordingly apportioned, or segmented, on a fair basis. Various formulas for levying these special assessments became institutionalized in law, such as the rules governing taxation by the front footage of adjoining lots and the principles underlying calculation of the percentage owed by public funds.[26]

But a segmented system of payment for city building was problematic in the case of widely shared public utilities such as bridges, lakefront breakwaters, and large-scale drainage projects. The battle over the Dearborn Street bridge illustrates the limits of the privatization of essential urban infrastructure. In 1834, town trustees constructed this first span over the Main Branch of the Chicago River to replace the unreliable ferry service. The wooden drawbridge was of a simple design, with two thirty-foot leaves that were opened by men pulling on iron chains. Its surface planking immediately began to deteriorate from the flow of heavily laden farm wagons from the south to the warehouses and docks on the north.

Without repair funds, local authorities were forced to make do as best they could to keep the passageway open. Five years later, the rickety bridge's condition had become so precarious that the aldermen ordered the structure demolished. Resentful of the North Siders' monopolization of the wharfing privileges, the South Siders awoke early to tear the bridge down and stayed late at the ensuing council meetings to oppose the construction of a new one. The controversy remained unresolved for a year until Ogden offered to loan the city most of the three thousand dollars needed for a low-cost replacement at Clark Street. Similar ad hoc arrangements of public money and private subscription financed other cheap bridges to connect the West Side to the south and north districts.[27]

The crisis of rebuilding after these primitive structures were swept away in 1849 reveals the beginnings of a swing in public works policy toward placing chief responsibility for environmental control in the hands of City Hall, not individual property holders. The voices demanding immediate action to reestablish passage between the three divisions also expose rising expectations for the minimum standards of urban life. Forced in the short run to revert back to riding ferries, an angry newspaper editor expressed the outrage of a community no longer willing to tolerate the indignities suffered aboard such flimsy conveyances:

> Yesterday the confusion and disorder at the ferry was disgraceful. The ferry boats for teams at Dearborn Street not being running, the rush at Clark Street was immense and it was really surprising that some accident did not result. Ladies have but very little chance in the melee

that ensues every time the boat lands; it is as much as a full grown man wants to do to elbow his way through the crowd. The boat is not large enough, to say nothing of its being a crazy, leaky concern.

Although Robin Einhorn argues that the outcome of the debate over paying for the new bridges represents a triumph of privatism, a more balanced interpretation tips the scale in the opposite direction. Mayor Woodward not only seized the initiative in formulating plans, he also held onto this position of leadership to advance the general welfare of the community. He effectively used City Hall's final authority over the location of the bridges to extort a one-third contribution from the businesspeople whose businesses lined the favored streets. If they refused, the mayor threatened to place these central arteries of trade on parallel streets where rival groups were willing to make the less-than-voluntary subscriptions. In June, a new bridge across Madison Street opened, followed two weeks later by one at Clark Street. In this sense, Woodward's power to impose the largest burden of expense on the general tax fund was a victory for the public sector.[28]

In either case, the advances Chicagoans made in gaining control over their environment were modest, especially in comparison to the long strides they were taking toward winning the urban crown of the midcontinent. Before 1849, the boosters focused their efforts and investments on constructing the basic technologies of an entrepôt city, leaving relatively little left to meet the needs of a frontier settlement undergoing mushroomlike growth. They were remarkably successful in channeling public and private investment into turning a flood-prone marshland into the great national pivot point of trade and transportation between the East and the West. Perhaps their greatest achievement was convincing so many others to believe in their vision of Chicago's promise, setting off a human wave of emigration to this strategic location.

In contrast, they were ill prepared to cope with the site's complex hydraulics of lake, river, and climate, which played such a crucial role in shaping the condition of its land. Initial hopes of simply paving over the wet ground ended for the most part in dirty shoes and annoying disappointment. And like the harbor project that caused lakefront erosion, the plank sidewalks had serious unintended consequences. The areas under the sidewalks, a convenient receptacle for wastes of all kinds, became infested with hordes of rats that virtually ruled the streets during the night. Conditions during the day were not much better. One pioneer recalled that "it was supposed that the sewage would settle in the gutters and be carried off, but the experiment was a disastrous failure, for the stench at once became intolerable."

These makeshift approaches to city building did not lock the urban infrastructure onto a set path of technological development. The low cost of wood and its high rate of deterioration from rotting in the mud ironically had the long-term benefit of keeping options open on the future direction of public works policy. After 1849, successive crises of damaging floods and deadly epidemics would force the community to refocus attention on drawing new plans for bringing the quality of the environment up to minimum standards of modern urban life.[29]

Venice of the West

In 1848, the transportation revolution began to remake Chicago. In only four years, it engendered completely new patterns of growth that overrode the original social and economic configurations of land use among its three divisions. A direct rail link to New York City was established in 1852, reducing a journey that used to take thirty days to a mere thirty-six hours. As its full effects kicked in, it boosted the influx of people and the expansion of trade to truly astonishing levels.

During 1853 alone, the thirty-nine thousand already in Chicago became sixty-one thousand. Overnight it came to be that the majority of Chicagoans were foreign-born. And over the next four years, these German and Irish immigrants would help erect ten thousand buildings, most of them balloon-frame cottages to house their families. By then, 120 trains were arriving every day, disgorging even more passengers and goods at the various depots strung along the river. New neighborhoods sprang up on the South Side and West Side, sprawling outward from the center. The river corridors too started taking on a new look as local manufacturers set up business on the waterfront among the shipping wharves and rail stations.[30]

Energy use in the budding city began to undergo a related revolution. A soaring rate of consumption stamped an indelible imprint on the environment. Consider that a lake steamer consumed six hundred to seven hundred cords of wood in a single round trip between Chicago and Buffalo. And it could make twelve to thirteen of these journeys during the seven-month season of navigation on the Great Lakes, consuming the equivalent of 234 acres of forest (and the work of forty lumberjacks) in an average season. To sustain an average of four steamship arrivals per day in 1845, an area covering nearly twenty-five square miles had to be cut clear of its timber. In comparison, a typical locomotive burned two cords a day. In the mid-1850s, the Illinois Central Railroad needed only three thousand cords a month, or about one hundred acres of woodland, to keep its trains running in the state.[31]

To meet the fast-rising demand for more power, heat, and light, Chicagoans, like their counterparts in Manchester, relied on the most readily available natural resources within their regional hinterlands. They both had access to abundant supplies of coal and horses, the two most important prime movers of the industrial city other than human labor. However, the environmental settings of these urban places were more different than alike, creating several significant contrasts in their patterns of technological adaptation. As we have seen, the cotton spinners took good advantage of the power of flowing water, an option virtually ruled out on the flatlands of the Midwest. What this region's peculiar topography and climate offered instead was a fairly steady wind on the Great Lakes and a seemingly inexhaustible stock of trees along the shorelines. Schooners with decks piled high with timber sailing along the shores of Lake Michigan became as ubiquitous as mill wheels turning on the hills of Lancashire. In both places an infrastructure of fuel yards, gasworks, and horse stables became commonplace fixtures of the built environment.

Chicagoans noticed almost immediately that the transportation revolution was shifting the pace of life into a higher gear. In October 1849 a journalist described the sights and sounds of this moving urban tableau:

> Our streets present an animated picture. Thronged with laden wagons, filled with busy people, vocal with the rattling of wheels, the rush of steam, the clank of machinery and many voices, goods gaily flaunting from awning posts and store doors, docks piled with boxes, bales and bundles of merchandise, warehouses like so many heart ventricles receiving the grain on one side, and with a single pulsation, pouring it out on the other into waiting vessels and steamers... the multitude of strangers whose arrival every packet bugle and locomotive whistle and steamer bell heralds, all these and more are now pictured upon every observer's eye and swell the diapason of busy life to every listening ear.[32]

Yet just beneath such effusive paeans to progress ran a darker undercurrent of doubt about the future of the flourishing entrepôt. Only in the final sentence does this subtext of anxiety break through the surface as the reporter sighs with relief, "How different from the listlessness and languor which pervaded the city but two months ago." The reporter left unspoken the reasons why the flow of trade had paradoxically been brought to a standstill at the very peak of the shipping season.

The unspeakable explanation was cholera, which had raged completely out of control, triggering panicked efforts to flee the city. The epidemic sickened a thousand people and claimed 314 lives in just thirty days. Officials had to establish the first public cemetery to handle all the bodies. The trepidation felt by boosters and doctors alike was more than justified: the disease returned the following summer to take a larger number, at least 450 victims, to their graves. Turning to the physicians for guidance, the community decided to entrust local government with the dual mission of purifying the water and draining the land. As leaders came to grips with the need for more holistic planning approaches to dealing with the city's delicate hydraulic ecology, the debate over policy formation would foster a second crisis of confidence that challenged the legitimacy of the nonpartisan, segmented system of the big property holders.[33]

Three case studies of selected sites help unpack the intricate interplay of energy and environment involved in Chicago's second round of efforts to build a city that was livable as well as profitable. The demands of a commercial crossroads like Chicago were different from those of an industrial center like Manchester, but no less essential to the city's growth and prosperity. The job of moving goods and passengers called for far greater amounts of work than did providing manufacturers with power and heat. After 1848, factories began to substitute products for a swelling home market that had previously been supplied by goods imported from the East. The waterworks is a good place to begin examining the subsequent linkages of town and country forged by sky-rocketing demand for the inorganic as well as the organic bounty of nature. During the nineteenth century, mechanical engineers considered the steam engine of the pump house the ultimate test of efficiency: coal in, water out.

The second case represents more a motion picture than a snapshot, that of horses in the streets. Keeping people and goods moving through the streets required a heroic plan for filling in the marshland to a level of several feet in order to raise the grade of the city high enough for proper drainage and sewerage.

A third location deserving close inspection is the brewery. Although at first glance an unlikely choice for the site of a case study, beer making brings together all the elements going into the social construction of technology better than any other manufacturing process. Manufactured in one of the most energy-intensive and science-based processes of the industrial city, beer also became the enduring symbol of the city's divisive political struggles over moral order.

The unique hydrology of Chicago posed a challenge to town planners that was almost exactly the opposite of those they had confronted in all their previous experience with engineering the environment. For most large urban centers, like Manchester and Liverpool, the key problem of water management was that of obtaining a sufficient quantity of uncontaminated drinking supplies. Nature seemed to take care of getting rid of wastes by sending them downstream and eventually out to sea. In contrast, contemporaries held an image of Chicago as a "New Venice" because of the canal-like branches of the river that ran through it. This analogy also reflected perceptions of a pattern of settlement that had grown along and outward from the river branches.

However, the setting of one city on a freshwater lake and the other on a saltwater sea made all the difference. Unlike Venice, Chicago could not depend on the tides and the currents to wash its wastes away in spite of the convictions of its tenacious water managers that the lake would automatically dilute the pollution to safe levels and that the city would always be able to count on a free, unlimited supply of pure drinking water from the same source—that all Chicagoans needed to do was stick their buckets in and pull out as much as they wanted.[34]

It was just about that simple for the pioneers and boosters before 29 April 1849, when the cholera epidemic began. While population densities remained low, the site's overabundance of water meant fresh supplies could be collected in several easy ways, from rain cisterns, shallow wells, the river, and the lake. The marshland initially helped to keep these sources uncontaminated. Organic wastes left in cesspools and privies or on the streets tended to sink into the ground, not flow away toward the watercourses. Edwin Gale recalled of his childhood in the early 1840s that the well water "was pleasant to taste [and] wholesome to drink." He also remembered families that worked as water bearers for those who could afford to have their supplies hauled from the preferred source, the lake. "With a hogshead placed on its side on a two wheeled cart, with a hole sawed in the upper surface to receive the contents of the long handled bucket," he wrote, "the boys would drive into the water, and standing on the heavy shafts fill the cask, which was emptied in barrels at our doors through a short leathern hose."[35]

In June 1842, the privately owned Chicago Hydraulic Company fired up a steam engine to pump water through two miles of mains made by boring holes in cedar logs. Gale reminisced:

> The event was celebrated by our proud, happy people with a glorious procession, followed by speeches and powder. We were quite vain of our enormous 24 horse power (h.p.) engine on the lake shore at the foot of Lake Street, to look after which Ira Miltemore had given up his steam sash factory on the South Branch. It was the boast of the town that

with it Ira could raise 25 barrels [790 gallons] of the crystal fluid per minute 35 feet above the lake, pumping our 1250 barrel [40,000-gallon] reservoir full in 50 minutes, besides grinding flour. . . . And how hilarious those aristocrats became, who had two story houses with pipes in the upper story, when incredulously turning an upstairs faucet, with fear and trembling, they saw the precious fluid trickle out.[36]

Admittedly, Chicago's entry into a new world of high energy use was less auspicious than its booster enthusiasm warranted. Fuel consumption was modest because the size of the engine was small and its hours of operation were limited to the business day. Still, Gale's amusing recollection misses the important meaning that the inauguration of the waterworks represented to the community: fire protection.

Three years earlier, the city built of wood had suffered its first great conflagration. Eighteen buildings had burned down in the heart of the fledging business district at Lake and Dearborn Streets. Only by blowing up another building in the fire's path had the people stopped the flames. In response, the city government had looked to an existing company, a paper creation formed by the same group of insiders who had given away the wharfing privileges. In 1841, the council had offered the company a contract for fire hydrants, underwriting the financial risks of building the works. The location of the waterworks' brick building and pier and its stem pipe along the Lake Street business strip indicates that the main concern of town planners was the safeguarding of commercial property, not public health. By the time of the cholera epidemic, the company had extended its leaky pipes another seven and a half miles to serve one hundred hydrants in the south and west divisions. Hooked up to the system were also about eight hundred homes and two hundred other buildings, or fewer than one out of every five structures served. The vast majority outside of this aristocracy of wealth, as well as rich and poor alike on the inaccessible North Side, had to make do with the traditional methods of collecting water.[37]

As the death toll from cholera mounted, however, so did popular pressure to reorder priorities, giving first importance to providing everyone with pure and abundant drinking supplies. In 1851, Walter Gurnee was carried into the mayor's office on a wave of support for a public waterworks. George Schneider, a crusading journalist on the *Staats Zeitung*, had led the campaign for municipal ownership, mobilizing the "Forty-Eighters" to vote in the local election. After Gurnee took office, a board of commissioners was duly set up, a water district was defined, and a respected engineer was hired from

New York City to take charge of the project. Four out of five voters affirmed their confidence in his plan in a second referendum on the issue.[38]

The outside expert, William J. McAlpine, proposed the construction of a much larger pump house at the northeast corner of the city, at the then beachfront intersection of Chicago Avenue and Pine Street (later Michigan Boulevard). Even before the public health crisis, the rapid deterioration of the once "decidedly pure and transparent" liquid coming out of the faucets exposed the error of putting the intake point only a hundred yards offshore in the backwater cul-de-sac of the harbor entrance. Its whirlpool effects often stirred up bottom turbulence to give the water a dirty appearance. Water quality also suffered badly from the unintended consequences of parallel larger-scale projects to begin draining the low-lying south division and installing sewerage there.

Whether the outfalls of these public water systems poured their pollution into the river or the lake, the result was the same. The piped water was contaminated with organic wastes that made it unfit for human consumption. By the late 1840s, moreover, a swelling population dependent on cesspools and privies had saturated the city's wet land, poisoning the shallow wells in backyards. The water that was pumped into the city center by the utility company exacerbated the problems of muddy streets, stagnate pools, and the insect populations that bred in them. The final irony of Chicago's hydraulic system was the way in which it created ideal conditions for the spread of a waterborne infection like cholera, once it arrived through the back door on a canal boat carrying emigrants from New Orleans.[39]

Popular understanding of the contagion and what to do about it was informed by the statements of members of Chicago's medical profession. Taking an active part in civic life from the start, a core group of these doctors, who had been trained in Eastern and European schools, had already established a local association, scientific journal, and medical school. Their role in shaping public opinion was clearly evident at the open meeting that was held a day after the flood to devise a defense against the dreaded disease.

The Saturday-night strategy session at City Hall was immediately dominated by the physicians. The meeting, led by merchant Walter Newberry and chaired by Mayor Woodward, had been called by prominent citizens. Dr. Brockholst McVickar spoke first on community responsibility to attend to the needs of the poor during such crises. Dr. Charles Dyer followed to reinforce this position, outlining plans for a city hospital and isolation wards in the three divisions. In contrast, no engineers were present to respond to requests for advice on overcoming the site's environmental problems. Without expert guidance from the engineers, the attendees had to defer the making of any recommendations on drainage and sewerage; instead, they set up a new committee to study the problem. Three of the five committee members were doctors.

In the meantime, a steering committee proposed a series of immediate reforms for cleansing the city that embodied the scientific theories of disease causation held by Chicago's leading medical practitioners. This group included such men as the first health officer, Daniel Brainard; the future head of Rush Medical College, Nathan Davis; and future mayor Levi Boone. In the absence of a specific, identifiable agent of infection, they took the commonsense approach that had been followed for the past four hundred years: residents should trust their noses; if it smelled rotten, it was bad for your health. The first line of defense, according to the miasma, or filth, theory, was to clean up the land and deodorize it with generous amounts of lime.[40]

Like their counterparts in England and especially the Chadwickians, Chicago's most influential doctors also advocated the purification of the city's water circulation system. At the Saturday-night strategy session, for example, Dr. McVickar had asserted that unpolluted drinking water was the single most important defense against the spread of cholera. Furthermore, he had taken Mayor Woodward to task as one of the directors of the Chicago Hydraulic Company, asking what steps were being taken to ensure its supplies against contamination. Thrown on the defensive, the mayor could only maintain that the quality of the water from the faucets was better than that of water from the carts. Such weak claims fell flat under the steadily mounting pressures of the cholera outbreak, throwing a desperate community into the arms of the doctors for a way out of the calamity.[41]

The doctors' claims of authority were tenuous at best except during temporary periods of this kind when the life of the city itself seemed to hang in the balance. Until specific agents or vectors could be linked to specific diseases, epidemiology lacked a solid scientific foundation on which to build internal consensus among medical practitioners. At the meeting, the biggest fissure in the American profession, between the contagionists and anticontagionists, found expression in the preemptive strike of the doctors who lobbied vigorously for an isolation-of-the-sick strategy. The defeat of their plan may have had less to do with protection of the public health than with concern for the economic vitality of a city built on trade. Raising the quarantine flag was equivalent to announcing that business was closed.

In June 1854, during the very worst of this ongoing human catastrophe, Dr. Dyer and fellow contagionists would finally get their chance, but the results showed just how thin knowledge was stretched in this field of medicine. The doctors organized themselves into an unofficial health board and rented a warehouse for use as an infirmary. "Hearing that a steamboat was coming into port with eighteen cases of cholera," Dyer reported, "we went out to the vessel and removed the patients to the improvised hospital. On viewing the sick, nine were decided to be beyond medical aid, and the remaining moiety were decreed to be favorable subjects for pathological skill; but, unfortunately, the nine upon whom we lavished all the resources of science died, and those who were esteemed to be about in *articulo mortis* all got well."[42] Under such baffling conditions, it is not surprising that Dr. McVickar and others assumed a middle-ground position of support for every reasonable remedy put forth by fellow professionals.

In Chicago, policy makers relied primarily on anticontagionist, or filth-based, etiologies in formulating plans to combat cholera and other illnesses that spread rapidly among the inhabitants. To early sanitarians like Dr. Nathan Davis, concern about the quality of the urban environment implicitly contained an ethic of social justice. His definition of modern medicine embraced a broad and dynamic sense of people's moral obligations to nature and each other. This holistic concept of public health and welfare included "the relations of man to the air he breathes, the earth he walks upon, and all the other elements around us. Hence the modern improvements in the construction of dwellings; the greater care to preserve pure air and good water; the reservation of ample parks, wide streets, and efficient sewers in all large cities, have not only prevented disease and lengthened the average duration of human life, but they have vastly enlarged the field of human happiness."[43] Davis and like-minded physicians helped shift public opinion in favor of municipal ownership of the waterworks. An increasingly large and diverse population demanded that the levers of environmental control be entrusted to the hands of public officials, not of private interests.

In addition to guaranteeing an abundance of pure water, the plans outlined by the outside expert, McAlpine, promised a more democratic distribution of its benefits. Open access to the hydrants and free drinking fountains—at least in the beginning—reflected the system's political origins in a community state of emergency. Although the engineer located the new pump house less than a mile north of the old one, he expected to find untainted supplies at the proposed intake point, which was twice as far, or two hundred yards, from shore. To further protect the wooden intake pipe from lake turbulence, he constructed a breakwater around its opening. This shield of stones and timbers faced toward the northwest, indicating that McAlpine took the prevailing currents into account when drawing his blueprints.

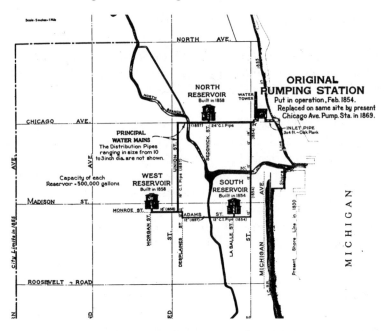

Figure 3.12. Chicago's original municipal water-supply system
Source: City of Chicago, *A Century of Progress in Water Works, 1833–1933* (Chicago: Department of Public Works, Bureau of Engineering, 1933), 35.

McAlpine's distribution plan did not depart from the previous system of mains, reservoirs, and service pipes, but it now covered all three divisions. Large cast iron mains carried the water under the river from the North Side to the west division and back across to the south, where the water filled a half-million gallon reservoir built with an impressive stone base and wrought iron top (see fig. 3.12). A standpipe hidden in the chimney of the works gave this basic network the capability of raising a stream of water eighty feet high.

Unfortunately, this was not enough to save the city from a second great fire in 1857, which took twenty-two lives and destroyed seven hundred thousand dollars worth of property in the business center. As figure 3.12 shows, the completion of the reservoir plan was then put on a fast track as the city council belatedly boosted the budget to upgrade the fire department and to purchase its first steam-powered pumper. More important, the distribution system was expanded threefold by the end of 1860, now serving a total of ninety miles of streets and four hundred hydrants. The 6,350 hookups completed in less than a decade's time and serving three-quarters of the dwellings within the water district represented a significant public works success.[44]

The centerpiece of the project was the coal-fired two-hundred-horsepower steam engine, the largest in the region. McAlpine projected ahead to meet the needs of a city of a hundred thousand people, a figure he estimated Chicago would reach in fifteen years. Actually, it would grow twice as fast, crossing the six-digit barrier by the end of the decade. In spite of this underestimation, McAlpine's calculations resulted in the production of a machine that had more than ample power for immediate purposes. Linked to a companion pump, its low pressure, single-stroke action could supply eight million gallons per day (mgd), or seven times as much as Ira Miltemore's twenty-four-horsepower machine. During its first full year of operation in 1855, the waterworks supplied an average of 2.4 mgd and operated six days a week during business hours. A mechanic remained on duty to stoke the boiler and start the engine if he heard the fire alarm. After the conflagration of 1857, a second, bigger engine and pump would be installed, giving the waterworks a twenty mgd capacity. The new gear was added mostly for use during a future fire emergency, however, since average consumption remained at less than five mgd at decade's end, well within the specifications of the original equipment.[45]

Even with a limited schedule of operation, the pump house required a regular supply of fuel. Compared to the difficulty of hauling coal and wood the short trip from the river docks to the waterworks, shipping it long distances to Chicago was relatively simple and cheap. The city's superlative geographic location and the availability of multiple modes of transportation made its market for energy fuels one of the most competitive in the United States. Like the rest of the nation, the rising metropolis of the midcontinent would rely primarily on wood for heat and power well into the post–Civil War period.

Lake shipping provided the first means of gaining low-cost access to extralocal stands of timber and more distant supplies of anthracite or hard coal. Just eleven miles south of the city was the region's second natural harbor at the mouth of the Calumet River. It became a favorite early destination for the lumberjacks after groves closer to Chicago had disappeared from the landscape. Large boats delivering Midwestern grain to the East carried coal as ballast on their return trips from ports on Lake Erie. Once they were thrown upon the market, a wide variety of coals from mines in the Appalachian Mountains and Ohio River Valley became available to fuel consumers. A full menu of different types was available, each type bearing the name of its origin: Lackawanna, Brier Hill, Chippewa, Newcastle, and so on.

After 1848, the canal and the railroad also opened up the market to new sources of competition. The water route created a highway for the soft, or bituminous, coals from mines dug into outcroppings in the Illinois River Valley and farther downstate along the banks of the Mississippi. A spreading web of railroads also fed a supply of energy resources into Chicago. But neither the water route nor the rail system had "coals at the heels of it" during the antebellum period.[46]

Almost from the beginning, local fuel dealers faced what quickly became a chronic condition of overstuffed markets and undercut prices. In 1841, the first load of coal carried into the city on the schooner *General Harrison* from Cleveland went to the North Side docks of Newberry and Dole. For the next two years while they slowly got rid of it, the merchants were stuck with this eighty-ton pile of bituminous left on consignment by captain-owner E. B. Ward. They and other fuel dealers had to overcome two major obstacles in finding buyers for coal. First, coal was priced higher than wood with an equivalent heat value. As a rule of thumb, the weight ratio for fuel woods and soft coals of equivalent heat value was two-to-one, a distinct advantage for the latter in terms of transportation costs, all other things being equal. But the close proximity of the timber more than compensated for the greater bulk of wood until the Illinois and Michigan Canal dramatically reduced this differential by opening access to outcropping seams less than a hundred miles away, near LaSalle.[47]

A second barrier to the marketing of coal still had to be removed: the technological limitations of fireplaces designed specifically for burning logs. The denser fossil fuel would not ignite and stay inflamed without higher grates with legs to increase the flow of oxygen. Anthracite coals, preferred because they yielded almost no smoke or ash when they burned, especially required different equipment. The difficulty in getting the hard fuel lit had earned it the name stone coal until Benjamin Franklin and others invented special equipment to get it to burn properly. Almost all of the original heat and power equipment imported to Chicago, however, was designed to consume wood. The city's first locomotive, for instance, was a used engine that had previously made the heavily forested run between Albany and Schenectady, New York. The new modes of transportation sharply increased the supply of fuel woods in the local market, but they also had the more important effect of tipping the economic scales in favor of converting to coal and purchasing new equipment that used it.[48]

By the time the municipal pump house was completed in 1854, this switch in fuel types had begun to make good sense for Chicago's largest energy consumers. The following year, the Illinois Central Railroad started buying coal-burning locomotives. This decision was forced in part by the railroad's own rapacious denuding of the forests along its routes, which drove up the price of cordwood. Also, company managers were attracted to the alternative

Table 3.1 Bituminous coal trade in Chicago, 1856

Origin of coal	Mode of transportation	Distance (miles)	Cost of coal/ton	Cost of transportation	Cost of delivery to Chicago
LaSalle, Illinois	Railroad	93	$1.93	$1.86	$3.79
Southern Illinois (DuQuin)	Railroad	500	$1.23	$5.00	$6.23
Ohio River	Canal to Cleveland	100	$0.95	$2.00	$4.95
	Lake schooner to Chicago	850		$2.00	

Source: J. W. Foster, *Report upon the Mineral Resources of the Illinois Central Railroad* (New York: Roe, 1856), 22–25.

fuel because its price was falling at the pithead and because it weighed less and occupied much less space on the train for the same amount of energy; with it fuel bills were slashed in half.[49]

The railroad also sent a geologist, J. W. Foster, to survey the fossil fuel resources of the state. Foster was optimistic about the future of the railroad's coal trade because "the great obstacle to the growth of Chicago, as a seat of manufacturing industry, is the high price of fuel." At the time, Chicago was paying 16 percent more than Pittsburgh and 9 percent more than Cleveland for coal. Although less than a tenth of the one hundred thousand tons consumed in Chicago came from local mines that year, Foster produced figures to show that the local mining firms were already beginning to undercut their out-of-state competitors (see table 3.1).

Foster's promise of a lucrative business for the railroad rested on a chemical analysis of downstate coals, which proved superior to those found in the LaSalle field. The southern seam, he stated, would make fine "steam coal" because it had less sulphur and fewer clinkers, it could be turned into coke, and it was more resistant to "slacking," or crumbling, during shipment. He was confident that the cost of mining would come down as consumer demand climbed for this valuable bulk freight.[50]

Foster could base such an encouraging report not only on the planting of a coal mining industry in the region but also on the recent establishment of several energy-intensive enterprises in Chicago, such as the municipal waterworks. The most striking case of a direct linkage between rural pithead and urban fuel burner coming on the heels of the transportation revolution was the coal-gas company. In 1850, this privately financed venture turned on the lights along the main streets of the city. Chicagoans never seemed to question that this urban service represented a private luxury, not a public necessity. By the end of the decade, the utility monopoly was prospering. It became the single biggest consumer of coal, turning fifteen thousand tons of it into eighty million cubic feet of illuminating gas. The next tier of large users fell into the pump house's range of eight hundred to one thousand tons a year. All the others in this group, including breweries and iron foundries, needed large amounts of both heat and power.[51]

Although the 1860 census manuscripts indicate that wood remained the common choice of smaller local manufacturers for heating purposes, coal was already the preferred fuel for powering steam engines. Thomas Dugall used 125 cords of wood for heating candle and soap boilers, and Henry Stienbeck burned 30 cords making earthenware pottery, but firms employing small engines fueled by coal formed a long list ranging from printing presses and coffee grinders to stoneworks and flour mills. At the same time, it cannot be assumed that forests of wood from the scrap piles of the city's extensive lumberyards did not continue to find their way into steam-boiler furnaces.[52]

On the eve of the Civil War, then, Chicago had largely overcome the obstacles that had stood in its way to becoming an industrial city. The census reports reveal that price levels based on heat values of wood and coal fuels had been more or less equalized. While Chicago manufacturers still might be unable to undersell their Pittsburgh competitors, they could hold their own in local markets, at least in terms of their energy bills. As the geologist had predicted, falling pithead costs and railroad rates were already making coal a profitable load for the Rock Island Line that paralleled the canal route to the closest mining area at LaSalle.

The LaSalle mining area turned out to be just the outer edge of a vast underground field that extended throughout two-thirds of the state. The rise of Chicago as an urban center was giving birth to a coal mining industry in the whole region. In Illinois alone, annual production in the twenty years from 1840 to 1860 went from 17,000 to 568,000 tons, requiring the labor of a thousand men. But the downstate seams of black gold along the Illinois Central were still too far away for the railroad's steam locomotives to compete against the wind power of the sailboats, which continued to bring in almost 70 percent of the city's coal supplies and over 60 percent of its cordwood.

Operators of schooners and steamers, canal boats, and railroads all wanted to move these bulk commodities to Chicago.

Glutted markets became the fuel dealer's watchword of despair as the supply on hand almost always outstripped the demand, depressing price levels and narrowing profit margins. In 1858, the Board of Trade lamented in its first annual report that "the year opened with a large stock on hand, which with a bountiful supply of wood, caused prices to rule low until the end of the shipping season." Things were no better next year, the Board confessed, because "Chicago will always be furnished with an abundant supply." Its environmental setting and commercial foundations combined to skew the classic supply-and-demand curve toward a buyer's market. Shippers involved in the grain trade had everything to gain by hauling the bulky fuel to Chicago rather than returning empty.

In a similar way, the railroads considered it profitable to carry wood and coal during the winter months when maritime navigation was suspended and farms lay fallow. After 1848, moreover, the railroads' all-year-round capabilities contributed to the emergence of a new wholesale commercial sector in the region as well as the rapid expansion of the traditional through-trade. But the lines were left with too many empty cars on the return trip to the city, again making wood and coal (and ice) attractive alternatives even if the carriers could only charge rates that left them with little or no margin of profit. Facing a chronic condition of overabundance, the fuel dealers of the city could find hope only in Chicago's ascendancy as the great crossroads of the nation. Of course, their lament was music to the ears of Chicago consumers of heat, light, and power.[53]

As early as the mid-1840s, the energy infrastructure began stamping permanent marks on the urban environment. One immediately noticeable effect was a decline in the quality of the air. City smoke not only grew thicker but now had the sulphurous odor of bituminous coal mixed in with the sweeter smell of hardwood. In 1845, an artist drew a panorama of the city looking east from the suburbs that depicts cows grazing in the foreground and plumes of jet-black smoke rising against the horizon. Three years later, the observant traveler John Peyton noted that "Chicago was already becoming a place of considerable importance for manufactures. Steam mills were busy in every part of the city... [and] large establishments were engaged in manufacturing agricultural implements.... A single establishment, that of McCormick, employed several hundred hands, and during each season completed from fifteen hundred to two thousand grain-reapers and grass-mowers."[54]

The river witnessed the most dramatic transformation, one that shattered any lingering fantasy of Chicago becoming the New Venice of the West.

Instead, the Chicago /River, this highway of commercial trade, was being turned into a diversified corridor of industrial activity and intraurban movement. Land use along its banks underwent vivid changes, from the appearance of energy-consuming factories like McCormick's, to the establishment of fuel depots, gasworks, breweries, tanneries, foundries, brickyards, and lumber mills. The use of the water in the river to carry away the wastes of these budding enterprises as well as the sewage of a swelling population also caused dramatic changes that destroyed the river's natural ecology.[55]

Housing construction followed jobs as industry spread down the South Branch toward the canal. Since workers had to live within walking distance of their places of employment, the south and west divisions boomed. In comparison, the North Side lagged behind. Cut off from the business center by more and more river traffic, it began to loose its luster as the best residential area. Its prestige suffered further decline because the older residential area was sandwiched between the city's first vice districts, the Kilgubbin on the banks of the North Branch at the fork, and the Sands on the new land formed by the accretion of sedimentation behind the harbor piers. In spite of a raid by municipal authorities in 1857 to burn down the Sands, a shantytown of vice and crime, the well-to-do began to gravitate to more convenient locations on the other side of the river along the lakefront promenade of Michigan Avenue. For both rich and poor, the sheer magnitude of the growth of the population made moving around the city increasingly difficult. A count of traffic crossing the six bridges on an average day in 1855 recorded 73,200 persons and 18,400 teams of horses.[56]

City of Ups and Downs

To sustain its success, Chicago would have to find a way of lifting itself out of the mud. If the skyrocketing climb of trade after 1848 did not force the boosters to rethink their designs for intraurban movement, the outbreak of cholera the following year left little doubt about the necessity of taking bold new directions in city planning. The planking of streets over marshland proved a miserable failure with costly unintended consequences. Besides the stenches, rats, and bugs being generated underneath, the pavement also became a source of injury to horses that stepped on rotten or loose boards. These problems had been regarded as annoying inconveniences, but the epidemic represented a human catastrophe that could not be so easily dismissed.

The doctors seized the opportunity to hammer home the point that the city needed to cleanse the environment. Within the broad spectrum of filth theories of disease causation, Chicago's medical spokespeople were attracted with obvious reason to the soil theories associated with the German scientist

Max Pettenkofer, who reasoned that wet ground was the seedbed for the spontaneous generation of the agents of human sickness. In the midst of the cholera crisis, Dr. E. McArthur explained, "One thing is certain. This disease develops itself most in the crowded and poorly ventilated parts of cities and large towns, in low damp places, and especially when stagnant pools and water-courses abound; making it the imperative duty of public authorities in such cities and towns to fill up and drain such places, or cause it to be done, whenever the disease prevails or is likely to prevail."[57]

Driven by the ongoing state of emergency, local officials drew up a novel master plan to drain the land, dispose of its sewage, and pave the city. The perceived requirements of public health went hand in hand with the equally pressing needs of private enterprise to forge a broad consensus in favor of reform in spite of the large costs involved in completing these infrastructure projects.

I take up the question of sanitation in the next chapter. Here I focus on the reconstruction of the built environment to facilitate street traffic. Admittedly this separation of land management from water management is artificial in the case of Chicago, but it helps to highlight horses as a crucial part of the city's energy system.

Until recently, urban historians have paid little attention to horses except as quaint but dirty nuisances that were replaced by mechanical substitutes such as trolley cars and automobiles. From an environmental perspective, however, horses and other animals were an integral element of urban nature and culture. Consider that the horse population of Chicago would reach eighty thousand by the end of the century. Theirs is not a story of technological determinism; rather, their growing numbers was emblematic of a symbiotic relationship between extralocal and intraurban modes of transportation. The more railroads, canal boats, and lake ships brought people and goods to Chicago, the more horses were needed to move them around within its expanding boundaries. By the mid-1850s, more than eighteen thousand wagons and carts were crossing the bridges each day; horses had already become vital to the commercial life of the city. In addition, feeding, equipping, and housing them were becoming major economic activities in their own right, reinforcing the spatial integration and intimacy between humans and animals. The horse ethos of the nineteenth-century city was as elaborate and complex as today's car culture. Moreover, the ubiquity of the urban horse created dynamic bonds of interdependence between town and country.[58]

An audacious scheme to raise the entire city by several feet grew out of the conundrum of how to design a drainage system that defied the laws of gravity. Since the business center was only two feet above water level, the ground could not be dried out simply by means of traditional methods of channeling the excess from higher to lower land. If the practical experience of the past had failed to teach this lesson, then frantically renewed efforts during the cholera epidemic hammered home the futility of trying to make water flow upward. In 1849, the city council declared State and Madison streets as the dividing lines in determining the direction of drainage for the south division between the river and the lake. The following year, it ordered the construction of V-shaped wooden box sewers in a vain effort to improve upon the open ditches that had already proven to be worse than useless. Still, as the pump house supplied more and more water to the city center, the drainage problem grew proportionately.

Concurrently, efforts by the county government to dry out one hundred thousand acres surrounding the city were meeting with much greater success. This project of wetlands reclamation was easier to accomplish in part simply because the designated areas were higher, from five to twelve feet above water level. Equally important, county officials had adopted a rapidly evolving institutional vehicle, the special-purpose tax district, to finance the large-scale project with general levies instead of special assessments. The origins of the Cook County Drainage Commission represent a classic case of the devolution of power over the environment under American federalism. In 1850, Congress gave away 11.5 million acres to the states in the Swampland Act. The Illinois legislature, in turn, transferred its share, almost 1.5 million acres, to the counties to be publicly improved or privately disposed of as soon as possible. Lacking guidance from Springfield, the officers of Cook County drew upon the Anglo-American legal tradition of what historian James Herget calls "ditch law" to create a commission to administer the plan. As the public health crisis deepened in 1854, Chicago would draw upon this model to create a similar special-purpose tax authority in which all property owners would be held liable for the costs of infrastructure improvements.[59]

Lacking expertise, however, Chicagoans seemed paralyzed by indecision about the best way to resolve the dilemmas of engineering their soggy environment. Following up the public meeting in March 1849, for example, Mayor Woodward took the occasion of his inaugural address to call for "immediate action": "The time has arrived when the adoption of a general, uniform system of drainage for our city is imperatively demanded." He outlined three different schemes for the aldermen's consideration. One was based on the seaport model of a few big masonry sewer mains with river outfalls that would depend on "tidal" fluctuations in lake levels to clean them out. A cheaper alternative was a grid of clay pipes just below the surface of the streets. Fresh water from the reservoirs of the Chicago Hydraulic Company would dilute the sewage and surface runoff and flush it into the river and the lake.

But the mayor's preferred plan was to embed a network of large brick tunnels deep underground to collect the wastewater. Pumping stations would presumably dispose of it at a safe distance from the population. Although the deep-sewers plan was admittedly the most costly option, the mayor believed that the promise of "comfortable cellars" made "deep drainage" the best investment in the future of the city. Other than falling back on special assessments and wooden box gutters, however, the council members did little to answer his call until the raging epidemic finally convinced just about everyone left alive of the urgency for action. Echoing the mayor's plea for a "general plan of sewerage" in May 1853, one of the newspapers declared emphatically, "We want no more wooden sewers in Chicago."[60]

After suffering through the most deadly season yet of cholera during the exceptionally hot, dry summer of 1854, a desperate city was ready to unite behind a comprehensive plan of environmental control. In a December mass meeting citizens agreed to ask the legislature to create a special-purpose tax district, which would be governed independently from the increasingly politicized municipal council. The result was the Board of Sewerage Commissioners, with a 1,200-acre jurisdiction covering most of the central city. The three-member board turned to the engineer who had been put in charge of the waterworks, Ellis S. Chesbrough. In 1850, he had arrived from Boston with four years of training in supplying water to that city but no experience in designing sanitation systems.

Chesbrough studied the little available literature on the subject and presented a fateful report in December 1855 laying out the city's options for disposing of its sewage. There were four choices of where to put the sewage, according to the neophyte expert:

1. "Into the river and branches directly, and thence into the lake."
2. "Directly into the lake."
3. "Into artificial reservoirs, to be thence pumped up and used as manure."
4. "Into the river, and thence by the proposed steamboat canal into the Illinois River."[61]

Chesbrough began by proclaiming that "the main object of the sewers is *to improve and preserve the health of the city*," but the objective of incurring the minimum tax burden emerged as the top priority by the time his report reached a conclusion. The board chose the first option primarily because it was the cheapest. "It would allow the sewers," the engineer reasoned, "to be constructed in such a manner as to take the utmost advantage of the natural facilities that the site of the city affords, and consequently, that the sewers may be less in extent and cost." The second option, of large, deep sewers, was rejected simply because they would be more expensive to build and maintain. And in similar fashion, the fourth option was dismissed as "too remote a contingency" at the time, especially since it would raise the price tag five-fold.

The third alternative was based on Chesbrough's reading of Edwin Chadwick's plans for London, and it was clearly the most advanced concept in terms of public health. However, it represented the greatest financial risk to the city in terms of initial costs, which the city might not be able to recoup by selling fertilizer to farmers at a profit. To be sure, the decision makers considered the possibility that their preferred choice "would endanger the health of the city, especially during the warm, dry portions of the year, and that it might fill up the river so much as to obstruct navigation." They believed, however, that they could depend on the freshets to cleanse the river and on the lake to dilute the sewage.[62]

The board's justification of the lowest-cost option was more than a little disingenuous. Collectively Chicagoans would be forced to spend a fortune raising the grade of their properties and lifting their buildings up high enough to make the sewers work by gravity. Chesbrough incorporated Chadwick's technological ideal of self-cleaning clay pipes in calling for an average land fill of eighteen inches in order to give the pipes a sufficient angle to create a natural flow toward river or lake outfalls. Actually, streets had to be built up five to eight feet—and in some cases fourteen feet—to achieve this goal. The dredging of the river to make it deeper supplied an initial source of fill, as did dirt excavated for basements, which now became possible.

The plan embodied a Jacksonian political economy that sought to contain the growth of the public sector as much as possible. In this case, the elite members of the commission, including the indefatigable William B. Ogden, were even willing to act against their own self-interest by shifting the heaviest financial burden onto the shoulders of the largest property owners. The proprietors of the one of the biggest buildings, the Tremont House, sought an injunction to defeat the plan. But a special session of the court quickly settled the matter by upholding the government's authority to set street grades.[63]

While this plan for lifting Chicago out of the mud deserves its celebrated reputation as bold and daring, it was not original. For the past two years, the construction of the joint Illinois Central and Michigan Central railroads terminal on the lakefront had been providing a conspicuous model for all to see. By far the most massive engineering feat in the city's brief history, the raising of two acres of submerged land above water level at the site of the original sandbar was virtually impossible to miss. After completing almost two miles of trestlework just offshore to Twenty-Sixth Street by the end of 1853, the Illinois Central had used its trains to haul in construction materials for the breakwater/terminal project. Workers had to hammer hundreds of wooden piles into the lake bottom, erect a seawall to enclose the space, and shovel in tons of earth and debris to fill it up.

The company had nearly finished building several massive structures on top of the landfill. The depot included grand passenger and freight stations, lumber and wood yards, and two mammoth grain elevators by the time of Chesbrough's report. If this striking example were not enough, then City Hall's more modest, albeit significant, public works project on the other side of the same site should have provided the crucial inspiration for the sewer planner: rather than adding land, workers had been cutting away the elbow where the fort had stood to widen and straighten the river channel and help create the kind of harbor needed for deep-draft lake steamers. The dirt removed was being dumped on South Water Street.[64]

Raising the grade solved several problems of city building simultaneously. Water lines and gas mains as well as sewer pipes could now be buried at least two feet underground. Furthermore, street pavement could now be laid on top of much dryer ground. The most successful and widely adopted method was called Nicholson pavement. Proven on trails outside the central business district on Western Avenue since 1847, this patented technique used four-by-six-inch wooden blocks set grain up. The ground was packed down and planks were laid on top. Then strips of wood were laid over the planks, and pine blocks were set between them to keep them in neat rows. Finally, a mixture of hot tar and fine gravel was applied to fill in the gaps. In July 1857, the completion of a stretch of Nicholson pavement on Lake Street made this commercial strip the pride of Chicago. "The attention of visitors," a local chronicler recorded, "was called to the wonderful pavement as soon as they arrived, and it was considered, with the water works and the grand view of the lake on Michigan Avenue, one of the sights of the city."[65]

Chicagoans embraced Nicholson pavement to accommodate their horses as much as their pocketbooks. Compared to stone or brick, the wooden surface was easy on the hooves of the animals. In addition, the edges of the blocks gave them ready-made places to get a grip when pulling their loads, especially during the icy winters.

Horses were such a ubiquitous part of daily life in urban and rural America that contemporaries rarely made a count of their constant companions. In a city with a well-deserved reputation for boasting about its growth in quantitative superlatives, the quantification of its emerging role as "probably the best horse market in the Union" proved an exception. "Until recently," the *Tribune* carped in 1855, "regular books of sale have not been kept by any of our sale stables and we cannot get an accurate number of horses sold here during the past season." The best the newspaper could come up with in its search for statistics was an estimate that 2,400 had been purchased at Mr. Eddy's, one of several businesses specializing in selling animals brought in from the country.[66]

Equal in importance to the size of this market was the type of horses being bred for its urban customers. As improved modes of transportation brought mounting volumes of passengers and goods to the city, the need for bigger, stronger animals to haul them around inside of it grew apace. Omnibus and streetcar companies, freight movers, construction firms, iron foundries, coal dealers, and beer brewers demanded draft horses to move their heavy loads. Beginning in the 1830s, breeders in the upper Midwest responded by importing Clydesdales from Scotland and Percherons from France. Isaiah Dillon became one of the most prominent breeders by bringing the famous Percheron "Canuck" to his stud farm near Peoria, Illinois. Many others set up similar operations in semirural communities outside of Chicago and handed out printed catalogs of their stock to dealers like Mr. Eddy.[67]

Paved streets and sale stables were two parts of an increasingly elaborate infrastructure that sustained the thousands of animals that kept the city in motion. Chicago was envisioned in its very first plat of the 1830s as a city of alleys. This plan to give over a significant amount of land primarily for the use of horses was continued without question through several additions and annexations. Suburban landscapes too showed sure signs of the close relationship between city people and city horses. Outlying areas contained not only breeding farms but also vast tracts of acreage devoted to growing hay, oats, and straw. These were carted to central outdoor markets and to feed dealers who distributed them to scores of commercial livery stables as well as hundreds of barns lining the alleys behind private residences and retail stores.

Between 1858 and 1860, a number of streetcar companies started operating their vehicles in the middle of the streets, adding another nine hundred animals to the city's nonhuman population within a decade. Horseshoers, veterinarians, and blacksmiths served their more immediate needs while manufacturers of goods ranging from whalebone whips to wagon wheels supplied their masters. Tanners and manufacturers of leather goods, including saddle and bridle makers, became especially important in the local economy, their industry growing in tandem with the city's meatpacking industry.[68]

By the time of the eruption of Civil War in 1861, Chicago was well on its way to overcoming it greatest natural liability, a waterlogged site. Although the raising and draining of the city would proceed for many years to come, Chicago now had a viable plan of environmental control. The uneven pace of these developments now became the most characteristic feature of the urban landscape. Since the decision to fill in property lots to grade level was left to individual owners, the central district soon presented a crazy quilt of ups and downs. The elevated streets, held in place by boards, were uniform, but the sidewalks varied in height, forcing pedestrians to climb and descend staircases several times to get anywhere. The new grade levels also triggered a wave of building moving. Some structures were jacked up while basements were built underneath, and others were relocated elsewhere before their lots were improved.

In an increasing number of cases involving the homes of the working class, the fulfillment of Chesbrough's plan would bring a significant worsening of conditions. These families would find themselves living in a pit with soil dampness and odors seeping in from below and street sweepings and runoff showering down from above. This problem would become especially acute on the near West Side, which Chesbrough had identified as the lowest-lying land within the sewer district. Better streets made the job of the workhorse much easier, however, helping to ensure the continuing rise of Chicago as the commercial hub of an expanding continental empire.[69]

On the eve of the Civil War, Chicago and Manchester were more different than alike. The English city was bigger and more integrated into a larger conurbation; it was also thoroughly industrial. Its giant factories with their belching smokestacks and polluting discharges had already spurred a comprehensive transformation of land use into separate spheres of business and housing, slums and suburbs. Moreover, the municipal government was actively involved in the political formation of urban space to reinforce residential patterns of exclusionary zoning by class and ethnicity/religion.

In contrast, the American city remained a hodgepodge of undifferentiated land uses sprawling across the prairie. While a central business district was beginning to emerge, the Topsy-like growth of the commercial entrepôt defied the rational rules of ground rents. Arriving in 1857 to start a dry goods store, Marshall Field found a city rising pell-mell in every direction. In comparison to the Manchester's Corporation, Chicago's local government was dangerously weak in both the power and the money available to shape the direction of urban growth.[70]

The Civil War would have profound, albeit opposite, effects on the two cities. While Manchester would suffer severe depression during four years of cotton famine, Chicago would triple its population. The latter city's nascent industrial base as well as its more fully developed commercial infrastructure would go full blast, bringing both prosperity and optimism. As in Manchester, however, success came with the price of smoky air, polluted water, and contaminated land. As Chicago took on a more industrial cast as Porkopolis, its land-use patterns began to resemble more closely those in Cottonopolis. Even before the outbreak of the war, Chicago was laying the foundation for its metamorphosis into an industrial ecology.

Munich on the Lake

The malt brewing industry provides a final case study of the ways in which the demand for more energy transformed the environment of Chicago. This ancient art underwent a complete change during the nineteenth century from a small-scale, seasonal activity for local consumers to a highly mechanized big business. Brewing involved the tightly controlled flow of organic liquids through a series of hot and cold vats and pipes. It used energy in a wide variety of ways: for heating and refrigeration, for powering mechanical systems that moved grains and pumped liquids, for the cleaning of equipment, and eventually for operating gigantic bottling plants as beer penetrated national mass consumer markets.

Brewers took the lead in using more and more energy to speed up the organic, thus fitting Alfred Chandler Jr.'s characterization of technological innovation. Mass production, the dean of American business history contends, was achieved first "in those industries where the processes of production required the application of heat and involved chemical rather than mechanical methods. Improved technology, a more intensified use of energy, and improved organization greatly expanded the speed of throughput and reduced the number of workers needed to produce a unit of output."[71]

The brewery offers an ideal site not only for detailing technological innovation within the industrial establishment but also for mapping changes in the city's energy infrastructure leading to and from the plant. Initially, in the 1840s, Chicago breweries were located near the lake, where they could secure fresh water and take advantage of the chilling winds. Before the establishment of the municipal waterworks in the early 1850s, the brewers had to dig their own wells and pumping systems. They also had to build their facilities close to the river harbor because they needed to truck in large amounts of heavy raw materials: fuel wood, coal, ice, and grain.

Street improvements too were essential for the sale and distribution of the breweries' highly perishable products to neighborhood restaurants and saloons. Since beer needed to be kept cool, deteriorated rapidly in transit, and soon went flat after its container was tapped, the location and size of the brewery depended on the number of customers in the immediate vicinity. In this respect, innovation in the city's energy system marched alongside tradition. Virtually every Chicago brewery maintained a stable of horses and delivery trucks. Drawing on English and German customs, these colorful vehicles and matched draft animals were important popular icons of the city streets. An early form of brand-name advertising, the beer wagon quickly became a distinctive feature of urban culture.

This study of the city's early breweries takes stock of their methods of operation, their links to larger systems of the urban infrastructure, and their consumer markets. The story of Lill and Diversey, Chicago's first beer makers and the most successful in the period before the great fire of 1871, illuminates these interactions of energy, technology, and the environment.

The German immigrants William Haas and Andrew Sulzer arrived from Watertown, New York, with equipment to start a brewery in 1833, the same year that Chicago achieved official status as a village, with 350 inhabitants. They selected a plot of land just north of the main settlement at the present site of the Water Tower. In those days, this location was on the edge of the beach.

At the lakefront Haas and Sulzer could secure an uncontaminated source of water and enjoy an unobstructed corridor of access to the cool breezes coming in from Lake Michigan. Their new brew house produced about six hundred barrels (of 31 U.S. gallons, or 70,400 liters, each) of ale and porter annually during the early years. As their consumer base swelled to 4,500 over the next six years, William Ogden saw an opportunity to share in the profits of this promising enterprise by helping William Lill buy out Haas and Sulzer.

The elevation of Michael Diversey from delivery driver to full partner in 1840, the year after the buyout, was symbolic of the growing importance of the great tide of immigration from northern Europe to the Midwest. Diversey was a thirty-year-old transplant from Germany, one of an advance wave of fellow Germans who would follow in his wake during the 1840s and 1850s. The Germans and the Irish would soon constitute a numerical majority in the boomtown. Known for their hardy drinking habits, they would fuel the expansion of the brewery to an annual output of about thirty-five thousand barrels (4,107,000 liters) during the Civil War decade.[72] Lill and Diversey put Ogden's money to good advantage by building a much larger plant on the site of the original brewery. Although the city's environmental features dictated the choice of location, demographic calculations guided the decisions on the size of the brewery.

To gain a better understanding of the brewers' dependence on the vicissitudes of nature, we must make a brief tour of their facilities. Our imaginary visit begins in the malting room located on the top floor of Lill and Diversey's four-story brick building, where the first of four basic steps in making beer was accomplished. Here, sacks of barley and hundreds of gallons of water pumped by hand or horse power were joined in a heated steep tank to germinate the grain, which then released enzymes that turn starch into sugar. The grain was then spread over a wooden floor to dry. After this malt was roasted and milled, it was ready for the second step, brewing. A big tub also situated on the upper floors was heated by a fire from below to extract the sugars and other nutritious elements from the mash.

After the cooking was completed, the resulting wort had to be cooled immediately to reduce the temperature enough for the start of the third step, fermentation. At Lill and Diversey, fans in large windows facing the lake blew air over pipes containing the wort as it was emptied by gravity into shallow, flat beds. The brewers followed English tradition by using yeast that rose to the top during fermentation. This organic process for producing ales and porters required only moderately cool temperatures of 55–65 degrees Fahrenheit. The final, fourth step involved pouring the beer into wooden barrels and distributing it to local saloons, groceries, and restaurants. Coopers made the barrels in a separate shop outside the brewery on a seasonal basis. The brewers also maintained a blacksmith shop and a horse stable for regular, weekly deliveries.[73]

In all except the last step, the brewer's art depended on the ability to regulate temperature, which controlled the rate of the various biochemical reactions. Armed with a thermometer, the maltster and the brew master could heat liquids to the right temperature easily enough by modifying the amount of fuel they added to the fire below the pots and by pouring hot or cold water into the vats. In these steps, however, Lill and Diversey had to keep around-the-clock vigilance over their unskilled workers to ensure even results. Cooling remained problematic in spite of rapid improvements during the 1830s and 1840s in the gathering and storage of ice.

Like the brewing industry itself, the ice business grew in tandem with the rise of the city. In Chicago and other northern urban centers, brewers became the chief consumers of ice, which was harvested in standardized blocks from nearby rivers and lakes. Lill and Diversey built two great icehouses before the Civil War as an alternative to expanding their underground cellars. In one of these buildings, the pile of ice stacked in the middle was twenty-five feet high and sixty feet square. Cold storage allowed brewers to make a "winter beer" for immediate consumption beginning in October and a "summer beer" in the early spring for use during the hot season. Yet ice was only so cold, and it had other drawbacks, such as excessive dampness that rotted the wooden buildings and promoted the growth of unwanted microorganisms.[74]

Nonetheless, Lill and Diversey's "Cream Ale" prospered as Chicago grew larger. Their silent partner, Ogden, recalled that "my brewery is the only thing that makes money without trouble." Even after the speculator sold out to Diversey in 1841, the brewery faced no significant competition for another six years.

Then, with Ogden's financial backing, John A. Huck opened Chicago's first lager beer plant and a German-style beer garden across the street. In contrast to ales and porters, lager beer was made from different strains of yeast that settled on the bottom. Introduced in Munich in the 1830s, lager beer was much more difficult and time-consuming to manufacture because primary fermentation required much lower, 32–46 degree temperatures for seven to ten days. The beer also had to rest in wooden casks—hence the name lager, or storage—at near freezing temperatures for long periods of aging and settling of impurities. The result was a cold, refreshing drink that was lighter in taste and color as well as more highly carbonated. With German neighborhoods emerging on the near North Side, Huck's business too prospered. Others soon entered the lager beer market, especially forty-eighters from Bavaria, who arrived well-trained in the brewing art. By 1860, the city directory listed twenty-two breweries of various sizes.[75]

During this period, Chicago beer makers seemed little inclined to introduce advanced equipment, let alone experiment with new techniques. On the contrary, they continued to follow long-accepted practices for establishments of comparable size. For the most part, they simply reiterated the technological evolution of the London breweries, which had grown to the large scale of more than one hundred thousand barrels a year with little mechanization. Lill and Diversey, for example, waited until 1856 before beginning to make the increasingly popular lager beer. With the sole exception of their building cold-storage cellars above ground, they were not innovators. Looking back a half-century, a close observer of the industry commented in the 1900s that "it is indeed surprising to note the tenacity with which the old, really primitive methods were adhered to." The testimony of Matheus Gottfried, a Bavarian-trained brewer who immigrated to Chicago in 1857, confirms the persistence of tradition. Some local beer makers, he reported, did not even use thermometers but relied on customary rules of touch: "blood heat," "milk heat," and "hot to the elbow."[76]

Until the 1870s, the brewing industry depended almost entirely upon age-old work routines of drudge labor and horse power. This was typical of industry in both the United States and Britain in the first half of the nineteenth century. A description of the energy system employed in London's breweries of the 1750s is equally appropriate for Chicago's a hundred years later. "Above all," historian Peter Mathias writes, "the need was for strong general laborers—to manage the sacks of malt, to mash the ground malt before the days of mashing machines, to clean out the utensils and the casks, to do the racking into barrels, to press the surplus yeast, and manhandle the casks into the stores or onto the drays—the 'drawers off,' 'stage-men,' and 'spare-men.'"[77] Lill and Diversey were conservatives, not progressives, in the adoption of steam power. The great London establishments had begun installing rotary engines as soon as they became available in the mid-1780s, replacing the horses that had been used to drive malt mills and water pumps. In 1828, John Beveridge of Newbury, New York, was the first to install a steam engine in an American brewery.

There is no evidence that Lill and Diversey made any attempt to mechanize their production before the 1850s. At the end of the decade, they had a single twenty-horsepower engine. They continued to rely primarily on an "organic machine" composed of fifty to seventy-five men and thirty-five horses. Once they installed the steam engine for milling and pumping, they began to make further use of the technology by attaching the engine to a mechanical elevator for lifting barley to the malting room at the top of the building. Yet this adaptation was hardly pioneering because these devices were well proven and in common use, especially in Chicago, the center of the grain trade. Until the post–Civil War decade, the brewing industry remained steeped in tradition.[78]

Within this context, those in charge of building the city's infrastructure took much more impressive strides toward giving Chicago an up-to-date, modern energy system. The shipping and railroad networks created by Ogden and other boosters represented the most important step in building a foundation for the growth of industry. For local beer makers, these transportation improvements meant significant advantages: they were at the heart of the grain trade and had access to highly competitive markets for coal, hay, and wood fuel. The railroads also helped them secure ample supplies of ice as urban growth forced the ice industry outward toward less polluted areas. In 1860, Chicago received almost 618,000 bushels of barley, of which only 1,225 bushels arrived by water. At forty-eight pounds per bushel, this harvest of nature represented a large load for the railroads—almost thirty million pounds worth. The city's brewers purchased about half of this amount, carrying it by horse-drawn vehicle from the rail yards to their storage bins. The railroads were also playing key roles in the creation of an analogous urban infrastructure of central wholesalers and neighborhood dealerships in cheap, soft coals from the Midwest. In short, the railroads turned Chicago from a regional marketplace into a national one, and it kept local brewers competitive by ensuring low prices for their supplies.[79]

In the mid-1850s, Chicago's initiative in raising the grade and paving the streets proved immensely beneficial to the beer makers. Streets improved with cheap but practical wood blocks were well suited for the city's horse-drawn vehicles, including wagons heavily laden with grain, ice, coal, and barrels full of beer. Efforts to pave the streets made steady progress up to the time of the great fire, when approximately one hundred miles of Nicholson pavement were in place.

These new road surfaces were concentrated in the business district and on the Near North Side, where most of the breweries were located. The brewers could take advantage of them for receiving supplies, although they still had to depend on the brute strength of their draft animals to make deliveries to about six hundred retail outlets along the alternately muddy and dusty dirt roads in most residential districts. With the city's output of beer rising to approximately 275,000 barrels, or 8.5 million gallons (32,175,000 liters), in the year before the great fire, the condition of the streets was crucial for the brewers, whose almost entire output was consumed locally. Taken together, the city's access to national markets, its infrastructure of environmental control, and the improvement of intraurban movement laid a solid foundation upon which to build mechanized, energy-intensive manufacturing enterprises.[80]

Conclusion: Gem of the Prairies

After 1848, the spectacular success of Chicago in attracting people and business wrought profound transformations not only in the city's built environment, but in its political culture and institutions as well. The flood of newcomers undermined the legitimacy of the segmented system by overwhelming its ability to respond to mounting needs for central planning. In many respects, the Jacksonian ideal of devolving political power directly into the hands of the property owners represented a utopian goal that was inherently unstable and doomed to collapse under the weight of external pressures and internal divisions. True enough, American federalism created a constitutional framework that seemed to support such an extreme privatization of public policy. Yet it also engendered national parties that acted as counterweights to this fragmentation of authority, rallying people around general principles and broad issues personified by presidential candidates.

The segmented system could not maintain an artificial suspension of partisanship for long before competition in state and national elections reasserted itself at the local level. Following the passage of the Kansas-Nebraska Act of 1854, the explosive issue of slavery in the territories triggered a major realignment of party politics, fueling its revival in the annual contests for election to City Hall.[81]

The downfall of segmented government had begun only two years after its triumph in the wake of the flood of 1849 and the ensuing cholera epidemic. While the privatization of public goods worked well enough for street improvements, it could not effectively provide infrastructure improvements that were of general benefit, such as bridges, breakwaters, waterworks, and sewer and drainage systems. If nothing else, the sheer growth of the population—it more than quadrupled over the next dozen years to over 110,000 in 1861—increased the demand for citywide plans of environmental control. The mounting public health crisis added an element of desperate urgency to the plans because this state of emergency threatened to choke off the very life of the commercial city. The coming of a national depression in 1857 would push local property owners and public institutions alike to the brink of bankruptcy, throwing the financing of infrastructure improvements into complete disarray for the next several years.

When the single-issue zealots of the prohibition movement stepped into such a volatile tinderbox of community tension to seize the reins of power in 1855, the fragile mantle of nonpartisanship was shed and the city's politics burst into a white heat of class, ethnic/religious, and ideological warfare. Led by Dr. Levi Boone, the forces of morality and nativism gained the upper hand after the Kansas-Nebraska Act split Chicago Democrats, who divided as supporters and opponents of U.S. Senator Stephen Douglas, the main author of the controversial legislation. Just a year earlier, in contrast, German, Irish, and American-born workers had rallied together to put one of their own, Isaac Milliken, into the mayor's office to fend off the temperance advocates' crusade to close the city's saloons.

Now Dr. Boone and his Law and Order ticket gained the upper hand. The council imposed an exorbitant license tax and the mayor beefed up the police department with nonimmigrant "special" officers to enforce the clampdown on drinking. On Saturday, 21 April 1855, the bitter conflict spilled over into the streets. The disturbance, known as the Lager Beer Riot, resulted in at least one death and many more injuries and arrests. A prohibition referendum was defeated in June, but partisan violence, intimidation, and fraud came to characterize the elections from then until the Civil War. The city's antislavery Democrats generally held the loyalty of the Irish, while the insurgent Republicans attracted a large share of the Germans.[82]

The final demise of the segmented system came in 1863 when the municipal ward map was redrawn to reflect the range of Chicago's neighborhoods, which were segregated according to class and ethnicity/religion. Not only did the sectional conflict reinvigorate two-party competition, several issues, both ongoing and novel, that called for citywide decisions stimulated the emergence of a full-blown, open style of urban politics. Two years earlier, a Board of Public Works, with elected officers, had been established to consolidate the administration of the municipal infrastructure, representing the first steps in this direction. In addition, the planning of future water and sewerage projects, the franchising of street railways, and the meeting of recruitment quotas for the Union Army were policy issues that contributed to the redefinition of the public interest in more inclusive, democratic terms.

In a country of universal male suffrage, each social group was expected to express its special identity and advocate for its self-interest in the political arena. The segmented system of the large property owners could not stand against an increasingly diverse and numerous populace. Although wealth and power remained synonymous, the diffusion of capital assets in an expanding local economy meant that no single group could dictate policy solely for its own benefit. The established commercial interests had to vie with the ascendant manufacturers, and the large developers had to contend with the one-third of the city's families that owned their own homes.[83]

In sharp contrast to Manchester, Chicago had no entrenched or cohesive elite to keep the formation of public policy within the tight-fisted grasp of a self-perpetuating oligarchy. On the contrary, widespread property ownership and voting rights among an immigrant majority engendered a completely different political culture and party institutions. The growing multiplicity of special interest groups would make consensus building an increasing difficult and problematic task, giving rise to a new class of ward-based professional politicians. Chicago experienced unprecedented prosperity during the Civil War; it could truly lay claim to the boastful title Gem of the Prairies. However, it remained an open question whose city it would become.

The bloody conflict would turn Chicago into a roaring boomtown; the postwar expansion would sustain the city's commercial development while amplifying its manufacturing sector into a position of dominance. But this mushroomlike growth of an industrial city would also spawn its first civic confrontation with the paradox of progress. The very success of its burgeoning stockyards appeared to threaten the invaluable health of the city's inhabitants. The *Chicago Times* gave perfect expression to the environmental dilemma facing contemporaries. In prefacing a story on the reform movement to get rid of the poisonous miasma rising from the river, a reporter asked rhetorically how "it may seem paradoxical to say that which is the very cornerstone of a city's prosperity should also prove the most important drawback to that prosperity.... Without the river, the city of Chicago would never have existed; with the river the citizens ... [find] it all but impossible to exist."[84]

CHAPTER FOUR

"A Fountain Inexhaustible"

Chicago and Environmental Profligacy

Introduction: "Ever-Lasting Purity"

On 25 March 1867, over twenty thousand Chicagoans came together to mark a heroic engineering feat: the tapping of Lake Michigan two miles out from shore. The largest crowd ever assembled in the history of the city lined up along a parade route to commemorate the completion of a brick tunnel from under the bottom of the lake to a pentagon-shaped island. The project had taken seven years from original concept to final connection between a new pump house and the "Two-Mile Crib," where fresh water entered the mouth of an intake pipe. The city was caught in the midst of yet another cholera epidemic, and the tremendous turnout of the citizens probably represented their collective sigh of relief as much as their joyful celebration. Embarrassment and ridicule would have followed if the effort had failed, but now the imminent arrival of pure water promised to release the community from the grip of anxiety that the constant state of emergency had produced.

Not only did people greet the success of the Two-Mile Crib with euphoria, they also showered acclaim on its seemingly brilliant and audacious designer, Ellis Sylvester Chesbrough. The chief engineer was also elated by this moment of triumph. A long line of dignitaries reminiscent of a medieval procession—complete with costumes and elaborate Masonic symbols—marched through the city center to the site of Chicago's glorious shrine to civic pride and environmental control. They had come to witness the laying of the corner-stone of an appropriately monumental water tower.[1]

A snapshot of the parade provides a revealing portrait of power and pres-tige in an urban society undergoing a period of unparalleled growth and prosperity. Brigadier General Arthur C. Ducat, the chief marshal of the event, was the first to pass the reviewing stand at Clark and Lake streets. Personify-ing the city's contributions to the Union victory, the temporary army officer and career insurance underwriter was followed by the apotheosis of local authority, the entire sixty-man police force. It was kept in step by a military band, which came immediately before the single largest group of marchers, the masons. One hundred and fifty strong, the masons represented not only the courageous bricklayers who had built the underwater tunnel, but all working men who had added to the city's success. Their high profile and their placement ahead of militia and municipal contingencies were signifi-cant, reflecting perceptions of their enhanced political strength in the new, ward-based system of government. Then the Dearborn Light Artillery, accom-panied by their two six-pound guns, and the Ellsworth Zouaves, attired in their fanciful uniforms and plumed hats, filed pass the review stand.

Next the various civic leaders had their turn taking credit for the promised improvement in the quality and safety of the drinking water. This train of local notables began logically enough with the mayor and the aldermen, but its order soon became a curious medley that reflected the anarchistic nature of the civil society. The private contractors were placed ahead of the federal judiciary. Then came the clergy; the press; ex-mayors; serving members of the boards of education, police, and public works; and more former pub-lic servants. Another blaring band separated them from a group of twenty teenagers forming the Quanenbos Collegiate Guards. The fire department brought up the rear, thus saving the marchers' shoes and boots from the droppings of its "powerful" teams of horses.

People in the crowd of parade watchers trailing behind the procession had to watch where they stepped as it proceeded to the North Side site of the dedication. DeWitt Clinton Cregier, manager in charge of the works and Deputy Grand Master of the Masonic Order, helped bury a time capsule under the foundation of the Water Tower. Following this formal ceremony were many speeches, and prayers, and tributes to the city's promise and to its man of the hour, the chief engineer.[2]

But the most revealing remarks were made the following day by Wilbur F. Storey, the influential editor of the city's largest circulation newspaper, the *Chicago Times*. "Yesterday was a great day for Chicago," he rejoiced. "We have the purest water in the world.... We have tapped the lake at a point where exists only ever-lasting purity." Storey barely attempted to disguise an orgasmic metaphor likening the construction of the tunnel shaft to male penetration of an innocent virgin. "In the whirlpool which eddies and circles tumultuously about the thither end of the tunnel," he declared, "the crystalline depths are as pure as the upper regions of space.... Hereafter, when one wants an emblem for chastity, for untainted lives, for immaculate actions, he will not say pure as the stars, but as the crystals which dance at the mouth of the tunnel. Thus: She died in the full flush of youth; she knew no evil; she was spotless, stainless as Chicago drinking water."[3]

Storey's gendered images of man commanding the (re)productive powers of nature for his own use were hardly original. Yet it is exactly in the commonplace of these Victorian attitudes toward the environment that we can find meaning to enable us to understand the false economy of Chicago's approach to water management and public health. True enough, the city stood at the center of a society busy exploiting the natural resources of the hinterland in the name of progress. And admittedly, it is hard to stand at the shores of Lake Michigan even today and not be impressed with its majesty and power. Nonetheless, an arrogant belief that there are no limits to the abuse of this great body of fresh water was bound to result in ever-greater costs in ecological damage and human suffering.[4]

Historians have long admired Chesbrough as "something of a hero ... a talented problem-solver," but from an environmental perspective, he must be regarded as just the opposite. For the most part, scholars have too readily reflected the narrow economic viewpoints of the engineers and businesspeople who have dominated the decision-making process. Like other Americans, historians have been easily seduced in our love affair with public works of enormous scale that dramatically demonstrate human mastery over the forces of nature—what David Nye aptly calls the "technological sublime." Sheer size has had a pivotal influence in determining which structures contemporaries would call engineering marvels, from the Chicago Two-Mile Crib, to the Brooklyn Bridge, the Panama Canal, and Hoover Dam. Only gargantuan creations that appeared to defy the laws of physics seem to have inspired the imaginations of American writers like Wilbur Storey to new heights of literary excitement. Scholars have further inflated Chesbrough's reputation by focusing their attention tightly on sanitation technology in isolation from other, interrelated aspects of water supply, medicine, and social policy.[5]

Environmental perspectives on the history of urban water management help create a broader context within which to make more balanced judgments of the policy makers in charge of this crucial area of public health and welfare. A few recent studies have begun to criticize those in charge of

Chicago's water system as myopic penny-pinchers. Yet few have attempted to assess the costs to the hydraulic ecology and the resulting price in terms of human misery, sickness, and death. From this more holistic point of view, Chesbrough's heroic plan and all those to follow that were based on his underlying assumptions about nature's unbounded resources were doomed to failure. The fundamental contradiction contained within the engineer's scheme was that of drawing on the lake for both a supply of drinking water and a source of fresh water to dilute the city's human and industrial wastes.

Ironically enough, Chesbrough soon began to see the fatal flaw inherent in his strategy to exploit Lake Michigan as a "fountain inexhaustible." In the days before standard engineering textbooks on urban sanitation had been written, touring other cities was almost the only way to learn about current techniques and practices. Significantly Chicago sent its chief engineer on such a tour in 1856, a year *after* he had formulated the master plan of sewerage and drainage. Traveling widely throughout Europe, Chesbrough recognized the leading role being played by England's Edwin Chadwick and his Sanitary Idea.

The American visitor could not help but be impressed with London's massive project of constructing intercepting sewers to keep pollution out of the River Thames. "Public sentiment in favor of sanitary reform," he noted in his follow-up report, "has been ... thoroughly aroused.... The feeling is becoming very general, that wherever practicable, sewage should not be allowed to pollute water courses of any kind." The engineer continued to defend his plan, but doubt and uncertainty had replaced the confidence expressed in the original report. He suggested that the present system could be easily modified by the construction of intercepting sewers leading to the lake at a safe distance from the city. Even better, he concluded, the ship canal could be deepened to flush the river clean with a constant flow of lake water. Chesbrough would spend the next quarter century in fruitless effort to make this plan work.[6]

"The River of Death"

Between the Civil War and the great fire of 1871, the extended debate among the civic elite on eliminating the river stench left no doubt that the city's water supply and sewage disposal systems were intimately coupled to the same source, Lake Michigan. At the height of the struggle to define water management policy in early 1865, the *Chicago Tribune* applauded proposals that "take into consideration the twofold subject of discharging the filth which finds its way into the river, and of furnishing the city with a pure water for drinking purposes." Or as the *Chicago Times* explained in simple, albeit nauseating, terms, "What the housekeeper poured into the sink one week, she was liable to get back through the hydrant [i.e., faucet] a week later. The tea seemed a not remote relative of the slop-bucket." To protect the city's potable supplies from such sickening thoughts and tastes, Chesbrough became the champion of the offshore crib plan.[7]

At the same time, however, he and almost all would-be sanitarians offering strategies to improve conditions continued to rely on Lake Michigan as a depository for the city's liquid wastes. While the "Lake Party" proposed that the wastes be dumped at a shoreline distant from the populated area, the "Mississippi Party," including the city engineer, advocated forcing the sewage through the Illinois and Michigan (I & M) Canal into the Illinois River Valley. Yet, with a few exceptions, even the latter group did not exclude using the lake as the final outfall for a significant proportion of the city's sewage. Purity would be restored neither to the river nor to the drinking supply. Policy makers, driven by intolerable smells and frightening epidemics, lurched from one technological fix to the next in a futile "search for the ultimate sink."[8]

As we have seen, the linkage between the two sides of urban water management had became evident in 1854, almost immediately after the pump house began delivering more than a million gallons a day to the low-lying peninsula forming the emerging central business district. Chesbrough arrived in that year to take charge of the public utility, and he confirmed that it made the city "in some respects worse off than before." The exacerbation of the drainage problem together with the seemingly endless recurrences of cholera at epidemic levels prompted city leaders to hire the waterworks engineer to devise a companion method of disposal. In the years leading up the Civil War, his designs for the first combined sewer and drainage system in the United States helped to get the south division business district out of the muck. East of State Street, the underground pipes he designed emptied directly into the lake. Sewers running downhill to the west dumped their contents into the South Branch and thus indirectly into the lake. The South Branch also received all of the sewage from the west division, which also ultimately found its way into Lake Michigan.

On the North Side, a gently rising topography allowed all the sewer outfalls to discharge into the Main Branch, avoiding further pollution of the North Branch. The liquor distilleries strung along this part of the industrial corridor posed a special problem. They found it profitable to keep attached feedlots crowded with cattle and pigs that ate the spent grains. Thus the river literally furnished an "ultimate sink" for the distillery companies. Within a few years, the sheer volume of sewage entering Lake Michigan effectively nullified the advantage of moving the waterworks more than a half mile north of the mouth of the Chicago River.[9]

Well before the war economy brought its own demands, loud complaints were being voiced about the quickly declining quality of the drinking supply. During the war, the river corridor would be completely overwhelmed with the discarded organic wastes of the meatpackers and the liquor distillers. During the dark winter of 1860–1861, for example, 272,000 hogs were processed in the slaughterhouses clustered along the South Branch. This number already represented an impressive eightfold increase compared to 1848, when Chicago came of age as a commercial entrepôt. But after the fighting began, demand skyrocketed because the Union Army had suddenly become a distant mass consumer. This virtually explosive rise topped out in 1862–1863, when 970,000 hogs—to say nothing of the herds of cattle—moved through an overloaded network of railroad and livestock yards.

Chicago's transportation advantages helped it take bragging rights away from Cincinnati, which had first held the moniker Porkopolis of America. Highly labor-intensive, meatpacking was only the most prominent of several industries undergoing structural transformation, becoming concentrated in urban centers, evolving in scale of operation, and supplying unprecedented numbers of new jobs for unskilled farmhands. A decade of boom times would parallel a spectacular threefold boost in the population, which shot past the three hundred thousand mark at the time of the great fire. By then, Chicago had become a full-fledged industrial ecology.[10]

At the opening of the 1860s, public discourse began to conceptualize the industrial city's paradox of progress in terms of its water supply. The smells emanating from the accumulation of rotting organic wastes in the river had exceeded some undefinable tipping point and were no longer tolerable. Its foul odors could not but stimulate nervous anxieties about infection with every breath of suspected poisonous air. The barely moving estuary was receiving the waste of tens of thousands of people and horses, which were disgorged out of fifty-four miles of sewer mains in the central area. Added to this were the liquid and solid remains of more than a quarter-million slaughtered animals. The sluggish waterway started offending not only the sense of smell, but also that of taste as the river pollution found its way to the intake pipe of the lakefront pump house. New levels of suspected contamination and actual sickness completed the conceptual circle between the lake's abundant supplies of pure water and its misuse as a supposedly safe depository for the city's escalating amounts of liquid waste. The following year, amendments to the city charter institutionalized this unified model of water management, consolidating the original waterworks and sewerage boards into the single Board of Public Works (BPW).

During the war period, the rapid expansion of Chicago drove policy makers to respond to the steady deterioration of the quality of daily life that resulted from the great odors arising from the river. In 1860, Chesbrough's recommendations initially focused on ways to remedy the contamination of the water supply by pollution coming from the river. He presented the city council with several options, including moving the works ten miles farther north, building purification facilities such as filter beds and subsiding reservoirs, and extending an intake pipe out from shore for a mile either on the lake bottom or under it. Becoming chief engineer of the new BPW a year later, he followed up his deep-water proposal by hiring a chemist to investigate the purity of the water at various distances from the beach. His analysis showed uncontaminated supplies at one and a quarter miles out in the lake.

At the same time, the assault of Chicago's befouled hydraulic environment on the senses of taste and smell was quickly reaching a crisis point. To ever more strident pleas and threats from the public and the press, the council responded by adopting Chesbrough's revised plan for an underground tunnel two miles long in order to ensure an extra margin of safety. The aldermen also employed the chemist to gather samples of river pollution in order to fortify their side in the blame game. They exploited his mantle of scientific authority in their attempt to point the public spotlight at the packers' trade wastes and away from the increasing volume of city sewage gushing into the waterway.

Amid well-publicized inspection tours by official "smell committees," in December 1862 the council passed a tough nuisance abatement ordinance. It not only forbade industries lining the river from dumping organic wastes into the watercourse, it also brought slaughterhouses, distilleries, and other facilities under the city's police power, permitting them to operate only if they complied with the law and qualified for a municipal license. Still, since expert studies and local laws did little to alleviate the immediate problem of sickening odors arising from the river, a crescendo of complaints kept the pressure on City Hall. If only the privileged voices of "merchants and others . . . made sick in their offices by exhalations" from the river could reach the inner sanctums of the aldermen, perhaps it would be enough to prod them to take more immediate steps of relief.[11]

As a stopgap measure, the council followed the chief engineer's advice to use the pumps at the Bridgeport end of the I & M Canal to create an artificial current to sweep the river clean. The pumps, which could force 108 million gallons of water per day into the canal, had originally been installed to keep enough water in the channel during the summer months when normal supplies from the Des Plaines River were insufficient. The city cut a deal with the canal commissioners in April 1862, agreeing to pay the cost of having the putrefying waters of the South Branch sucked into the water toll road.[12]

Relieved citizens now observed that the pumps reversed the normal flow of the river, bringing in relatively fresh lake water to replace the stinking mess being flushed down the canal. Although historians dispute the origins of this discovery, the evidence seems in favor of those, like James O'Connell, who argue that Chesbrough knew exactly what the pumps could achieve in environmental control. The engineer saw their use as a cheap short-run solution, especially compared to the time and expense of digging a drainage channel deep enough to create a constant current of water propelled by the force of gravity. Over the next few years, Chicago boosters would attempt without success to get Washington to fund the deep-cut drainage plan, which they disguised as a plan for a national defense highway for moving warships between the Atlantic and the Gulf. In the meantime, the pumps provided some mitigation, slowing a deteriorating situation and keeping it from getting far worse.[13]

If the human-made currents in the industrial corridor seemed to give a temporary reprieve to the senses, they were not sufficient to keep widespread fears of plague arising out of the river's polluted waters from assuming apocalyptic proportions. During the 1850s Chicago had become a human incubator of infectious microbes. Like other populous industrial cities, it suffered from a long list of endemic diseases that could suddenly flare out of control without apparent or consistent explanation. In 1863, for example, erysipelas, a streptococcus-type bacterium that causes an irritating and disfiguring facial skin infection, spread through the river districts with frightening speed. Dr. E. Andrews plotted the geographic pattern of the disease, producing what is possibly Chicago's earliest medical map (see fig. 4.1).

Andrews's research showed that the "epidemic clung to the river," which could only further reinforce popular notions linking polluted water, bad air, and lost health. The doctor adopted the language of biblical revelation to give emphasis to his prophecy of divine retribution. "No city can be bathed in a putrid air with impunity," he warned ominously, "and if Chicago shall neglect to make a thorough removal of its filth, it will be infallibly scourged with these pestilences which through all time have smitten cities that commit sins against cleanliness and pure air." The miasma emanating from swelling amounts of animal manure, urine, blood, and offal and other animal parts being thrown into the river was widely believed to be the immediate cause of the erysipelas outbreak.[14]

The epidemic of 1863 provided the most visible evidence of the onset of a full-blown public health crisis. The following year, inhalations of river

Figure 4.1. Medical map of Chicago, 1863–1870
Source: City of Chicago, Board of Health, *Report of the Board of Health of the City of Chicago for 1867, 1868, and 1869, and a Sanitary History of Chicago from 1833 to 1870* (Chicago: Lakeside, 1871).

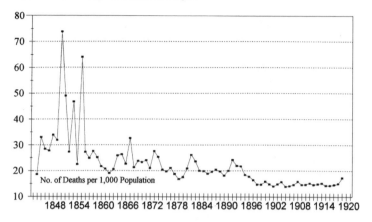

Figure 4.2. Chicago mortality, 1843–1920
Source: City of Chicago, Department of Health, *Annual Report* (1911–1918).

stench and perceptions of disease causation combined to push middle-class businessmen to the breaking point. Articulating their outrage, the eminent lawyer Edwin C. Larned exclaimed in the daily press: "That a city of nearly two hundred thousand inhabitants . . . should quietly permit a river running through its entire limits to be converted into a gigantic sewer . . . here red with blood, there slimy with grease, and black with filth and putrid matter, turning what is in itself a noble and beautiful object into a sight so foul and loathsome as to excite only thoughts of a 'River of Death,' is a matter of profound astonishment." In 1866, the death rate would rise to the state-of-emergency level of 32.2 persons per thousand when cholera swept through the city (see fig. 4.2). A second epidemic, of smallpox, was also causing alarm bells to ring. Scarlet fever, dysentery, diphtheria, measles, and typhoid fever were also raging at high levels.

Larned exploited his personal influence among members of the Board of Trade to leverage the city council into setting up an ad hoc group of politicians and businessmen from the two institutions. The resulting joint committee was charged with recommending a public works plan for permanently keeping the Chicago River clean. In soliciting expert testimony on the best way to resolve the crisis, the committee eagerly turned to the advice of the engineers while shying away from the prescriptions of the doctors.[15]

The Civil War coincided with the nadir of the authority of medical science in the public discourse that was the context of the formation of environmental policy in Chicago. Perhaps the doctors' utter helplessness during the killer epidemics of the preceding decade had undermined the public's faith in their power to protect the body's health and to heal it when it was sick. Or perhaps the intuitive realization that the city had become a perpetual reservoir of sickness and death undercut their influence. In any case, popular skepticism about the special knowledge of physicians was reflected in the council decision of 27 March 1861 to abolish the Department of Health.

But the Chicago Medical Society, led by Dr. Nathan Davis, fought back. "I know of no city except Chicago," Davis protested, "with a population of 110,000, that has neither a Health Officer, Board of Health, nor any other official sanitary organization." The civic denouncement of the profession had been bad enough, but it turned into open ridicule when the mayor, hotel owner F. C. Sherman, responded by appointing his police bodyguard as the "Acting Health Officer."[16]

Only mounting concern about the rise in smallpox cases during 1863 goaded a reluctant council to reinstate the office of the city physician. As a gratuitous insult, however, the aldermen demanded that he pay out of his own pocket for all drugs dispensed and slashed his proposed salary by 40 percent, to only six hundred dollars a year. Although they heeded the medical community's call for a new "Pest House" in which to isolate smallpox patients, they persistently rejected its appeal during the war years that they set up a public system to keep accurate records of the city's births and deaths. In 1867, in the wake of the 1866 cholera epidemic, the Department of Health would finally be restored, too late to participate fully in the search for an ultimate sink.

During the 1860s, the engineers in charge of water management seem to have acted without paying serious attention to the opinions of Dr. Davis and his colleagues in the Chicago Medical Society. One pioneering study of Chicago's environmental history found that "engineers and health officials played complementary roles, but they seldom collaborated to control pollution." Two projects under the supervision of the engineers illustrate the limitations of their approach to solving environmental problems. In large part, the narrowing of focus that these projects represent was the result of the need to meet political demands for fiscally "practicable" proposals for large-scale public works projects.[17]

Eager to please their municipal sponsors, the engineers responded by breaking down the region's complex hydraulic ecology into separate parts. From such a myopic point of view, a remedy for removing putrefying wastes in the stagnant South Branch had no foreseeable consequences for the quality of the city's drinking water. In June 1863, Chesbrough shepherded his deep-water project through the council to counteract the evil of river pollution reaching the pump house's intake pipe. Just four months later, however, the engineers in charge of the I & M Canal decided that the easiest way to empty the channel at the end of the navigation season was simply to reverse the Bridgeport pumps. Pushing the rotting effluvia from the canal and the South Branch into the lake, they added significantly to the risk of the drinking supply becoming contaminated. Water customers believed they could taste the difference.[18]

Members of the Army Corps of Engineers were plotting simultaneously to solve the perennial problem of silting at the mouth of the harbor, but they did not bother to take into consideration Chesbrough's plans for a lake tunnel. While the local authority was digging the underwater conduit and building the massive crib on the lakefront, the federal agency was equally busy extending the pier another one thousand feet in the direction of the island station (see fig. 4.3). The pier blocked the lake's prevailing currents along the shoreline to the south, having the unintended effect of rerouting the natural path of the river's flow to the east in the direction of the two-mile intake pipe. Looking back in 1877, Chesbrough could see what a shortsighted error it had been to fragment the environment into disconnected, manageable pieces:

> At the time the construction of the lake tunnel was determined upon, careful examinations were made and no evidence was obtained that the effect of the river could be perceived more than about a mile and a quarter from the shore; but as the repeated extensions of the piers extended the mouth of the river into the lake . . . ultimately [it] . . . extended much farther out, and thus carried the sewage where the currents of the lake would lead it much nearer the "crib" or entrance to the tunnel.[19]

In contrast, the doctors had a more holistic approach to the urban environment that stemmed from their primary focus on human health rather than infrastructure projects. The organic nature of their subject, the body, inherently defied the kind of technical subdivisions the engineers had found so useful in imagining ways to gain greater control over the physical world. The Chicago engineers had ignored the fact that the city as a natural system is one of our oldest and most enduring metaphors of the workings of the urban infrastructure. Edwin Chadwick and his American followers were only the latest in a long line of sanitarians who drew parallels between the body's circulatory systems and the city's technologies of environmental control of the water and the air. Chesbrough had encountered Chadwick's Sanitary Idea and had admired it, but he had been willing only to modify, not to discard, his original vision for environmental control.[20]

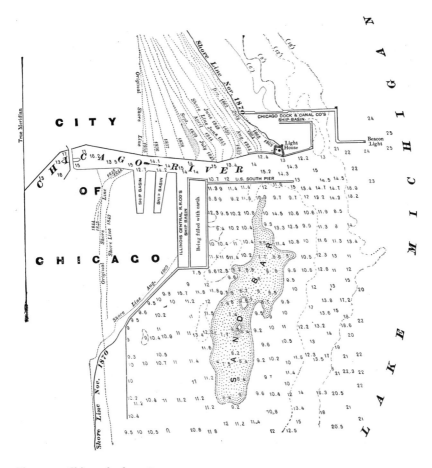

Figure 4.3. Chicago harbor, 1870
Source: A. T. Andreas, *History of Chicago*, 3 vols. (1884–1886; reprint, New York: Arno, 1975), 2:72.

The mysterious nature of the doctors' most formidable enemies, fast-spreading infectious diseases like cholera and smallpox, contributed to the broad perspective that diseases had miasmatic etiologies. Dr. Davis's multi-faceted battle plan of employing environmental services to defend the public health was typical of the medical community's platform of sanitary reform. Davis was already the author of one of the earliest comprehensive plans of water management, dating back to 1850. When City Hall summoned him fifteen years later, once again during the height of a cholera epidemic, a co-ordinated system of delivering pure drinking supplies and removing waste-water remained at the core of his public health strategy. He reiterated the admonition that the city must aggressively speed up expansion of the sewer network to catch up to the pace of the laying of water mains in new, outlying districts.

In Chicago, this uneven, beltlike gap in the infrastructure created a developmental process of environmental destruction. Too much water saturated the land and contaminated the groundwater before sewers were built. The ring of suburban areas was waterlogged as a result of the fundamentally different methods of financing the two utility services. On the one hand, the waterworks was a legacy of the segmented system. Annual service bills were unconscionably lucrative to city coffers, while the heavy fixed expenses of construction and hookups were financed separately by municipal bonds and special assessments. On the other hand, the sewer system was a part of the ascendant citywide system of government. Only the fees for building hookups could be collected directly from property owners. The original geographical concept of a special-purpose tax district also helped to establish the sacrosanct precedent of paying for these extensions from general property taxes.[21] While fat profits from the waterworks encouraged extension of its services, tight budgets from tax receipts restrained construction of city sewers. Dr. Davis wanted the city to execute a much more proactive program to force home owners enjoying water services to hook up to the sewer system.

Davis also called for a full array of supplemental countermeasures, including a significant expansion in local government's police powers over the environment, and he recommended beefing up the bureaucracy to enforce compliance with these regulations. While health inspectors would safeguard the land from overflowing privies and accumulating slaughterhouse wastes, patrol boats would protect the water from riverfront polluters and midnight dumpers. In addition, Davis envisioned a public sanitation department to keep the streets clean and to remove the garbage and ashes from the alleys.[22]

Of course, the aldermen's half-hearted measures to implement his package of reforms could do little to stem the spread of the cholera outbreak. In November 1865, the council's belated appeal to the medical community to reconstitute a Board of Consulting Physicians came almost a year after the key decisions had been made on the choice of policy options for cleaning up the river. Although the doctors' concepts of health, disease, and nature were clearly evident in the planning debate, they were conspicuously absent in the shape of its outcome.[23]

Between January and March 1865, a plan for the design of Chicago's new ultimate sink was hammered out in a fierce political struggle among the businessmen, engineers, and politicians. The close infighting among them to gain control over the governance and financing of the public works project elicited a wide-ranging discussion about a surprising number of proposals for managing the city's hydraulic ecology. Historians have frequently listed the options outlined by the chief engineer—in the 1860s, Chesbrough advocated a deep-cut canal plan with add-ons: auxiliary channels to create an artificial current through the North and South Branches with water pumped out of Lake Michigan—but they have not gone beyond his reports to ask if other plans were a part of this civic debate. Actually, several additional models held popular attention, at least briefly, as credible alternative schemes for the sewerage and drainage of the city. The recovery of at least two of these forgotten plans sheds light on contemporary attitudes toward the urban environment and its energy system.[24]

The initial assault in the reform battle was set in motion just three days after the new year by a group of businessmen who had long before passed the point of tolerating the river miasma. An angry Edwin Larned organized what came to be known as the Committee of Thirty after the politicians had turned the promise of the joint committee into a dead end of frustration. The reformers' manifesto announced their determination to take direct political action. It conveyed a fascinating mix of concerns about physical states of sickness and well-being, the environmental quality of civic life, and the commercial prospects of the city. "The present foul and corrupt condition of the waters of the river and the lake," they protested in a revealing passage, "not only impairs the comfort of the citizens and injures the reputation of the city, but threatens the most serious danger to the public health and prosperity." The businessmen hoped to get a steamroller of popular support in motion behind a full-scale proposal for a combination of an ultimate sink and industrial corridor development. Adding the momentum of expert authority to their insurgency, they enlisted some of the city's most respected engineers, such as Roswell B. Mason, the master builder of the Illinois Central Railroad and of its massive landfill project near the mouth of the river.[25]

One version of the Lake Plan, the committee's Calumet Plan, envisioned a canal running nine miles southeast from the emerging meatpacking district on the South Branch to the Calumet River (see fig. 4.4). Steam-powered pumps would draw fresh water into the Chicago River that would then be flushed, with its load of pollution, back into Lake Michigan at a presumably safe distance away from the city's drinking supply. As figure 4.4 shows, the Calumet Plan also had the highly touted advantage of embracing private values while acknowledging the necessity for large-scale public works projects. This early model of a planned industrial district promised rich profits for landowners, shippers, and manufacturers. The main designer was none other than the president of the BPW, John G. Gindele.

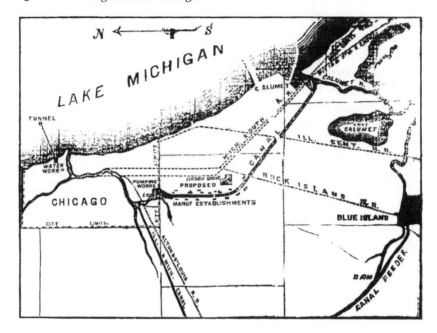

Figure 4.4. Calumet Plan
Source: *Chicago Times*, 16 January 1865.

The engineers' blueprints were given legislative construction by the Committee of Thirty in the form of a proposed enabling act that the committee anticipated introducing in the following month's session of the state legislature. Larned, Wirt Dexter, and other attorneys drafting the bill, however, rebuffed democratic values. Their proposal specified that an independent governing board would not be elected by the people but appointed by the judges of the circuit court. Nonetheless, this Chicago River Commission would be empowered to issue up to $3 million in municipal bonds and conveniently shift the burden of collecting the taxes to pay for them to City Hall. To finance the ongoing operations of the new agency, the business leaders' bill imposed what amounted to a sliding scale of user fees, or "drainage licenses," on the companies dumping wastes directly into the waterway.[26]

One example of a Mississippi River Plan forgotten by history represented a viable alternative to Chesbrough's deep-cut canal proposal. The Des Plaines Plan was the brainchild of scion William B. Ogden and was designed by William Gooding, "one of the ablest engineers in the state," according to the *Chicago Tribune*. Ogden and Gooding's vision projected a sanitary channel separate from the shipping lane and dedicated to environmental control.

Chicago's top booster argued that this option had the dual benefit of quick relief and low cost in comparison to any scheme involving the I & M Canal, which was financially tied up in London bond houses and bogged down in shipping commitments that largely precluded construction work during the warmer seasons when it could be performed. Instead, Ogden welcomed the coming of spring as the ideal time to dredge a drainage ditch from the headwaters of the South Branch westward across the soft, soggy soils of Mud Lake to the Des Plaines River about seven miles away. This endpoint was ten to fifteen feet above the level of the lake, but the city's supreme promoter promised that the deepening of the riverbed would result in a substantial saving of time and expense as opposed to the alternative of cutting through solid rock at the geological summit of the canal's route.

Yet Ogden's plan, like Chesbrough's and most others, included a mechanism for periodically flushing the river's polluted wastes into Lake Michigan. A controlling works could be built, Ogden reasoned, so that "when the Des Plaines was raised six to ten feet by flood, its waters would sweep into the lake with force, cleaning out and deepening our river and harbor entrance most desirably." Recalling the great flood of 1849, he stressed the urgency of accepting his proposal in time to harness the natural freshets of early spring. Ogden believed he had found a way of purging the river stink that was free of cost, but he did not consider the price that would be paid by the people who would suffer from drinking contaminated water.[27]

There was little attempt to disguise the self-serving motives embedded in the various plans put forth by the municipal reformers. Ogden was the major owner of the Mud Lake wetlands. The Des Plaines Plan would enhance the value of the speculators' properties since the sanitary channel would conveniently supply a means to drain them at public expense. In a similar way, Gindele's inner circle of venture capitalists held options on choice parcels of land along the proposed route of the industrial canal. A legacy of the booster era, large gray areas remained between the public and private sectors at war's end. In spite of the fierce competition among the promoters of the various schemes, they never challenged each other's right to reap personal profits from public works.[28]

In sharp contrast, the formation of the Committee of Thirty triggered the opening salvo in a naked battle between local businessmen and city politicians for the reins of power. Meeting on the same evening as the Committee of Thirty, 3 January 1865, the aldermen made it perfectly clear that they had no intention of letting go of their prerogative to set water management policy. They called the special session to draw attention to the fact that they had prepared their own plan for environmental reform, which they had already translated into an enabling bill for submission to the state legislature. Suddenly reviving the report of the moribund joint committee, City Hall approved its recommendations for pursing several options, including the authorization of $2 million in additional municipal debt; pursuit of the Des Plaines Plan; the construction of the auxiliary canal on the South Branch proposed by Chesbrough; and the appointment of a panel of consulting engineers. As the ensuing conflict would bring out, however, neither side was deeply committed to any particular planning design or administrative structure for the project.[29]

Instead, the heart of the contest between the city council and the business community was for political control of the money machine that would pay for the urban infrastructure. The winner of this intense struggle would determine who set the capital budget on public works spending as well as the proportional amounts of taxes to be levied on property owners and licensed businesses. On the surface, the challenge mounted by the Committee of Thirty reflected a lingering resistance to the replacement of the segmented system by neighborhood wards. Underneath the policy debate, it also exposed a continuing opposition to democratic forms of popular government.

Although the new ward system of elections was only two years old, the municipal corporation as an institution had a long track record of success in upholding public authority against private rights. Speaking for the city's nascent professional politicians, City Comptroller S. S. Hayes denounced the businessmen's initiative as a bald usurpation of power. On 17 January, he attended the second open meeting of the business leaders' committee. Boldly taking the offensive, he called its proposal for an appointed commission a "direct insult to the Board of Public Works ... and a direct insult to the people of Chicago who have elected that Board."

Hayes drew upon the republican shibboleth of "no taxation without representation" to demand that any sanitation plan come under the jurisdiction of officers chosen at the polls. He called for the adoption of a substitute bill that left planning and administration vested in the BPW, but it was defeated. Another politician, Alderman C. Holden, then moved to attach a referendum proviso to the bill, but the motion was ruled out of order. The businessmen were determined to remove decision-making power from the urban masses and their local representatives. Taking the side of the Committee of Thirty, the *Chicago Tribune* castigated the city's politicians for their do-nothing "tortoise policy." The Republican newspaper warned Hayes in particular that he "had better move with" the business leaders, "or he may be run over." In a rare case of agreement with its partisan rival, the *Chicago Times* lent the weight of its editorial influence as well to the business leaders' cause.[30]

Three days later, the city council launched a counteroffensive to push back the juggernaut of public opinion mounting behind the reform movement. Meeting again in special session, the aldermen marshaled the two other members of the BPW to attack President Gindele's claim that the board was overwhelmed with work. Furthermore, they asserted that it was the city's only authorized agency of water management planning and administration. Alderman Holden then introduced a bill similar to the one rejected by the Committee of Thirty, protesting against the committee's perversion of "the principle of local self-government of the people." Holden's resolution provided for the appointment of a panel of consulting engineers to decide upon the best plan that did not exceed a $2 million cap on spending by the BPW.

Holden now added political muscle to the proposal in order to wrestle the initiative away from the business leaders. He proposed that a lobby of elected officials would be dispatched to Springfield to condemn the Committee of Thirty's bill as a dangerous breach in the safeguards protecting the taxpayers of the city. The City Hall lobby was also charged with ensuring the passage of its alternative legislation. Several aldermen attempted to preempt the planning of the project by proposing specific designs for the cleaning up of the river. After extended debate, however, all of the politicians except one, George W. Gage of the downtown First Ward, rallied together to present a united front in the looming confrontation with the business leaders.[31]

In the highly charged partisan atmosphere of the state capitol, the businessmen were no match for the politicians. The Committee of Thirty's bill was defeated, but the final showdown sparked the passing of a flurry of public and private laws to deal with Chicago's emerging industrial ecology. The centerpiece of this burst of legislative creativity remained the bill the city council sponsored in order to retain its hold on the reins of power over large-scale water management projects. To fortify the legitimacy of their authority, two more engineers, Mason and Gooding, were added to the BPW as acting members in matters concerning the river cleanup. Party loyalty's advantage over business influence was embodied in provisions that shifted the ultimate cost of the drainage project onto the freight being shipped through the state-owned I & M Canal.

By approving Chesbrough's deep-cut plan, the lawmakers were able to justify funding it as a fulfillment of the original design of the waterway. The legislature claimed that it was simply making good on promises that had had to be deferred during hard times. With the London bondholders scheduled to be paid off in 1872, the legislature easily finessed its way around any problems with them that Ogden presumed would otherwise be insurmountable. The canal improvement act created a second lien of traffic tolls that would underwrite up to $2 million in new municipal bonds. The city council still awaited the report of its panel of experts, but the attractive deal worked out in Springfield would prove irresistible to just about everyone. The politicians would keep control of large-scale public works projects while the local taxpayers and the polluting industries on the riverfront were being given a virtual free ride in getting rid of the city's liquid wastes.[32]

Chicago's business leaders had private plans to reduce the river stink in the business district as well. The big packers and railroads joined hands to create the Union Stock Yard and Transit Company. They planned to move the slaughterhouses away from the city center to a single 320-acre site on the Southwest Side, just outside the city limits at Thirty-Ninth Street. This suburban location was chosen because it was beyond the settlement line but close enough to the Chicago River for the slaughterhouses to continue using the waterway as an ultimate sink. The new stockyards would encompass a portion of the South Fork of the South Branch, making the Calumet Plan the logical choice of the Board of Trade–inspired Committee of Thirty.

At the same time, the largest and most efficient firms also favored environmental regulations that would impose uniform standards on Chicago's entire dressed beef industry. In this way, they hoped to use the power of the state to put the fly-by-night operators who were giving them a bad reputation out of business. These goals help explain why the leading firms lined up to support the passage of another law, which directed the city council to appoint a health officer who would be charged with enforcing a stringent set of cleanliness rules on the meatpackers and the manufacturers of by-products such as soap, lard, and tallow, both within city borders and beyond them in a four-mile cordon sanitaire.[33]

The following month, the blue-ribbon panel of engineers declared the I & M Canal deep cut the best plan, closing the policy debate and opening the way for the plan's implementation. The five experts, including Chesbrough, Mason, and Gooding, had reduced "a great number of communications" that offered ideas into three "general plans." The other two plans were for a system of intercepting sewers and a pair of auxiliary "cutting canals" from the lake to the two branches of the river. The panel argued in favor of its choice because it was the only "self-acting"—that is, gravity-fed—design, it kept the river wastes out of the lake, and it had the lowest effective cost to the city in spite of having the highest price tag. The construction phase would take an estimated three years, but the engineers reasoned that the Bridgeport pumps would fill the gap if the city enforced the nuisance regulations against industrial dumping.[34]

The engineers knew full well the danger the river water posed to the purity of the drinking supply, but all of the options presented significantly increased just this kind of risk to the public health. They focused tightly on the single goal of creating a constant current in the stream in order to remove its polluting wastes, "which have given Chicago a world wide fame for its vile odors." The result was a myopic vision of environmental control that looked at only one side of the inherently interdependent relationship between sewage removal and water supply in Chicago. Using some undisclosed formula, the experts determined that 258 million gallons of lake water a day would be needed to flush the river every forty-eight hours, an amount about two-and-a-half times greater than the capacity of the Bridgeport pumps. To achieve the same current with the proposed auxiliary canals, reversible pumps would "force the filthy waste out [into the lake], or the lake waters in." The engineers designed an intercepting sewer system that assumed a final outfall in the lake. They did not pause to consider sending it somewhere else, such as to outlying fertilizer farms or into the I & M Canal.

In the case of the deep-cut plan, the engineers designed a series of locks that would enable them to simulate natural freshets. These artificial waves, they proposed, "could be suddenly discharged into the Chicago River, making a strong current to the lake."[35] They had chosen the biggest, most environmentally damaging option for getting rid of the river stink. Here was a chance to build a dramatic public works project that would permanently reverse a river, turning it into a huge drainage ditch plugged into an inexhaustible source of "ever-lasting purity."

In contrast to the experts' cavalier and shortsighted approach to water management, they expressed more circumspect and realistic attitudes toward their limitations in engineering the industrial city. Unless the city council strictly enforced a no-tolerance manufacturers' waste policy, they warned, all of the money and effort spent on public works "will only mitigate the evil." The experts singled out the distilleries on the North Branch since its waters were free from city sewage and its rate of flow would be only marginally affected by the deep-cut project. The city council faced the choice of either forcing the distilleries to stop dumping their feedlot and factory wastes into the river or bearing the extra half-million-dollar expense of cutting an auxiliary canal along Fullerton Street to the lake in the near future.

Not only did it cost an estimated twenty thousand dollars annually to operate steam-driven pumps, the engineers predicted gloomily that their expert ingenuity would be more than offset by human greed. "The proposed canal," they anticipated, "would probably encourage and increase to a very great extent filthy discharges into ... the river from establishments that would be most probably nuisances of themselves to their neighborhoods."[36] In this respect, the engineers reinforced the doctors' case in favor of an activist administration that would take a broad view of government's duty to exercise the police power in the name of the public health and welfare.

Ironically, the engineers expressed serious concern about energy conservation even as they showed a gross disregard for the environmental protection of Lake Michigan. However, this stark contradiction was not as apparent as it seems. They did not worry about the depletion of fossil fuels while ignoring the value of pure water. It is doubtful that they bothered at all to take the conservation of natural resources into consideration. Instead, the issue was the drain on city budgets and ultimately taxpayer pocketbooks caused by the expense of coal to keep the pumps running. And like their preference for the deep cut's "self-acting" mechanism, the engineers held the belief that they had a way to harness nature to the pumps free of charge. They contended that putting windmills on the beach was worth a try; or maybe the lake's tidal motions could be put to work in the service of the city.[37]

Almost exactly two years later, at the grand dedication of the Water Tower on 25 March 1867, a mortar was set as its cornerstone that represented something more than the human will's conquest of the natural world. Pump house chief Cregier was cementing the symbiotic relationship between the politicians and the engineers as his trowel sealed a time capsule under the monument. Imagery of triumphalism also adorned the speeches Chicago's leaders presented that memorable day. "We have the water pure from yonder glittering reservoir made by God brought to our houses by the genius and industry of man," Mayor John B. Rice declared in typical fashion. Singing praise to the builders of the public works masterpiece, Rice called it "the great storehouse of the city's health." But he reserved the highest adulation for Chesbrough, "a man whose name is heralded throughout the scientific world because of this great achievement and whose fame rests upon a foundation so broad and deep that it will endure for ages."[38]

This oratorical deification of the chief engineer went hand in hand with a political rhetoric of self-congratulation. The mayor and other elected officers celebrated their own Olympian sagacity in sponsoring a public utility that would enhance the prosperity of the city while paying for itself by way of customer fees and special assessments. City Hall could take credit, according to Rice, not only for the anticipated drop in public and private health bills, but also for "the increase of the working [man's] ability, and the moral and intellectual advancement of the entire population attendant upon the improvement in their physical condition."[39]

The deep-cut project now under way held a similar promise of delivering big payoffs to local politicians and their partners, the civil engineers. The Two-Mile Crib and tunnel project managers had spent $2.5 million in jobs and contracts over a four-year period. The construction of Chicago's new ultimate sink would eventually cost over $3 million and take six years to complete. By then, the great conflagration of 1871 would force water management priorities to shift in the direction of fire prevention. The engineers would seek to accommodate the political needs of elected officials to resolve this different kind of state of emergency, thus creating opportunities for professional advancement as well.

"Legitimate Objects of the City's Care"

Members of the medical profession were conspicuously absent from the speakers' stand at the Water Tower, but they had good reason to rejoice nonetheless. Not only was there the promise of pure water, the doctors had just helped move a bill through the statehouse reestablishing the Department of Health, which would fall under the control of a board of physicians. Passed two weeks earlier over the opposition of the penny-pinching city council, the Chicago Medical Society–sponsored legislation had prevailed because it was backed by elite business groups such as the Board of Trade and the Mercantile Association.

The municipal reformers had closely copied a model law enacted during the cholera epidemic in New York City a short time before. Fear of the deadly disease motivated elites in both cities to petition for higher taxes to pay for better public services—between August and December 1866, almost a thousand Chicagoans had perished. Embodying the lessons of the war experience, the innovative acts represented a start toward a more activist government armed with sweeping police powers to safeguard the health and welfare of the industrial city. "In the history of public health in the United States," Charles Rosenberg notes in a seminal study, "there is no date more important than 1866, no event more significant than the organization of the Metropolitan Board of Health."[40]

The bloody conflict also had the ironic effect of setting in motion the rehabilitation of the expert authority of the medical profession. Public opinion was turning around less because of the surgeons' skill in binding the soldiers' wounds than because of their ability to save them from succumbing to infection afterward. The sanitary work of the doctors and nurses behind the lines had earned them new respect among both the male officers of the troops on the battlefield and the female organizers of the sanitary fairs on the home front. Equally important, the knowledge gained about saving lives gave American physicians a badly needed dose of self-confidence. A generation of seasoned medical veterans returned to the cities with a positive image of themselves as skilled specialists in preventing disease from spreading among large populations. They also brought back powerful weapons of statistical analysis to bolster their social status as scientists and professionals. During the postwar period, they would bring these quantitative tools to bear in the next round of the fight to win political influence on a par with that of the engineers in the formation of public policy.[41]

In Chicago, the first head of the Department of Health, Dr. John H. Rauch, exemplified the new urban sanitarians. Born in 1828 in Pennsylvania, he attended the state university, obtained a medical degree, and joined the research team of the nation's most prominent scientist, Harvard geologist Louis Agassiz. In 1857, he moved to Chicago to accept a position on the faculty of the Rush Medical College. Two years later, he became one of the founders of a related spin-off, the Chicago College of Pharmacy. Rauch served the Union cause throughout the war, rising to the prestigious position of medical director of the Army of the Potomac. Coming home, the doctor immediately began applying the lessons of the battlefields to the neighborhoods. In addition to taking charge of a massive cleanup campaign, he started a movement to create a system of public parks.

In the decade following the war, Dr. Rauch led Chicago doctors in the institutionalization of the medical community as a participant in the decision-making process on public health and environmental control. From his official position as superintendent of sanitation, he spearheaded two key reforms that engendered widespread belief in the special, expert authority of his profession: He undertook a careful survey of the city's hydraulic infrastructure to produce a detailed statistical correlation between the quality of life and the risk of disease in each ward. He also directed a crusade to vaccinate every schoolchild against smallpox because he knew it would produce tangible, indisputable results.

The sanitarian matched his leadership in municipal reform with a commitment to promote medical education and professionalism. In 1872, he helped establish the American Public Health Association. Four years later, he was elected its president. The following year, he was instrumental in the organization of the Illinois State Board of Health, which he then directed until his retirement in the mid-1890s.[42]

Over the course of his impressive career, however, Dr. Rauch's generation of physicians faced much higher barriers to professional recognition and political influence than the engineers. During the Gilded Age, the lack of a satisfactory theory of disease causation imposed the single greatest restraint on popular acceptance of medicine as a science. Painfully aware of the shortcomings of miasmatic theories, doctors and biologists throughout the Atlantic community were engaged in a wide-ranging search for a new paradigm that would enable the identification of individual agents of particular diseases. Doctors, and ministers as well, also suffered as a result of broad cultural changes that tended to divide society into separate spheres according to gender. While the engineers' work building cities cast them in heroic masculine roles, the doctors' job of caring for the sick put them in the domestic realm of subservient women. The sanitarians' vocal expressions of concern about society's moral and ethical duty to the less fortunate classes reinforced impressions of them as sentimental and feminine. The growth of women's political activism in these areas of public health and welfare may have further strengthened the shackles keeping medical practitioners from achieving a status of authority equal to that of the civil engineers.[43]

Yet, in contrast to their sinking reputation during the antebellum period, doctors now encountered a receptive public willing to pay attention to their advice on the best ways to improve the quality of urban life. The complete difference in the responses to Dr. Rauch's call for the removal of dead bodies from the public cemetery just before and just after the war illustrates the newly won respect for the medical veterans in the public sphere. In 1858, Rausch had lent his professional authority to a group of middle-class protesters who lived near the city burial ground on the beach just across the city limits at North Avenue and Clark Street. Despite the doctor's endorsement, their not-in-my-backyard (NIMBY) petitions had fallen on deaf ears in the city council.

But the city leaders were ready to listen eight years and sixteen thousand corpses later, when the doctor published an updated version of his paper on the urban geography of the living and the dead. Dr. Rauch argued that the error of placing too many decaying, disease-ridden bodies so close to populated areas was compounded by the fact that they had to be put in shallow graves since the water table was only three or four feet below the surface at the lakefront. Sounding warning bells about vitiated air and contaminated water, he asked the city council, "where was the Health Officer?" The council chose to answer him this time: they took his advice and had the coffins relocated and the burial ground converted into park land. In a similar way, Dr. Rauch soon obtained what Dr. Davis had long been denied, an official registry of births and deaths in the city.[44]

A string of quick victories like these stimulated a heady sense of optimism among Chicago physicians that they were witnessing the birth of a new politics of public health and sanitation. Between 1865 and 1868, for instance, the aldermen approved generous appropriations for garbage scavenger services and sewer extensions, passed the tough nuisance abatement and license ordinance, erected an isolation hospital, and supported Dr. Rauch's campaign to require that every schoolchild be vaccinated.

Chicago suddenly became a beehive of sanitary activity. During Dr. Rauch's first year in office, 7,769 loads of ashes were carted away; 8,192 privy nuisances abated; 12,281 dead animals removed from the streets; 10,653 manure heaps eliminated; and 1,859 orders issued to landlords requiring them to connect their buildings to the sewer system. All together, the Department of Health issued over thirty-five thousand notices. This fury of cleanliness seemed to work: cholera did not return to epidemic levels and death rates fell dramatically, from a peak of 32.6 down to 23.7 per thousand people.[45]

Riding this wave of success, the chief health officer launched a comprehensive sanitary survey of the city. He correlated statistics of disease and environment, plotting social and geographic patterns of causation. A follower of the soil moisture theory of Max Pettenkofer, the doctor drew links between such factors as sewer pipes per ward and cholera cases, population densities and mortality rates, and surface elevations above lake levels and health conditions of the districts. The importance of this study and of a follow-up report three years later in 1873 cannot be stressed too much because they established the scientific foundation upon which the medical professionals would build their authority as public health experts.

The methodologies Dr. Rauch introduced, rather than his conclusions, are what mark this historic divide. Quoting a well-known textbook on the subject, the doctor declared that "an accurate basis of facts, derived from a sufficient amount of experience, and tabulated with the proper precision, lies at the very foundation of hygiene, as of all exact sciences." The public's need to know Chicago's vital statistics, he argued, had to take priority over the boosters' need to suppress bad news about the city's health status.[46]

Dr. Rauch was equally emphatic about the moral imperatives of environmental justice in the formation of public health policy, or what he called the "sanitary duties" of the city. His research documented the gap in the provision of sewers between the rich and the poor neighborhoods. His statistical analysis, moreover, drew a positive correlation between good drainage and good health. "As a general rule," he found, "sewerage is wanting where the poorer, and especially foreign portion of our population live, and as a necessary consequence, owing to their condition, they are compelled to resort to our public charities for care and treatment, thus making the difference in the ward mortality still greater."

Rauch was especially concerned about the extraordinary death rates of children under five years old. These infants accounted for 54 percent of the mortality in the city compared to 41 percent in the nation as a whole. He did not oppose good drainage in the well-to-do sections, but he insisted that priorities be set on the basis of sanitary need, not political clout. The health officer asserted that "the drainage of the poorer parts of the city, where population is dense, should be the first care of the municipal authorities. Those living in such districts are least able to control the conditions that affect health, and, therefore, are legitimate objects of the city's care."[47]

Like other city bureaucrats, however, Dr. Rauch found that his sense of social justice soon came up against the limitations on public-sector activism that were being imposed by an emerging political culture of urban growth. To be sure, the inauguration of a neighborhood-based system of wards in 1863 represented a major victory for popular government over the privileging of private property that had been the case under the segmented system. Yet the struggle for control of the municipal purse strings was far from over, as we have seen in the effort to settle on a public works plan to get rid of the river stink. Compared to those in other American cities, Chicago's first generation of professional politicians were caught in an especially tight vise, between the exploding demands of a population that had tripled in size in a single decade and the relentless pressures of the taxpayers to keep their bills to a minimum. And in complete contrast to Manchester, universal male suffrage and widespread home ownership made these taxpayers a significant proportion of the voters in working-class as well as more affluent wards. The tax base was expanding, but municipal revenues lagged far behind the immediate need for better public services and infrastructure extensions.[48]

Over the course of the Reconstruction decade, the struggle between the politicians and the taxpayers resulted in a quid pro quo of low-cost government. By 1885, this informal contract would give Chicagoans the lowest per capita taxes of the nation's big cities. As long as the city council kept a tight lid on general taxes, the business elite generally abandoned the effort to monitor the daily administration of local government. Property owners large and small also retained control over special assessments to finance a wide range of infrastructure improvements, from sidewalks to street lights. To further safeguard the taxpayers, Chicago followed many American urban centers in imposing constitutional limitations on the size of the city's municipal indebtedness.

In exchange, the aldermen were given a relatively free hand to disburse the jobs and contracts that financed the party's money machines. These prerogatives helped turn them into ward bosses who reigned supreme within their own fiefdoms. At the citywide level, the single most important source of power became the council's finance committee, not the mayor's office, because the finance committee determined the annual budget. A political culture of fiscal conservatism and constitutional limitation was fostered by affluent people's fear that the urban masses of foreign immigrants and poor people would tax them to death. The shocking exposure of the first big city boss, New York's William M. Tweed, seemed to confirm all of their worst suspicions about these "dangerous classes."

On the contrary, however, the working classes supported the politics of urban growth, with its centerpiece, low-cost government. A large proportion of the city's working-class people had bourgeois aspirations to become home owners. At the time of the fire, a recent study estimates, about one in five adult males owned real estate in Chicago. Keeping property taxes as low as possible was one of the prerequisites of this version of the American Dream. The second was a flexible means of financing infrastructure improvements that allowed property holders to defer the attainment of these amenities until they could afford to pay for them. Special assessments seemed ready-made for this pay-as-you-go ethic of upward social mobility on the installment plan. Working-class home owners added sidewalks, sewer hookups, and so on gradually as their mortgages were paid down. This fiscal system of low general taxes and optional special assessments not only allowed entry into the real estate market for many Chicagoans, it also provided them security against being literally taxed out of their homes in the future.[49]

Department heads like Dr. Rauch may have owed their appointments to the chief executive, but they depended on the inner circle of aldermen on the finance committee for their funding. The apparent success of the new breed of public health experts in preventing a return of cholera epidemics after 1866 had the ironic effect of undercutting their efforts to create the "sanitary city."[50] Political support for Dr. Rauch's ethical vision of the "sanitary city" faded as the threat of epidemic crises receded into the past. He had helped put the medical community on a new footing in the formation of public health policy, but the path remained a narrow one. The initial burst of activism to clean up the city settled down to day-to-day bureaucratic routines of fighting for budget appropriations, issuing nuisance abatement notices, inspecting food venders, negotiating scavenger contracts, and tracking down the sources of errant "vile odors" polluting the air.

The glaring gap between available resources and unmet goals confronting the Department of Health was emblematic of a fiscally anemic public sector. The political formation of urban space in Chicago left some neighborhoods without a fair share of sewer extensions, regular garbage pick-ups, health inspectors, and a host of other municipal services. As Dr. Rauch's studies graphically illustrated, local government's chronic state of poverty was reflected in a landscape that was becoming more deeply divided into separate spheres of riverfront slums and lakefront suburbs. The catastrophic fire of 1871 would sharply accelerate the pace of this process of spatial segregation.

"Somewhere Out in the Prairie"

The conflagration spurred massive changes in settlement patterns, transforming Chicago from a commercial city into an industrial one. The rebuilding accelerated preexisting patterns of both outward physical expansion and internal social reorganization of land use. During the 1860s, this spatial metamorphosis had involved finding room not only for a threefold increase in population but also for an even more remarkable sevenfold boost in the amount of capital invested in industrial facilities. The sudden upsurge in the construction of slaughterhouses and liquor distilleries along the riverfront was indicative of the robustness of the manufacturing sector. William Cronon's "nature's metropolis" of meat, lumber, and grains was the context of equivalent exploitation of the earth's in organic resources: iron, coal, and clay. Between the fire and the onset of the depression of 1873, industrial production would skyrocket another 137 percent. Just keeping up with this boom in terms of providing hydraulic infrastructure and urban services posed a formidable challenge to the public sector. The private sector too faced a great trial: that of turning the fastest-growing big city in the Western world into a place for building communities as well as making profits.[51]

The single greatest makeover of the urban environment occurred in the central business district (CBD). In *The Limits of Power*, Christine M. Rosen gives a comprehensive analysis of the ways in which businessmen redeveloped this area. Their buildings had burned down in the great fire but the reasons for Chicago's ascendancy as the gateway to the West were undiminished. Most of the rail network and the industrial plant were untouched, helping to account for its phoenixlike rise from the ashes. In the CBD, almost all housing, especially ramshackle workers' homes on the south and west sides, was replaced by commercial structures.

The new commercial structures were built on a larger scale with more substantial building materials. Individuals like Palmer Potter were also able to turn the disaster to personal advantage. Heavily invested in properties along State Street, which runs north and south, he was able to leverage offers of credit to turn the axis of the city center ninety degrees from its original, east-to-west direction along Water and Lake streets.[52] However, while the commercial interests' campaign for a fireproof CBD achieved success, their efforts to prevent the return of noxious industries to the riverfront failed.

In the face of the paradox of progress, Chicago's policy makers balked at upsetting private vested rights. "Chicagoans both disliked and could not live without dangerous and polluting manufacturing activity," Rosen confirms. Following the lead of the meatpackers, some of the city's fastest-growing heavy industries took advantage of the fire to move to more spacious tracts of land. Cyrus McCormick's farm tool factory, the Columbian Iron Works, and various bridge, rail, and steel mills relocated on the southwest edge of the river's industrial corridor. But most manufacturers insisted on returning to their existing sites. They defeated the Board of Health–proposed ordinances that were aimed at cutting down the amount of trade waste being dumped into the river. Real estate developers had even fewer limits in planning residential communities on the flat land that seemed to stretch forever on the south and west sides of the city.[53]

The rise of Packingtown and Hyde Park represents a pair of classic case studies in the response of local business leaders to a common problem, explosive urban growth. The two residential *quartiers* were just a couple of miles away from each other, yet they were worlds apart (see fig. 4.5). In terms of the quality of daily life, the two communities came to starkly portray environmental inequality and social segregation by class and ethnicity/religion.

The origins of the Union Stock Yards illustrate the interplay of jobs, housing, and environment in the development of the industrial districts of the city. Contemporaries were well aware that slaughterhouses were undesirable neighbors that should be as isolated as possible from other built-up areas. The river stink hammered home this point, encouraging the meatpackers to relocate their scattered facilities from the congestion of the central city to a much larger remote site where transportation and processing could be efficiently coordinated and consolidated. Even before the fire, according to a *Chicago Tribune* article of June 1864, promoters had planned to put the new facility "somewhere out on the prairie, beyond the line ever to be reached by the expanding city."[54]

But it did not take long for people seeking work to start building stores and houses across from the entrance to the new mecca of jobs. "Already something of a village has grown up around the yards," the newspaper reported only eighteen months later, "and the smoke of scores of chimneys may be seen rising from the vicinity."[55] As in Ancoats, then, housing construction followed the building of factories because low wages forced employees to live close enough to walk to work.

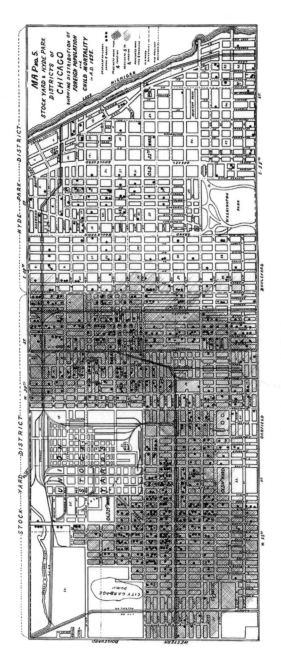

Figure 4.5. Bushnell medical map of Hyde Park and Stockyards districts, 1898

Source: Charles Bushnell, "Some Aspects of the Chicago Stock Yards," *American Journal of Sociology* 7 (1901–1902), map no. 5.

Note: Dots indicate infant deaths; shading indicates immigrant population.

The site selected by the planners of the stockyards represented a compromise between economic advantages and environmental drawbacks. Their choice incorporated several calculations aimed at reducing the cost of business. These factors included a distance from the commercial core of at least five miles, close proximity to existing trunk lines, and free access to the Chicago River for unrestricted dumping of huge amounts of organic waste. The business leaders' choice proved to be a good one: they could process three million animals annually by 1870, just five years after opening.

The biggest trade-off was that the slaughterhouses were located on low-lying wetlands. Workers had to install thirty miles of sewers and drains in the marshy ground before they could begin construction of the buildings and pens. But the meatpackers considered this investment a small price to pay. Large savings continued to accrue year after year from the disposal of their waste by-products at virtually no cost in a channel of the city's industrial corridor.[56]

The locational advantages of the site for the dressed beef industry proved to be disadvantages, however, for the workers of Packingtown, or Back of the Yards, as the area came to be called. The health and well-being of the people living in housing built upon a swampy marshland were inherently at risk in the absence of the environmental improvements that were the essential infrastructure of the nineteenth-century city. Dr. Rauch had identified some of these very areas as the lowest-lying in the whole city. Without paved streets and sidewalks, storm drains and sanitary sewers, and pure water and indoor plumbing, the quality of life was bound to suffer. To be sure, in the United States the law of real estate encouraged land sales and home ownership, while in England landlords held virtually perpetual tenure, but unfortunately the results for the built environment were more similar for the Back of the Yards and Ancoats than they were different.[57]

To a significant extent, the political decision to pay for environmental improvements with special assessment taxes rather than general property levies accounts for slum conditions in Chicago. The landlords of rental units in the industrial districts had the same incentives as their counterparts in Manchester to favor this method of financing. By simply refusing to pay for these so-called public utilities, they kept their costs to a minimum. Would-be home owners among Chicago's working classes also favored this funding approach.

In Packingtown, the collective choices of landlords and home owners produced internal patterns of spatial segregation. The most recent immigrants lived closest to the slaughterhouses while more seasoned workers earning higher wages moved toward the south and west, as far upwind as possible.

Yet there was no escape from the stenches and smells, the mud and manure. The garbage dumps and railroad tracks acted like ghetto walls to keep Packingtown's inhabitants trapped within its borders.[58]

In complete contrast, the planners of Hyde Park promised its prospective residents a location with all the natural advantages of the open lakefront. Enhanced by a full array of modern amenities, the suburban development proscribed factories, warehouses, and low-class saloons. The creation of this preserve for the city's elite was attributable almost entirely to the work a single individual, Paul Cornell. After arriving penniless from downstate in 1847, the twenty-five-year-old had risen quickly to become one of Chicago's prominent attorneys. In addition, he had turned his avocation of horseback riding to profitable ends by scouting along the shoreline south of the city limits for potential sites for an exclusive residential community.

Within six years he had found what he was looking for. He purchased a three-hundred-acre parcel about seven miles from downtown that included a mile and a half of beachfront. He platted his property between Fifty-First and Fifty-Third streets and erected a first-class hotel, which immediately became "a favorite resort for the sporting people of the city when they desired a little diversion," a contemporary recalled. But the key to the success of Cornell's project was a strategic decision to trade sixty acres of his precious land to the Illinois Central Railroad in exchange for a commuter station. The station acted like a gatekeeper that allowed only the most affluent to join the informal social club of men riding inside the stylish railcars for their daily trip to work. As historian Ann Keating points out, "The cost of commutation tickets helped to determine the class of residents who could afford to live in an area."[59]

Cornell used a litmus test of wealth and status to filter out all except an elite group of insiders from admission to charter membership in the community. Naming the subdivision Hyde Park to conjure images of London's fashionable district, he kept its initial list of permanent residents under tight personal control. The developer not only limited investors in his schemes to close friends and relatives, but also allowed only a small circle of handpicked candidates to become home owners. Like their counterparts in Victoria Park, the pioneer settlers of Hyde Park could afford the costs of engineering the environment to conform to a shared vision of a suburban ideal. In addition to installing the usual array of infrastructure improvements, they had their houses built on stone or brick foundations to lift them above the unhealthy dampness of the city's low-lying land. In 1861, Cornell tightened his grip on the future of the budding community by organizing other developers of upscale residential enclaves on the South Side. Together, they were able to have this lakefront district separated from the rest of Lake Township, the area that would soon become Packingtown. But even Cornell could not control the tumultuous pace of urban growth all around him.[60]

The ways in which Cornell used the power of the state to protect his vision of an ideal suburban community provide insight on the corresponding failures of City Hall to safeguard the residents of Packingtown from the rapid environmental degradation of their neighborhood. As a lawyer and real estate speculator, Cornell found that he could play the public roles of municipal reformer and local official to achieve private ends. Threatened by the war-fed expansion, he envisioned an elaborate system of parks and boulevards that would form a buffer zone to protect Hyde Park residents from undesirable residents and businesses.

Because Cornell's personal resources were finite, he turned to the state, with its virtually unlimited powers to tax and to expropriate land for public purposes. In 1866, Cornell joined forces with Dr. Rauch and other urban sanitarians, and together they drafted a series of bills to establish three park authorities for the Chicago area, each with the full powers of an independent municipal corporation. The proposals were so pathbreaking in terms of creating special-purpose tax districts and overlapping jurisdictions that Cornell had to become a lobbyist in Springfield for the next couple of legislative sessions before he could get the lawmakers' approval. In a similar way, the doctor led a referendum campaign at home to gain final approval of the plan.[61]

In 1869, the governor duly appointed Cornell to the South Park Commission, a position he would hold for the next thirteen years. Now armed with an array of powerful city planning tools, he and his colleagues quickly spent the agency's first two hundred thousand buying land, digging it up, installing drains and water lines, and planting a nursery with sixty thousand young trees. They also hired the well-known designers of New York's Central Park, Olmsted and Vaux, to disguise their *cordon sanitaire* in an attractive gown of natural foliage. By 1875, the busy public authority had assembled over a thousand acres of land with eleven miles of interconnected roadways for pleasure riding and safe passage through and around working-class neighborhoods to the city center. South Park (now Washington Park) and the boulevards formed a virtually impenetrable barrier to maintain class and ethnic/religious segregation.[62]

Cornell also assumed the part of an elected official to seal off his lakefront reserve from the massive amounts of pollution that were suddenly being generated after the stockyards opened in 1865. He seemed especially skilled at making use of the nuisance abatement powers of local government. In 1867, for example, when the Northwestern Fertilizing Company obtained a charter to operate just south of Hyde Park, Cornell countered immediately by having the township boundary extended all the way down to the bottom of the county at 138th Street. Then he became entangled in a protracted public nuisance case against the fertilizer company. First, he took advantage of a village form of government to strengthen the police powers of Hyde Park. Then he launched an attack to put the fertilizer plant out of business. In a well-publicized showdown, Cornell stood on the tracks to stop the trains that had been carrying two hundred tons of animal offal a day through Hyde Park. By 1871 he had hounded another foul-smelling rendering operation to the other side of the Indiana state line.

In a story well told by Louise Wade in her book *Chicago's Pride*, the "perfumery war" has the high drama of the battle between David and Goliath. And as in the case of this biblical fable, there was never any doubt about the ultimate outcome: Cornell's victory was complete. By 1880, his unrelenting pressure had forced the packers back into the yards, where seven of the industry's nine fertilizer plants were now located. The railroad would be forced to retreat too, literally rerouting its tracks to the Northwestern Fertilizer Company around the lakefront suburbs. The new line would be built straight through the working-class neighborhoods of Lake Township. Packingtown would end up with both the rendering plants and the offal trains.[63]

In comparison to Cornell's resoundingly triumphant approach to the politics of growth, City Hall's efforts to improve environmental conditions in Packingtown ring hollow. The packers fiercely resisted the city authorities' hesitant attempts to stop the annual dumping of hundreds of tons of animal parts into the river. The businessmen complained that they would not be able to compete with rivals in other cities. Moreover, the meatpackers banded together and threatened to move elsewhere, which was no small matter considering that they were already Chicago's largest employers.

Popular pressure to do something about the awful state of the river prodded elected officials to at least sue the packers for noncompliance with the 1865 nuisance abatement and license ordinance. But even when it finally won the test case establishing its police powers over the albatross in 1878, the city had achieved only a pyrrhic victory. For those living in the Back of the Yards, the ruling of the state supreme court had come much too late. Packingtown had already become one of the most concentrated toxic zones in industrial America, a densely populated slum drowning in a lethal dose of air, water, and ground pollution.[64]

While Hyde Park and Packingtown represent polar extremes of private development schemes around the time of the fire, the urban landscape in between conformed, more or less, to these patterns of land use and spatial

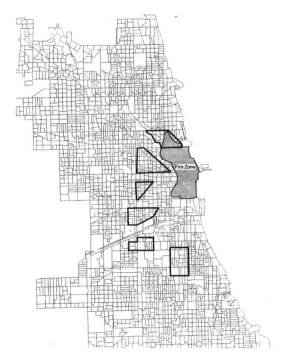

Figure 4.6. Postfire working-class residential construction
Source: Data from Homer Hoyt, *One Hundred Years of Land Values in Chicago* (Chicago: University of Chicago Press, 1933).

segregation. The reorganization of the CBD added to the demand for new sites for working-class cottages on the fringes of the built-up area in all three divisions. These hot zones of house-building activity started about three miles out (see fig. 4.6). The city's land-use patterns began to look more and more like those of Manchester. Chicago was becoming an industrial city. Factories provided thousands of new jobs, and working-class housing and institutions clustered around them. Many working-class neighborhoods took on the distinctive identities of their immigrant populations. At the same time, the actual environmental and imagined moral pollution emanating from these factory zones created powerful incentives for people to move as far away from them as they could afford. The laying of streetcar lines between the CBD and outlying suburbs closely paralleled the rise of the industrial sector.

Farther out, homes for the well-to-do along the steam rail lines complemented this new construction within the city. Forced to find temporary lodging after the fire, affluent Chicagoans discovered distant villages like Evanston and Highland Park on the Northwestern line, and Austin and Oak Park on the Burlington route. Many never came back, but instead gave these exclusive communities their first wave of significant growth. Although still restricted to a relatively small upper crust, suburbanization after the fire established social trends that strongly reinforced spatial patterns of segregation by class and ethnicity/religion. As private decision makers expanded the city's area of residential settlement and industrial development, the collective result compounded the massive problems of rebuilding the public infrastructure in the burnt-over district. City officials would have to make tough choices in ordering priorities, deciding between upgrading badly overtaxed networks of sewer pipes and water mains in the built-up areas and extending them to the new subdivisions.[65]

"The Fountain Head of All the Corruption"

The American political culture of federalism, local self-rule, and universal male suffrage helps account for Chicago's politics of growth. Compared to their English and continental counterparts, during the nineteenth century urban centers in the United Stated acted as nearly autonomous city-states in most areas affecting the environment. They had long grown accustomed to expecting their contacts with the capital in Washington, D.C., to be limited to the receipt of pork-barrel appropriations for locally inspired economic development projects. The politics of growth directed by the city's ward bosses combined low-cost government with a democratic strategy of providing municipal services to anyone willing to pay for them. The ward bosses also wanted to expand the budgets and patronage of City Hall, and large-scale public works projects and continuous extensions of the networks of pipes and mains fit right in with their plans. The highly decentralized structure of government also meant that Chicago was virtually free to give top priority to promoting commerce and industry without fear of intervention by state and federal authorities.[66]

This laissez-faire approach meant that market forces were given relatively free reign to determine land-use and settlement patterns. Ideas about class status, ethnic/religious character, and moral order acted as powerful filters for separating the rich from the poor in the choice of housing and neighborhood amenities. The political formation of urban space reinforced these patterns of residential segregation. In Chicago a combination of low property taxes and payment for municipal utilities in the form of special assessments and service fees played a major role in dividing the haves from the have-nots. In the polluted environment of the industrial city, the American version of privatism gave new meaning to the notion of being in poor health. Forced by low incomes into the toxic zones bordering the riverfront and surrounding the factories of heavy industry, working-class people truly lived in a world apart from the members of the upper crust and their enclaves lining the lakefront.[67]

The emotional and economic trauma of the great fire of 1871 set off a naked struggle for the reins of power at City Hall that would persist for nearly a decade. A prolonged state of emergency sharply intensified class conflicts that were already being played out in the civic arena as the rivalry between the Democratic ward bosses of the immigrant workers and the Republican citizen reformers of the respectable elements. A second, lesser fire three years later further exacerbated this crisis of political authority, exposing deep-seated tensions between social classes and the closely related identities of ethnicity and religion. With suffrage widespread, some of the conflict was channeled into local election campaigns, but it also spilled over legal boundaries and into the streets, spawning disruptive demonstrations, violent confrontations between laborers and factory owners, and mass boycotts.

The rapid rise and fall of fusion and third parties was emblematic of this period's tumultuous upheaval of partisan loyalties, class consciousness, and ideological identities. They also were indicative of the politicians' desperate search for a common cause or platform that they could use to build an enduring majority coalition (see table 4.1).

In the heated civic contests that followed the Civil War, the largest ethnic group, the Germans, often provided the crucial swing vote that tipped the election results this way and that among the parties. The battle for City Hall was a battle over both the style of civic life and the quality of neighborhood life. The Germans actually formed a highly diverse group that divided into

Table 4.1 Mayors of Chicago, 1865–1887

Years in office	Name	Affiliation
1865–1869	John Rice	Republican Party (Reform)
1869–1871	Roswell Mason	Citizens' Ticket (Reform)
1871–1873	Joseph Medill	Fireproof Ticket (Reform)
1873	Lester Legrand Bond	Eclectic Coalition (Ring)
1873–1876	Harvey Colvin	Combined Bummer Ticket (Ring)
1876–1879	Monroe Heath	Republican Party (Reform)
1879–1887	Carter Harrison	Democratic Party (Ring)

Source: Weston A. Goodspeed and Daniel D. Healy, eds., *History of Cook County*, 2 vols. (Chicago: Goodspeed Historical Association, 1909).

different-sized blocks of voters depending on the issue at stake in each campaign. When incumbent Republicans demanded temperance in 1873, for example, boss Anton Hesing led most Germans back into a winning alliance with the Democrats' Irish-Catholic boss, Daniel O'Hara. In other elections, however, Germans split their votes along ideological, religious, and class lines. The relatively widespread property ownership in Chicago compared to European cities opened the possibility of cross-class alliances among the taxpayers to resist the professional politicians' attempts to inflate the budget. Tightly clustered on the North Side in an area now known as Old Town, the German community had the highest rate of property ownership, at 27 percent of its male population.[68]

The stakes were high not only for gaining control of the machinery of the city's government, but also for determining the social equity and environmental justice of its policies, and results hinged on the outcome of the partisan contests. Three related crises of class conflict that arose as a result of the fires and played out in the arena of civic life illustrate the ways in which widespread voting and property ownership shaped political culture in Chicago.

The first battle was the now well-known drama in the streets between the small home owners of Germantown and the large property owners of the CBD, who had gained control of the city council after the first catastrophe. At issue was a "fire-proof" building code that would have effectively priced working people out of the housing market. In January 1872, a mass of angry Germans marched from the North Side to City Hall to oppose the proposed ban on wooden structures within the municipal boundaries. The protestors surrounded the building, and their threatening demonstration of power intimidated the council into drawing in the boundaries of the fireproofing requirement. The requirement embraced only the new CBD in the final act, leaving builders in the residential neighborhoods free to construct cheaper, balloon-frame houses that were light enough to do without expensive foundations.[69]

A second controversy erupted in the council chambers shortly after the second fire, in 1874, which also pitted small and large property holders against each other. At issue was the distributive justice of water main and fire hydrant improvement projects. In the wake of the new crisis, a self-proclaimed elite formed the Committee of One Hundred in response to the insurance underwriters' threat of an embargo of Chicago property. Renamed the Citizens' Association, this organization of "best men" became the first permanent civic group of its kind devoted to municipal reform in the United States. It invented the lobby tactics of the special interest group, and it was devoted to institutionalizing low-cost government in municipal charters, state laws, and court decisions. The association also put pressure on city council to upgrade the waterworks system to the standards set by the insurance industry for the CBD.

But the aldermen from the wards of the small home owners held up passage of a bill giving priority to downtown commercial property. They demanded a greater share of construction projects. The ability of the Democratic ward-based ring to frustrate the policy agenda of the Republican business elite inspired the elite not only to organize the Citizens' Association but also to search for class-bridging issues that could forge the taxpayers into a solid block of voters.[70]

In the midst of these local political battles, another kind of calamity, a national economic panic, handed the Republicans a ready-made common cause to bridge the class divide: low-cost government. As the depression deepened, bottom-line questions of setting public spending priorities within severe budgetary constraints crowded out other issues, giving the reform rhetoric of the Republican Party an edge at the polls. Demands among the large landowners to keep taxes down had been sounded simultaneously with the switch to the ward system of elections. Hard times now gave their insistent refrain a heightened, shrill resonance that penetrated across class barriers of social and physical distance to reach working-class taxpayers. Historian Richard Schneirov brilliantly illuminates "the reason for the fall in taxes" after 1875. It was "an open secret in the city: scandalously low and inequitable tax assessments. Chicago property holders, particularly those holding corporate property, made their peace with machine politics by utilizing corruption and the selective non-enforcement of laws to minimize their taxes."

Furthermore, the large real estate holders also helped ensure low tax bills by devolving the task of assessing property to three separate townships insulated from the city council. The township system encouraged its independently elected officials to compete against each other in reporting the lowest valuations; an early case of what economists call the race to the bottom. The city's property lists would not reach the boom levels of prefire 1871 until 1898, according to Schneirov.[71]

In 1875, during the depths of that decade's long depression, the Citizens' Association pressed the taxpayers' revolt to the limits of reform by spearheading a movement for a new municipal charter aimed at reigning in the professional politicians by shifting the balance of power from the ward-level aldermen to the citywide mayor. The newspaper of the respectable classes, the *Chicago Tribune*, beat the rhetorical drums of its editorial page for the crusade. "The Common Council is the fountain head of all the corruption that has disgraced the city of Chicago for years," the editor, a Republican stalwart, carped, "and it has been impossible under the present city charter for the people to protect themselves against the ring which has been formed." The municipal reformers were successful in getting a new charter, but party leaders would soon turn their intent to opposite effect, making the mayor's office into a political plumb.[72]

Once the Democrats learned that the quid pro quo for victory at the ballot box was a pledge of low-cost government, they were able to exploit other class and ethnocultural issues to put together a majority coalition. In 1879, a majority of voters would finally resolve the political crisis by uniting behind the seasoned U.S. congressman Carter H. Harrison. Upper class mugwumps and small property holders would join with trade unionists, Germans liberals, and Irish nationalists to elect him mayor for four successive two-year terms. While he possessed impeccable credentials as a true-blooded American—including having a recent president in the immediate family—it was Harrison's expression of cosmopolitan attitudes that made him the first truly popular chief executive of Chicago. Harrison became the city's first master of the politics of ethnic and class accommodation.

The Democrat also toed the line on low-cost government. Despite the city's strong economic revival, property assessments continued to drop during his administration. By 1885, Chicago was dead last in per capita taxation among the nation's thirteen largest urban centers. But Harrison's keen political skills were of absolutely no use in coming to grips with the city's environmental problems, especially its fragile hydraulic ecology.[73]

During this period of intense class and ethnic/religious conflict, large public works projects figured prominently in the civic discourse that collectively gave definition to the political culture of the industrial city. Their technological scale and geographic scope seemed to express symbolically republican ideals of equality, community, and uplift. Like the celebration at the Water Tower in 1867, the dedication of the deep-cut canal four years later presented elected officials an excuse for another full-blown public ritual to showcase their faith in the democratic value of technology and its heroic engineers.

Expanding infrastructure networks gave shape to the configurations of power in Chicago in a second important way. With tight constitutional limitations clamped on the municipal budget, the politicians ran the waterworks and sewer department like a private business for their own personal and partisan benefit. The "pump-house gang" would become as well entrenched as the corner fire and police stations as a bastion of patronage and clout in local lore. After 1875, moreover, the city council quickly came to depend upon its water management utilities to produce an annual surplus of cash profits that bankrolled the council's slush fund for pet projects.[74]

The enormous scale of the deep-cut drainage project, whose completion had long been awaited, justified the decision of the Board of Public Works (BPW) to pull out all the stops to mark this milestone in the city's history. On 16 July 1871, the *Chicago Tribune* trumpeted the opening of the gates at Bridgeport a full week ahead of the official celebration. "Relief cannot come too soon," the editorial panted, in spite of the size of the inflated final bill for the ditch-digging job, which had climbed past the $3 million mark. Just forty-eight hours later the newspaper proclaimed with a sigh of relief that "the bad odor has entirely disappeared already." By then, the initial rush of water into the I & M canal had reached Joliet. Dispatches from there reported what "has all the appearance of a freshet from heavy rains. No unpleasant smell thus far." What turned out to be unusually favorable climatic conditions helped the canal drain water out of Lake Michigan at a rate of more than a half-billion gallons a day, or about four times the maximum output of the Bridgeport pumps.[75]

But the boat pilots sounded a discordant note, objecting that the new, faster currents made their horses work harder to get upstream. Some had to add a fifth animal to offset the force of the flow. Although the *Tribune*'s editorials shamelessly dismissed their complaints, the paper's editors now admitted to having reservations about the dual use of the waterway for both shipping and sanitation purposes. But keeping the influx of lake water sufficiently strong to cleanse the river took priority because "if the boats lose time coming up stream, they will gain time when going down the current; so there will be some compensation for the evil complained of." Whatever the size of the boat pilots' lobby, it was smothered under a blizzard of 2,300 invitations to the inaugural event sent by William H. Carter, president of the BPW. Not only did he invite those on the numerous laundry lists of local dignitaries and leaders, official summonses went flying out to a far-flung array of fellow politicians at the city, county, state, and federal levels.[76]

That 1,500 leaders and other citizens showed up for a ceremony to dedicate a sewer project was a testimonial to the democratic spirit that Chicagoans embedded in large-scale technologies of environmental control. Illinois governor John Palmer and other eminent Americans, such as General Philip H. Sheridan and Boston Brahmin Francis Adams, lent their respectability to the occasion. The fact that engineer Roswell B. Mason had been elected mayor as a reform Republican was further evidence of the prestige associated with the civil engineers and their big infrastructure projects. Anticipation of free liquor at public expense undoubtedly helped swell the size of the crowd of citizens eagerly boarding the four boats provided for the party.

The BPW had transformed coal barges into sightseeing yachts by hastily tacking on upper decks and generously packing aboard cases of whiskey, champagne, and beer. Commenting on the ensuing public spectacle, a reporter observed wryly that "it is characteristic of Americans . . . when they do not have to pay for what they eat, to act as if they had to provision themselves for a starvation period of a week, and to drink all they can." Perhaps the celebrants were preparing themselves for what was to come that day because they could not expect to escape their water bound journey without hearing the obligatory minimum of speeches from the project's political sponsors. As the currents washed them downstream, the citizens called upon the appropriate spokespeople, starting with their chief benefactor, the president of the BPW.

Carter aroused immediate applause by giving voice to the deep cut's symbolic meaning as a major victory in the age-old struggle to harness the forces of nature to the uses of civilization. "The universal sentiment today," he announced, "is that it is a complete success, and the experiment has triumphed, and the river is clean." Most deserving of the public's praise, he declared, were Mason and his fellow engineers William Gooding and E. B. Talcott. A similar rhetorical theme in the speeches of the aldermen and other popular orators reinforced the message that the drainage ditch represented the conquering of nature by technology. Of course, elected officials also deserved credit for enabling the engineers to bring their expert knowledge to bear in this Herculean mission of environmental control. Francis Adams stood up to pronounce his encouraging, albeit restrained, judgment that Chicago was "typical of the progress of the age."

Rising to the occasion, local politician John C. Dore gave the best-honed civic sermon of praise to human ingenuity in altering the natural world in more and more powerful ways. "I know of no other instance," he crowed, "where the current of a river has been so changed as to flow in a direction exactly opposite to the course it has been accustomed to." He called the engineers of this modern-day miracle "magicians" who "have given us pure air and pure water, and the light of the sun has never been denied us." Yet, Dore saved the ultimate compliment for an even more exalted concept, "the science of engineering." "Throughout the civilized world," he sang, engineering "is continually accomplishing wonders, proving feasible things apparently impossible." Dore assured everyone aboard that the particular marvel they were privileged to witness in style would advance the loftiest democratic goals of the entire city population. By reducing river miasmas and thereby boosting public health, he decreed in a visionary leap of faith, "Chicago ought to be one of the healthiest cities in the world."[77]

Just ten weeks later, the hammer blows of the catastrophic Chicago fire, business panic, and a second damaging blaze began presenting city officials with just the opposite kind of reality. Widespread homelessness and deprivation sounded a different public hymn, a dirge that was recorded by the sharp jump in mortality during this prolonged state of emergency (see fig. 4.2). After 1871, the competing needs of fire reconstruction and new development added to the high levels of stress over the questions of who paid for and who benefited from public spending.

As the depression deepened in the mid-1870s, the cost of government rose to the top of the political agenda. With a firm lid sealed on the municipal budget, the aldermen had few opportunities to tap traditional sources of patronage: city jobs and contracts. To fuel their party machines, Chicago's ward bosses came to rely mostly on less legitimate means: they accepted bribes and sometimes extorted payment in exchange for not enforcing the law. They would overlook crimes of vice, lawbreaking by saloon owners, and building code violations, and they instructed the police to crush strikes with brutal force. There is little reason to doubt that the money generated by dishonest practices furnished a large part of the funds used to sustain the party organizations. For example, Richard C. Lindberg has made a careful investigation of the police department and its corruption by City Hall. He found that "the ethnic coalition that guided Chicago's political destiny in the late nineteenth and early twentieth centuries was composed of liquor men, gamblers, and resort keepers who viewed politics as a means to an end. The police of this period strengthened the numerous 'mini-machines' that flourished in the sprawling corridors of the inner-city wards."[78]

However, historians have missed another lucrative source of money flowing through the hands of the professional politicians, the so-called surplus funds of the water and the sewer departments. The charter reform of 1875 consolidated these patronage-rich operations under the mayor's control in a new Department of Public Works (DPW), along with street paving and scavenger operations. Strapped for patronage sinecures, the mayors had to carefully dole out their few precious appointive positions to high-profile members of their various constituent groups of supporters. Harrison, for example, picked General Herman Lieb of the liberal German faction to head up the waterworks, while trade union leader Joseph Gruenhut was made a health inspector. But Harrison also took advantage of the DPW as a new source of unskilled jobs to strengthen his hand in cutting deals with the ward bosses.

Nonetheless, the true center of power remained the city council's finance committee because it continued to control the municipal budget.

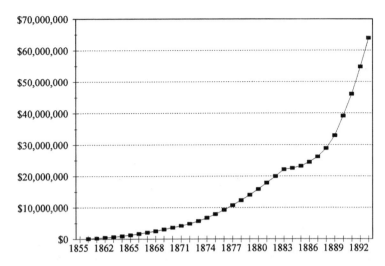

Figure 4.7. Cumulative surplus in Chicago waterworks fund, 1855–1893
Source: Data from Louis P. Cain, *Sanitation Strategy for a Lakefront Metropolis: The Case of Chicago* (DeKalb: Northern Illinois University Press, 1978), 143, tables 24–25; City of Chicago, *Annual Reports* (1855–1894).

Maintaining the business-oriented practices of the previous commissioners and board members, the aldermen set the fees for water and sewer hookup and service to generate a stream of revenue into the surplus fund. After the council members gained control of the DPW in 1876, the profits gushing from the waterworks alone were so large that the expansion of the two public utilities became essentially self-sustaining, no longer needing general tax subsidies or municipal bond issues. The profits poured into the special account under the control of the all-powerful finance committee (see fig. 4.7), whose policies shifted the effective cost of city government from the large property owners to the domestic utility customers. And the structure of its water rates rewarded needless waste by some consumers while others were forced to adopt conservation measures.[79]

The sheer growth rate of the city, of course, created a fundamental demand for more of this essential and irreplaceable commodity. In 1869, only two years after the dedication of the Water Tower, officials attended a groundbreaking ceremony for a second pumping station on the booming Southwest Side. And insurance underwriters left the council little choice but to comply with their demands for more fire hydrants and water pressure. But it did not take long for the penny-pinched politicians to learn how to exploit these public necessities for personal and partisan advantage.

The massive loss of water underground that resulted when the tremendous heat of the great fire melted thousand of lead stopcocks and pipe joints, for example, taught the aldermen an important lesson. They learned that a waterworks with an underground distribution network that chronically leaked was good for City Hall. True enough, allowing the needless loss of a third to a half of the total water supply created dangerously low hydrant pressure and serious inconvenience. But it also was guaranteed to arouse persistent public demand for more stations, engines, pumps, and mains. In other words, low water pressure meant more patronage jobs and fat contracts for the professional politicians to exploit for their own ends.

This politics of waste, then, squandered both natural and financial resources for corrupt purposes. To assess the environmental costs in the case of the waterworks requires several measurements. We need to define what constitutes a sufficient supply of water on a per capita basis and to find indicators of the extent to which utility service was made available to the city's inhabitants. Moreover, we need to know when the engineers in charge of the system became aware that underground leaks posed a serious problem because they caused water shortages and low pressure. Finally, we should analyze the alternatives the experts proposed for solving this technological challenge and what their influence was in the formation of policy.

By any measure, the increase in the amount of water provided for Chicago outpaced even the virtual stampede of newcomers into this mecca of industrial jobs. By 1885, as figure 4.8 shows, the average amount of water consumed had risen to almost 125 gallons per capita a day (gcd), while the average total output of the waterworks was fast approaching 100 million gallons a day (see fig. 4.9). Other statistics also demonstrate a general trend toward making service more readily accessible to a greater proportion of the population (see fig. 4.10). These general averages are admittedly crude indicators that mask tremendous variation in the availability and consumption of city water from neighborhood to neighborhood, and from inhabitant to inhabitant, but they are the only statistics available to historians. Although daily gallons-per-person statistics do not differentiate between industrial, public, and domestic uses and do not take waste into account, they still provide a useful measure of change over time.

Contemporary social standards of a minimally adequate supply also changed in concert with the increasing size and complexity of the industrial city, and for many reasons accepted standards of water consumption varied greatly between American and European cities. In 1876, for example, Chicago civic leader and local historian William Bross suggested a standard of 30 gcd, while seven years later, John Bateman of Manchester reported a

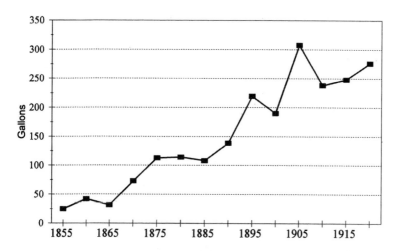

Figure 4.8. Average daily per capita water consumption in Chicago, 1855–1920
Source: Data from City of Chicago, Department of Public Works, *Annual Report* (1935),
57b.

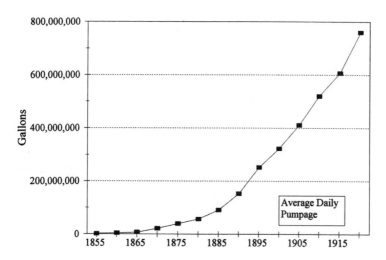

Figure 4.9. Daily water consumption in Chicago, 1855–1920
Source: Data from City of Chicago, Department of Public Works, *Annual Report* (1935),
57b.

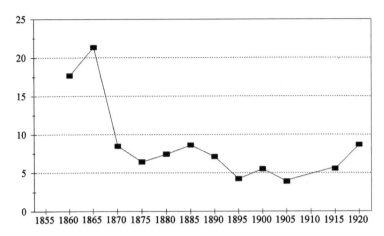

Figure 4.10. Number of persons per tap in Chicago, 1855–1920
Source: Data from City of Chicago, Department of Public Works, *Annual Report* (1935), 57b.

more spartan 22.5 gcd, with only 15 gcd estimated for domestic use. By 1890, the U.S. Census indicated that average water consumption in 225 cities was just under 90 gcd. Ten years later, water use in industrial cities in the United States with universal meter systems converged around a level of 100 gcd. If this figure is taken as standard for big cities at the end of the nineteenth century, then Chicago had already reached the standard level a quarter-century earlier.[80]

If we measure standard consumption in this liberal way, all of the water pumped in excess of 100 gcd after 1875 represented waste. For the environment, the major costs were the extra water and coal consumed and the air pollution created by the engines in the pump houses. At the very least, profligate water use meant the diversion of limited resources from the meeting of other needs in a democratic society that promised distributive justice. In this case, the duty to promote the public health and welfare required an equitable sharing of the benefits of the water management system among all the city's inhabitants.

A huge amount of money was wasted just for the unnecessary fuel consumption and construction work related to the underground leaks in the water system. Those dollars could have been better spent, for example, upgrading the infrastructure in the older, more crowded districts and extending it more quickly to newer suburban areas. In 1874 the stalemate in city council over funding waterworks improvement projects clearly indicates that the aldermen were acutely sensitive to their constituents' pressing demands for the urban necessities of pure drinking supplies and sanitary drainage. The sum of the dollars wasted and the money in the surplus fund represents the amount water customers were overcharged. And the diversion of some of these surplus fees to unrelated purposes poses another set of troubling questions regarding social equity. The city council was unfairly forcing all utility customers to bear a share of the property owners' burden of paying the costs of city government.

In 1875, consumer protests about utility overcharges prodded the BPW into publicly acknowledging that wasted water had become a serious problem. Aldermen fielded the complaints from constituents and asked the still semi-independent agency to respond. While defending the rates as the lowest in the country, the BPW admitted that repairable fixtures and profligate habits had driven the price of service up by 66 percent to one cent per one hundred gallons. The report pointed to leaks in pump valves and pipe joints and to defective plumbing. But "the greatest waste of all," according to the BPW, was the custom of the typical Chicago household of leaving the kitchen faucet open during the winter to prevent pipes from freezing and during the summer to keep food and drinks from spoiling.

The BPW proposed a technological remedy, the use of water meters, which could cut down waste by effectively addressing the problems of physical infrastructure and social behavior simultaneously. Meters should be installed universally, the report recommended, or "whenever practicable," because they would pay for themselves by reducing the operating costs of the utility. Service charges based on consumption carried a built-in incentive to conserve by closing faucets and fixing the plumbing. They also more equitably distributed the cost of running the utility than did the current system of flat fees based on the number of faucets and the classification of users according to a mind-boggling system of categories ready-made for corrupt purposes. However, the BPW had only 1,200 meters in place, on some of its biggest customers, leaving almost all of the fifty thousand other buildings it served subject to the fee-assessment system. The report called for a gradual, phased-in conversion and suggested giving priority to the placement of meters on all buildings that were not private residences.

Universal metering also had the major benefit of providing the only practical way of locating leaks in the underground network of distribution mains and service pipes. By strategically installing similar recording devices on the various arteries of the system, the waterworks could make an accounting of the water between the pumping stations and the consumers. Leaks could be tracked down by comparing the gaps between in the amounts supplied through the mains and those registered on customer meters.[81]

184 :: *Creating Industrial Ecologies*

But the ward bosses on the finance committee had no intention of threatening their lucrative politics of waste by following the recommendations of the BPW. When the division was reorganized a year later as the DPW and placed under the direct budgetary control of the city council, the aldermen promoted the engineers to its top positions. Chesbrough became the commissioner and Cregier moved up to become the chief engineer. Appealing for universal metering, they spoke with surprising openness about the political hurdles they had to overcome in convincing the politicians. The first great barrier was the fear that the fountain of cash income would turn into a drain of treasury accounts. "If meters could be universally introduced, they would undoubtedly prevent waste, but unfortunately," the engineers admitted, "an extended use of these meters under such circumstances would materially decrease the revenue and, perhaps, render the Water Department of the City no longer self-sustaining."[82] Left unstated were the rich opportunities for "boodle," or graft, that the flat-fee system made possible for the local lawmakers who annually redefined the special categories of consumers and set their rates. This system left room for the water assessor to extort bribes from customers in exchange for reducing the rate classification of their buildings and undercounting the number of their faucets.

The second reason the city council wanted to maintain the status quo was fear of losing the extra jobs and contracts produced by a waterworks operated to squander up to one half of its supply. Putting an annual price tag of fifty thousand dollars on this profligacy, the engineers warned of mounting costs ahead. "The alarming yearly increase in the leakage and waste of water has reached such an extent," they cautioned, "that it implies additional cost to the City for pumping, and if not remedied, will shortly necessitate a large additional outlay for engines and machinery, in order to supply the demand under an emergency." This was exactly the goal of the council's politics of waste.

Chesbrough and Cregier tried to reassure the aldermen that they could set the meter rates to generate just as much total revenue. They also pointed out that cities across the nation and in Europe were adopting meters as the best way to reduce waste. But the finance committee consistently refused to pay for more meter installations or to readjust rate schedules to promote conservation in the years to come. Under the Harrison administration, the DPW would add a measly 250–300 meters a year in a city undergoing another wave of building construction and swelling land values.[83]

Probably the only solace left the municipal engineers from the complete politicization of the DPW was an inner sense of satisfaction from steady gains in energy efficiency. Each new generation of hardware for the pump house got better at using dirty boiler coal to produce clean drinking water. After courageously helping to save the Water Tower station during the great fire, Cregier personally designed a much larger steam engine and companion pump with a capacity of thirty-six million gallons per day. Popular magazine *McClure* was soon advising its well-heeled readers to visit the rebuilt pump house to see "what is said to be the largest engine in the world, priced at an expense of $200,000 and which pumps 2,750 gallons of water at each 'stroke.'"[84] Two years later, in 1876, a smaller matched pair of fifteen-million-gallons-per-day engine pumps the engineers had selected for the West Side station came on line, and in 1884, a second pair raised its capacity twofold (see fig. 4.11).

Although the original "Old Sally" engine was still running, the engineers cut fuel consumption by half on average (see fig. 4.12). Economic savings, of course, were dependent on the price of coal, which generally fell in Chicago's glutted fuel markets. In anticipation of their takeover of the public utilities after the charter reform of 1875, the aldermen began pressuring the BPW to switch from the more expensive but cleaner anthracite to the dirtier bituminous.

After that, the politicians made the public pay the price in added air pollution for their sweetheart deals with favored fuel dealers. In 1876, for example, the council would dole out contracts for almost seventeen thousand

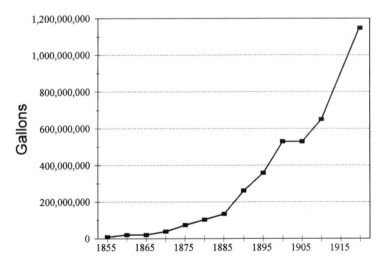

Figure 4.11. Capacity of waterworks in Chicago, 1855–1920
Source: Data from City of Chicago, Department of Public Works, *Annual Report* (1935), 57b.

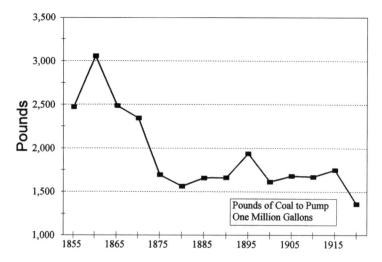

Figure 4.12. Fuel efficiency of waterworks in Chicago, 1855–1920
Source: Data from City of Chicago, Department of Public Works, *Annual Report* (1935), 57b.

tons of soft coal. Nonetheless, greater engine efficiency and less expensive coal accounted for a 37 percent cut in the basic cost of operating the waterworks. This achievement gave the engineers something positive to take pride in during the regime of the ward bosses. In sharp contrast, the public praise showered upon them at the dedication of the deep-cut project took only four years to come full circle back to a civic maelstrom of finger-pointing and an angry clamor for the next technological fix to purge the city of the frightening return of the river stink.[85]

By 1876, the engineers in charge of the reorganized DPW were painfully aware that the drainage and ship canal had already been overwhelmed because of population and industrial growth. Under some climatic and seasonal conditions, it was too small to create a current strong enough to sweep clean all the branches of the river. But it worked well enough to kill the fish downstream. At Ottawa, Chicago's wastewater was reproducing an all-too-familiar stench that was "a most intolerable nuisance. It poisons the air, and affects the health of all who are compelled to breathe it."

More and more often, conditions were not much better within the city. Under the not infrequent natural condition of low lake levels, the current of water into the canal was sufficient for neither sweeping the river clean nor diluting what was sent down the canal enough to render it harmless. After opening the deep-cut canal in 1871, the engineers had optimistically dismantled the Bridgeport pumps and sold them off for one-tenth their original cost. But complaints by Ottawa, Joliet, and other Illinois River towns in the state legislature caused Dr. Rauch to intervene on their behalf. He favored reinstalling a set of pumps to ensure a minimum daily flow of 650 million gallons a day. Dragged into compliance by a state law in May 1881, the city would go two-and-a-half times over budget and fall two years behind schedule in building the new pumping station. It did not take that long for the engineers to admit that the deep cut had virtually no effect in ameliorating the stench in the North Branch.[86]

High lake levels and inflated expectations of relief in 1871 had helped contemporaries whip themselves into a false euphoria of civic triumphalism in the battle for environmental control. Yet even the most enthusiastic supporter of the deep-cut project, the *Chicago Tribune*, had only been able to claim that "the waters of the North Branch appear to be clearing up."[87] Actually, they were getting much worse, and for two reasons besides the construction upstream of a continuous ribbon of riverfront factories and working-class neighborhoods.

First, very little water from the North Branch was pulled into the I & M Canal simply because the Main Branch and South Branch were much deeper and wider. Also, private developers intervened in unanticipated ways that eventually proved disastrous for the city. As soon as the canal project was finished, William Ogden and John Wentworth followed through with the Des Plaines Plan. They set dredging equipment to work digging a big ditch from the Des Plaines River back toward the city, across their large holdings of suburban marshlands, to the western edge of the Chicago River. Since the Des Plaines River is nine feet higher than the lake, water draining into the "Odgen-Wentworth Ditch" (OWD) tended to flow eastward toward the South Branch and the Bridgeport opening of the I & M Canal. After filling the canal to capacity, this runoff had the effect of greatly reducing the amount of foul water sucked into the artificial waterway from the other branches of the river.

Worse, heavy rains could cause a current to gush from the OWD that was strong enough to reverse the flow of the Chicago River in the direction of the lake. In March 1875, storms put the city at risk of flooding in just this kind of scenario. Recalling memories of "the experience of 1849," the *Chicago Tribune* now admitted that the new canal had unintended consequences of its own that endangered public health and safety. It too could cause flooding in the city because "in spring time and times of heavy rain," the paper confessed, "so much water runs into the new canal by underground channels from the land on both sides . . . that its force overcomes the fall of 3 feet in 30 miles and the water turns the current back into the Chicago River."[88]

As the newspaper predicted, the raising of the city grade saved the CBD when the flood tide came ten days later. Yet low-lying neighborhoods bordering the industrial corridor on the north and southwest sides suffered. Although property damage was limited, there was good reason to suspect that the filthy water had washed out to the water intake pipe. The flood of 1875 thus ended any lingering doubts that the deep-cut canal was a dismal failure in achieving its two main goals of ending the river stink and protecting the drinking supply.[89]

Two years later, the freshly anointed Chief Engineer of Public Works Ellis Chesbrough, revealed just how little he had learned in over twenty years as the main architect of Chicago's water management plan. True enough, he could proudly display statistics showing the tremendous growth in the scale and scope of the infrastructure under his supervision. Moreover, he ably defended the cost-benefit compromises that had decided such questions as how much to spend burying the sewers deeper and raising the grade higher to offset an unacceptable risk of flooding. This calculus also provided a reasonable apologia for the utter lack of support for an alternative, intercepting-sewer plan of sanitation. But he continued to recommend stopgap remedies to patch up past mistakes. Resorting to his original blueprints, he proposed cutting a canal along Fullerton Avenue to alleviate the problem of sewage stagnating in the North Branch.[90]

Chesbrough's fixed conception of the endless bounty of nature blinded him to the fundamental flaw of his master plan to engineer the delicately balanced hydraulic ecology of Chicago. He still had not decided whether its ultimate sink should be the lake or the river. This indecision goes a long way in explaining why the sewage effluvium was allowed repeatedly to befoul the drinking supply. His design of the Fullerton Avenue Conduit provides a perfect case in point of the ways in which his inability to imagine a more harmonious relationship between the city and the environment put the public health at great risk, this time more than ever. The submerged tunnel was equipped with built-in screwlike propellers that could spin in either direction. "The conduit," he explained, "has been located as to be capable of serving as an outfall into the lake." Chesbrough seemed incapable of seeing that this would mean disgorging 10.8 million gallons an hour of highly polluted wastewater at a point on the prevailing southerly currents less than five miles away from the Two-Mile Crib.

The only certainty that seemed unshakable was Chesbrough's belief that the lake was "a fountain inexhaustible, lying at our very feet, requiring us only to provide a means for drawing from its boundless resources." With public works technology of sufficiently gargantuan scale to exploit the lake to the fullest extent, somehow all of the city's sanitation problems would be solved. The curative powers of the lake's fresh water would automatically protect the public health by properly diluting and purifying the stream of pollution gushing out of the conduit before it reached the intake pipe. In a similar way, he also insisted that an intake tunnel that was twice as long would certainly place the drinking supply far beyond any possibility of contamination by the sewage pouring out of the industrial city. Moreover, he envisioned a limitless supply of fresh lake water fixing the shortcoming of the sanitary canal if only it had a much deeper deep cut, turning failure into "one of the greatest [public] works of the nation."

Chesbrough would resign his office to pursue consulting work two years later. But many other civil engineers in Chicago were ready to take up his banner of the technological sublime with its seductive appeal of public works projects of heroic scale.[91]

Conclusion: Chicago and the Politics of Growth

From 1879 to 1885, the party bosses, led by Mayor Harrison, made full use of the politics of urban growth to consolidate their grip on City Hall. While bringing a period of relative political stability, this system of low-cost government, corruption, and waste came at a heavy price. The evidence of popular and expert science kept mounting that Chicago was being put at risk of imminent environmental calamity from deadly epidemics and catastrophic floods. Chesbrough's close protégé DeWitt Clinton Cregier comfortably fit into the shoes of his old boss when he moved up to become the commissioner of the DPW. He too based the city's water management policy upon a false assumption of unlimited supplies of free natural resources like fresh water and clean air. Perfectly personifying the politicization of the municipal engineers, Cregier faithfully defended Chesbrough's master plan even while it was collapsing under the accumulating weight of experimental proof that pollution spewing out of the river and sewer outfalls was contaminating the drinking supply.

In the absence of more holistic perspectives on the emerging industrial ecology, Cregier adhered strictly to the politically correct approach of engineering the environment piecemeal, lurching from one improvement project to the next. The choice of "practicable" alternatives offered by the municipal engineers remained locked within a narrow set of policy parameters. Although the commissioner routinely expressed concerns about waste to the aldermen, his seemingly brave calls for conservation were meant to fall on deaf ears. Unquestioned loyalty to the Democratic Party and the administration's politics of growth, the career bureaucrat knew, was the essential prerequisite to keeping his job and gaining approval of his budget requests.

Policy makers continued their project-driven assault on Chicago's fragile hydraulic environment. They ignored all the telltale signs that this approach was bound to trigger a cascading series of human-made natural disasters. But until their arrival, an official state of denial created a convenient illusion that City Hall, despite its profligate waste, represented a democratic engine of urban growth and prosperity.

Still, nagging doubts about the administration's reassurances that the city was safeguarding the public health seem to have motivated Chicagoans to redouble their efforts to study the quality of the drinking supply. Although faith remained unshaken that the lake was a reservoir of "ever-lasting purity," fear kept building that the faucet water had become a source of life-threatening filth. Employing a wide variety of experimental methods, the investigators steadily assembled an irrefutable case that the city was on the brink of a tragic outbreak of contagious disease.

During Harrison's inaugural year in office, the Chicago Academy of Homeopathic Physicians and Surgeons sponsored the first of these scientific reports. In November 1879, Dr. T. W. Williams and his colleagues collected water samples to test for the standard chemical indicators of whether the drinking supply was likely to contain dangerous, disease causing agents. But the doctors also employed an underwater diver to examine the lake bottom from the shoreline to the Two-Mile Crib. What he found was a microenvironment completely different from that of nonurbanized areas of the lakefront. On each side of the river's mouth, the diver observed, "there is a slimy deposit or growth on every natural thing in or about the harbor which I have not noticed anywhere else upon the lake."

The diver waited until a storm blew in from the southwest to follow an underwater stream of raw sewage from the outfall pipe at Twenty-Second Street to the intake pipe. He verified that some of its daily thirty-five thousand gallons of wastewater were contaminating the city's drinking supply. Having repeatedly seen river water reach the crib, the diver went into its well to discover at the bottom "about ninety-five cubic feet of a substance, which has been deposited there, by the lake water. It has a soft, velvet-like feeling, but I do not know what its appearance is." On the basis of his research, the diver predicted that the North Branch cutting canal would be a "stupendous failure" because "it would drive the fifth of that stinking stream into the lake and to the crib."[92]

The contrast between the Chicago Academy's dire report and the Harrison administration's meaningless reaction to its own inspection of the Fullerton

Conduit a few months later could not have been more complete. The mayor, the commissioner of the DPW, aldermen, reporters, contractors, and "friends of everybody" crammed aboard a tugboat for a junket to celebrate the successful completion of another public works project. But unlike the good weather that greeted the grand party at the opening of the deep-cut canal in 1871, a steady rain and freezing wind dampened the normally jocular spirits of the mayor and his entourage.

Entering the North Branch, a newspaperman noted that the "scenery was rich," but it was not rich with nature. Canadian geese and other migrating birds had long ago lost their favorite places for resting and feeding. Instead, the industrialized landscape of the river was alive with "large numbers of men . . . at work upon the vessels which were laid up at their respective docks, caulking their sides, repairing their railings, hulls, and rigging." Above the Division Street bridge, the factories lining the banks became unbroken canyon walls, except for a giant rolling mill and a huge distillery near Fullerton Avenue at the end of the raw, wet ride.

Once inside the shelter of the pump house, Mayor Harrison made it perfectly clear that he wanted to talk about anything but the possible repercussions of the present engineering project on the environment and health of the city. Huddling around the warmth of the steam engine, the official inspection party watched as "an immense volume of [lake] water came pouring out of the tunnel into the North Branch, stirring up the filthy bottom until the filth and corruption rose to the surface, covering it with a thick, bluish scum. A fairly swift current was formed, extending southward toward the mouth" of the river. The mayor immediately deflected any questions about this disturbing result by engaging the contractors in a technical inquiry on the design of the pump wheels.

When the machine operator reversed the direction of the pumps for the first time, "it looked as though the whole North Branch might be pumped dry in twenty-four hours." Rather than discuss what the wastewater being dumped into the lake might mean for the safety of the drinking supply, Harrison raised concerns about the durability of the equipment. He concluded the inspection tour by making the case for hiring an extra worker at City Hall to be a wind-direction observer who would inform the machine operator whether to run the pumps in or out.[93]

News that something was terribly wrong occasionally arose from within the city government in the form of special Department of Health reports to the aldermen. One of Harrison's key strategies of coalition building was the appointment of men of impeccable social standing and professional respectability to high-profile positions, men like Dr. Oscar C. DeWolf, who served as commissioner of health from 1877 to 1889. In early 1881, DeWolf's inspection tour of a low-lying area just south of the commercial district uncovered the horror of slums in Chicago. Overshadowed by the Palmer House and several other big hotels, "the entire block of houses stands over a reeking swamp, some four inches in depth of kitchen and water-closet filth."

Conditions inside six overcrowded "tenement houses" on Wabash Avenue were equally bad. The landlord charged exorbitant rents but neglected to keep the plumbing in repair. In one of these formerly elegant homes, a resident blamed the omnipresent sewer gases for the death of a child on one floor and the serious illness of another in a different apartment. "From a sanitary point of view," Dr. DeWolf warned portentously, the whole block represented "a plague spot, awaiting only the balmy breezes of summer to fan into full force the destroying power of the gases which occupy it from basement to top story."[94] Without certainty as to how to forestall epidemics, Chicagoans' fear of a coming public health calamity kept rising with each announcement of higher annual mortality rates.

Just after Thanksgiving Day in 1882, doctors sounded the alarm about a sharp increase in the number of new cases of deadly intestinal and lung diseases. Although the *Chicago Tribune* echoed their call to purify the city, it also criticized them for being unable to agree upon the exact identity or cause of the rampantly spreading, life-threatening "fever." The paper's editors suspected environmental factors and listed just about everything as potential carriers, with one significant exception, the water supply. Reflecting popular anxieties at the same time, they exposed a subconscious paranoia that the mysterious invisible enemy, "the real cause of disease, may be in our drains, our back yards, and our alleys. It is bad now. Unless we clean up, it will rapidly grow worse ... and our gates will be wide open for the admission of a monster."[95]

In 1884, a new kind of scientist, the "microscopist," began to put a face on that frightening enemy by identifying the tiny living organisms called bacteria. A Professor Long, whose first name is lost to history, and his students at the medical school had been testing water samples for the past three years. In addition to conducting the standard battery of chemical tests, the researchers had also subjected the samples to biological examination. "These results are not such that I like to report," the professor disclosed, "for they indicate an unwholesome condition of our water."

Professor Long's investigation had located the most polluted waters in the river near the stockyards, but the greatest danger to the drinking supply, he contended, was the Fullerton Conduit. The pumps forced the heavily contaminated organic wastes of the North Branch into the lake regardless of which direction the currents were running. Declaring this city policy an "evil," the scientist advised the public that the only available way to protect their health was to boil or filter their drinking water before consuming it. The report of Professor Long's research in the popular press might represent the first time the science of biology rather than that of chemistry was evoked as the basis of expert authority regarding the quality of the Chicago water supply.[96]

But general acceptance in Chicago of the germ theory of disease causation was at least a decade away. The discussion at the 4 August 1884 meeting of the Chicago Medical Society explains the preemptive timing of the publication of the story on Professor Long just a day earlier. Widespread anxiety about a cholera outbreak had brought the doctors together to discuss preventive measures, but discord remained the hallmark of medical discourse on epidemiology. The first speaker, Dr. I. N. Danforth, stated firmly that "cholera cannot yet be said to be a disease produced by any specific germ." However, the next participant, Dr. W. T. Belfield, was equally emphatic that "in all cholera cases there has been found a special organism in the intestine."

Turning from the current dispute over theory, the doctors looked to their veteran sanitarians for guidance in mounting a practical defense against the scourge. In a letter, Dr. Rauch stressed the need to keep river water from reaching the Two-Mile Crib. Dr. Davis drew on his long experience to advise his colleagues on the most humane ways to treat their patients. Without a new consensus on the nature of disease, the medicine men had to resort to their default position on public health policy: clean up the environment. Although this time the dreaded contagion from Europe did not reach the city and the general mortality rates declined for the year, Chicagoans had little reason to feel any safer.[97]

By 1885, the city had become a powder keg of social and environmental crises. On the one hand, tensions between business and labor were on the verge of violence. A mass movement was gaining strength among the working classes around the demand for an eight-hour day. Labor leaders had set the date of 1 May 1886 for a showdown, a general strike to win this common cause.[98] On the other hand, disturbing evidence kept accumulating that the failure of city's water management strategy was increasing the risk of environmental disaster. The engineers' large-scale drainage projects had not succeeded in tipping the delicate hydraulic balance of the metropolitan area's flat marshlands permanently away from the lake. Heavy rains could reverse the flow in the public canal and the private channel back toward the city, putting it at risk of flooding. And polluted water from the river's mouth, the sewer outfalls, and the Fullerton Conduit raised the chances for contamination of the drinking supply with deadly microorganisms into the realm of the highly probable. Nervous anticipation of social disorder and fear of a public health catastrophe fed on each other, creating extreme states of anxiety and denial in the public sphere.

The impending state of emergency promised to tear Mayor Harrison's coalition asunder and thus to bring a period of relative political stability to an end. The politics of environmental profligacy that sustained the party organization had the paradoxical consequence of limiting policy options in ways that threatened to spell disaster for those in charge of City Hall. Consider the dilemma confronting Commissioner Cregier of the DPW. In 1884, he faced the urgent need to begin planning ahead for new pumping stations, under-the-lake tunnels, and intake cribs while contending with a distribution system that wasted one-half of its total supply. Over the past year, the DPW had hooked up 7,684 new house-service taps but installed only 276 meters. The council was happy to hear his expert recommendations for spending to expand the infrastructure. His dutiful recitation of the waterworks' contribution of $136,900 to the surplus fund was also welcomed as music to ears of the ward bosses.[99]

The politics of growth meant that the commissioner could only pay lip service to conservation of natural and financial resources. Cregier's plea for universal metering presupposed defeat. "While the most reliable and efficient means of preventing waste, and bringing the consumption of water within reasonable limits, is a resort to a general use of meters," he conceded, it "is believed that a rigid and adequate house to house inspection, properly carried out, would go far to remedy the evil."[100] Of course, no one was expected to take this idea so seriously as to create a small army of city plumbers who would go around issuing certificates of efficient housekeeping.

On the contrary, Cregier and other City Hall insiders could count on the political bosses in charge of the finance committee to pursue policies based on the false economy of nature's limitless free gifts. In the two decades following the Civil War, big infrastructure projects had become ingrained in the political culture of Chicago. They generated patronage for the ward bosses, and they also inspired in the public mind dramatically appealing images of the technological sublime. It would take a real state of emergency to jar policy makers out of their comfortable pipe dreams of achieving complete social and environmental control. Then the inhabitants of the city would begin to learn the price they must pay for believing that they were still living in a self-renewing natural world instead of a highly toxic industrial ecology.

Just this kind of unnatural disaster had already begun to strike Manchester with increasing ferocity and cost to life and property. In the early 1850s, that city suffered the first in an escalating series of floods. Although floods were an accepted risk in a city built at the junction of three rivers in a valley long known for torrential downpours, these disasters were different. They were less the result of the forces of nature than the unintended consequences of the forces of production. The industrialization of nature in Manchester involved not only the city, but the entire regional conurbation stretching up to the headwaters of the rivers. After a half-century of the waterways being hemmed in with factories and filled up with rubbish, storm surges overflowed into the crowded factory districts of the working classes.

Like Chicago's politicians, Manchester's city officials initially assumed a posture of denial, attributing the damaging overflows simply to acts of God. As each emergency grew worse than the last, however, the floods forced local and national authorities to reexamine the impacts of the industrial city on the environment. Extending over a twenty-year period in Manchester, this stumbling process was marked by drift, default, and stalemate. Policy makers had to learn that plans relying on piecemeal engineering of the environment were inherently deficient. Eventually they began to invent more holistic concepts of water management as well as novel approaches to conserving river basins.

Chicago too would have to suffer from unnatural disasters before it would adopt similar regional perspectives on its hydraulic ecology. In both places, experts such as engineers, doctors, and scientists played increasingly important roles in designing ever more complex plans of environmental control. But mediated by very different political cultures and institutions, the formation of public policy in the two cities would produce very different results.

CHAPTER FIVE

"The Hardest Worked River"

Manchester and Environmental Catastrophe

Introduction: The Holmfirth Catastrophe

In the winter of 1852, heavy rains caused the first notable flooding in Manchester and Salford. Almost two weeks of steady downpours preceding the great deluge of 4–5 February had provided plenty of warning that the ground was already saturated throughout the Mersey-Irwell Rivers Basin (MIRB). "It was not a matter of surprise," a writer at the local newspaper dryly noted, "that all the mountain streams should be converted into torrents." Once the big rains came, though, most Mancunians seemed transfixed into a state of disbelief by the disaster unfolding before their eyes. True enough, local heroes appeared, as they often do in the midst of such emergencies, to undertake daring rescues and other selfless acts of bravery that seemed to defy the power of the rivers' irrepressible currents. Yet the general response of city officials and ordinary citizens alike was emotional paralysis in the face of the awesome power of nature.[1]

Flooding in the city itself remained restricted to isolated areas of the lowest-lying land. On Wednesday afternoon, the Irwell began spilling over its banks above the central business district, inundating Salford's Peel Park and Crescent districts and Broughton's scattered farms and homes on the opposite side. By evening, these zones were under six feet of water, and during the height of the storm, around midnight, the river rose to thirteen feet above its seasonal norm. The more industrialized Medlock River overflowed too, covering the shantytown on its right bank known as Little Ireland and spilling into adjoining riverfront factories and warehouses near Great Marlborough Street. The Irk submerged a still largely vacant area that would soon enough be designated as the New Town for the city's beleaguered Irish-Catholic minority. With no loss of life or widespread damage, Manchester escaped relatively unscathed. Even another heavy accumulation of over 1.3 inches on Sunday, which again "converted" Broughton "into a large lake," seems to have been endured with a stoic sense of fatalism.[2]

The real trouble occurred at the milldams high above the valley towns, in the Pennines. Here amid the full intensity of the two-day deluge, the hills' innumerable rills, brooks, and streams mounted an onrushing violent assault on the dams' earthen walls. The three descending dams of Manchester's brand new waterworks withstood the test. But a similar type of dam less than ten miles away, on the other side of the divide, near Holmfirth, did not. The bursting of the Bilberry Reservoir above the town became the first humanmade "natural" disaster in the modern era to achieve the status of a national tragedy. Although it did not directly affect Manchester, an examination of this devastating blow helps to set a baseline against which to measure contemporary response to analogous states of emergency in the textile center.[3]

What struck such a deep chord of sympathy throughout England was the immediate realization that the great loss of life in the Holmfirth flood had been entirely preventable. This was definitely not an act of God. Ninety-one people had died needlessly because everyone had seemingly been frozen in place watching a reservoir they all knew was defective overload and give way, just as predicted. Built in 1837 about three miles above the town of six thousand inhabitants, the milldam had been plagued by technical and financial problems from the beginning. When the embankment was nearly completed, its site was found to contain an underground stream, and its planners realized they had made a crucial error. They attempted to fix the leaky foundation, but a shortage of funds led them to make the fateful decision to literally cover up the problem. They believed that as long as they kept the water level low enough, the three-hundred-foot span of the dam would be strong enough to contain the six-acre lake filling up between the long, narrow ridges behind it. Testimony at the coroner's inquest revealed that the whole community knew the dam was defective because they could plainly see two large leaks in its wall "as big as a man's arm" in addition to the one at the base, which was "as big as a man's leg."[4]

Even with its floodgates fully open, the reservoir started filling to far above safe levels at a dangerous rate of 2.85 million gallons per hour (mgh) on Wednesday evening. The manager of the water power venture exclaimed frantically to the many watchers trekking nervously up the hill from the town, "It is going to burst! It is going to burst!" Yet neither he nor anyone else at the dam had "the presence of mind or sufficient knowledge" to act to save it or even to warn those below before it was much too late.

The dam had a final, fail-safe system. A vertical brick pipe had been erected to a height several feet below the top of the wall to prevent water from spilling over it and causing it to collapse. Over the years, however, the stream that had been left to run unchecked under the foundation had been steadily eating away at it, so that now the embankment was slightly lower than the mouth of the escape drain. Anyone with a sledgehammer could have saved the day by simply knocking a few layers of bricks off the opening of the pipe. Instead, water began spilling over the top of the dam about eleven o'clock. Still the alarm was not sounded. Almost two hours of suspended belief elapsed before the watchers finally started scrambling down the hill, yelling frantically, "Run for your lives!" Many of these would-be heroes were themselves swept away in the midst of their belated mission. The death and destruction that followed in the wake of the flood was particularly severe because a huge section of embankment resting on top of the defective foundation had given way all at once and sent an avalanche of water, mud, and rubble barreling down the narrow canyon and right through the center of town.[5]

The Holmfirth flood evoked two universal reactions that bridged class and geographic boundaries to produce a massive aid effort on a national scale. The worthiness of the survivors was never in doubt because the "dilapidated state" of the dam was, according to the *Manchester Guardian*, what had caused "this amount of havoc and destruction, never perhaps, paralleled in England." The Victorians' impressive army of private volunteers quickly organized subscriptions to relief funds for the victims. The spirit of community expressed by these charitable groups in cities across the county seemed to pervade all levels of society. Special collections were raised at neighborhood parish meetings while the wealthy held pompous ceremonies of self-righteous display in the town hall chambers of London, Birmingham, and Manchester. These occasions provided platforms for those gathered in each location to exhort their fellow citizens to help shine their particular city's sterling reputation for generosity, reinforcing a strong cultural penchant for pride in and attachment to place.

In addition, this horrific tragedy created a national sensation that drew the curious by the tens of thousands to see for themselves. Holmfirth—the little that was left of it—was inundated a second time by "witnesses" who swarmed between the flattened dam and the ruined town. Coming at the worst time, of course, these well-meaning tourists represented another sign of the indelible impression the needless cataclysm stamped on the national conscience.[6]

If only briefly, the paradox of progress engendered by the industrial city was plain for all to see. In their greedy haste to harness the forces of nature, the milldam operators had unwittingly created a monster that had struck back with a vengeance. Although the Holmfirth disaster was seemingly remote from Manchester's immediate needs in the aftermath of its own local flooding, the latter city's decision makers would soon be facing the same kinds of moral and legal dilemmas as those presented by the collapse of the milldam. Who was ultimately responsible for such unnatural disasters and how should the guilty be made to pay for them? An equally perplexing set of questions revolved around the relationship between government and business in terms of enacting preventive measures to protect the public safety and welfare. Troubling issues were also raised within the private sector.

Urban Victorians may have had little trouble raising money for such worthy recipients as the victims of such emergencies, but they had considerable difficulty figuring out how to spend it. After the immediate relief need was met with food, blankets, tents, and so on, the question became who deserved aid for long-term support or property losses. On the one hand, for instance, the factory owners who had built the defective dam hardly qualified for welfare to underwrite the cost of rebuilding their cotton mills and dye houses, especially when hundreds of families had been left indigent and homeless by the flood. On the other hand, these cotton mills and dye houses had employed thousands of people who were now out of work. And what about the loss of livelihood suffered by destitute farmers left without livestock or equipment and desperate shopkeepers confronting shelves full of spoiled goods? In the near future, moreover, charity administrators would have to deal with the ethics of disposing of the surpluses that remained in the special relief funds.[7]

The Next *"Heavy* Flood"

For both Holmfirth and Manchester, the interrelated problems of determining responsibility for the unintended consequences of industrialization and assigning institutional authority to fix them stymied the formation of environmental policy for a generation. In the case of the burst dam, the coroner's inquest marked only the opening act in a theater of denial that would play a very long engagement in various courts of law. In the case of Manchester, public discourse on flooding focused on identifying causes and formulating responses to prevent future occurrences of the problem. The debate also raised novel moral questions of distributive and environmental justice. The bifurcation of urban space into affluent garden enclaves and working-class slums meant that the burden of the disasters fell disproportionately upon the inner-city poor. And the repeated return of increasingly furious storm surges for more than two decades gave continuity to the evolution of conceptual approaches to the problem of water management in the Mersey/Irwell watershed. Following this long travail of political wrangling, failed remedies, and human suffering helps illuminate the ways in which contemporaries responded to the creation of the world's first regional-scale industrial ecology.

Before the flood of 1852, the inhabitants of Manchester/Salford had received at least three clear warnings of the growing risk of catastrophe resulting from the effort to control the basin's water in pursuit of progress. The first and most obvious sign of impending disaster was simply the historic increase in the number of floods in the first half of the century. The six inundations noted by Richard Proctor probably resulted less from rising levels of precipitation than from changing patterns of land use as the city experienced rapid growth.[8] Until the 1780s, the population had remained under fifty thousand, and the people had lived in a relatively compact area with a quarter-mile radius. Moreover, the settlement was located on the highest ground, a pie-shaped wedge sitting between the Irwell, Irk, and Medlock rivers. Even as the population multiplied fourfold to 400,000 between 1801 and 1851, the lowest-lying areas remained largely devoted to farming and grazing. Newspaper accounts of flooding in 1829, 1833, 1837, 1840, and 1843 confirm that the urban community suffered little property damage and no loss of life on those occasions.

Several other factors also combined to mitigate the effects of the cloudbursts before the first great calamity of 1852 struck the city with unprecedented force. Retrospective analysis shows that fewer obstructions, smaller volumes of surface runoff, and less upstream debris and riverbed sedimentation all contributed to keeping most of the water from these storm surges between the steeply sloping banks of the three rivers. Nonetheless, the significant rise in the frequency of flooding provided contemporaries with ample notification of the potential for disaster that lay ahead as a result of the accumulation of human interventions that were steadily reducing the carrying capacity of the waterways.[9]

The local scientific community furnished town planners with a second source of invaluable information on the growing risk of catastrophe caused by the altering of the physical hydrology of the rivers. Founded in 1781, the Manchester Literary and Philosophical Society was one of the earliest formal groups devoted to the pursuit of knowledge about nature. Furthermore, it served as an institutional bastion of social and cultural prestige for the city's Dissenting Liberals, the merchants, manufacturers, and professionals rising in fortune with the expansion of the Atlantic cotton (and slave) trade. Along with Dr. Thomas Percival, John Dalton was a charter member of the society and would become one of the outstanding leaders of science and technology during the Age of Industry. Although best remembered for working out the chemical table of elements, this professor of natural philosophy also helped lay the basic foundations of meteorology. In 1799, he delivered a paper to show nature's economy; it had the long-winded, albeit self-explanatory, title, "Experiments and Observations to Determine Whether the Quantity of Rain and Dew Is Equal to the Quantity of Water Carried Off by Rivers, and Raised by Evaporation; with an Inquiry into the Origin of Springs."[10]

Forty-five years later, a young civil engineer named John Frederic Bateman, a thirty-four-year-old homegrown product of the Moravian community, revisited Dalton's essay to bolster the theoretical calculations of scientific speculation with the hard facts of systematic observation. At the February 1844 meeting of the "Lit and Phil," Bateman respectfully affirmed his predecessor's veneration for the "beautiful system of nature," but tactfully complained about the critical lack of accurate data. With the recent floods in mind, he explained his pioneering efforts to devise a reliable method of recording the quantity of rainwater falling on the ground. "The measurement of a single flood may be omitted," he warned, "and yet that flood may send down as much water in a single day as would pass off in two months of ordinary weather."

Bateman drew upon his experience as an apprentice milldam builder to highlight the ways in which changes in the land were defeating its built-in mechanisms for regulating the pace of surface runoff. Reflecting on his work in the hill country, he pointed to the widespread practice of draining its bogs and swamps for agricultural purposes as a major contributor to rapid surges in river levels in the valleys below. The construction of reservoirs, he explained, helped to counteract the downside of progress as well as to ensure a steady, year-round source of power for downstream mills. In addition, these artificial lakes provided Bateman just what he needed to formulate precise answers to the questions raised by Dalton's hypothetical "imagining."[11]

Despite its own methodological shortcomings, Bateman's investigation established the first solid foundation for the study of hydrography. The difficulties he encountered in gathering reliable data on rainfall during his first job as a professional surveyor illustrate the primitive state of contemporary understanding of the weather and its role in the ecosystem. In 1833, he went to work for the renowned millwork and factory designer, William Fairbairn, on a waterpower project on the Ban River near Ulster, Ireland. By surveying the acreage draining into the reservoir and then sampling the amount of precipitation distributed over this watershed, he was be able to identify several key aspects of water's circulatory cycle between the atmosphere and the land.

Most important, perhaps, Bateman's strategically placed rain gauges settled an old argument over whether more precipitation fell on the valleys or the hilltops. The overwhelming evidence from several different tests left no doubt in his mind that the amount of rain increased proportionally with the elevation. A second major finding grew out of the engineer's ability to calculate how much of the rain found its way into the rivers by comparing the amount falling into his gauges against the volume collecting behind the earthen embankments he was becoming expert in building. The correct answer was that approximately two-thirds of the rain found its way into the rivers, with the remainder either soaking into the subsoil or evaporating into the air.[12]

However, Bateman was painfully aware of troubling inconsistencies in the numbers, complaining that "it was difficult in that country to find persons to attend properly to the gauges." Leaving aside his unstated racism, the problem was real enough within a cultural context of little training in or experience with precise standards of scientific measurement. "A rain-gauge, except in the hands of a philosophical observer," he recalled some years later when he was in a more generous mood, "was a thing unknown. All was guess or 'rule of thumb.'" Nevertheless, Bateman returned to Manchester determined to replace guesswork with statistics by enlarging the scope of his research.[13]

Although it is easy to imagine that the young professional's long, detailed report on his findings put most of his audience to sleep, his analysis of the flood of less than four months earlier should have stirred them back to attention. He had carefully recorded the story of the October 1843 storm from the vantage point of one his current test sites, the Entwistle Reservoir on the Irwell River above Bolton. Under flood conditions, the proportion of rainfall becoming surface runoff had climbed to over 90 percent, sending a surge of water down the river at ten times its average rate of flow. Bateman hammered home his concerns about the risk for much more severe consequences by drawing a distinction between a "continuous downpour" and a "*heavy* flood." The October storm represented the former, having dumped five inches of rain on the region over the course of ten days. Knowing that half that amount could fall in a single day, Bateman predicted a future that included tidal waves twenty to forty times larger than the normal flow rushing through the valley.[14]

Apparently the membership was impressed enough by Bateman's cautionary tale to support his concluding plea for additional research. The society sponsored the establishment of more test sites and related experiments on the best way to standardize the measurement of rainfall. These studies laid the groundwork for the establishment in the early 1860s of a national network of weather stations. Bateman's investigations also helped him rise rapidly as a local, then national, then, eventually, international expert in building urban water-supply systems using gravity-fed chains of upland reservoirs. In Manchester, for instance, the municipal government soon put him in charge of construction in one of the largest such projects of its time, in the Longdendale Valley above Stockport. The engineer proposed to capture the surface runoff of eighteen thousand acres of the Pennines behind a chain of three embankments spanning one of the MIRB's other tributaries, the Etherow River.[15] The experience gained in the process of building the waterworks supplied a third source of useful information about the grave risks involved in the effort to harness the forces of nature.

The timing of Bateman's study of hydraulic science and engineering could not have been more opportune. In the first half of the 1840s, Manchester's paradoxical position as a shock city was expanding as it reached new levels of social crisis. While the young professional was making his reputation in the august chambers of the Lit and Phil, Léon Faucher, Fredrick Engels, and Dr. Richard Howard were gathering documentation for their exposés in the underground hovels of the needy and sick. On one thing they could all agree: there was an appalling lack of attention to providing a population approaching four hundred thousand people with an adequate supply of potable water. "All the medical witnesses agree," Bateman testified, "that the large rate of mortality by which Manchester is distinguished is greatly owing to its destitution of water." A private company piped well water on an intermittent basis into less than a quarter of the 46,577 households in the borough; it offered standpipes in the street to another quarter for the same few hours of service a day. And even this relatively clean water often became spoiled because without constant service, both groups of householders were forced to put their supplies into storage vessels that they did not know were contaminated.[16]

The other half of the households depended on a variety of traditional sources, but these were all badly polluted with the waste products of industry. "The rain water," a local history notes, "was so much blackened by soot that it was like ink, and useless even for cleaning purposes until it had been allowed to settle or had been filtered; the river water was even worse." Increasing crowding in the central city districts meant that shallow backyard wells were also poisoned with human wastes. The parliamentary inspector H. P. Holland found that "the water from the pumps is foul, probably from filth filtering through the soil into the wells. . . . The inhabitants are poor and wretched;

and it is no matter of surprise that the mortality among them is above twice the average amount."[17] In the midst of an economic depression, malnutrition and deprivation, in combination with bad water, account for a significant proportion of this ghastly toll.

In August 1842, the desperation of Lancashire's textile workers had spilled out into the streets, sparking a true state of emergency. Reviving the frightening specter of the Peterloo Massacre, the civil disorders were variously known as the "Big Six-Week Turnout," the "Plug Plot," or the "Food Riot," according to different memories of the mass protest against hunger. There is no disputing that large numbers of textile operatives marching under Chartist banners had gone from mill town to mill town calling out their brothers and sisters. To forestall their replacement with countless others starving for work, the mechanics had removed the plugs from steam-engine boilers, bringing the factories to a halt. Decades later, workers recalled getting free food along the way from sympathetic bakers, publicans, and shopkeepers as gestures of class solidarity. One witness remembered, however, that a Mrs. Charles Smith had been roughed up and her dry goods store looted of its bread, flour, and potatoes. This exceptional act might have been a case of revenge since her husband was a hated boss at one of the big mills.[18]

In any case, the workers in the street sounded a literal and symbolic wake-up call to Manchester's ruling elite: action to meet needs for basic urban infrastructure like a waterworks could not be put off much longer. Over the next several years, the Chartist cause would continue to mobilize working-class power in the political arena. The traveler Léon Faucher captured the gnawing sense that a social explosion was impending when he wrote, "amid the fogs which exhale from this marshy district, and the clouds of smoke vomited forth from the numberless chimneys, Labour presents a mysterious activity, something akin to the subterranean action of a volcano."[19]

By the middle of the decade, outside pressure was also building up on city officials to decide on a plan to provide the burgeoning city with an abundant supply of pure water. Lord Lyon Playfield's national inquiry on the urban question had cast an unfavorable light on Manchester's completely inadequate approach to both water supply and sewage removal. Yet the city's Liberal elite had always ignored such political challenges from the top and the bottom with impunity. Its perception of a true threat to its power came from a different direction, from entrepreneurs seeking franchises from Parliament to supply more water in response to the city's pent-up demand. Once started, the scramble for water rights in the MIRB forced everyone with an interest to join in the contest, including the existing waterworks, milldam owners, canal companies, would-be utilities, and, of course, the Manchester Corporation.

At the end of the wrangling, in September 1847, the Corporation emerged victorious, but at a very heavy price.

To secure the exclusive franchise for a municipally owned waterworks, the town council agreed to pay a king's ransom in compensation to the other entities that had a vested interest in the catch basin's water rights. Perhaps the most generous sweetheart deal went to the primarily local shareholders of the existing utility company. To buy them out, the city became obligated to pay them an annuity in virtual perpetuity. This expense helped keep the fledging public enterprise in the red for several years, but it did not become a significant financial restraint on infrastructure planning after that. The water promised to the mill owners in the Etherow River Valley proved much more crippling to the city as it tried to keep up with the needs of a growing metropolitan area. Waterpower site operators secured a parliamentary amendment assigning them more than half of the water captured behind the dams, an amount equivalent to fifteen million gallons per day (mgd). For the next quarter-century, according to the officials' spokesmen, the remaining amount, nine to fifteen mgd, would be insufficient to supply working-class homes with indoor plumbing.[20]

Unprecedented in scale, the public works project became a source of both on-the-job education in hydraulic engineering and influential advances in waterworks technology. Several important inventions, for instance, made the pipelines safe enough to withstand the tremendous internal pressure of the water racing through them. Manchester's Dr. Angus Smith cooked up a new method of lining the iron conduits, a tarry coating that prevented corrosion and reduced friction by as much as 40–50 percent. Local engineers designed bigger, stronger pipes and joints and devised a whole series of ingenious control valves. Consider the "self-acting closing value": it could detect a break in the line, shut off the water, and send an alarm signal to the reservoir watchman. In building dams for water supply rather than mill power, Bateman worked out ways to harness the force of gravity for the task of purifying the flowing liquid. Although the hills above the embankments were comparatively free of peat, the discoloring residues in the rainwater of what peat there was were removed by a succession of weirs and slots in the streams. Bateman also installed drain valves at various heights in the dams to siphon off the purest water. Finally, he learned that the three descending reservoirs acted like gigantic settling tanks. He drew the cleanest water out of the lowest reservoir for delivery to the city.

However, the construction of the municipal waterworks was anything but an unmitigated triumph of technological progress. In October 1849, a *"heavy* flood" caused a catastrophic collapse of the Woodhead Reservoir, the uppermost site at 680 feet above sea level. Sending 130 million gallons of water cascading down the valley, the dam burst was the result to two miscalculations. First, Bateman had not followed his own advice about building in extra capacity for an act of God that could not be foreseen. He had originally calculated a maximum flow into the reservoir of 20.2 million gallons per hour (mgh). But a storm the previous July with over twice that rate convinced him to revise the plan by raising the height of the embankment from sixteen to twenty-four feet. It was not enough: the twenty-four-hour downpour in October 1849 peaked at over one hundred mgh, filling up the dam and sending water fatally over the top. The second mistake was far more serious and costly in the long run. Bateman's original survey of the base of the reservoir seemed to indicate the presence of an ideal subsoil of solid boulders that could withstand the tremendous pressure of the water behind the dam. But the engineer was mistaken: just below the surface of the shallow crust of solid boulders was a treacherous fault line of millstone grit. This unstable base contributed to the disaster by undermining the dam as the weight of the stormwater built up behind it. Looking back twenty years later, Bateman would admit that "the Manchester district is a very difficult one in which to make reservoirs. It is the most difficult district, which I ever had to deal with."[21]

The failure of 1849 was a lesson the engineer would never forget; he was one of the few who were well prepared to meet the next "*heavy* flood." In 1852, Bateman ensured that the three dams under his supervision were appropriately equipped with emergency flood devices at each stage of construction. He anxiously dashed from one to the other, but they were never in imminent danger of having water spill over the top. Unfortunately, the same kind of painstaking precautions had not been taken in Holmfirth. Bateman's timely reports supplied city leaders both great relief from worry about the safety of their reservoirs and useful information on the meteorology of the storm.[22]

Equally important, a letter published a week after the flood in the *Manchester Guardian* provided an urban analogy to the engineer's insightful analysis of the ways in which drainage improvements in the upland moors were accelerating the rate of surface runoff. Writing anonymously, the "Inquirer" asked why so little attention had been given in the policy debate to "the obstruction of the watercourses" within the city. He also questioned the wisdom of permitting alterations of the riverbanks since those alterations effectively negated the natural protection against flood surges afforded by their steep, sloping sides. Among the encroachments he listed were the "erection of vertical walls at the sides which contract the space for the natural flow when the water rises to a certain height; fixing piers in the river bed to support bridges; and, though last not least, constructing arches over the entire water-course which are not sufficiently capacious to allow the water to pass freely under them after heavy rains." If these impediments were the cause of "serious damage of property, and injury to health, and even to the destruction of human life!" the writer gasped, then "is it not the duty of any public body to remove such obstructions, or to prevent the creation of new ones?"[23]

"Rivers of Sewage"

These and other pressing questions of flood control quickly got mired in a political morass over much larger decisions on water supply and sewage removal policy. Inaugurating service from the Longdendale reservoirs only a year earlier in 1851, the municipal waterworks had immediately tripled the amount of water reaching the city to eight to nine mgd. But this figure still remained at least one to two mgd short of estimates of what it would take to provide every dwelling with a water closet in addition to meeting the soaring demands of existing domestic and industrial consumers. To bring the city into conformity with the standards of Chadwick's sanitary movement, the Corporation faced the possibility not only of spending a minimum of £250,000 extra on infrastructure, but also of losing the entire revenue from its privy scavenger service. Obsessed with turning a profit, the city council stubbornly resisted public health reform, in part by disclaiming authority to regulate the rivers and their contents. The issues raised by the "Inquirer" simply got buried under the mountains of rhetoric in the ensuing middle-class infighting between the low-tax business elite and the true-economy sanitarians.[24]

In sharp contrast, local officials in Salford found ample sources of police power to order riparian owners to undertake flood prevention projects. In Manchester's little sister community, Salford, the problem with the Irwell was centered near a low-lying peninsula known as the Crescent, which formed a natural flood plain. Frequently inundated in the past, these marshy areas on both the Salford and the Broughton sides of the river had long been given over to the pasturing of animals, the disposal of rubbish, and other marginal uses. But urban growth was encroaching upon the river's built-in drainage mechanisms in Salford just as it was in Manchester. The expansion of the adjoining city centers was putting tremendous pressure on property owners to subdivide these wetlands and develop their riverfronts.

In addition, parallel growth patterns in the mill towns upstream were causing additional human and industrial pollution to flow into the valley. For example, manufacturers dumped an estimated sixty-nine thousand tons of coal ashes and cinders annually into the waterways of the MIRB. Heavy rains like the ones in February 1852 helped flush these wastes downstream to Salford and Broughton, where they collected at the sharp bend of the Irwell across from Peel Park. At the next meeting of the town council, Alderman Jenkinson stated that the resulting "bank was an encroachment on the river" that, "by throwing the water on the Salford side, injured the Crescent bank." He also reported that the landlords on the Broughton side, the Humphrey Booth Charity trustees, were willing to comply with the council's directives issued in the name of "the conservation of . . . the river."[25]

On the Manchester side of the Irwell, political attention remained focused on water supply policy until the heavy damage caused by floods in 1856 and 1857 pushed the "Inquirer's" questions back to the top of the municipal agenda. As we have seen, the city council purposely rigged the rates for indoor sanitary services so they would not have to lay water mains and sewer pipes in the slum districts near the rivers' industrial corridors. But the Corporation's chief spokesman, Town Clerk Joseph Heron, argued that river conservancy was the primary reason for restricting the vast majority of inhabitants to the use of backyard privies and cesspools. "If the use of water-closets in the city became general," he asserted, "the state of the rivers into which they must be discharged . . . would, in fact, become neither more nor less than open sewers." A second compelling reason for adopting a policy of spatial segregation by class (and ethnicity/religion), according to Heron, was that most Mancunians lacked enough innate intelligence and moral rectitude to operate a toilet properly.[26]

However, this unjust policy did not go unchallenged. Soon after the water was turned on in 1851, local sanitarians organized the Manchester and Salford Sanitary Association (MSSA) to contest Town Hall's blatantly discriminatory rates, which were aimed at carving the physical and social geography of the city into separate spheres. Rooted in paternalistic traditions of Christian duty and charity to the poor, the MSSA would become a permanent lobby on behalf of a better urban environment. The opponents of the council shared an almost religious faith in Chadwick's vision of the sanitary city. Fueled by a powerful blend of medical science, social statistics, and moral fervor, they were driven more by physical metaphors of the city as a living organism than by political images of an egalitarian society. As scholar Christopher Hamlin explains, the Sanitary Idea "was an ingenious political construct. . . . It would unite widespread middle-class concerns with local amenities, central government concerns with economic and social order, and evangelical visions of a coming world of morality, decency, and cleanliness. Could anyone possibly object?" In effect, the council decision to make water closets prohibitively expensive in the homes of the working classes represented just such an objection.[27]

In the battle for municipal reform, the MSSA attempted to refute Town Hall's policy of spatial segregation and to gain acceptance of a comprehensive system of environmental engineering. In most ways, its first annual report of 1853 closely resembled Dr. James P. Kay's classic account of the slums, complete with a dire warning about these breeding grounds of disease spreading their deadly infections to affluent commuters from the suburbs. The MSSA took exception to Kay's call for moral uplift, however, by demanding a universal system of indoor plumbing as the first priority of public health reform. This small but dedicated band of reformers offered a much more holistic alternative to water management that included ways to respond to the "Inquirer's" subtle appeal to save the rivers. Sensitive to the criticism that this policy alternative would cost too much, the sanitarians defensively replied, "but if we look at the subject in its true light—first, as affecting the health of the people; secondly, as to its value as an article of manure; and thirdly, as to economy of removal—it has been proved over and over again, and it appears almost useless to repeat it, that in every respect we should be gainers by the adoption of this system."[28]

The sanitarians offered visionary blueprints of a sanitary city that would have a complete technology of water supply, sewage treatment, pollution control, and flood protection. Rather than blame the victims for their own extraordinary rates of sickness and death, the MSSA's members drew support for their position not only from Chadwick's crusade, but also from the technical expertise of national engineer Robert Rawlinson. His authority was based on the statistical data he had complied while conducting investigations of environmental conditions in several Manchester suburbs. Although Manchester had scorned Parliament's innovative Public Health Act of 1848, Broughton, Altrincham, and other communities had adopted its provisions. In response to their applications for official surveys, Rawlinson had become their duly appointed commissioner three years later. Committed to the Sanitary Idea, he provided local reformers with both expert testimony and practical plans for cleaning up the pollution of the rivers.[29]

To counter Heron's argument that a universal system of water carriage would cause insufferable river pollution, the sanitarians pointed to longstanding official acquiescence in massive industrial contamination of the waterways. Moreover, the city had already permitted thousands of indoor toilet and outdoor privy connections to the drainage pipes. As a result, according to Rawlinson, "a semi-liquid compound is formed, an accurate idea of which no written description can convey. A thick scum coats the surface [of the rivers], upon and over which birds can walk; the putrid carcasses of dead animals, dogs, cats, etc. float and rot in the midst; fermentation takes place rapidly, as large bubbles of gas may be seen escaping, and a thick vapour hangs over the entire area." True enough, to annually dump into these "rivers of sewage" an additional sixty-five to ninety thousand tons of human excrement now being carted away would make the rivers even less tolerable. But the MSSA disarmed its critics by calling for intercepting sewers to divert all of the city's liquid wastes away from the rivers and to recycling farms. The reformers, moreover, demanded that the public sector take charge of river conservancy, remove artificial obstructions, and dredge the river bottoms and pave them over to reduce silting in the future.[30]

Although the reformers may have won the policy debate in the realm of public opinion, they were no match for the entrenched elite in the political arena of local government. In fact, the MSSA foreswore any type of activism other than "moral suasion." The main strategies of the group were the mass distribution of tracts, an endless series of lectures, and a tireless round of "visitations" by middle-class women to the homes of the poor. At the association's second annual meeting in 1854, the Lord Bishop of Manchester applauded these efforts because they were helping to "raise the moral tone of the working man, enableing him to work out his own improvement."

The self-perpetuating inner circle of big merchants, manufacturers, and landlords that controlled election to the city council had every reason to join in the praise of the MSSA's nonconfrontational politics of cooperation. The do-gooders' work among the poor posed no threat to the business elite because stiff property qualifications kept voting restricted to less than the 20 percent of the adult male population. Taking the support of the reformers for granted, the city council sought most of all to appease the large ratepayers by keeping the expenses of the public sector as low as possible.[31] As in Chicago, then, low-cost government became the quid pro quo of political legitimacy. In both cities, this approach to local government reinforced spatial patterns of environmental inequality in spite of the different motives of Manchester's business elite and Chicago's ward bosses.

Even the return to a state of emergency from severe flooding could not budge the council from its stand in favor of reinforcing spatial patterns of segregation by class and ethnicity/religion. Manchester Liberals were facing serious challenges to their civic leadership from within the top ranks of non-Anglican society for the first time. People from the best families, including former mayor John Potter, were splitting apart from the Free Traders and Radicals. In 1857, the ejection of Richard Cobden and John Bright from their seats in Parliament formally signaled the schism. In the midst of this infighting among the middle classes, the council drew up blueprints of environmental control that were aimed at holding together a low-cost-government coalition of the large property owners and the shopocracy of small retailers and artisan homeowners. The council's defense of the privy system had the effect of exempting landlords in working-class districts from the significant expense of installing plumbing and paying municipal hookup fees. The scavenger bills they had to pay instead were minimal since the city got around to cleaning out the disgusting pits an average of only twice a year.[32]

The spatial zoning embodied in Manchester's water management decisions significantly limited the council's policy options in dealing with the next round of back-to-back floods. In 1856 and 1857, mill owners' accusations that the Corporation was itself responsible for causing heavy property damages jarred local officials into taking notice of the pressing need for some kind of central plan of river conservancy. But they had to continue to treat river conservancy as an isolated problem separate from other aspects of public health and sanitation in order to defend their politics of exclusion. In the deluge of August 1856, several days of saturating rains were once again followed by an extraordinary downpour. Bateman reported that at the Longdendale reservoirs the final rainfall exceeded the 1852 record of 2.5 inches in a twenty-four-hour period by more than half an inch. The most serious danger shifted this time from the Irwell River to the smaller and more confined Medlock.

The "Inquirer's" questions had fallen on deaf ears. Both the public and the private sectors had added major new obstructions that made the rushing waters overflow their banks. Next to Little Ireland, the city had paved over the river, forcing it through a quarter-mile-long culvert that proved much too small to handle flood surges. Just above this impediment, three mill owners had installed weirs and floodgates that they inadvertently left closed during the height of the emergency. All of these encroachments acted like dams when river levels began climbing rapidly, diverting the water into the factories lining the banks and into the houses behind them. Although the city escaped without loss of life, the daily newspaper predicted that the ultimate price tag of the flood "will be a very large sum."[33]

Sued by the mill owners, the city government could no longer afford to ignore the need to establish a public authority over the rivers. Its knee-jerk defense was to attempt to kick the entire legal liability for and financial cost of the floods back onto the owners of the private property bordering the riverfronts. The council introduced a bill in Parliament to divide the regional watershed into tiny segments to create a system equivalent to the special-assessment arrangement for assigning the costs of street and sidewalk improvements. Riparian owners would thus be required to pay for the city's plans for deepening and paving the riverbed. But the owners kept the Corporation's bill bottled up in the national legislature while vigorously prosecuting their damage suits in the local court. Led by the influential Birley family, the factory owners contended that the city's culvert caused the backup of the Medlock and their ensuing losses. The judiciary agreed with the property owners, awarding £4,500 in the case of the J. & W. Bellhouse mill, for example. Painful financial reminders like this helped turn the council's attention to the need for a master city plan of environmental control over the rivers.[34]

Another flood almost exactly one year later, in August 1857, hammered home the undeniable point that river levels and the costs of damage to private property would both continue to escalate with each succeeding emergency. In 1856 the level of the Medlock had set a record, three feet higher than the level recorded during the 1852 storm surge. In 1857, the high-water mark on the Medlock was four feet higher still. The water was fourteen feet deep in some buildings in 1857; Little Ireland all but disappeared under it. Moreover, the force of the current in the tightly confined river was more powerful and destructive in 1857 than ever before. At the low point of the riverbank, near Brook Street, the swollen stream slammed into the retaining wall of an indigo dye works and washed it away. The pressure of the water rushing into the building was so great that it lifted a stone tank weighing ten tons and carried it along for several feet. A little farther downstream, the boiler house of the Bellhouse mill was wrecked, and the wall of Birley's nine-hundred-loom weaving room was knocked down, ruining everything inside. This kind of catastrophic loss occurred over a more extensive area than ever before, stretching from the upper Ancoats/Holt Town District to the municipal culvert at Oxford Road.[35]

The city's first flood fatality added special urgency to the effort to put public works programs into place that would correct the rivers' loss of carrying capacity as a result of artificial obstructions and silting. An eighteen-year-old boy had drowned when he fell out of a boat and was carried away helplessly under the swift currents. The frustration at the unnatural calamity quickly turned into angry denunciations of the town council. Cautioning against a rush to judgment, the *Manchester Guardian* disingenuously let others point the finger of blame. "We can only say," the paper equivocated, "we heard . . . a general and strongly expressed opinion that the time had arrived when the Corporation would be compelled to deal broadly with the questions of weirs, bridges, etc.; any powers that might be requisite being obtained as speedily as possible." The MSSA was more explicit, sending the aldermen a memorial reminding them of its often-repeated concerns about the undersized culvert and the silt accumulating behind Birley's weir. Its annual report bristled with self-righteous indignation because the sanitarians "consider the use of the Rivers of Manchester as open common Sewers to be one of the monster nuisances of the City."[36]

Thrown on the defensive, the local government assumed a more cooperative posture in working with the riparian property owners to reach agreement on a flood protection plan for the Medlock River. Already stung by the defeat of their Medlock River bill in the previous session of Parliament, the council members slyly hid behind the excuse that this legislative roadblock deprived it of jurisdiction over the river channel and its contents. The maneuver flushed out a representative of the landowners' group who came forward to negotiate a compromise. An agreement was reached that the local government and the landowners would unite behind the proposals of City Surveyor James G. Lynde for dredging the waterway and raising the bridges, but a majority of the council balked at the idea of paying for the plan from the general fund. Even the return of a state of emergency in December 1860 could not budge the council from its penny-pinching position. Riparian owners, it kept insisting, would have to bear the entire cost of the flood protection project.

Nevertheless, the relatively minor deluge of December 1860 served to remind both sides that the problem would only grow worse in the absence of a general plan of environmental control. While the mill owners had been building stronger, more waterproof retaining walls, they could not defend themselves from the water overflowing into the adjoining streets and backing up into their basements through the sewers. The impasse was finally broken three years later when the council established the River Medlock Committee and the private interests conceded that they would have to underwrite at least a portion of the project. The council now agreed to pay one-half out of the general fund as Lynde's cost estimates had more than doubled to £30,000. In 1865, a bill embodying this formula was duly passed by Parliament. But Manchester would soon pay a much greater price for its eight-year delay in reaching a consensus behind the need for a more comprehensive approach to the problem of river conservancy.[37]

"The Great Flood"

During the next round of crisis and response, urban reformers began to reconceptualize these local catastrophes within the larger regional context of an increasingly industrial ecology. Led by experts like John Bateman, they drew much stronger links not only between flood protection and pollution control but also between water management and environmental justice. The repeated failures of Manchester's public officials to prevent the disastrous inundations combined with widespread concern about the rapid degradation of the nation's waterways to bring the intervention of Parliament. The findings of its investigating committees left little doubt about the need to establish new levels of administrative supervision over the MIRB.

Fearing a loss of local autonomy and an additional tax burden, however, the city's civic elite lobbied against every reform proposal to create just this type of authority. At the same time, they took the Janus-faced stand of disclaiming responsibility for safeguarding the city against the next natural disaster without the help of such a regional agency for river conservancy. Manchester's big property owners and manufacturers continued to give greater priority to their own narrow pecuniary interests than to the community's health, safety, and welfare.

Despite the frequency of emergencies in recent times, the flood of the Irwell River in mid-November 1866 seemed to throw the people of Manchester/Salford into a numbing state of disbelief, just as the Holmfirth tragedy had done. Two days of heavy rains and swelling rivers gave people plenty of warning, a local newspaper reported, "but none seemed to have been fully prepared for the floodtide of disaster and discomfort which was to follow. Previous experience seemed to give no criterion of the disastrous result. A vast area of a busy city submerged by the accumulating and fast flowing waters of an overcharged river was one of the last of the evils contemplated." The Medlock too overflowed its banks, submerging factories and homes at several places. Rainfall in the hills far exceeded the amount coming down in the valleys, putting Bateman's Longdendale reservoirs to their severest test. Overwhelming every emergency discharge device, water briefly spilled over the top of the Torside and the Rhodes Wood dams, but the engineer's designs ultimately withstood this supreme test.

The Medlock and Irk overflowed their banks, but the most serious problems involved the Irwell, the largest of the three waterways. Altogether 1,100 acres were inundated on either side of the river's serpentine path through the twin cities of Manchester and Salford. Large sections of Salford, the Broughton District of Manchester, and the upstream suburb of Pendleton were swamped under three to eight feet of water. "There extended one huge lake of turbid water," an eyewitness vividly recalled, "rushing irresistibly along, carrying with it in its course everything which it was capable of rooting up or dislodging from its place. It was a truly magnificent sight to those who could from some point of safety stand and take in the panorama of seething waters which lay stretched out before them. But to those who had life and property at stake, it was a day of disaster and never-ceasing anxiety and dread."[38]

As the fast-rising currents made at least two thousand people homeless and four people drowned while trying to escape, the twin cities had to mount large-scale rescue and relief efforts for the first time. Early in the day, the mayors took charge of organizing city workers and heroic private citizens to help save families stranded on rooftops and to find temporary shelters for them in public buildings and churches. Although hundreds were drawn to the bridges and other observation points by the spectacle, there seems to have been no shortage of volunteers willing to come to the aid of the refugees.

As the waters receded, scenes reminiscent of Holmfirth were repeated. Hordes of curious witnesses roamed the devastated areas and put money in specially marked boxes to aid the victims. The police conducted systematic surveys of the destruction in preparation for a meeting at Town Hall to organize the relief effort, but Manchester's officials had instructed them to limit this census to only the very worst cases. For example, the officers ignored several hundred buildings severely damaged by dampness and counted instead a mere 166 houses and 81 shops in the Strangeways District near the Crescent that were wrecked beyond repair. The report further restricted its accounting of the suffering to that of the poorest occupants of these structures, many of whom had been made completely destitute.[39]

The Town Hall meeting exposed sharp conflict over the ethics of charity for the flood victims. In contrast to the discussion following the Holmfirth disaster, questions were immediately raised about the worthiness of the recipients. Hardliners claimed that it was immoral to give handouts to anyone but the most "necessitous" who would otherwise be reduced to public burdens as paupers. The discussion, led by Mayor Robert Neill, initially underscored the need for close scrutiny of the disbursements to protect against freeloading and fraud. Consider the Reverend Canon Richson's assertion that great evils that would takes years to overcome had resulted from giving charity to unemployed factory workers impoverished by the Cotton Famine during the American Civil War. Echoing these sentiments, the mayor reasoned that a small shopkeeper facing ruin because of a £50 loss should be given only £20, while any surpluses in the fund should be divided among the city's churches. Reverend Richson then offered a formal resolution embodying these sentiments, putting disbursements under the tight-fisted control of a small executive committee.

In contrast, the rector of St. Matthias in Salford took a liberal stand because he believed the suffering was widespread and would last far beyond the immediate relief of the flood victims. One of the council leaders, Alderman Grundy, even argued that the petit bourgeois homeowners in Lower Broughton were worthy of aid if it could be given to them discreetly so they could avoid the stigma of becoming known as charity cases. The Reverend G. S. Allen also appealed for generosity toward all of the five thousand inhabitants of this hard-hit area who had to return to waterlogged, foul-smelling dwellings. Others claimed that the planning of contingencies for a surplus would be self-defeating in raising funds. They suggested, for example, giving a little more than £20 to the shopkeeper with the £50 loss. The mayor of Salford, H. D. Pochin, added his own to a swelling chorus of voices calling for giving away all of the £5,000 subscription proposed for the two communities. In the face of this opposition, the Reverend Canon Richson withdrew his resolution, leaving the executive committee to proceed in raising and dispensing the entire relief fund.[40]

Ethical questions of social justice lay at the heart of the wide-ranging policy debate on long-term environmental-control solutions that followed on the heels of the great flood. In large part, fear of death from cholera was the motivating force driving public discourse toward the linkage of flood protection, pollution control, and water management. The return of the horrifying disease to epidemic levels in London had already galvanized the MSSA to revive its campaign for a water-carriage system of sanitation. On a national level, the latest public health crisis encouraged Parliament to study the condition of the country's major rivers, including the Mersey-Irwell watershed. Reflecting the heightened awareness of the industrial city's impacts on nature, one newspaper editorial lamented, "England is no longer a pastoral country, and she bids fair to become rather a land of sewers than a land of streams."[41]

On a local level, the arrival of the parliamentary investigators again bolstered the position of the MSSA in its campaign for a holistic approach to environmental reform. In 1867, Robert Rawlinson, returning as chairman of the first Rivers Pollution Commission, chastised the municipal government for denying indoor plumbing to the working classes in the city while extending it to the affluent classes in the suburbs. His support helped the sanitarians to prod the council to appoint a part-time medical officer of health almost two decades after the passage of the benchmark Public Health Act authorized the creation the office. The gasworks chemist Dr. John Leigh was selected as the first medical officer of health because his appointment would not add any extra cost to the budget.

The policies of the Corporation came under much closer scrutiny a year later with the arrival of a second commission, which was charged with making a full-scale report on the MIRB. A nationally respected scientist and local son, Edward Frankland, directed its work, including a remarkably detailed survey of 10,500 industrial sites in the watershed. Armed with various chemical tests, the commission also sought to distinguish between pollution caused by factory wastes and that caused by human sewage. Professor Frankland hoped to prove his pet hypothesis that the natural flow of the rivers was insufficient for self-purification, and his experiments included taking water samples at strategic points along the entire lengths of the watercourses for analysis in the laboratory.[42]

When the commission arrived in Manchester in June 1868, the accumulating record of dismal failures threw Town Hall onto the defensive. Added to the city's dithering policy on flood protection and its lack of progress in reducing an extraordinary infant mortality rate were the shortages suffered by its highly touted waterworks, which cut off service for half of each day. Even the compliant Dr. Leigh had opened his first annual report a few months earlier with the damning admission that "Manchester has long had an unenviable reputation as one of the most unhealthy towns in the kingdom. Its death-rate has always been high, much higher than that of many other considerable towns, and largely in excess of the general death-rate of the kingdom."

One of the purposes of the investigation was to gather statistical evidence on the local government's management of the water supply and sanitation system (see table 5.1). As the critics of the council's hard line against Chadwickian systems pointed out, these numbers meant that the residents of the central city were condemned to live with the equivalent of a twenty-five-acre cesspool filled, on average, with sixty thousand tons of human waste. To them there was no need to look further to account for the city's status as the nation's leading death trap.[43]

Nonetheless, Manchester's ruling elite remained steadfast in upholding the privy system as the only way to save the rivers and continued to blame the poor for their own ill health. Unwavering adherence to this official position seems to have been the obvious quid pro quo for the selection and subsequent appointment of Dr. Leigh to the full-time job of medical officer of health with a salary of £500 a year. True, the doctor recognized the sufferings of the working class: "A large part of my life has been spent amongst the poor of Manchester," he reported in his inaugural address to the council. "I have seen much of, and painfully felt, the misery and destitution brought into the very many homes by these diseases, the calamities entailed by which I desire earnestly and strongly to bring before you." And he was not insensitive to the fact that half of the city's children died before they reached five years of age and that three-fifths died by age ten, an appalling proportion. Yet he held the mothers responsible for the tragedy. He asserted that their "outdoor occupations . . . and the unfavourable influences to which children are subjected—such as improper food, the administration of opiates, exposure to wet and cold, and especially to infection, with the respiration of a vitiated atmosphere—sufficiently account for this."[44]

In testimony before the commission, the benighted town clerk, Sir Joseph Heron, supported the doctor's position, pinpointing the worst plague spots as those occupied by either the "vicious classes," or the city's favorite

Table 5.1 Manchester sanitary census, 1868

Housing		Water supply		Sanitary services	
Annual rental value	Number	Inside water service	Outside standpipes	Water closets	Privies
Under £10	52,700	31,500	2,078 (21,000 dwellings)	0	30,700 (52,700 dwellings)
Over £10	17,300	17,300	0	10,000	7,300
Total	70,000	48,800	2,078 (21,000 dwellings)	10,000	38,000 (60,000 dwellings)

Source: "First Report of the Commissioners . . . The Pollution of Rivers (Mersey and Ribble Basins)," vol. 1: "Reports and Plans," *Parliamentary Papers* (1870): vol. 40, 454–64.

scapegoats, the Irish Catholics. Public officials were blameless, he insisted, because "no sanitary arrangements that can be made will to any very large extent, I believe, affect the condition of those classes—it is something that is beyond the reach of mere sanitary legislation. Manchester is not, as a whole, an unhealthy town."[45]

This well-worn official line of defense became threadbare then snapped under the weight of the scientific evidence the experts piled up in the course of the inquiry. On the one hand, Frankland could praise the Corporation for adopting an upland reservoir system of water supply since he was convinced that the rivers were simply too overloaded with pollution for self-purification to make their waters safe for human consumption. Reinforcing his hypothesis of disease causation, he attributed the city's escape from the ravages of the recent cholera epidemic to the municipal waterworks. On the other hand, he could censure the council for the "fallacy" of its claim that the privy system of sanitation did not contribute significantly to the lethal contamination of the rivers. By conducting a series of chemical tests on samples drawn above and below the city, he was able to amass overwhelming evidence to the contrary. Although in theory dry conservancy meant less river pollution than water-carriage technology, he concluded,

> the marked distinction between the two methods which is thus asserted, disappears however when we inquire into their practical working. The privy system is in reality both wasteful and offensive. Neither the cesspool nor the ashpit is water-tight, and their liquid contents soak into the land around them. Sewers are necessary whether water closets exit or not; and chamber slops with most of the liquid excrement and other house drainage find their way into them notwithstanding the existence of a privy. And that which is collected in the privy tanks or cesspools is occasionally so soaked with rain water and at best so imperfectly dried up by the added ashes, that for the abatement of a nuisance it becomes necessary to give these middens connection with the town drains. The liquid part here too, therefore, drains away, and the remainder, while fouled for any other purpose, becomes of very little value agriculturally.[46]

The parliamentary commission was also willing to make a direct assault on the stance taken by the city's powerful manufacturing interests. Organizing their own self-defense group, the Millowners Committee lobbied against any intervention by the national government that might end the unrestricted dumping of "trade pollution" into the rivers of the Mersey-Irwell watershed.

Since these unfortunate by-products of a £100-million annual business posed no threat to humans, the group warned, imposing limitations would only serve to undercut England's competitive position in world markets. Although Frankland conceded that such a "great evil" of loss of business was to be avoided, he upheld the fundamental right of those living near a river to equal enjoyment of water free from the deleterious effects of pollution.[47]

Frankland and his fellow investigators identified two types of industrial wastes that warranted public control. Relying on his laboratory tests for support, the scientist highlighted the potential health hazards posed by the massive amounts of toxic chemicals coming out of the city's factories. For example, his analysis of a typical textile finishing plant with 250 workers, the Kinder Printing Company, showed that it annually poured 500 million gallons of polluted water into the river, including 19 tons of liquid arsenic containing almost 8 tons of the poisonous metal. In this diluted form, a person would have to drink 138 cups of the factory's wastewater to consume a fatal dose, but he believed no amount of the deadly substance should be allowed in the river. The second type of pollution calling for government regulation also came from the dye, bleaching, and printing plant: the solid matter contained in its liquid discharges amounted annually to 664 tons, plus an additional 220 tons in suspension. These kinds of solid wastes, the parliamentary report concluded, contributed significantly to the flooding in Manchester and Salford by silting up the rivers and making the waters overflow their banks.[48]

In forging links between pollution control and flood protection, the commissioners drew heavily on the river studies of John Bateman. He had been asked by municipal officials to prepare an independent study of the recent disasters in anticipation of a national investigation that would again cast the officials in an unfavorable light. The engineer was not as accommodating as Dr. Leigh, however; he had a growing reputation beyond the local community to protect. Four months after the commission hearings in October 1868, Bateman submitted his report to the council's newly formed Irwell Flood Committee. Taking core samples of the riverbed, he had found that silting was an important cause of the increased frequency and severity of the city's states of emergency. Sedimentation was accumulating at a rate of two to three inches a year, he noted, raising the bottom of the Irwell to between four-and-a-half and nine feet higher than its original depth. In the worst case, a ramp-shaped wedge seventeen feet high had built up behind one of the mill weirs. In addition to ever larger amounts of human sewage and industrial wastes, the engineer estimated, a minimum of thirty-three thousand tons of coal ashes and cinders were thrown into the Irwell each year. "The river is," he declared, "'the hardest worked river in the world.' It has unfortunately been considered the proper receptacle for everything which could not be otherwise conveniently disposed of,—for quarry rubbish, surplus excavation and especially for the ashes and refuse of the various manufactories upon its banks."[49]

The council members charged Bateman with finding not only the reasons for the floods but also the remedies to safeguard the city in the future. This was the one area where Mayor Neill had welcomed even the outside commission to join with local experts in making recommendations. In the two years since the great flood of 1866, the local engineers had prepared a plan to construct a storm tunnel near the Salford Crescent through which extraordinary surges would be diverted to an outfall below the convergence of the Irwell and Medlock rivers. Bateman concurred that the overall concept of the project was valid, although he disputed its design specifications, contending that the tunnel would be too small to handle the enlarged volumes of water now draining into the Irwell during the heaviest rainfalls. He also suggested cutting a new channel to straighten the river and shorten it from 7.1 to 4.7 miles in the built-up districts, digging it deeper to increase its carrying capacity, and inclining its bottom more sharply to speed up the flow.

He warned, however, that the implementation of all these proposals and similar efforts finally under way to reengineer the Medlock would soon be rendered useless by new silting. Steps had to be taken to reduce dumping and to remove private weirs and other obstructions. On the basis of his broad perspectives on river-basin hydrography, he came to the inescapable judgment that Manchester's self-serving defense of local autonomy had to yield to the greater need for a regional authority. "I cannot close this Report," he bravely proclaimed,

> without drawing attention to the importance of establishing a Conservancy Board for the whole basin of the Irwell, whose duty it should be to protect the river from the injury it is sustaining by its being made the common depository for all refuse material.... The interests of all the land and property owners in the valleys through which the river and its tributaries run are all dependent upon the suppression of the great and crying evil which has so long existed, and no works which I or any one else can devise will long continue effective unless it can be prevented.

Issuing its report two years later in 1870, the Parliamentary commission reached exactly the same conclusion.[50]

Yet, the elite insiders in charge of Manchester's municipal government refused to reconsider their position in spite of the fact that they were putting the twin cities at tremendous risk of disaster from the inevitable next big downpour. For the next several years, the council would refuse to negotiate in earnest with Salford about sharing the costs of the storm tunnel, would oppose Salford's efforts to create an agency for the conservancy of the MIRB, and would join with the Millowners Association in lobbying against a national rivers pollution act. When Parliament finally passed such a bill in 1876, Sir Heron could boast that he had helped encumber its enforcement provisions with so many grandfather clauses and other loopholes that neither the city's Corporation nor its factories had anything to worry about.[51]

The most sanitary reformers could get from the council as a result of the policy debate during the late 1860s was a commitment to replace the open cesspools and privy middens with a pail-closet system of dry conservancy. But even this minor concession was motivated more by the lure of turning losses into profits for the city's troubled scavenger service than by a desire to improve the lives of the vast majority of its citizens. With the installation of Dr. John Leigh in the new office, public discourse over the city's sanitation policy was effectively brought to a close for a generation. To be sure, the members of the MSSA continued to send memorials to Town Hall, but their genteel tactics of moral suasion made little headway against the more weighty pocketbook concerns of the property owners.[52]

Although the pail closets marked a small advance in the quality of daily life in the industrial districts of the city, they represented no departure from the council's policy of allowing environmental inequality in the name of low-cost government. Even under the best of circumstances, these backyard accommodations were no match for the comfort and convenience of indoor plumbing, and compared to the public sector's estimated share of the costs for a Chadwickian water-carriage system, dry conservancy kept spending on sanitary services to the residential districts of the working classes to a minimum.

Local officials even hoped to turn reform into profit. They set up a shop to build the new-style outhouses and then ordered landlords to pay for them. In addition, the council erected a highly mechanized processing plant to turn the city's solid wastes into commercial-grade fertilizer. Located on the edge of Ancoats, the Holt Town facility incorporated several significant technological innovations to make a competitive product from a bizarre recipe of human excrement, horse manure, slaughterhouse offal, and coal ashes. At the same time, the council remained steadfast in its position that the city had neither the fiscal nor the natural resources to supply working-class homes with indoor plumbing.[53]

Manchester could have well afforded to begin closing the gap between the slums and the suburbs during the economic boom that followed the Cotton

Famine. Perhaps the best evidence of the flushness of these times was the Liberals' sponsorship of a monumental new town hall, a secular cathedral to rival the grandest churches of the Anglican Tories. The stark contrast between the lavish spending of over a million pounds on this superfluous status symbol and the miserly expenditures on public health reflected the depth of class prejudice among the city's ruling elite. "This sense of values seems to us now somewhat perverted," a local historian commented from the safety of the 1930s, "but we must remember that at that date the Council was only representative of the middle class, and the middle class suffered much less from the insanitary state of the city than did the working class."[54]

The council's constant refrain that the waterworks had reached the limits of the reservoir system also stands in stark contrast to the disposition of the supplies already available. While the Corporation supplied mill owners on the Etherow River with 14.2 million gallons per day, the metropolitan area was receiving a slightly smaller amount, or 13.5 mgd. The council could have found other ways to supply the mill owners, especially considering the technological advances that had recently produced a new generation of steam engines. Finally, in 1870, the city paid £50,000 to buy back 4.6 mgd from the manufacturers. In a similar manner, railroads could have been substituted for some of the canals, which had been built at the turn of the century and consumed a proportion of the watershed's resources equivalent to 24.4 mgd.[55]

Even within the constraints on the system of delivering water to the city, adjustments could have been made between provision of water to city and suburban domestic consumers and to their industrial counterparts, whose use accounted for one-third of the demand. The council's sliding schedule of water rates strongly favored the largest users over the smallest by charging the latter as much as thirteen times more per gallon. Given a gravity-fed system of delivery, there were no economies of scale to justify this differential. Furthermore, water taxes were paid by every household regardless of services received, creating a strong case for the argument that equity and justice demanded that every city resident receive a full share of the benefits of this public utility. The mothers of the central city were not blameworthy; rather, they were the principal victims of a cruel class system that placed disproportionate burdens on them in the never ending, uphill struggle to clean their homes and care for their children.[56]

"The Most Disastrous Flood"

On 14 July 1872, nature seemed to strike back at Manchester with a vengeance for neglecting its need for unobstructed watercourses during storm surges.

To be sure, policy makers had reluctantly taken some half-hearted measures to restore the carrying capacity of the Medlock by correcting the results of previous shortsighted public works projects. But the Corporation's reluctance to interfere with the rights of riparian property owners had resulted in the introduction of more and more artificial intrusions that impeded the flow of water through the city. The reasons for the council's stubborn refusal to order their removal were as much economic as ideological; it simply did not want to pay compensation to mill owners for their submerged weirs and riverbank encroachments. The same penny-pinching motives held town officials back from agreeing to let the city bear its share of the costs of constructing the Irwell storm tunnel and of payment of damage claims by those downstream of its outfall should such claims arise. Instead, the officials spent a fortune of political capital on behalf of the Corporation and the manufacturers in blocking reforms in Parliament for regional river conservancy and urban public health. Weather conditions and human contrivance combined to make the subsequent state of emergency "the most disastrous flood" of the century.[57]

What made this flood unique was the city's location at epicenter of the tempest. Four days of intense thunderstorms "rarely seen except in the tropics" swelled the three rivers to their full carrying capacity; then came the great deluge. Beginning at about one o'clock on Saturday morning and "lasting for more than thirteen hours, the rain fell in Manchester so heavily that occasionally (especially during the night) one almost imagined that a waterspout had broken over the city." Bateman's rain gauges collected 10.4 inches of rainwater in the two days preceding the torrent; that rainfall created the equivalent of an astronomical fifteen inches of runoff during the twenty-four-hour peak period of the torrential downpour. In comparison, Bateman had measured 6.4 inches at the hilltop Longdendale reservoirs during the peak of the 1866 thunderstorm. The result was a veritable tidal wave of over two hundred million gallons an hour barreling down the Medlock. The engineer believed that it "far exceeded any previous records, either on this river or any other in Great Britain."[58]

Nature's fury alone would have wreaked havoc on the city since the maximum carrying capacity of the channel was 46.3 mgh. But beginning about four miles upstream from the town center at Medlock Vale, a series of obstacles retarding the currents made a bad situation much worse. Each of these weirs and bridges acted as a dam holding back a huge volume of water and debris until it burst, sending a tidal wave down the river to smash up against the next impediment. Even the fortified walls of some of the factories hemming in the channel were not strong enough to resist this kind of hammering. Besides the tragedy of one fatality, the most painful and gruesome cost of the flood was the disinternment of at least seventy bodies from the Roman Catholic section of the Philips Park Cemetery. The town fathers had prescribed spatial segregation even in death: since the 1865 dedication of the public graveyard, they had reserved the high ground exclusively for Protestants while assigning Catholics—most of Irish origin—to the low-lying flood plain next to the river. The flimsy retaining wall that the city council had erected on the sandy soils of the riverbank after similar incidents in 1866 and 1869 was undermined by the floodwaters and washed away along with the recently buried coffins and bodies.[59]

Property damage and human suffering were widespread along the Medlock's entire course through the city. Water that overflowed the banks submerged homes and shops from the working-class district of Ancoats to the Duke of Bridgewater's wharves at Castlefield, where barges were lifted and deposited on land far from their moorings. The worst flooding occurred in the Chorlton-upon-Medlock area, where the river reached a high-water mark twenty-one feet over the normal seasonal level. As in the Salford/Broughton flood six years earlier, a newspaper observed, the Medlock "along the whole course has been one vast expanse of water." Unfortunately, there are no reports on the exact number of people displaced by the disaster, but there was a momentary rediscovery of the slum in Manchester. As journalists and other witnesses surveyed the damage, they were struck by the utter squalor of those forced by poverty to live near the river and in the shantytowns hugging its banks. Reviving shock-city images of a decent into hell from the 1830s, an editorial cried out,

> It is impossible on the basis of the dry details, which have appeared in our own and other newspapers, to realize in all its horrors the misery and destitution produced in countless homes by the recent floods. ... Probably the feeling, which will take precedence of all others in the mind of the visitor, will be one of amazement at the fact that hovels such as those which abound in the neighborhood ... should be allowed to exist for the shelter of human beings. ... To the right and left are low dark openings ... more the passages of a mine, and these are the dens in which about a dozen and a half families are huddled. ... Indeed, the tales of misery to which the explorer listens become monotonous, as there is necessarily but little variety in a misfortune which has reduced thousands to absolute destitution.[60]

Various community and religious groups' sympathy for the victims produced several spontaneous acts of charity to organize relief funds. Emblematic of the city's political culture, however, was Mayor Booth's quick attempt to bring this volunteerism under centralized control. Still, at the subsequent meeting in his Town Hall quarters, he left no doubt about his sincere desire to help the needy. When complaints were immediately raised about the abuse of aid money for liquor and so forth, the mayor declared that expressions of such sentiments were inappropriate.

But the mayor was overruled and overwhelmed by the real chief executive of the municipal government, Town Clerk Heron, who decisively took charge of the proceedings. Thrown on the defensive by reaction to his gross mismanagement of the memorial park, he denounced any criticism of the Corporation as out of place and counterproductive. Justified anger and resentment ran deep among the Catholic minority, which held him personally responsible for the ghastly debacle, but he hid behind the excuse of the unprecedented fury of the storm and retorted that the city was doing all it could to recover the bodies and clean up the foul-smelling mess left in its wake. Incredibly, he struck back by righteously heaping blame on the flood's victims for hindering the work of the scavenger department in order to exploit opportunities for begging. Deprecating the charity efforts of local groups, he abruptly terminated the meeting with an announcement that a relatively small sum of £2,000 would more than suffice to aid all worthy recipients. Nonetheless, even an officer as imposing and powerful as Sir Heron could no longer choke off public discourse on Town Hall's failed approaches to flood protection and river conservancy.[61]

For the first time, the daily press was willing not only to publish letters critical of these policies but also to write stinging editorials of its own. Manchester's leadership became subject to more open attacks in large part because of a consensus on the reasons why Salford had escaped a repeat of the 1866 calamity in spite of flood tides six feet higher on the Irwell River. The Broughton Bridge had been the primary contributing cause of the earlier disaster because a huge lake had formed after a barrier of debris had jammed up against its massive masonry buttresses. Since then, those buttresses had been replaced with much thinner columns. According to the *Manchester Guardian*, the new supports "caused so little obstruction to the current that no backwater whatever is observable." Of course, the low-lying lands on the flood plain near the Crescent suffered from the usual sewer backups that filled basements.

In 1872, Salford endured no widespread flooding comparable to the Medlock's spilling over its banks at several points as it snaked its way through Manchester. The "lesson" that had to be learned, the *City News* lectured public officials, was "that all artificial obstructions, such as weirs, dams, and low or narrow bridges should be avoided altogether, if possible, or if permitted, should be scientifically constructed in accordance with the peculiar requirements of the current." The weekly paper hammered home its point by reminding the civic elite of the paper recently presented by the "well-known geologist" E. W. Binney to the Literary and Philosophical Society. The expert had laid out overwhelming evidence that sedimentation building up behind the weirs posed an ever greater risk to the public's health and safety by blocking the "natural flow" of the river.[62]

Still, Manchester officials refused to enact reforms until yet another damaging flood exactly five years later, on 15 July 1877, jolted them into acknowledging that simple denial would not make these unnatural disasters go away. During the interim, the town clerk and councilmen had been anything but passive; they had worked energetically to achieve goals pointing in just the opposite direction of river conservancy. As Sir Heron diligently lobbied Parliament on behalf of the Corporation to dilute the rivers pollution bill, his only regret was that the manufacturers outdid him in inserting language that shielded their respective prerogatives from the authority of the national government.

Heron's other major project was to secure vast new water rights in the Lake District, over a hundred miles away. Under an ambitious scheme proposed by John Bateman, one of the district's most remote and untouched meres would be transformed into a gigantic reservoir linked to the city by a great pipeline. However, the council had no intention of using the water to meet working-class residents' need for indoor plumbing. On the contrary, the waterworks project was aimed at supplying anticipated growth in demand by industrial and suburban customers. After a depression reduced their consumption following the passage of the enabling legislation in 1879, the council delayed completing the project until the local economy had fully recovered fifteen years later.[63]

After suffering through the July 1877 state of emergency, the city council finally began to move toward the adoption of more inclusive approaches to river conservancy that embraced both flood protection and sewage treatment. Three years earlier, its River Medlock Improvement Committee had proposed the building of a single-purpose overflow tunnel similar to that envisioned in the stalled scheme for diverting storm surges on the Irwell. However, the measure was doomed by a patently obvious design intended to benefit the committee chairman, who just happened to own a mill immediately below the proposed the intake point. Instead, the council called once again upon Bateman to draw plans for both "the safe passage of storm water" and "the complete interception of the drainage of the city."[64]

In September 1877, the aging and ailing engineer presented blueprints for a comprehensive system of environmental control on a metropolitan scale for the Medlock River basin. Working together with City Engineer Lynde, Bateman made his single most important contribution when he reconceptualized the storm tunnel into an intercepting sewer that would convey wastewater to a treatment facility five miles below the built-up area. An upstream reservoir would regulate surges from heavy rainfalls while a deepened and straightened riverbed free of weirs and other obstructions would keep currents contained within the embankments. The Bateman-Lynde plan also outlined a parallel project for the Irwell and Irk rivers that would feed water into the main drainage pipe leading to the sewage plant. The report underscored the generous financial terms offered in the updated Public Health Act of 1875 to help strengthen the position of reform advocates against the predictable counteroffensive by the fiscal hardliners. To further disarm the hardliners, the engineers warned that the Rivers Pollution Act of 1876 made intervention by the national government inevitable in the absence of local initiative.[65]

Over the course of the following year, Manchester took positive steps toward reaching an agreement with its surrounding townships on a metropolitan plan of river conservancy. With the ever-present threat of the central authority imposing solutions from above, the suburbs shared a common incentive to work with the city. By joining together, they hoped to keep political control of the massive public works project as well as to spread its costs among all of the affected communities in the two main river basins. In October 1878, the first real progress was made when Salford agreed to Manchester's stringent, albeit fair, terms for apportioning the costs of the now modified Irwell plan for a combined storm tunnel and interceptor sewer. Four years later, the twin cities would begin construction on this public works project. In contrast, the city had less success in bringing the suburbs on board for the Medlock plan after they began calculating their respective shares of its £563,000 price tag. With a slowdown of the regional economy, the political will for environmental reform also seemed to lose momentum and stall.[66]

Conclusions: Manchester and the Politics of Exclusion

Although further progress awaited the rise of a new movement to jump-start an economic recovery, the Bateman-Lynde plan represented a major achievement in coming to grips with the industrial ecology of the region. By embodying flood protection and pollution control in a single infrastructure, the engineers recast the debate over policy options in more holistic and realistic terms. States of emergency resulting from the MIRB's hydrology could no longer be ascribed fatalistically to acts of God alone, conveniently exempting public officials and riparian owners from responsibility. As the frequency and severity of the floods increased after 1852, so too did understanding of the human interactions with the environment that made them unnatural disasters.

Urban reformers in England drew upon both traditional and new sources of knowledge in formulating novel concepts of river conservancy consistent with an industrializing society. On the one hand, they applied time-honored metaphors of nature's economy and bodily health to the city as an anthropomorphic system requiring unimpeded circulation of pure fluids and clean air. On the other hand, a wide range of experts opened new approaches to explaining the geology, chemistry, biology, and thermodynamics of an environment undergoing rapid and profound change. In the case of Manchester, John Bateman deserves special credit for leading this process of education on the ways in which the forces of production were reshaping the forces of nature in the region's watershed. Perhaps only a practical engineer like him could have gained the respect of the city's civic leaders and prompted them to consider any plan for river conservancy other than the least expensive alternative.[67]

The fundamental reason for the quarter-century delay in undertaking environmental reform in earnest was not lack of knowledge but a political culture of rigid hierarchy and privileged authority. A tightly restricted franchise and a self-perpetuating oligarchy reinforced discriminatory patterns of segregation by class and ethnicity/religion in the real estate market. This politics of exclusion, in turn, encouraged the ruling elite to put their pocketbook interest in keeping taxes to a minimum ahead of their moral responsibility to safeguard the health, safety, and welfare of the whole community. There is no need to question the sincerity of their belief that the moral failings of the poor were the cause of the conditions in the slums. However, we should still ask why they refused to take accepted remedial actions, such as removing the weirs, to reduce the unequal burden of the floods on those living near the rivers.

Some contemporary commentators and later historians have sought to excuse Manchester's public officials on the grounds that the dilemmas of water management and river conservancy were so complex and elusive that they lay beyond the ability of reasonable men to respond in any way other than with postponement. As early as the 1850s, however, Bateman and other experts had begun offering practical solutions that held real promise of addressing these admittedly difficult problems. Rather than offer an apologia for an urban regime of social stratification and geographic exclusion, commentators and historians should hold the officials to account for the environmental injustice of the enormous gulf in the quality of life between the riverfront slums and the garden suburbs.[68]

The subsequent story of the implementation of the Bateman-Lynde plan adds further evidence consistent with these conclusions. As we will see, the 1880s would mark a changing of the guard for the local ruling oligarchy. The passing away of the original generation of Manchester Liberals coincided with the final realization of universal manhood suffrage, which spawned partisan politics in municipal elections. The business community, perceiving a crisis of economic decline, would mobilize working class voters in support of its golden remedy, a ship canal to bypass Liverpool. However, the city's sewage threatened to turn the proposed docks and turning basin into a gigantic cesspool that would be constantly stirred up by ship propellers.

Suddenly, the lack of a sanitation system for the entire metropolitan area loomed as a major liability to the future of the city. As historian Alan Wilson explains, "the decision to implement an intercepting sewage scheme for Manchester was clearly a direct response to the decision to build the ship canal." Over the course of the decade, the town council would take the initiative in prodding the surrounding suburbs into conformity with its master plan of water management and river conservancy.[69]

The industrialization of nature that caused the flooding of Manchester was often obscured by the paradox of progress that produced so much material wealth. Spanning a generation, these recurrent states of emergency represented painful reminders of the massive transformation of the region's hydrology by the forces of production. Equally important, if not more so, in forcing policy makers to confront the need for novel approaches to the problems of environmental control were the unpredictable outbreaks of frightening epidemics. Although experts were unable to pinpoint the exact etiology of these deadly diseases, their suspicion that polluted drinking supplies were responsible had led by the 1840s to Chadwick's Sanitary Idea. His metaphor of the city as a natural system gave public health reformers a comprehensible concept that could be translated into practical policies of water management. London's success in limiting the spread of cholera provided a trans-Atlantic model for other urban centers. Sanitarians in Manchester as well as in Chicago held city officials to account by comparing local mortality rates with those in the world's largest metropolis. Although the politics of low-cost government acted as a powerful restraint on the building of water supply and sewage disposal systems, a more or less effective technology of environmental control had long been available to urban planners.

In sharp contrast, the pollution of the air by the engines of production posed a more insidious and enigmatic threat to the health and welfare of the city's inhabitants. On the one hand, the coal smoke pouring out of chimneys was ubiquitous in the industrial city, obvious for everyone to see and smell.

On the other hand, to demonstrate that it harmed humans, let alone figure out a way to get rid of it, proved elusive. There was no doubt that diseases of the lungs killed and disabled at least as many people as those of the intestines. Tuberculosis, or "consumption" as it was called by the Victorians, was the single greatest cause of death in the nineteenth century.

But comprehending the role smoke played in these illnesses seemed beyond the grasp of medical science. Most experts and lay people alike intuitively believed that clean air was preferable to dirty air. Real estate agents took advantage of this commonsense understanding when they sold property in the suburbs. Yet some authorities continued to maintain that sooty carbon particles in the lungs had a positive, prophylactic effect against infection by dangerous miasmas.

The problem of smoke emissions from burning coal was as baffling to the engineers as to the doctors. The rise of modern industry without this fossil fuel is unimaginable. It was so central that it defined the period: the "Age of Steam," the "Age of Energy." The entire thrust of Western civilization toward the final conquest of nature depended upon coal-based technologies, but the paradox of this progress was that more and more air pollution enveloped the cities and suffocated life inside them. To the engineers, smoke going up the chimney represented waste from inefficient combustion. They would invent one "smoke-eating" device after another but none of them really worked. Even more discouraging, every incremental gain in reducing bad emissions was more than offset by a greater increase in the rate of fossil fuel consumption.

To illuminate the dilemmas facing the industrial city in the battle for clean air, I now shift my attention from the waterworks to the brewery, for it was inside this particular site that the use of energy first reached new levels of intensity. Beer making represents a prototype of the transformation of industry from the use of traditional, labor-intensive methods of hand work to that of energy-intensive systems of mechanization. By carefully examining this metamorphosis of the brewery into a mass-production food factory, we can come to understand the reasons that more and more smoke came belching out of the city's chimneys. We can also begin to gain insight into the reasons that doing anything to alleviate air pollution became so problematic that the situation defied contemporary solution.

CHAPTER SIX

The Technological Construction of Industrial Ecologies

Introduction: "A Veritable City within a City"

After spending a lifetime as a brewery worker, Hermann Schluter wrote a book about his experience in America. It closely paralleled the industry's history. He recalled that "the farther west the German immigration went, the farther west extended the beer-brewing industry." Published in 1910 by the United Brewery Workmen of America, the book reveals his identity as a union organizer and labor leader. No friend of capitalism, Schluter was nonetheless impressed by the tremendous growth and total transformation of the business of making beer in the half-century following the Civil War. "In a few decades," he explained, "industrial development turned the log-houses and insignificant equipment in which American brewing at first had its home into gigantic establishments with masses of buildings, factory works, stables, and warehouses constituting a veritable city within a city."[1]

Schluter was not exaggerating when he characterized as revolutionary the change in the sheer size and organizational complexity of this urban site of industrial production. From a timeless, rural ritual of storing the harvest, making beer became one of the most capital-intensive, energy-consuming, and technologically sophisticated business enterprises of the modern city. One illustration in a trade journal provides a graphic verification of the writer's depiction. It supplies not only a bird's-eye view of a typical example in Chicago, the Schoenhofen Brewery, but also annotated labels of the factory's buildings. Located at Eighteenth Street and Canalport Avenue, the brewery made about 180,000 barrels or almost 5.6 million gallons (21,121,200 liters) of beer annually at the time of the World's Fair.

Reflecting Schluter's imagery, this figure illustrated a story of fabulous success. Having come from humble origins, Peter Schoenhofen had sold 8,457 barrels (992,344 liters) in 1867, his first year as a sole proprietor. Although the illustration shows that his brewery had grown to become one of Chicago's biggest by 1893, its output represented less than 7 percent of the 83.2 million gallons (314,945,280 liters) of beer made locally during the year. The steady expansion of consumer demand and the perishable nature of this food product created room for a wide range of firm sizes from specialty shops to gargantuan establishments several times larger than Schoenhofen's.[2]

This brewery was composed of at least twenty buildings arranged in three clusters, each of which covered several city blocks and stood in the shadow of a tall smokestack. In between were two major thoroughfares busy with horse-drawn vehicles. Railroad tracks ran along the eastern side where the grain elevators stood, and the shipping docks were on the opposite side next to the bottling department. Each cluster housed a major functional part of the manufacturing process: malting, mashing and brewing, or fermenting and storage.

A fourth scattered group of buildings handled packaging and distribution. It included sales offices, horse stables, feed and wagon barns, cooperage and blacksmith shops, barrel washing and racking rooms, and pasteurizing and bottling plants. In addition to the three great belching chimneys, the huge cold-storage "refrigerator," the ice-machine building, and the other massive structures of the brewery's energy system formed a fifth distinctive feature of this industrial tableau. Less visible were the miles and miles of electric wires, conveyor belts, and pipes of all kinds. Through them was pumped the gas, water, steam, ice water, wort, fermented substances, brews, and liquid wastes that collectively wove together all the different kinds of machines running and work going on inside.[3]

In environmental perspective, this sprawling site of production can be seen as a microcosm of the industrial city as an energy system. It is one of the most important and least understood aspects of the urban environment, especially in terms of its role in creating pollution problems. A closer look at the technological and scientific transformation of beer making helps to reveal the underlying sources of the pollution of the city's air, water, and land, and the ways in which both organic and mechanical forms of power were essential to the rise of modern cities with their massive populations, teeming commerce, and booming factories.

As we have seen in the case of Manchester's Bridgewater Canal, transportation improvements began in the 1760s to facilitate the relocation of manufacturing from rural sites in close proximity to traditional sources of material and energy to urban centers where labor and coal supplies were abundant. Traditional forms of energy—flowing water, heat given off by burning wood, and the work of humans and animals—now competed against an expanding array of machines powered by fossil fuels. The coming of industrialization required innovation and the elaboration of the energy system on a vast scale. Coal yards grew alongside hay markets, machinists worked next door to blacksmiths, and teamsters hauling ashes and manure passed beer wagons making their weekly deliveries to the thousands of saloons, restaurants, hotels, and groceries peppered across the urban landscape.

Both the shapes on the ground and the movement in the streets that made up the city's energy system became ubiquitous parts of its daily life. In Chicago popular culture owed as much to the city's Irish teamsters as to its German brewers, for instance. Complicated networks of gas lines, steam pipes, and electrical wires transmitting energy from central stations also played an increasingly influential role in shaping and giving direction to urban growth. By the end of the nineteenth century, energy applied to new technologies would be expanding physical boundaries, transforming the city into the metropolis. Equally important, the growth of an energy-intensive society within this ballooning space would help spur the ascendancy of a culture of consumption.[4]

A transnational comparison of the malt brewing industry in Chicago and Manchester provides a useful illustration of the causal connections between the development of the industrial city and that of its energy system. The 1890 U.S. census confirms the brewing industry's leadership in mechanization. It shows that it had the highest ratio of capital (that is, machinery) to labor among Chicago's ten leading industries. The scientific and technological makeover of the brewery also fueled the expansion of a rural empire of barley fields and hops groves. Like other industrial sites, moreover, the brewery depended upon an urban infrastructure of energy leading to and from it.[5]

Although the brewery was a leader in manufacturing, it represents a typical case of the processes of industrial change. In a highly uneven fashion, hands and hooves were being replaced by machines consuming fossil fuels. Mechanization took command little by little over the course of the nineteenth century.[6]

Rather than one technology replacing another in a linear, progressive fashion, each part of the energy system occupied an evolving economic niche of its own while being interdependent with the other parts. Old and new—draft horses and refrigeration machines—coexisted in symbiotic relationships. To be sure, demand for mechanical technologies based on fossil fuels rose at such an incredible rate that organic systems may have appeared to be in decline. Yet the two grew in tandem, and often in complementary ways. For example, Manchester's spinning machines kept an army of hand weavers busy for years; it took the power loom a half-century to gradually reduce their numbers until they were a small band of high-end arts-and-crafts workers.

The uneven, interwoven nature of change in industry and in the city's energy system highlights the need to balance conventional perspectives according to which technology drives history with contrasting approaches that place emphasis on the social construction of technology. Focusing attention on the "consumption junction" in the case of beer making means giving agency to the customers with their taste preferences. And in the American case, there is no doubt that popular taste had a powerful feedback effect on the brewery's methods and products. To stay in business, immigrant beer makers had to learn that Chicago's German and Irish immigrants, as well as its native-born residents demanded unique types of brew. "The demands upon beer in this country," a prominent trade journal reported, "include a brilliant luster in color and clearness ... exceptionally strong effervescence and a marked hops flavor, together with a vinous character and as pale a shade as possible."[7]

Preference for this ice-cold champagnelike drink engendered several major technological innovations in brewing practice in the United States. In German Chicago, "scientific brewing" came to have the ideal meaning of complete mechanical and environmental control of internal space within the brewery. Ever-greater inputs of heating and cooling, pumping and power promised to change beer making from an erratic process of biochemical guesswork into the production of a uniform, standardized product. Consistent delivery of a high-quality drink was the golden key to brand-name success in local and national markets.

In contrast, beer sales grew in Manchester at a more sluggish rate than in Chicago. According to historians of the condition-of-England question, workers apparently found other things more attractive to buy as their incomes finally began to edge upward during the final quarter of the century. Certainly local brewers offered little that was new or different, such as lager-style beers, to capture some of this added disposable money. In Britain, then, less marked changes in energy consumption should be expected than in the United States.[8]

In the larger social context, the liquor question remained a hotly contested aspect of contemporary life in both the United States and the United Kingdom.

Prohibition continued to have currency in religious, civic, and political discourse during the Victorian and Progressive eras. Although this debate over alcohol lies outside the boundaries of this book, it too helped shape technological alternatives, energy patterns, and business strategies within the brewing industry. In the United States, where prohibition forces were gaining political momentum, the brewers created new products and packaging in order to backpedal away from the saloon, which was becoming an untenable social institution. Although the brewers and their business allies also fought back in the political arena, they proved less effective than their better-organized counterparts in the United Kingdom. In large measure, however, the ethnic cast of the beer industry in the United States was the knockout blow that forced it to its knees after America entered World War I against Germany.[9]

A balanced approach to the study of the city as an energy system requires equal attention to the technological construction of industrial ecologies. On the one hand, the markets the brewery created for barley and hops, coal and ice helped reshape the countryside. The hops growers with their kilns invariably left a landscape denuded of trees in their wake. And coal mines in southern Illinois and Indiana brought heavy industry and immigrant workers to these farm zones.

On the other hand, Schoenhofen's brewery represented shapes on the ground that helped define the urban landscape as unmistakably industrial. The architecture of his brewery spoke a distinctive ethnic language. Its Romanesque Revival style (*Rundbogenstil*) embodied a German civic consciousness by disguising efficient, functional spaces with imposing false facades. Schluter's impression that places like this represented a "veritable city" reflected an insider's view of someone who knew how all the pieces of such a far-flung group of structures worked together.[10]

Creating a mosaic of large and small firms within the city, the brewing industry was complemented by an even more common fixture of urban life, pubs and saloons. In 1891, Manchester had 4,830 of them; Chicago put its count at 7,000 two years later. Coming in innumerable shapes and styles, they were often the most—and sometimes the only—imposing structures in the immediate neighborhood. Men were the almost exclusive inhabitants of both the buildings for making and those for consuming beer, as well as the occupants of the beer wagons moving back and forth between them. This gender divide in social and physical space, of course, had its own influence on the makeup and ideology of the prohibition and antisaloon movements.[11]

The energy system of the industrial city had pronounced impacts on the quality of its air, land, and water. The brewery offers an opportune test case because of its pioneering role in the development of artificial refrigeration, which became the single largest consumer of electricity by the 1920s. Emissions of visible smoke and invisible gases from burning coal, which made it harder to breath, posed the foremost threat from energy-consuming industries like beer making. Urban land was becoming increasingly crowded with the undesirable waste by-products of commerce and industry. Removal of the tons of manure, ashes, and garbage generated every day required its own infrastructure of public regulations, scavenger services and workers, special equipment, and disposal sites. In addition, the design problems related to street paving and drainage had as much to do with the need for cleaning technologies for horse-drawn vehicles as with the need for construction standards for handling traffic loads. The breweries also generated large amounts of organic wastes, just like Chicago's stockyards and Manchester's textile mills. Here I will focus attention mainly on the powerhouse. To the extent that the brewery's pattern of burgeoning energy use is an indicator, the city's air was indeed suffering a rapid deterioration in quality as a result of coal emissions.[12]

This case study of the brewery calls for a detailed examination of the energy infrastructure that underpinned the industrialization of beer making. The individual stories of the mechanization and environmental control of the three major stages in the manufacturing process contribute to a fuller understanding of the root causes of urban air pollution. The first step, malting, illustrates the environmental links between urban markets and rural resources. The next step, mashing, highlights the mechanization of production, the substituting of machines and fossil fuels for animal and human power. The third step, fermenting, focuses attention on the science of industrial technology, the turning of coal into ice. The brewery became the prototype of not only the sanitary kitchen but also the environmental control of interior space.[13]

Pasteur's Brew

A basic change in popular taste from a preference for ale and porter to one for lager beer goes a long way in explaining the origins of a twenty-year period of scientific and technological revolution in the brewing industry. Demographic shifts, especially the influx of large numbers of German and Irish immigrants, account in part for new taste preferences in the United States. In Chicago, for instance, the number of German-born residents increased dramatically during the Civil War decade from twenty-two thousand to fifty-two thousand; the number of Irish residents doubled to forty thousand. Imported German culture set new standards for urban life in terms of expanding the types of public venues in which consuming alcohol was socially acceptable.

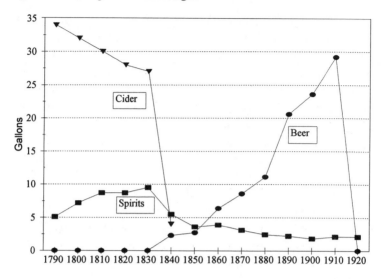

Figure 6.1. U.S. annual per capita alcohol consumption, 1790–1920
Source: Data from W. J. Rorabaugh, *The Alcoholic Republic: An American Tradition* (New York: Oxford University Press, 1979); and George B. Wilson, *Alcohol and the Nation* (London: Nicholson and Watson, 1940), 331–34.

Native-born Americans' reform movements for temperance and prohibition also played an important part in the reorientation of the nation's drinking habits. In attempting to curb overindulged appetites for strong distilled liquors like whiskey and bourbon, some reformers advocated the consumption of beer and wine as an acceptable substitute. The emergence of the urban middle class with its strident emphasis on respectability may have added further social pressure for a shift away from alcohol abuse. In any case, the per capita use of distilled spirits began to decline after 1830, at the same time that lager beer began its climb toward becoming the country's most popular alcoholic drink (see fig. 6.1).[14]

An equally important cause of technological innovation in the brewing industry was consumer demand for the quality associated with brand-name products. In the post–Civil War period, manufacturers that could offer a standardized product found rich rewards by expanding their markets to a national scale. The rise of Chicago's dressed beef industry is probably the best-known story of marvelous business success resulting from consumer desires for reliable food products of consistent quality. Although impossible to quantify, this preference is familiar today to every interstate motorist who stops at fast-food chains rather than local restaurants. McDonald's or Burger

King may not have the best cuisine, but the traveler knows exactly what to expect in terms of menu, quality, service, and facilities. In contrast, that little roadside diner may have great homemade pie, or its greasy food may be inedible and its washroom out of order. In many respects, the transformation of some breweries, like Pabst and Anheuser-Busch, into big businesses closely paralleled the achievements of meatpackers like Armour and Swift in gaining national brand-name recognition.[15]

In the cities of postbellum America, neither butchers nor bartenders could promise to serve their customers products with the same consistent quality. As we have seen, the brew master lacked basic knowledge about the biochemical reactions involved in making beer, and his ability to control them with heat and cold was very limited in any case. Unwanted microorganisms and other impurities could ruin the beverage at virtually every step of the way from the brewing of the mash to the tapping of a keg at the bar. His unrelenting problem of quality control was significantly exacerbated by consumer preference for lager beer over darker, virtually opaque ales and porters. Before the 1860s, an industry historian points out, "the appearance of beer was not important [because] it was served in stone mugs. Where it was drunk from thin, clear glasses it must please the eye as well, it must be brilliant in color and lustrous in clarity. For the American, it must be sparkling."[16]

Impurities that clouded the beer during the final, resting stage of fermentation were especially troublesome. Another major difficulty in making lager beer was the steady loss of its carbonated effervescence during racking, shipping, and tapping. Rich rewards indeed awaited the brewer who could solve these problems and offer a standardized product to the nation.

The case of Lill and Diversey reflects the vital importance of placing an internal history of technological innovation within larger social and cultural contexts. Its Cream Ale was Chicago's favorite brand of malt liquor at the time of the 1871 fire, when the brewery burned to the ground across the street from the Water Tower. However, the brewing industry seemed more tethered by tradition than driven by the inner logic of the machine to the frontiers of technological innovation. Perhaps this loyalty to customary practices should come as no surprise during the period when the market for beer was almost exclusively local. Lill and Diversey, for example, could gradually ratchet up its operations in tandem with the growth of the city's population without having to take potentially costly risks by trying unproven methods. Brewing a quality product in the traditional way was difficult enough.

Profit margins were apparently sufficient to turn the city's oldest brewery into a bastion of business conservatism. For Lill and Diversey, the result was stagnation during the 1860s while others raced ahead to meet changing cultural patterns. At the opening of the decade, it sold 3,320,722 liters of ale and porter but only 821,380 liters of lager beer. Coming late to the lager market, it failed to respond adequately to the shift in consumer taste. The brewery was operating with at least 30 percent unused capacity. Ten years later, it was making virtually the same total amount of beer, 4,318,112 liters, despite a nearly threefold increase in Chicago's population. The brewery was not rebuilt after the fire.[17]

Between 1870 and 1890, a combination of scientific research and technological innovation helped brewers meet the demand created by American popular taste for lager-style beers. Revolutionary ways of brewing beer by highly mechanized, energy-intensive methods grew alongside the traditional processes of small-scale producers. Like most other historical events, the dramatic metamorphosis of the brewing industry in the United States had deep roots in the preceding era. In this case, scientific controversy over the basic nature of fermentation had engaged Europeans in lively debate since the beginning of the century. In addition, the introduction of new technology in the form of the steam engine had opened a wide range of potential heat and power applications. Once brewers made an initial commitment to employ steam technology, innovation seemed to follow in an orderly progression toward more and more intense use of this form of energy.

But this logic of mechanization makes sense only in the larger cultural context of the search for an exceptionally light, highly carbonated lager beer that could hold up during shipping and handling across a vast continent. Brewers in Germany followed an equally logical but different course of innovation in order to meet the taste preferences of their customers, one that involved much less standardization for a national market and hence less mechanization of production. Nonetheless, Germany retained the crown as the world's largest producer of beer, and its people remained the greatest consumers of the drink.[18] In big American cities like Chicago, both emerging national-scale firms and thriving local ones continued to co-exist. Rather than moving along a single linear path of progress, the U.S. brewing industry grew in multiple directions, creating a diverse pattern of technological alternatives and consumer choices. Most other industries followed this pattern.

If we had stood in front of a brewery in the 1860s or early 1870s, we would have witnessed a parade of scientists, including possibly Louis Pasteur, going in and out. Fermentation was not only one of the most fundamental processes of organic chemistry, it was also a critical part of the making of beer and wine. But it remained poorly understood; scientists continued to disagree about its elemental nature and how it worked. Was fermentation the result of the spontaneous generation of yeast germs whenever sugar was present, or did the yeast germs come from the air? Was yeast animal or vegetable? And what made some fermenting liquids go bad and not others? To find the answers, which would revolutionize beer making, we need to turn from Chicago and Manchester to Paris, France.

Louis Pasteur set out, single-handed, to accomplish what the entire French army had been unable to achieve, the defeat of Germany. Hoping to restore the national pride of his humiliated country, he sought revenge against its ancient foe through the power of science. "Our misfortunes inspired me with the idea of these researches," he wrote six years later. "I undertook them immediately after the war of 1870, and have since continued them without interruption, with the determination of perfecting them, and thereby benefiting a branch of industry wherein we are undoubtedly surpassed by Germany." Once he reached his goal, he would reveal an ingenious way for France to counterattack and even the score. "I am convinced," he reported, "that I have found a precise, practical solution of the arduous problem which I proposed to myself."[19]

Pasteur, of course, had been trying to perfect not a secret weapon for the military, but a way of making a superior beer. In what would quickly become a landmark of science, *Études sur la bière*, the Frenchman proudly announced that he had discovered "a process of manufacture, independent of season and locality, which should obviate the necessity of having recourse to the costly methods of cooling employed in existing processes, and at the same time secure the preservation of its products for any length of time." The term *biotechnology* had not yet been coined; Pasteur's project represents one of the very first attempts to put pure science into the service of industry. Almost as an afterthought, the scientist suggested that his research might also illuminate the "etiology of contagious diseases." It would do much more than that: it would help establish the foundation of modern germ theory.[20]

The Frenchman's work on fermentation and the related applications of the German scientist Carl Linde's investigation of thermodynamics would fundamentally transform brewing from a labor-intensive craft to an energy-intensive food-manufacturing process. On the basis of Pasteur's research findings, engineers would construct an automated, artificial environment within which the organic chemical processes of beer making could be regulated with scientific precision. They would build a system that was completely closed from the time the barley entered the malting room to the moment the keg or bottle was sealed, a system that finally allowed the brewers to reach Pasteur's goal. They would now be able to offer their customers a product of consistent quality and taste, one that could become highly profitable in local and even distant markets by building consumer loyalty to a brand name.

The Frenchman had understood that the only way to reach this goal of satisfying consumer demand was to take a pragmatic approach in designing his research project. Starting with the bottom line of popular taste, he would have to work his way back up the chain of the manufacturing process, solving problems and hopefully making new discoveries along the way. "Thus it becomes a matter of extreme importance," he revealed, "that we should have an exact knowledge of the causes and nature of the changes which affect our produc[t], and it may be that this knowledge will lead us to regard the conditions of the brewing industry from a novel point of view, and bring about important modifications in the practices of the trade."

The scientist had done his homework. He had traced the history of the alcoholic beverage as far back as 450 B.C., when Herodotus had made reference to the "barley wines" of the Egyptians. In those times it had taken about eight days to make a barrel of ale or porter; consumers had about an equal time after tapping it to enjoy it before it went flat or spoiled. Methods of making these types of brown-colored, low-carbonation drinks had remained basically unchanged since then, with one crucially important exception, the production of lager beer.[21]

With the coming of the railroad in the 1840s, beer makers in the southern regions of Germany began exporting the new drink, which the French called German, or Strasbourg beer. "The preference of the public for this kind of beer and the increased facilities [of transportation] that such a beer affords the trade," Pasteur reported, "are the two reasons why its manufacture has so greatly increased. In Austria, Bavaria, Prussia, and other Continental countries this new method of brewing is almost exclusively adopted." His interviews of the proprietors of Parisian cafes and review of trade journals convinced him of German predominance in the trade: "That such a superiority does exist is admitted as a fact by the majority of beer drinkers."[22]

The economic promise of the fashionable new drink for his country's farmers, manufacturers, and tradespeople seemed virtually unlimited. By the time of the Franco-Prussian War, aggregate figures for England and Wales were more indicative of the important contribution the brewing industry could make to a national economy because the spread of the factory system there and its linkage by rail and canal had already created an urban network. Producing 25,390,000 barrels (4.16 billion liters) of malt liquor, British brewers directly employed about 40,000 workers and generated almost £60 million in retail sales. For the government, a tax on each bushel of malt brought in £6.5 million. Perhaps another 75,000–95,000 farmers were involved in growing the 1,334,000 acres of barley and 66,000 acres of hops, to say nothing of the land and workers devoted to raising lesser amounts of sugar, corn, and other ingredients of the organic beverage.

When other major factors related to the beer business are taken into consideration, we can begin to a get a sense of the scale and scope of the industry that Pasteur hoped to turn to France's advantage. Foremost would be the pubs themselves and the men and women working in them. In addition, there were the many vehicles transporting the bulky commodities from farm to market, the virtual army of horses moving the beer through the city streets, and the vast agricultural infrastructure needed for breeding and maintaining these animals. Other inputs included the coal fueling the breweries, and the forests of wood being turned into barrels.[23]

Harvesting the Sunlight

Ironically, it was the Germans and their emigrant settlers in American cities who would embrace Pasteur's ideas with almost religious reverence. The United States and Germany would most fully reap the rewards of adopting energy-intensive methods of scientific brewing. In the United States, the rise of the great urban breweries went hand in hand with the environmental transformation of the countryside. The story of barley, the main ingredient of beer, closely parallels that of wheat, well told by William Cronon in his seminal book *Nature's Metropolis*. In the case of both crops, the energy of the sun embodied in the plants was transmuted into marketable agricultural commodities sold in the pits of the Chicago Board of Trade. Figure 6.2 displays the impressive growth in Chicago's consumption of barley, with about

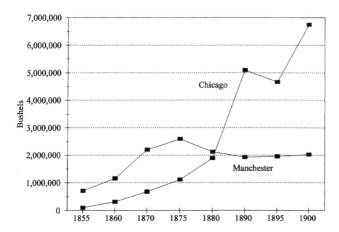

Figure 6.2. Manchester and Chicago barley malt consumption, 1855–1900
Source: Data from Parliamentary Papers, House of Commons, *Sessional Papers* (1831–1901); and Chicago Board of Trade, *Annual Report* (1850–1921).

90 percent going to local breweries and maltsters. Its supplies came from the upper Midwest, the Great Plains, and western Canada. Farmers could grow an average of twenty-three to twenty-six bushels annually per acre. A brewer of lager beer used about 2.75 bushels of the malted barley to make a barrel of beer (31 U.S. gallons, or 117.34 liters). In 1892, Chicago breweries' production of 2.28 million barrels (267.5 million liters) accounted for the use of almost 250,000 acres of land.[24]

For Manchester, comparative figures were smaller but not insignificant. Brewers of ale used two bushels of barley malt per barrel (36 U.K. gallons, or 166.66 liters). Its supplies came mostly from areas nearby, including Yorkshire and Lincolnshire. After British law lifted the ban on ingredients other than barley malt in 1880, some brewers began using rice and sugar in an effort to produce a lighter, more highly carbonated drink. In 1891, for example, Manchester's breweries added 9.4 million pounds of sugar to 99.15 million pounds of malt. This was equivalent to the output of eighty thousand acres of land.[25]

Rather than embellish Cronon's tale of a sack of wheat's journey from farm to market, I will focus here on three different stories of environmental interaction between rural production and urban consumption. Compared to barley, delicate hops vines require far more energy-intensive cultivation, harvesting, and processing. Coal, and later oil, was another essential ingredient in the making of beer. A third contribution of the hinterland were the draft horses and the food and bedding needed to sustain them in the city. Complementing the flow of farm-raised animals into the city was a human migration of men and their families: employment related to horses offered a relatively easy and familiar way to make the transition to urban life and labor.[26]

The story of hops represents a moving picture of production that cut a trail of soil and timber exhaustion from the Atlantic to the Pacific over the course of the nineteenth century. First grown for profit by the Puritans of Massachusetts, this valuable, albeit demanding, crop would migrate in stages to upstate New York in the early 1800s, to Wisconsin in the middle of the century, and to California in the closing decades. The typical farmer sowed only a few acres of the crop because it required so much handwork during the growing phase and meticulous attention during the harvest. Traditionally the vinelike plants were trained to store the energy of the sun by growing along sixteen-to-twenty-four-foot wooden poles assembled teepee-style. These had to be replaced every three to five years. When the hops cones matured, they had to be picked at just the precise moment and immediately heated to fix their peak bitter flavoring, which would offset the sweetness of the malt. Added to the wort, the hops would also act as a natural preservative, retarding the growth of undesirable bacteria in the brew.

Unlike farmers in England, Americans constructed primitive, wasteful kilns in hill banks that burned logs instead of charcoal. In a pattern repeated from one side of the continent to the other, rising costs and declining quality from depleted soils and wood supplies in one area led to the economic eclipse of hops cultivation in that location by production in fresh fields and forests farther west. In 1880, for example, New York was still leading in hops production, but only because it had far more acres in hops than any other state; California devoted less area to hops cultivation, but was harvesting twice as much per acre.[27]

The energy flows involved in the cultivation of hops illustrate the complex social and environmental interplay of town and country created by industrial production. The linkages between Chicago and Wisconsin in the decades following the Civil War can serve as an example. "The rise of production in the Badger State," the author of *Tinged with Gold* writes, "can only be described as meteorlike." The state's production, centered in Sauk County, soared during the 1860s from 135,600 to 385,600 pounds. By 1880, Chicago consumed about one-third of the 3.5 million pounds reaching its warehouses, making it the nation's second largest market for the crop.[28]

While the sunlight stored in plants moved toward the city's breweries, animal manure and human hands traveled in the opposite direction. Each acre of hops required about a quarter-ton of organic fertilizer, which came in large part from draft horses living on suburban breeding farms and in urban boarding stables. Moreover, the need to harvest the hops at just the right moment created an annual out-migration of "city pickers" to supplement the "home pickers." Each year, about eight thousand Chicagoans, mostly young women, boarded special trains to join about twice as many rural workers in gathering in Wisconsin's crop. The city dwellers enjoyed a working holiday— sleeping in tents, eating around campfires, and joining in nocturnal dances and hootenannies.

Although they got a brief respite from Chicago's dirt and disease, the city pickers did not escape air pollution. The crudely built wood-burning kilns kept them and everyone else in the vicinity enshrouded in clouds of pungent smoke. In the early twentieth century, oil and gas pipelines from the city would fuel more efficient technology on the hops farms of the West Coast. Gradually, cultivation would become concentrated in the Yakama Valley, Washington, where favorable climate and soil conditions combined to produce the optimum yields.[29]

Chicago's insatiable demand for fossil fuels created a much more important case of the industrialization of the countryside. Coal, of course, represents the stored energy of sunlight from millions of years ago. What

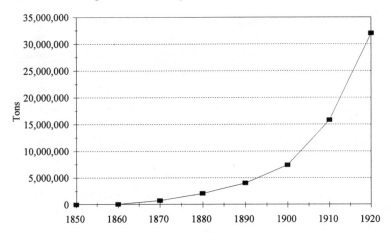

Figure 6.3. Coal consumption in Chicago, 1850–1920
Source: Data from Chicago Board of Trade, *Annual Report* (1850–1921).

Midwestern coal shared with hops was a skyrocketing market triggered by the Civil War's boom-time economy (see fig. 6.3). However, the environmental and economic links between underground coal seams and firebox doors, between rural production and urban consumption was fundamentally different. The coal shipped from each mine retained its geographic identity despite the bulk amounts of the fuel extracted, transported, and distributed. This was in contrast to the individual farmer's sack of wheat or barley, which became an undistinguishable commodity blended together with the contents of countless other sacks in the city's gargantuan grain elevators. Various combinations of physical and chemical properties met specific needs for different lump sizes, heat and light qualities, waste residues, and delivered costs. Blacksmiths across the nation preferred "Blassburg" semibituminous coal from Pennsylvania because of it was virtually flameless, and gave off an intense, steady heat.

In the mid-nineteenth century, everybody from home owners to railroad executives became coal experts. Consumers were offered a broad range of fuels, whether premium anthracite from Pennsylvania, quality furnace and smelting "Brier-Hill" coal from southeast Ohio, or substandard "poor-man's coal" from nearby Braidwood, Illinois. "In fact," notes James MacFarlane's handbook on America's coal regions in 1873, Chicago had "a stock of every variety of the best coals produced in the United States for all the various uses."[30]

The Civil War sparked not only a brief energy crisis, but also a rapid expansion of coal mining in the Midwest and a related rise in energy-intensive industries in the region's cities. Moreover, heavy-handed occupation of the

Pennsylvania coalfields by the U.S. Army set the tone of labor-management relations for a generation. By the time of Chicago's great fire of 1871, a glut of cheap fuel was fast transforming the commercial entrepôt into a major center of manufacturing and food processing as iron and steel works, machine shops, and breweries took advantage of the sharp competition among lake, rail, and canal shippers of fuel supplies.

Although Pennsylvania's anthracite had reached the city through the Great Lakes during the 1840s, abundant and cheap supplies of fuel wood had dominated local markets during the antebellum era. The demand for wood would reach a peak in the region at the end of the 1860s, and the fuel would remain the nation's leading source of energy for another fifteen years thereafter. During the war, however, fuel shortages, the constant extension of the railroads, and the opening of large mines within one hundred miles of Chicago began to make Illinois's bituminous, or soft, coals an increasingly attractive alternative. Over the course of the 1860s, the city's geographic and transportation advantages helped boost local coal consumption from 775,000 tons to over two million tons. An industrial revolution was clearly under way in the metropolis of the West.[31]

At the same time, however, the obvious preference of the city's factories, utilities, and railroads for the cheapest fuels had a noticeable downside: air pollution. MacFarlane warned that "it is indeed but too evident that, compared with the coal produced in almost any part of the Allegheny coalfield, that of Illinois is very inferior. Its disadvantages are its feeble heating power, the extraordinary quantity of sulphuret of iron it contains, and the large amount of clinker, ashes, soot, and smoke produced."

Chicago's civic elite, who formed the Citizens' Association in 1874, soon put air pollution on their agenda of municipal reform. After initiating private nuisance suits against the most notorious offenders, they turned to City Hall to demand the achievement of what was quickly becoming an unattainable goal, clean air. In 1881, they successfully lobbied the council to pass the nation's first urban antismoke law. The ordinance declared the emission of "dense smoke" a public nuisance punishable by a fine of five to fifty dollars. Over the next three years, police and health inspectors made four thousand visits to factories, issued two thousand warnings, and prosecuted several suits. But this vigorous campaign seemed to make little if any difference in air quality, and enforcement of the law lapsed. Ravenous demand for more energy simply overwhelmed environmental reform efforts.[32]

The markets connecting boiler furnaces in Chicago to coal mines in Illinois turned both places into polluted industrial landscapes. By the early 1870s, geologists had pretty well defined the boundaries of the state's 36,800 square miles of productive coalfields (see fig. 6.4). The three great seams underlying nearly 75 percent of the state varied greatly in quality from north to south. Yet they were all at shallow depths, on horizontal planes, and without drainage problems, making them relatively cheap to mine. "There is, perhaps," McFarlane suggested, "no other area of equal extent in the United States where coal is so easily obtained with a moderate expenditure of capital."[33]

In the postwar decade, fast-rising urban demand stimulated the greatest activity on the northeastern edge of the field, closest to Chicago, and the southwestern area, bordering the Mississippi River across from St. Louis. In the LaSalle and the Will-Grundy-Livington districts near Chicago, the three seams were two hundred to four hundred feet below the surface and were four to nine feet thick. What this coal lacked in quality because of its lower carbon and higher impurities content, it made up in price because of cheaper production and transportation costs. Classified generically as steam coal, it generally cost only half as much as hard coal from the East and was used mostly to power railroad locomotives and factory boilers. And, as MacFarlane noted, the working classes also relied on it to heat their homes in spite of its rotten-egg odor and smoky emissions and messy loads of clinker and ash that had to be removed.[34]

The exploitation of fossil fuels in northern Illinois turned frontier landscapes into industrial ecologies. The sprouting of mines and mine towns on the prairie was the most obvious manifestation of the links between town and country. At the dawn of the period of mushroomlike growth in Braidwood in 1865, a contemporary observed "nothing but a sea of tall grass, or in winter a boundless field of snow, reaching out to meet the horizon, with scarcely a cabin intervening." A year later, the new town sent ten thousand tons of coal to Chicago; eight years after that, the mines were pouring out this amount every five days. The processing of coal, like the processing of hops cones, was done at the site of harvest before the product was sent to the city. Mountainous collections of material from the mines, including waste coal, took shape on the flat land. As the mines opened the deeper seams, steam engines were brought in to raise the black gold. The coal was then crushed, washed, and sorted by size into shoots that filled the waiting railroad cars.

Dense clouds of black smoke, invisible gases, coal dust, and rock grit were thrown into the atmosphere, despoiling the pastoral nature of the countryside. Water quality also suffered because toxic chemicals continuously seeped from spoil heaps and gob piles into nearby rivers and streams. Screening and washing the coal for urban markets added to the problem of water pollution. Moreover, the swelling number of humans in the towns and their mine

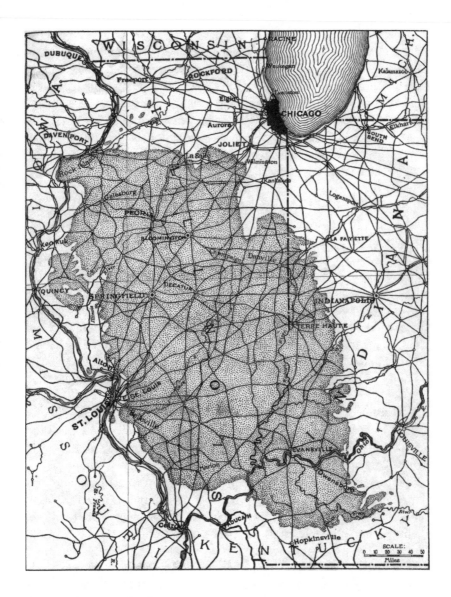

Figure 6.4. Eastern coal region
Source: Chicago Association of Commerce, *Smoke Abatement and Electrification of Railroad Terminals in Chicago* (Chicago: McNally, 1915), 14.

mules, horses, and other animals added their own pollution burdens to areas otherwise characterized by scattered, low-density populations. Though the concentration of industrial sites of production did not approach that in the city itself, local clusters of mining activity made these areas distinctly different from comparable areas that were devoted entirely to farming.[35]

An army of industrial workers invaded rural Illinois after the Civil War, lured by good wages and cheap prices for homestead lots in the boomtowns of the coalfields. In 1860, the state counted just over a thousand miners, a number that increased to almost twenty-six thousand men and boys over the next quarter-century. The ethnic origins of the miners and their families were quite different from those of the farm population. Initially drawing first and second generation Welsh, Irish, and Scottish immigrants, Illinois mines gradually attracted more and more newcomers from southern and eastern Europe. Although just 6 percent of Braidwood's 691 miners came from the continent in 1870, this proportion climbed to 29 percent of the town's 2,138 mine workers over the next ten years. Mostly Slovaks, Poles, and Italians, the continental Europeans helped create truly multiethnic communities that changed not only the dynamics of labor organizing but also the social and political landscape of the region. At the constitutional convention of 1870, lawmakers influenced by immigrant mine workers established Illinois's first mine-safety regulations in this "disaster prone industry."[36]

The railroads hauling the coal between the pits and the city were another key agent of the environmental transformation of the countryside. As early as 1870, twenty trains a day were leaving Braidwood for Chicago. True enough, cars full of barley, hops, and other farm products continued to move across the prairies. But coal became king, the transportation companies' single most important source of freight payments. Beginning in the anthracite fields of Pennsylvania, the companies either bought up the mines or sought to control them by carving up territories in which noncompetitive monopolies could operate.

Compared to stationary engines, locomotives and tugboats were heavy polluters. The locomotives first stood idle, and when they were loaded with fuel to get them started, they threw out thick plumes of smoke, soot, and ash as they struggled to overcome inertia. Unlike the emissions rising from the tall chimneys of the factories, the pollution pumping out of railroad and riverboat stacks suffocated people and befouled their clothes at street level. Although locomotives caused the most annoying nuisances at the ends of the lines in populated areas, they crisscrossed the nation hauling heavily laden cars and leaving long trails of airborne pollution in their wakes. As Chicago demanded more and more energy, the number of coal trains increased, contributing to the environmental degradation of both urban and rural America.[37]

The spread of storage and distribution facilities for energy-related products also added to the making of the industrial city. Fuel yards strung along the rail lines and the riverfront were the physical manifestations of this infrastructure of energy. They varied widely in size and range of services from convenient neighborhood stores carrying wood, coal, hay, and feed to centralized depots with gigantic piles of a particular type of fuel. In 1880, the city directory listed 115 coal dealers who sold 1,857,000 tons to local consumers and 528,000 tons to customers beyond the city limits. Twenty-nine were large enough to be incorporated companies, and twenty-two operated yards at two or more locations. Yet most dealers were like Canadian-born Napoleon Barnett, who had started a coal, coke, and wood yard the year before at 3121–25 South Cottage Grove on the South Side. By buying directly from the mines, he was able to offer relatively low prices and build up his business within five years to twenty-five thousand dollars in annual sales.[38]

The chronic glut of coal on the Chicago market inspired some of the larger dealers to form associations and exchanges in a futile series of attempts to set minimum prices. While the handful of anthracite wholesalers achieved some success, the ready availability of acceptable substitute fuels invariably undercut their efforts. A coal-trade expert lamented that "severe, and in some respects, unreasonably bitter competition, carried sometimes beyond the boundaries of wisdom, or the simple rules governing supply and demand, had left quite a large supply of eastern bituminous coal on hand at the beginning of 1884." The result was a significant price cut from $3.65 to $3.40 a ton.[39]

In spite of skyrocketing demand for energy, this type of atomistic competition kept downward pressure on every aspect of the coal business, especially worker wages, mine safety, and transportation charges. The externalization of pollution costs—damage caused by smoke emitted into the air and ashes thrown into the river or street was not factored into the price of the coal—engendered similar market forces that encouraged purchase of the cheapest, dirtiest types of fuel.[40]

The mass of residential, commercial, and industrial customers, both rich and poor, relied on the horse to haul their fuel supplies from dealer yards to basement bins. Only the largest users, like Schoenhofen's brewery, had their own railroad sidings. Of the three stories told here of harvesting the sunlight, the horse as energy system represents the most complex symbiotic relationship between town and country, people and nature. These draft animals were living things that required uninterrupted flows of the energy of the sun that was stored in food and bedding that had grown in farm fields.

Horses also needed constant attention and care from human custodians. This close working relationship made horses, not dogs, man's best friend before the 1920s, when Henry Ford's Model T became a leading icon of the Machine Age. Until then, horses were a pervasive part of daily life and culture, taking on intricate class, ethnic, and gender meaning.[41]

On one side of urban society, the Irish became predominant as Chicago's teamsters, hauling the barley, hops, and coal to the breweries, while the Germans introduced the decorated beer wagon as a new form of brand-name advertising. On the other side, a city dweller's horse and carriage became the most conspicuous sign of wealth and prestige. "The acme of comfort and social progress," local historians observed in 1895, "is considered by most men to be attained when their circumstances are such that they can afford a carriage, and enter the magic circle of the driving public." Indeed, they believed that "there is no surer sign and better evidence of the growth and progress of a city and the financial solidity of its citizens than the means and methods employed by them in traveling, either on business or pleasure."[42]

Only an elite few could join the "magic circle," but a great many in the city and the country depended on horses for their livelihood. An ubiquitous part of urban life, horses were rarely counted, so historians must make educated guesses about their numbers. Chicago probably had seven to ten thousand horses at the time of the great fire, and their number rose to a peak of seventy-seven to eighty thousand in the first decade of the twentieth century. Transportation historian Clay McShane calculates with more precision that it takes about four acres of land to feed one horse. Each animal consumes about three tons of hay a year and a variable amount of oats, depending on how hard it works. McShane estimates an annual average of sixty-three bushels of oats. Breeding and raising horses thus required considerable additional farmland. During the Civil War, Chicago became a major market for horse sales, boosting Illinois ahead of Ohio as the leading state for breeding the animals. By 1870, Illinois had 881,500 farm horses worth more than $62,000,000; the number exceeded a million animals by the time of the next census, ten years later.[43]

Though only a fraction of these were raised for Chicago, the extra-large city horse filled an important market niche during the war years. The story of the Dillons' farm of French Normans, or Percherons, illustrates the growing attention breeders paid to the urban market. Moving from Ohio in 1823, this Quaker family of seven brothers and their father arrived in Tazewell County, where they raised their English-bred draft horses for their farms. In 1857, they brought the first Percheron stallion, Old Louis Napoleon, into Illinois to improve their stock. Soon they were selling his male offspring for sums equal to his purchase price of $2,000, and transforming themselves from farmers into breeders. Six years later, this new source of prosperity funded the family's move en masse to new farms near Bloomington, at the crossroads of the Illinois Central and Chicago and Alton lines.

The Dillons were initially mocked at state fairs by farmers who called their huge animals bulls without horns. But at the important agricultural showcases held in Chicago in 1865 and 1866, derision began turning into admiration for the tremendous strength and endurance of the horses. The ideal of the athletic racing horse gave way to one that matched the physique of the stocky, 1,700-pound offspring of the Dillons' prize stallion. Because of its tireless stamina, each Percheron was more than a match for two ordinary-sized horses in work output. Urban as well as rural demand soared, prompting the Dillons to import additional Percheron studs and to build generously proportioned sales barns on their five farms. Special trains for buyers from Chicago complemented mail-order catalogs for more distant customers. By 1882, the Dillons' annual sales figures were $109,000.[44]

A significant number of the Dillons' horses were loaded onto railroad cars, bound for buyers in the Chicago area. Draft horses were an essential part of the energy infrastructure of the industrial city. Their crucial role in moving people and goods by pulling streetcars has inspired historians to label these turbulent places streetcar cities with good reason. The largest employer of work horses, the transit companies helped reshape not only the city's land-use patterns, but also its political, social, economic, and cultural boundaries. Between 1870 and 1890, the expansion of Chicago's streetcar lines brought a corresponding increase from 1,000 to 8,300 animals employed, in addition to the 2,500 workers needed as drivers and caretakers. Omnibuses and hackney cabs rounded out the means of moving the still select group of passengers who could afford the fares but not membership in the "magic circle." The mass of working-class commuters and shoppers remained pedestrians.[45]

Even larger numbers of draft horses were employed in a myriad of jobs transporting goods within the city. In 1890–1891, showy Percherons and Clydesdales distributed more than two million barrels of beer to Chicago's retail outlets. The increase of freight shipped on the railroads meant commensurate growth of the teamster traffic in the streets. Some firms specialized in transferring goods between depots while others provided express and delivery services. A wide range of local businesses, from coal dealerships to department stores, maintained their own stables of horses and wagons. In today's world of personal automobiles, it's hard to imagine a time when the streets were clogged with commercial delivery vans. Everything from the luxury purchases of the carriage trade to the everyday commodities purchased

Table 6.1 Chicago North Side horse infrastructure, 1892

Type of structure	Number
Private stables—residential and commercial	2,450
Horseshoeing/blacksmith shops	39
Public stables—livery and boarding	34
Wagon and carriage shops	18
Feed and hay stores	10
Breweries with stables	10
Street railway barns with stables	7
Milk depositories with stables	6
Riding academies with stables	2

Source: Rascher Map Publishing Company, *Fire Insurance Maps of Chicago* (Chicago: Rascher Map Publishing Company, 1892), vol. 2, plates 112–226.

from the butcher, grocer, and milkman went from store to residence in these horse-drawn vehicles.

Accommodation of city people's dependence on city horses required an entire system of physical structures and land uses intertwined with those devoted to directly meeting human needs. To gain a sense of the nature of the seamless integration of animals and humans in Chicago, I counted the buildings devoted to horses using 1892 fire insurance maps. The area surveyed covered three square miles from Chicago Avenue to Fullerton Avenue and from the industrialized riverfront to the gentrified lakefront. Table 6.1 summarizes the findings.

Census figures show that about ninety thousand people lived in this built-up area of the North Side. The large number of private stables also stands out. The deep, narrow lots with alleys and barns at the back reflect the city's original plat. While the survey does not disclose whether a horse was inside each backyard barn, anecdotal evidence points in that direction. "Having a deep lot," local historians wrote of the "man of small means" in the mid-1890s, "he is tempted to build a small stable, and there keeps an inexpensive horse and vehicle, both cared for by himself and boys, in many instances without employing outside help." The desire to join the "magic circle" helps explain the tens of thousands of privately owned horses and carriages actually counted when a wheel tax was imposed after the turn of the century. This great demand for "auto-mobility" also goes a long way in helping to link the era of the horse-drawn vehicle to the coming success of the Model T.[46]

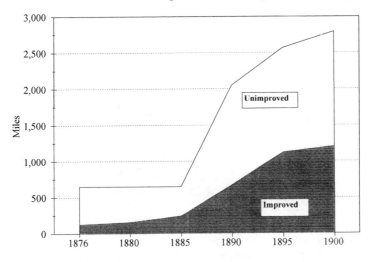

Figure 6.5. Street improvements in Chicago, 1876–1900
Source: City of Chicago, Department of Public Works, *Annual Report* (1876–1901).

Like any ground transportation technology, city horses and carriages had their own system of paved and railed roadbeds. Chicago had 650 miles of streets within its 36 square mile area before the annexation of 1889, which raised the total to slightly over 2,000 miles. Wooden blocks were the paving material of choice while the horse remained the king of the road. The city shifted from pine to cedar block pavement during the mid-1870s. According to a Department of Public Works report, the latter "is smooth, noiseless, pleasant to drive on, and when covered with gravel affords a good footing for horses." The department's 1888 report commented unfavorably on the more expensive and stylish stone blocks in the central business district. They had drawn "numerous complaints" because of the "wear and tear upon vehicles and horseflesh, and the attendant noise." Cedar blocks lasted only five to seven years, but the special-assessment system of street improvement taxation helped make this comparatively cheap paving material the overwhelming choice of property owners, only a minority of whom opted to have the pavement installed on their streets (see figs. 6.5 and 6.6).[47]

The street railways represented an important mode of urban transportation in spite of their limited geographical coverage and middle-class ridership. They racked up their own statistics in the millions by compiling the number of passenger miles covered by their cars. The rails allowed the horses to pull several times as much weight as that of a passenger vehicle designed

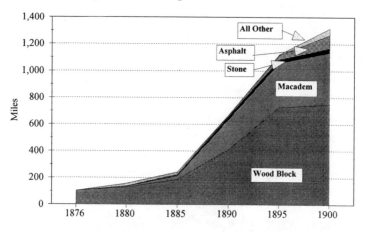

Figure 6.6. Street paving types in Chicago, 1876–1900
Source: City of Chicago, Department of Public Works, *Annual Report* (1876–1901).

for street pavement. Nonetheless, normal-sized horses tired in a half-day or less, requiring the drivers and conductors to help in the hard work of switching animals at the car barns.

In the early 1880s, transit companies began installing a mechanical substitute for a horse's power, the cable system. Chicago's system, which eventually became the second largest such network, was based on the urban utility idea of central-station technology. Like coal-gas plants and waterworks, powerhouses delivered energy through fixed distribution lines, in this case the underground cables that gripmen on the cars grabbed hold of with special devices to make the cars move forward. Ten years later, the electric overhead trolley cables would follow with much larger impacts on the city's spatial and social geographies. These transit technologies were harbingers of even greater changes in the city's energy system from the use of organic sources to that of fossil fuels: from horses to automobiles.[48]

In the post–Civil War period, the horse played a crucial role in creating a unique type of urban space, the park and boulevard system. Driving on special paths inside city parks became a ritual of elite society. In Chicago, the managers of the three park districts laid down miles of these showcases-in-motion for the true members of the "magic circle." Not satisfied with the constraints of proper decorum on these paths, the park boards gained additional authority to build and police connecting ribbons of well-groomed boulevards, where the spirited trotters and their proud owners could pick up speed.

Chicago's elite erected another special institution of horse culture that became the pinnacle of urban society's summer season. Started in 1883, the

Washington Park Jockey Club racetrack on the South Side adjacent to Hyde Park instantly became a special space for the wealthy to conspicuously display their consumption. A club memoir captured the spirit of the place. For the high stakes "American Derby" the following year, the author remembered, "there were Sulkys, Teams, Four-in-Hands, Broughams, Longhorns, Dog Carts, Tallyhos. Along came the gay blade driving his spanking team and atop a spiffy vehicle glistening with nine coats of Valentine varnish."[49]

If owning a horse was the dream for most city dwellers, the pollution problems generated by these animals were something they wanted to keep out of sight, smell, and mind. Historians conclude that each city horse created an average of twenty-two pounds of manure a day. When we multiply that figure by the tens of thousands of animals, the scale of the solid waste removal task begins to take shape. Clearly horse in the city posed a multifaceted threat to human health. Thousands of decaying carcasses of overworked and underfed animals were left in the streets each year. Mounds of manure became the birthplace of veritable plagues of disease-carrying horseflies at a time when only a few homes had any kind of protective screening. In the summertime horse manure baked on the streets, then was ground up by wagon wheels into a fine powder that polluted the air, clogged the lungs, and covered surfaces with germ-laden dust.

Given the formidable downside of the city horse as an energy system, it's easy to understand why contemporaries welcomed mechanical substitutes as a godsend of technological progress. Beginning in the 1880s, city dwellers had new options for transportation in the form of centrally powered mass transit vehicles and self-contained bicycles and "horseless carriages." Although draft animals retained significant meaning in urban culture for a long time to come, even after their utilitarian role diminished, they began to fade in importance after the turn of the century.[50]

By then, the relationship between town and country had undergone considerable evolution since the period immediately following the American Civil War. Urban consumers were still harvesting the energy of sunlight stored in crops, animals, forests, and fossil fuels, but the quantities and the mixes shifted in step with changing patterns of demand. In Chicago and Manchester, competing modes of transportation and chronic gluts of coal from nearby mines fostered fast-growing and highly fluid markets for energy fuels. The brewers of the two cities were emblematic of industry's insatiable demand for more energy. The mechanization of production was the driving force that ultimately boosted consumption of its farm-raised ingredients of barley and hops. Brewers installed more and more machines to heat and cool and move the liquid drink in line with Pasteur's scientific formulas of quality control. The mechanization of the brewery as a microcosm of changes in the industrial city's energy system suggests that the sheer increase in coal consumption would make difficult any gains in the battle against air pollution other than a slowing of its rate of damage to the environment and public health.

Mechanizing the Organic

For the brewers, Pasteur made his greatest scientific contribution by demonstrating that organic agents in the air caused sugar to ferment and food to rot. Once Pasteur had dismissed the possibility of the spontaneous generation of life, he had focused new attention on harmful microorganisms in the air and in brewers' yeast as the sources of the problem of spoilage. The scientist suggested protecting the wort from contact with the air and using only pure strains of yeast. Moreover, pasteurizing the beer, or heating it inside its container, just before shipping would kill any remaining germs and ensure that product quality would not deteriorate before the beer was consumed. The new science underpinned a fast-growing sense of mastery over the technology of brewing. Energy-intensive mechanical processes replaced labor-intensive work routines. Engineers, scientists, and brewers participated in the mechanization and integration of malting, brewing, and fermenting within a completely controlled internal environment in order to make a product of consistent quality and taste.[51]

Recognizing the historic preeminence of London's porter breweries, Pasteur crossed the Channel in September 1871 to undertake at first hand a scientific study of their mass production methods. The emergence of London as the first large city in the modern era had already witnessed the parallel growth of the great breweries to unprecedented size. As early as 1800, the Samuel Whitbread brewery surpassed the 200,000-barrel (32.7 million-liters) mark in annual production.[52] Completing an estimated thirty million retail transactions a year through five hundred pubs and one thousand other customers, this business enterprise had established a true mass consumer market.

Introducing the microscope into Whitbread's gigantic plant, Pasteur soon identified the most likely source of problems in the multistep process of making beer. Samples drawn from the production line showed that it was at the fermenting stage that the product was at the greatest danger of contamination and infection by potentially ruinous "microscopic parasites." These "germs," Pasteur claimed in a defensive tone, caused "diseased ferments ... which are acid, putrid, viscous, bitter, or otherwise unpalatable, a consideration of commercial rather than scientific importance."[53] The Frenchman probably felt a need to couch his findings in pragmatic terms because the managers of the brewery initially denied having any problems. "At first," Pasteur related, "the English brewers returned somewhat vague answers to our questions; however, after what had taken place, they doubtlessly recognized the fact that a mutual understanding between a savant and a practical man may often be of considerable advantage to the latter, and in the end they confessed to us that they had stowed away in their brewery a large quantity of beer which had gone bad in cask a fortnight or so after it was brewed." London's beer makers ultimately disclosed that as much as 20 percent of their product was unsellable, a huge loss considering that each of the five largest firms was producing an average of nearly 17 million gallons (77.3 million liters) a year.[54]

Pasteur's on-site investigation directed the agenda of his research on the biochemistry of fermentation when he returned to his laboratory at the École Normale Supérieure in Paris. He had pinpointed two places where the organic liquid was especially vulnerable to infection. The first and more obvious source of trouble was the yeast itself. The microscope proved particularly useful in distinguishing between normal yeast cells and "diseased ferments." Brewers had long suspected that bad yeast could defeat their labors. The prevailing custom was to supply each other, as the need arose, with new batches of this essential substance that turned the freshly brewed, sugar-laden liquid, or wort, into a carbonated alcoholic beverage. Pasteur conducted a series of experiments that confirmed that yeast was a plant, a "living being."

These findings also reinforced his position that miasmatic theories of disease were wrong. The Frenchman admitted that he took "malicious satisfaction" in this work of "demolishing" and "annihilating" the contentions of his academic opponents, including one of Germany's leading authorities, Justus von Liebig. "We should gain but little from the use of a yeast uncontaminated by any foreign germs," he declared, "if natural organic substances had the power of organizing themselves by means of spontaneous generation. . . . Theories of this kind are warmly advocated, but, to our thinking, rather from sentimental considerations or prejudices than from any basis of serious experimental proofs."[55]

The identification of a second source of infection, polluted air inside the brewery, also helped to advance Pasteur's alternative—germ theory. "All these diseased ferments have a common origin," Pasteur insisted. "Their germs, infinitesimal and hardly perceptible as they are, even with the aid of the microscope, form a part of the dust conveyed through the air." The risk of contamination was particularly acute at the very start of the fermentation stage. The wort had to be cooled to a temperature low enough for the yeast to be added without causing nearly explosive results. In a practice that had changed little since the time of the Egyptians, the ale and porter brewers poured the wort into large, shallow trays in an effort to reduce the temperature by about a hundred degrees as quickly as possible. Steam, condensation, and a rich, organic medium made the rooms containing these "cooling squares" perfect breeding grounds for parasitic bacteria.

But it was much harder to demonstrate that the air contained contaminants than to show that unwanted bacteria were growing in a liquid. In the laboratory, Pasteur was left to prove the negative; that is, the absence of spontaneous generation in a completely purified environment. He had previously designed experimental apparatuses to create such a completely enclosed system. While some of these containers had remained free of infection for over twelve years, others had shown unmistakable signs of life due to undetected contamination. Pasteur confessed that these experiments were the most frustrating aspect of his work since he could never be absolutely sure that his meticulous procedures to eliminate every possibility of microorganic infection were flawless. Despite some time-consuming setbacks, however, he was confident that he had found the fundamental reasons why beer went bad and equally certain about the ways to remedy the problem.[56]

In designing a counterattack on the harmful enemies of beer, Pasteur acknowledged that he first had to return to the bottom line of popular taste. Having identified many different species and strains of yeast, he knew that each would produce a drink with its own distinctive qualities. Simply developing the apparatus and procedures to generate a pure strain of brewers' yeast would not be enough; he would have to select a strain that could pass the supreme test of consumer approval. These requirements led the scientist back to the Germans' lager-style beer. With a new sense of appreciation, he turned his efforts to unlocking the secrets behind its superior taste and greater stability during shipping. The Germans used a radically different kind of yeast that fermented at the bottom of the cask at much lower temperatures. If the beer was kept near the freezing point, it could be shipped to distant markets without necessarily losing its freshness or taste. Pasteur estimated that it took about two pounds of ice to make a gallon of lager-style beer and transport it to the point of sale.

Pasteur now realized that achieving precise control of temperature was the key to retarding the growth of unwanted bacteria in the organic beverage from its most vulnerable stage of fermentation to its final destination, the beer drinker's glass. A product made by these methods, Pasteur concluded, "possesses a flavour and delicacy which cause it to be held in higher esteem by consumers than beer produced by means of other ferments." The Frenchman believed that he had found the way to strike back at the Germans. He pondered not only the prospect of selling this cool, refreshing drink in existing domestic markets, but also the grand vista of virtually unlimited consumer demand in the hotter climates of Europe's fast-spreading empires.[57]

As the final test of his scientific work, Pasteur constructed two small devices to brew the perfect beer. The first was essentially an industrial version of the laboratory flasks he had used for isolating a pure strain of yeast within a completely closed and sterilized environment. In spite of his effort to reassure the practical brewers that "all this may be done in considerably less time than we have taken to describe it," his method proved cumbersome and time-consuming. It would soon be replaced by the easier technique of cultivating a pure strain from a single cell. Dr. Emil Christian Hansen, who developed the new method in the Carlsberg brewery in Copenhagen, Denmark, was emblematic of a general transition in the operational management of the brewery from the guild-trained brewmeister to the university-trained chemist. Precise measuring instruments and testing laboratories would begin to replace the traditional reliance on touch, smell, and taste.[58]

The second piece of equipment Pasteur built, a fermentation chamber, also marked a historic break with the past. The scientist understood that by purifying the air and the vessels used in this critical phase of brewing, and "by employing a perfectly pure ferment [yeast]...we have it in our power to prepare a beer which shall be incapable of undergoing any pernicious fermentation whatsoever." Sensitive to the practicalities of the business, he attempted to justify the extra time and expense involved in his methods with the promise of a better product and less waste. Pasteur's claims would merit approval by skilled advertising copywriters. With persuasive rhetorical flourish, he asserted that any added costs "were largely compensated by the superior quality of the beer, which is stronger and has greater fullness on the palate, whilst the aroma of the hops is preserved to an extent never found in beers brewed by the ordinary process."[59]

Like most hucksters' promises past and present, Pasteur's mouth-watering appeal ran far ahead of its composer's ability to deliver the goods. In the spring of 1875, he tried out his novel methods at Tourtel's brewery in Tantonville, then he shipped his brew on an ordinary, unrefrigerated train about three hundred miles back to Paris in the heat of the summer and stored the bottles for a few months in a warm cellar. When he finally opened one of the bottles, he was disappointed to find that the beer had a horrible "yeast-bitten flavour and defective clarifying powers." Speculating that contamination during the making of the pure yeast was the most likely cause of the problem, he could still declare a partial victory in the "remarkable keeping properties" of the foul-tasting drink.[60]

Although Pasteur's brew failed the ultimate test, his scientific findings would trigger a far-reaching revolution in the industrialization of the production of foodstuffs for a swelling mass market of urban consumers. Gradually over the course of about twenty years, the brewers would take the lead in expanding upon his scientific findings and improving upon his primitive devices. In biochemistry they would perfect the cultivation of pure strains of yeast, raise standards of quality control, and make major advances in reducing waste. In technology they would construct a closed system of production within which the environment and temperature could be controlled with the same precision as in the most exacting laboratory experiment.[61]

Among German-American brewers, Pasteur's findings quickly engendered an ideal of scientific brewing. Consider that the leading trade journal, *The Western Brewer*, not only published the results of the most recent scientific advances, but also harped tirelessly about the sacred duties of the practitioner to implement them without delay. By 1879, the German-owned, Chicago-produced publication was singing praise to "Louis Pasteur, The Eminent Chemist ... the great Pasteur—to whose studies, experiments and researches the brewing trade all over the world is so much indebted." The subsequent story, about the importance of using only pure strains of yeast, was soon followed up by entreaties to brewers to buy a microscope. Over the course of the next decade, the journal continued to publish discussions by eminent authorities on virtually every aspect of the implications of Pasteur's science for the "modern brewer."[62]

Now that brewers in American cities knew the causes of and remedies for poor quality in beer, some of them took the lead in implementing a steady, progressive series of innovations to produce a standardized consumer product for a national market. To meet popular demand for the cold, light, bubbly drink, brewers applied increasing amounts of energy in the form of heat and refrigeration in order to gain more precise control over the biochemical reactions involved in the making of their product. This more intensive application of energy changed the outward appearance of the brewery as well as the work routines inside.

A quick tour of a new-style brew house illustrates how mechanization helped the brewer achieve the kinds of control necessary for producing a standardized product. The mash tub, for example, was completely redesigned. Beginning with the lowering of steam coils into the vessel, brewers made further adaptations of steam technology to heat and stir the mash in a consistent, uniform manner. Thus machines replaced the men who used to stir the kettle night and day. A false bottom made of metal grating facilitated access for an array of pipes to fill, drain, and clean the container. Temperature regulators automatically activated hot-water and steam jets embedded in the bottom and the walls of the closed tub, power rakes stirred the mash, and various pumps sprang into action to move the contents, including the thick mass of spent grains, which were then dried, processed, packaged, and sold as animal feed.

The wort was pumped to another enclosed kettle, where similar methods of steam heating were applied. After the hops were added and the mixture was cooked, the wort was no longer drained into shallow, open-air beds for cooling. Instead, it was fed through an elaborate system of coiled pipes that were submerged in refrigerated tanks. To aerate the wort properly while avoiding infection, this entire apparatus was placed inside a sealed cabinet and supplied with filtered air.[63] German-American brewers also took the lead in perfecting refrigeration machines, a technology that would eventually cause a profound change in the nutritional standards and diet of the nation.

Like Pasteur's work on fermentation, the search for an appropriate science and practical technology of refrigeration was international. During the 1860s, several experimental devices were tested in U.S. and European breweries. They were all based on the same general principles, which are still employed in our modern-day refrigerators and air conditioners. In the 1840s, the English scientist Michael Faraday had proposed that if a gas was compressed into a liquid, cold would be produced when the liquid was allowed to expand and evaporate back into a gas. Thirty years later, Carl Linde, in Munich, worked out the theoretical formulas for testing the efficiency of existing machines, thus opening the way for a new generation of refrigeration hardware. The thermodynamic concepts were simple enough, but actually designing an efficient compressor, finding a safe and effective liquid coolant, and building a system of pipes and valves that could withstand unprecedented pressures required twenty years of effort. Brewers and would-be refrigerator makers also used trial-and-error methods to determine whether the machines should be used to make ice or to equip cold-storage areas and brewing gear with pipes of cooled liquid.[64]

The race to produce a standardized beer for a national market created a certain logical goal for technological innovation, but it did not result in a singular solution, a one best way of uncontested, maximum efficiency. On the contrary, a range of designs for the scale, equipment, and organization of the brewery continued to compete successfully right up to the time of

Table 6.2 Chicago brewery firm size, 1866–1886

	Number of firms		
Number of barrels	1866	1877	1886
150,000–200,000			1
100,000–150,000			0
75,000–100,000		1	3
50,000–75,000		1	2
30,000–50,000	2	3	6
20,000–30,000	2	0	1
10,000–20,000	3	4	2
5,000–10,000	6	2	4
1,000–5,000	6	4	4
Under 1,000	1	5	7
Total	20	20	30

Source: *One Hundred Years of Brewing: A Supplement to the Western Brewer* (Chicago: Rich, 1903), 422; *Schade's Brewers' Handbook* (Chicago: Western Brewer, 1877), 26; *Wing's Brewer's Hand-Book of the United States and Canada: A Supplement to the Western Brewer* (New York: Wing, 1880–1886), 43–45.

Prohibition. In the case of refrigeration machines, for example, several companies emerged in the early 1880s that developed this technology using very different approaches. Each machine offered advantages in some areas in exchange for weaknesses in others. For instance, some compressors achieved a high efficiency but only by incorporating valves that tended to leak. Other machines consumed more fuel but were less prone to breakdown, and so on.[65] Brewers too made a range of choices based on different formulas for calculating cost savings, reliability, convenience, and aspirations for reaching extralocal markets. Traditional methods continued alongside new inventions, often with complementary effects.

Although some breweries grew to enormous proportions, diversity remained the single most distinctive characteristic of the industry. As table 6.2 shows, one-half of the city's thirty breweries in 1886 produced less than ten thousand barrels (1,173,400 liters) a year; seven of those made less than one thousand barrels (117,340 liters).[66] Rather than the inner logic of the machine driving it in a linear progression toward scale economies, technological innovation helped maintain a highly fluid range of business options, including firm size, extent of mechanization, and use of alternative energy systems. Upstart brewers could adapt new improvements to meet the competitive dynamics of the market just as readily as the biggest, most established companies. In this regard, the brewery seems representative of American industry.

The mechanization of beer making revolutionized not only the apparatus of the brewery but its work routines as well. The timing of this technological transformation and the organization of brewery workers into unions was not coincidental. "The mashing process," an industry historian recalled, "used to be back-breaking labor, compounded of lugging and hauling, pumping, grinding, stirring, boiling, digging out spent grains, etc., and a constant source of anxiety to the head brewer who depended upon his senses of sight, smell, taste, and feeling to judge the condition of his mash and wort." As the assured quality made possible by laboratory testing replaced the unpredictable results of former days, the brew master no longer needed to drive his workers around the clock with relentless determination. In the late 1870s, workers began protesting their low pay, the extremely long hours, and their quasifeudalistic vassalage to their bosses, who often forced them to live close to the brewery in prepaid boarding houses and tenements. Even the tradition of providing workers with unlimited free beer began to take on the appearance of an evil capitalist plot. The brewers, according to labor militant Hermann Schluter, "promoted drunkenness among the men and sought to degrade them in order that they might exploit them and use them up more freely." Of course, the bosses did not make concessions easily; it took a decade of persistent and at times violent labor agitation to secure recognition of the workers' unions.[67]

The mechanization of malting illustrates the ways in which energy-intensive infrastructure spread throughout the brewery. On 1 April 1887, Louis C. Huck, son of Chicago's pioneer lager brewer, dedicated a three-story building that boosted his capacity from seven hundred thousand to over a million bushels a year. The processing plant was designed to house new machines recently perfected in France that germinated the barley within a self-contained system. An inventor in his own right, Huck was the first maltster in the United States to import the "Saladin" machine and the first in Chicago to incorporate refrigeration machines. "Pneumatic malting," the *Western Brewer* exalted, "means the absolute control of the conditions of all air supplied to germinating barley, and its consequent modifications of growth." Superseding the old steeping tanks and rooms, tube-shaped drums with screws turning inside supplied the barley with filtered air prepared with precise levels of humidity and temperature.

A single operator replaced the legions of workers formerly engaged in the arduous tasks of spreading, raking, and shoveling the wet grain on the floor. The pneumatic machines were also equipped with mechanisms for automatic loading from the storage elevators and unloading to the finishing kilns. Huck had redesigned these a few years earlier to take advantage of similar technologies for regulating the quality and flow of air to produce a superior, "very pale" malt. To substitute machines for human workers, he supplemented an eighty-horsepower steam engine with a bigger one-hundred-horsepower prime mover that also ran electric lights in the new malt house.[68] Huck's spirit of innovation was greatly admired by a self-conscious business community devoted to "scientific brewing."

Taken together, technological changes inside the brewery accumulated to a point where the industry's outward expression also underwent a metamorphosis. The adoption of ever-larger vessels, an expanding energy infrastructure, new methods of refrigeration, and more power machinery and control mechanisms eventually required the help of professional engineers and architects. As iron framing replaced wooden beams to support the tremendous weights of the liquid containers and the ice, the new buildings became more vertical in design. Although gravity still played an important role in moving liquids within these five-to-eight-story structures, powerful pumps facilitated the erection of separate buildings for each of the basic steps: malting, brewing, fermentation and storage, and packaging. In the 1880s, the success of some brewers in reaching a national market turned their neighborhoods into industrial landscapes, places of mass production. The new-style energy-intensive brewery had truly become a "city within a city."[69]

Rather than eyesores, however, some breweries became objects of urbanity, style, and civic pride. During the 1870s and 1880s, the engineering and architecture of breweries evolved into specialized fields. This process of professionalization centered in Chicago, creating what architectural historian Susan Appel calls a golden age of brewery building, one that produced highly decorative building facades in the best Victorian style. "Visually," Appel states, the brewery became "a striking architectural element of the city at the same time that it provided efficient spaces in which to pursue a growing business."[70] In addition to becoming icons of industrial progress, some brewing plants provided their neighborhoods with German-flavored beer gardens. These imposing factory complexes may have added to a city's image and civic pride, but few people actually wanted to live next door to one of them. Breweries not only were a source of air pollution and nauseating smells, but also brought annoying street noise and congestion.

Creating Industrial Ecologies

As a microcosm of the city's energy system, the brewery illuminates the transformation of urban places into industrial ecologies. Pasteur's science of microbiology solved problems by encouraging the use of energy-intensive methods of applying more heating, cooling, and power to the process of making beer. More consistent quality and brand-name advertising helped spur rising consumer demand, fueling the growth of some breweries into large-scale sites of production. The technological construction of society in this case meant changes in the land, air, and water in both town and country. Scientific brewing spurred the expansion of the farming of crops, the raising of animals, and the mining and transportation of coal in rural areas. It also fostered the erection of distinctively industrial building complexes and fueled the proliferation of saloons and pubs and other places of popular amusement.

The burdens of the pollution that resulted from this industrial growth fell disproportionately on the inhabitants of the factory zones. In both Chicago and Manchester, manufacturing plants often came first to relatively unpopulated areas, then were followed by cheap housing to accommodate the pedestrian workers, while their employers were able to escape to suburban retreats. The growth of Manchester's Ancoats and Victoria Park represents an early example of this process of allocating residential locations. Chicago's Packingtown and Hyde Park were also typical of the bifurcated land-use patterns that came to define the physical form of the industrial city.

As the cities became more built up and demarked into districts, most manufacturers could not afford the extra costs of operating at their edge in spite of cheaper land prices there. Still, they often had a wider range of choices in deciding where to place their businesses than their workers did in deciding where to live. Did the owners consciously decide to site their factories in the poor and immigrant neighborhoods, compounding the pollution problems there? Before taking up the question of whether Chicago manufacturers violated the principles of environmental justice by using discriminatory criteria in making locational decisions, it is worthwhile to determine whether they and others considered coal smoke to be harmful to human health and well-being.

Members of the post–Civil War generation considered air pollution more a regrettable nuisance than a direct cause of sickness and disease. Because the smoke caused property damage, Chicago passed an antismoke ordinance; it was the first large American city to do so. The law was aimed not at improving public health by reducing air pollution, but at penalizing those individuals who flagrantly disregarded normal procedures for operating their coal-burning equipment. Public health reformers in the United States did not begin to draw a direct link between smoke and disease until after the turn of the century.[71]

An extensive review of *The Western Brewer* confirms that factory managers discussed the "smoke evil" in the idiom of engineering and technology, not medical science or environmental protection. Since most of the visible black emissions from coal-fired furnaces were the result of incomplete combustion, the main arguments in favor of making improvements were framed in terms of efficiency and fuel savings. Consider the coming of the oil pipeline to Chicago, which could have led to a significant reduction in air pollution. Compared to coal, which had to be shoveled into the furnaces and was sometimes added in excessive amounts, the liquid fuel could be fed automatically into the furnaces in just the right amount. In February 1890, Chicago's Phoenix distillery took the lead and converted its boilers so they could receive crude oil instead of Illinois's soft coal. The journal provides a detailed report on the savings in fuel bills and labor costs, but mentions only in a footnote the elimination of visible smoke emissions that resulted from the conversion.[72] It would take another fifteen years before Chicago women would mount a grassroots antismoke campaign aimed at improving both public health and environmental quality in the city.

Industries with polluting smokestacks should not be judged guilty of knowingly contributing to the spread of diseases caused by bad air, but can we discover a pattern of discriminatory locational decisions nevertheless? Using city directories, I have plotted a series of maps showing the locations of the city's new breweries in discrete periods spanning the years from just before the 1871 fire to 1910, when the prohibition movement was beginning to see success (see fig. 6.7). The most consistent pattern to emerge in the site choices of the brewers indicates the primacy of access to transportation.

The breweries clung to the riverfront industrial corridor and the railroads' trunk lines coming into and out of the city. As some of these factories grew to gigantic size, they consumed immense quantities of heavy bulk commodities that were transported along those routes: grains, hops, coal, and ice. The river also served as a convenient place to dump the stream of wastewater pouring out of their plants. Fortunately for Chicagoans, the breweries did not rely on the river for their source of water, the other crucial ingredient in the making of this increasingly popular drink of the working classes. The bigger plants turned to artesian wells as their primary source of pure water, which freed them to move closer to rail and shipping lines. At the same time, the continuous extension of the city's water and sewerage systems allowed small-scale operators to give greater priority to other factors, such as proximity to niche markets and cheap rental space.[73]

Unfortunately, we cannot measure the class, racial, and ethnic composition of Chicago's neighborhoods with the same precision with which we can

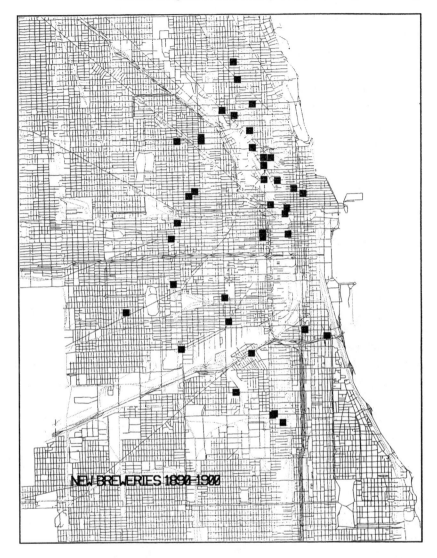

Figure 6.7. New brewery locations in Chicago, 1890–1900
Source: Data from contemporary city directories.

map the locations of its breweries. In the 1890 census, the ward level is the smallest unit of statistical data. Among the few social variables reported, the proportion of people who were foreign-born probably furnishes the best indicator of class status. A lack of economic and political empowerment can also be reasonably inferred for the wards with a large percent of immigrants.

With only thirty-thousand African-Americans in a city of a million people, any effort to link race to industrial location is practically meaningless.

Generally, mortality rates for both infants and people of all ages climb in tandem with the percentage foreign-born in the wards. Closer analysis of the medical causes of death shows that waterborne diseases account for most of the fatalities. Inadequate water and sewerage facilities in these poor neighborhoods were the factors most to blame for the higher mortality rates. How much air pollution from factory smokestacks contributed to the death rate is impossible to assess with accuracy.[74]

Plotting the locations of the breweries against the census data yields inconclusive results. In 1890, the wards with the most immigrants or the worst housing tended to have more breweries than the wards with the largest proportion native-born or the best housing.[75] A parallel study of 1910 data yields similar results. Yet the logic of access to transportation, not intent to discriminate, best accounts for these geographical patterns. Maps from fire insurance companies and Hull-House clearly show that some of Chicago's worst slums were located next to its rail and shipping depots, where cheap hotels and rooming houses for sailors, vagrants, and jobless men were located.

The case for a violation of environmental justice by the beer makers is also undercut by the fact that some of the city's big breweries remained in prestigious residential districts along the lakefront. On the Near South Side at 23rd Street, the city's greatest beer factory, the Conrad Seipp Brewery, literally cast a shadow over the city's most exclusive addresses on Prairie Avenue. And on the North Side, other beer makers remained close to Germantown, sandwiched between the increasingly fashionable Lincoln Park area and the emerging Gold Coast. Of Chicago's sixty-three breweries in 1910, no more than five were operating in any single ward. At the same time, the beer makers did not choose remote suburban sites because they were too far away for their horse-drawn wagons to make regular weekly deliveries within the city. If brewing beer was a typical smokestack industry, a reasonable case can be made for the contention that factory managers in general were not guilty of discriminatory practices in the location of their facilities.[76]

This retrospective analysis of environmental justice cautions against imposing current standards of ethics on the past. Historians must use extreme care to define the status of medical knowledge, to order the chronology of land-use and settlement patterns, and to understand the motivations of the decision makers. The vast majority of factory owners did not consider the impacts of their chimney emissions on health because they did not believe that coal smoke made people sick. In our test case of the brewers, locational decisions do not seem to have been noticeably influenced by discriminatory motives. On the contrary, close access to both transportation facilities and commercial customers seems to account best for their choice of sites. Other industries, of course, had their own lists of criteria and priorities for making locational decisions.[77]

Conclusions: Technology, Culture, and Society

By the time of the great British buyout of Chicago breweries and saloons in 1889–1890, the industrialization of beer making in the United States was virtually complete. Hermann Schluter was not guilty of hyperbole when he expressed a sense of awe about the revolution in the scale and scope of the business in a single generation. Guided by Pasteur's science, German-American brewers became pioneers on the technological frontiers of the mechanization, refrigeration, and sanitation of the production line. To reach this pathbreaking goal of internal environmental control required greater and greater inputs of energy. Machines and fossil fuels replaced the power of humans for the most part, but synergy rather than linear progression best characterizes the nature of the resulting changes in the energy system of the beer factory.

The brewery was a leading representative of a general transformation of industry during the Gilded Age that led to profound and interrelated alterations in the urban and the rural environment. The railroad—itself a voracious energy consumer—connected coal mines and breeding farms in the country to smokestacks and horse stables in the city. In a similar way, pasteurized beer produced in the high-tech brewery was linked to the spread of low-tech iceboxes in home kitchens. Both places, as well as the city streets between them, became sites of more intense energy use.

To the extent that technology drives history, the city's energy system formed the infrastructure of an emerging consumer society. Its increasing reliance on vast quantities of energy for production and consumption contributed to better standards of material well-being. The quality of the beer served in Chicago improved tremendously in the quarter-century following the Civil War. But the downside of industrial progress was having to live within an environment made worse by it.

In the 1890s, urban energy consumption would begin to climb even more steeply as a result of the implementation of new central-station technologies. In the case of electricity, overnight conversion from cable to trolley cars led the way in the wiring of the city for innumerable lighting and power applications. In the case of coal gas, a revolution in production methods turned the fossil fuel from a relatively expensive source of energy for lighting into a relatively cheap source of energy for heating and cooking. Modern utility plants often installed the most efficient, and hence least polluting, coal-burning equipment.[78] Nevertheless, urban demand for energy would grow at such prodigious rates that the absolute amount of smoke particles and toxic gases going up the smokestacks would far exceed the decrease in emissions made possible by these technological gains. Chicago's breweries also enjoyed tremendous success while contributing increasing amounts of pollution to the city's air, water, and land.

This case study of the technological construction of society helps account for the decline in the environmental quality of urban life. Yet it needs to be balanced with an assessment of the influence of consumer demand and popular taste on the city's energy system. To make this assessment, in the next chapter I compare the relationship between consumers and producers, between beer drinkers and brewery managers in the United States and the United Kingdom. Perhaps city dwellers were willing to trade clean air for better beer. The links between material wealth and environmental degradation in the paradox of progress were neither direct nor easy to discern. The diffuse nature of air pollution made these relationships especially obscure to ordinary people. Though the technological construction of society helps account for the decline in the city's environment, the social construction of technology would have little impact on the environment until reformers began to question the effects of the industrial city's energy system on public health and the quality of everyday life.

CHAPTER SEVEN

The Social Construction of Industrial Technology

Introduction: The Stillbirth of the Bacterium Club

In 1876, thirteen men met to form a new association dedicated to the advancement of science and industry. Led by Horace T. Brown, the founders of the monthly dining group were all chemists who worked for various breweries in Burton-upon-Trent. Its hard well water helped make it a place renowned for high-quality pale ales: Bass, Allsopp, and Worthington. Besides the rarity of their employment in English brewing companies, most of these scientists also shared an exceptional education in Germany or by German-trained teachers. The occasion that brought them together was equally remarkable, the publication of Louis Pasteur's *Études sur la bière*. "At once producing a profound impression," Brown recalled forty years later, "the Frenchman's research promised to mark a great divide between the previous period of hidebound practice and the coming age of scientific brewing."[1]

But Brown and his fellow members of the Bacterium Club would have to wait almost a quarter-century for the rest of England's beer makers to start crossing over from traditional to modern methods of production. In sharp contrast to their German and German-American counterparts, British brewers largely ignored Pasteur's findings, scorned university-trained experts, and rejected lager-style beer as an unwanted foreign intrusion. Even within the small island of enlightenment of Burton's brewers, the scientists had to wage an uphill struggle against apprehension and distrust. The Worthington brewery, for example, resisted Brown's pleas to set up a laboratory for several years "due to fear that the display of any chemical apparatus might suggest to customers ... the horrible suspicion that the beer was being 'doctored.'" The company's directors finally granted his request, but only after he promised to keep all the windows covered in order to prevent anyone looking inside.

Finally in the mid-1890s, the industry initiated a concerted effort toward the institutionalization of scientific brewing. By then, however, it found itself badly behind. English brewers would be forced to play catch-up to the far more advanced quality-control and production technologies of the Americans and the Germans.[2]

In the brewing industry, then, Pasteur's breakthrough on the causes of spoilage did not lead to any inevitable results. Since brewers in England and the United States had equal access to this scientific knowledge, what accounts for their diverging paths when it came to industrial technology and related business strategies of distribution and marketing? Scholars disagree over the extent to which science and technology drive history. They also argue about the meaning and importance of the social construction of technology. Some, taking a top-down approach, tend to limit agency to the businessmen and engineers in charge of industry, while others start at the bottom, giving ultimate power to consumers.[3]

A comparison of the two countries offers an opportunity to examine this dynamic tension between producers and consumers. Did the beer makers dictate what the public got to drink, or were they ruled by their customers, their customers' taste preferences, and the larger cultural context that defined society's attitudes and public policies related to alcoholic beverages? In the hands of American (and German) brewers, Pasteur's research became a powerful, albeit flexible, tool that was used in a variety of ways to meet the current demands of a highly competitive marketplace. In the United States, popular taste did drive technology to a significant extent.

But in the United Kingdom, instead of responding to customer preferences, brewers choked them off. The retarded growth of scientific brewing in Britain reflected cultural orientations within which the privileges of class and elite reactions against the industrial city took precedence over the sovereignty of the consumer. England's brewers pursued a business strategy aimed at capturing market share in their retail outlets, called tied houses. These pubs were owned by the brewers and leased to tenants, who had to agree to sell only the landlord's brands of beer. Satisfying customer taste preferences took second place behind cutting real estate and financial deals to monopolize these outlets.

Clinging to tradition, British brewers remained rooted to craft-based practices. Their parochial perspectives were remarkably resistant to innovation in any form. According to historian E. M. Sigsworth, "German methods of beer brewing, Pasteur's discoveries, and Hansen's work upon yeast wrought no revolution in the British industry." In this case, the social construction of technology meant a much slower transition to energy-intensive methods of production.[4]

The London Porters, Burton Ales, and Neighborhood Tied Houses

The striking differences between the United States and the United Kingdom underscore the complexity of the interplay among diverse groups of actors in the social construction of science and technology. The brewing industries in the two countries represent polar extremes in the dynamic interaction between producers and consumers. British brewers "were conservative men," a business historian explains, "each carefully preserving, often very secretively, established, empirical practices which had been handed down to them." Horace Brown's experience fits this interpretation. "Certain rigid rules had been laid down for the guidance of the brewer and maltster," he remembered, "which were assumed to have been so far sanctified by experience and tradition that to throw the least doubt on their general applicability laid one open to the terrible charge of being a 'theorist.'"[5]

If we accept the agency of the consumers, we also have to face the possibility that these brewers were more or less hapless victims, hostages of popular taste. And there is plenty of evidence that the vast majority of beer drinkers—members of the working classes—were themselves conservatives in private life and clung tenaciously to their neighborhood pubs and strong porters. Moreover, hundreds of small-scale brewing enterprises throughout the country—not just the big London operators—continued to thrive by catering to the preferences of these customers, who appear to have remained loyal to the familiar tastes and narcotic effects of their traditional local products.[6]

An assessment of the British brewing industry's reception of Pasteur's science, then, will require close attention to the interplay between producers and consumers within the larger contexts of the nation's business and popular cultures, an approach that will make it possible to clearly and unambiguously measure British brewers against their American counterparts. This transnational comparison illuminates the highly uneven pace of industrialization. Leads and lags within each industry as well as between different countries were typical, making generalizations difficult. Here I will remain focused on the interrelated creation of energy-intensive consumer societies and industrial ecologies.[7]

The test, of course, is not who makes the best beer. Regardless of what kind of drink consumers preferred, every brewer aspired to gain better control over the quality and consistency of the product. The ability to deliver a drink that customers could depend on time after time to meet their expectations of how it was suppose to taste was the beer makers' ultimate goal. Pasteur's understanding of fermentation and his insights into the use of heating and cooling to control the organic processes of brewing offered them a set of extremely powerful tools with which to reach for this ideal. The rapid translation and dissemination of the Frenchman's findings meant that the brewing industry in each country enjoyed a relatively even playing field on which to begin adapting the new knowledge to its particular needs and its customers' demands.

According to the industry's leading historians, T. R. Gourvish and R. G. Wilson, at the heart of the problem was a gradual but inexorable change to a preference for lighter, less alcoholic drinks and the obstinate refusal of London's great brewers to respond in any way other than by trying to stifle the competition. Gourvish and Wilson argue that because of this clear failure of leadership, London's brewers did not sustain their previous roles as the world's foremost sponsors of science and technology. The business historians suggest several reasons for this loss of momentum, including the changing attitudes of a new generation of managers and the sheer multiplication of their number to a point where decision making was effectively paralyzed.[8]

Most important, perhaps, the great enterprises of London fell behind because their directors neglected the business of brewing and instead became obsessed with playing the real estate game. For the fifty years before 1830, the top dozen firms had commanded 75–80 percent of the city's market, and they were determined to keep a stranglehold on it. They diverted more and more of their resources to gaining direct control of their retail sales outlets, the tied houses. Rather than paying attention to the brewery, the fountainhead of their wealth, they became managers of the brewery's profits, preoccupied with buying and leasing pubs. They attempted to lock competitors out and force patrons to choose among their own limited range of brands.

With the population of the city nearly doubling to four million between 1830 and 1870, the brewers could fool themselves into believing that a steady if sluggish rise in sales figures reflected sound business judgments. In fact, the absorption of market share, not additional consumer demand, accounts for a large part of the growth of the big porter breweries during this period. Their gains mostly represented losses on the part of very small-scale, publican brewers who were unable to keep up with the more exacting standards of quality that increasingly sophisticated urban consumers insisted on.[9]

Pasteur's observations of London's brewers in 1871 lend support to Gourvish and Wilson's claim that the industry's business culture had changed so that instead of being the spearheads of technological innovation these brewers were the rearguard of the scientific status quo. Since England did not contain a single lager-beer producer, the visitor from France assumed that its people must have a "decided preference" for traditional brews. Yet he strongly suspected that conservatism on the part of its leading establishments was at least partially responsible for the complete absence of the fashionable new drink that had so quickly won over the continent. "Even in the event of public taste demanding a 'low beer,' " he speculated, "English brewers will hesitate a long time before converting their breweries. Such a conversion would impose upon them expenses and difficulties of a very serious nature."

Chief among these, according to Pasteur, were the costs of either retrofitting existing facilities or erecting new ones after finding suitable sites for their location. Given the steady flow of profits from their comfortable oligopoly, Whitbread and the others could well have afforded to construct new breweries incorporating the most up-to-date equipment and building materials, but instead they poured this rich stream of cash into London real estate, spending a fortune on pubs. By 1886, 70 percent of the pubs in England and Wales had become tied houses, a proportion that would rise to 95 percent at the time of World War I.[10]

Over the course of this period, London brewing became a reactionary backwater of old business practice, acting as a drag on the spread of scientific methods throughout the British brewing industry. Making porter was the easy way out because it required the least amount of quality control. "As a result of the use of high-roasted malts," Gourvish and Wilson point out, "it was dark and cloudy. ... Essentially it was a weaker, inferior stout, easily produced in bulk and ideally suited to the soft well-water of the capital. Because of its opaqueness it was not difficult for publicans to adulterate, and brewers themselves were adept at mixing and fining returns with fresh porter." Whitbread's managers furnish a typical example of resistance to Pasteur's science. Although they purchased a microscope in the wake of his revealing investigation, they held out for over thirty years, until 1903, before establishing a laboratory to put it in.

Other examples of hostility to science abound. J. M. Hanbury, a director of another great London establishment, admitted at the end of the century that his firm had hired its first trained chemist only a few years earlier even though the brewery's output exceeded twenty million gallons (90.92 million liters) a year. Hanbury was himself shocked by the ignorance of his fellow directors. When asked about "malt diastase," a basic term that had been used in the trade for over sixty years, one of Hanbury's colleagues replied in an irritated tone, "What the devil are you talking about?"[11]

The main result of this hidebound business culture was that the industry was suffering economic stagnation at the very time when Pasteur's science was handing it a golden opportunity to create new products and revive waning consumer demand. From 1831 to 1876, an overall rise in per capita beer consumption helped fuel an anemic 1.74 percent annual rate of growth, slower than that of any other major British industry. This pattern peaked in the 1870s, an extraordinary decade when real gains in the disposable income of the working classes went unmatched by access to other mass-produced goods and services. After 1880, working-class people drank less beer and spent more of their money on other consumer goods and popular amusements.

In spite of the resulting flattening of sales, the industry responded neither by building science-based lager beer plants for the domestic market nor by trying to open new outlets abroad for their current line of products. As Gourvish and Wilson put it succinctly, "Exports can virtually be ignored. Never shipping more than around 3 percent of output," the brewing industry "is the only major British industry in which the focus is almost entirely insular." The big players seemed little interested in meeting the demands of consumers and instead remained fixated on funneling their profits into mergers, acquisitions, and a variety of dubious financial schemes.[12]

However, this interpretation loses a considerable amount of its authority when we widen the lens of analysis to view the situation from a national perspective. It is a fundamental mistake to focus narrowly on London because the railroad created an increasingly unified national market in the second half of the nineteenth century. If the managers of the city's breweries were slow to meet shifts in consumer demand, other beer makers were poised to rush in and fill the gap. To a large extent, the business history of the industry is a tale of two cities: of Burton-upon-Trent and the rise of its pale ale brewers, and of London and the fall of the porter makers. "Shifts ... in taste 130 to 150 years ago are now difficult to pinpoint with accuracy," an expert suggests cautiously, "but the evidence suggests that mild and then pale ales made increasing inroads into the traditional porter market."[13] The statistics of Burton's mushroomlike rise over the next thirty years, from nine breweries making 2.5 million gallons (11.36 million liters) to twenty-six making 88.5 million gallons (402.3 million liters), is perhaps the best indication that consumers were turning away from dark porters and toward lighter beers.

Like the German lagers in the United States and on the continent, the unique light ale of provincial producers like Bass, Allsopp, and Worthington owed its spectacular success to the coming of the railroad. Beginning in 1839, the railroads revolutionized the distribution of this highly perishable commodity, allowing the Burton brewers to invade the porter makers' previously safe and lucrative market with a distinctly different, high-quality product at a reasonable, albeit premium, price. The new transportation link to London cut travel time to a half-day from the week that had been required for the journey by canal, and it reduced shipping costs by 75 percent. Equally important, the railroad effectively put an end to the adulteration of beer: the bargemen had gotten into the habit of regularly drinking substantial portions of their cargo along the way and refilling the ravished containers with canal water.[14]

The pale ale makers of Burton furnish an important contrast to London's conservative business culture. The link between the Burton brewers' support of science and the type of beer they produced was not coincidental. The light, clear nature of their ale created a need for higher standards of quality control, especially as glassware came into common use. They began hiring chemists in the 1840s also because they did not know that the problem of bad beer was being caused by the canal workers.

A business culture more receptive to science was reinforced by the competitive market strategy of the Burton brewers, who concentrated on building consumer loyalty to their brand names by selling their products in the so-called free houses, which were not tied to specific brewers, rather than diverting profits into buying a chain of retail outlets. For the Burton brewers, as for their American counterparts, the search for a consistent standard of taste became the linchpin of business success.

Yet even here the members of the Bacterium Club had to overcome the company directors' deeply rooted opposition to scientific expertise and technological innovation, a hostility that must be attributed to national cultural and business orientations. Horace Brown contended that a staggering proportion of the ale made by traditional methods went bad after it was shipped from the brewery even without the intervention of the bargemen. He believed that this spoilage was the single most important reason for the directors' acquiescence to the involvement of the chemist and, eventually, to the presence of his laboratory. Initially working at home, Brown conducted experiments that disproved the customary wisdom that atmospheric electricity and occult "vital forces" were to blame for bad beer. But the established array of chemical tests failed to reveal the causes of the problem.

In frustration, Brown turned to the microscope. "The immediate effect," he reported, "was that of a ray of light piercing the darkness and illuminating a new path into the unknown." Embracing Pasteur's science, he began making solid contributions that not only reduced spoilage but increased profits. He characterized the ensuing decades of the 1870s and 1880s as the "halcyon days" of the Burton breweries. Yet he remained painfully aware of just how exceptional they were within the larger context of England's business community.[15]

From a more balanced, national perspective, then, a mixed picture of the British brewing industry emerges of both innovation and conservatism in the reception of Pasteur's science. While the views of Gourvish and Wilson are overdrawn, there is some truth to their portrait of London's influential role in shaping a national business culture. Equally important, however, was that a parallel adherence to tradition among the working classes also sustained a vibrant popular culture. Their loyalty to local brewers and regional tastes acted as a buffer to protect against the oligopolistic strategies of the nation's largest beer makers. Moreover, the central role of the pub in the social, economic, and recreational life of the people ensured that the industry would continue to enjoy a healthy stream of revenue and an opportunity to make a profit.

Yet popular culture was not static; it found expression in changing patterns of drinking habits and taste preferences. Beer makers such as those in Burton, Dublin, Manchester, and other provincial centers who proved most responsive to these shifting consumer trends were rewarded with success.[16] The causal links between the success of these firms and their leadership in adopting Pasteur's science are significant. The technological implications of the Frenchman's work helped them meet consumer demand for products that met the ideal of consistent high quality. In the final analysis, then, the dynamic interaction of producer and consumer in the British brewing industry presents a complex, albeit not atypical, case study of business history.

The British Invasion of Chicago

A comparative perspective on the British and American brewing industries sheds additional new light on the social construction of science and technology. Businessmen and their culture can be regarded as one distinct group of actors in a more inclusive concept of society. The dogged resistance to science by London's big firms is instructive in this regard. These industrial leaders show how consumer desires can be deflected, even derailed by a determined oligopoly or monopoly. Since beer was a basic staple of working-class diets—in fact, the single largest expenditure in their food budget—the brewers could more or less force the masses to take whatever was offered to them.

The London business leaders' strategy of gaining control over the places of consumption, the public houses, further solidified their grip on this captive market. Within the craft-based tradition, moreover, the large-scale porter and ale makers were able to reach higher standards of cleanliness and deliver a perishable commodity at an acceptable level of quality with greater consistency than private and on-site publican brewers. In a limited sense, then, the big breweries were able to satisfy the demands of consumers for standardized, brand-name products better than their smaller competitors. Even Pasteur had to acknowledge what had been achieved with customary modes of production in London's largest enterprises. "When we review the operations of the brewer's art," he admitted, "we are surprised by the comparative perfection to which that art has been brought by the laborious experience of years, and the more so when we consider that, as regards the question of the diseases of beer, the brewer has never been guided by any such rigorous principles as those which we have explained in this work."[17]

Nonetheless, the power of popular taste should not be underestimated. In a period of acute social tension, the definition and protection of cultural identity became one of the most important manifestations of class formation. The advent of middle-class humanitarianism turned the pubs into one of the pivotal social battlegrounds of the Victorian Era. Their working-class patrons rallied against the attacks of the moral crusaders and mounted a tenacious defense. They guarded the sanctity of these semipublic spaces and, perhaps, everything connected to them, including their customary types of drinks: dark porters and strong ales. In the first twenty years following the completion of the rail connection between Burton and London in 1839, the slightly more expensive pale ale became fashionable among the city's more affluent beer drinkers. It "looked good—unlike the somewhat murky porter—in the new glassware which was everywhere replacing the old pewter drinking vessels," Wilson remarks. "Burton ales became increasingly the accepted drink of the Victorian middle and skilled artisan classes."

This choice may have further reinforced the loyalty of the working classes to their traditional brews. During the next twenty years, however, economies of scale, shrinking transportation costs, and reduced spoilage allowed the Burton brewers to offer attractive wholesale discounts that significantly narrowed marginal differentials in price. The tremendous success enjoyed by these beer makers as well as by Guinness during this period largely resulted from an irreversible shift in the preferences of the masses of working people for brand names associated with a consistent standard of high quality. After 1880, the craft-based porter brewers faced stagnation and decline in the face of this change in popular taste toward the superior products of their more science-based competitors.[18]

In comparative context, the business culture of the British brewing industry was tradition-bound when measured against its counterparts in Germany and the United States. In these countries, scientific brewing gained virtual cult status, preparing its leaders to meet the unprecedented challenges of an emerging consumer society. The idealization of science and technology fostered adaptivity and improvement, a spirit of innovation readily in tune with the changing demands of the marketplace. In the case of the United States the sense of confidence gained from this belief in the power of science and technology helped the industry formulate ingenious business strategies. It broadened the appeal of the breweries' products while making them more socially acceptable at the same time.

Chicago offers a useful vantage point from which to examine the transformation of the American brewing industry. The city's surging immigrant population and its central location as the nation's transportation hub made it a prime target for nearby brewers in slower-growing Milwaukee, Cincinnati, and St. Louis. Beer makers in Milwaukee, like Fred Pabst and Joseph Schlitz, were especially alert to take advantage of the sudden opening created by the great fire of 1871 to get a permanent foothold in Chicago. Less than a hundred miles away, they quickly established commercial beachheads: semi-autonomous distribution centers complete with their own icehouses, stables, and local sales forces. Others, such as St. Louis's Anheuser-Busch soon followed, making Chicago one of the most competitive marketplaces for the loyalty of beer drinkers in the United States.[19]

In 1889, a significant new player entered Chicago's already crowded brewing industry, the British syndicates. These investment vehicles sought to buy up the city's breweries and saloons and consolidate them into the same kind of oligopoly that had been established in London. England's large breweries had already been capitalized into common stocks, although management remained within a closed circle of personal and family relations. Now the syndicates publicly offered shares in the American ventures on the basis of the expectation of big dividends from the highly profitable Chicago wholesale price of eight dollars per barrel and a tax loophole on overseas earnings. Chicago Brewers, Limited, sold £400,000 worth of stock and bought two companies with annual sales of 206,000 barrels (24.174 million liters) and the capacity to make 315,000 barrels (36.96 million liters).

Over the next three years of frenzied acquisitions at inflated prices, the syndicates gained control of many of the city's largest brewing and malting enterprises. In 1890, they would pay the princely sum of three million dollars for Peter Schoenhofen's business. They would also buy up the city's biggest brewery, Conrad Seipp, and its biggest maltster, L. C. Huck. But after spending almost twelve million pounds, they still only commanded just over half of the city's output. Their market share was actually far less because extralocal brewers such as Pabst and Anheuser-Busch intensified their sales campaigns, and new beer makers joined the contest for consumer loyalties.

Facing stiff competition, the syndicates triggered a beer war that cut wholesale prices to less than half of the customary amount. While the consolidations achieved some savings, they did little to alleviate the overcapacity of either the syndicates' own plants or those of their rivals. As the anticipated profits vanished in the price war, the heavy burden of debt and dividend payments began to sink the British ventures. In desperation, they applied the tied house strategy, dropping another six million dollars for saloon properties. But American competitors again stymied any gains, matching this move simply by opening more neighborhood bars, beer gardens, and meeting halls. Unlike Boston and some other cities, Chicago had no limit on the number of liquor licenses. With the coming of the World's Columbian Exposition in 1893, for example, it issued seven hundred new saloon permits, bringing the total to over four thousand. The national depression that followed the fair's temporary uptick in local beer sales continued to erode the value of the syndicates' common stocks, sending some of them into bankruptcy. Final defeat in the beer war came in 1899, when the British courts declared the tax break on overseas profits illegal.[20]

The failure of the British invasion of Chicago reflected the emergence of not only a more openly competitive industry, but also more highly adaptive producers and consumers. Both contributed to a fluid social construction of technology that allowed the ready filling of new market niches and accommodation of changing lifestyles. Below, a case study of one large and one small brewery illustrates the ways in which scientific brewing offered producers a flexible array of technological tools with which to meet the shifting exigencies of the marketplace. A look at the rapid growth in demand for bottled beer shows how consumers shaped production techniques and work routines inside the factory.

The Brands were one of Chicago's most successful brewer families. Led by forty-eighter Michael Brand, it had been one of the first on the North Side to rebuild on the ruins of the old after the October 1871 fire. Six years later, father, nephew, and three sons moved the business from the Water Tower area to a spacious thirty-acre property along the North Branch of the Chicago River. The new Lion Brewery with a capacity of one hundred thousand barrels (11.74 million liters), included tenements for workers and featured an artesian well that fed an artificial pond where thirty tons of ice could be harvested in a day.

Reflecting the rapid pace of technological change, the Brands installed a refrigeration machine in 1883, about six years after this revolutionary innovation was first tested in Chicago. In 1889, they again took the lead by selling their booming business to the British-owned United States Brewing Company during the first great wave of syndicate buyouts. Michael retired, and his nephew Rudolph became an officer of the besieged new firm. "The trouble with the brewing situation," Rudolph complained in the midst of the beer war, "is that the Chicago breweries have a capacity of about 9,000,000 [barrels] and a market for only 2,800,000."[21]

Nonetheless, Michael's sons poured some of the family's profits into yet another brewery venture next door to the old one, on ten acres of land they had not sold to the syndicate. In 1898, they hired the renowned architect Louis Lehle to supervise the construction of the new facility. By now, he was designing standardized plants that had equipment installed with an initial capacity of one hundred thousand barrels a year and space alongside for a second, parallel production line. By the turn of the century, the principles of scientific brewing had led to a general consensus on proper methods of production and the machinery needed to achieve its ideals of high quality and consistent taste.

The Brands, of course, were not the only Chicago brewers to accept inflated buyout offers from the British syndicates then turn around to use some of this money to compete against them. In fact, some local venture capitalists with no experience in making beer hired experts like Lehle to erect breweries in anticipation of being bought out by foreign investors. On the basis of Pasteur's science, the industry had created an elaborate infrastructure of architectural and engineering firms, brewer schools, and so on that made the establishment of a London-style oligopoly virtually impossible.[22]

Science and technology remained a flexible tool that could serve a variety of different purposes even in small enterprises. In 1883, Joseph Junk, another German immigrant, built a small brewery that produced a modest 5,500 barrels (442,900 liters) during its first year of operation. When he died four years later, his wife, Magdalena, took over, becoming the only woman brewer in Chicago. She must have been successful because she decided to expand in the midst of the British invasion. In 1890, she built a new boiler house and installed a refrigeration machine, which helped to bring annual sales up to nearly 25,800 barrels (3.03 million liters).

The Junks had kept their initial investment costs relatively low by avoiding both the high prices and the potentially fatal risks involved in installing experimental machinery like refrigerators. Instead, they had taken advantage of the high level of technological efficiency that had already been achieved in the natural ice business. By the 1880s, a sophisticated system of harvesting tools and steam-driven equipment supplemented men and horses in gathering, transporting, and storing the heavy, perishable commodity and delivering it to urban markets.

The Junks let industry leaders like the Brands absorb the costs of making early improvements to their breweries' machinery. By the end of the decade, refrigerator manufacturers and other equipment makers could offer reliable, reasonably priced units that were downsized to a scale suitable for a small brewery like the Junks'. During the 1890s, Magdalena added a four-story cold storage facility and doubled the brewery's output. She and local brewers like her made choices among technological alternatives. This allowed their enterprises to find profitable economic niches in a highly competitive market.[23]

By 1890, the ingenuity of American brewers in adapting the technological innovations and scientific discoveries of the past generation had enlarged the range of ways to make beer. In some cases, improvements in one area were counterbalanced by losses in others. Energy-intensive mechanization, for example, helped brewers cut labor costs and produce large quantities of a consistent product for sale in a national market. Yet these savings were offset by the added expense of shipping and marketing. In other cases, technological innovation gave a clear advantage to either national or local brewers.

On the one hand, new inventions such as mechanical refrigeration helped big brewers like Michael Brand and Peter Schoenhofen make a standardized, brand-name product that could reach distant markets and retain its quality. On the other hand, the ability to cultivate pure yeast spread quickly throughout the industry, from top to bottom. This helped small brewers who could not afford full-scale mechanization but could easily introduce the use of pure yeast to eliminate the most common cause of bad beer—the kind that could ruin reputations and put a local brewer out of business. In this case, advanced methods probably most helped small, local brewers like the Junks, keeping them competitive by giving them a low-cost way to make a large gain in quality control. Small brewers, moreover, benefited from the industry's growing array of professional support services, which aided them in accessing the full range of available alternatives.[24] The final result of the revolutionary change of technology set off by Pasteur's science was that the industry became overbuilt. Its excess capacity began to outpace even the rapid rise in Chicago's population and its thirst for beer.

The Repackaging of Mass Consumption

In the 1890s, America began to undergo a sea change as it passed from the Victorian Era to the Machine Age. The emergence of an urban industrial society was painful, especially for the guardians of morality who led strident nativist movements against vice and in favor of racial segregation and prohibition. The saloon—the classic site of male, working-class anarchism—became one of their favorite targets. Suburbanization, the rise of new commercial amusements like the movies, and the growing strength of moral crusades against public disorder sapped the vitality out of these neighborhood bastions of the workingman.

Nevertheless, the saloons' loyal patrons rallied successfully to defeat the increasingly well-orchestrated efforts of the temperance reformers to shut the establishments down. In the heated atmosphere of ethnocultural politics leading up to World War I, defending the right to a drink brought the immigrants of Chicago and other cities together in a political coalition for the first time. At the same time, the brewers saw privatization of beer drinking as a way to distance themselves from the mounting problems and sinking image of the saloonkeeper. They responded by refocusing their sales efforts toward the home market.[25]

In the 1890s, scientific brewing helped the industry respond to changes in the lifestyles and taste preferences of urban society. Faced with cutthroat competition, Chicago brewers turned in new directions, from the public saloon to the private home. Bottled beer offered them a way to take advantage of the redefinition of social relationships between the sexes and the classes that was occurring in the emerging urban culture. Although this historic change in popular culture was most apparent in the new types of nightspots and other commercialized amusements springing up in the city, its roots were seated deep within the private realm of domestic life.[26]

If brewers could penetrate the home market, they could potentially double their customer base. The saloon remained an exclusive male preserve, and many of the newer semipublic amusement venues were still regarded as indecent places for respectable women. Packaging beer in bottles for use in a private setting seemed to offer a convenient and socially acceptable alternative. For the more affluent middle class, home delivery service was a common feature of daily life. The already familiar beer wagon blended in with the horse-drawn trucks of the grocer, butcher, iceman, and other fresh food vendors that plied the paved residential streets and alleys of the well-to-do. Advertising strategies like Pabst's "Blue Ribbon" label and his purchase of luxury hotels and restaurants sought to attract the attention of this of this new, upscale, family-oriented customer.[27]

True enough, putting beer in bottles was not a new idea, but it remained a very minor part of the business until the cultural crisis of the 1890s. As early as the 1850s, for instance, Chicago had two bottlers, whose enterprises were devoted exclusively to repackaging other brewers' products. They would import barrels of beer from Pittsburgh and other eastern places and simply use a rubber tube to drain the liquid into pint-sized glass containers. To seal the bottles they used hand labor to jam in a cork, secure it with a wire cap, and cover it with a foil wrapper, giving the finished package an appearance similar to today's champagne bottles. But the beer's quality had suffered greatly because of the vicissitudes of being shipped in barrels for long distances, the loss of carbonation, and the high probability of contamination during filling. Beer bottled in this way was for immediate consumption.[28]

Between 1870 and 1890, American brewers made use of Pasteur's science to overcome these problems and achieve his goal of engineering a standardized product that could reach distant markets. The most significant advance in this direction was made early in the period by Adolphus Busch of St. Louis. He was the son-in-law of the owner of a typical local firm, the E. Anheuser Brewing Company. In 1873, only two years after the French scientist published his first preliminary report on fermentation, Busch became possibly the first American to pasteurize beer inside sealed bottles. Because St. Louis was strategically located at the southernmost border of beer making, and the weather was hot and the cost of ice high below this imaginary line, Busch had a strong incentive to experiment with new methods of packaging the perishable drink. The South represented a huge untapped market for beer, which he sought to supply by putting the drink into bottles.

The ascendancy of the soon-to-be-renamed Anheuser-Busch Company to the top of the industry by the end of the century is testimony to the improvement in quality achieved by heating the beer in the bottle to kill any germs inside before shipping it, especially into a torrid climate like that of the South. The company's product, the king of the brand-name bottled beers—Budweiser—also made significant inroads in the cities of the North, including Chicago, about 250 miles away.

In 1889, the great annexation expanded the area of Chicago from 36 to 196 square miles; Chicago added two hundred thousand people to become the second largest city in the country. This year marked a distinct turning point in the reorientation of the Chicago brewers toward a mass market of home consumers. In addition to the British invasion and the ensuing beer war for the saloon trade, the year saw the bringing of a huge new customer base of working- and middle-class residents under municipal jurisdiction.

State local-option laws permitted previously dry communities to keep the saloon out, but not the beer wagon. After losing a court case, even Evanston—home of the national headquarters of the Woman's Christian Temperance Union—could not stop Chicago liquor dealers from making residential deliveries. Telephones made the private enjoyment of alcoholic beverages more convenient and discreet by saving consumers the potential embarrassment of being seen in a liquor store. Bottled beer was perfectly suited to meeting the greater emphasis of urban society on a more intense domestic life in which men and women spent more time together.[29]

Advertisements for bottled beer played on these emerging cultural trends. While commercial appeals were designed in the hope of influencing behavior, they also reflected it without going too far outside currently acceptable social norms. One ad, showed a mixed group of young adults enjoying a summer picnic along a waterfront. The well-heeled couples are gathered around a table drinking from bottles that came from a wooden case prominently placed in the middle of the foreground. Another ad, for the Rheingold brand, depicts an obviously modern woman sitting behind the wheel of an automobile. In her hand is a glass of beer from a bottle positioned to the side of the seat. This ad and most others includes a telephone number for delivery service. In the 1890s, consumer demand for bottled beer went hand in hand with the revolt against Victorianism, whether in the privacy of the home or in the limelight of the new, respectable entertainment spots like Midway Gardens, designed by Frank Lloyd Wright.[30]

During the preceding decade, the volume of sales of bottled beer had remained low compared to sales of keg beer, but profit margins were high. In the case of Pabst, for example, the net gain from selling beer in bottles was two and a half times larger than from marketing it in barrels. With the beer wars intensifying in cities like Chicago to a point where profits were being squeezed out, brewers had a strong incentive to formulate new business strategies. While some tried consolidation schemes to reduce the competition; others, like Fred Pabst, took the lead in developing marketing plans based on bottled beer.

In 1890, Pabst helped shepherd a bill through Congress that would allow brewers to use a pipeline to pump beer directly from storage vats to bottling plants. To ensure the full collection of excise taxes, federal law had previously required that the beer be put in barrels first, even if they were only being carried across the street. The pipeline act still compelled brewers to maintain completely separate structures for brewing and bottling, but the reform meant that the beer could now remain unexposed to germs within an internally closed system until it was safely sealed inside the bottle.

At the same time the big brewers were plotting to revise the national tax laws, nature was conspiring in a paradoxical way to help the small beer makers. For two winters in a row, 1888–1889 and 1889–1890, warm weather created an unprecedented ice famine. As a result, according to the standard history of the subject, by 1891 "nearly every brewery was equipped with refrigerating machines. It was claimed that more were employed by brewers at that time than by all other users."[31] Being forced to buy into an expensive energy system may not appear to have been a blessing to small brewers like Magdalena Junk, but converting to this key technology represented an essential preliminary step in gaining a competitive edge over their bigger, national rivals.

The ice famine occurred at an opportune time when refrigerator manufacturers were well prepared to meet the emergency. For a quarter-century they had been accumulating valuable experience, mostly inside the brewery. Magdalena Junk and other local brewers could choose among several successful designs and sizes that offered well-tested and fuel-efficient service. After installing these steam-powered machines, they began to enjoy immediate savings in the cost of labor because they no longer needed someone to handle the natural ice; they would save on future outlays as well because they would not need to build the much stronger and larger storage houses that could support the weight of the ice at the top where it had proven most effective.[32]

But even more important, perhaps, access to refrigeration technology set the stage for the small brewers to enter the bottling business for themselves. According to a *Handy Book* for brewers, bottling involved at least ten steps, from soaking the bottles to applying their labels and wrappers. While the guidebook advised managers to position workstations no more than an arm's length apart to create a human assembly line, it also listed equipment manufacturers that could mechanized the entire operation. One machine, for example, could handle forty bottles a minute, or twenty-four thousand in a ten-hour day; a bigger one could fill twice as many. "One of most remarkable of modern machines," another trade publication boasted, "is a combination of a corking, capping, and wiring machine performing the entire work mentioned automatically, and saving a great amount of time and labor."

Moreover, rapid improvements in electrical technologies, especially small motors, gave brewers even more flexibility to combine traditional and innovative methods. Access to this wide range of choice helped local brewers undercut the national companies, which had to spend more on administrative overhead, advertising, and transportation. "Strange as it may appear, and contrary to the established rules of manufacturing," the *Handy Book* exclaimed, costs "are usually greater in large bottleries than in small ones."[33]

The response of the American brewing industry to consumer demand for beer in bottles provides an ironic, final example of the complexity of the social construction of technology. The very success of its efforts to mechanize the bottling plant helped to shut its doors. Repackaging alcohol in a way that appealed to middle-class women seemed to pose a powerful new threat of moral decline, especially to the prohibitionists who were already convinced that drinking was America's greatest social evil.

To be sure, women in working-class neighborhoods had long been accustomed to drinking beer with their lunches and suppers. It was common for them to get a beer pail filled at the back door of the corner saloon or to send one of the children to fetch it. But these traditions came under severe attack after the publication of William T. Stead's scathing indictment, *If Christ Came to Chicago*. The evangelical tract by the English visitor to the world's fair of 1893 galvanized the city's guardians of morality. They began to mobilize tremendous political and social pressure behind demands for the complete segregation of women and children from the corrupting, evil influences of the saloon. Led by women, this reform movement to protect families gained additional momentum by linking alcohol abuse to the big brewers and their conspicuous sales promotions. Thus the industry's new marketing campaigns, which boosted the consumption of beer to record levels, ultimately backfired when the prohibitionists achieved their goal during World War I.[34]

In the American brewing industry, then, technology was largely shaped by consumers, their taste preferences, and the cultural context that defined society's attitudes toward drinking alcoholic beverages. At most, innovation gave short-term, marginal advantages to national over local firms, and to bigger over smaller ones—or vice versa. But these gains proved temporary and canceled each other out over time as beer makers adjusted and adapted to new conditions. Even the rapid diffusion of mechanical refrigeration did not lead to an inexorable decline of the natural ice industry. On the contrary, the two energy systems reinforced each other, creating a synergetic relationship. The growing availability of bottled beer and other fresh foods fueled demand for home iceboxes, which in turn created a mass consumer market for the ice business. In 1910, the trade association of the industry confirmed that

> every family within the range of a delivery wagon now has its own
> ice-box, and can keep beer at a palatable temperature, and when once
> a family tries the experiment, and finds how pleasant and harmless

it is, the habit is almost sure to become fixed. Curiously enough, the development of the bottled beer business is decreasing the "growler" or bucket trade. The workingman's family in the cities is getting into the custom of keeping bottled beer on the premises, instead of sending to the nearest saloon for a pail of draught beer at meal times.[35]

In this and other cases examined here, technology was a flexible tool in the hands of the American brewers, who shaped it in a diverse variety of ways to meet the current demands of the market. In response to a changing culture, the brewing industry turned toward bottled beer and direct sales to consumers. The social reconstruction of technology in this case meant the birth a virtually new industry.

The bottling plant was a precursor to Henry Ford's energy-intensive mass-production assembly line. As direct sales became more important, brewers adjusted by altering basic recipes, installing special carbonation machines, standardizing the bottle cap, and refocusing advertising campaigns to highlight the advantages of drinking in more intimate, private settings. Even the breweries' horses had to adapt to new routines as their drivers began making unexpected stops at private residences to deliver cases of bottled beer. In 1914, the industry in the United States enjoyed another record year of sales, 60.8 million barrels (7.13 billion liters), but it would prove to be its last. The wartime emergency and a misguided patriotism that turned against everything German finally gave the upper hand to the moral crusaders in their long battle for prohibition. Over the next five years, they succeeded in closing not only the saloons but the breweries as well. Ultimately no amount of technological innovation could save them from a society determined to outlaw the drinking habits of its people.[36]

The Rebirth of Scientific Brewing in England

In 1894, Horace Brown and other British pioneers of scientific brewing established the Institute of Brewing in England. The importance of this national association cannot be overestimated. The Institute acted like a wedge, opening up the industry to the latest scientific, technical, and managerial innovations. Besides creating a forum for collaboration among businessmen, scientists, and engineers, it published a journal that made the fast-paced flow of international information on brewing readily accessible for the first time. In both obvious and subtle ways, the association helped not only to professionalize the role of the chemist in the brewery but also to legitimize the chemist's position of authority in the organizational structure of these increasingly large and complex firms.

The rapid transformation of the industry in the two decades following the founding of the Institute sheds light on the persistence of traditional practices during the previous period, when the Bacterium Club was stilted and unable to grow into a national association. Without the support of industry leaders in London, repeated efforts to establish scientific brewing had been stillborn for a quarter-century. In the 1890s, for example, when regional branches of the Institute helped spur the inauguration of schools of brewing in Manchester and Birmingham, London's breweries refused to hire their graduates, dooming these projects. Similar initiatives to start a training program in the city a few years later also failed because the industry's business leaders rejected proposals calling for the industry to contribute a relatively modest sum of thirty thousand pounds to get a school started.[37]

But the directors of the big breweries could not completely deny the seriousness of the challenges facing the industry; rather, they were forced to become more receptive to new ideas. England's prohibitionist movement was delivering politically damaging blows in the form of higher taxes and restrictive licensing regulations. Moreover, the working classes were dispensing their own kind of economic punishment by drinking less beer and by changing their social habits and spending less time at the pub. In the resulting tightening of the market, brewers confronted more intense pressures of competition to satisfy the consumers' desire for consistent, high-quality products of the type each one of them preferred.[38]

Reflecting these demanding conditions, the papers delivered to the various regional branches of the Institute underscored two major interrelated themes in the period leading up to World War I. First, by the turn of the century, lighter, less alcoholic ales had gradually replaced porters as the most popular preference of the working classes. A general consensus existed among professionals at these trade association meetings in favor of customary pale ales with their delicate secondary fermentation in the cask. Yet they had to admit that the public had a different taste preference, for bottled beer. "A certain class of the public in the large towns," one member reported, "has now learned to like this hastily prepared carbonated beer; and there was an enormous trade to be done in it." He explained about bottled beers:

> Notwithstanding their lack of a certain amount of character, the chilled and filtered bottled beers produced have met with such appreciation as to induce so many brewers to adopt one or other of the various systems hitherto in operation, [which] surely proves the existence of a great and increasing demand for a lighter, cleaner, and more easily digestible beer than the ordinary running ales or the quickly-produced stock beers

hitherto offered to the public. . . . The fact that this bottled beer with all its drawbacks is in such demand, should surely convince brewers that improved methods are essential if the trade in "draught beer" is to be maintained.[39]

Other papers confirm that market pressures presented the industry with the challenge of meeting consumer demand for lagerlike ales. "The public will no longer tolerate beer which is not perfectly bright," a typical paper argued, "and having found it possible to get consistently bright beers in good condition, they will insist upon having them either in cask or in bottle. I believe that the unreliability of draught beers in respect to condition and brilliancy has been a chief factor in stimulating the demand for bottled stuff, a fact which so many breweries deplore in making up their balance sheets."[40]

Meeting this shift in consumer demand set the agenda of the second major theme of the Institute's papers, adopting modern methods of production while preserving traditional quality of taste, that unique character of British ale. Horace Brown cogently summed up the goal in 1897 when he declared that "the combination of the two systems, limited maturation, and cold storage with its attendant filtration and carbonation, give a beer which, if consumed within a reasonable time, is as near perfection as anything can be." In practical terms, this meant importing American and German machinery and training programs. In the years that followed, many reports describe the ways in which the British brewing industry was engaged in a process of technological catch-up in a race to satisfy the taste preferences of their customers.

Pilgrimages by Institute members to the breweries of the United States and northern European countries became common. By the late 1890s, an intense use of energy in the form of refrigeration had been incorporated by these nations' brewers. Refrigeration was adapted not only to fermentation but also to virtually every other stage of production, from malting to yeast purification and storage, to aging and finishing, and finally to packaging in both barrels and bottles. "As a result of my observations in America," English brewer Hugh Abbot stated, "I am convinced that the bottling methods there in vogue are superior to our own, though it is questionable whether the brewing methods there obtaining are anything like as good as ours. The case may be stated, however, that in most American breweries the beer varies only with the quality of the original product," that is, the original ingredients. In other words, the Americans' use of science and technology allowed them to make a beverage that met the ideal of a consistent standard of quality.[41]

The records of the Institute leave no doubt that before the catastrophic interruption of the World War Britain's beer makers made great strides toward this goal. In this case, the social construction of technology meant adapting modern methods of production to the particular demands of customers for light ales with traditional tastes. Yet the existence of the tied houses that put a virtual stranglehold on the consumption side of the equation cautions against taking this interpretation of technological change too far. Consumers can exert a dominant influence on the forces of production only when consumers have freedom of choice, as in Chicago, where the brewers were in a wide open competition for loyal customers.

More monopolistic conditions limit the power of buyers to direct the course of technological change. Sellers can assume a take-it-or-leave-it posture. Only when enough consumers decide to spend their money elsewhere can they collectively regain some measure of influence in shaping industrial technology. The striking differences between the United States and the United Kingdom presented here underscore the complexity of the interplay among diverse groups of actors in the social construction of science and technology.

Conclusions: Energy, Environment, and the City

In broader perspective, the advent of assembly-line brewing raises difficult and important questions about the technological construction of society. Like Andy Warhol's paintings of soup cans, images of standardized bottles of pasteurized beer clattering along endlessly in sterile packaging plants pointed toward the homogenization and packaging of society itself. When coupled with modern advertising and new forms of mass media, technology began to influence consumer culture in unprecedented ways. Connections between the natural world and the manufactured product become more and more obscure. Ask a city child were food comes from and the most likely answer will be, "The supermarket." Knowledge that most food grows on farms has been lost as the commodification of nature recasts even basic organic substances like fruits and vegetables as shrink-wrapped, genetically cloned products.

The industrialization of beer making was typical of the transformation of production methods during the second half of the nineteenth century. Sometimes called the Second Industrial Revolution, the era was characterized by ever greater use of mechanized tools, energy from fossil fuels, and scientific and technical experts. As we have seen in this case study, not only did the number of barrels of beer increase by leaps and bounds, but so did the amount of coal burned to produce each one.

The more intense use of energy meant more air pollution. The exponential rise in Chicago's coal consumption gives a rough index of the scale of this problem (see fig. 6.3). Although each smokestack and residential chimney added only a relatively small amount of smoke and gases to the air, the cumulative effect was a fundamental ecological change in the atmosphere and climate enveloping the city. Breweries were joined by other energy-intensive establishments, including steel mills, chemical plants, oil refineries, and electric utility companies, as technological and economic leaders during the period leading up to the World War.

Together these establishments expanded the spatial dimensions of urban areas, new and old, to metropolitan size. The loss of handworkers' employment to the machine was more than offset by increases in the number of new jobs, making industrial cities magnets drawing a mass migration from the countryside. More people generated more liquid and solid wastes as well as greater amounts of bad air.

While the built environment and population density of the conurbation of Manchester continued to increase at a steady pace, Chicago grew faster. Roughly doubling in population every ten years to reach well over a million people by the time of the World's Columbian Exposition of 1893, Chicago became the shock city of the western hemisphere.

One out of five Americans visited the fair, and an equivalent share of European elite society also came to see Chicago. What they found was not all that different from Manchester in its moment as a shock city, except everything was bigger. The buildings were taller, the hotels were grander, the factories had ballooned into "veritable cities," the slums seemed to stretch forever, and the streets were dirtier, noisier, more chaotic. What was less evident to outside observers was the commensurately greater scale of the city's pollution problems. Most visitors traveled by boat or train or rode on the new elevated line along State Street from downtown to reach the fairgrounds just south of Hyde Park, along the lakefront.

Significantly, the intrusive steel structure of the elevated line was used to reinforce the invisible boundary between the respectable and the dangerous classes. Like most tourists, its passengers traveling to the fair avoided the sprawling neighborhoods of working people because they were deemed unsafe. Even the adventuresome who went to the stockyards were guided through a highly insulated and sanitized showcase, a make-believe disassembly line. Only a few stayed long enough to grasp the profound implications of the environmental transformation of the industrial city as it grew to metropolitan proportions.[42]

Nonetheless, the swelling size of industrial ecologies like those of Chicago and Manchester caused a significant deterioration of the quality of daily life. In some cases, quantitative gains brought higher levels of pollution. In Chicago, for example, population increases meant more sewage pouring into the lake, adding not only to the risk of epidemics but also to the number of victims in each one. In a similar way, the remarkable rise in energy use enlarged and thickened the shroud of bad air engulfing urban areas. Hyde Park was no longer safe from black soot and toxic gases, which rained down on the community after being carried from upwind smokestacks stretching along the southwest industrial corridor of the Chicago River.

In other cases, the aging of central-city dwellings and factories made the environmental conditions of everyday life worst of all. In Manchester, for example, the dilapidated, fifty-year-old houses that Engels had seen in the 1840s were now twice as old. Many of these jerry-built structures had suffered water damage from the floods that made them unfit for human habitation even by contemporary standards of decency. As one resident recalled, "The damp got into the walls and foundations of the houses, and for years hardly a dry or healthy habitation could be found where the waters had full play. Sickness and a high death-rate were of course only a natural consequence, and newcomers avoided Lower Broughton almost like a plague spot."[43] In a similar way, the older some of the manufacturing equipment and steam boilers in the factories became, the more waste by-products they dumped into the environment. Chicago also had its decrepit housing stock and obsolete factories. True enough, better dwellings and more efficient power plants were being built, but they all added their share of pollution to the already overburdened industrial ecologies.

For most Victorians, the paradox of progress posed so succinctly by Tocqueville represented an impossible dilemma, an enigma with no solution. Yet his juxtaposition of material wealth and environmental impoverishment contained a critique of industrial capitalism that could inspire reform. During the nineteenth century, such a reaction against the commodification of nature took shape in a cultural movement called Romanticism. In England, artistic giants including William Wordsworth, John Ruskin, and William Morris condemned the city as a technological monster, but they equally abhorred the idea of political activism. Most members of the middle classes who were willing to get involved in municipal reform believed that immoral behavior was the root cause of slum conditions. Only under the pressure of recurring emergencies such as epidemics and floods were these moral suasionists pushed into taking concrete environmental control measures. The Victorians' most significant response to the development of the industrial city was social and geographical segregation into separate spheres by class and ethnicity/religion.

Toward the end of the century, however, new types of urban reformers who promoted new concepts of reform emerged. Calling themselves Progressives, they espoused direct action and a complete makeover of the industrial city into the city beautiful. Reversing cause and effect, they believed that slum conditions were the root cause of immoral behavior. Rebuilding the physical environment of the cities, they asserted, would create corresponding gains in social uplift and moral order.

The American novel *Looking Backward* was emblematic of the shift from moral to social environmentalism. Published in 1889, this book about a utopian city of the future was an instant best-seller. Reading it became the "aha" experience for a generation coming of age; it provided a roadmap for reform activism and urban planning. Just four years later, Daniel Burnham's White City area of the Columbian Exposition appeared to turn this literary fantasy into tangible reality. Its beauty, order, and efficiency embodied the idealistic promise of the coming city of the Machine Age.[44]

Technology had profound impact on organization of space both within the city & more rural areas. That said, culture (specifically attitudes toward science) mediated the impact of technology in that it determined how new science sources of energy were adopted. But still not clear to me how deterministic this process was. Culture might impede adoption of technologies, but is it only a matter of time before they're adopted & have subsequent impact on organization of society & space?

PART TWO

Reforming
Industrial Cities

CHAPTER EIGHT

Introduction

Public Health and the Politics of Environmental Reform

Introduction: From Hygeia to the Garden City

At the 1875 meeting of the Social Science Association in Brighton, Dr. Benjamin Ward Richardson presented his version of utopia, "Hygeia: A City of Health." A proponent of Edwin Chadwick's sanitary idea, Richardson envisaged its gospel of cleanliness in elaborate detail. Richardson's plans specified everything from the architectural design and interior décor of the middle-class home to the minimum width of residential streets. The physician was an exemplar of a new breed of experts, what Nancy Tomes calls "domestic sanitarians." During the 1870s and 1880s, some of them would medicalize the house by drawing organic analogs of health between human bodies and the physical structures they lived in. These "building doctors" created a "private side of public health" that tended to erase lines not only between the inside and the outside of physical spaces but also between the urban reform ideologies of moral and social environmentalism. Inspiring lively debate on both sides of the Atlantic, Dr. Richardson's utopian plans became one of the origins of urban progressivism. "Hygeia" would help municipal reformers envision the slums in novel ways as a problem of bad housing and poor neighborhood design rather than of depraved people.[1]

A quarter-century later, this evolving civic discourse on the metaphorical relationship of body, house, and environment would reach a climax with the publication of Ebenezer Howard's equally visionary "Garden Cities of

Tomorrow." A member of the London Radicals, Howard would go beyond previous spatial concepts of town planning to propose a regional-scale "Social City... a group of slumless smokeless cities." Howard's emphasis on solving the problems of substandard housing and health-impairing pollution in congested central city districts was significant. It accurately reflected contemporary perceptions of the top priorities of urban reform as well as their preferred solution, suburban deconcentration. In between, Edward Bellamy's *Looking Backward* and Daniel Burnham's world's fair would solidify a widely held ideal of the city of the future around the goals of health, beauty, order, and efficiency.

The shift in spatial perspective from Richardson to Howard was full of meaning for the outcome of Progressivism. As Lewis Mumford points out, Richardson's plan put one hundred thousand people on four thousand acres, whereas Howard's contained only thirty-two thousand residents on six thousand acres. While the goals remained the same, the vision changed from an urban to a suburban ideal. The Victorians' notion of separate spheres was reformulated on much larger dimensions into a strict separation of housing from industry and commerce. In the 1890s, the advent of rapid transit, automobiles, and new energy systems held promise of turning utopian dreams into concrete reality. Encouraged by the new technology, reformers increasingly came to look upon the city as the site of a physical and social pathology of overcrowding. In contrast, the garden setting of the suburbs would allow for the reparation of individual bodies and minds while restoring the family as the central unit of society. Consider that Frank Lloyd Wright called the product of his domestic architecture "a city man's country home." By World War I, Howard's vision had become one of the cornerstones of twentieth-century urban planning.[2]

Recently, however, some historians of women in the city have recast his influential vision of the garden city into one of a confining prison of gender subordination. According to them, secret plans to subjugate women in physically isolated, gilded cages were embedded in the suburban ideals of Howard, Wright, and their apostles. Elizabeth Wilson charges that "a new anti-urban ideology developed in the nineteenth century, a central, but largely unacknowledged, aspect of which was a fear that women escaped patriarchal control in large urban centres.... What I am saying is that aside from the explicit and stated aims of doing away with slums, ill health and so on, there was a hidden (perhaps unconscious) agenda which was about the control of women." She quotes with approval H. Blake's analysis that "'the layout of the Garden City, with its clear separation between work and the home and its single family housing... reinforced trends of women's dependency on men and the cultivation of an ideal family of a working man, a dependent wife and child.'"[3]

Tomes and other historians of the domestic hygiene movement have firmly established the gendered nature of Victorian social roles and interior space in the home. Tomes shows how the turning inward of health concerns to the private household placed a disproportionate burden of responsibility on women, who fulfilled the traditional role of safeguarding both the health of the family's bodies and the cleanliness of its living quarters. In an analogous way, some spaces, such as the kitchen, children's nursery, and bathroom, became associated with female housekeeping while other parts of the house, such as the cellar, the plumbing, and the roof, were male zones. Moreover, Annmarie Adams, in her study of England's middle-class homeowners, demonstrates how the building doctors usually represented domestic spaces as female bodies. She too found that the turning inward to the private side of health had the effect of shifting the focus of civic reform away from changing destructive personal behavior and toward ameliorating unhealthy environmental conditions.

For Tomes and Adams, the immediate and widespread acceptance of germ theories among domestic sanitarians was pivotal in making the boundaries between the inside and the outside of the body, the home, and the environment seem more and more transparent. According to etiologies of disease based on miasmatic theories, physical distance from the sources of visible filth and bad smells provided security from sickness. But germ theories' invisible world of microorganisms eroded confidence that this was enough to protect the health of the family. Adams posits that "evidence from the 'inner world' of the home demonstrates that many of [John] Ruskin's 'anxieties of outer life'—the spread of infection, the rationalization of knowledge, scientific theories of sexual difference, the emancipation of women—continually invaded the late-Victorian middle-class home and were managed there by Victorian women; in this respect both the house and the housewife were vital 'part[s] of that outer world,' as Ruskin feared."[4]

In both the United States and the United Kingdom, this blurring of spatial boundaries on the quality-of-urban-life question was one of the taproots of Progressivism. It eventually spurred the formation of reform movements to clean up the central city slums and to promote, as one Manchester activist demanded in 1889: "healthy lives, healthy homes, and healthy surroundings." Tomes's insight on the tensions between the private and the public sides of health in the Victorian city also sheds light on the problem of the chronology of municipal reform between the time of Richardson and the time of Howard. On the one hand, she suggests that the turn inward toward domestic hygiene in the 1870s and 1880s resulted from frustrations in efforts to make progress beyond Chadwick's water and sewer systems. On the other hand, Tomes and others show that popular education on "house diseases" helped tilt civic debate on urban reform from a concentration on personal behavior to a focus on social environmentalism. In other words, the rediscovery of the slums in the 1890s was rooted in the domestic sanitation movement of the preceding two decades.[5]

As the subject of reform shifted from behavior to the environment, the reformers first focused on the environment within the home, so this study of environmental reform begins there. Of course, the streets remain important in this context both as the environment immediately in front of people's homes and as the primary means of moving masses of people and goods around burgeoning urban areas. Next follows a return to the waterworks and their companion, the sewerage system. In this case, germ theories led to the transfer of expert authority in the formation of public health policy from the engineers to the doctors and from the chemists to the microbiologists. Finally, the selected site for examining the air will move up and out of the brewery smokestack to encompass the entire shroud of pollution covering the metropolis. Here reformers faced their greatest challenge in the face of modern society's dependence on an ever more intensive use of energy. Rather than resolving the paradox of progress, the Progressives' suburban ideal simply gave it a different form. Metropolitan sprawl would require so many automobiles that the promised advantages of a garden environment would be nullified by bad air and highway congestion.

Bodies, Houses, and Cities

Attention to the origins of Progressivism first needs to focus on the chronological links between the concentration on domestic hygiene and that on bad housing, and between municipal housekeeping and neighborhood design. How did Victorian representations of health influence the course of urban reform during the succeeding era? What were the gender, medical, and political dimensions of the project to rebuild unsanitary residential districts and to improve the quality of life within them? What were the spatial and environmental implications of germ theories? How—if at all—did the new world of the infinitely small microorganism change perceptions of larger spaces such as metropolitan areas and regions? Moreover, what was the relationship between cleaning up the slums of the city and constructing the garden cities of suburbia?

A comparison of Manchester and Chicago provides some tentative answers to these questions (see fig. 8.1). Daniel Rodgers's *Atlantic Crossings* demonstrates

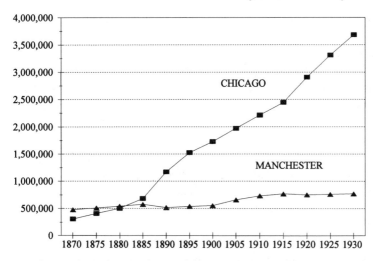

Figure 8.1. Population of Manchester and Chicago, 1870–1930
Source: Data from U.S. Bureau of the Census and Alan Kidd, *Manchester*, Town and City Histories (Keele, Staffordshire: Ryburn/Keele University Press, 1993).

the value of viewing the Progressives within a transnational context. In the English Cottonopolis, a native son, social worker Charles Rowley, led a grass-roots mobilization in the worst slum. In 1889, seven years after the founding of his Ancoats Recreation Movement, Rowley helped organize a single-issue pressure group, the Healthy Homes Society. In the American Porkopolis, Jane Addams moved that same year into the midst of the port of entry for European immigrants. Like the Mancunian, she would become a champion of environmental justice and a spearhead of reform in cleaning up the slums. Both were intimate and active members of the Arts and Crafts Movement, which had been inspired by the Romantics. Rowley and Addams also shared an optimistic faith in the ability of experts to solve contemporary problems with the powerful tools of science and technology.[6]

In spite of their many shared perspectives and values, however, the contrasts in their reform campaigns highlight major differences in the two countries' cultures of gender politics and related conflicts over the authority of experts. The social roles assigned to doctors, clergy, scientists, architects, and engineers had decisive consequences for the two Progressives' battle for municipal reform. The different reception of Pasteur's research in the U.K. and U.S. brewing industries underscores the importance of society's attitudes toward science and technology. In terms of urban public health, germ theories were rapidly disseminated on both sides of the Atlantic, but their reception in Manchester and Chicago produced very different reform outcomes.[7]

Progressives in the two cities were typical in putting housing reform at the center of their project of social uplift. To expose the roots of the Progressives' rediscovery of the slums, Nancy Tomes suggests that germ theories were pivotal in shifting perspectives on the metaphorical representation of body, house, and environment into naturalistic terms. Certainly the representation of the British city as a natural or organic system had become a standard trope by the second half of the nineteenth century. In the 1850s, Edwin Chadwick had known he could draw upon these now conventional images to build a convincing case for sanitary reform. He had reasoned that the proposed network of water and sewer pipes was just like the body's circulatory system of arteries and veins.

In the United States too, at least some reformers were envisioning city plans in domestic, bodily terms at the same time. For example, when Horace Bushnell of Hartford, Connecticut, proposed the construction of a public park, he called it the "outdoor parlor" of the city. In the gendering of the Victorian dwelling, the formal parlor was considered the face of house, the place of first and most lasting impressions. For Bushnell, a conservative Protestant minister, according to Peter Baldwin, "the park would be a feminized form of public space, a way of extending female values outside the home." For both Chadwick and Bushnell, this kind of municipal housekeeping or ordering of public space promised moral dividends because it would inspire uplifting patterns of behavior among the degraded masses.[8]

The Victorians' miasmatic theories of disease had conceived of sickness as primarily caused by the improper disposal of the body's wastes. This created a corresponding set of three circulatory systems of consumption and removal. The invisible nature of disease-causing germs had the effect of dissolving borderlines that had previously separated the body, the house, and the city into distinct physical spheres. No longer could the middle-class family count on its suburban home with its surrounding garden and wall to protect it from deadly invasion by unseen microorganisms. Now not only did poisonous bodily wastes have to be cleansed immediately from the body to stay healthy, they also had to be efficiently purged from the house and the surrounding area.

In the 1880s and 1890s, fear of sickness and death, especially of vulnerable infants, reached new levels; it became probably the single most powerful force driving the middle classes to clean up the slums. Dreadful epidemics of typhoid fever replaced cholera as the most high-profile public health menace. Popular publications on domestic hygiene sounded the alarm: germs were everywhere! They could sneak in through the water taps and the sewer pipes, they could float in on a particle of soot, and they could even hitch a ride on horseflies following delivery vans from central city stables to backyard picnic tables. Deprived of their basic senses of smell and sight in the battle against disease, the middle classes had to assume that they were at environmental risk of being in bad health. Germ theories taught the lesson that residential segregation from the "fever nests" of the slums was a false barrier against the hordes of microscopic foes permeating the city's water supply, garbage heaps, and polluted air.[9]

As their sense of the safety provided by the spatial cordon sanitaire eroded, the middle classes began refocusing concern outward from the private to the public side of health and housing reform. Their preoccupation with battling diseases in their own houses helped smooth this perceptual transition from domestic to social environmentalism. Immensely popular utopian fantasies like Edward Bellamy's *Looking Backward* also helped Ebenezer Howard and many others imagine how the city beautiful could create the good society. For young idealists like Rowley and Addams, the place to start this project in environmental and social engineering lay not in making citywide plans or building grand parkways, but in bringing the congested slums of the central city up to standards of common decency and health. The idealists played key roles in bridging the gap between the classes by organizing political activism around living and working conditions in poor residential districts. While drawing on the familiar tropes of the organic city, their reform campaigns also contained radically new concepts of social welfare and environmental justice.

Social Environmentalism, Urban Masses, and Moral Order

What was novel about the Progressive Era and what made its reform of cities different from that of the Victorian Era has been the subject of much study by academic historians and social critics. Rodgers underscores the intensification of print communications, personal contacts, and trans-Atlantic travel among urban reformers in the United States and Europe. What they discovered they had in common was deep concern about the social and environmental problems of the industrial city. They also agreed on the need to shift their emphasis from moral suasion of the individual to physical improvement of the individual's surroundings. This "positive environmentalism" represented an original turn in the tactics of reform, according to Paul Boyer, although the ultimate goal remained largely the same: "the moral order of the urban masses." The Progressives moved in different directions from the Victorians in part because of the failures of the Victorians' reform methods. From the

1840s to the 1880s, reformers had had literally tens of thousands of personal contacts with slum dwellers to deliver tracts, sermons, and aid, but those contacts had not proven effective in changing their individual habits and social behavior.[10]

Besides recognition of the dead-end prospects of previous approaches, urban Progressives were driven by idealistic hopes that a healthy environment would arouse uplifting moral impulses within the city's inhabitants. This "search for order" relied heavily upon the expert advice of a rising generation of college-educated professionals to aid in the social engineering and the planning of the physical layout of the modern metropolis of the twentieth century. "Whatever the strategy," Boyer contends, "the underlying conviction remained constant: the behavior and morality of the urban masses could surely be influenced for the better by changing or upgrading their housing. Here was a fundamental beginning point for the positive environmentalism of the Progressive years."[11]

Women's political activism was also essential in the launching of the new reform movement. It became much more public and affected the course of civic debate on houses, neighborhoods, and cities. Boyer and others have neglected almost entirely to listen to these women's voices and to identify their influence in shaping the outcome of reform. Elizabeth Wilson and H. Blake, for example, do not take seriously the very women they are championing, but instead turn them into helpless victims. The suburban ethos was not a conspiracy of sexual oppression; rather, it was the product of a complicated mix of ideas from both genders. In a similar way, men and women alike were enamored with the latest science and technology, which spread rapidly through a myriad of professional and popular channels. Germ theories were discussed widely not only in medical and engineering societies, but in women's and civic clubs as well. Between 1880 and 1900, house doctors and popularizers of germ theories undermined the confidence of middle-class families that they were living in good health.[12]

During the Victorian era, shifting spatial perspectives on bodies, houses, and cities within a familiar discourse of organic analogs played an important part in the reorientation of urban reform. The refocus of attention on the physical conditions of domestic hygiene also had the effect of shifting related questions about the sources of moral corruption. The site of moral failing had been the individual behavior of the poor; now it was the production of an unhealthy urban environment by the city leaders. Reversing cause and effect, urban reformers saw improving the slums in novel ways as a problem of rejuvenating entire neighborhoods rather than condemning isolated buildings as unfit for human habitation. Moreover, they had learned from this approach that tearing down exteriors only exacerbated the perceived evils of overcrowding within. After 1890, Manchester and other cities became involved in building public housing projects both inside and outside of their congested cores.

At the same time, however, middle-class families were moving farther away to new-style suburbs on the expanded edges of the metropolis. Changing perceptions of spatial relationships fostered new ideas about gender and place. As Margaret Marsh observes, "it was not until the last years of the nineteenth century" that gender and place "began to merge, creating a new suburban ideal that recast domesticity to include men and reshaped the suburbs to emphasize family togetherness." Chronically high infant mortality rates and recurring epidemics in the slum districts remained a salient reason to get as far away from the central city as practicable. Germ theories helped not only to dissolve spatial barriers between the inside and the outside of the home, but also to reinforce middle-class anxieties about moral and bodily infection by the poor. In sharp contrast to Wilson and Blake, Marsh posits that the new-style suburbs embodied "masculine domesticity" in the form of an intensification of family life and emphasis on child rearing. She interprets the opening up of the interior layout of the house as evidence of the blurring of gender roles. Women became more involved in the public side of health, moral, education, and environmental reform, while men devoted more time in the private realm of the family.[13]

If germ theories informed settlement patterns and the housing reform strategies of the Progressives, it also helped redirect the search for abundant supplies of pure water for the city and an "ultimate sink" for its liquid wastes. Failed policies of the past showed that simply adding greater distance between one's home and the source of impurities did not translate into lower health risk. Securing safe water was not the same as achieving added personal security by taking advantage of new transportation technologies that increased the physical separation between the slums and the suburbs. Modern water management had to encompass the natural boundaries of the hydrological region. The effort to design supply and sewerage systems for the industrial metropolis engendered original ideas about the conservation of natural resources such as river watersheds and lake basins.[14] Germ theories reinforced an environmental ethic of returning human and toxic wastes to a "natural" state. Beginning in the 1880s, the identification of specific microorganisms with specific infectious diseases provided public health officials with a much better set of indicators of water quality. Now they could

accurately measure the efficacy of various technologies for filtering and purifying the drinking supply. The shift in authority from the inorganic to the
organic sciences had equally profound, albeit less well-known, impacts on
the treatment of sewage.

The fast rise of organic chemistry and microbiology caused a major breakthrough in the ways reformers approached the question of how to safely
dispose of the organic wastes of the industrial city. Rather than advocating
costly and ineffective chemical treatments, the new science suggested that
"clever microbes" could be put to work eating the sewage and rendering
it harmless. In fact, they proclaimed, Chadwick's sanitary idea of pouring
sewage out on the land involved the same processes of bacteriological di-
gestion. Under the control of the scientists and engineers, this time- and
land-consuming natural transformation could be speeded up and confined
to much smaller, industrial sites.

Manchester and Chicago both became leaders in experimenting with biological methods of sewage treatment, but their different cultures of science
and technology produced very different political outcomes. While the authority of science and medicine played a powerful role in shaping water
management policy for the Mersey-Irwell Rivers Basin, the engineers continued to rule supreme in drawing up plans for Chicago's water and sewage
systems. In both cases, Progressive ideas about nature conservation attracted
the attention of the respective national governments to the planning of the
environmental control of water on a regional scale.

The air pollution generated within industrial ecologies posed health risks
even more inescapable than contaminated water for the residents of the
metropolis of the twentieth century. Spurred by soaring energy consumption, cities seemed locked in Tocqueville's paradox of progress. More and
more inputs of energy into breweries, street vehicles, and commercial buildings helped improve the quality of some aspects of urban life, but at a price
of dirty air. Scientific verification of the old adage that sunlight kills germs
added medical urgency and moral obligation to the lifting of the suffocating
pall of bad air from the city. Unfortunately, reform efforts to reduce the visible particulates of smoke had the unintended consequence of legitimizing
increasing emissions of invisible toxic gases. Making incremental gains in
the battle for clean air and facing exponential rises in energy consumption,
reformers could only hope to slow down, not reverse the process of environmental decay. Acidic fumes that rose from tall smokestacks in the city
centers would continue to reach the suburbs until deindustrialization shut
them down many decades later. The bad air coming out of the exhaust pipes
of automobiles still follows us from downtown into our ever more distant

suburban enclaves, degrading the very thing we hope to preserve, the natural beauty of the garden.

Health, Habits, and Habitations

For working-class residents of the central city, there is no question that the quality of life underwent significant change during the Progressive Era. In Manchester, the "reconditioning" of privately owned housing stock proved much more important than the token social housing projects. The replacement of outdoor privies with water closets, and back-to-backs with "through houses" marked the greatest advance. The Corporation supplied fewer than a thousand dwellings; in contrast, seven thousand back-to-backs were converted and another three thousand demolished. Higher standards of construction also expanded the top end of the scale of housing choices for better paid workers.

In a similar way, conversion of Manchester's horse trams to vehicles employing electric traction between 1901 and 1903 increased opportunities for workers to live beyond walking distance from their jobs. Commuters could travel up to three miles from the center for a penny, and most paid half that amount for shorter rides. Perhaps the most important indicator of conditions of life in the slum districts, infant mortality rates, showed steady if slow improvement. However, the extent to which public policy as a whole, let alone housing reform, accounts for these gains is very difficult to separate out from a highly complex array of factors that determine individual and public health.[15]

Offsetting the gains in physical health were losses in the form of broken bonds of community in Ancoats and other working-class neighborhoods. What seems to have been missing from middle-class reform discourse is a sense of place as a social organism, a symbiotic group of people helping each other cope with daily life. True enough, Howard and his Fabian supporters eventually built some communal kitchens and wash areas, taking them outside of the private residences. But the garden city model of Letchworth was drawn along the lines of a rustic bourgeois utopia.

Working-class culture was rooted in identity of place and in tight webs of kin and social relationships. When the next great wave of slum clearance hit Ancoats in the early 1930s, university-trained sociologists were there to record the human toll from the forced dislocation of hundred of families. Over half of the group of 460 households interviewed had lived in Ancoats at least ten years, and some had been there for generations. Of the 185 families who had moved in less than five years before, two-thirds had at least one parent who had grown up there. A majority of households had relatives in the immediate vicinity. These uprooted families complained that the Corporation's higher rents meant less money for food, and they dreaded the commutes from their physically stark and socially sterile housing projects on the outskirts of town. "They knew the [old] neighborhood," the study reported, "and the cheapest shops which often allowed them to buy 'in the back of the book' [on credit]; they had networks of friends there that would now be lost." For them, suburbia was anything but ideal.[16]

Exactly how to calculate the pluses and minuses of the Progressives' housing reforms remains an open question. One the one hand, as Lord Woolton of the Manchester University Settlement noted in 1937, the reconditioning approach had ultimately done little to provide a better quality of life within jerry-built structures more than a hundred years old. "They were patched up and given a longer lease of life," he remarked, but "the general appearance of the area was sordid and ugly." New housing in suburban settings unquestionably furnished people who had been living in slum buildings with a healthier environment. On the other hand, Woolton was impressed that "the greater majority of families visited in the survey were certainly not slum-minded. The obvious effort of the majority to keep the dilapidated houses as decent as possible, applying fresh paint to decayed wood and new paper to walls whose crumbling plaster would hardly hold it, are sufficient proof of this."[17]

The legacy of the Progressives' suburban ideal of the garden city still poses daunting, unanswered questions. In *Flesh and Stone: The Body and the City in Western Civilization*, Richard Sennett provocatively asserts that today's sprawling megalopolis has completely pacified our bodies within sensory-deprived, motorized, media-dazing spaces. Like his acknowledged mentor, Lewis Mumford, Sennett puts this process of the alienation of human nature from the built environment in broad context. His search for "master images of the body" sheds light on the ways in which those images became embedded in domestic architecture and urban design at the dawn of the twentieth century. "We are beginning to see the city as a conscious, living organism," American reformer Frederic C. Howe exalted in 1913, "which the architect and engineer . . . the administrator and the dreamer can build and plan for the comfort, convenience, and happiness of people. In a big way, city planning is the first conscious recognition of the unity of society."[18] Guided by new visions of the suburban ideal, social engineers used powerful technologies—the automobile, electricity, telephones—to transform nature into the distended but ordered spaces that most people now live within. Sennett challenges us to reimagine the spatial and metaphorical relationship of bodies, houses, and cities. He suggests that fresh perspectives may be a prerequisite for redrawing the line between the public and the private sides of being in good health.[19]

CHAPTER NINE

The Environmental Justice Movement in Manchester

Introduction: Charles Rowley and the Rediscovery of the Slum

The 1880s laid the seedbed of a new type of urban housing and environmental reform among both the working and the middle classes. While Charles Rowley was nurturing a grassroots movement in the inner city, the domestic sanitarians were planting novel ideas about health and disease among the more affluent homeowners in the suburbs. True, neither slums nor efforts to improve them were new. Anthony Wohl counts at least forty Parliamentary acts between 1840 and 1880 on the subject in his appropriately titled book, *The Eternal Slum*. Yet, he concludes, "neither party was deeply committed to housing reform, and neither party until the mid-1870s embraced it as a major part of its programme." At best, lawmakers learned what did not work. What changed over the next decade and led to the first truly effective housing reform legislation was the result of a fruitful combination of working-class empowerment and alterations in middle-class perceptions of the spatial and metaphorical relationships among body, home, and city.[1]

In the previous decade, Manchester Liberals had suffered a crisis of confidence. Local economic depression had slowed the city's growth, causing a slight drop in the number of people living within its boundaries, from 347,000 to 344,000. At the same time, both the economy and the population of the larger metropolitan area had been making steady gains over an ever widening expanse of territory. The process of industrial reorganization was turning Cottonopolis into a more deconcentrated, albeit integrated, conurbation. During the decade, the area's population had risen from 815,000 to just under a million people. Compared to the big increases over the course of the past century in the city center, Manchester proper seemed to be headed straight for the abyss of urban decline. Distressed civic leaders responded with a bold vision of economic development: they would build a ship canal to bypass Liverpool and bring its lucrative dock facilities to the foot of the city. Although historians discount the value of this public works project as an engine of urban growth, they have no doubts about the pivotal significance of its impact on local politics and sanitation policy.[2]

The seeds of a grassroots movement for housing reform in Ancoats would be planted in the organization of the working classes behind the ship canal scheme. To realize their dreams of a port of Manchester, local promoters faced an uphill battle in Parliament. These businessmen had to convince the legislature to approve not only the project itself but also its relationship to regional designs for cleaning up the Mersey-Irwell Rivers Basin (MIRB). The town council had long resisted the national governments' efforts to gain its cooperation in reducing the pollution of the rivers. Now, however, the success of the ship canal depended on supplying its turning basin and docks with water clean enough to meet an acceptable standard of toleration. The business leaders turned to the major trade unions in an effort to present Parliament with a unified front. Facing hard times, the unions gave the project enthusiastic endorsement because it promised jobs and legitimacy. This mobilization of the city's working classes provided valuable political experience on the eve of national reform legislation that would grant universal manhood suffrage in 1884.[3]

The weight of the workingman's vote in the local arena was amplified in a second important development related to the ship canal project. Driven by fears of decline, city officials had reversed their position on annexation and were taking the initiative in prodding the surrounding districts into conformity with their master plan of water management. The municipal corporation exerted its leverage as the sole supplier of essential utility services to force these outlying communities into agreeing to amalgamation. The city added a large numbers of workers to its poll books in 1885 when it absorbed the inner belt of communities, including both workers neighborhoods and the exclusive gated community of Victoria Park. A much larger consolidation of the outlying suburbs followed five years later (see fig. 9.1).[4]

Figure 9.1. Manchester annexations
Source: Alan Kidd, *Manchester*, Town and City Histories (Keele, Staffordshire: Ryburn/Keele University Press, 1993), 199.

Over the course of the 1880s, then, the enfranchisement and mobilization of the working classes finally gave birth to partisanship in local elections. Local advocates of housing reform were finally handed the political weapon they needed to pry open the city's closed, self-serving circle of merchants and manufacturers. In 1890, Town Hall would change hands from the Liberals to the Tories for the first time since the inauguration of the modern municipal government over a half-century earlier. The empowerment of Manchester's workers generated a groundswell of protest against slum conditions that the city council could no longer afford to ignore.

Evidence of this objection to the politics of exclusion emerged simultaneously with the extension of voting rights to the mass of working men. In 1884, J. H. Crosfield was elected to the council from the Ardwick district, immediately adjacent to Ancoats. He not only pressured the medical officer of health, Dr. John Leigh, to undertake a new survey of the industrial districts, but also prodded his colleagues into establishing the Unhealthy Dwellings Committee. Even with the most favorable spin put on the statistics, Dr. Leigh's report showed a wide gap in annual mortality rates between the slums and the suburbs. In Ancoats, there were nearly twenty-eight deaths per thousand, while in the district containing Victoria Park, the rate was only eleven per thousand. The medical officer of health faithfully reiterated standard dogma about the moral failings of the poor, but he also argued that

> Ancoats is a district requiring, I think, distinct and special consideration. Though a part of the old township of Manchester, it is really a somewhat outlying portion of the city, and has received but scant justice.... It is a compact block of cottage houses, most of them of the meanest character, housing some 48,000 of the most industrious people in the world.... It has not a single road or street enabling that vast population to communicate in a fairly straight line with the city with which its business chiefly lies. A series of zigzags, along narrow streets and courts, form its avenues to the city. Every year adds to its dismal character and lessens the enjoyments of its inhabitants. I remember the time when the Medlock rippled along its border, its banks clothed with trees and shrubs, a picturesque stream along which the weary worker might stroll with pleasure; low, black and polluted, it pursues a sullen course between walls of brick and stone, receiving every few yards tributes which take the gladness from its waters.

Still under the regime of the Liberals, the council gave Dr. Leigh only ten minutes to make his report. Moreover, the incumbent leading party was strong

Figure 9.2. Charles Rowley
Source: Ford Madox Brown,
c. 1890, as reprinted in Kenneth
Bindiner, *The Art of Ford Madox
Brown* (University Park:
Pennsylvania State University
Press, 1998).

enough to have Crosfield, that embarrassing representative of the working classes, defeated in the next local elections.[5]

Although Crosfield lost his council seat, Charles Rowley was building a stronger, more enduring movement from the bottom up in neighboring Ancoats. Born in 1840, he grew up there in a struggling family of thirteen children, but his father was no ordinary workingman. A picture-frame maker by trade, the elder Rowley opened his own shop, and it became a favorite of pre-Raphael painters like Ford Madox Brown. During the 1850s, he was also a leader of the movement for adult education, helping to establish mechanics institutes with two of the city's radicals, the publishers John and Abel Heywood. His frail and sickly son, like many other children of the slums, did not attend school. Unlike them, however, young Charles gained a wonderful education from a home library rich in the Romantic literature of the day as well as from his father's extraordinary guests. These contacts led to entry into the literary clubs and social activities of Arts and Crafts luminaries such as John Ruskin and William Morris. In addition, young Rowley attended religious classes at the nearby Bennett Street Sunday School of St. Paul's Church, where he eventually became one of the teachers. But at age thirty, he had a breakdown, and doctors ordered him to get out of the inner city (see fig. 9.2).[6]

For the next five years Rowley received a different kind of education in class relations and spatial segregation that would alter the course of his life. Seeing at first hand how affluent Mancunians lived gave him a whole new perspective on the slum. He recalled that "some of us are driven out of the city because we are not physically capable of living in its dirt and noise; others leave for mere pleasure and comfort and that suburban isolation which to most natures is deadly, however respectable it may be. Suburbs become the homes of coddled conceit and degeneracy." Returning home in 1875 with a sense of mission, he ran successfully for the city council on a platform of "sanitation, social reform, and education." As a Sunday school teacher, he did not arouse the suspicions of the Liberals. But getting elected proved to be the easy part compared to coping with his reception at Town Hall after the other council members found out about his intentions.[7]

Contemporaries and historians agree that Manchester had the most rigid and hierarchical political culture of any industrial city in the period before universal manhood suffrage was granted by Parliament. Within the closed and self-perpetuating circle of the city council, each committee chair acted as a virtually autonomous dictator. As Rowley soon learned about the committees, "this policy of exclusion led to curious results. You hardly dared to criticise, let alone find fault with such august bodies. The secrets were as the secrets of a regiment or of a Cabinet Council."

While Rowley's advocacy of public baths fit within acceptable parameters of middle-class reform, his call for a public meeting hall in Ancoats cast him beyond the pale as a dangerous radical. "I cannot forget the anger of the older members of the council that day at such an audacious proposal from so tiny and so new a councilor," he remembered. "One of the leading men, Alderman Grundy ... tackled me personally one day after ... and the wonder is that I came away alive. His rage was real, almost despairing, for he saw in such proposals the beginning of the end of the old regime." Rowley persisted in getting funding for his project, the New Islington Hall, but he was targeted for defeat at the next election just like Crosfield would be a few years later. Shunned and thrown out of the citadel of power, he took a new tack in a career of selfless devotion to improving the quality of life of his working-class neighbors.[8]

In 1878, Rowley started something original that would contribute to the creation of an institution that would be copied in hundred of cities on both sides of the Atlantic, the social settlement house. Drawing on his wide network of friends, he organized a series of cultural events in Ancoats. The recreation movement was based on Rowley's belief that working people would enjoy high culture as much as the well-to-do if given access to it. As he put it, Ancoats deserved the "good stuff" as opposed the "indifferent stuff." He began by mounting an art exhibit, then a series of musical concerts and educational lectures on Sunday afternoons. At the newly dedicated New

Islington Hall, the eminent chemist, Professor Henry E. Roscoe, delivered the first talk, on coal-pit explosions. As part of the series presentations were made by literary and artistic notables of the day, including George Bernard Shaw, G. K. Chesterton, Ford Madox Brown, Sir Charles Halle, and the Brodsky Quartet.[9]

Drawing large audiences of between four hundred and one thousand people, this class-bridging effort was successful in large part because of Rowley's irresistible enthusiasm and magnetism. As one contemporary remarked, "he was a man with an extraordinary personality which made him unique as a chairman, and which attracted great men in every walk of life." Tongue-in-check, George Bernard Shaw confirmed that "no matter on what spot on the globe you may happen to be, you are never safe from a summons to Ancoats. . . . It is my firm belief that ninety nine percent of the deaths that have occurred within the last quarter century among the public-spirited men of this country are due to diseases of which the seeds were planted in untimely journeys to Manchester. Rowley is the only man alive who could induce any sane man to go to Manchester unless he had urgent and lucrative business there."[10]

The positive response of the community convinced Rowley that the achievement of urban reform would come only when a political base was built from the ground up rather than with the traditional, paternalistic top-down approach. Rowley was strongly influenced not only by his searing experience on the city council, but also by the trade unionists and cooperators working within the community. Rowley wrote, for example, of Arthur Acland, who had become an early supporter of the recreation movement. "One of his methods," Rowley recounted, "was to come among us, stay in our cottages, and meet us all on equal terms. His view evidently was that you must go forward for yourself to the people to help them, by knowing them." Now armed with the vote, the men attending Rowley's events helped broaden the focus by making politics a frequent topic of discussion and debate.

The recreation movement formed new channels of legitimacy for democratic expression outside of the trade unions. Over the course of the decade, the range of cultural events and social services Rowley sponsored continued to expand. In 1889, these various programs were given institutional form as the Brotherhood of Ancoats, which soon had over two thousand dues-paying members. Rowley's social work also served to build an organizational platform for launching a political movement to clean up the slums. Simultaneously, the Healthy Homes Society announced its inaugural event, a lecture by Dr. Aldred on the "Laws of Health." But without the sympathy and support of the middle classes, these voices of protest may have fallen on deaf ears at Town Hall.[11]

"The Bitter Cry of Ancoats"

During the Progressive Era, bridging the social divide between the classes was often a prerequisite to success in the political arena. Charles Rowley's autobiography offers revealing insight into the reasons a groundswell of protest from inside the slums awaited the arrival of a new wave of anxious concern about those areas from those living in the suburbs. After his recuperation outside the central city, he realized that the quality of everyday life within the urban neighborhood appeared normal to the relatively isolated slum dweller. It was the common condition of the industrial city. "The memories of the squalor and the potency of the odours of those appalling, stinking slums can never be effaced," he wrote, "We had been living next door to them all our lives, and yet were not aware of their bestial condition." As a child in the 1840s, Rowley could still escape to the countryside, but thirty years later there was no easy exit from the urban environment.

In 1878, another native son of this area lamented:

> The Broad Green has disappeared, the orchards of the Hopwoods and, the granges of the Traffords, the green lanes, the bright woodlands have been covered over by the habitations of man. The little hamlet is now a mighty hive of industry. The hand of the Ancoats artizan stretches forth to the ends of the earth. Whilst we glory in the progress and prosperity of the present we may regret the disappearance of the clear stream, the green lanes, the merry songbirds, the smokeless sky that made fair and beautiful the old Ancoats that has for ever passed away.

Rowley too bemoaned the industrialization of nature in terms reminiscent of Tocqueville's paradox of progress. Ancoats "had been a veritable Klondike for over fifty years. The gold, however, had gone, but the debris, human and otherwise, was left," he observed.[12]

Looking back, the reformer confessed that the mobilization of Ancoats did not happen until outside agitators arrived. His extraordinary life allowed him to bridge not only between social classes but also between their different spatial points of view. He reasoned that "it is, of course, as difficult to see ugliness as it is to see and appreciate beauty. Until you see the horror of your surroundings nothing can be attempted. I fear that much wild talk was indulged in by us about black smoke, the far worse noxious vapours, the unsanitary areas, and the hundred and one things which are either cause or effect, or both, of our worse town conditions." Although memoirs by members of the working class from this period are rare, they generally support his testimony.[13]

The domestic sanitarians and popularizers of germ theories shifted middle-class perceptions of both the private and the public sides of health. By refocusing attention on the spatial dimension of being in good health, they helped formulate novel concepts of social environmentalism. Urban reform began to be perceived not so much as solving the problems of individual buildings and personal habits as responding to a crisis of entire residential zones. These zones were now considered the original sources of self-destructive and antisocial behavior. The policy implications of this reversal in the causes and the effects of slum conditions could not have been more complete.

Consider the 1868 testimony in of the true chief executive of the Manchester Corporation, Sir Joseph Heron, to the Royal Sanitary Commission on the reasons the city had the highest death rates in the kingdom. According to the town clerk,

> The districts where mortality in Manchester is greatest, are two; one is chiefly occupied by what you may call the vicious classes, the haunts of thieves and prostitutes and all people of that class, and there is another district, which is mainly occupied by the Irish. No sanitary arrangements that can be made will to any very large extent, I believe, affect the condition of those classes—it is something that is beyond the reach of mere sanitary legislation. Manchester is not, as a whole, an unhealthy town.[14]

Rowley believed in just the opposite approach, social environmentalism. In 1885, the upstart from Ancoats gave expression to a mature theory of urban reform in his first publication, *Social Politics*. Rowley was irate at Heron's self-serving behaviorist approach. Modestly labeling his own twenty-page pamphlet a "paper for discussion," he blasted Heron: "One other bogey shall have my protest as often as I can get it in, and that is the bumptious axiom that you cannot make people good or happy by Act of Parliament." Identifying himself as a Christian socialist, he denounced the apostles of Social Darwinism, who were producing a "world of devils," where people did as they pleased for "greed's sake." Instead, he demanded environmental justice as the necessary first step toward the moral uplift of the individual. Pointing to Ancoats, he argued that "the actual expenditure of life is as patent as it is scandalous.... About six children are sacrificed each week in Ancoats alone— that is, six more die than would die if they and their parents had fair play. ... I wonder what the founder of Christianity would say about these figures."

Until these conditions changed, he asserted, the suburban middle class had no right to complain about alcohol abuse or other forms of self-destructive behavior.[15]

Rowley called for the strong hand of the State to curb the excesses of a laissez-faire system that had virtually destroyed the natural environment inside as well as outside the cities. He declared:

> Revolution is needed in regard to the crimes against decent living, which are committed by interested criminals. All people whose work produces noxious effluvia should be compelled, and there should be no exceptions, to deal with noxious matter where it is made. No body of men should be allowed to destroy, say Phillip's or Queen's and Peel Park, not to speak of thousands of acres of lovely country to the west of Widness, and many other parts of England. Everybody who pollutes a stream, in any way whatever, by a water closet, a dye works, or in any fashion, public or private, should be considered a molester of his kind, and treated as such. And so with scores of cases, prevention is the key-note to strike, and then we should have little to repair.[16]

While Rowley was spearheading reform, the momentum of public opinion was moving behind him toward social environmentalism. An early sign of the shift was the changing attitudes toward slum dwellers. In 1878, an expose on "Ancoats Roughs" reflected this turn in civic discourse away from portraits of Ancoats residents as subhuman criminals to depictions of them as unfortunate victims worthy of public support. Walter Tomlinson stated that he wanted to test the conventional wisdom of the city press that a respectable person could not visit the district without "risk of abuse, a broken head, or something infinitely worse." What he found in Ancoats during his Eastertime visit reinforced environmental images of "houses mean, small, and of all degrees of dinginess and squalor; yet, it is pleasant to see in many of them a feminine pride of housekeeping which has induced a supreme effort in the way of brightness and cleanliness in honour of the time." What he failed to encounter was anyone posing a personal threat to his safety. "The fact is," he declared, "the people of these districts are generally regarded by ignorant people as roughs, on account of their rough clothes and rough speech[. But they] are in the main, harmless, fairly decent hard-working fellows."[17]

On a much larger scale, the women of the Manchester and Salford Sanitary Association (MSSA) also added to a fundamental reformulation of the causes and effects of slum conditions. The "Ladies' Branch" of the city's mainstream reform group, originally founded in 1862, launched an initiative in 1886 to divide the city into thirteen subdistricts along parish lines, each with its own "Lady Superintendent" in charge of coordinating the volunteers, whose "chief work is house to house visitation; a willing hand extended to help in trouble and sickness, with a word of sympathy, coupled with good and sensible advice, which though it often falls on deaf ears, yet sometimes bears good fruit." Emblematic of the transition in Victorian attitudes, these Christian do-gooders came armed with tins of soap, which had to be sold and could not be given away free.[18]

Peaking in the mid-1890s, this project swelled into a veritable invasion of moral suasion and maternal sympathy. In 1893, the city's 19,300 slum dwellings received 38,400 visitations, or an average of two per household. Typical of the help offered were cases in which a widow was aided in finding a job washing clothes; a nurse and a loaf of bread were sent to a mother having problems giving breast milk, and a city inspector was persuaded to put pressure on a landlord to fix clogged drains. Although the impact of the resulting encounters on either patrons or recipients, let alone on public discourse, defies precise measurement, there can be little doubt that they made a contribution in bridging the spatial and social gap between the classes. By humanizing the slum dweller, the visitations helped create sympathy and support for more aggressive reform measures.[19]

In Manchester, muckraking journalism served as the catalyst for the crystallization of changing spatial ideas about health into a reform campaign to clean up the slums. In 1887, the expelled councilor, J. H. Crosfield, fired the first salvo in an assault to topple the regime of the Liberals entrenched in Town Hall. In *The "Bitter Cry" of Ancoats* he sought political revenge. He used the medical officer of health's statistics to indict the city council for criminal neglect of the public health, and in a series of letters to the newspapers, he hinted at the existence of a cover-up of the city's appalling mortality rates. "I do not suppose," he suggested, "that Dr. Leigh has had instructions from his committee to draw it as mild as possible in reference to the death rate, but I must say that the whole truth is not apparent."

On the one hand, Crosfield pointed to an undercount in the nearly eight thousand annual fatalities listed by the health officer. For instance, his report failed to include the 1,500 deaths that occurred in the city's hospitals and workhouses. Crosfield's calculations of the overall death rate for Manchester pushed Dr Leigh's figures from twenty to twenty-five per thousand. On the other hand, he argued that the boundaries of the medical districts prevented the creation of an accurate picture of the most concentrated pockets of poverty, such as District No. 1 in Ancoats. "I will not lay myself open to criticism by surmising what the death rate thus arrived at would be" in the worst districts, argued Crosfield, "but I am quite sure the comparison then between the highest and the lowest percentages would form a ghastly indictment against somebody. It can be caused only by a departure from the laws, natural and divine, to which we owe reverence.... We have in this city an annual holocaust of nearly 6,000 persons. The horror increases and the darkness deepens as you look further into this field of the dying and dead. ... The extinction of 6,000 lives, long before their due time, is a very serious matter, and surely ought to be accepted as an intimation that something has gone wrong."[20]

Over the next two years, the "bitter cry" of Ancoats would grow into an undeniable chorus of support for social and environmental justice. The broad public response was, in part, the result of Crosfield's strategy of building on the uproar caused by the publication of *The Bitter Cry of Outcast London* in 1883 and its popularization in William T. Stead's *Pall Mall Gazette*. Triggering widespread debate in the press and in Parliament, this exposé of slum conditions even reached Queen Victoria, who pressured Parliament to undertake an investigation. "Perhaps the greatest value of *The Bitter Cry*," Anthony Wohl states, "was that it went beyond the usual description of the *external* features of the streets, courts, and alleyways to a powerful and accurate portrayal of the overcrowding *within* the houses." In contrast to the situation in London, the problem in Manchester was too many bad houses densely packed together rather than too many people living inside each one. Yet, the furor set off in the capital city helped the entire nation rediscover the slum as a problem that would take bold new approaches to solve, including large-scale public projects to compensate for the failure of the private sector to build an adequate supply of affordable, decent houses.[21]

Crosfield's attack served as a spark of a reform movement by raising enough questions to justify demands for yet another, more comprehensive study of the neighborhood. The results of the original report exploded like a bombshell, blowing away current assumptions about housing reform and opening up civic discourse to new approaches, and his polemical style had a moral and political appeal that cut across class boundaries. The middle-class MSSA sponsored the new investigation, which was published in 1889, two years later. The researchers, led by Dr. John C. Thresh established a new standard for the scientific study of the city's environmental conditions. By measuring, counting, and calculating in minute detail, they discovered that the actual annual death rate in the Ancoats district was more than two and a half times higher than Dr. Leigh's average figure. Some blocks and dead-end streets reached astronomical rates of eighty to ninety deaths per thousand each year. These figures meant that five to nine people were dying in the slums for each fatality suffered in the suburbs. "We find in this district," Thresh claimed, "an almost entire absence of everything which makes a locality healthy, and the presence of everything which tends to render it unhealthy."[22]

Thresh's inquiry went beyond previous descriptive models of social and physical conditions to assess the administration of public health services in the industrial slum. Bordering on the Engels genre of the radical critique, his report accused Town Hall of shameful hypocrisy in the blatant neglect of the pail-closet system of sanitation. In theory the technology and its support system of inspectional services and health regulations were adequate, but in practice they were both meant to fail. "The present system or want of system," Dr. Thresh wrote, "is a disgrace to any civilised community. . . . In all our investigations in the Ancoats districts, though we have frequently met the inspectors in the leading thoroughfares, and have seen them evince a good deal of curiosity as to our movements, we have never on any occasion had the pleasure of meeting one in any of the filthy passages or courts. . . . To read [the health code], and then to visit No. 1 District, Ancoats, almost drives one to the conclusion that the whole system of inspections so far at least as that district is concerned, is intended to be a farce; and so it would be were not the results so tragic." In many cases, the pail closets had deteriorated after twenty years of use to a disgusting state of disrepair.[23]

The charge of official wrongdoing struck a particularly telling blow because it came hard on the heels of a closely related scandal in the operation of the pail-closet refuse processing plant. During the housing investigation, recently fired workers from the Holt Town facility revealed that they had been frequently ordered by their supervisors "to have a breakdown" in order to create an excuse to unload the machines' raw contents into the Medlock River just above Ancoats. An embarrassed town council initially issued pleas of innocent denial. But surreptitious observations in the middle of the night from a rowboat in the heavily polluted stream confirmed the secret dumping. Public exposure forced the secretive committee in charge of scavenger services to admit that the harmful practice had been a regular part of Manchester's dry conservancy system from the very beginning. "We have it appears," one exasperated reformer protested, "had twenty years of slipshod government; the 'Health' Committee (save the [quotation] mark!) has for twenty years converted our rivers into an open sewer." Taken together, the Thresh report and the Holt Town scandal provided the populist movement of the slum dwellers just the kind of political ammunition it needed to put city officials on the defensive.[24]

In Ancoats, the shock waves of these exposés set off a groundswell of popular protest in sharp contrast to the aftermath of previous studies of the slum. Mass rallies were held and petitions gathered to demand greater equity in the distribution of public resources. In April 1889, for example, Rowley and 3,653 others sent a memorial to the city council to back up the proposals of the Thresh report for slum clearance, social housing, and smoke abatement. Resting their case on grounds of environmental justice, they declared that "according to the last published accounts, the capital expenditures for public improvements in Manchester since its incorporation has been £1,404,640, but in the extensive and densely-populated district of Ancoats only a very inconsiderable portion of this has been laid out." With the power of an aroused and organized constituency behind it, the voice of the working class could no longer be ignored by elected officials.[25]

In July 1889, the Thresh report served as the foundation for the launching of the Healthy Homes Society. John Sanders, a member of Rowley's Brotherhood, took charge of organizing this "new mission to the slum." "Our formula was," he reflected several months after the work began, to go "right to the people, to their very doors." With his approach of grassroots organizing around a single issue, he sought not only to mobilize the slum dwellers but also to change the course of public policy. Building on Rowley's work to empower the residents of Ancoats, the Healthy Homes Society supplied a focal point for reform activism. "Our first lecture," Sanders boasted, "was attended by 300, and there was not a single bonnet visible or a single person 'dressed up' in the whole crowd." Over the course of the first year, over eight thousand people attended the organization's meetings. A significant number of city council members found it politically expedient to attend as well, and three of them became officers of the organization. In 1890, the Healthy Homes Society would become the springboard for the return of Rowley to Town Hall, accompanied by several other reform candidates.[26]

During this critical period of political realignment, the MSSA briefly flirted with the democratic idea of organizing the working classes to promote their own welfare. In 1890, the middle-class reform group reported:

> It has been found desirable to secure the co-operation of earnest, intelligent working men, and they having acquired a knowledge of the laws of health themselves convey it to the cottage homes with which they are familiar. In this way, people who derive little permanent benefit from being 'talked at' (as they frequently describe it) at public lectures, are led, often by practical illustration, to see the advantages of cleanliness, order, ventilation, etc. By these agencies men are influenced who, as a rule, cannot be reached by the Mission Women of the Ladies' Branch of the Association as housewives are, the practice of visiting courts and

alleys, and holding impromptu meetings there or in other suitable places in the open air, being essential men's work.

Bridge building across class lines led to sponsorship of organizations similar to the Healthy Homes Society in Hulme and Chorlton-on-Medlock.[27]

Although the MSSA quickly drew back from the specter of a politically autonomous working class, it continued to seek ways to broaden the base of support for environmental reform. Most important, the reform group took the lead in 1891 on the issue of cutting the gas rates of the municipally owned utility. Rather than generating big savings for the benefit of the property owners in the form of smaller tax bills, lower utility rates would lead to the wider use of gas as fuel and to the reduction of air pollution from coal-burning domestic hearths. The MSSA campaign was endorsed by the Healthy Homes Society, Rowley, and other working-class representatives in the city council. They succeeded in getting a token cut, but fell short of making gas competitive with coal. Nonetheless, this middle-class initiative helped to strengthen the common cause of environmental justice for central city residents, who remained pragmatically focused on improving the quality of life in their neighborhoods.[28]

From Clearing Slums to Building Suburbs

In Manchester, the year 1889 became pivotal in moving civic discourse on housing reform from a focus on individual behavior to an emphasis on social environmentalism, from the private to the public side of health. A decade of anxious concern about the role of the dwelling place and its immediate surroundings in the etiology of bodily disease had the effect of blurring the spatial and metaphorical boundaries between them. The widespread diffusion of germ theories with their invisible agents of infection also helped erode confidence that physical distance would effectively safeguard the family against ill health. As these borderlines between inside and outside became more transparent, perceptions of cause and effect, in turn, shifted from personal morality to public policy.

This new understanding formed the conceptual foundation of Dr. Thresh's report and the movement it triggered for environmental justice. At one of the first meetings of the residents of Ancoats on housing reform in February 1889, he paid lip service to the conventional wisdom that considered dirty air and overcrowding two of the basic ingredients in the making of the slum. A third factor was needed to explain the antisocial behavior and unhealthy dwellings found there. The first two, he reasoned, "operate, but unequally; for the character and habits of the people depended to a great extent on their surroundings. They could not improve the mental and moral condition of the people till such property as he had referred to was destroyed and replaced by something better." The reconstruction project Thresh envisioned went beyond the provision of decent housing to encompass the redesign of entire neighborhoods. To improve the quality of daily life, these plans needed to incorporate a broad array of health-generating amenities, such as open "breathing spaces," public baths, and free libraries.[29]

In May 1889, the Liberal regime finally began to abandon its politics of exclusion and to make amends for its part in sustaining the slums of the central city for the previous half-century. Stripped of its defenses by the Thresh report and facing an aroused electorate in the upcoming elections, the city council announced this historic sea change in public policy. The report of its Unhealthy Dwellings Committee embraced an inclusive concept of social environmentalism that bridged the spatial borderlines of residential communities segregated by class and ethnicity/religion. Although it took pride in its first four years of work, the committee acknowledged that much bolder approaches were needed. Enforcement of the building and health codes was simply not enough. Manchester still had between ten and twelve thousand back-to-back row houses, a design long condemned for its lack of through ventilation, but since 1885, fewer than seven hundred houses of all kinds had been cited for code violations. Only sixty buildings had actually been demolished and another 180 closed as unfit for human habitation.[30]

Now the councilmen endorsed Dr. Thresh's proposals for a positive environmentalism. They called for the active involvement of the municipal corporation in wholesale slum clearance and construction of replacement housing. The committee report buttressed their position with figures of the profits from the existing projects committee members had visited in Liverpool, Glasgow, and Edinburgh. Moreover, the councilmen announced the steps they had already taken to purchase several parcels of land in Ancoats and other industrial neighborhoods. The committee concluded by asking the council to signal its approval of this policy reversal by adopting a long string of enabling parliamentary legislation on housing stretching as far back as 1851. For the Liberals, however, the long overdue start in a new direction was too little, too late; they were kicked out of office the following year by housing reformers running under the Conservative banner.[31]

Reform discourse about model housing and neighborhood design moved from the private to the public arena. Pressure from a coalition of middle-class reformers and working-class protest groups kept Manchester's belated efforts to ameliorate the environmental conditions of the slums on track. Housing reform took several forms, including strengthening of the building code to force landlords to upgrade existing properties, conversion of back-to-backs into single-family homes, and retrofitting of dwellings with indoor plumbing. Moreover, the city council followed up on the social housing plan, cautiously expanding it in incremental steps over the course of the decade. Local authorities became engaged in clearing slum areas, widening and straightening streets, and erecting housing projects.[32]

Equally important in closing the gap in urban amenities between inner districts and outer suburbs was the decision to reverse course on the dual, class-based system of water management. After years of dithering, the city completed a major public works project in 1892 that brought large new supplies of fresh water from over a hundred miles away in the Lake District. Informed by germ theories, the champions of the new public health made the triumph of Chadwick's water-carriage system of sanitation over the dry conservancy alternatives all but inevitable. With the death of Dr. Leigh in 1888, the way was opened for a change in policy. Two years later, the council declared that all new residential construction must include indoor plumbing, and in 1892 it ordered landlords to retrofit existing housing with this modern convenience. The landlords' resistance to paying the costs of conversion was initially met by public subsidies, but in 1906 the council ended these payments and stepped up the pace of enforcement. Prompting the conversion of existing dwellings at an average rate of two thousand a year, the new policy eliminated the dual standard of sanitation between the rich and the poor by the end of World War I. While large differences remained between the quality of life in the slums and that in the suburbs, the battle for municipal reform in Manchester had led at least to the rectification of the most glaring instance of class discrimination in the political formation of urban space.[33]

Conclusion: "Healthy Lives, Healthy Homes, and Healthy Surroundings"

The new politics of social environmentalism helped change the course of urban policy and planning, but reform remained confined within the limits established by the traditional context of municipal capitalism. Manchester's political culture of privilege and authority still set tight constraints on the use of the public sector for purposes other than those that could turn a profit. In the case of sanitation, the pail-closet system had always been a loser. It failed on all counts. It did not generate surplus income, prevent the befouling of the rivers with human wastes, or help overcome the city's image as one of the most polluted and unhealthy places in the country. Because the council was forced by the ship canal enterprise and the national government to install a complete network of intercepting sewers and treatment plants, its decision to convert waste management in the slum districts to a water-carriage system could easily be justified as good economics. However, the water rates set by the council continued to discourage the use of running water in the home, keeping Manchester's average residential consumption low compared to that of American and other British cities. Bathtubs remained a luxury, perpetuating a humiliating hardship for working people. The fact that George Orwell could still document the lack of this modern convenience in painful detail during the Great Depression represented a dismal failure of public policy.[34]

At the same time, the Corporation started a new enterprise to reap profits from its additional sources of supply in the Lake District. A year before the water was even turned on, the council won approval from Parliament to create a hydraulic power system that required huge volumes of the liquid to be conveyed in a separate, underground network of high-pressure pipes. By 1900, cheap business rates encouraged local industries to use over 150 million gallons of water a year to run machines while the high price of residential service precluded the vast majority of Mancunians from taking a bath in their own homes. Under the regime of the Tories during the Progressive Era, expansion of efforts to advance social welfare were circumscribed primarily because the tradition of paternalism persisted; thus the era saw no great departure from the tenets of the new Liberalism.[35]

During this period, the town council found that its management of new electrical technologies was a more powerful tool than housing reform in the reordering of urban space. Here traditions of municipal ownership of public utilities laid the foundation for the integration of slum and suburb into a more unified metropolis. The annexations of 1885 and 1890 had tripled the territory of the city in addition to boosting its population by 50 percent to just over a half-million inhabitants. The advent of electric light and power, telephones, and trams tended to burst the bounds of previous settlement patterns while weaving the communities more closely together. Older suburbs lying closer to the city center became more built up and urban in character; new enclaves of the well-to-do were established at the practical commuting limits of the new transportation technologies. In the 1880s, for example, the settlement line of working-class housing began to surround the guarded walls of Victoria Park. Rows of terrace-style houses and more moderate strips of cottages were erected all around the gated community, gradually tarnishing its image as the city's most prestigious residential address. Outside investors completed the transformation of Victoria Park into an inner-city neighborhood in 1899 when they announced plans to construct 650 row houses on an iron grid plat of streets. The social elite relocated to the edges of the enlarged metropolis, to places like Didsbury, Fallowsfield, and Altrincham. Town Hall also built a tramcar suburb, but this model community was designed for the working class.[36]

The public discourse over the environmental plan of the Blackley Estate marked the climax of housing reform in Manchester during the Progressive Era. Between 1899 and 1903, the city council became a forum for civic debate over the design of the 203 row houses that would be erected on a 239-acre tract of open land on the far north side of the 1890 annexation. This experiment in community building embodied many of the same ideals that Ebenezer Howard incorporated in his vision of a garden city. Important lessons had been learned from the early projects in Ancoats. The council had to design not only sanitary homes but also attractive sites, or people would object to living in them. The first project, at Oldham Road between Spittal and Bengal Streets, had been a five-story square with a playground space for children in the middle. The *City News* description of it was in accord with a consensus of public opinion: the project was a "civic barracks . . . the buildings look monotonous and uniform." Several smaller efforts followed that produced conventional-looking two-story, row-house "cottages." Public officials also learned that high land values in the central city precluded the possibility of reaping even a modest return for their ventures in municipal capitalism. Not only was land cheap in the suburbs; there they had greater freedom to coordinate designs for housing, neighborhoods, and transportation into one overall plan.[37]

If the construction of the Blackley Estate was the high-water mark of housing reform, it also marked the limits of the public side of social environmentalism. Closely resembling the best privately built suburbs for people of modest income, it proved too successful. Real estate developers complained bitterly about unfair competition, and especially about the advantage local government had in securing lower rates of interest for long-term financing. Although the town council went ahead with a similar sized project, the Temple Estate in Cheetham Hill, in 1908, they acquiesced to the developers' demand that they end the suburban project. Instead, policy makers revised the building code to upgrade minimum standards of design and materials for private housing. New homes had to have open space all around them, damp-proof foundations, more windows and better ventilation, and fire-retardant roofs, for instance. Town Hall also continued to move forward in getting landlords to retrofit existing housing with indoor plumbing and to convert back-to-backs into through houses. By the outbreak of World War I, however, the slum districts of the central city remained basically intact. A real attack on them awaited the direct intervention of the national government during the interwar years.[38]

Charles Rowley had mounted a new type of reform movement, but the long-established channels of political culture and institutions narrowed its potential for effecting fundamental change. Despite the success of the Ancoats Brotherhood and the MSSA in building bridges, the divisions between the classes remained wide and acted as a powerful restraint on the achievement of Progressive ideals of social and environmental justice. Manchester's traditions of low-cost government and municipal capitalism created additional barriers that further retarded momentum toward these goals. A comparison of Rowley's efforts and Jane Addams's similar campaign to clean up the slums of a Chicago neighborhood helps expose the ways in which political structures shape the course of reform. As Addams would learn, the ward bosses had already built extremely strong organizations from the bottom up. Uprooting their corrupt regime of patronage and graft would be no easy task. But Addams, like Rowley, was a formidable driving force; she too seemed undaunted by obstacles in the path toward improving the quality of life of the working classes of the industrial city.

CHAPTER TEN

The Environmental Justice
Movement in Chicago

Introduction: Jane Addams and the Ward Boss Revisited

In 1893, London's muckraking journalist William T. Stead came to Chicago and stirred up a hornet's nest of moral ferment and civic activism. First at an open meeting at the Central Music Hall in November, and then later in a book, the evangelical crusader asked his receptive audiences to imagine what it would be like "if Christ came to Chicago." What Stead found during his several months in the city was a biblical Sodom of commercialized sin and political corruption. Sparking the formation of the elite Civic Federation to purify City Hall, he also triggered a much broader mobilization of religious institutions that rallied to his cry for a social gospel. The Englishman's influence in the creation of a reform movement in Chicago was emblematic of the trans-Atlantic reach of Progressivism. Stead's impressions of Chicago were also typical of the two-way nature of this evolving discourse on the social and environmental problems of the industrial city.[1]

For Stead, Jane Addams and her four-year-old settlement house were a model of the social gospel in action. "Hull House is one of the best institutions in Chicago," he exclaimed, "not merely because of the humanitarian influences which it radiates around the district in which it stands, but because it will become a training ground and nursery for multitudes of similar institutions speedily to spring up in all the great cities of America." Inspired by Addams's open-arms approach to helping her neighbors, Stead's version of Progressivism drew an analogy between the domestic household and the urban community. Only by adopting the direct and inclusive approach of Addams, he argued, "can we hope to reconstruct the human family, and restore something approaching to a microcosm of a healthy organization in every precinct of the city.... The healthy community is that of a small country town or village in which every one knows his neighbor, and where all the necessary ingredients for a happy, intelligent and public-spirited municipal life exist in due proportion." After also reviewing the work of Toynbee Hall and other pioneering settlements in Great Britain, the editor of the London *Pall Mall Gazette* declared Hull-House the ideal reform vehicle of positive environmentalism.[2]

Chicago served Stead as a source of inspiration in a second important way: it helped him to envision the city of the future. After seeing the Court of Honor at the World's Columbian Exposition, the writer joined Dr. Benjamin W. Richardson, Edward Bellamy, and other contributors to the popular contemporary genre of the urban utopia. In a chapter titled "In the Twentieth Century" that is tacked onto the end of his book, Stead imagines that "Chicago had become the ideal city of the world." Daniel Burnham's White City of 1893, he wrote, had aroused a great "civic revival" that transformed the "black city" into the city healthy and humane. Chicago would surpass New York when a great ship channel from the Atlantic Ocean to the Gulf of Mexico turned the Midwestern city into the nation's greatest port.[3]

Perhaps the Englishman overstayed his visit because he too came to believe that Lake Michigan represented a "fountain inexhaustible." He too became enamored with the technological fix of intense energy use to solve all the social problems of the industrial city. His suggestions for environmental engineering in the name of the moral order of the masses incorporated the city's plans for a large-scale drainage canal to permanently reverse the flow of the Chicago River. "The descending volume of the surplus water of the lake," he explained, would drive "immense" electrical turbines. "The tapping of this great reservoir of costless power corresponded with the great moral and social upheaval which, following the civic revival, enabled citizens to accomplish many things which otherwise would have been beyond their reach."[4]

Neatly resolving the paradox of progress, Stead's utopia on the lake embodied many of the World Fair's most attractive features: cleanliness, order, beauty, and efficiency. He and other visitors were impressed by the ways in which Daniel Burnham had planned buildings, streets, and landscapes to produce a sense of visual unity and grand but human scale. The papier-mâché fantasy of 1893 left an indelible impression on many who strolled the grounds. They walked away convinced that such an uplifting environment could be built in the real city with equally positive effects on personal behavior and moral values. While waterpower would run Chicago's industrial machine, municipal utilities would sell gas so cheaply that the burning of coal would be outlawed. Smokeless, clear skies would shine germ-killing sunlight on the playgrounds, schoolyards, parklands, and recreational facilities liberally sprinkled throughout the neighborhoods. In such a moral geography of environmental justice, Stead surmised, the prominent philanthropist Mrs. Bertha Palmer would become the first woman mayor of a big city.[5]

Although men kept women out of elective office, they could not keep City Homes Association head Jane Addams out of City Hall. As one of the most celebrated leaders of urban Progressivism, Addams has been the subject of a continuous stream of scholarship that has followed the main currents of postwar historiography. Beginning with a 1960 essay by Anne Firor Scott, the story has been told several times of the social worker's campaign to depose the city's most powerful and corrupt politician, Nineteenth Ward alderman Johnny Powers. During the same period in the early 1890s when she was creating her settlement house, Powers was establishing a dubious reputation as the leader of the city council's pack of "gray wolves"—so-called for their predatory approach to government.

Addams orchestrated an insurgency movement in order to rectify the appalling lack of sanitary and health services in a neighborhood crowded with poor immigrants. But after hard-fought campaigns in 1896 and 1898 during which male candidates stood in for Addams, the reformer seems to have lost not only the immediate objective at the polls but also the enduring contest of historical interpretation. Scott, for example, reasons that "as a practical matter there was no use waging another opposition campaign. Powers held too many cards . . . he proved too tough a nut to crack." From the narrow perspective of electoral politics, scholars have been left with little choice except to conclude that reformers' revolts against the machine were exercises in futility.[6]

In contrast, the application of the wider lens of an environmental approach to the study of Addams's campaign to clean up the slums offers an opportunity to gain fresh insight into the political formation of urban space and the related process of spatial segregation by ethnicity, class, and race. The reformer looked at her defeats at the polls as just the beginning, not the end of the battle to hold City Hall to account for the conditions of the working classes in the industrial city. She scorned any accommodation with Alderman

Powers, declaring in 1900 that "the protest of Hull-House against a man who continually disregards the most fundamental rights of his constituents must be permanent."[7]

The Education of an Urban Environmentalist

This story of Jane Addams's education as an urban reformer begins in 1889, when she moved into one of Chicago's poorest, most run down neighborhoods, just west of the Loop, or central business district. Her first lessons consisted of direct observations in what was also one of the oldest, most built-up sections of the city and was now serving as an immigrant port of entry because of its close proximity to the central business district.[8]

Although the great fire of 1871 had started just a few blocks away from Addams's new home, Hull-House, the settlement and most of the West Side had escaped the conflagration. Many of the wood-frame tenements, some dating as far back as the Civil War era, had been constructed on the low-lying land bordering the river, several feet below the artificially raised street grade. Subject to frequent flooding, sewer and privy overflows, and falling debris from the streets above, the backyards and alleyways of Johnny Powers's Nineteenth Ward were virtual dumping grounds for the city's liquid and solid wastes. Hull-House was located in the center of the city's riverfront wards, an area corresponding to its industrial corridor and Packingtown (see fig. 10.1).

The community's location just across the river from the many apparel and department stores in the Loop also made it a convenient site for the sweatshops that were intermixed with the factories and the garment manufacturers on the west end of the central business district (see fig. 10.2). All three depended on an abundant supply of the cheap labor provided by the immigrant men, women, and children who moved into these slum areas because that's where jobs were most readily available. Appointed as chief factory inspector of Illinois in 1893, Hull-House resident Florence Kelley began learning how to turn casual impressions that conditions were substandard into systematic studies of environmental injustice. Over the next few years, Kelley and Addams applied these powerful tools of research to produce a series of surveys and maps that would lay a solid foundation of social science upon which to build a compelling case for municipal reform. The two Health Department maps reproduced here were inspired by their pioneering work (figs. 10.1 and 10.2).[9]

The Hull-House women's headlong plunge into the ring of electoral politics also helped them to make rapid advances in their understanding of how money and power worked together in the construction of a social geography

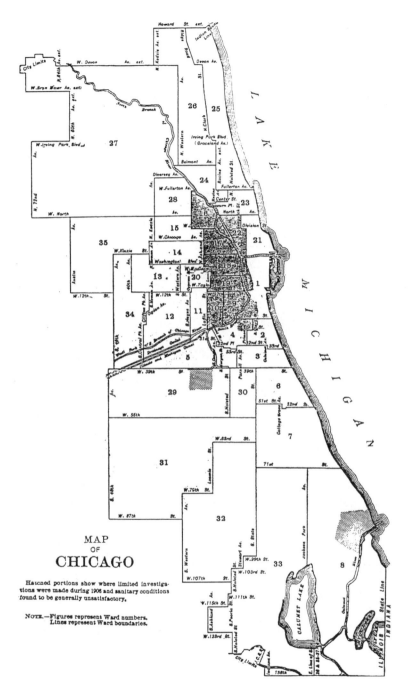

Figure 10.1. Unsanitary districts in Chicago, 1906
Source: Chicago, Board of Health, *Annual Report* (1906).

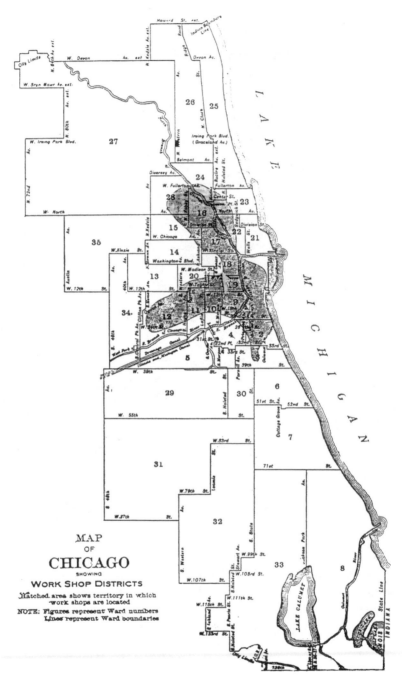

Figure 10.2. Workshop districts in Chicago, 1906
Source: Chicago, Board of Health, *Annual Report* (1906).

of inequality. Of first importance was Chicago's fragmented structure of government, which allowed each alderman to rule virtually supreme within his own ward. Powers, for example, held undisputed command over as many as 2,600 payrollers, a number equal to one-third of the ward's voters. These city jobs formed the taproot of his power. They gave him a broad-based organization of loyal voters and campaign workers who simply could not afford to deviate in any way from the party line. Dependent upon the alderman for their livelihoods, many residents considered him the chief benefactor of the neighborhood, not its most malevolent exploiter.

Each alderman also exercised nearly absolute authority over the enforcement of public regulations and the distribution of city services within his ward. A weak mayor, strong council form of government left chief executives with few instruments of power other than the force of their personalities to discipline renegade aldermen or pressure them to get back into line behind administration policies. Mayors were more likely to be held hostage to the ward bosses who controlled the all-powerful finance committee of the council. As one of its members, Powers exercised extraordinary influence in the municipal government. Only by giving free rein to the aldermen within their own fiefdoms did a few mayors, like the Carter Harrisons, father and son, achieve some success as leaders of the city.[10]

In her battles against Powers at the ballot box, Addams faced a particular kind of machine rule. The Chicago machine has been characterized as a political party that "has a tight, hierarchical organization, includes party agents at the grassroots level, and systematically distributes patronage among its members." This type of partisan mobilization based on ward-level factions rather than a central dominant figure has been the most common form of urban regime in the United States. Chicago varied from the norm in the extremity of its fragmentation of power. The highly decentralized structure of government made the party organizations prone to especially vicious forms of internal competition, strife, and betrayal. The devolution of power into the hands of the aldermen and the ward committeemen in Chicago effectively precluded the building of the kinds of coalitions among traditional groups of reformers that were replacing machine rule with progressive administrations in other places. But the entrenched positions of the ward bosses were not entirely immune to subversion.[11]

The very structural fragmentation that erected a nearly insurmountable barrier to a consolidation of power opened a special door of opportunity for women to participate in the public arena. As Kathryn Kish Sklar brilliantly shows in her biography of Florence Kelley, "Chicago offered women's organizations ideal conditions for expanding their power through civic action.

Government and labor were stymied; women and children were suffering; and both working-class and middle-class families were potentially threatened by disease." The political paralysis of the city's badly splintered labor movement allowed women to fill the resulting power vacuum as "class-bridging activists."[12]

Sklar's crucial insight on the gendered dimensions of Chicago politics sheds light on Addams's explanation of the sources of the ward boss's grassroots support in terms of class rather than ethnicity. In January 1898, as she launched her second campaign to unseat Powers, she delivered a progress report on her education as an urban reformer to a meeting of the Ethical Culture Society. She argued that poor people have very different needs and standards from those of the middle and upper classes: Their "sense of just dealing comes apparently much later than the desire for protection and kindness. The Alderman is really elected because he is a good friend and neighbor."[13] In other words, the secret of his success was an ability to perceive and respond to their desperate need for help, and in the minds of many working-class people, giving a man a job on the city payroll was the best help anyone could offer.

The only way to defeat Powers, Addams learned, was to beat him at his own game of paternalistic benevolence; but whereas his benevolence was cynical, hers would be real: Hull-House would offer social welfare programs that would significantly improve his constituents' everyday quality of life. The social worker understood that to achieve this goal she would have to expand the class-bridging efforts of Hull-House beyond its walls to reach directly into the dwellings, public spaces, and workshops of the district. This lesson had been driven home by the recent struggle with the alderman over control of the ward garbage inspector in the run-up to the 1898 elections. Powers had initially regarded the mayor's appointment of a woman to this post as something of a joke, but he realized his mistake when residents began noticing the improving condition of the neighborhood. Since the position was by that time protected by civil service rules, the alderman was forced to go to elaborate lengths and to spend valuable political capital in the council to get it cut entirely out of the budget.[14]

After again suffering humiliating defeat at the hands of alderman Powers in the local elections, Addams adopted a new strategy of reform that sought to address the most basic of working-class environmental concerns, a decent place to live. She decided that a sustained attack on housing problems was one of the best ways to put Chicago's women of affluence into the service of the poor. In launching this campaign, she drew upon the rich heritage of the work of English sanitarians and housing reformers as well as the technical skills

Florence Kelley, Julia Lathrop, and other social investigators were currently accumulating as they mapped the physical conditions of the slums. Another Hull-House resident, Edith Abbott, recalled that they were also influenced by other Progressives' initiatives in this direction, including Charles Booth's massive study of working-class London and Jacob Riis's revealing photographs of New York City.

The first step in the Chicago campaign was the creation of an institutional vehicle of reform, the City Homes Association. Having secured financial support from Anita McCormick Blaine and other rich patrons, Addams proposed to turn impressionistic descriptions of the slums into scientific proof of bad housing. She crossed not only class but also gender lines, bringing in Stanford University professor Frank A. Fetter to conduct the investigation during the summer of 1900 and Robert Hunter to write up the results. The results of the groundbreaking study appeared the following year as *Tenement Conditions in Chicago*.[15]

The report laid a solid foundation upon which to build among the urban middle class a convincing case for remedial action. Although Kelley's work for the U.S. Department of Labor had established that Chicago did in fact have slum conditions, her survey was more demographic than environmental in nature. Her findings were both too narrow in geographic scope and too broad in relevant categories of enumeration to reveal the underlying causes or the full extent of the city's housing problems. In contrast, the City Homes investigation was carefully designed to describe the physical conditions of the home and its immediate surroundings in exhaustive detail. To achieve their goals, the reformers chose to focus their efforts tightly on a few representative working-class neighborhoods rather than taking a citywide census or depending on a sensational account of the very worst area, Packingtown. Every aspect of the physical environment in the three sample districts, which contained forty-five thousand people, received attention, from the quality of the light and air inside the buildings to the arrangement of sanitary and drainage facilities outside of them. An extensive collection of maps and photographs helped paint a vivid picture of human misery and squalor.[16]

The investigation left no doubt as to the existence of a housing problem in Chicago. Calculations based on the sample data estimated that seven hundred thousand people, or 40 percent of the city's inhabitants, were living in conditions below contemporary standards of decency. The report established a reliable baseline against which Abbott and her colleagues at the University of Chicago's influential school of sociology would measure environmental change in the central city for the next thirty years.[17]

Moreover, the investigation made important strides in shifting public discourse—at least among the middle classes—from an ethnic-based to a class-based mode of social analysis. At least since the rise of the Know-Nothings in the 1850s, the politics of nativism and ethnocultural division had been a staple of the American party system. The impulse to blame immigrant groups for the city's social problems was deeply rooted in English traditions of xenophobia, especially in relation to Irish Catholics. We saw those traditions at work in Manchester, where civic leaders drew on them to heap blame on the victims for their own poverty, slum conditions, and extraordinary rates of sickness and death. America's own traditions of racial slavery and prejudice also played a role in giving legitimacy to this virulent kind of political discourse. In sharp contrast, Addams and her allies cleverly undermined popular stereotypes of the immigrant. First they conflated the heterogeneous populations of the districts into uniform zones that they called, for example, Little Italy, Poletown, and the Jewish Ghetto, and then they demonstrated that geography, not ethnicity, accounted for different conditions in these neighborhoods.[18]

More important, the City Homes report inaugurated a political discourse that sought to assign responsibility for slum conditions in conceptual terms that rested upon a nexus of money and power. Consider that 44 percent of the families in the Hull-House district had to use outdoor privies, which had been banned by city ordinance for over a decade. The privies were visible for all to see, so only a conspiracy of property owners and public officials could explain such a blatant violation of the law.

Reformers identified three underlying causes of environmental injustice. First, of course, the "slum landlords" put personal profits ahead of the social welfare. Second, the municipal authorities were also to blame for substandard housing conditions. The report asserted that "official neglect and corrupt politics" went a long way in accounting for such unlawful conditions as "unpaved and unclean streets, dangerous sidewalks, [the lack of] garbage disposal and removal, rubbish and refuse upon open spaces, the outlawed privy vaults, houses unfit for habitation, damp basement dwellings, overcrowded, dark, and unventilated rooms," and so on. Finally, the third culprit, public indifference, had to share responsibility for the wretched state of municipal administration.[19]

Addams and the women of the City Homes Association hoped the report would serve to spark a movement for reform, but they were realistic in anticipating a long, uphill struggle to overcome the combined forces of the ward bosses, property owners, and building contractors who profited from shoddy construction methods. The reception of the study confirmed their prediction that it might take a "Ten Years' War" to win over public and official opinion to the cause of environmental justice for the working class. Addams, Blaine, and other reformers used the study to good effect in a series of lectures to arouse the attention of the well-to-do, building pressure on the politicians to enact the model tenement reform bill drafted by the City Homes Association.

In many respects, the preparation of the bill represented the culmination of the environmental reformers' education. The proposed law called for a significant expansion of the scope and range of the city government's police powers over the built environment. Its regulatory authority would be extended to cover all buildings with two or more dwellings as well as every aspect of their environmental quality, including light, ventilation, and sanitation. Minimum standards of construction would require contractors to install a water closet in each apartment and at least one sink on every floor. For the first time, the city would bring housing under the protective umbrella of significant fire safety rules. Equally important, the ordinance spelled out plumbing and building codes in exacting detail in order to eliminate large gray areas that could be left to the interpretation of inspectors and contractors. In a similar way, the city's enforcement powers would be beefed up through careful attention to administrative procedures and prerogatives. Finally, the new law went beyond previous efforts to ban the outdoor privies of existing buildings; now they would have to be replaced with modern toilets.

In April 1902, their agitation seemed to have done its work when no less a power than the chairman of the finance committee, William Mavor, introduced the new health and building code for the council's consideration. But the proposed ordinance was immediately sent to the judiciary committee where the aldermen expected it to be soon forgotten and permanently buried.[20]

Only the intervention of an unplanned and unwelcome event, an outbreak of typhoid fever, revived the reform measure from its resting place deep in the vaults of City Hall. Few other causes could so effectively mobilize public opinion as this particular dread disease. By the 1900s, the presence or absence of typhoid had become the litmus test of public health among the medical profession and the urban middle class because doctors and scientists had firmly established that the cause of this horrible intestinal ailment was bacteria, or germs, that were usually spread by water contaminated with human wastes.

Although a relatively small proportion of the total disease-related deaths in the city were among the well-to-do, typhoid fever loomed large in the minds of members of the more affluent classes. Their residential enclaves afforded no protection from the dreaded germs, which insidiously infiltrated their homes through the water taps. In sharp contrast, social exclusion and compulsory isolation spatially insulated them from the masses of common people who were afflicted with the much more prevalent and equally fatal contagious respiratory illnesses, such as pneumonia, bronchitis, and, worst of all, tuberculosis. In this case, the perspectives of class analysis help shed light on the social construction of health and disease.

When the number of typhoid fever cases began rising ominously in July and August 1902, fear quickly galvanized Chicagoans into commencing a shrill chorus demanding action on the part of the city authorities. Suddenly the reformers were presented with a unique opportunity to steer an alarmed and motivated public into their movement for environmental justice. Jane Addams was determined not to let this strategic moment slip away in her ongoing battle against John Powers and the ward bosses.[21]

"An Inquiry into the Causes of the Recent Epidemic"

During the next phase in the campaign to better the living conditions of poor people in Chicago, Addams went on the offensive, shifting tactics from investigation and analysis to accusation and exposure of official malfeasance. The mysterious accumulation of typhoid fever cases in the Nineteenth Ward presented a challenge to social as well as medical science. Although the ward contained one thirty-sixth of the city population, it accounted for one sixth of the deaths from the disease. With the tenement house report in hand, Addams jumped at the chance to turn social science into a political weapon. She immediately launched a follow-up investigation aimed at drawing direct casual links between the physical conditions of the slum and the extraordinary suffering of its inhabitants. Although the inquiry failed to prove an environmental etiology of the disease, it did uncover what appeared to be an institutionalized system of corruption among landlords and officials.

Naming names and leveling formal charges of wrongdoing, the women of Hull-House triggered a process of public exposure that took on a life of its own. Their reform campaign revealed layer after layer of a deeply ingrained conspiracy to reap personal profit and partisan advantage at the expense of the poor. This unfolding scandal would briefly open a window on the mechanisms by which class and power worked to build urban landscapes of exclusion and inequality. What Addams ultimately exposed was an urban political culture of unbridled capitalism; Chicago was "a city on the make."[22]

In both a literal and a metaphorical sense, the Hull-House women's 1903 report on the epidemic represents a historic crossroads in the struggle for environmental justice in Chicago. First, the inquiry itself embodied a pivotal shift

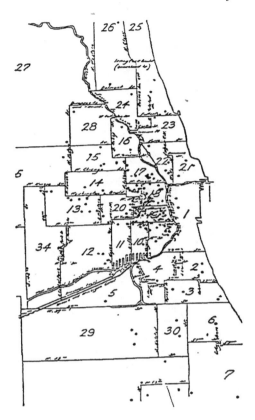

Figure 10.3. Spot map of typhoid fever deaths, August 1902

Source: Maud Gernon, Gertrude Howe, and Alice Hamilton, *An Inquiry into the Causes of the Recent Epidemic of Typhoid Fever in Chicago, Made by the Residents of Hull-House* (Chicago: City Homes Association, 1903), frontispiece.

in scientific paradigms of disease causation from miasmatic, or filth-based, models to germ theories. Since the ward was only a small part of the distribution area served by the water intake points that were the most obvious source of the typhoid fever outbreak, contaminated drinking supplies could not explain the strange pattern of clustering (see fig. 10.3). A door-to-door survey of two thousand buildings also failed to prove a direct correlation between bad plumbing and location of those who had gotten sick (see fig. 10.4). Addams called upon Hull-House resident Dr. Alice Hamilton to bring the relatively new methods of bacteriology to bear on the mystery, and Hamilton reached what seemed to be the definitive conclusion: houseflies carried the disease.

To contemporaries, however, this change from a miasmatic to a germ theories of disease etiology represented an easy transition in conceptual models. Perceptions of the two theories were mutually reinforcing: both bolstered middle-class convictions about the need to clean up the slums. Whether the cause of the contagion was noxious vapors or infected bugs, the remedy

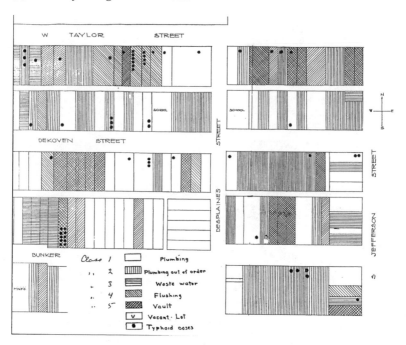

Figure 10.4. Detail map of typhoid fever epidemic, 1902
Source: Maud Gernon, Gertrude Howe, and Alice Hamilton, *An Inquiry into the Causes of the Recent Epidemic of Typhoid Fever in Chicago, Made by the Residents of Hull-House* (Chicago: City Homes Association, 1903).

remained the same. Addams was more determined than ever to gain passage of the proposed tenement bill, which established minimum housing standards and administrative procedures to enforce them. Her tactics turned again to direct action, which sharply distinguished her approach to urban environmentalism from the academic orientations of the male-dominated departments of sociology. Now armed with useful information, she reentered the political arena to undercut the sources of the ward bosses' strength at the grass roots.[23]

The frightening surge in typhoid fever cases in July 1902 took the city by surprise because the heroic engineering project to reverse the direction of the Chicago River permanently away from the lake was supposed to guarantee safe drinking supplies. Two years earlier, when the dual-purpose sanitary and ship canal finally opened, politicians and leading daily journals such as the *Chicago Tribune* had proclaimed "the city at last is freed from the growing menace of a contaminated water supply." The few dissenting voices among the medical practitioners of the new public health fell on deaf ears until

3 August 1902, when the newspaper revealed in a startling Sunday headline: "Typhoid Reaches Epidemic Stage." Now, the *Tribune*'s editors confessed to their chagrin that "the entire water supply is of inferior quality. The only consolation is that if it were not for the drainage channel the water would be inconceivably worse than it is now. It would be rank poison."[24]

Most doctors and public health officials immediately blamed the city's water supply. Heavy rains during the preceding three months of spring, they believed, had purged massive amounts of human wastes from sewers that emptied directly into Lake Michigan. Chemists and bacteriologists verified the presence of dangerous levels of microorganisms at all four of the city's intake points along the lakefront. Despite the health department's advice to boil the water, the epidemic continued to take its toll. The health department recorded 177 deaths during August; ten times that number probably contracted the disease, which had a fatality rate of about 10 percent. One indication of widespread public alarm was the near hysteria as the opening day of the new school year approached. On 2 September, the children learned about a new prerequisite for admission: children must carry their own supply of water. The Board of Education had responded to the parents' anxieties by turning off the drinking fountains. This "bottle brigade" of a quarter-million students represented the front lines in the battle against typhoid. Echoing the warnings of the medical experts, the Reverend W. A. Bartlett of the First Congregational Church urged his audience to boil the water and pray.[25]

Dr. Alice Hamilton, whom Addams had asked to undertake an investigation of the sources of the contagion, was a member of the new breed of university-trained medical scientists who was particularly adept in the emerging field of microbiology. But she was more; her gender and background helped ensure that she would put these professional skills in the service of society. Hamilton recounted in her autobiography:

> I came back from Mackinac to find Chicago in the grip of one of her worst epidemics of typhoid fever. . . . As I prowled about the streets and the ramshackle wooden tenement houses I saw the outdoor privies (forbidden by law but flourishing nevertheless), some of them in backyards below the level of the street and overflowing in heavy rains; the wretched water closets indoors, one to four or more families, filthy and with the plumbing out of order because nobody was responsible for cleaning or repairs; and swarms of flies everywhere. Here, I thought was the solution of the problem. The flies were feeding on typhoid-infected excreta and then lighting on food and milk.

Drawing on the recent breakthroughs in epidemiology made during the Spanish-American War, Hamilton studied the suspected disease carriers in the laboratory. "It was a triumph to find the typhoid bacillus," she wrote, "and it explained why the slums had so much more typhoid than the well-screened and decently drained homes of the well-to-do."[26]

Hamilton, Addams, and the women of Hull-House played a major role in mobilizing public support for tenement house reform. As early as mid-August, health department maps had identified a "plague spot" in the Jewish immigrant neighborhood at the south end of the ward. Having found a ready-made scapegoat, Health Commissioner Arthur Reynolds implied that greedy Jewish street peddlers were selling rotten fruit, which he blamed for the epidemic. He sent the department's inspectors, armed with cans of kerosene, swarming into the "Ghetto" on a mission to seek and destroy the suspect produce and dairy products. Addams could not yet openly refute this resort to a politics of ethnic division because her project to link bad plumbing to social geography was just getting under way.

Hamilton's preliminary report to the Chicago Medical Society, however, helped to refocus the public's attention on sanitary conditions in the working-class district. Whether one believed in the older filth theories of disease causation or the newer germ theories, Chicago's middle and upper classes could agree on a commonsense remedy, cleaning up the slums. "Cleanliness is not only next to godliness," the *Tribune* preached in familiar terms, "but it is the only safeguard against typhoid fever. Typhoid fever is the result of lack of cleanliness." After attempts by council leaders like William Mavor to shift the blame to the mayor's office evoked little response, the aldermen decided to resurrect Addams's buried reform proposal.[27]

By mid-December, most of the aldermen seem to have been converted to the cause of environmental justice. They voted overwhelmingly in favor of the proposal by an unexpected margin of forty-seven to seven. "The long delayed and disputed 'tenement house' ordinance" received such unified support from the politicians that every maneuver on behalf of various special interests was beaten back. The only significant exception was a grandfather clause limiting application of the new, higher building and plumbing standards to future construction. The new housing code can be judged only as a major victory for the forces of reform in the battle against the machine: it not only raised minimum standards of decency, but also changed the administrative institutions of government to achieve the new goals. The triumph of the reformers was short-lived, however, because the party bosses had a hidden agenda to pervert the housing code to their own personal and partisan ends.[28]

The ward bosses' unanticipated about-face was motivated not by conversion but by the cunning and deceit with which they cynically betrayed the public trust. The aldermen had determined that the reform bill could be turned into a piece of "made-to-order 'four-flush' legislation," according to historian Thomas Philpott. "A four-flush law," he explains, "was one which politicians passed for the purpose of soliciting graft in return for *not* enforcing it." Contractors were soon lining up to pay tribute to the party bosses, who were all too willing to sell exemptions from the new law for the right price. The law's "greatest weakness," Edith Abbott confirms, "was the failure on the part of the authorities to make any genuine effort to enforce" it.[29]

Addams and her coinvestigators, still in the midst of writing their inquiry on the epidemic, were not easily fooled. They had heard too many stories from frustrated residents about complaint after complaint to the health department that had brought no results. "The explanation rife in the neighborhood," the women learned, "is that the inspector is 'fixed.'" The voices of poor immigrants were was rarely recorded, but the Hull-House study leaves little doubt that these people were taking active steps to improve the quality of their physical surroundings, even though these steps were being thwarted. The house-to-house visitors found "a touching eagerness 'to have something done about it.' They encountered a general feeling of anxiety and helplessness, and in some instances bitterness and indignation that life had been needlessly endangered and lost." Even the most persistent tenant protesters, the investigators found, were rendered powerless by health officers who stamped their formal complaints "nuisance abated," in spite of the fact that absolutely nothing had been done. The accumulation of these anecdotes of corruption convinced Addams to set a trap to ensnarl slum landlords and city inspectors in a web of careful documentation of their official misconduct.[30]

Waiting until just after the municipal elections in April 1903, Addams sprung the trap in a brilliantly conceived counteroffensive to gain maximum publicity for the typhoid fever inquiry, the report of which became a political weapon in three ways. First, it posed questions about environmental justice in concrete terms. The published version of the inquiry was muckraking journalism at its sensational best. It revealed every detail about seven specific cases of grievous wrongdoing except the names of the landlords and the ward's two health inspectors, teasing the press in a footnote to obtain them at the Hull-House. The women also hand delivered a special copy with the names filled in to Mayor Harrison. Scrambling to catch up with the fast-breaking story, the newspapers were soon disclosing names and demanding that City Hall investigate the charges. This attention in the daily press helped ensure a wide readership for the short, twenty-page pamphlet among affluent and influential Chicagoans.

Second, it hammered home its goals on behalf of poor people by linking their fate to the general welfare of the community. The report made explicit the links between bodies, neighborhoods, and the larger urban environment. Playing on middle-class fears of infection by the lower strata of society, it warned that "the river wards cannot be isolated from the other residence portions of the town." The Nineteenth Ward, readers were informed, served as the city's central origination point for home delivery vehicles and produce peddlers. "With all these go the houseflies," the report ended ominously, "bearing, as we may believe, the typhoid germ."[31]

Third, the reformers' attack on official corruption won widespread public attention because they had successfully chosen test cases that would explode like bombshells in midst of the professional politicians. The first slumlord name leaked to the press was that of former alderman John Nagel. For over five months, the Hull-House women charged, the inspectors had known that the main sewer pipe in one of his buildings at 324 South Halsted was broken and that the basement was therefore filled with human waste. In addition, a toilet on the second story "was clogged, so that on the floor there was a puddle which the woman daily swept down the front stairway. This liquid filth also seeped through the ceiling and dripped down on the floor below, occupied by a Greek." Yet, none of the five tenant complaints sent to the health department via registered mail had even shown up in the department's records.

In a similar way, the reformers built a high-profile case against the University of Chicago as one of the ward's largest and most negligent landlords. Ironically, the Hull estate had given large amounts of rental property to the university in order to fund a biology laboratory. Hoping perhaps to deflect the main attack, the health department joined in, accusing the university of "bluffing" and "bulldozing" every effort to bring its buildings into compliance. In only a few days, the Hull-House report achieved its political objective of kicking the movement for environmental justice to the front pages of the daily press. Now charge and countercharge by city officials ducking for cover would give the growing scandal a public life of its own.[32]

"Destructive of Government and Justice Alike"

Over the course of about two years of intense political struggle, the women of Chicago led the reform battle to reshape the contours of city government's active involvement in the formation of urban space. Between April and July 1903, Hull-House directed the campaign to unmask before the Civil Service Commission (CSC) the ways in which City Hall interacted with property owners in defining the quality of the built environment. Addams highlighted how the politicians played a vital part in erecting a social geography of class division between the riverfront and the lakefront zones. She also orchestrated a chorus of testimony before the commission that drew upon her women's network of civic and charitable organizations as well as her academic connections.

The explosive contents of the typhoid report cracked the insiders' code of silence and revealed that owners and public officials were engaged in an open conspiracy to reap mutual profit from the misery of those forced by poverty to live in the slums. Eventually the women helped to implicate not only the health department, but also the fire, building, street, and police departments; the city attorney's office; the boiler inspection bureau; and the local improvements board. Paying no attention to protecting the public health and welfare, City Hall was corrupt from top to bottom.[33]

Addams's strategy of focusing public attention on the dishonesty of carefully selected landlords and inspectors was a logical and effective way to launch the struggle for environmental justice. The *Tribune* framed the question at the outset of the battle, "Is Hull-House right or not?" and Alderman Nagel's knee-jerk reaction of blaming the tenants and the Hull-House women played right into Addams's hands, helping to define the issues of the political debate in clear, simple terms.

The immediate target at City Hall was the supervisor of the two accused inspectors, Health Commissioner Dr. Arthur Reynolds. He had gained a good reputation for bringing the modern methods of bacteriology to the department after the city's previous and worst episode of typhoid fever a decade before. Now he was thrown on the defensive by the Hull-House report and by the reactions of the press and of the mayor, who held him publicly to account while back pedaling away from any personal responsibility.

Isolated and hurt by Harrison's desertion, Dr. Reynolds struck back, leveling two of his own blockbusters at the status quo. He revealed the administration's deep secret about the strange clustering of the epidemic in the Nineteenth Ward. In his startling disclosure he blamed the water department for causing a fatal foul-up at a pumping station. For three full days, raw sewage had been allowed to pour into the local area's drinking supplies, causing at least seventy-one needless deaths. Almost equally unnerving was the doctor's allegation against University of Chicago president William Rainey Harper, who was portrayed as the ward's largest and most recalcitrant slumlord. Dr. Reynolds told reporters why he held the city's leading educator personally responsible for the substandard condition of the housing units owned and managed by his institution. When the health commissioner confronted him about the mismanagement of the Hull estate properties at a social event some time before, Harper showed only cold indifference to the plight of their poor tenants. He rudely turned to break off the conversation and abruptly walked away without saying a word.[34]

The first round of charge and countercharge triggered a political chain reaction and unleashed a firestorm of accusations against the city's party leaders. At the same time, Addams kept adding fuel to the flames by marshaling a parade of witnesses before the public. By the time the CSC finally convened on 4 May 1903, the Nagel case was reaching a stage of political meltdown that the ward bosses could no longer contain. In this instance, the paper trail extended far beyond the inspector to entrap top bureaucrats and key jurists in the web of documentary evidence of their corruption. Hull-House's intervention on behalf of the tenants in Nagel's buildings had produced two suits resulting in fines against the negligent owner. But the court had later remitted both fines upon the request of Chief Sanitary Inspector Andrew Young. In his own defense, Young disclaimed any improper influence, explaining that the policy of the administration was to rescind all fines against property owners after their buildings were deemed to be in compliance. Mayor Harrison now appeared to take the high road by reversing course on this policy and declaring a crackdown on slum buildings.[35]

But the fallout from the Nagel case continued to expose the administration to new charges of corrupt practices. Hull-House documentation pointed to yet another way in which the ward bosses had institutionalized environmental injustice for the city's working classes: the use of the "stay book," a pernicious device to stymie tenant rights on behalf of the property owners. Under pressure, Dr. Reynolds had revealed the existence of a secret log containing a long list of health department suits that, as a courtesy to one sort of political sponsor or another, had never been prosecuted. Of the 365 stay orders listed by the newspapers, about two-thirds had been requested by the health commissioner and his secretary, and one-fifth by one of sixteen different aldermen. John Powers' name appeared ten times, putting him near the top of the councilmen's list. The names of judges, former city workers, influential party figures, and a member of congress also appeared in the stay book, as did that of former city sealer Fred Eldred, one of the slum landlords targeted in the Hull-House report.[36]

This phase of the graft scandal reached a climax in early July with the appearance of the sanitary bureau's two top managers before the CSC. Young and his deputy John S. Kelly had to answer not only for the stay book and other dubious record-keeping practices, but also for new charges that their inspectors were using retaliatory tactics to intimidate witnesses. Both men vigorously denied any wrongdoing, staunchly defended their inspectors, and aggressively justified the customary practices of the department. Pressed by the commissioners, Kelly conceded that granting over five years of delays in enforcement might seem excessive, but he still maintained that "there must have been a good reason for granting such an extension." He also admitted that at the request of any alderman his office would defer the process of bringing violators into compliance "because we feel that" an alderman "has the interests of his constituents at heart and is responsible." As he waited for the hearings to close, Dr. Reynolds took a similar stand to defend his reputation. Lashing out in all directions, the doctor exclaimed, "I have had great trouble holding myself in for three months. Hull-House has been scouring the town for a year" to come up with "nothing but complaints, faked up as a rule, and with no substance."[37]

The accumulating evidence left little doubt, however, about the answer to the question posed by the *Chicago Tribune*: Hull-House was right. The overwhelming weight of the testimony Addams brought into the public arena supported her political objective of linking the causes of environmental justice and municipal reform. Even more compelling perhaps was the remarkable metamorphosis of the Nineteenth Ward in the short time since the report of the inquiry was issued. City officials and property owners alike had taken advantage of the deliberately slowed pace of the official proceedings to clean up the neighborhood. The university, for instance, had decided to install sanitary plumbing in all its buildings, finally coming into compliance with the law. "A widespread movement is going on in recent weeks," a reporter observed in early June, "of abolishing ancient nuisances which had enjoyed immunity."

One Hull-House resident took note of the vital difference city government could make in determining the quality of life in the industrial city. "You could hardly recognize the old haunts of filth," she declared. "They are stirring things up there, and the owners are compelled to obey the ordinance in many cases. The result is a veritable transformation and hundreds of plague spots have been made innocuous." Health department statistics comparing the work of the same group of inspectors before and after the release of Addams's report further highlight the importance of the political culture of a city (see table 10.1). In Chicago, that culture had allowed the ward bosses to turn the city government into a private business for their own personal and partisan profit, at the expense of their working-class constituents.[38]

In late July, the movement for municipal reform entered a new phase, jumping into higher gear as Chicago's male civic and party leadership attempted to reassert control over the political process. The shame of the slums

Table 10.1 Sanitary Bureau nuisance abatement activity, 1902–1903

	April–June 1902	April–June 1903	Increase
Number of inspections	5,136	6,987	1,851
Number of nuisances abated	4,105	6,408	2,303
Percentage abated	77.9	91.7	

Source: *Chicago Tribune*, 31 July 1903.

had become a full-blown crisis marked by the spreading scope of the corruption investigation and the exposure of an urban regime perverted to the core. Testimony volunteered by union plumbers had suddenly opened the eyes of businessmen to the alarming possibility that the same political culture of unfettered capitalism that usually worked in their favor could also work against their interests. The plumbers had brought to light a cunning conspiracy between inspectors and contractors to steal from property owners by falsely charging them for labor and materials that were not put into the construction of their new buildings. Gathering additional affidavits from the union, the Citizens' Association, the oldest men's civic group, led the way. At the end of the month it announced that criminal indictments were being filed against five health inspectors, including Assistant Chief Kelly.

The bribery probe uncovered fundamental differences in gender perspectives on the urban environment. Reflecting their personal interests as some of the city's largest property owners, the big landlords tried to shift the focus of attention from the city government's role in maintaining existing housing conditions and toward its role in overseeing future construction. Yet the new round of revelations had an effect similar to that of the women's campaign. Public demand continued to mount for structural reforms that both strengthened public authority over the built environment and established professional standards for the delivery of vital urban services.[39]

In some respects, the 22 July 1903 release of the CSC report on the health department helped to keep Addams's reform movement from being sidetracked by the Citizens' Association. The report advanced her political objective to tie much stronger checkreins of accountability on the municipal bureaucracy. Lambasting the urban regime, the commission found regarding the health department that "there is either an unintelligent direction of the important work of the department, or an intentional effort to leave the records in such an incomplete shape it would be impossible to place responsibility where it belongs." The roots of boss rule were so deeply embedded in the political culture that "citizens have been taught to believe that laws could be evaded if proper influence was used." Addams's appeal for environmental justice for the slum dwellers must have also gotten through to the commissioners because they flatly refuted the inspectors' pious claims that they bent the rules only to help the struggling, poverty-stricken homeowners. "The people who own the poorest properties," the panel retorted, "are not generally poor people. In most instances, they are persons of ample means . . . who could afford to make improvements. . . . But these are not matters for the health department. The balancing of the public health as against private interests, considerations of real estate values, are not within the scope of its authority and are destructive of government and justice alike."[40]

In other respects, however, the thrust of the CSC report was to stop the cause of environmental reform far short of reaching its goals. The commissioners labored mightily to reach the ultimate judgment that the department might be found guilty of mismanagement but not of corruption. Mayor Harrison also hoped to use the report to steer the women of Hull-House into a political dead end by putting a Band-aid on the systemic flaws they had uncovered in the structure of public administration. Assuming the mantle of progressive reform, he exonerated Dr. Reynolds and assigned a clerk to help him keep better records of housing complaints.[41]

But Harrison badly underestimated the strength of the public's seething anger and resentment against machine rule by the ward bosses. The courage displayed first by Addams and then by the union plumbers seems to have triggered the release of an avalanche of pent-up grievances against the mercenary urban regime. Over the coming months, for instance, stenographers subjected to sexual harassment blew the whistle on their tormentors and water department workers fired for not paying tribute to the party came forward to demand justice.

On a larger metropolitan scale, the environmental impacts of water management policies twisted by the ward bosses for their own ends punctuated the political crisis with painful reminders that the middle and upper classes also paid a heavy price for a regime riddled with corruption. With the coming of warm weather, Chicagoans braced for another season of water shortages despite the fact that they lived in the city with the world's greatest waterworks in terms of its pumping capacity and its virtually unlimited supply of this most essential commodity.

During 1903, affluent Hyde Park suffered from chronic low pressure. Stung by the tragic cover-up in the pump house, Chief Engineer John E. Ericson vented his simmering frustrations directly to the public in an appeal for reform along the lines of efficiency and scientific management. The ratepayers, he pointed out, could enjoy an immediate $1.8 million savings in the annual operating expenses of the waterworks, to say nothing of much larger long-term reductions in capital costs.[42]

In August, an outbreak of typhoid fever in the suburban enclaves of the well-to-do along the North Shore hammered home Addams's frightening warning that there were no safe havens from the infectious diseases breeding in the filth and squalor of the riverfront wards. Once again, pollution-laden storm water had been flushed from sewers into the lake, contaminating drinking supplies. And just as in the recent water shortages, a respected and influential expert stepped forward to point an accusing finger at the politicians.[43] Guided by a new generation of experts, the more the middle classes looked, the more they saw a political system that had run amuck.

In September, municipal reformers continued to mobilize influential members of the public for a final assault on City Hall, but the knockout blow was delivered by a minor payroller who led investigators straight to the mayor's office. The official in question, John W. Gildea, had been enjoying a coveted patronage post as chief janitor. Now he was caught up in the corruption scandal for taking penny-ante kickbacks. Ironically, his crime involved contracts for bottled water that was provided to the offices of elected officials. Facing certain dismissal from his job by the CSC, Gildea broke the party insiders' code of silence, striking back hard with accusations of serious misconduct on the part of Harrison and river ward boss John H. Sullivan. The mayor had ordered that all city plumbing work be given to the Sullivan, in direct violation of laws barring members of the council from participating in municipal contracts.

Harrison sought high ground by immediately denying any knowledge of Sullivan's ownership of the Union Plumbing Company. His position began eroding just as quickly, however, as the public learned more about what must be considered the single most outrageous plot uncovered by the graft investigation. One of Sullivan's disgruntled employees came forward to charge that the company was using its city contracts as a front to hide a nefarious plan to make illegal water hookups. For weeks, the newspapers had been reporting the discovery of more and more of these illicit connections, which allowed consumers to use city water without ever having to pay for it. Providing a list of these secret hookups, the plumber explained that "it was easy to do the work without permits as the tapping wagon supplied by Ald Sullivan to the city at $3 per day was used after the city work was done. As the wagon had the city's name on it, no policeman ever would think of questioning the right of workmen who tore up the street."[44]

Harrison sounded the retreat in late September 1903, when he signaled the surrender of the professional politicians. With the attack on the politicians threatening to spin completely out of control, the leadership voiced their anxiety with a shrill cry. The mayor declared, "This hall is full of 'graft' big and little.... If I could fire all the men I suspect of 'grafting' they would be jumping out of every window." He took the lead in offering major concessions to municipal reformers in a desperate effort to prevent the rapid deterioration in his position from becoming a complete rout. On 2 October, Harrison began throwing out accused ringleaders in the police, public works, and health departments as the first big step in placating public opinion. The firings continued over the next six weeks, ultimately reaching Chief Inspector Andrew Young, who became the eleventh and final inspector swept out of the seventeen-man office.

As the mayor's dismissal of this sixty-five-year-old bureaucrat marked the end of the housecleaning at City Hall, the aldermen stepped forward to support Harrison's efforts to recapture the political initiative. Equally desperate to contain the unfolding scandal, the ward bosses finally committed the city council to fixing the administrative machinery. They set up a special committee, headed by the honest and well-respected Ernst F. Herrmann, to overhaul the record-keeping practices of the administration. One result would be a model plumbing code that would endure for a quarter-century.[45]

The removal of Young seemed to clear the way for Addams to claim final victory over the ward bosses with the installation of her handpicked candidate, Charles Ball, as the new chief inspector. She and the City Homes Association had persuaded the top manager of New York's tenement house bureau to move to Chicago in anticipation of his appointment. But still tasting the bitter pill of defeat, the politicians engaged in a stubborn rearguard action to forestall reform for as long as they could. Even though the sanitary engineer had earned the top score on the civil service exam, the post was given the following March to none other than Charles Clarke, who had scored eleventh in a field of thirteen and was one of the two inspectors originally identified by the Hull-House inquiry. The sixty-two-year-old payroller was declared the winner on the basis of an obscure technicality that gave preference to Civil War veterans.

Addams had to mobilize the women of the Nineteenth Ward once again to hurdle the latest roadblock thrown by the politicians into the path of environmental justice for the working class. Clarke proved an especially inept prop of obstructionism, blundering into one statement after another that was damaging in the court of public opinion. He conceded, for example, that he did not enforce the ban on outdoor privies because "law is ... purely a matter of custom. It was not the custom to enforce that particular law in that particular neighborhood, and so I didn't enforce it." Such self-incriminating statements allowed the CSC to override his claim to entitlement and certify Ball for the position. Thrown back on the defensive, party leaders found a much stronger bulwark of resistance in the form of a friendly local judge who forced the New Yorker out of his job on another legal technicality. Reformers would have to wait for almost another year before their appeals reached a successful conclusion in the state supreme court. Ball finally took his place at the end of February 1905 and would remain on the job for the next twenty-three years.[46]

Addams must be declared the victor in her two-year campaign against the ward bosses: she achieved her immediate goal of linking environmental justice and municipal reform. The physical conditions of the Nineteenth Ward did get noticeably better as city services were distributed more equitably. Illegal privies were removed, streets and alleys paved, sidewalks built, dilapidated buildings razed, and garbage removed. The settlement workers' efforts also brought about permanent changes in the structure of city government that helped modernize the city's inspection services and make them more accountable to the people. The arbitrary discretion of individual officers was replaced by standard administrative procedures, which were institutionalized in minute detail in housing, plumbing, and health codes. The installation of an honest and efficient expert at the head of the sanitary bureau also marked a big step forward in the delivery of essential public services to those who needed them most. Taken together, the reforms spearheaded by Addams and her allies represented significant movement toward the realization of a progressive vision of the industrial city.[47]

Conclusions: The Political Culture of Unbridled Capitalism

Revisiting Jane Addams's battle against the ward boss from an environmental perspective helps refocus attention on the political formation of urban space. City government plays a central role not only in the physical construction of the built environment but also in the day-to-day maintenance of the quality of life within it. This study of power and money, moreover, goes a long way in explaining one of the most important characteristics of the modern city, spatial segregation by class, ethnicity, and race. The window opened by the graft investigation illuminates some of the ways in which the public sector was intimately involved in creating these geographies of inequality. In some wards city inspectors held landlords strictly to account for compliance with health and building codes, while in other wards officials made no effort to enforce these laws in spite of tenant complaints of gross violations. Some neighborhoods enjoyed clean streets and alleys while other residential districts had to endure insufferabe manure and garbage heaps that had been left by city neglect to accumulate for years.

Addressing questions of environmental justice also lends strong support to scholars like Terrance McDonald, who contend that existing models of urban politics are inadequate. For example, Jon Teaford posits that urban regimes in the late nineteenth century achieved an "unheralded triumph" of city building, but he fails to ask for whom they achieved it. Or consider Allen Davis's seminal study of the settlement house movement, *Spearheads for Reform*. After providing an account of the defeat of Hull-House at the ballot box similar to Anne Scott's, Davis lays out a full chapter on municipal reform that concentrates exclusively on efforts to curb the twin evils of vice and police corruption. Admittedly, this approach helps expose important ways in which government and society have interacted to create a distinctly urban sense of moral order. Yet Davis unwittingly cast doubts on the underlying motives of the social reformers because American crusades against sin and drink have usually been fueled by Waspish attitudes of prudery and nativism. Deflecting attention from the workings of class and power, the representation of municipal reform as a battle over morality invariably provokes a debate on ethnocultural politics and the meaning of pluralism. In this discourse, as McDonald points out, liberal sympathies have often combined with functionalist modes of analysis to undercut the standing of the reformers while boosting the image of the bosses as cosmopolitan defenders of toleration.[48]

The alternative approach taken here suggests ways to bring not only the state but gender back to the center of the study of the city's political culture. As Maureen Flanagan, Kathryn Sklar, and other scholars of urban politics have demonstrated, the women had different agendas from those of the men. The story of Addams's battle against the ward boss is consistent with their assessment of the strengths and weaknesses of women's political activism during the Progressive Era. The belated entry of the Citizens' Association highlights the gender gap in the environmental concerns of the members of the middle and upper classes. Addams called upon traditional notions of domesticity, health, and welfare to build class-bridging bonds of political solidarity among women. Transforming the maternalist role into "public housekeeping" helped her overcome the problem of residential segregation that made "it easy for even the most conscientious citizen of Chicago to forget the foul smells of the stockyards and the garbage dumps, when he is living so far from them."[49]

Men remained aloof from Addams's campaign to clean up the slums until they perceived a direct challenge to their own sense of prerogative in the local real estate market. The plumbers' disclosure of a conspiracy between the professional politicians and the building contractors caught the attention of the business elite and their allies on the editorial boards of the city's major newspapers. Their support proved pivotal in briefly tipping the balance of power in favor of the cause of environmental justice, but their loyalties swung back in the old direction as soon as the politicians had resolved the immediate crisis. Without a much more sustained and unified effort to provoke a shift to an urban political culture based upon notions of social welfare, the limits of reform were quickly reached.

In the absence of such a sea change, Chicago's ward bosses had little difficulty adjusting to the new configuration of environmental policies and services. Power stayed rooted in the council finance committee, which effectively hobbled Ball by cutting his budget and staff to a minimum. The politicians simply moved their base of operations from the health to the building department, which became the new den of thieves for loyal patronage workers. In this case, the reconfiguration of government institutions had little impact on the city's political culture. Chicago remained "a city on the make" in spite of the inroads made by Jane Addams on behalf of environmental justice for the working classes.[50]

A comparison of the movements for environmental justice in Chicago and Manchester underscores the crucial importance of political culture in the formation of urban space. In many respects, the goals of Addams and Rowley were remarkably similar: clean up slum neighborhoods and improve housing conditions so they will meet contemporary standards of decency. Moreover, they employed many of the same tactics of reform, such as muckraking journalism, use of expert authorities, grassroots organizing, and coalition building across class and gender lines. Perhaps these common aspects of their campaigns should come as no surprise since the Progressives engaged in a vigorous trans-Atlantic exchange. The Hull-House settlement and the Ancoats Brotherhood were major crossroads in this traffic of activists and visionaries. Emerging out of their positive environmentalism was a broad consensus in the United States and Europe on the need for higher standards for minimally decent housing and neighborhood design.

Most important, the political establishments of the two cities forced reform into narrow channels that greatly limited its outcome. Both Chicago and Manchester enacted structural reforms that strengthened government's regulatory powers to control land use in the industrial city. Health codes imposed greater duties on landlords. Building and plumbing codes imposed tighter restrictions on the construction of new residential units. The Progressives could take pride in these accomplishments, which gradually helped to improve the quality of urban life. However, the reforms the two cities enacted never seriously threatened the supremacy of the property owners' authority in managing existing dwellings or building new ones. Manchester's tentative inroads into social housing had the potential for fundamental change, but the city made a quick retreat as soon as the real estate interests sounded the alarm. Since their taxes remained the primary source of financing for the municipal corporation, property owners retained dominant control over its institutions and administration. Not only were they the largest stakeholders in city government, they were also major contributors to the local party organizations. Paying homage to the idol of low-cost government and protecting the prerogatives of private property continued to define the parameters of urban politics.

Although slum conditions continued during the Progressive Era, reformers could declare final victory in the long war against epidemics caused by waterborne infection. As we have seen, germ theories of disease gave sanitarians powerful new ways of attacking the problem of contaminated water supplies. Armed with microscopes and petri dishes, they could now see and identify their enemies, then develop effective weapons to combat them. They proposed several sanitation strategies, each with its own strengths and weaknesses. Given the great costs involved, these diverse plans became the subject of intense civic debate about how to define a new relationship among public health, water management, and environmental protection. The ensuing battles for reform in the two cities offer further proof of the pivotal role of political culture in shaping the outcome of Progressivism.

While the formation of both land and water policy was mediated in the context of local politics, geography required much more. Addams and Rowley organized their campaigns for public health and better housing in the neighborhoods and in the cities of which they were a part. As the advocates of the new public health took reform to the next level, their work encompassed the much larger boundaries of the metropolis, the region, and even the nation. As we have seen in the case of the Manchester floods, sanitarians had to draw up water management plans that were in harmony with the natural hydrology in order to achieve their purposes. This inescapable prerequisite for engineering the environment brought extralocal units of government into the political equation of reform. For both Manchester and Chicago, the intervention of the national government had a significant impact on parochial political cultures.

CHAPTER ELEVEN

"Monstrous Waste"

Water Supply in Chicago and Manchester

Introduction: The Great Chicago Flood of 1885

On Sunday, 2 August 1885, Chicago suffered an environmental disaster, a flood of veritably biblical proportions. It started the night before with gale-force winds coming off the lake, and then in the early morning hours the deluge began. "It rained so hard and so incessantly," the *Chicago Daily News* quipped tongue-in-cheek, "that the city might have floated out to the [water intake] crib if it had not been kept in place by some of the big buildings." But the unprecedented storm, which dumped almost six inches of rain over the next twenty-four hours, was no laughing matter. As the sewers filled and their outfalls in the Chicago River sank below fast rising currents, large areas of the city began flooding. By noon, the water was flowing back into basements, rats by the thousand were scurrying for higher ground, immigrant Chinese and other families living in downtown cellars were being forced into the streets, and storekeepers were making frantic efforts to save their merchandise. Low-lying areas just to the north and southwest of the city center were completely inundated and were under two to three inches of water. New breakwaters in suburban Hyde Park were washed away and streets above recently built sewers collapsed, some sinking by as much as three or four feet. Thirty-six hours after the downpour began, it finally ceased, only to return later that evening for an intense, albeit brief, reprise with a pounding hailstorm.[1]

In the apparent absence of any loss of life, city officials initially greeted the storm as a blessing in disguise. The superintendent of sewers set the tone, singing the flood's praise because "the 420 miles of sewers will be purged of all the filth that accumulated during the hot spell, the river will be cleaned and, as a consequence, the public health will be vastly improved." Neither he nor the man in overall charge of Chicago's water management, Commissioner of Public Works DeWitt Clinton Cregier, believed that the massive amount of sewage swept into the lake posed a threat of the contamination of the city's drinking supplies. With thirty-three years experience stretching back to the building of the first municipal waterworks, Cregier was confident that the strong northeasterly winds had kept the human and industrial wastes belching out of the river's mouth confined close to shore and away from the intake crib two miles out into the lake. Health Commissioner Oscar DeWolf added his voice to the chorus, radiating "jubilation" over the thorough cleansing of the city.[2]

Others, however, were less sanguine about the safety of the city's supply of drinking water in the days immediately following the storm. Fears that the flood's ultimate result might be a horrible epidemic were fueled by three unsettling stories receiving coverage in the daily press. The first undercut confidence in the authority of medical experts like Dr. DeWolf. On Thursday, his public health report detailed the appalling mortality statistics for the previous month. He had recorded 1,493 deaths during July. Over three-fifth of them were of children under five years old, and 689 of infants under one, including 326 victims of cholera. Typhoid fever, another disease associated with filthy conditions and polluted water, had taken 79 lives.

The second frightening news item gave warning of a major outbreak of cholera in France and Spain. While this threat was more distant at the moment, it was no less a cause of anxiety to Chicagoans, who could vividly remember patterns of the deadly scourge crossing the Atlantic. In fact, the specter of a contagion just over the horizon was probably the single most powerful spur to civic action in the nineteenth-century city.[3]

On top of these two causes of apprehension, the third story triggered a full-blown policy debate over public health in Chicago, marking a major turning point in the history of the city's water management and urban reform. Just three days before the great downpour, the city fathers had undertaken an official investigation of the water supply, but had made a complete mockery of it. Led by Mayor Carter Harrison and his top aides, the mission to gather water samples at the Two Mile Crib had turned into an excuse to beat the heat for "the representatives of the city government, a few other citizens, and almost everybody else who had heard that a junket was to occur." Two tugboats were required to ferry the swollen party and its ample provisions of alcohol to the island station.

Even the sympathetic reporter from the Democratic organ, the *Chicago Times*, could not restrain himself from portraying the "so-called investigation" in the terms of a screwball comedy. He observed that after collecting some water samples, "everyone congregated in the stone foundation to the lighthouse and the beer, which a prominent brewing house had furnished, was tapped.... Ald Dixon had found a fishing pole and was singing out of a south porthole; Dr. DeWolf was trying to convince Dr. Wickersham that cholera was imminent, and Carter Harrison was talking. The rest were drinking beer.... If the trip to the crib had any purpose it was carefully concealed."[4] This ridiculous farce might have passed quickly from public attention, but given the uneasy mood of crisis suddenly created by the storm, the junket now came back to haunt the mayor. For the remainder of the month, public debate raged over water management policy and planning.

The issues raised in the aftermath of the catastrophe illuminate basic dimensions of the struggle for urban environmental reform during the Progressive Era. Most provocative, the storm's awesome power to wreak havoc in the city forced Chicagoans to question their commodification of nature, including the Great Lakes as a limitless reservoir of "everlasting purity." Fresh perspectives on the conservation of natural resources challenged both the practical efficiency and ethical morality of Chicago's political culture of profligate waste.

Closely related, germ theories of epidemiology contested the authority of experts on the ways disease was transmitted among bodies, homes, and surrounding neighborhoods. Doctors and scientists came into conflict with engineers and promoters of big technology projects. For several years before the flood, "microscopists" and medical school researchers had been experimenting with bacteriological indicators of water quality to supplement the standard chemical tests. Now this science entered the civic arena for the first time as a source of authority municipal reformers used to undermine the entrenched positions of their opponents. The angry backlash against Mayor Harrison's harmless junket, caused by the flood, exposed the political context within which the policy debate on pure water and sewage disposal took place. Urban regimes shaped the outcome of these debates in part by privileging the authority of some experts above that of others; in effect, narrowing the options to a single predictable conclusion.[5]

Chicago: Digging the "Big Ditch"

To explain the reform of water management policy in Chicago during the Progressive Era requires that we give top priority to the study of political culture. In this case, the examination of local politics must be put in an environmental context that includes contemporary ideas about nature as well as closely related notions of society's relationship to it. In particular, we need to shine a spotlight on local elected officials because they acted as the ultimate gatekeepers of reform, bending the alternatives laid out by various contentious groups to their own personal and partisan purposes.

Recent work on the Progressive Era based on Jürgen Habermas's theoretical concept of the public sphere reinforces the proposition that the politicians should be placed center stage. The entry of women's, labor, professional, and other organized groups into a more pluralistic, open debate over the coming city of the twentieth century did not weaken and diminish the politicians' position. On the contrary, the new urban politics of coalition building that began emerging in the mid-1880s solidified and enlarged their role. They became power brokers, managers of the process of decision making on the public works projects and social welfare programs that collectively defined the quality of the urban environment.[6]

Water management policy had been shaped not only by the power of general cultural values but also by specific economic interests. By the time of the flood of 1885, Chicago had become a bifurcated city of riverfront and lakefront. Living at a safe distance from the toxic zones of the industrial corridor, the city's more affluent inhabitants condemned poorer Chicagoans to make their homes in those river districts, with disastrous, even tragic results. Whether the power brokers accepted or rejected the policy recommendations of the experts and their reform-group allies depended ultimately on calculations of partisan gain. The politicians were one special interest group, and their economic interests were rooted in the jobs and contracts that strengthened their party organizations. They did not hesitate to ignore the expert recommendations of their own water and sanitation engineers whenever they clashed with their own self-serving goals.

However, the catastrophic flood of 1885 spawned a pervasive state of emergency that was beyond the ability of City Hall to paste over with facile assurances. Leading the agitation for reform was the Citizens' Association, a powerful group of Chicago's top businessmen and professionals. Acting as a shadow government, the city's elite now confronted Mayor Harrison, who was serving an unprecedented fourth two-year term. In the wake of the thinly veiled burlesque of his administration's investigation of water quality, the

Citizens' Association launched its own independent study. The chair of its drainage committee, Ossian E. Guthrie, gathered a much smaller group consisting of the "well-known microscopist" B. W. Thomas and four members of the press to accomplish the task.[7]

Disclaiming scientific precision, Guthrie declared that a commonsense approach of sight and smell was enough to prove that polluted discharges from the river were reaching the crib. His group performed its test a week after the mayor's trip, and Guthrie was right in claiming that the unaided senses could detect contamination of the city' drinking supply. "The water around the crib was as different as possible, when it was viewed by the municipal junketers," one of the journalists confirmed. "In place of the blue, pellucid depths into which the Mayor on that memorable occasion peered with enraptured gaze was a frothy, neutral-tinted mass of water which resembled nothing so much as a sheet of the dirty sky struck with a club and writhing in mortal convulsions."[8]

Looking beyond the colorful rhetoric, the reporter's observations are important because they highlight the ways in which variations in the weather could dramatically alter Chicago's hydraulic conditions. The mayor's entourage had visited the crib on a perfectly calm day when there was virtually no current in the river; now there was a strong flow of water pouring out of the river's mouth, and the prevailing seasonal winds from the southwest were pushing it deeper into the lake. The river was already "tinctured with an unhealthy yellow—suggestive of stinks," and these tainted waters could be distinguished from the lake's waters as many as six miles out from shore. There were no visible signs of contamination in water collected in a bottle at the crib, but Guthrie argued that "this proved nothing; the sewage was there, though not apparent to the naked eye."[9] Both he and Thomas had seen enough to be convinced that the city's water supply was seriously compromised. With a zeal fueled by the alarm over the threat of a cholera epidemic spreading from Europe, Guthrie enlarged the scope of his fieldwork to embrace the entire drainage basin of the metropolitan area.

The change in focus from political to natural hydrological boundaries marked a major step forward in urban environmental planning. Only five years earlier, Guthrie and the Citizens' Association had issued their first report on Chicago's drainage and sewerage. The businessmen had been motivated by the return of intolerable conditions to the city center. "The river stinks. The air stinks. People's clothing, permeated by the foul atmosphere, stinks. ... No other word expresses it so well as stink. A stench means something finite. Stink reaches the infinite and becomes sublime in the magnitude of odiousness," the *Chicago Times* complained. Its recommendations, however, had been confined to suggestions regarding the area within municipal borderlines.[10]

Reviving the association's drainage committee in 1885, Guthrie gave it a new charge on the basis of the news accounts of the extent of the flood. Investigators would have to expand their research to encompass the entire natural catch basin of storm runoff. On the basis of this enlarged geographical concept, the committee's report rejected Ellis S. Chesbrough's master plan of environmental engineering. Guthrie now saw his dual-purpose drainage-and-ship-canal design as a potential cause of conflicts in function as well as in jurisdiction between the national and the local government. On the precedent provided by the state's agricultural drainage districts, the report called for a large-scale sanitary channel. And the businessmen were not the only ones who had been questioning the engineer's sanitary strategy.[11]

Employing a wide variety of experimental methods, the investigators steadily assembled an irrefutable case that the city was on the brink of a horrendous outbreak of contagious disease. Not long before, Professor John Henry Long of the Chicago Medical College had begun to test water quality with microbiological tests as well as by assessing chemical indicators.[12] The flooding of large sections of the downtown district, then, served as a catalyst of reform activism, not its original impulse. This dramatic demonstration of the failure of Chesbrough's plan handed policy makers a golden opportunity to try fresh, more environmentally and socially progressive approaches to water management. The Citizens' Association deserves credit for leading the search for a better sink for Chicago's massive amounts of human, animal, and industrial wastes. Its follow-up report to Guthrie's inspection tour confirmed his informal observations.

A chemist named M. Delafontaine verified Guthrie's preliminary judgment that sewage from the river was reaching the intake crib. After testing samples of tap water a few days after the flood, the scientist concluded that "our hydrants supplied us with an article hardly less foul than the Chicago River water. This was the most disgusting sample that ever came to my notice. It was a mine of putrefaction products and bacteria. Quite often, doctors disagree; but, if there is a point on which hygienists are unanimous, it is the importance of preventing the pollution of drinking water by town sewage; therefore, it is our duty to devise forthwith, the means of improving the quality of our deteriorating water supply." The elite group put the authority of its expert consultants, like Delafontaine, to good effect in its campaign for public health reform.[13]

The new muckraking journalism played a powerful role in the Progressive Era. The *Chicago Tribune* kept the story in front of the public over the next month, highlighting the activities of the drainage committee and firing a constant barrage of editorial venom at the Democratic mayor. Among those joining the chorus demanding reform was Dr. Frank W. Reilly, a nationally respected sanitarian and writer who was currently serving as an editor for the *Chicago Morning News* and was a member of Guthrie's committee. His voice added a sense of urgency to the public health crisis. At the end of the month, the Citizens' Association brought its publicity campaign to a climax by issuing a list of recommendations, including a call for a blue-ribbon study commission.[14]

But in this battle for municipal reform leading to the creation of the Sanitary District of Chicago in May 1889, the authority of science continued to take a backseat to the expertise of engineering. At first City Hall simply dismissed the reformers' complaints as hysterical exaggeration, and in the absence of any of the predicted epidemics, the politicians smugly assumed that official reassurances about the city's good health would soon silence their critics. Nonetheless, the Citizens' Association and its influential allies at mainstream papers, such as the *Tribune*, the *Daily News*, and the *Morning News*, kept up the pressure for reform. A typical editorial demanded "the creation of a commission of competent engineers" to study all the issues surrounding water management policy.[15]

Although the storm turned Mayor Harrison's junket to the crib into a public relations debacle, it also presented him with a chance to refurbish a badly tarnished image. His knee-jerk reaction to the Citizens' Association report was defensive. Denying that there was any novelty in its recommendations, he fell back on long-established appeals to low-cost government. "What is the use of discussing plans now?" he carped, "We have no money to carry them out; barely the power of taxation for current expenses [and] no power to tax for great public improvements."[16]

But the reformers' call for further study presented the mayor a graceful way out of the mess, especially since the deluge was a natural disaster. In October, the mayor orchestrated the appointment of the Drainage and Water Supply Commission. By including both sides of water management, it seemed to promise a holistic approach to environmental control. In addition, Rudolph Hering, one of the nation's leading sanitation engineers, was put in charge of a wide-ranging group that included in-house and outside experts on law, geology, sewage treatment, and water supply.

The fact that not a single medical expert served on the commission is telling. However, it is doubtful that the presence of physicians and biologists would have fundamentally altered the decision-making process. Expert scientific opinion of the time reinforced the proposition that dilution was not only the cheapest but also the safest way possible to dispose of Chicago's sewage. The years between 1880 and 1900 represented a highly contentious, transitional period in the history of medicine. Although germ theories of disease were gaining ascendancy over miasmatic models, uncertainty prevailed in every aspect of the new science, including its basic concepts, methods of testing, and practical implications in terms of prevention and treatment.

If anything, the discovery of germs in urban water supplies added weight to traditional arguments in favor of traditional approaches to cleaning up the environment. Reviewing the debate between Dr. Robert Koch and other medical experts on the cause of cholera, for example, a typical newspaper editorial penned in the midst of Chicago's public health crisis summed up contemporary understanding. "Through these innumerable discussions, however, there is being firmly established a general consensus, which was long since formulated by the *Daily News*: Cleanliness is the best preventive of cholera."[17]

The injection of germ theories into the policy debate opened an opportunity to depart from the previous pattern of crisis and response, but the results were essentially the same. The engineer's report of January 1887 listed the same alternatives and recommendations laid out by Chesbrough thirty years earlier. The only significant difference was that the environmental engineering would be on a much larger scale. Like Chesbrough, moreover, Hering let the bottom line of cost dictate the commission's recommendation. When the commission calculated that a drainage canal would cost only half of the fifty-eight million dollars estimated for an alternative infrastructure of intercepting sewers and treatment plants, its experts concluded that the more expensive project was "entirely impracticable." Their conclusion lamely echoed those of so many engineering studies of the past.

Hering argued that if a drainage channel were big enough, it would preclude any need to consider alternative measures to protect the water supply. Ignoring the scientific findings of the microscopists, he assumed that the lake was a source of everlasting purity; the commission rejected the idea of water filtration plants out of hand.[18]

In most respects, the plans reported by the Hering Commission closely resembled those outlined by the Citizens' Association committee. The overlapping membership of the two groups goes a long way in accounting for this consensus. Both proposals recognize the basic contradiction of using the lake as the source of the city's drinking water as well as the sink for its sewage. And both groups envisioned a metropolitan-sized drainage plan that would be managed and financed by a separate, special-purpose tax district. Finally, both groups advocated making the blueprints of the drainage channel flexible enough that the state and national governments would later be able to expand the waterway into a Lakes-to-the-Gulf ship canal.[19]

From his position on the Illinois State Board of Health, the indefatigable Dr. John H. Rauch added further support to the engineers' proposal to dig a new, larger drainage canal and use lake water to dilute the city's wastes. He directed a comprehensive study of water quality as Chicago's sewage moved downstream. The recent state of emergency, he remarked bitterly, had finally pried opened the pocketbooks of the city's power elite to make this type of scientific research possible. Gathering more than a thousand samples, Rauch applied the current indirect methods of chemical analysis to confirm that dilution worked. In the test for free ammonia, for instance, the reading of polluted water at Bridgeport stood at 26.56, but had fallen by half by the time it reached Lockport twenty-nine miles away, and had diminished to a "safe" level of 0.41 at Ottawa, eighty-one miles downstream. The only remaining question among sanitary reformers, then, was to decide how much water would have to be diverted from Lake Michigan to dilute the sewage of a metropolis whose population would soon exceed two million. In addition, reformers faced the formidable political task of achieving the passage of an enabling act in the state legislature.[20]

In spite of Chicago politicians' opposition to the sanitary district plan, the civic elite was not to be denied. In early 1887, the aldermen quietly closed down the Hering Commission after it issued its preliminary and only report. In Springfield, moreover, the city delegation gave the mugwumps' initial enabling legislation an unenthusiastic reception, contributing to its defeat. Undaunted, the sophisticated lobbying machine of the Citizens' Association sprang into high gear and rammed the needed act through the legislature two years later. This was a remarkable achievement considering the novelty of its proposal to create a special-purpose tax district on a metropolitan scale. Chicago also had to overcome the opposition of downstream legislators. It had not taken them long to make the obvious deduction that the Illinois River Valley would be turned into a massive conduit for the city's human and industrial wastes.[21]

Emerging as the chief advocate of the drainage channel was an engineer, Lyman E. Cooley, whose lifelong preoccupation came to be the promotion of a vision of a great river highway of commerce stretching from the Atlantic Ocean to the Gulf of Mexico. Trained at Rensselaer Polytechnic Institute, he had joined the faculty at Northwestern University in 1874 and had worked on both the Citizens' Association and the Hering Commission investigations. Cooley would put his considerable technical, literary, and political talents to good effect in steering the enabling bill through the legislature.

Cooley had a missionary zeal for the technological fix. He believed that engineers like himself could improve upon nature. When he set off the first dynamite charge to commence construction a few years later, he would declare the building of the artificial canal an important step in the forward march of civilization in conquest of the continent: "Man's creative intelligence can remedy Nature's caprice, restore the ancient outlet; and even more, extend through the continent from fog bank to tropic breeze, as though it were the sea, joining coast, lake, and river systems in one whole, as is not possible elsewhere on earth."[22]

After the drainage bill sponsored by the Citizens' Association and its their Republican allies was defeated, the engineer set out to win support from downstate and city Democrats. To sweeten the bill for these lawmakers, Cooley held out the promise that the ship canal would be a mighty engine of economic growth and development for the entire valley. The pioneering and recently completed linked ship canal and industrial park in Manchester, England, served as a convincing model of success. The dimensions of the twenty-eight-mile waterway would be enlarged to allow full-sized oceangoing vessels to pass through the Illinois channel. Cooley also held out the promise that the federal government would eventually take over the much larger task of completing the transcontinental shipping lane.[23]

To bring Chicago Democrats on board, Cooley made three concessions that virtually guaranteed City Hall's continued control of the water management system. Hering's proposal for a metropolitan water-supply board to parallel the drainage district was dropped, ensuring that the waterworks and its huge profits would remain firmly in the hands of the aldermen. Second, the transformation of the drainage channel into a deep-water ship canal promised to shift a large share of the tax burden of the project from the city to the state and national governments. Most important, at-large elections by all of the voters within the sanitary district's sprawling boundaries would be conducted to choose its nine-member governing board of trustees. The unique jurisdiction, which cut across normal political borderlines, and the obscure nature of the posts were a sure recipe for getting voters to cast their ballots in favor of their respective parties' entire slate of candidates. This does not mean that no men of high caliber and honest intentions were chosen by the party professionals to served as trustees, but only that all of the candidates had to pass the litmus test of partisan loyalty.

"There was a wild scene of disorder when the Speaker announced that the bill had passed," the *Tribune* reported on 25 May 1889, "and ... Professor Cooley was the happiest man in Springfield." However, Cooley's joy was cut short when he quickly became embroiled in what became a nasty two-year political battle to save his grand vision of a deep-water canal. Chicago's elite reformers turned the first election into a high-profile event by putting up what they called a Citizens' slate of candidates who were nonpartisan. The campaign for "competent and intelligent" men to manage the huge public works project, worth an estimated fifteen million dollars, attracted the support of Chicago's leading businessmen, including Marshall Field, Lyman Gage, and Andrew McNally. While excitement within the Republican Party collapsed in the face of the defection of the party's big contributors, the Democrats, under the nominal leadership of Mayor Cregier, joined the race in earnest.[24]

Not everyone was convinced that the party would provide the most qualified candidates. Typical of the charges against the party regulars were the *Tribune's* allegations that they would create a dangerous army of ten thousand patronage workers, doubling the price tag of construction. "If small-fry politicians, party hacks, gambler-based officials, brassy, gabby demagogues, boodle jobbers, or ignoramuses are elected trustees," the newspaper warned, "the cost of the work to the taxpayers of Chicago will come up to and surpass even Mayor Cregier's extravagant ideas." With the election of all six Citizens' candidates and three Democrats in December 1889, the triumph of the forces of municipal reform seemed complete.[25]

Cooley was soon engaged in open political warfare with the board of trustees in spite of his well-deserved appointment as chief engineer. The controversy revolved around the efforts of the majority bloc of nonpartisan reformers to scale the project back to the original design for a drainage channel. Concerned about the costs and practicality of a dual-purpose waterway, the board instructed Cooley to draw up blueprints with specifications that virtually excluded the possibility that the waterway would become a ship canal. By now obsessed by the dream of completing a heroic engineering project, the engineer stalled for time while plotting behind the scenes to unseat the majority bloc on the board.

After waiting for almost a year for Cooley to submit a report, the six trustees from the Citizens' Association met secretly to plan a preemptive strike of their own. In a surprise move, they fired the chief engineer at the 10 December 1890 meeting. "Clearly, this official," President Richard Prendergast charged, "thinks he is superior to the board." Also turning on him, the *Tribune* hinted darkly that Cooley was a secret agent of the party bosses, who would turn the drainage project into a gigantic boondoggle. The editorial also addressed the policy question at issue: should public health or commercial development take priority in the planning of the waterway? The newspaper declared in exasperation that although the ditch was "a big one," it was "still a ditch. Unfortunately for Mr. Cooley it did not strike him in that light."[26]

The struggle between Cooley and the nonpartisan trustees revealed the environmental implications of giving priority to either the ship canal or the sanitary channel. The engineer had indeed been preparing a report, but not the kind of geological survey of the route desired by the board. Instead, the engineer was writing a stinging rebuttal not only to the policy goals of the reform bloc of trustees but also to the technical opinions of his critics in the Army Corps of Engineers. Finished in August 1890 and published the following May, *The Lakes and Gulf Waterway* was the first of several polemical books Cooley published that combined technical expertise and booster spirit. He railed against the conservatism of the trustees, stating that "the project has too much vitality... to be killed off by any set of men. The great projects of the world have been carried out by their friends, and a mistake is made when such enterprises are entrusted to unfriendly and pessimistic agents."

In a similar way, he attacked his fellow engineers who doubted the utility of a transcontinental shipping lane with a depth of fourteen feet. Captain W. L. Marshall of the Army Corps of Engineers called instead for a more modest waterway with a five-to-seven-foot draft, which would accommodate over 90 percent of the boats and barges plying the lower Mississippi River. Cooley charged that the Corps's experts, like Marshall, had made one "astonishing error" after another for at least a quarter-century.

Shortsightedness and professional jealously were to blame. In Cooley's opinion, "the idea that expenditures that satisfy present needs may be made in harmony with a policy of unlimited growth and development... is antipodes of the pessimism that runs through the last official report of the local Army engineer. This need not be attributed to anything more than the natural conservatism of the official mind toward a bolder and more useful project from an unauthorized source."[27] Cooley, of course, did not confine his protest to print; he took his case to the state legislature in Springfield as well.

In the spring 1891 legislative session, the engineer promoted a bill to abolish the current board of trustees. He also enlisted support to defeat an amendment sponsored by the reform trustees to downsize the project and return to the original design of a drainage channel. The ensuing debate showed that Cooley's plan required the withdrawal of an enormous amount of water from the lake in order to maintain the depth of the Illinois River during seasonal periods of low water, but the resulting flow of 4.5 million gallons per minute would create currents dangerous to navigation in the Chicago River and the artificial canal. The only way to offset this hazard was by enlarging the depth and width of these channels enough to slow the speed of this great volume of water to safe levels.

In contrast, Prendergast stated on behalf of the trustees that half as much lake water and half as many pumping engines could meet Chicago's public health needs. Moreover, he pointed out, Cooley's plan would require huge added costs for buying expensive riverfront property in the heart of city, for constructing the canal, and for replacing all of the bridges along the route. Cooley rallied city and downstate commercial interests to defeat the sanitary district amendment, but he could not muster enough votes to unseat the governing board. Moving openly into the Democratic camp of the ward bosses, he began preparing for a final political showdown with the nonpartisan trustees.[28]

In less than a year, Cooley orchestrated a virtual coup d'état by cobbling together a new majority. Although all six Citizens' trustees kept their nonpartisan pledges, ill health and the strain of constant political infighting took its toll. First, a Democrat resigned, followed by two Citizens' members of the board, setting the stage for a special ballot for replacements in the November 1891 elections. Unlike their performance in the contest a year earlier, elite reformers were unable to unite behind a coalition ticket. Only Ossian Guthrie ran as an independent, and he was badly defeated. Running as a Democrat, Cooley won one of the three empty positions; two Republicans won the other seats.

This outcome seemed to favor the reform coalition. The *Tribune's* editors, for example, believed that "the two Republican members-elect will doubtless cooperate with the Citizens' members ... and Mr. Cooley ... will find himself acting with the minority and powerless to obstruct." But in Chicago politics, appearances are often deceptive. In this case, the other two new trustees turned out to be Democrats in disguise. Cooley demonstrated his total control of the board at its very next meeting. In December, the two new members joined Cooley, the two regular Democrats, and a turncoat Citizens' trustee previously affiliated with the Democrats in a significant test vote.

The new majority shelved the current plan and decided to begin anew the process of route selection. With the resignation of another Citizens' trustee in January, the board was completely reorganized. It became a rubber stamp, approving whatever Cooley wanted as chair of the engineering committee. Most important to the politicians was the number of men who could be put on the public payroll. Cooley accommodated them by changing the method of construction. Under the original "wet" plan, powerful steam shovels on barges would do the main work of digging the channel. The floating machines would also load the earth onto flatboats, which could then easily dispose of it in the lake. In contrast, Cooley's "dry" plan of construction required hundreds of unskilled men. Under his command, this army of patronage

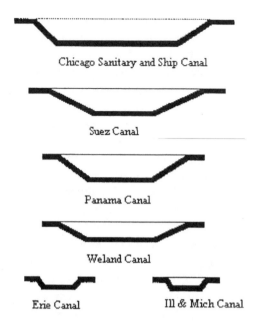

Chicago Sanitary and Ship Canal

Suez Canal

Panama Canal

Weland Canal

Erie Canal   Ill & Mich Canal

Figure 11.1. Comparative canal dimensions
Source: City of Chicago, Public Library and Department of Sewers, "Down the Drain: Chicago's Sewers: The Historic Development of Urban Infrastructure," http://www.chipublib.org/digital/sewers/history4.html. Reproduced with permission.

workers took eight years to complete the biggest earth-moving project in history, a technological precursor to the Panama Canal (see fig. 11.1). But unlike the Central American waterway, Chicago's sanitary canal was never a route for ocean-sized ships.[29]

It is probably impossible to calculate the proportion of the eventual price tag of almost fifty million dollars that was spent making the channel deep and wide enough to accommodate navigation for deepwater vessels as opposed to digging a more reasonably sized channel. What is known with certainty is that the final cost was almost twice Hering's estimate and not all that far from the projections for a main drain/sewage treatment plan. Whatever amount of money went into digging the twenty-eight-mile channel to a depth of twenty-four feet and a width 140 to 160 feet to accommodate oceangoing vessels was a total loss. Neither the state nor the national government was willing to pay the astronomical amount it would have taken to dredge 328 miles of the nine-foot-deep Illinois River. Once the digging was completed, the rush of water through the Chicago River and the canal created such a strong current that the barge captains experienced serious difficulty controlling their cumbersome vehicles.[30]

After all of the rhetorical vitriol, moral outrage, and expert testimony, the new plan of water management represented a missed opportunity. What finally emerged was essentially a rehash of Chesbrough's defective designs, but on a much larger and more environmentally damaging scale. Not only were the lessons of the two earlier cycles of crisis and response largely ignored, but the accumulating experience of other cities was rejected as well. Engineers like Hering, who knew better, caved in to political and economic pressures to give top priority to the short-term calculations of lowest fiscal cost and highest political payoff. An expert on European sanitary practices, Hering must have known that diverting Chicago's swelling quantities of human and industrial waste to sewage treatment facilities or at least to a relatively harmless outfall far downstream of the built-up areas was anything but "impracticable."

It is reasonable to suspect that Hering knew his plan would pose a real threat to the ecological balance of the Great Lakes. He estimated that the amount of lake water needed for dilution of Chicago's untreated sewage was 6.5 billion gallons per day. The artificial waterway became a gigantic drainpipe that represented the only major outlet of the lakes other than their natural one at Niagara Falls. Although this amount of water equaled only 5 percent of the total amount flowing over the falls, it would be enough to lower the water level of not only Lake Michigan but also the entire interconnected system by four to six inches. Only Lake Superior, which is higher than the other four lakes, would escape immediate environmental damage.

Major Thomas Handbury of the Army Corps of Engineers had anticipated this damage to the Great Lakes. At the 1887 Interstate Canal and River Convention in Peoria, he warned about the likelihood of a drop in lake levels of about this amount. Two years later, the city's engineering community, including Lyman Cooley, held a seminar that fully vetted the potential that the water diversion would have a significant environmental impact on the Great Lakes. The issue would remain moot, however, until the Corps began systematic measurements after the sanitary channel was opened.[31]

Equally important, the opportunity to establish an institutional linkage between sanitation and water supply was lost as well. The decision for a giant scale drainage channel meant a summary dismissal of interrelated concerns about safeguarding the city's drinking supplies. Policy makers did not create an agency for dealing with water supply that would be analogous to the metropolitan-wide sanitary district, a failure that would soon result in new public health crises and more unnecessary deaths. What had started by moving in promising directions toward the gaining of an environmental perspective on urban water management ended up by legitimizing the inherent flaws of Chesbrough's original sanitary strategy. It did not take long for these contradictions to become painfully evident.[32]

Chicago: The Politics of Health, 1890–1900

Between 1890 and 1893, Chicago suffered its worst epidemic since the pre-Civil War period (see table 11.1). The timing of this outbreak of typhoid fever goes a long way in explaining what appears to have paradoxically been the city's least discussed public health crisis. The city had just beaten New York and other urban rivals in a national contest to host the World's Columbian Exposition in 1893. In part, this success was the result of a rare political truce that allowed Chicagoans to impress Congress with a united front of bipartisan cooperation. Now the sudden appearance of the dreadful contagion threatened to ruin all the grand hopes of the elected officials and elite civic groups that were busily engrossed in promoting, planning, and managing the fair.[33]

Whether the city's leaders were guilty of a conspiracy of silence, a "cover-up" as one historian has charged, is difficult to prove.[34] But there is no mistaking their fears that a public health crisis could result in cancellation of the fair, an event that promised major benefits to almost every local group. Consider the defensive tone of Health Commissioner John D. Ware as he

Table 11.1 Typhoid fever in Chicago, 1885–1914

Year	Number of deaths	Mortality rate (per 10,000)	Year	Number of deaths	Mortality rate (per 10,000)
1885	496	7.46	1900	337	1.98
1886	483	6.86	1901	509	2.91
1887	382	5.03	1902	801	4.45
1888	375	4.67	1903	588	3.18
1889	453	4.84	1904	373	1.96
1890	1,008	9.16	1905	329	1.69
1891	1,997	17.38	1906	370	1.85
1892	1,489	12.41	1907	372	1.82
1893	670	5.35	1908	332	1.58
1894	491	3.75	1909	271	1.26
1895	518	3.79	1910	300	1.37
1896	751	5.26	1911	241	1.07
1897	437	2.93	1912	175	0.76
1898	636	4.08	1913	249	1.06
1899	442	2.72	1914	167	0.69

Source: City of Chicago, Department of Health, *Annual Report* (1911–1918): 1432.

rebutted charges regarding danger from polluted water. "During the winter," he retorted in his annual report of 1891, "foreign journals commenced an attack on Chicago and the contamination of its water supply, and highly colored and much distorted statements were printed, apparently for the purpose of belittling the greatness of Chicago, and injuring the attendance during the World's Fair." In the face of thousands suffering from typhoid, Dr. Ware claimed that the chemists testing city supplies had not found any "unusual amount of contamination" and that "the water was pronounced as good as any water ever supplied to the city."[35] The commissioner might have denied the magnitude of the state of emergency because he knew that very little could be done in the short run to improve the city's system of water supply and sewage disposal (see fig. 11.2).

The timing of the outbreak of typhoid fever was more than just an unfortunate coincidence; it was directly linked to political compromises on the city's sanitary strategy that kept control of the water department in the hands of the ward bosses. Hering had called for not only the drainage channel, but also a series of new pumping stations and intake tunnels to alleviate chronic water shortages caused by low pressure in several outlying neighborhoods. He had been careful to build political support by making a disingenuous argument in favor of giving the best-served area, the central business district, top priority in the expansion program.

The council had responded quickly to approve this expensive project, but it had chosen to disregard all of Hering's suggestions for decreasing the pollution of the lake with sewage over the next three years, despite their moderate projected cost. Four of the five proposed projects would have improved the Chicago River by diverting storm water to other waterways and by sending stockyard wastes directly into the Illinois and Michigan Canal. The fifth and perhaps most important proposal was for the construction of interceptor sewers parallel to the shoreline on the South Side to prevent massive amounts of pollution from pouring daily into the lake. There is every reason to believe that completion of these short-term projects between 1887 and 1890 would have completely forestalled or at least significantly diminished the severity of the typhoid epidemic.[36]

The city council's decision to second-guess the engineers was representative of a political culture that subordinated expert knowledge to the self-serving needs of politicians. The single most powerful group of elected officials, the finance committee of the city council, controlled the water fund. They insisted on a flat-rate system of fees rather than the use of meters, thus maximizing the bottom line rather than the social welfare. The rates were structured to guarantee the huge annual surplus that fed the slush fund the

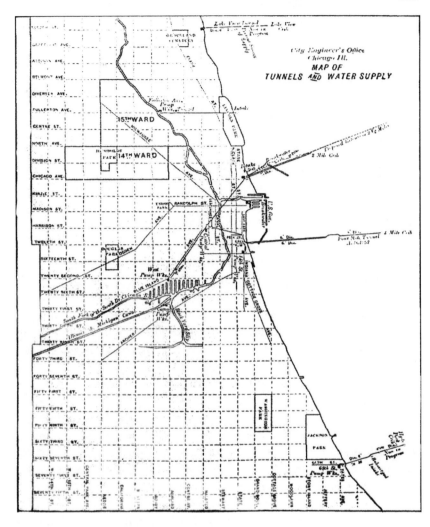

Figure 11.2. Chicago waterworks, 1892
Source: City of Chicago, Department of Public Works, *Annual Report* (1892).

aldermen spent mainly on pet projects and other purposes unrelated to the water supply. As table 11.2 demonstrates, the size of this pool of profit was grossly disproportionate to the amount of money actually required to meet the expenses of the waterworks.

The rate structure established by the council contained at least two types of inequity that significantly penalized the great majority of residential consumers. The sliding scale of rates was constructed in such a way that those

Table 11.2 Chicago waterworks revenues, 1893–1913

| | | Cost ($) | | | | "Surplus" | |
| | Total | | | | | Amount | Profit ratio |
Year	revenue ($)	Salaries	Fuel	Other[a]	Total costs	($)	(%)
1893	2,950,000	252,800	250,000	63,200	566,000	2,384,000	421.2
1903	3,690,000	277,900	392,100	275,000	945,000	2,745,000	290.5
1913	6,500,000	403,200	437,000	780,000	1,620,200	4,879,800	301.2

Source: City of Chicago, Department of Public Works, *Annual Report* (1893, 1903, 1913, 1914).
[a]Includes repair, maintenance, and new construction other than that of the distribution system.

who could least afford to pay for water were charged the most for each unit of this necessity of life, while large commercial and industrial consumers that could best afford to pay were charged the lowest unit price. Furthermore, the use of the surplus for supposedly municipal purposes kept the tax bills of the relatively small number of politically connected property owners low at the expense of the mass of utility customers.

The day-to-day operation of the water department under the direction of the city engineers also advanced the goals of the politicians and their party organizations. While the amounts involved in the maintenance, repair, and expansion of the waterworks were small compared to those in the slush fund, they still represented a sizable contribution to the local economy. Two of the main expenses were fuel to run the pumps and wages to pay the workers who kept the machinery operating smoothly. Both offered innumerable opportunities for partisan advantage: the politicians could turn jobs into patronage plums and reward favored party supporters with lucrative coal and oil contracts. Given Chief Engineer Cregier's unwavering loyalty to the Democrats, it is not hard to imagine that one of his unofficial duties was to accommodate the mayor and aldermen in these matters.

Cregier had little choice. Elected officials alone held the power to offer the municipal engineers tangible rewards, completing the symbiotic circle of mutuality between the two professions. In return for the politicians' legitimation of their authority as experts, the engineers played an essential part in helping the politicians sustain and nourish their party organizations. One need not look for a corrupt conspiracy or hidden graft to show that the engineers learned how to submit their reports in politically correct terms and how to respond appropriately to the rejection or modification of their recommendations. For Cregier, the ultimate award would come in 1889, when he would be slated for the mayor's office.[37]

Looking through the broader lens of political culture, we can now begin to see how the Progressives used germ theories to challenge the authority of the municipal engineers in the formation of public policy. In Chicago, the typhoid epidemic of 1890–1893 triggered another round of public discourse that raised troubling questions about prevailing approaches to water management and public health. The growing stature of the microbiologist as expert gave new importance to the politics of health, affecting the powers of the mayor's office, the scope of the chief executive's duties, and decisions regarding the appointment of a health commissioner.

For the most part, the debate over the causes of the typhoid outbreak was disguised within a less threatening discussion about an impending outbreak of cholera. Even if the first line of defense, a strict quarantine, failed to halt its spread from Hamburg, Germany, to the Midwestern city, blame for the resulting crisis could be cast elsewhere, on foreigners and federal officials. Yet fear that its appearance in Chicago would force the cancellation of the world's fair created a pretext for sounding the civic alarm and mounting a major cleanup campaign.

The participation of doctors and academics in the ensuing debate exposed deep divisions within the scientific community about the nature of disease and the best ways to prevent it. Official reaction was also revealing, showing some of the basic reasons why the aldermen maintained tight control over not only the Department of Public Works but the Department of Health as well. A closer look at the struggle to gain acceptance of germ theories of disease helps to uncover some of the power relationships that determined the answers to questions of environmental justice and equity in the distribution of public health services.

Initial responses to the news of the European epidemic of cholera in late August 1892 embodied the traditional miasmatic theories of disease causation. Pleas for a citywide cleanup reflected those older notions that dirt furnished the seedbed for disease. "Cholera is born of filth," the *Tribune* declared, "It lives upon filth. It is spread by filth. The first duty of cities, therefore, is to clean up." The strident editorial emphatically demanded a fullscale assault on filth in the urban environment because of "the danger of cholera, which if it comes here next year, will ruin the business of the Fair."[38]

Municipal officials also endorsed this approach. Within a few days, Health Commissioner Ware had announced plans to mount "a supreme effort to put every street and alley in the populous districts into such condition that

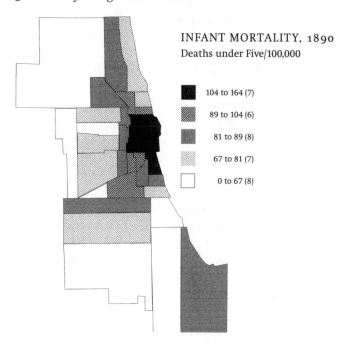

INFANT MORTALITY, 1890
Deaths under Five/100,000

- 104 to 164 (7)
- 89 to 104 (6)
- 81 to 89 (8)
- 67 to 81 (7)
- 0 to 67 (8)

Figure 11.3. Infant mortality in Chicago's wards, 1890
Source: Data from U.S. Bureau of the Census, *Vital and Social Statistics*, vol. 7
(Washington, DC: U.S. Bureau of the Census, 1890), pt. 2, pp. 161–81.

the city as a whole may laugh at cholera and all other zymotic plagues of
filth origin and sustentation."[39] Direct evidence that the threat of cholera
became a code for the real typhoid epidemic is lacking. But Ware's inclusion
of "zymotic plagues" seems like an oblique reference to the latter disease, a
conclusion reinforced by his list of the wards in greatest need of cleansing.
They constituted a crescent-shaped zone of contiguous communities on the
West Side just across the river from the central business district. These areas
bordering the industrial corridor were the very ones suffering the highest
death rates (see fig. 11.3).

Before the great annexation of 1889, the aldermen had kept tight control
over sewer extensions. They had insisted that these improvements be paid
for out of general revenues rather than by means of special tax assessments,
which had long been the accepted way to pay for other infrastructure such
as street paving, sidewalks, and gas lighting. After 1890, sewer extensions
joined the list of improvements funded by special assessment, once again

raising the price that building owners had to pay to take advantage of modern sanitation technologies and their potential benefits to health. In that year, the Department of Health counted forty to fifty thousand outdoor privies, many of them in the backyards of tenements like those investigated by Jane Addams and the women of Hull-House.

Although housing historians make the well-taken point that the special assessment system cut initial costs for working-class families struggling as new homeowners, that conclusion does not speak to questions of social justice and good public health policy. Even when service extensions were paid for out of general revenues, landlords had been reluctant to pay for hookup fees and the cost of indoor plumbing in the boarding-house districts of the Near West Side and other areas immediately adjacent to the central business district. The city possessed ample police powers to require building owners to make these improvements, but they were rarely exercised. The politicians' acquiescence to these deplorable conditions represents a betrayal of their working-class constituencies and belies any notion that the ward boss was their friend and protector.[40]

As the city council awarded lucrative contracts for the cleaning up of the city, some doctors and scientists used germ theories to present a very different analysis of the causes of epidemics. On 26 August, a reporter interviewed Dr. W. L. Tallman, who had just returned from Europe, where he had conducted an investigation of the cholera outbreak. He observed of Chicago that "everything about this city seems to invite the germs and bacteria of cholera—the filthy condition of the alleys, the excavation of streets, allowing noxious gases to escape, and above all the health-destroying water the citizens are supplied." Although the doctor's diagnosis contained a confused mix of miasmatic and germ theories, he was certain that boiling the water was the single most urgent prescription that must be followed to forestall the development of a plague in Chicago.[41]

The journalist's knee-jerk reaction was to reject this advice and defend the purity of the city's drinking supplies. After eliciting a favorable testimonial on water quality from a Dr. Gilmore, the reporter derisively concluded that Dr. Tallman's "talk about the 'necessity for boiling the water' and 'filtering it through cotton' would have been well enough at the time of the city's greatest affliction from the floods of last spring, but just now it is fol-de-rol and fudge. It is calculated to cause an unjustifiable scare ... and to incite to needless worry and expense. . . . There is no city on the face of God's green earth that has a better water supply." Physicians who took a position similar to Dr. Tallman's at the next meeting of the finance committee were greeted with the same cynical dismissal. The aldermen were more concerned about the city's image and about the risk of frightening away visitors to the world's fair than they were about the health of their constituents.[42]

In the early 1890s, growing acceptance of germ theories began to change the politics of health in fundamental ways by giving the medical community a powerful new source of authority. Rapid advances in the science of microbiology gave them a sense of self-confidence that miasmatic theories could never inspire. American medical experts may have lagged behind their continental counterparts in adopting germ theory, but its triumph within professional circles was clearly evident at a special meeting of the Chicago Medical Society on 10 September 1892, when the association met to discuss the cholera threat. A panel of three doctors, including a bacteriologist, contended that "cholera is caused by a definite, well recognized germ.... The disease breaks out only in persons who have in some way or other put these germs into their mouths." They advised that cooking all foods thoroughly and boiling liquids like water and milk were the only truly effective means of protecting individuals from infection.

After hearing the society's official report, the doctors paid deference to their venerable emeritus leader, Nathan S. Davis. His recitation of the traditional nostrums—quarantine, environmental cleansing, and personal hygiene—only served to underscore the pivotal timing of the meeting. The momentum of the paradigm shift was beginning to turn public discourse on health in new directions. Significantly, several municipal department heads attended the meeting, as did representatives of the Municipal Order League, a women's reform group involved in establishing public baths and promoting other municipal housekeeping measures.[43]

During the following months, Dr. Frank W. Reilly emerged in the public sphere as the leading champion of germ theory. Although he was not a young man, his dual careers as a public health official and journalist made him particularly well suited for his role as a Progressive reformer. Born in Bolton, England, in 1836, he had moved with his family to Chicago when he was twenty years old, and after receiving training in local medical schools, he had joined Sherman's army as a surgeon. After the war, he set up a practice in the Irish Catholic neighborhood of Bridgeport and soon fell under the influence of Chicago's first great sanitarian, John H. Rauch. In 1872, Reilly left for New York City to start a journal titled *Hygiene*. For more than a decade, he drifted between journalism and public health work as a sanitary investigator and quarantine inspector.

Reilly then returned to Chicago, becoming publisher and editor of the *Chicago Morning News* at the time of the great flood of 1885. Because he was a doctor, his muckraking editorials on Mayor Harrison's water management policies caused the administration acute political embarrassment. In addition, he served as a member of the drainage committee of the Citizens' Association during the public health crisis following the flood. In 1891, he was Dr. Rauch's hand-picked successor as secretary of the Illinois State Board of Health.

From this office, Reilly wrote a devastating critique of the city's handling of the typhoid epidemic, *Zymotic Diseases in Chicago, 1890–1892*, which was transformed into a highly visible exhibit at the State of Illinois building at the world's fair. It graphically refuted Commissioner Ware's lame explanations and placed blame for the contagion squarely on germs that were contaminating the city's water supply. The importance of this pamphlet cannot be overstressed because it represented the opening salvo of a barrage of criticism informed by the new science that openly contested City Hall's approach to public health.[44]

Although elected officials helped stave off a boycott of the fair on account of health risks, they could not stop the groundswell of concern about drinking the tap water supplied by the municipal utility. On the one hand, the fair's directors prudently avoided any signs of open conflict with the local government. On the other hand, they made a well-publicized decision to award a drinking water concession to a company in Waukesha, Wisconsin, which laid a pipeline 126 miles from its underground springs to the exhibition grounds. Moreover, a filtration plant was erected to purify the water taken from the city mains. Some of the harshest censors of Chicago were foreign visitors to the exposition. If William Stead was the most influential of these outside observers, he was certainly not alone in being struck by Chicago's "river of death," its stockyard stenches, and its air pollution.

Professional medical opinion joined in the condemnation of the city's water management strategies, lending support to Dr. Reilly and germ theory. For example, the editor of the *British Medical Journal* reinforced the notion that science was providing convincing evidence of the failures of engineers to solve the problem of public health crises caused by waterborne diseases. The Englishman was appalled at the way the city polluted Lake Michigan with its own wastes. The doctor pronounced:

> If it be the policy of your rulers to persist in fouling this magnificent source of water supply by continuing to pour this mass of sewage into it, in the vain belief that they can rely upon the currents or reversing engines, or winds, which always go wrong. . . . If they are determined to do that; if they won't carry all their water cribs out four miles, insist

upon their having subsidence and filtration . . . it is criminal to give [the water] to the poor, who cannot buy artificial water and who cannot always boil their water.[45]

Germ theories pointed to the conclusion that no technological fix could restore the lake to a condition of everlasting purity; alternative strategies would be needed to safeguard the public's health from its polluted waters.

The crescendo of complaints about the city's public health policies created enough pressure to force the politicians to reorganize the health department. In 1893, the incoming administration of John Hopkins acceded to demands to install professionals who could bring the department up to modern scientific standards. The mayor appointed one of the new breed of experts, Dr. Arthur Reynolds, as commissioner of health, and Reynolds in turn persuaded the council to fund the previously unfilled position of assistant commissioner in order to make room for Dr. Reilly. In the "awakening" of the department, Reynolds later recalled, "Dr. Reilly's work stands out head and shoulders above all concerned. . . . He had an inventive and orderly mind and he had a genius for organization."[46]

The first order of business was adopting nomenclatures of disease and water quality tests and other statistical measures that met international standards. Next in importance was building and staffing a municipal laboratory. Competent bacteriologists were hired to test milk, but they soon extended their experiments to study an increasing variety of infectious diseases. Dr. Reilly was able to implement the object of his and other doctors' previously ignored pleas: systematic evaluation of the water supply using both chemical and biological tests. He also helped implement a public education campaign on health and hygiene, beginning with a boil-the-water campaign in the daily press.[47]

From their new positions of authority, these public health experts challenged water management policies that were based on the engineers' assumption that the lake could be relied upon to dilute the city's sewage and render it harmless. Between 1894 and 1896, the department's physicians and scientists came to just the opposite conclusion. Before accumulating sufficient statistics on the quality of the water, they too had accepted the engineers' recent solution of placing the water intake cribs twice as far from shore. Commissioner Reynolds, for instance, had argued that this solution was cost effective. Putting a price tag of five thousand dollars on each human being, he calculated that the cost of 2,153 deaths in 1892 from typhoid and diarrheal diseases was more than three times greater than the $3.5 million cost of a four-mile tunnel.

A year later, the department took a more cautious position in its annual report. "It is a well-accepted fact in connection with disease etiology," it announced, "that very many pathogenic microorganisms can be transmitted by drinking water, and at times when the state of the lake water rendered it unfit for consumption, the alarm has been sounded and the people notified to take such steps as might be considered best to purify the water."[48]

In 1896, the department reversed course completely in spite of the opening of a four-mile crib and the closing of the two intakes closest to shore. The daily water tests were showing that the drinking supplies were "usable" or "good" only 19 percent of the time, as opposed to "suspicious" 48 percent of the time and outright "bad (pathogenic)" the remaining 33 percent of the time. "There is an area of continually contaminated water along the lake front," warned the department's bacteriologist, Dr. Adolph Gehrmann. It usually remained less than two miles offshore, but it could extend at least twelve miles into the lake. "To attempt to obtain pure water by locating cribs beyond this line of permanent contamination leads to a false security," the director of the city laboratory now advised, "because at one time the area of contamination may be determined as extending a certain distance into the lake, at another time it may have receded, or again, it may have extended to a much greater distance."[49]

In a special report to the medical community, Dr. Reilly laid out the implications of the conclusion that the lake was permanently polluted. He pointed out that the sewage of about three hundred thousand people within the city limits was pouring from sewer outfalls directly into lake. On the North Side, the drains were spaced at half-mile intervals beginning four miles from the city center, while a similar set of outlets on the South Side started only 2.75 miles from the Loop at Twenty-Second Street. Moreover, the residential suburbs along the North Shore used the lake as their ultimate sink, and the booming industrial Calumet District, sweeping south of the city along the bottom end of the lake, also posed a danger to Chicago because of its poisonous mixture of industrial and human wastes.

Even if the drainage canal prevented any further discharges from the river, the assistant commissioner reasoned, the engineers' plan was fundamentally flawed. "Raw" water taken untreated from Lake Michigan would continue to cause sickness and death. Referring back to the Hering Commission, he reiterated its call for a system of intercepting sewers along the lakefront. But Reilly went much further, contradicting the report's rejection of sewage treatment and water filtration plants on the grounds of cost. The doctor proposed building both types of facilities as essential for protecting the health of the city.

Once scientific research had established that the lake was dangerously and permanently polluted, the logical conclusion was that the contaminated water must be purified. Both sewage treatment and water filtration were already well established in Europe. By the mid-1890s, microbiologists and engineers there were well advanced and were putting a second generation of equipment on-line now that they had a much better way of measuring water quality according to bacteriological as well as chemical standards. Special experimental stations contributed to this rapid progress in understanding the ways in which chemicals and microorganisms interact with various types of polluted water. In the case of sewage treatment, the sanitary experts were developing an early form of biotechnology by putting bacteria to work eating organic wastes, including many kinds of disease germs.[50]

In 1896, Reilly's mobilization of the medical community and reform groups resulted in the creation of the Pure Water Commission. The politicians, however, consented only to the recommendation that intercepting sewers be constructed, and then only along the South Side, the residential district of the well-to-do.[51] While this project was undoubtedly worthwhile, the council's decision suggests two important questions. The first is the question of social justice: the plan called for the main drain to run under Thirty-Ninth Street until it emptied into the South Fork of the river in the midst of the Packingtown and Bridgeport neighborhoods. The second is regarding the curious resistance of the aldermen to the building of water filtration and sewage treatment plants. City Hall would stubbornly hold out against not only the growing weight of expert opinion in favor of such technologies, but also against the steady pressure of the federal government.

During the 1890s, nonetheless, the reception of germ theories began to affect the public discourse on the urban environment, challenging the underlying assumptions of City Hall's politics of health. Rapid progress in identifying the specific agents of disease boosted the social status and authority of the new breed of scientists and medical practitioners. On the basis of their experimental findings, these experts came into conflict with the engineers, who had long worked together with the politicians to promote the interrelated causes of property development, government expansion, and professional careers.

Chicago's engineers continued to believe that Lake Michigan was an inexhaustible fountain of everlasting purity while the scientists were coming to just the opposite conclusion. In their studies for the sanitary district they helped confirm the theory that dilution was an effective means of rendering sewage harmless to health. But they were also becoming increasingly convinced that in practice the massive amounts of human and industrial wastes pouring into the lake were overwhelming this natural process of purification. Additional steps were needed both to ensure the safety of the city's drinking water and to reduce the amount of raw sewage being returned to its ultimate source of supply.

In this way, the new public health promoted a distinct environmental perspective that emphasized the conservation of natural resources. To be sure, historians of medicine have shown convincingly that germ theory had the effect of reorienting the profession from the effort to clean up the city to the treatment of sick individuals. However, this shift in therapeutic approach does not fully account for the impact of the germ theories of disease causation on prevention strategies, especially those aimed at illnesses known to transmitted by contaminated water and air. As Joel Tarr has shown in his pioneering essay "Disputes over Water-Quality Policy: Professional Cultures in Conflict," the environmental perspectives of the new sanitarians were shared by many others, giving rise to the conservation and efficiency movements of the Progressive Era.[52]

In Chicago, the controversy between science and engineering remained problematic until the opening of the drainage channel in 1900 and the outbreak of another epidemic of typhoid fever two years later. The latter crisis would convert most of the city's engineers to the epidemiologists' position, but the politicians would stand firm, rejecting their recommendations for the next quarter-century.

Manchester: Preserving "One of the Sweetest Glens"

In Manchester, consumer demand for more water paradoxically arose in the midst of environmental crises resulting from the presence of too much of it. Between the catastrophic floods of 1866 and 1872, the city suffered a drought that severely reduced the amount of water available from its upland reservoirs. Service had to be restricted to eight to twelve hours per day and factory owners had to cut their usage by half. Town Hall looked to Chief Engineer John Bateman to end the shortages that were squeezing the profits out of its utility business and out of the cotton mills, which were dependent on abundant supplies of soft, clean rainwater.

Bateman's ambitious plan to build a pipeline one hundred miles to a remote lake won almost unanimous approval locally, but provoked howls of dissent across the nation. The protesters rallied support for the preservation of nature in the face of the rapacious encroachments of the industrial city. Drawing upon the recent precedent of the creation of Yellowstone National Park in the United States, they laid the groundwork for the emergence of novel approaches to environmental protection during the Progressive Era.

The movement to save Lake Thirlmere would eventually lead to the creation of the National Trust in 1895.[53]

Business profit, not public health, was the prime mover driving the scheme to secure a much larger source of supply. The cost of constructing the Long-dendale system in the hills behind the city had climbed far beyond Bateman's estimates because of the area's unanticipated geological problems, but the waterworks had met his promise of supplying about twenty-five million gallons per day. During the yearlong drought that began in August 1868, however, Bateman could only deliver eighteen million gallons per day by drawing down the reservoirs. Town Hall's expectations of fat profits from the utility had evaporated in the years that followed. Now Bateman proposed a heroic public works project to bring twice as much water, fifty million gallons per day, to Manchester.[54]

Reflecting dominant cultural orientations, the chief engineer's views expressed a commodification of nature. Bateman believed that rainwater, the "natural produce" of the hills, was the same as the commercial crops of the flatlands, like cotton and wool. "I never could see the wisdom of the view which would confine the supply of water to the towns or places which lay within any particular watershed," he explained. "Where the water was most abundant it was generally the least wanted." In the 1850s, his work on a thirty-five-mile conduit from Lock Katrine to Glasgow had proven the feasibility of this kind of long-distance project. During the following decade, Bateman had drawn up plans for a gigantic 180-mile water line from Wales to London and an equally fantastic train tunnel under the English Channel. When he was hired by Liverpool in 1873, he recommended that the city enter into a joint venture with Manchester to tap Ullswater in the Lake District. But the all-powerful chairman of Manchester's water committee, John Grave, was dead set against any cooperative venture with the archrival port city.[55]

Gaining his key support for the large-scale project, Bateman convinced the city council to go it alone in order to secure a water supply large enough to preclude shortages in the foreseeable future. In 1877, after two years of debate it followed his advice and purchased an eleven-thousand-acre estate in the Lake District. Chairman Grave and Chief Engineer Bateman had changed the site for two important reasons. Lead mining above Ullswater raised questions about the quality of its water supply, and a fortuitous dispute among the heirs of the estate surrounding Thirlmere offered a rare opportunity for an outside buyer to gain control of that entire property. Bitter experience in the Longdendale District had taught local officials the lesson that once property owners found out about the Corporation's public works plans, they would blackmail it with extravagant prices for land parcels and use rights.[56]

Bateman and Grave were spellbound by the noble scale of the project. From Bateman's point of view, the opportunity to reengineer an entire lake basin from its primordial natural state into a technological fountain inexhaustible represented a dream come true. His topographical surveys confirmed that the site formed a ready-made reservoir and catch-basin in a place where rainfall averaged eighty inches a year, or twice the average in the Longdendale watershed. Located five hundred feet above sea level, Thirlmere was long and narrow, making it relatively easy to dam the lake and to drain its water all the way to Manchester using only the force of gravity. A human-constructed embankment—one hundred feet high and eight hundred feet across—would raise the lake's level by fifty feet and increase its size from 328 to almost nine hundred acres.

From the perspective of Manchester's elite, the imperial scale of this public works project also appealed to civic pride and local boosterism. Crucial was bringing Town Clerk Sir Thomas Heron on board. His tireless support would prove decisive in Manchester's coming battle in Parliament against the rest of the nation.[57] Perhaps the only major miscalculation made by Bateman and Grave was that of underestimating the size and determination of the opposition.

Marching under the banner of the Thirlmere Defence Association, the protesters demanded the protection of this environmental sanctuary of pristine beauty from the utilitarian demands of the industrial city. Led by the Lord Bishop of Carlyle, the association enlisted the participation of not only members of the upper crust but also representatives of the middle-class intelligentsia, such as John Ruskin and Octavia Hill. Against the city's assertion of its right to protect the public health, the protesters declared a superior claim to the necessity of saving the nation's few remaining havens of unspoiled nature. As one editorial put it, "The plan represented the most monstrous piece of vandalism of which this self-satisfied nineteenth century has been guilty. As a precedent sure to be followed—unless some terrible accident should humble the self-confidence of daring engineers—it threatens to originate a system under which whatever beautiful scenery, whatever healthful resorts are left in England, will be defaced and despoiled for the real or supposed advantage of those monster aggregations of houses miscalled cities, which are the embarrassment and reproach of modern civilization."[58]

The two Mancunians' plans had been based on the mistaken assumption that few would care about one of the remotest spots in the fashionable resort area. Bateman, as a surveyor, and Grave, as a long-term vacation-home owner, both knew that Thirlmere was a hidden lake located on the northern side of the resort area, farthest from the streams of railroad and coach tourists coming from points to the south. In contrast to Ullswater, with its goodly number of lakefront cottages, Thirlmere had few human inhabitants, and they were far outnumbered by the Herdwick sheep they tended. Inheriting the animals' medieval grazing or "stint" rights with the purchase of the estate, Alderman Grave technically became Lord of the Manor of Legburthwaite and Wythburn.

What Grave and Bateman didn't anticipate was how many people cared about the lake precisely because it was relatively secluded and untouched. The association's call to arms rang out:

> There is no valley in the District which is at once seen by so many visitors, and is so entirely free from modern erections out of harmony with the surroundings. The western shore of the mere is perhaps the most beautiful we have: it is not the simple grassy slope that borders so many of our lakes, but a series of bays divided by little rocky headlands, crowned with dwarf trees, and rich in wild-flowers and ferns. . . . The outlet of the lake must be reached on foot, and, combining as it does certain elements of severity and grandeur, with the charm of a lonely and picturesque loveliness, forms one of the sweetest glens in Cumberland.[59]

The Thirlmere protestors set off a wide-ranging debate on environmental protection, at least in the popular press. The city's champions were caught off guard, but they quickly recovered their ability to mount a vigorous defense of the pipeline project. By one estimate, the Manchester lobby would have to spread at least thirty-eight thousand pounds around to ensure final passage of an authorizing act in Parliament. Of course, the city's advocates took the high ground by maintaining the position that the water was absolutely necessary for the protection of the public's health and welfare. Responding to the Lord Bishop's protest letter to the *Times*, Alderman Grave claimed that "the trade of the [Manchester] district is to be paralyzed and the growth of population stopped by the want of water. . . . Do these sentimentalists know what they mean by ridiculing the wants of trade? They mean the denial of a primary necessity of life to a working population."

Grave boldly asserted that the man-made project would actually improve nature, making the site both more attractive and more accessible. "But I should think he [the Lord Bishop] knows, if his followers do not," the civic spokesman argued, "that Nature has been at work for ages in destroying her own primitive and untouched beauty. Perhaps he prefers the swamps and bogs which Nature always tends to make wherever she has a chance and never removes again.... All that ground will be again submerged, while the rocky banks where they are steep will retain the same character."[60]

Against the well-oiled Manchester lobby, the self-appointed guardians of Thirlmere made the case for balancing the needs of the industrial city with the preservation of the natural world. Octavia Hill, a housing and open spaces reformer, tried to distance their cause from accusations that it represented an untenable stand against public health for the urban masses. Conceding that "all men must have good and abundant water," Hill posited that the real question was where Manchester was going to get it. In her opinion, it should not come from the Lake District. She asked rhetorically:

> Are the men who say their embankment, with a few boulders scattered about, will rival in beauty Raven Crag itself, who ask us to rejoice that they propose to submerge fields in the valley and pull down gray stone walls,—who finally tell us they scorn the form of the lake as moulded by rainfall and streams in long ages, and seem to see no value in the flowers of its swamps and no charm in its little-frequented bridle-paths,—are these the men to whom we are going to commit one of the loveliest lakes and valleys our England owns?[61]

In 1877, the argument over Thirlmere moved into Parliament, which took up Manchester's authorization bill. The settlement that was reached two years later reflected an institutional structure of centralized power and a complementary political culture of aristocratic hierarchy and social privilege. Although the project was approved, the national legislature imposed a stringent set of conditions on Manchester for the environmental protection of the land crossed by the pipeline. Lobbyists for the great landlords along the route had received a sympathetic hearing from the lawmakers. Almost the entire length of the aqueduct would have to buried underground and the right-of-way restored by landscape gardeners to its original appearance. Affected property owners were empowered to supervise the planning and execution of this construction work. Moreover, any disputes arising from the project would be placed under the jurisdiction of national administrative officers.[62]

Manchester: The Politics of Capital and Labor

Although it had pushed the bill through the national legislature as a pressing necessity for the protection of the public health, Manchester's civic elite felt little urgency about building the big, expensive water project. At the moment of the political triumph, consumer demand from the mills began to fall off with a slump in trade. Certainly, the elite had no intention of using the water to improve the quality of domestic life for the vast majority of the city's inhabitants. Even nature in the form of the next round of drought-related "serious inconveniences" during the summer of 1884 could not budge the council to initiate a construction project that would takes years to complete. By October, the Longdendale reservoirs were down to one-sixth full, requiring another period of restricted, half-time service the following month. Yet only a token start of work on the dam and pipeline was made in January 1885 because, according to Sir John Harwood, "Manchester and the surrounding district suffered from a depression in trade such as had not been experienced for many years, and this had the effect of checking the demand for water which had previously taken place as the result of increased trade and population."[63]

What is conspicuously missing from the alderman's semiofficial history is the story of how it took a massive uprising of the city's unemployed to kick-start construction work on the project. With the passage of the third great reform act of 1884, which extended suffrage rights to working-class males, factory slum zones like Ancoats became hotbeds of radical agitation. The civic elite's ship canal project had helped not only to arouse mass political participation but also to legitimize it. The businessmen and trade unionists had built this class-bridging "Lib-Lab" coalition on what historian Ian Harford calls a "producer ideology." The following year, the number of unemployed grew to thirty to forty thousand workers, adding urgency to the passage of an authorizing act for Manchester's "Big Ditch."

Although parliamentary approval was secured in August, stalled efforts to finance the ship canal strained the Lib-Lab alliance to the breaking point. The radical Social Democratic Federation led the mobilization of the working classes. On its behalf, William Morris accepted Charles Rowley's invitation to give a lecture on socialism. With strongholds in Ancoats and Salford, local leaders of this direct action group began organizing gatherings of the people in the streets in the tradition of Peterloo and the Plug Riots.

After a Social Democratic Federation demonstration in London's Trafalgar Square turned into the Black Monday riot of 8 February 1886, social tensions threatened to explode in Manchester. When the federation announced plans to hold two Sunday demonstrations of Manchester's unemployed in support of their London comrades, the police force of five hundred men braced for trouble. The meeting on the morning of 28 February took place without incident, but later in the afternoon a crowd of at least fifteen thousand people poured out of Ancoats and clashed with the police at several points.

Although the group at the next rally was only half as large as the afternoon crowd and was peaceful, it was big enough to keep the city gripped in a fearful, state-of-siege mentality. The following month, the Thirlmere project began in earnest. With the completion of a railroad siding and warehouse at Windermere, Mancunians began arriving by the hundreds to become diggers, or navvies, as they were called. The timing of the mass demonstrations and the appearance of the construction jobs was not coincidental, in spite of the selectivity of Sir Harwood's memory. In contrast, it took nearly two more years before work commenced on the ship canal.[64]

The two public works projects kept huge armies of navvies going for the next several years of hard times. The larger ship canal project employed 16,000 diggers in addition to 6,300 horse-drawn wagons, 173 locomotives, and 97 steam shovels. Although not all of the workers came from the pool of Manchester's unemployed, the benefits to the local and regional economies were immense. The ship canal cost about fifteen million pounds, and the water-supply pipeline poured another three million pounds into the area's economies. To reduce technological and environmental risks associated with the pipeline project, Bateman's master plan called for the construction of a sequential series of five conduits, each with a carrying capacity of ten million gallons per day. Adopting methods in common practice on the continent, albeit novel in England, city engineers used pipes with plain ends, which were coupled together with special collars. In January 1894, the ship canal opened to traffic, and by August the Thirlmere reservoir had built up enough water for a final connection to be made with Manchester's distribution network.[65]

Nonetheless, Town Hall hoped to keep the water turned off for as long as possible in order to forestall the start of its obligation to pay for the public works project. Like the commencement of construction, the opening of the tap was driven more by popular anger and official paranoia than by concern about sanitary or environmental reform. Middle-class consumers' complaints about poor water quality had accumulated to the point that the town council believed it would be blamed for any ensuing outbreak of an epidemic. Because it had held off the start of pipeline construction for seven years, the council was forced to suck the Longdendale reservoirs as dry as possible to supply the Corporation's suburban and industrial customers. Now an official tap-opening ceremony was hurriedly put together for 12 October at Thirlmere.[66] Little of the newly available water flowed into the slum districts and jerry-built houses of the working classes, however.

In the midst of the transition from Liberal oligarchy to "Tory democracy," traditions of class discrimination and spatial segregation remained the bedrock of Manchester's political culture. Although it was difficult to dislodge, this exclusionary approach to decision making was being steadily eroded by new currents of social environmentalism and working-class empowerment. By 1894, the forces of urban Progressivism had succeeded in shifting the direction of the policy discussion on water and sanitation services, but the reformers were not strong enough yet to implement new policies.[67]

The reasons behind Town Hall's decision two years earlier to reverse course from its insistence on pail closets for the working classes helps explain the snail's pace of conversion from that discredited system of waste removal. Manchester had backed into the choice for universal indoor plumbing after eliminating all the other alternatives. After the passage of the manhood suffrage act in 1884, an accumulation of internal and external pressures kept undercutting the stance of the diehard supporters of the status quo. By then, the conversion from privies and cesspools to pail closets was virtually complete but the council had precious little to show for its sanitary strategy in terms of either public health or river conservancy (see table 11.3).[68] In the 1890 housing code ordinance, the Progressives gained a proviso for mandatory indoor plumbing in new construction. This victory encouraged the representatives of central-city districts and their Progressive reform allies to keep up the volume on the case for requiring landlords to get rid of backyard privies and to install water closets inside each of their tenants' homes.[69]

By then, the Liberals had finally been overthrown, having been shaken by an inbred political culture that spawned insidious scandals of sweetheart deals and personal aggrandizement. A look at one of these self-destructive episodes illustrates the ways in which the Progressives' belief in social environmentalism changed the city's political culture. This scandal on the health committee exposed how the Liberals' regime of secrecy and arrogance had led to its own criminal corruption. Like Jane Addams's reforms, structural changes then enacted by Mancunians pried open the powerful

Table 11.3 Manchester pail closet conversions, 1873–1888

Year	Number of pail closets
1873	696
1875	5,026
1880	59,931
1885	65,000
1888	66,499

Source: Alan Wilson, "Technology and Municipal Decision-Making: Sanitary Systems in Manchester 1868–1910" (Ph.D. diss., University of Manchester, 1990), 127.

council committees to greater public accountability in policy making and administration. Under the new-style Tory democracy, the bright light of civic revelation about the years of secret dumping at Holt Town would dissolve whatever final defenses were left standing for the old pail-closet system.

In 1885, this bombshell of news about corruption inside the health committee rocked Town Hall's crumbling facade of moral authority. The superintendent of the night-soil department, Henry Whiley, had become caught in a web of conflicting interests, ghost payrollers, and sweetheart contracts. Whiley had started working for the Corporation in 1865 and within a decade had risen from sanitary inspector to administrator of the pail-closet system and its Holt Town processing plant. While he held this position, he was also attempting to keep his land and building company from going under during the hard times of the mid-1880s. Although he ultimately escaped indictment for his mismanagement of public funds, the notoriety of the case helped plunge his private business into bankruptcy.

The investigation also attracted the attention of the public and provoked it to cast a disapproving glare on the committee, which not only paid Whiley a generous salary of six hundred pounds a year, but also furnished him with a nice house and paid the bills for its upkeep. These extras were the equivalent of a payoff or bribe to buy his silence and his complicity in the nefarious practices at the Holt Town facility, where thirty to sixty tons of human wastes were being poured every day into the Medlock and Irwell rivers. The exposure of this scandal became the final blow that shattered the credibility of the ruling party's sanitary strategy of dry conservancy. The appalling conduct of the committee proved so embarrassing to the ruling elite that the sanitation services had to undertake reorganization, undergo a cosmetic makeover, and be renamed the Cleansing Department.[70]

In 1886, a more focused investigation of the streams of wastewater generated within the city demolished any remaining claims by public authorities that they were speaking in the name of river conservancy. Dr. Charles A. Burghardt made a presentation to the Literary and Philosophical Society on his study of "The Pollution of the River Irwell and Its Tributaries." For two years he had been collecting and analyzing water samples above, within, and below the city limits. The scientist surmised that the poor quality of the Irwell's water was "almost entirely due to pollution of the Irwell by its tributaries, the Irk and the Medlock, the sewage being mostly that poured into the rivers by the Manchester sewers." Although he did not know yet about the massive dumping at Holt Town, he measured its effects, and attributed them to the textile mills. "I cannot draw any other conclusion than this," he told the members of the Lit and Phil, "that about ONE-HALF the total pollution of the Irwell ... is due to manufacturers' waste waters—in other words, avoidable pollution."[71] Over the next few years, the accumulating weight of expert opinion in favor of the water-carriage system of sanitation flattened the arguments of the few remaining stalwarts of the old guard.

In 1885, national approval of the ship canal project furnished the initial impetus to clean house at Town Hall and bring in a new generation of key administrators. With a sixty-foot descent and four locks from the turning basin at Trafford to the estuary above Liverpool, the thirty-six-mile-long artificial highway would need as much water as it could get to keep its extrawide channels full. The time for intercepting sewers and main drains on a metropolitan scale had arrived, and with it a new city surveyor, John Allison, and consulting engineer, J. Bailey Denton. Both favored a conversion to universal indoor plumbing as part of the overall plan of water management for Greater Manchester.

Like their Chicago counterparts, the Manchester engineers expanded the geographical boundaries of their blueprints outward from the artificial municipal borders to create natural drainage districts. Dusting off the Bateman-Lynde plan of the mid-1870s, the planners envisioned a unified network of main drains leading to a treatment plant near the turning basin of the ship canal. This hydraulic system encompassed many suburban communities around Manchester, especially those upstream to the north, which had no choice except to use the Irwell River as their sink for sewage. In 1888, the chairman of the canal project, Lord Egerton, would take the lead in persuading the suburbs to accept a great consolidation of the Manchester conurbation.[72]

Reinforcing the efforts of the engineers, the doctors who succeeded Dr. Leigh as medical officer of health added their professional backing to calls for social justice and environmental reform. Dr. John F. W. Tatham, who assumed the office in 1888, had come from Salford after winning it over five years earlier to Edwin Chadwick's sanitary strategy. He helped push through ordinances in Manchester requiring water closets in both new and existing housing. Six years later, he was replaced by Dr. James Niven, who took up the battle against the passive revolt of the landlords in opposition to paying the cost of installing plumbing in their rental properties. "When I came to Manchester in 1894," Niven remembered, "the pail-closet system had failed very largely to do what had been expected of it. The narrow passages and courts were again such as Mr. Leigh described them: the air oppressive and malodorous, urine trickling onto them from within the closet chambers, their surface full of rises and falls from defective and soaking drains, and the surfaces imperfect, so that foul liquid was soaking into the soil."

In return for calling for a water-closet system, Dr. Niven received strong support from the senior engineer in charge of sanitation. The engineer's official report buried the old pail-closet system under an avalanche of statistics regarding economic inefficiency. It simply made no sense to go to all the trouble of collecting the waste of thousands of people a day only to dump it in the river upstream of where most of them lived.[73]

As the momentum of expert opinion within Town Hall shifted irreversibly against the pail-closet system in the late 1880s and early 1890s, outside pressures limited the council's options to a single choice: universal indoor plumbing throughout the entire metropolitan area. Desperate to save its system of environmental inequality, the city council had pursued a plan to transport the excess pail-closet wastes in special trains to incinerator stations located in the suburbs. But suburban residents had retaliated successfully with not-in-my-backyard (NIMBY) campaigns to keep them out. The surrounding suburbs were not the only extralocal political units hemming in Manchester's freedom of choice to set environmental policy. The 1879 Rivers Pollution Act had authorized the creation of administrative boards with jurisdiction over areas defined by natural river basins. In contrast to that of the Sanitary District of Chicago, the authority of these boards was restricted to regulatory oversight of local governments within each of their districts. The knee-jerk reaction of Manchester Liberals had been to fight the establishment of the Joint Rivers Authority as a threat to local self-government. But once it became an accomplished fact in 1887, they found ways to turn the agency to their own ends as a powerful tool of urban imperialism.

The great amalgamation of Manchester in 1890 represented the climax of sanitary reform during the Progressive Era. The city gained 120,000 people and almost doubled in size by adding seven thousand acres (see fig. 9.1). Since the first presentation of the Bateman-Lynde plan, the suburbs had resisted this complete capitulation in the struggle over the formation of a comprehensive strategy for cleaning up the river basin. They had feared not only the loss of community identity but also the added burden of infrastructure costs. The creation of the Joint Rivers Authority had signaled that in the absence of local initiative the national government would impose a Chadwickian solution. In 1891 Parliament passed the Local Government Act, which reaffirmed its commitment to administrative oversight by regional-scale boards whose jurisdiction was based on both customary county borderlines and the boundaries of natural river basins.

Pushed by the ship canal project and pulled by the national government, Town Hall now found itself in the position of chief advocate of a metropolitan-scale scheme of intercepting sewers and treatment plants. Using its leverage as the sole supplier of essential public utilities, such as water and gas, to the suburbs, it left them little choice between accepting annexation and facing a cutoff of services. Manchester also exploited its considerable power within the Joint Rivers Authority to confront the suburbs with a second ultimatum: either become a part of the city's master plan or bear the entire cost of building a separate system of water management that could meet the Joint River Authority's standards of purity for effluent discharges into the rivers. Only Salford was self-sufficient enough to hold out against its neighbor.[74]

Manchester's triumph over the suburbs committed it to the implementation of a comprehensive solution for sewerage but not to a conversion from a pail-closet system to a water-closet system. In fact, Town Hall had already earmarked the Thirlmere water for use in a new venture in municipal capitalism, the creation of a hydraulic power system. Water sent through special high-pressure pipes could run machines ranging from small hand tools to giant dock cranes. The council was already heavily invested in the Ship Canal Company—for five million pounds—and it hoped that sinking more public money into this power technology would help guarantee the canal's financial success. Along the banks of the canal was the Trafford Park Industrial Estate, perhaps the world's first large-scale planned district of its kind. The estate was designed to complement commercial activity with facilities attractive to new manufacturing enterprises. Power offered at bargain-basement rates would help lure such American companies as Westinghouse, Kellogg, and Ford. The hydraulic system would also ensure that a significant volume of Thirlmere's pure water would flow into the ship canal.[75]

The exposure of the clandestine dumping at Holt Town upset the council's carefully laid plans to save the pail-closet system in working-class neighborhoods. After the suburbs rebuffed the attempt to build incinerators in their communities, Town Hall had only one other option left if it was going to keep the pail-closet system, a retrograde resort to sewage farms. In 1886, the council had purchased a six-hundred-acre estate at Carrington Moss and had laid a railroad line to it from Holt Town. Although much of the human waste was processed into fertilizer and Whiley's operation transported sixty tons to the farms each day, he was still left with an excess of about thirty-six tons collected each day.

The great amalgamation only made matters worse by adding waste from another thousand privies and pail closets to this unwanted surplus. The council tried to expand its sewage farming but failed because the available land proved unsuitable for this purpose. Moreover, the cost of collecting and transporting the semisolid wastes was high compared to moving it in liquid form through pipes by gravity. If economic computation of costs and benefits was not enough to persuade the council to adopt indoor plumbing, then political calculations of working-class votes tipped the scales in favor of this policy choice.[76]

Reluctantly backing into the decision for water closets in 1892, the Tories cast the move as a progressive step forward not only for public health but also for good government. By finally bringing Manchester in line with national standards, local officials placated the working classes, vindicated the medical community, and appeased the long-frustrated Manchester and Salford Sanitary Association. Since the cost of conversion would be borne primarily by the landlords and their tenants, the new council majority claimed that the Corporation would save money by closing out a losing business venture. The council quietly wrote off the over £212,000 already spent on the pail-closet system.

The ratepayers, however, loudly complained about the switch in sanitary strategies. Gaining the ear of Parliament, they halted Town Hall's plan to offer landlords a small subsidy as an incentive to convert their properties. Thwarting the council at the national level, they also resisted it at the local level by simply refusing to comply with the new policy. Ten years later, 105,800 of the city's 151,500 sanitary closets remained unchanged (see fig. 11.4).[77]

During this period, the council deferred responding to this challenge to its authority even though it had ample power to force the property owners

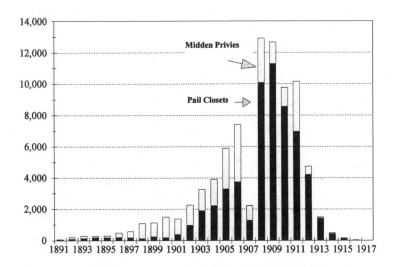

Figure 11.4. Conversions of midden privies and pail closets to water closets in Manchester, 1891–1917

Source: Data from Alan Wilson, "Technology and Municipal Decision-Making: Sanitary Systems in Manchester, 1868–1910" (Ph.D. diss., University of Manchester, 1990), 127.

to obey the law. Manchester's political culture had changed little with the Tories' overthrow of the Liberals. To the ruling elite, the suffering of the working classes was still of less concern than the pocketbooks of the ratepayers. Environmental inequality and spatial segregation were deeply ingrained in a society structured according to the belief that class and ethnic/religious conflict were eternal. One of Manchester's leading reformers later attributed the slow pace of conversion to the callous attitudes of the political establishment toward the slum dwellers of the central city. Looking back from the vantage point of the 1930s, she asserted:

> The story of main drainage in Manchester does not reflect credit on the council. That one of the richest cities in England and one of the largest, should have been behind much smaller towns like Salford and Leeds, in tackling a prime necessity for health, speaks little for the foresight or even for the humanity of our forefathers. . . . It was an outstanding case of "penny wise and pound foolish policy." That property owners and ratepayers' associations, in their shortsighted zeal for saving the rates and their own pockets, may not always be the best judges even of their own interests and certainly not of those of the community as a whole, is clearly proved in this instance.[78]

Equally important in Town Hall's acquiescence to landlord resistance was the basic failure of the Corporation's sewage treatment plant to meet minimum standards of purity for wastewater effluents. The Davyhulme facility that opened in tandem with the ship canal in 1894 used chemical precipitation to separate the solids from the liquids. This method, however, had major shortcomings. It generated huge amounts of semisolid sludge that had to be disposed of either by spreading on the land or by loading onto ships for dumping at sea. Both choices involved great expense.

More problematic, the liquids spilling out of Davyhulme into the turning basin still contained intolerable levels of organic matter that underwent malodorous putrefaction. This contaminated water did not pass the chemical tests of effluent quality set by the Mersey and Irwell Joint Committee, successor to the Joint Rivers Authority. Until the experts came up with a better method of purification, hooking up more water closets to the sewers would only make a bad situation worse.[79]

By the end of the year, Manchester's triumph of water management—Thirlmere, the main drain, and Davyhulme—had become a political and environmental nightmare. Backed by the national Local Government Board, the Mersey and Irwell Joint Committee threatened to cut the Corporation off from access to money for all of its various public works projects. The polluted waters pouring out of the sewage treatment plant also endangered the value of its major investment in the ship canal. Rather than being a pump primer of economic development, the projects were beginning to suck the treasury dry. Town Hall might be forced to spend a fortune in a futile effort to meet the joint committee's minimum standards of waste-water quality while losing money operating a toxic waterway no one would use.

Hanging in the balance was the city council's promise that it would use the additional supply of water from Thirlmere to improve the quality of domestic life. The residents of over one hundred thousand houses were being denied modern plumbing. How they would express their disappointment in the streets and at the polls was a troubling source of concern for elected officials. They must have felt squeezed between the demands of the national government on one side and the expectations of the grass roots on the other. This pressure soon became unbearable, cracking the council and its secretive committees wide open and setting the stage for the development a new style of democratic discourse in the formation of public policy.

Even by European standards, the average daily usage of water per person in Manchester was low. In the mid-1880s, before the addition of the Thirlmere pipeline, the waterworks delivered up to 24 million gallons a day, or about 66.3 gallons per capita. In contrast, Chicagoans were each consuming an average of 135 gallons daily, over twice as much. At the turn of the century, Manchester's waterworks yielded 32 million gallons a day or about 50–55 gallons per capita. Chicago's production was a whopping 187 gallons a day per person, still more than three times as much as Manchester.[80]

Although Manchester had narrowed the gap, its discriminatory class policies, high level of industrial use, and hydraulic power system made the amount of water available for domestic use in the slum districts seem greater than it was. There is no doubt that the conversion from pail to water closets marked a major victory for public health and environmental justice. As Medical Officer of Health Dr. Niven understood, the coming of the indoor toilets served as the vanguard for the complete reconstruction of houses' pipes and drains. "It thus came about," he wrote, "that most of the foul matter formerly soaking into the ground near houses has now been diverted into the sewers, while at the same time the subsoil has been rendered dry."

Still, some houses remained without water taps, and occupants were forced to collect their supplies in buckets from standpipes in the street. Until the mid-1930s, moreover, most family dwellings were denied a bathtub. A special tax of ten shillings on bathtubs in low-cost housing turned this modern convenience into a luxury enjoyed by only a fortune few among the working classes. The extent to which the relative shortage of water and lack of indoor plumbing accounts for Manchester's abysmal record of public health is unknown, but there is no doubt that it made keeping bodies, houses, and neighborhoods in the central city clean much more difficult.[81]

Conclusions: Political Culture and Environmental Reform

If Manchester's political culture legitimized keeping a tight lid on the use of the Corporation's water, Chicago's encouraged opening the valves of the city's pumping stations full throttle. But in the opening decade of the new century, Progressive reformers challenged the authority of Chicago's elected officials to set urban environmental policy. On the matter of water management policy, an unbridgeable gap opened between the professional politicians of City Hall and the local and outside experts, including engineers, scientists, and medical specialists involved in public health, whose consensus was growing. Against accumulating evidence to the contrary, the ward bosses and the sanitary district engineers found it advantageous to adhere to the increasingly outmoded idea that the lake was a fountain inexhaustible that could be tapped with impunity as both a source of drinking water and a tool with which to render raw sewage harmless by dilution.

In the case of the waterworks, the city's policy of prodigal waste became notorious, the subject of ridicule by its own engineers as well as panel after panel of outside consultants. Nonetheless, the city council refused to take any steps that might endanger the flow of obscene amounts of money into the surplus account of its water fund. As early as 1874, the Chicago Board of Public Works had bemoaned "the monstrous waste of water," calling it "a reflection upon the moral sense of those guilty of it." The board exclaimed in its annual report of that year, "It appears to be impossible for many people to understand that water, unlike air, is not a free commodity and that no one is entitled to use more water than he pays for."[82]

Three years later, Chief Engineer Cregier had recommended taking the logical step, from curbing the behavior of individual wrongdoers to controlling the consumption habits of whole populations. He had not only identified the problem of excessive waste but also suggested an appropriate remedy, universal metering. But the politics of growth meant the subordination of the engineer's concerns under the aldermen's insistence upon a steady flow of profits into the water fund.[83] During the Gilded Age, the wanton waste of water was seen largely in moral terms; during the Progressive Era, it became more a matter of open conflict between the authority of experts and that of politicians.

During the 1890s, water department managers' traditional deference to the politicians began to weaken as the managers were drawn more fully into extralocal professional communities. An obsession with efficiency became a virtual religious faith among American engineers, making the elimination of waste the litmus test of professional competency. This cult of efficiency, which came to be one of the hallmarks of Progressivism, inspired an entire generation of American municipal reformers. Calls for water filtration by public health experts like Commissioner Reynolds and university scientists from the microbiology labs reinforced efforts to reverse the insatiable demand for more water. On the basis of bacteriological findings, these experts had concluded that the lake was permanently contaminated with disease-causing germs. Water treatment plants offered the only reliable technology that could ensure the safety of the drinking supply. However, given the huge amount of water pumped in the city, 323 million gallons a day in 1900, the cost of constructing filtration facilities and sewage treatment plants would be extremely high. For the politicians, the risk of a taxpayer revolt was even higher.[84]

As Chicago's extravagant use of water came to greater public attention, the engineers took the lead in speaking out in favor of universal metering. By conducting field tests with a new type of measuring instrument called a pitometer, they confirmed previous estimates that between one-half and two-thirds of the total pumpage was being wasted. As the water supply system became larger and larger, moreover, the number and difficulty of its technical problems grew apace, making a shift in emphasis from expansion to conservation more attractive to those held responsible for the city's chronic shortages in the midst of plenty. By the end of the decade, the crusaders for efficient use and conservation of resources found a champion within the administration, City Engineer John E. Ericson. For the next quarter-century, Ericson would lead an uphill battle to convince elected officials to close out their slush fund and bring Chicago into conformity with national standards.[85]

Between 1901 and 1907, municipal reformers mounted a sustained campaign to prompt the city to operate the water department in a businesslike manner. But in the end, the politicians prevailed in producing just the opposite result: the amount of surplus in the water fund was significantly enlarged. The city officials had little difficulty in getting around laws that prohibited the transfer of funds from one account to another. For example, a new boat for the harbormaster was charged to the water fund because he was occasionally called upon to help the municipal laboratory gather water samples. A comparison of water fund levels at five years before and after 1906 shows that the ratio of revenues to operating costs remained about the same, close to four to one. Yet the amount of annual profit jumped almost a million dollars, from $2.90 million to $3.84 million. Over the course of the decade, the cumulative surplus would amount to more than $23 million.[86] By maintaining the water fund, the city's elected officials perpetuated a politics of waste. They refused to appropriate money for meter installations or underground repair work, but they spent freely on expanding the network of pumping stations and distributor mains. The policy created a self-sustaining system of patronage jobs and contracts. With fewer than 10 percent of Chicago's water consumers hooked up to meters in 1924, even the tireless Ericson would wonder if it was still worthwhile "to keep hammering at it any longer.... There seems to be no limit to the capacity that should be provided in order to give proper service under such conditions. One cannot carry water in a sieve without plugging up the holes."[87] The engineer's lament pointed to the supreme power of the professional politicians in the formation of environmental policy in Chicago.

A comparison of Chicago and Manchester highlights the ways in which political culture played a configurative role in shaping water supply and sanitation strategies during the Progressive Era. In Chicago, universal male suffrage and extreme devolution of power had engendered a ward-based system of leadership. The aldermen usually reflected the class and immigration status of the rank and file of their districts. Coming from humble origins, they made politics a career path of upward social mobility. They considered the municipal government a money machine that produced profits for their own gain and that of the party organization. They exploited their position both directly to extract illegal payoffs from various schemes and indirectly to engage in corrupt practices involving sweetheart deals, campaign contributions, and special favors. Chicago aldermen had a well-deserved reputation as "gray wolves" preying on the body politic.[88]

In Manchester, restricted suffrage and a strong central government had produced a very different political tradition. Although they had revolted against an entrenched oligarchy, the Liberals had established a similar regime of elite rule and class and ethnic/religious exclusion. The members of the town council often served multiple terms, but they did not consider politics to be a professional career. Instead, they projected a sort of aristocratic noblesse oblige, a sense of duty to maintain social and moral control over the unwashed urban masses.

These chauvinists of commerce and industry, unaccountable to the public until the third enfranchisement act of 1884, applied their ideology of free trade to the administration of local government. They became the Corporation, a vehicle for the promotion of private and public economic development. They used their business acumen to maximize the monopolistic privileges of municipal capitalism in order to minimize the tax bills of the ratepayers. Town Hall reinforced existing patterns of land values by intentionally denying infrastructure improvements and public services to the central-city slums while extending them to the garden suburbs of the well-to-do. They justified this unequal allocation of resources by condemning poor people—especially Irish Catholics—as moral degenerates who deserved to suffer stunted lives and early death in unhealthy homes and degraded surroundings of their own making.

Although Manchester and Chicago were more different than alike, both were urban imperialists. In pursuit of growth and power, each underwrote large-scale projects for engineering the environment to create a great metropolis. During the 1880s, the fascination with big technology boosted the municipal engineers to the zenith of their influence in the formation of public policy. The big ditches promised to enlarge the two cities' commercial hinterlands, and the major annexations at the end of the decade expanded their political boundaries. In each case, the city government's control of essential public services provided the leverage to force or attract surrounding communities into giving up their individual identities of place.

Blurring the distinction between urban and suburban, the historic consolidations helped bring the political and the environmental boundaries of the industrial city more in line with each other. The creation of even larger special-purpose water districts—the Sanitary District of Chicago and the Mersey and Irwell Joint Committee—gave further recognition to the hydraulic geography of environmental control. Although driven by imperial visions of wealth and grandeur, these various reforms set a solid foundation of opportunity for the application of germ theories to public health, especially the prevention of waterborne diseases. As we shall see in the following chapter, however, Chicago and Manchester would have to resolve the conflict inherent in using their new canals both as shipping lanes and as ultimate sinks.

CHAPTER TWELVE

"Clever Microbes"

Sanitation Science in Manchester and Chicago

Introduction: The Great Manchester Sewage Crisis of 1896

In September 1896, the town council of Manchester confronted a crisis of decision making in uncharted waters of science, technology, and medicine. A national body, the Local Government Board (LGB), and a regional agency, the Mersey and Irwell Joint Committee (MIJC) were pressing the local government to choose a method of sewage treatment. The LGB was threatening to cut off funding for all public works projects, and the MIJC was suing the city for not meeting its standards of wastewater quality. The council was being forced to act, but it was adrift in a sea of conflicting recommendations from engineers, chemists, biologists, and doctors. "The question was surrounded with great difficulty, and probably there would be opposition on all sides" a member of the town council's rivers committee, Nathaniel Bradley, reported to the full council. "The Committee," he explained, "in great measure depended upon expert and scientific evidence, and were largely dominated by officials and professional advisers. That must necessarily be so from the very nature of the thing." Seeking shelter from the political storm, the council committee proposed constructing a fifteen-mile conduit that would not only dump the sewage into the tidal estuary above Liverpool, but also fall outside the jurisdiction of the regional bureau of watershed conservation.[1]

In sharp contrast, Chicago's process of constructing its "ultimate sink" was virtually free of interference from outside agencies of government. The Sanitary District of Chicago was essentially autonomous because it had been given its own power to tax and borrow. Moreover, the special-purpose district was granted authority to operate the twenty-eight-mile sanitary channel between the Chicago River and the Illinois River Valley. Although the U.S. Army Corps of Engineers formally exercised jurisdiction over inland waterways, it had never acted to strangle the city's growth with regulations. On the contrary, it had always acted to help Chicago by sponsoring various improvement projects. The state and federal governments had an unbroken record of facilitating the growth of the city.[2]

In both Chicago and Manchester, policy makers attempted to combine sanitation and transportation into their plans for engineering the environment. Manchester's ship canal depended on the city's main drain for the water to keep it filled. While the main did satisfy this purpose, an unintended consequence of the canal's reliance on it was the transformation of the turning basin into an insufferable cesspool. The parallel installation of a sewage treatment facility, the Davyhulme plant, next to the canal had failed to bring relief, and the water treated there failed to meet the minimum standards of purity set by the MIJC.[3]

In the case of Chicago, the original goal of improving public health had also been transformed but with full and open volition. Lyman E. Cooley had turned the reformers' plan for a sanitary channel into a plan for a Lakes-to-the-Gulf superhighway of commerce. Although the artificial river was made much wider and deeper in accordance with Cooley's plan, little money was left for other infrastructure projects needed to safeguard the drinking supply from sewage contamination. An unintended consequence was the epidemic of typhoid fever that struck the city less than two years after the product of Cooley's grandiose scheme opened with tremendous fanfare and great expectations.[4]

In each case, the relatively new and fast-evolving science of bacteriology became increasingly central to the policy debate over sanitation strategies. Over the past decade, germ theories have received considerable scholarly attention in the interrelated areas of epidemiology and urban water supply. However, historians have given much less consideration to their role in revolutionizing the other side of water management, the treatment and disposal of human and industrial wastes.[5]

By the mid-1890s, contemporaries involved in the search for the ultimate sink were closely following experiments in the United States and Great Britain using "clever microbes" to treat wastes. On both sides of the Atlantic, the

Progressives were well-versed in the newest trends and inventions that were part of the effort to ameliorate the worst environmental conditions of the industrial city. Pressured from above, Manchester's officials made a thorough study of the contact beds of William Dibdin in London, the septic tanks of Exeter, the intermittent filters of Salford, and the theories of biological sewage treatment being developed at the Massachusetts Experimental Station. And in 1893, Owens College (now the University of Manchester) established a department of bacteriology. During the same year, Chicago underwent a complete makeover of its public health department that included the establishment of a bacteriology laboratory.[6]

A comparison of the reception of the new science in the two cities shows that institutional structures and political cultures played a pivotal, perhaps even decisive, role in shaping the formation of public policy related to sanitation technology. As Christopher Hamlin reminds us in his pioneering essay on London's sanitarian William Dibdin, the issues facing the decision makers of the Progressive Era were not simple questions of scientific progress. On the contrary, they "were much more complicated: they were political and pragmatic, concerned as much with appearance as with substance, and as much with persuading people as with purifying sewage."[7]

The contrast between the strong arm of regional and national authorities in the United Kingdom and the "weakened springs" of the federal government in the United States could not have been more complete. While Manchester found no safe haven from the pressure from above, Chicago functioned as a virtual city-state, defying with impunity Washington's feeble efforts to enforce the law for over a quarter of a century. True enough, the city councils in both cities fostered environmental inequality and social discrimination in the name of low-cost government. Yet this rhetorical trope had little effect in either place on the outcome of the application of bacteriological science to sewage disposal.[8] Instead, political cultures and institutions gave definition to the authority of science in the decision-making process on sanitation strategies. The politics of aristocratic hierarchy and deference in Manchester privileged the special knowledge of scientists in the formation of sewage disposal policy. Rivers committee member Bradley's sense that "the very nature of the thing" put the policy question in the hands of scientific advisors reveals the basic assumptions underlying this type of political culture.[9] And in a similar manner, the various governmental bodies and parliamentary commissions gave legitimacy to the authority of science by calling prominent representatives from the academic community to give expert testimony on policy questions.

In many cases, the officials and the scientists were from the same social stratum. In the Progressive Era, a classical education in pure science remained an honorable degree for members of the upper class trained at Cambridge and Oxford. The relatively centralized structure of government and society created a political framework that pointed Manchester toward decisions on sanitation technology that were based on the authority of science.[10] In Chicago, on the other hand, a politics of anarchistic growth and individualism largely relegated scientists and doctors to the sidelines of policy formation. They were excluded from most inner circles of decision making on water management and large-scale public works projects, especially compared to the municipal engineers, whose technical methods and bureaucratic style had become an integral part of urban political culture during the Gilded Age. Those claiming authority based on the sciences of medicine and biology were forced to play the role of outside critics, warning the public of impending public health disasters caused by flawed sanitary strategies. The officials in charge of Chicago's sanitary district would fight a quarter-century campaign against the tide of scientific opinion in spite of the city's research community's leadership in the study of bacteriological methods of sewage treatment.[11]

Chicago and Manchester invite comparison for three important reasons in spite of their very different cultural frameworks and environmental settings. First, unlike cities located downstream from sources of pollution, these two are richly endowed with pure water for their drinking supplies. Second, traditional approaches such as land filtration on sewage farms that might have worked for smaller places were simply impractical for these two sprawling industrial giants. The factories of the two urban centers produced massive amounts of organic and chemical liquids that added a significant burden to the system of sewage disposal, and although Chicago's 1890 population of nearly one million was about twice that of Manchester, the populations of both were big enough to require large-scale technologies to solve their sanitation problems. Finally, each cities' search for an ultimate sink was complicated by the ambitious goal to turn a canal intended, in part, for that purpose into an engine of economic development, a busy shipping lane.

Manchester: The Politics of Deference

The September 1896 report of the Manchester council's rivers committee outlined the contours of the politics and science of sewage disposal in the heavily industrialized Mersey-Irwell watershed (see fig. 2.4). The normally secretive proceedings of this powerful committee were forced into the open by imminent judicial rulings. The county police court was expected to help enforce the MIJC's effluent standards by hitting the municipal government where it hurt, with a fifty pound fine for each day the Corporation failed to comply. Reminding the council of his thirty-one years of service, committee chair Alderman Joseph Thompson admitted that he felt trapped and defeated, caught between the proverbial rock and a hard place.

On the one side, the MIJC was turning the screws on compliance with what it had set almost three years earlier as the city's minimally acceptable "limits of impurity." The exasperated Alderman Thompson now admitted that the best efforts of the engineers and the scientists in charge of Davyhulme had failed. Technology designed to use chemicals to precipitate most of the solid matter out of the liquid had neither filtered out nor killed off the organic matter responsible for causing the horrid smells of putrefaction in the ship canal. Instead, the sewage treatment plant had generated a mountain of sludge. The city had to buy a thousand-ton steamer to haul the semisolid wastes out to sea. Even more problematic, Thompson lamented, the key expert in defining a series of chemical indicators of wastewater quality for the regional agency, Sir Henry E. Roscoe, was also the city's top advisor in charge of the sewage treatment plant. This chemistry professor, who held public positions as a member of the Parliament, the MIJC, and the faculty of Owens College as well as his dual role as private consultant, possessed veto power over any plan for sewage treatment.[12]

On the other side, the LGB was insisting on land filtration on sewage farms as the final step of wastewater disposal regardless of whatever novel sanitation strategies the city might adopt. The most promising of these strategies were based on germ theories. Their enthusiastic advocates claimed that bacteria could be put to work "eating" organic waste, not just deodorizing it like some chemicals. But in 1896, the LGB remained unconvinced by the biologists' explanations that sewage farms simply represented a primitive, inefficient form of this natural process of purification. The LGB also had the power to hurt the Corporation in the pocketbook—in this case by holding its ability to borrow for public works projects hostage to the national governing body's demands.

Alderman Thompson recounted the committee's dismal and frustrating experience in trying to meet the LGB's demands. Following the advice of Manchester's veteran city surveyor James G. Lynde, the committee had obtained parliamentary approval to buy 213 acres in suburban Carrington and Flixton, along the banks of the Mersey River. But when Lynde retired only two years later, Sir Roscoe and Lynde's replacement, T. de Courcy Meade, using the same hole-boring tests the former surveyor had employed, found the land completely unsuitable. Since then, the committee had been unable to find a reasonably priced parcel of land that was big enough for such a large-scale sewage farm.

The only way out, the Thompson concluded, was to adopt the committee's new plan for a tidal conduit. It would convey the twenty-six million gallons of effluent reaching Davyhulme each day to an outfall point of tidal flow at Randle's Sluices, about three miles above Runcorn. The ship canal could be supplied, Thompson proposed, with fresh water from the Lake Thirlmere aqueduct. Besides having the bottom-line advantage of being the lowest-cost option, he argued, the conduit scheme would allow Manchester to escape the jurisdictional reach of the MIJC, which ended at the point of tidal flow.[13] For Thompson, this alternative had deviously delightful prospects of turning a bitter political defeat into a final, glorious vindication.

Over the following year, the report generated a storm of public debate that exposed the various ways in which different groups of Progressives understood the new science of bacteriology and the role it could play in reducing the shocking urban mortality rates, especially among infants. At the time the chairman made his surprise announcement about the tidal conduit plan, the council was undergoing a historic shift from its first to its second generation of ruling Liberals. Ever since the extension of voting rights to most working-class men in 1884, the public space of political discourse had been becoming more open and contested.[14]

A broadening of the suffrage after Manchester's especially acute case of elite rule had profound impacts on the political culture within the town council. The old regime of committee chairs like Thompson was being replaced by a less elite group of leaders that had a much higher rate of turnover. And if nothing else, suburban annexation was adding many new faces to the council while diluting the power of its committee chairs.

Two of the most influential Progressives of the era, Sidney and Beatrice Webb, recorded their impressions of Manchester in the midst of this tumultuous civic debate on the links among health, science, and the environment. They observed that "the abler administrators have no pretension to ideas, hardly any to grammar: they are merely hardheaded shopkeepers, divided in their minds between their desire to keep the rates down and their ambition to magnify the importance of Manchester as against other cities." The Webbs believed that the tasks of city government had outgrown its organizational structure. Lending support to the thesis offered here, they observed that "the different parts of the machine are out of joint; it rumbles on in some sort of fashion, because it is pushed along by outside pressure."[15]

The Webbs' skepticism perfectly captures the spirit of the age in challenging those in positions of authority. During the Progressive Era, reformers pitted expert against expert in a lively exchange of ideas over the best ways to improve city life. At the 3 September 1896 meeting of the town council, for instance, objections were immediately raised after Thompson introduced the committee report. Sir John Harwood demanded time for a thorough vetting of its recommendations. A venerable leader with a political and social stature to match Thompson's, Harwood was chair of the water committee, hero of the Thirlmere aqueduct project, and a member of the MIJC along with Thompson.

Mayor Lloyd expressed surprise that Thompson was reverting back to the old days when the committees routinely expected the council to rubber-stamp their proposals. Acknowledging the tactical blunder, the committee's supporters sought cover behind the excuse that the MIJC's prosecution of its suit against the city had forced their hand. They quickly accepted Harwood's face-saving offer to sponsor a special meeting that would be held one week after a copy of the report was delivered to every member of the council.[16]

The one-week intermission gave both sides time to prepare their speeches for a wider public than the council membership. Alderman Thompson delivered a well-rehearsed lecture on the current status of the science and technology of urban sanitation. Taking the audience step-by-step through the various methods of sewage disposal let the alderman establish his technical expertise and his command of the legal aspects of the policy question. After laying the option of land filtration to rest, the committee chair accurately called Dibdin's biological work promising but still experimental. The London scientist had been among the first to discover that the layer of bacteria on top of contact filter beds was doing most of the work of purification. "The whole process as to ... call in the use and assistance of bacteria to do the work which land could do better ... succeeded very fairly, but it must be remembered that those experiments [have] only been on a small scale." Thompson cited cost as the reason this approach was ruled out, leaving only the tidal conduit option. Pulling out all the stops, the chair then produced a letter from Sir Roscoe that endorsed the committee's recommendations over his own experimental projects at the Davyhulme facility.[17]

Although Meade, the engineer, fell in line behind the committee chair, his report confirmed that a milestone of technical understanding was being reached regarding the bacteriological basis of sewage purification. In August 1895, Roscoe had converted some of his mechanical sand-filtration beds into biological ones, more or less duplicating Dibdin's work in London. Meade clearly understood that the "slime deposit on the sand constitute[s] the real filtering material in the waterworks filter." He even conceded that Dibdin's studies showed that wastewater effluents, especially when already treated by chemical precipitation, could be purified to meet any standard of wastewater quality. The engineer was helping to translate Dibdin's scientific experiments into a practical technology that would result in "the oxidation of organic matters, both those in suspension and those in solution, through the agency of living organisms. It is the preliminary establishment and subsequent cultivation of these organisms which is to be aimed at in the scientific process of purification by filtration."[18] Nevertheless, Thompson did not have to distort Meade's encouraging report to portray this scientific breakthrough in sewage disposal as largely unproven and its ultimate costs as incalculable.

Reflecting the relative novelty of the application of germ theories to wastewater treatment on a large scale, the opponents of the tidal conduit plan did not propose the new method or any other technology as an alternative policy approach. Instead, they seemed content to lambaste the river committee for incompetence. Sir Harwood led a small chorus of councilors in attacking the committee for spending the ratepayers' hard-earned money on "scientific will-o'-the wisps." Wrapping themselves in the sacred banner of low-cost government, the opposition sanctimoniously tore apart the committee's cost estimate of £265,000 for the tidal conduit and doubled the price tag. But without proposing any other course besides outright defiance of the governing agencies, the opposition was outvoted by a three to one margin. The rivers committee was authorized to gain parliamentary authority for a right-of-way for Manchester's new culvert.

Marking a sea change in Manchester politics, the plan's local opponents made their case to the community at large. They had lost the battle inside the council, so they joined with lobbyists for downstream interests to rally the small property owners. Together they forced a ratepayers' referendum on the national authorization act. In December 1896, qualified voters rejected a plan endorsed by their elected representatives on the town council for the very first time on an important policy issue. Outside pressure must have felt far more intense to local policy makers after this unprecedented political defeat at the hands of their own constituents.[19]

The new idea of linking bacteriology and sanitation technology attracted a tremendous amount of attention from urban Progressives in 1896. In many respects, Professor Roscoe saved the day for the town council in his dual role as private consultant to the Corporation and public servant to the MIJC. The chemistry expert helped persuade the regional agency to give the city one year to come up with a complete plan of wastewater treatment and disposal that could meet the agency's "limits of impurity." During that interval, Dibdin's theories appeared to sweep the field in the scientific community, until only practical questions of engineering and management remained. Working with bacteriologists from Owens College, Roscoe experimented with various materials for the contact filter beds, such as coke, gravel, and cinders. It was here inside the spongy, black coating where the "clever microbes" were at work that theory, practice, and politics came together in the effort to shape public opinion and policy.

While Town Hall went through the civic rituals leading to the re-adoption of its tidal culvert plan in September 1897, urban sanitation reformers were meeting in nearby Leeds to take stock of the rapid acceptance of bacteriological theories of sewage purification. The engineers, chemists, biologists, and civic activists assembled at the Sanitary Congress no longer questioned germ theories; instead, they now sought ways to work out its implications in practical terms for cities and the environment. William Dibdin gave an update on the "scientific basis of sewage treatment," but most papers focused on more technical issues: sludge cake removal, filter bed materials, and septic tank design. Dr. Sims Woodhead summed up the situation in Manchester by stating simply that the city "did not know what to do with its sewage."[20] In 1897, the authority of science was much more contested terrain in the public arena of Manchester politics than in the elite convention on sanitation studies.

Still, germ theories played an important role in shaping what became a surprisingly well-informed and wide-ranging public debate on sewage disposal. Far more than they had the year before, the sides staked out on the council floor spilled over into the daily press, spawning a lively discourse of expert against expert, and one insider version against another. Most fascinating was the way in which the Davyhulme experiments became a popular metaphor for scientific and technological progress while the tidal conduit became an icon of a "policy of despair," in the words of an opposition council member. The chief spokesperson of the ratepayers, Dr. R. M. Parkhurst, similarly alluded to it as "a scheme at once of panic and of despair."

However, the best expression of the industrial city's faith in scientific progress and native know-how came from a letter writer with the perfect pen name, Technologist. To him, the sewer-pipe plan was a "most humiliating confession of defeat upon a point of technology, a confession of defeat which Manchester—the representative of Lancashire intelligence and grit—should never make ... On a question where our position in the forefront of scientific advance is concerned, I venture to enter my protest against the policy of 'funk' embodied in the culvert scheme."[21]

Within this politically charged atmosphere, bacteriological science was cast as a shining beacon of knowledge that could lead the city from the dark pessimism of the council chambers to the bright light of the healthy city of tomorrow. On 24 September 1897, Dr. Parkhurst took the politicians to task for giving up too easily on the Davyhulme experiments at the first general meeting of the ratepayers on the issue. If the experts failed using the original chemical precipitation methods, he asked rhetorically, "Had science made no advance from 1888 to 1897? Had it not made a daily advance: was it not hourly advancing?" In more reasoned tones, other opponents used newspaper columns and speaker podiums to educate the public on the theory and practice of biological methods of sewage disposal. Over the next month leading to a climactic final vote of the people, the press also supplied detailed and informative stories on the new science, including graphic accounts of visits to Davyhulme and academic-sounding articles on "the scientific aspects of sewage purification."[22]

Letters by academics on both sides of the issue underscore the point that the authority of science and technology remained contested terrain in the 1897 policy debate in Manchester. In this wide-ranging discourse, chemists rather than biologists still held center stage as the voice of authority on standards of water quality, but the main focus of attention increasingly became the studies of the biological filter beds in London, Manchester, and Salford and similar field experiments in England and the United States.

Although a few experts hid behind fictitious names, such as Chemist with a Vengeance, most proudly announced their professional and institutional affiliations. It is reasonable to suppose that they believed such official titles of authority carried political weight in the policy debate on urban reform. The experts lined up against the river committee made good use of germ theories to offer the public an attractive and ingenious alternative to the culvert scheme. The science of bacteriology promised not only to solve a major problem of the industrial city, but also to advance the Progressive ideal of the conservation of natural resources at the same time.

In the end, Dr. Parkhurst's mobilization of the protest vote proved decisive. In addition to their arguments against defeatism and for faith in science and technology, opponents of the council's plan raised legitimate questions about the effects of diverting so much water from the ship canal.[23] In contrast, the council's position rested on too thin a base of legalistic and bureaucratic politics. At the meeting of the council at which the culvert scheme was to be approved, river committee stalwart Saxon was more open than his absent chairman had been in disclosing the committee's motives. Politics, not science, was the driving force behind the body's policy priorities. After paying ritualistic homage to low-cost government, Saxon admitted regarding the culvert plan that "the greatest reason of all, however, was that it took the [rivers] committee out of the jurisdiction of the Mersey and Irwell Joint Committee, and they were consequently freed from their excessive requirements as to purity."[24] Such a rational was not strong enough to carry the weight of public opinion needed to prevail at the polls.

In what at first seemed a decisive development, two separate referenda on funding the project that were held at official meetings of the ratepayers delivered a crushing defeat to the politicians. Resentful of this challenge to their authority, the council members reverted back to intrigue behind closed doors at the Town Hall. Digging up an obscure provision known as the Borough Funds Act, which had been used only once before, in 1878, to underpin support in Parliament for the Corporation's Thirlmere aqueduct plan, the council majority insisted on yet a third vote.

This time, the appeal to the general electorate backfired. On 31 October 1897, Mancunians voted 49,069 to 20,528 in opposition to the council's culvert plan. No one could question the finality of this overwhelming rejection of its policy choice. In a dramatic gesture of defeat, if not despair, Chairman Thompson and his fellow members resigned their positions on the rivers committee. The city government was thrown back to square one in its effort to find a way to meet the persistent demands of the MIJC and the LGB that it find a method of sewage disposal that could meet their standards of wastewater quality.[25]

Under different leadership, Manchester emerged in 1898 as a champion of the new science of bacteriology. The process of elimination had left it as the only viable alternative to the old science of sewage farms. In the heat of his defense of the culvert plan, Alderman Thompson had conceded that chemical precipitation had failed to produce an effluent acceptable to either the governing boards or the ship canal company. Furthermore, sanitary experts' fast-growing consensus behind biological solutions gave the reconstituted rivers committee the confidence it needed to make a commitment to a specific course of action.

In this rapidly changing area of research, the various field and laboratory experiments left little doubt that the scientists were headed in the right direction. Although the precise details of an appropriate technology remained to be worked out by trail and error, the path of knowledge opened by Dibdin and company now seemed not only the most promising but also the only rational sanitation strategy. Reflecting the swift diffusion of the new science among urban reformers, Parliament responded positively to the plea of Manchester's representatives that it create a royal commission on sewage disposal. The representatives hoped the commission would undermine the LGB's stand on land filtration as well as supersede the MIJC's stringent wastewater quality requirements of for the industrial city with a more lenient single standard for the whole nation.

The choice of yarn merchant Sir Bosdin T. Leech as the new chair of the rivers committee was equally important in turning Manchester into an outspoken advocate of biological methods of sewage treatment. Along with fellow Liberal councilor Harwood, he had been the most responsible for steering the ship canal proposal through the town council. This considerable achievement had earned the merchant knighthood and a directorship of the transportation company. Now he was asked to use his considerable political skills to convert the city's governmental overseers into apostles of the new science.

Leech had less difficulty persuading the court to grant another three-month extension to continue the filter bed experiments than convincing the council to adopt a posture of compromise with the extralocal agencies. At its regular meeting after the court ruling on 6 April 1898, the chairman deflected calls for confrontation and took a firm stand in favor of cooperation. In sharp contrast to Thompson, Leech asserted that members of the committee "were distinctly of the opinion that biological filtration presented at once a less costly and more effectual means of filtration than any other." He asked for funding to support this ongoing bacteriological research on four acres at the Davyhulme plant in the expectation that full-scale conversion of its thirty acres of filter beds would follow as soon as practicable. In the spirit of compromise, he accepted Harwood's suggestion that the city also comply with the demand for land filtration by purchasing the required two to three hundred acres while pushing forward at Davyhulme with maximum speed. Apparently unable to accept defeat, the embittered supporters of the culvert plan staged a walkout to deny a quorum for a vote on Leech's amended proposal.[26]

Nonetheless, the Leech-Harwood compromise plan contained the elements of a resolution of the city's conflict with its regulatory overseers. First Leech rallied the needed majorities to proceed with plans for a small-scale operational test of the bacteriological method of sewage treatment. Then he turned to foster a new partnership with the regional and national agencies. By adopting a specific technology and by embracing germ theories, Leech effectively shifted the burden of scientific proof back to those agencies. The city could now ask whether it had their official sanction to scale up the experimental station into a fully operational facility. On 12–13 January 1899, the showdown came at a crucial hearing of LGB. At issue was Manchester's petition for a loan of £160,000 to construct twenty-six acres of additional filter beds that would use biological methods of sewage purification.

The city's solicitor, member of Parliament Balfour Browne, came well armed with the powerful authority of experts to bolster his case for the new science. He strove to demonstrate that Manchester's bacteriological filtration system would enable the city to more than meet the MIJC's minimum standards of effluent quality. Gilbert John Fowler, a chemist and bacteriologist at Owens College who was emerging as the effective director of the Davyhulme experiments, supplied the board with technical data. In addition, Browne brought along several heavyweight reinforcements from the scientific establishment, including professors Percy Frankland and W. H. Perkins.

Browne may have best captured the historic meaning of the hearing when he coined the term *clever microbes*. He observed that "sewage disposal at one time was simply a matter of engineering ... and it is only recently that this matter has passed out of the hands of the chemists and passed into the hands of the biologist, who will tell us ... that the method, and the only method, of disposing of sewage is by the bacterial method." Although the hearing examiners grilled the experts on the clever microbes' efficacy in eating industrial wastes, the LGB seemed more retrospect in its insistence on land filtration as the only way to solve the problem.[27] The biology-and-land package looked increasingly attractive as a face-saving way out of the interagency conflict for all three public institutions. In less than a year, each level of government agreed to the compromise plan, ending the policy standoff over urban sanitation and watershed conservation.

Responding to concerns about Manchester's strong brew of so-called trade wastes, Leech sponsored the empanelment of yet another group of experts. In October 1899, their recommendation that the use of biological septic tanks could entirely replace chemical methods of precipitation was accepted by the LGB as part of a package deal that included the thirty acres of bacterial contact beds for the second stage of effluent treatment. In exchange, the city agreed to purchase land for a final stage of land filtration if that was required to meet national standards in the future. Chairman Leech had made no secret of his expectation that the city would never have to spend a penny actually building sewage farms, but in heavy-handed fashion, the LGB finally forced him to acquiesce, at least symbolically, and buy the land. After two years of unrelenting bureaucratic pressure, the politics of deference had prevailed in shaping sanitation policy in the industrial corridor of the Irwell and Mersey rivers.[28]

Under pressure from above, the town council had become highly motivated to find an ultimate sink for Manchester's rapidly swelling volumes of wastewater. Between 1896 and 1900, the highly charged political struggle over science and technology policy spilled over into the larger arena of popular opinion. Urban reformers embraced germ theories as modern and progressive, and they seemed eager to adopt biological methods of effluent treatment as a step forward toward the future. The notion that bacteriology offered a new source of authority to challenge the old also may have appealed to some political activists.

To be sure, Alan Wilson's assessment that the city's sanitation policy was driven by considerations of lowest cost has much to recommend it. He posits, for example, that the referenda of 1897 rejecting the council's culvert plan was a simple protest against higher taxes during a period of depression.[29] Yet this victory for hard-pressed ratepayers was equally a triumph for the new science and for the faith people had in its power to solve the environmental and social problems of the industrial city. In the case of Manchester, the authority of experts helped steer policy formation toward a science-based approach to problem solving.

Chicago: The Politics of Defiance

In sharp contrast, the authority of scientists held a tenuous place in American political culture, especially compared to the nearly sacred space reserved for the engineers in the planning of large-scale infrastructure projects to improve the quality of urban life. In spite of growing confidence in the science of bacteriology during the Progressive Era, the city's doctors and academics would remain frustrated, ignored and isolated on the fringes of decision making. As they came to see the urban environment as a world teeming with microbes, they kept pointing to the fatal flaw in the city's sanitary strategy. Yet the engineers were able to retain their privileged positions by proposing ever bigger technological fixes that generated more and more jobs and contracts for the politicians to dole out to their constituents.

Just after midnight on 17 January 1900, a special train pulled out of Chicago carrying a contingent of public officials on a secret mission to Lockport, about thirty miles to the southwest in the Des Plaines and Illinois river valleys. They were racing to beat an injunction that they expected would be issued later that day by the U.S. Supreme Court. The managers of the Sanitary District of Chicago (SDC) were headed for a dam that controlled the water level in its brand new ship canal and drainage channel, the $33 million waterway that, under the control of the politicians, had become the world's biggest earth-moving project.

Reaching their destination before noon, the officials ordered the dam's "bear trap" doors lowered, sending a rush of water down the Illinois River. The opening of the canal was so hurried that unfinished construction projects five miles downstream at Joliet were swept away in the ensuing flood, putting the city in sudden danger of inundation. Nonetheless, the SDC officials felt relief that they had won their race with the attorney general of Missouri, who was heading for Washington to ask the high court to stop the operation of the canal before it got started.

This triumph was short-lived, however. Seeking an injunction, Missouri's legal counsel claimed that Illinois and the SDC had no right to pollute natural streams and rivers that flowed from one state to another. He scored an important initial victory by convincing the national court to accept original jurisdiction in the nuisance case between the two states: the justices agreed to hear Missouri's claim that Chicago's sewage posed a serious public health threat to St. Louis and every community downstream that drew its drinking supplies from the Mississippi River.

This strange birth of the sanitary canal in the midst of conflict was symptomatic of a widening circle of controversy that swirled around Chicago's water management politics and policies, which grew in number and scope over the next forty years. This giant-scale project had environmental implications that expanded outward from metropolitan to regional, national, and international jurisdictions.[30]

The opening of the canal had several different meanings for contemporaries, but none of them anticipated the deepening involvement of the national government in the formation of Chicago's water management policy. Contemporaries speculated on the implications of the project for public health and the quality of the urban environment. Civic boosters like the editors of the *Chicago Tribune* predicted that the public works project represented a technological fix for waterborne epidemics even while medical experts cautioned people to continue boiling their drinking water. In St. Louis, of course, perceptions were literally and figuratively reversed. The improvement in Chicago's environmental conditions meant deterioration of the quality of life in their city.[31]

Cooley and the managers of the SDC expressed hope that the completion of the project represented the dawn of new era of economic development for Chicago. Boasting that "the Chicago Sanitary and Ship Canal is one of the greatest artificial waterways ever constructed," the trustees petitioned Congress to appropriate $25 million to turn the 328 miles of the Illinois River from Joliet to the Mississippi River into an artery of commerce for ocean-going vessels. The memorial also asked for official sanction for the withdrawal of 4.5 million gallons per minute (gpm) from Lake Michigan because "it is not possible to produce such a waterway without this water supply."[32]

But the basic incompatibility of transportation and sanitation as dual functions of the canal became immediately evident. As soon as the waterway opened, the downstream currents became a hazard to navigation, repeating the effect of the 1870s "deep cut." Observers noticed a current of about three

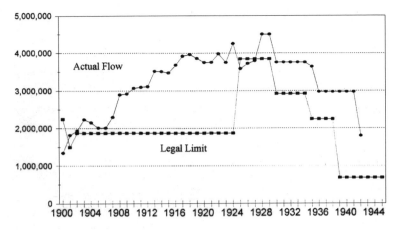

Figure 12.1. SDC water withdrawals (gallons per minute)
Source: Data from Walter Smith, comp., *Stream Flow Data of Illinois* (Springfield, IL: Department of Public Works and Buildings, 1937), 168.

miles per hour in the Chicago River, or more than twice the safe limit of 1.25 miles per hour set in the permit granted by the secretary of war in his capacity as the regulator of the nation's shipping lanes. In May 1901, the secretary ordered a reduction in the withdrawal of Lake Michigan water to 1,875,000 gpm upon the recommendation of the Army Corps of Engineers. Chicago simply defied his authority (see fig. 12.1).[33]

Although this formal restriction threatened the dream of a transcontinental water highway, the setback seemed only temporary. Congress soon earmarked six million dollars for the Corps to help dredge the Chicago River so it would be large enough to cut the speed of the current to safe levels. This support encouraged the SDC to place first importance on selling its industrial sites along the canal, offering a variety of incentives to buyers, such as cheap building materials and electrical power. Cooley and the politicians put their responsibilities for the metropolitan area's public health in distant second place.[34] The typhoid fever epidemic of 1902 made the costs of this strategy painfully evident. This state of emergency kick-started Jane Addams's environmental justice movement and solidified medical experts' belief in germ theories of disease.[35]

Among those investigating the causes of the latest epidemic was Edwin Oakes Jordan, an assistant professor of bacteriology at the University of Chicago. He had been trained at MIT and the Massachusetts Experimental Station, where the most advanced work on biological methods of sewage treatment was being conducted in the United States. His article in the December

1902 issue of the prestigious *Journal of the American Medical Association* expresses a comprehensive understanding of the environmental implications of the paradigm shift in the etiology of disease. Jordan immediately acknowledged the benefits of the drainage channel, praising it for the reduction of typhoid fever deaths since its opening to the lowest rates in the history of the city.

He was equally quick, however, to take the channel's planners to task for their failure to divert all of the city's sewage away from the lake and into the waterway. "Through a lack of foresight and coordinated endeavor on the part of the responsible authorities," he complained, "a large part of the sewage system of Chicago remains at this date unconnected with the Drainage Canal.... It is certainly singular that the present situation should not have been foreseen and guarded against. The excuse for ... pour[ing] fresh sewage into the lake for upward of three years after the completion of a great and enormously expensive sanitary undertaking can hardly be adequate." Jordan produced a map showing that sewer outlets were still flushing the wastewater of over a quarter-million people into the lake (see fig. 12.2). He concluded that this was the source of the problem "since there seems to be no instance on record where a large city possessing a pure or purified water supply has experienced an epidemic of typhoid fever of the proportions of the one that has just visited Chicago."[36]

The problems highlighted by Jordan had been anticipated by the SDC trustees, but ignored as they pursued their single-minded obsession with the ship canal. Both the Hering Commission of 1887 and a similar Pure Water Commission of nine years later had put a system of lakefront intercepting sewers at the top of their respective lists of immediate goals. Although the city had finally begun to implement these recommendations in 1898, the problem of the pollution of Lake Michigan was much larger and extended far beyond municipal borders. As Jordan showed, quality was especially problematic for public supplies from the Sixty-Eighth Street intake crib in Hyde Park because of its close proximity to the burgeoning industrial zone that was sweeping around the bottom of the lake.

Cooley and the other planners of the SDC had given consideration to this area, called the Calumet District, from the start, only to defer action until after completion of the main channel. Then they figured out a plan to divert an additional 1.8 million gpm from Lake Michigan. Prevented by the harm to navigation from withdrawing water through the Chicago River, they now became enthusiastic about digging a second channel to drain the additional lake water through the Calumet River to the main channel at Sag (see fig. 12.3).

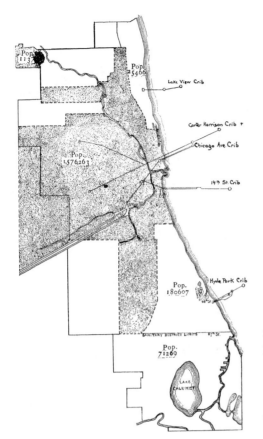

Figure 12.2. Sewer outfalls in Lake Michigan
Source: Edwin Oakes Jordan, "Typhoid Fever and Water Supply in Chicago," *Journal of the American Medical Association* 39 (December 1902): 1563.

The main goal of the "Cal-Sag" project was to guarantee the presence of deep water in the Illinois River. In addition, the promoters highlighted the potential boost in the agency's revenues from the extra water. They proposed a hydroelectric power plant that would benefit from a commensurate increase in the flow of water. Of course, they also held up their plan as the best way to prevent sewage from reaching the city's water intake cribs.[37]

Jordan believed that this type of approach was doomed to failure. On the basis of germ theory, he reasoned that all plans must incorporate the assumption that Lake Michigan would remain a source of pollution, not purity, into the foreseeable future. "No one familiar with the general sanitary history of water supplies can expect that all chances for water pollution will cease with the completion of the sewage system," he concluded. The bacteriologist explained that as many as 172,000 typhoid germs could be found in just

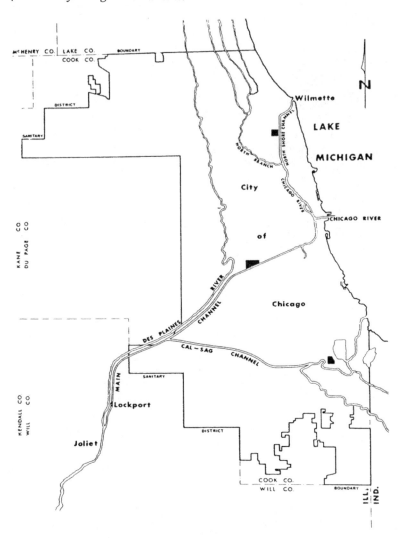

Figure 12.3. Sanitary district channels, 1917
Source: Louis P. Cain, *Sanitation Strategy for a Lakefront Metropolis: The Case of Chicago*
(DeKalb: Northern Illinois University Press, 1978), 67. Copyright © 1978 Northern
Illinois University Press; used with permission.

one cubic centimeter of urine. A single passenger on a cruise ship or bather on
the beach could cause the next crisis. Yet, Jordan reasoned, the real threat was
rapid industrial and suburban growth, which made problematic any water
management plan based on the use of the lake without the employment of
some method of purification.

The scientific revolution in the theory of disease causation led Jordan inexorably toward an environmental ethic of conservation. A dual approach of water filtration and sewage treatment for inland lakes and streams seemed like
the only hope for eliminating the crises of epidemics caused by contaminated
water supplies. Jordan concurred with the plan to expand the SDC to integrate
the North Shore and the Calumet District into the metropolitan system. But
he sharply disapproved of the gigantic canal building scheme for the industrial district because it would still leave the Hyde Park water intake vulnerable
to contaminated supplies. Jordan thought a two-million-dollar water filtration plant would be far less expensive and far more effective in protecting
the public health than the estimated twelve-million-dollar Cal-Sag project.

Moreover, Jordan calculated that it would cost only $8.5 million to install
filtration works to guard the water supply of the entire city. Underscoring the
lessons of the current epidemic, he warned against repeating the flawed strategy of the main channel. "It would prove most discouraging," he predicted,
"to discover after the expenditure of seven or eight million dollars for the
construction of a drainage canal for the Calumet region that the pollution of
the Hyde Park water supply from towns in Indiana south of the Calumet and
from other sources was still so great that the amount of typhoid fever in that
portion of the community served by this supply remained excessive." State
lawmakers listened to the engineers, not the scientists, during the following
legislative session. They approved the SDC's package of enlarged boundaries,
navigation locks, and hydroelectric facilities.[38]

In contrast, the authority of science played a more influential role in the
judicial arena, where the St. Louis case finally reached the Supreme Court
in 1906. Speaking for the court, Oliver Wendell Holmes Jr. expressed a professional's sense of appreciation for the awesome intellectual challenges facing those in charge of protecting the public health. Yet he also confessed a
layman's sense of bewilderment and perhaps frustration with the technical
jargon of the new, highly specialized fields of bacteriology and epidemiology.
The contradictory evidence presented by a long train of experts on both sides
of the case had produced over a thousand pages of testimony.[39]

In the end, the court accepted the premise that presence of the "bacillus of
typhoid" was the litmus test for determining the factual evidence in the case.
Justice Holmes concluded that St. Louis was unable to prove its case against
Chicago. "We assume the now-prevailing scientific explanation of typhoid
fever to be correct," he announced. "But when we go beyond that assumption,
everything involved is in doubt." What effects Chicago's discharges had on
the public health of the Missouri city could not be determined. Echoing
the conservationist ethic of the new public health, Holmes stated that "the

evidence is very strong that it is necessary for St. Louis to take preventive measures, by filtration or otherwise, against the dangers of the plaintiff's own creation or from other sources than Illinois. What will protect against one will protect against the other."[40]

The ruling demonstrated not only the court's willingness to incorporate germ theory into constitutional law, but also the limits of judicial intervention in the formation of urban environmental policy during the Progressive Era. To be sure, the court set a precedent for the future simply by accepting jurisdiction of the case. Holmes had no doubt that industrial cities' impact on the nation's water, land, and air went far beyond their political boundaries. The Chicago–St. Louis dispute, he said, presented "a question of the first magnitude: whether the destiny of the great rivers is to be the sewers of the cities along their banks or to be protected against everything which threatens their purity."

At the same time, however, Holmes worried that accepting Missouri's nuisance complaint would set off an avalanche of similar petitions, with cities suing each other under the guise of states in order to get original jurisdiction before the high court. Hoping to forestall such an occurrence, the jurist drew a distinction between the case at hand and more ordinary nuisance complaints. This controversy, Holmes reasoned, was a rare exception because "the nuisance set forth in the bill was one which would be of international importance,—a visible change of a great river from a pure stream into a polluted and poisoned ditch." By holding St. Louis to the "strictest proof," however, the court could rule that the city had not established its case. In effect, the judiciary decided to leave the formation of public health and environmental policy at the local level.[41]

Nonetheless, Chicago's overweening ambition set the stage for the unexpected intervention of extralocal forces in the city's environmental policy. In 1907, the SDC's presumption that it could take as much water from the Great Lakes as it wanted ran into stiff resistance for the first time from an unlikely source: the Canadians. Just two years earlier, they and the Americans had set up the Inland Waterways Commission (IWC) to hammer out the terms of a treaty for the boundary waters, including the establishment of the proportional shares of water each country could use at Niagara Falls for the purpose of generating electricity. Chicago's artificial waterway made the work of the commission much more difficult because it represented the only major outlet of the lakes other than the natural one at Niagara Falls. Now Chicago's withdrawals had to be calculated into the formula for dividing the water between the two countries.[42]

The IWC was originally sympathetic to Chicago's sanitation problems. It was willing to acquiesce in a diversion of 4.5 million gpm in spite of the significant damage to navigation on the Great Lakes and the cost of lower lake levels, which was estimated at over fifty million dollars annually. The commissioners became upset, however, when they found out that the SDC was asking permission from the U.S. government for an additional 1.8 million gpm for its Cal-Sag project.

In a cautiously worded statement, the commission attempted to draw a line that would permanently set a limit on the city's use of water to dilute its sewage. Granting Chicago the diversion of 4.5 million gpm, the IWC declared that this was an amount that would, "with the proper treatment of the sewage from areas now sparsely occupied, provide for all the population, and ... will therefore suffice for the sanitary purposes of the city for all time." During the two years of hard bargaining at top levels of government to hammer out the final Boundary Waters Treaty of 1909, Chicago's demands for more water became an international embarrassment that helped stiffen the resolve of federal officials to force the sanitary district to comply with its permit limit of 1.875 million gpm.[43]

In Chicago, however, the managers of the sanitary district were laying plans that depended on a diversion of lake water more than three times as great. Led by Robert R. McCormick, the agency continued to place first importance on becoming an engine of economic growth with sanitation services as a by-product. In a 1906 pamphlet promoting the ship canal, McCormick promised that "the enterprise of the District will be the means of promoting Chicago as a greater manufacturing community. It will eventually make the Sanitary District, primarily intended to furnish Chicago with a pure water supply, a self-supporting tax body. It will produce a revenue vastly in excess of maintenance charges."[44] But the SDC's hopes for a 5 percent return on its fifty-million-dollar investment put the public health at risk. The agency's decision in 1907 to build the Cal-Sag canal rather than adopt Jordan's conservationist strategy of water filtration and sewage treatment reveals its dereliction of its primary duty.

This case also exposed the duplicity of the engineers. Rudolph Hering was hired to go before the IWC to refute his own report. As he labored to prove that a further diversion of 1.8 million gpm was the best plan for disposing of the industrial district's sewage, the engineer had to gloss over several potentially fatal problems, including federal government restrictions, environmental damage from an additional drop of eleven to thirteen inches in the level of the Great Lakes, and the likelihood that storm water would overtax the capacity of the canal, contaminating Chicago's water supply with toxic chemicals and biological pollution.

Moreover, Hering had to disregard his own calculations of the engineers' litmus test of economic efficiency: cost. He argued in favor of the canal project with its projected $15.5 million price tag over sewage treatment facilities that would cost an estimated $4.8 million. The payoff, Hering claimed, would be a constant flow of revenue into agency coffers from hydroelectric power and industrial development along the ship canal. Hering gave priority to economic growth over public health. "There is no money return from the sprinkling filters," he concluded, "as their product has no value. But there is a return from the dilution project, because the flow of 4,000 cubic feet per second can drop 66 feet and develop 22,500 efficient horse-power.... This cost comparison alone would decide which project is the most desirable one for the citizens of Chicago."[45]

The SDC's decision in favor of a new canal in 1907 came in the face of the opposition of the federal government. Just two months after the IWC's January 1907 report on Chicago, Secretary of War William Howard Taft served notice that the national government intended to press its case against Chicago's blatant defiance of its authority. There is little question that the Canadians pushed the secretary to act. In denying the SDC's petition for permission to reverse the Calumet River, Taft cited an 1899 act of Congress that completely prohibited the making of changes in any navigable waterway without the approval of the federal chief of engineers and the authorization of the secretary of war.

Under this law, General A. Mackenzie had duly submitted a strong condemnation of Chicago's sanitation strategy because of its negative impacts on navigation in the Great Lakes. While Taft was willing to concede that the public health of great cities had to be given serious consideration by the national government, he reiterated his predecessors' disclaimers dating back to the original permit of 1899. Only Congress had the power to authorize the withdrawal of lake water for any purposes other than navigation. "Added to this," Taft pointed out, "is the international complication which is likely to arise in the threatened lowering of the lake level in the ports and harbors and canals of Canada."[46]

Since Chicago remained stymied in its efforts to secure the needed legislation, Taft and the SDC agreed to let the courts decide in the conflict over the city's withdrawal of water from the lake in defiance of the national government. In September 1907, the secretary issued a permit for the construction of the Cal-Sag canal, but barred the district from taking any additional water from the lake. In return, the following month the local agency sent a team of construction workers to a prearranged place along the route where federal agents could observe them digging. This created the pretext for a test suit. The national government then sought an injunction against the SDC in the federal district court of northern Illinois for taking more water from Lake Michigan than its permit allowed.

Until construction began four years later, however, the federal government seemed reluctant to press its case. Its original petition had not asked for a preliminary or immediate injunction, and the case languished. In the meantime, Cooley, now acting as a private consultant to the district, began lobbying in Washington for permission from Congress and the secretary of war to withdraw 4.5 million gpm from the lake. But strong and frequent protest by the Canadian government, together with accumulating evidence from the Corps of Engineers on the lowering of the Great Lakes, helped persuade both branches of government to reject Cooley's appeals.[47]

The SDC's obsession with the ship canal turned the agency into one of the worst polluters of Lake Michigan. In 1902, it responded to the limits imposed by the federal permits with a project for dredging the Chicago River. The only way to slow the river while maintaining a withdrawal of 4.5 million gpm was to make it wider and deeper. The Army Corps of Engineers underwrote the effort, in which decades of sewage deposits from the bottom of the river were dug up and dumped either into landfills along the lakefront or directly into the lake. Although city ordinances required that all refuse be dumped at least a mile beyond the two-mile water intake cribs, the federal government was not subject to local law. To cut costs, the Corps barges simply dumped their foul cargo at the nearest, most convenient locations just to the east of the mouth of the river.

It was impossible to measure the extent to which this dumping was responsible for the steady deterioration of water quality during this period, but health department officials had no doubt that it was contributing to a dangerous rise in the water supply's bacteria count. The decision in favor of the Cal-Sag canal in 1907 meant even greater amounts of human and highly toxic industrial wastes would worsen the quality of the city's water supplies. The dredging of the Calumet River would continue for over a decade during the construction of the canal, endangering the public health in order to bring in profits for the sanitary district.[48]

It should come as no surprise that in the years following these 1907 decisions on water management policy, the city suffered rapid deterioration of water quality as well as chronic water famines because of low pressure. In October 1908, the city bacteriologist, Dr. Joseph F. Biehn, wrote to the SDC to alert it to the fact that bacteria counts in tap water had reached pre–drainage canal levels of two thousand per cubic centimeter. Army Corps expert Colonel W. H. Bixby, with the concurrence of the sanitary district's chemist, Dr. John Lederer, warned that the dilution method was fast approaching its maximum limit in the canal. Both called for sewage treatment. Health Commissioner Evans agreed that "the water has not been up to standard for some time, although it has been safe."[49]

Evans persuaded Mayor Fred Busse to sponsor a Lake Michigan Water Association composed of Illinois and Indiana authorities to coordinate plans for reducing the amounts of pollution entering the lake. In work that confirmed Army Corps studies, the Water Association's scientists followed streams of sewage discharges from the Calumet area at least seven miles into the lake. In the early part of 1909, the group's findings again raised questions about Chicago's sanitary strategies, including the latest plan for constructing the Cal-Sag canal. "The City of Chicago," a newspaper exclaimed in the new language of germ theory, "is hemmed in by a belt of water a mile wide so poisonous that if a drop of it is injected under the skin of a guinea pig, the pig will die. The city is literally besieged by colon bacilli. There are billions and trillions of them off the lakefront and they are only waiting for a favorable opportunity to invade the city. When they do, that invasion will be more tragic than an attack of a hostile army."[50]

In the fall of 1911, the predicted invasion arrived, a wave of typhoid fever sweeping over the South Side district served by the Hyde Park pumping station. The mortality figures were low compared to previous epidemics of the disease (see table 11.1), yet there was no doubt in the mind of Health Commissioner Dr. G. B. Young that drinking water contaminated with sewage was responsible for the twenty-nine typhoid deaths during the worst month, of August. Now that the city was partitioned into four distinct sectors, each supplied by a different intake crib, he reported, water quality statistics could be correlated more precisely with public health records. His analysis of the spatial patterns of typhoid pinpointed the Hyde Park district as the one with disproportionably high seasonal rates of the disease. The fact that this area was largely residential and suburban in nature compared to the congested neighborhoods downtown persuaded the doctor that pollution from the Calumet River or other sewage outlets along the bottom of the lake, rather than poor hygiene on the part of the area's residents, was the source of the problem.

Dr. Young had a hard time convincing anyone else in authority that polluted water was causing the illnesses. "For several years practically no attention was given to the water as a persisting factor in the situation," Dr. Young explained. Other public officials seemed complacent because the drainage channel, the completion of the intercepting sewers, and a much improved milk supply had cut fatalities from typhoid to a couple hundred a year, or less than 1 percent of the total deaths. In important respects, the politics of profligate waste had left the commissioner with no ammunition with which to meet the threat other than the old resort to a boil-the-water campaign. He had neither filtration plants to purify the water nor sewage treatment facilities to keep dangerous germs out of the lake.[51]

Without these modern technologies to ensure a healthy and ample supply of water, the doctor decided to try an experimental but exceptionally promising new approach, adding chlorine as a disinfectant. First, however, he had to get past the finance committee, which had to agree to make an appropriation to pay for the necessary equipment and the supplies of hypochlorite. The aldermen were not so worried about the cost but feared "that the hypochlorite might be tasted and the discovery of its use give rise to unfounded distrust of the general water supply." They finally gave their approval after the doctor cleverly got them to take a taste test of treated and untreated water to make sure they could not tell the difference.

In March 1912, the city began adding the bleaching power at the two intake cribs off Sixty-Eighth Street. The number of typhoid cases dropped dramatically, especially compared to the incidence of the disease in the three territories served by different water intakes. Making a chart of these contrasts, Dr. Young asserted his conviction that it was not possible that "any one studying this sheet can escape the conviction that waterborne typhoid in Chicago must still be reckoned with as a factor of considerable importance in determining the city's rate [of mortality]."[52]

The new science of bacteriology gave public health experts like Dr. Young confidence in chlorination in spite of the fact that it represented a virtually untested, radical departure from past practices. Although the commissioner had less than three years of experience to draw upon, his decision to add a potentially poisonous chemical to the drinking water of a large urban population entailed far less risk than might otherwise be supposed. Chlorine in the form of bleaching powder had been used as a disinfectant for over a century, and many researchers had shown that it was an effective agent for rendering sewage harmless to human health. But before the general acceptance of germ theories in the early 1890s, the chemical and biological reactions involved in this process had eluded precise understanding. Without such an understanding, scientists had refrained from taking the risk of adding the highly poisonous substance to drinking water. Instead, they had restricted their experiments to the treatment of organic wastes in the hopes of reducing their danger to public health.

In 1908, Chicago had become the first place to attempt chlorination of sewage on a commercial scale. The consistent opposition of extralocal authorities to the city's massive withdrawal of lake water had forced the SDC to acknowledge that the limits of the dilution method would soon be reached even with permission to use the full 4.5 million gpm allowed in its state charter. Chief Engineer George M. Wisner pointed out that "careful study shows that immediate action is necessary . . . [because] the water available for dilution is not sufficient to properly dilute the sewage wastes coming from the large manufacturing concerns."[53]

The most obvious place to begin experimenting with sewage treatment was at the stockyards, which produced over six million gallons of wastewater a day. A crude but effective chlorination plant was soon achieving "spectacular results," according to its young manager, George A. Johnson. This success led almost immediately to Johnson's retention by a waterworks in New Jersey. In desperate straits, it was searching for a quick technological fix to solve its recurring failure to meet legal standards of water quality.[54]

In 1909, the courtroom drama in a case between Jersey City, New Jersey, and its utility company became a national forum, establishing overnight the legal and scientific authority for the chlorination of public water supplies. The city had brought the case because of the company's failure to meet its contract obligations to deliver at all times a supply of water that was "pure and wholesome and free from pollution deleterious for drinking and domestic purposes." Rather than undertake a costly and time-consuming effort to build a filtration plant, the utility hired Johnson to install a chlorination facility at its Boonton reservoir. The city objected to this unproven approach, but a long train of scientists and engineers testified on behalf of the novel practice. The overwhelming weight of expert opinion came down on the side of Professor J. J. Flather of the University of Minnesota, who, also calling the results "spectacular," presented the court with evidence of a reduction in bacteria counts from two hundred to six hundred per cubic centimeter to four to six per cubic centimeter.

After accumulating over three thousand pages of evidence on the chlorination method, the court ruled in favor of the chemical treatment of the drinking supply. The decision stated that "it is an effective process, which destroys in the water the germs the presence of which is deemed to indicate danger, including the pathogenic germs, so that the water after this treatment attains a purity much beyond that attained in the water supplies of other municipalities. The reduction and practical elimination of such germs from the water was shown to be substantially continuous."[55]

Later in the year, several of the witnesses involved in the case presented their findings to a meeting of the American Water Works Association. Reflecting the shift in the authority of experts, the doctors, not the engineers, now led the discussion. In any case, there was little disagreement between the two professions because bacteriological tests could now supply such powerful and convincing evidence of the efficacy of various sanitation technologies in eliminating the threat of waterborne disease. Professional meetings and publications ensured a rapid dissemination of information on the new, relatively low-cost method of disinfecting public water supplies; adaptation by major American cities followed with equal speed.[56]

In this context, the decision for chlorination by Chicago's Commission of Health in March 1912 was neither particularly risky nor especially bold. Johnson's stockyards experiments had shown that very small amounts of chlorine killed bacteria, including the germs that caused typhoid fever, cholera, and diphtheria. On the basis of his fabulous results, the engineer had even been able to convince his fellow experts that the effluents of Packingtown's infamous Bubbly Creek sewer were safe to drink. Professor Flather was among those visiting the experimental station. "I confess as I drank the water I had the sewer in back of me in mind," he recalled, "but it was pure, and I had sufficient confidence in scientific results to be able to drink it with satisfaction." The SDC's chief engineer went a step farther by drawing the conclusion that chlorine could be used directly to disinfect the water supply. "It is perfectly practicable in accordance with modern sanitation," Wisner wrote in 1911, "to provide an emergency treatment which will protect the health of the citizens in this district. Sterilization by use of hypochlorine of lime, in small amounts, is the proper remedy."[57]

A year later, Dr. Young contended that his statistical analysis of the sharp reduction of typhoid fever cases in the Hyde Park district indicated "conclusively that the hypochlorite treatment was a large factor." By 1918, Chicago's entire supply would be protected by the chemical additive with correspondingly gratifying results in bringing the incidence of waterborne disease down to unprecedented levels. With only thirty-eight deaths from typhoid during the entire year, the disease was virtually eliminated as a significant public health danger. In the future, occurrence of the disease would be limited to minor outbreaks in highly localized areas.[58]

While Chicago's politicians joined in applauding the triumph of the new public health over typhoid fever, they continued to reject its conservationist ethic in favor of perpetuating their own self-serving politics of waste. The same scientists and engineers who championed chlorination were also advocates of water filtration plants. They saw the two as integrated parts of an array of technologies designed to protect the public health by improving the quality of the environment. Even the most outspoken apostle of chlorination, George Johnson, warned that "the use of hypochlorites cannot be considered as a substitute for filtration." Chicago's water may have been made safe, but its quality remained low in the absence of filtration plants. Complaints were commonly made about its turbidity and poor taste due to the chlorine as well as the industrial chemicals that were being dumped into the lake.[59]

Some form of sewage treatment also seemed like the only practical way to reduce the amount of lake water illegally withdrawn to dilute Chicago's industrial and human wastes. By 1911, the SDC's own chief engineer was arguing that planning for treatment facilities needed to begin in the near future to avert the flooding and public health disasters that followed the region's inevitable storms and heavy rains. But Wisner, like most other expert engineers, then came face to face with the huge extra cost of processing the extraordinary amount of water used by the city.

The combined output of the city's pumping stations had already reached an average of over a half-billion gallons a day (see figs. 4.8 and 4.9). "The use of water in Chicago today, as stated by the Department of Public Works, is extravagant and wasteful," Wisner reiterated. The "large volume of water makes the question of sewage disposal more expensive by increasing the size of settling tanks and sewers, and the pumping. . . . Metering the water service throughout the city is the only remedy to prevent waste." The more fresh water the city pumped out of the lake, the more wastewater the sanitary district would have to process in its treatment plants. But the surplus profits generated in the water fund by keeping 90 percent of the city unmetered meant that the ward bosses would permit no serious effort to curb the city's profligate consumption of water.[60]

Without any effective outside pressure from the state or federal government until the mid-1920s, Chicago's ward bosses continued to promote their own self-serving interests at the expense of the health of the people and the environment. In a reflection of traditions of localism, the federal suit against the SDC was buried for almost a decade by the district court judge, Kenesaw Mountain Landis. In spite of their status as national officers, district court jurists like Landis often acted to protect local and regional interests. In this instance, the Chicagoan indicated that he would eventually issue the injunction, but he conveniently kept the case off the docket until his retirement in 1922, about the time of the completion of the Cal-Sag channel. As one of the lawyers in the case recalled, "Judge Landis . . . in somewhat characteristic fashion refused to decide the case. . . . It is believed that because he felt the situation should not be changed during the war, he refused to enter the decree." In harsher terms, Chief Justice William Howard Taft castigated the lower bench for an "inexcusable delay." The case was assigned to a new judge, and the district court then issued the long-anticipated injunction. In June 1923, it limited the withdrawal of water to the 1.875 million gpm set in various permits dating back to the turn of the century.[61]

Conclusion: Political Cultures and Science and Technology

By the early 1900s, germ theories of disease causation had triumphed over previous approaches in both Manchester and Chicago.[62] Also in both places, the biological basis of sewage purification had come to be commonly understood. Although the new science was widely accepted, the technology of wastewater treatment and disposal that would make the best use of this knowledge remained to be worked out. Closely related were questions of political culture because the costs of conducting experimental studies and of installing large-scale facilities and operating them year-round would be significant. For Manchester, a politics of deference meant complying with the rulings of the regional and central agencies while searching for ways to reduce ongoing expenses. For Chicago, a politics of defiance entailed disobeying the orders of the national government while enhancing the self-serving goals of the politicians. Nonetheless, both cities would play a key role in the development of an advanced technology, the activated sludge method, which remains in general use today.

Unable to budge Chicago's ward bosses on water filtration, young sanitary engineers working for the SDC had come up with chlorination as an alternative solution for delivering drinking water free from dangerous germs. Although phenols dumped into Lake Michigan by steel makers meant extra-heavy doses of hypochlorite were required to protect the public health, the politicians believed they had found the perfect answer to the demand for pure water. Chlorination would prevent future epidemic crises from waterborne disease without endangering the surplus fund. At the same time, Chicago's policy makers stubbornly refused to install even a single water filtration station or large-scale sewage treatment plant. Despite overwhelming scientific evidence to the contrary, the politicians in charge of Chicago's water management system continued to act on the assumption that they could always count on the Great Lakes for unlimited amounts of water.

In the case of Manchester, the main challenge facing scientists and engineers was reducing the costs of sewage treatment and disposal. After 1901, various technologies were strung together to produce a more or less acceptable effluent, but the bill kept mounting for dumping the sludge at sea. As more and more working-class homes were finally allowed to install indoor plumbing and were hooked up to the main drain, the Davyhulme facility fell behind in adding enough new capacity to handle the ever larger quantities of wastewater to be processed. Open septic tanks were installed because they proved more effective than contact beds in reducing the amount of sludge; this pointed the way toward using bacteria more efficiently to consume the waste. However, these gains were more than offset by the sheer increase in the volume of wastewater to be purified.[63]

In 1912, Professor Fowler of Owens College visited the Massachusetts Experimental Station and observed studies of aeration of sewage in bottles. Returning home to continue this line of inquiry, he enlisted two of the Corporation's engineers, Edward Ardern and W. T. Lockett. Rather than separating the solids from the liquids as the first stage of the treatment process, they found that if they allowed the microorganisms to accumulate in the sewage, they would purify it much faster and more completely. Some of this "activated sludge" could then be added to the next patch of raw sewage, producing even better results. Moreover, the much-reduced waste by-product had pecuniary value as fertilizer. News of the breakthrough at Manchester, first published in 1914, spread with remarkable speed throughout the professional community on both sides of the Atlantic.[64]

In less than a year, Dr. Fowler was providing advice on how to duplicate the new method to sanitary engineers in Chicago and Milwaukee and at the University of Illinois at Urbana-Champaign. Information on the results of the work were reported in technical trade journals and discussed at meetings of the regional professional organization, the Western Society of Engineers. The SDC's Langdon W. Pearse quickly began tests at the Packingtown station, but large-scale trials that advanced the science and technology of activated sludge were conducted only in the other two cities. Over a relatively short period of three years, Manchester, Urbana, and Milwaukee became international leaders. They established the new method as far superior to all previous methods of sewage treatment and disposal.[65]

In contrast, Chicago would lag farther and farther behind, stubbornly holding onto notions of the fountain inexhaustible in the formulation of its sanitary strategy. In 1922, the SDC would open its first sewage treatment plant in the heavily industrialized area of Calumet. There it would use older technologies rather than taking advantage of the new method. Only the direct intervention of the U.S. Supreme Court three years later to enforce the district court's injunction would finally begin to bring Chicago up to modern standards of water management. Almost twenty years more would pass before the city came into basic compliance with the court's orders on sewage disposal, though it did install its first water filtration plant.[66]

Comparative studies of Manchester and Chicago lend strong support for the assertion of Daniel Rodgers that Progressivism took shape within a trans-Atlantic context. The ascendancy of germ theories provides an especially useful test case because its timing closely parallels the rise of the impulse for urban reform. European medical practitioners may have been ahead of their American counterparts in adopting microbiological approaches to disease causation, but their academic colleagues appear to have kept abreast of the rapid development of bacteriology in Chicago and elsewhere in the United States.

Beginning in the early 1880s, scientists from Chicago's medical schools had applied the lessons of the microscope to answer questions about the safety and quality of the water supply. And with the establishment of the Massachusetts Experimental Station in 1893, important research findings had begun flowing back to Manchester, informing that city's debate over sanitation policy. The movement of information and people across the Atlantic in both directions made the search for improved methods of biological treatment and disposal of sewage truly international. There was no gap between the two cities in the state of knowledge about this area of science, technology, and medicine. Emblematic of this process were the direct interchanges leading to the discovery of activated sludge by experts in both the Manchester and the Chicago areas.

A comparative approach also reinforces Christopher Hamlin's claim that political culture played a crucial role in shaping public health and sanitation policy during the Progressive Era. This transnational case study illuminates the ways in which decision making was affected by sharp contrasts in the expert authority of science and technology, the structure of government and society, and the style of partisan organization and mobilization. For Chicago's ward bosses, environmental reform was seen in terms of public works projects that generated patronage. From their point of view, bigger was better. This priority often received enthusiastic support from ambitious engineers like Lyman Cooley who were using the public sector as a stepping-stone to professional and social status.[67] Together they created a political culture of urban reform that depended on the natural environment to pay the final price as a virtually free and unlimited commodity. In the case of water management, improvements in the quantity of the supply and the removal of sewage came at a cost of significant damage to the ecology of the Great Lakes and the Illinois River.

For Manchester's Liberals, environmental reform was put in this context of the city's prospects as a place for entrepreneurs to make money. Since abundant supplies of soft rainwater were essential to the textile industry, the town council secured Thirlmere as a savings account against shortages anticipated in the future as a result of economic growth. When business contracted instead, the council delayed construction of the pipeline because it had no intention of responding to the "bitter cry" of the residents of Ancoats and other slums for housing reform and environmental justice. This remained so even after the extension of the vote because the Liberals' regime had become such a closed hierarchy of power that they arrogantly turned a deaf ear to the demands of the working classes until threatened with massive demonstrations of civil unrest.

In a similar way, Town Hall backed into sanitary reform for central-city districts after exhausting other alternatives that would have perpetuated its cruel policy of spatial segregation. The decision for universal indoor plumbing resulted less from Progressive ideas of social environmentalism than from the city's traditional political culture of municipal capitalism, which had led to the ship canal plan and the Corporation's heavy investment in its success. Only as a by-product of the environmental challenges posed by this project would central-city residents eventually enjoy some real gains in the quality of their daily lives.

If the Progressives made little headway in establishing an ethic of environmental protection, they could claim big gains in understanding the etiology of infectious disease. On the basis of germ theory, scientists devised a new set of biological indicators of water quality. These, in turn, led to more effective technologies of water purification and sewage treatment. To be sure, there is irony in the fact that the liquid that fulfilled the new definition of purity was an artificial product containing chemical additives like chlorine. Nonetheless, mortality rates, especially for vulnerable infants, went down dramatically. In this case, a success of urban environmental reform marked a major improvement in the quality of daily life.

The application of germ theory, of course, was not restricted to waterborne diseases. The Progressives were also concerned about bad air and the ways in which it robbed people of their health and well-being. The identification of the number-one killer, tuberculosis, as a bacterium that could be transmitted through the air was one of the most valuable early medical discoveries of germ theory. Advances like this encouraged urban reformers to redouble their efforts in the battle for clean air.

Having learned from their campaigns for pure water, the reformers began to understand that environmental control of air pollution also required regional, even national solutions. Reduction of the problem in one locality only seemed to transfer it to another. Moreover, the reformers learned that the spread of invisible toxic gases rising out of the smokestacks was practically boundless and that the contaminants could fall back to earth as acid rain. In this case, the Progressives confronted the paradox of progress head on and came up against an emerging culture of consumption that was dependent on an ever more intense use of energy.

CHAPTER THIRTEEN

"Invisible Evil"

Pollution and Class Politics in Manchester

Introduction: Smoke and Sickness

The Smoke Abatement Exposition of 1881–1882 in London marked a propitious moment in urban environmental reform. The event attracted over 115,000 people before it was moved to Manchester, where it drew another 31,000 visitors. These attendance numbers mirrored the sponsors' sense that the long-running, frustrating movement to reduce atmospheric pollution had reached a crossroads and was now heading in new, more promising directions. The convention was more than just a dazzling display for an international array of heating, lighting, cooking, and power-generating hardware. Each device was subjected to a battery of standardized tests for fuel efficiency and smoke emissions. Yet the exhibition was not a tradeshow; it was a classroom created by an activist for housing and open spaces, Octavia Hill, and Dr. Ernest Hart of the National Health Society. By purposely setting a sliding scale of admission rates, they attracted large audiences to a series of popular-science lectures, aimed at the working classes, on the most up-to-date methods of heating and ventilating the home. While the final report rejoiced in the popular success of the event, it also expressed a realistic awareness of the complexity of technological solutions as well as the limits of current scientific and medical knowledge.[1]

Reformers had three important reasons for believing that they were turning a historic corner and would be making substantial gains in improving the quality of urban life. Technological innovations offered one promising avenue by making possible the replacement of innumerable smoke-producing devices with a few relatively clean, large-scale central generating stations. Charles W. Siemens of the United Kingdom was leading the way in transforming manufactured coal gas into an economically competitive source of heat and power as well as illumination. And in 1880, Thomas A. Edison of the United States had developed a practical system of incandescent lighting. Finally, the less smoky mechanical stokers, gas engines, coal grates, and other advanced devices displayed at the exposition had the chance of actually being adopted by the city's fuel consumers.

Four years earlier, another leap forward had been made in the emerging field of bacteriology when Robert Koch finally isolated a specific germ that caused a specific disease. His discovery opened a new era of medicine and public health because doctors could now begin drawing causal connections between respiratory disease and air quality. A crescendo of great, distressing fogs in London over the previous decade presaged a third critical sea change in social perceptions of the smoke evil and the political will to do something about it. The recently enacted Public Health Act of 1875 incorporated new powers for private individuals as well as public officials to take action against flagrant violators of pollution standards. Taken together, the technological, scientific, and sociopolitical directions of change raised expectations among city dwellers that the tide of environmental reform was now turning in the right direction.[2]

Historians have largely denied the importance of the Smoke Abatement Exhibition and its sponsors. In a pioneering essay that draws a sharp distinction between town and country in Europeans' efforts to identify and reduce the impacts of acid rain, for example, E. Schramm dismisses urban reform, positing that "its political imagination ... only extended to technological solutions, especially smoke prevention measures, such as better fuel economy, use of improved smokestacks and ovens, electrification, etc. In contrast to that of the urban movement, the foresters and biologists saw the limits of a technical solution to the smoke problem." Only these scientists understood the paradox that reform measures to reduce the visible black coal soot belching out of home and factory chimneys would increase toleration of the invisible noxious gases spreading into the atmosphere. Schramm notes that policy makers largely ignored or suppressed the impressive findings of the plant researchers about the harmful effects of acid rain from distant, tall smokestacks. Still, he champions the biologists' broad ecological perspective as against the myopic vision of the smoke abatement crusaders.[3]

What the historian ignores in this environmental retrospective is an appreciation of contemporary perceptions of the appalling human and social costs resulting from urban air pollution. Missing is an accounting of their concerns about horrendous mortality rates among the inner-city poor from respiratory diseases, as well as about stilted lives, self-destructive behavior, class conflict, and even race degeneracy. Urban reformers—at least those in England—were not so much unaware of the limits of their campaigns for clean air as they were willing to accept them if improvements could be made in the public health and welfare.

To these environmentalists, the wide diffusion of harmful emissions into the countryside seemed preferable to their currently heavy concentration in the most densely populated areas of the city, especially during recurring episodes of deadly fog. Faced with the emergence of an energy-intensive consumer society, they could realistically hope only to keep a bad situation from getting far worse. Even if the smokeless city remained a futuristic ideal, the influence of urban reformers in shaping the formation of public policy on air quality standards deserves careful reconsideration.[4]

A close examination of air pollution reform in Manchester reveals a community making pragmatic choices in confronting the modern dilemma of the rising consumption of energy and the declining quality of daily life. Manchester had become the first shock city of the age of industry and remained a classic Dickensian Coketown a century later. As local historian Shena Simon lamented in 1938,

> We cannot say that Dr. John Leigh's "dark canopy which hangs as a pall over the city" is a thing of the past, or something dimly remembered by the very old. Sometimes it has been the overhead darkness, which requires complete lighting-up for houses, business premises, and vehicles at midday, when the city has literally been under a roof of soot, but without mist, visibility at street level being the same as at night. Other times the city has been wrapped in choking sulphurous (SO_3) fog, composed of mist, a natural phenomenon met with in the open country and at sea, but here laden with soot.[5]

Despite Manchester's ultimate defeat in its battle to replace bad air with good, its leaders never retreated from the front lines of the nation's assault on this seemingly intractable problem. Some of the industrial center's most eminent scientists, doctors, and engineers devoted their professional expertise to the effort to secure victory over the original causes of environmental pollution. In addition, the city's amateur botanists and town gardeners volunteered in the early 1890s to launch a bold mission into unknown territory to advance understanding of the linkage between acid rain and public health. Contrary to Schramm's depiction of urban reformers, Mancunians helped to identify many of the most chronic unintended consequences of industrial progress for the natural world and for its single most important organic resource, human beings.[6]

Gas and Germs

If exceptional killer fogs galvanized public opinion in favor of remedial action in London, the ordinary daily weather was sufficient to mobilize civic action on behalf of smoke abatement in Manchester. The environmental setting of Cottonopolis created just the right conditions for maximization of the deleterious impacts of air pollution caused by burning fossil fuels. It is situated at the bottom of a crescent-shaped amphitheater of coal-laden hills facing southwest toward the Atlantic Ocean. With its surrounding conurbation of mill towns, Manchester and Salford were subject to the full effects of the area's industrial ecology. From one of the hills, Dr. Leigh vividly described the microclimate of smog. "On the finest day," he wrote during the year following the exhibition, "the vista is obscured by a column of haze, the accumulated density of which terminates the view by an apparent wall of fog. The smokey envelope of the town is very well seen from a distance of four or five miles in the country, particularly on the approach of evening, when the slanting rays of the sun give a remarkable definition to the black, cloudy covering, and indicate very distinctly the site and general boundaries of Manchester."[7]

The burdens of a valley location were greatly exacerbated by climatic conditions that made the area one of the wettest places in the kingdom. The rain coming down would combine with the discharges going up to produce what Mancunians aptly called the "blacks." London journalist Angus B. Reach, one of the first to conceptualize the region as a unified textile district, had sketched his impressions of the railroad corridor leading to the "Queen of the cotton cities" in 1849. A quarter-century later, another newspaper from London returned to the subject by contrasting that city's environmental endowments with the shortcomings of the northern conurbation. While the article conceded that Manchester's superabundance of rain gave it a superior water supply, the contrast turned invidious when it came to air quality. "Pure air they rarely get in their homes," the *Daily News* lambasted, and "analysts say that no trace of ozone can be found in the atmosphere of Manchester. The rivers and brooks which run about the city are black and turbid; there is little pure green in the gardens; the flowers and vegetables must be washed after they are gathered."[8] Such outside criticism was hardly necessary, however, to make residents aware of their environmental disadvantages.

The development of local perceptions of the downside of technological progress paralleled the earliest adaptation of the steam engine to the factory. With the installation of the first Boulton and Watts engine in Peter Drinkwater's cotton mill in 1789, Mancunians began tinkering to attain more complete combustion and hence a reduction in the amount of unburned carbon escaping up the stack as soot. But like so many similar would-be improvements that followed, the price paid in lost power and increased fuel costs soon led to their rejection. On the contrary, the textile makers embraced the steam engine as a new source of power and an economical alternative to waterpower. By the turn of the century, there were thirty-two steam engines with 430 horsepower adding visibly to a rapid deterioration of air quality. Local authorities reported that "the increase of... steam engines, as well as the smoak issuing from chimnies used over Stoves, Foundaries, Dressers, Dyehouses, and Bakehouses, are become a great Nuisance to the town unless so constructed as to burn the Smoak arising from them which might be done at moderate expense." Needless to say, very little was done to impede the growth of industry during the next four decades of extraordinary expansion and prosperity. By 1840, Manchester/ Salford mills had over two hundred engines generating ten thousand horsepower and consuming a million tons of coal a year.[9]

The record success of its merchants and manufacturers that made the textile district the horror and wonder of the world also made it the center of urban reform. In 1842, thirty members of the ascendant elite, including Mayor B. Houldsworth and factory designer William Fairbairn, formed the Society for the Prevention of Smoke. They applied their characteristic approach of scientific experimentation and quantitative methods to the study of coal-fired boilers. What they discovered was that a perfect combination of fuel, temperature, and air could produce complete, virtually smokeless combustion. But neither they nor countless others who came after them for the remainder of the century could find a practical way to bring these three basic elements into equilibrium for sustained periods of time. For example, something as elementary but essential as opening the furnace door to shovel in more coal allowed cold air to rush in, lowering the temperature below optimal levels and resulting in a release of carbonous emissions. Every invention aimed at solving a problem with one of the elements seemed to come at the price of creating an imbalance in the other two. In addition, the intense heat inside the fireboxes could turn even the best smoke-eating devices into expensive piles of junk in short order. Finally, low pay, onerous work, and employer indifference largely precluded the establishment of the training necessary to turn the furnace stoker into a highly skilled technician.[10]

At the same time, the reformers recognized that incorporation of the best available equipment and practices could make a difference by ameliorating what had come to be perceived as an unacceptable degradation of the quality of daily life. In 1844, Manchester enacted one of England's first antismoke laws. It stated that "every Furnace employed or to be employed in any Mill, Factory... or other Buildings used for the Purposes of Trade or Manufacture... shall, in all Cases where the same shall be practicable, be constructed so as to consume or burn the Smoke arising from such Furnace." Municipal records indicate that officials briefly prosecuted the most blatant violators of the nuisance regulation, but that enforcement efforts soon became paralyzed.

The quandary facing magistrates was the accused offenders' not unreasonable defense that the various smoke-reducing machines were costly to install, wasteful of fuel, and prone to breakdown. As Member of Parliament John Bright testified as he successfully led the opposition to the insertion of a similar proviso in the landmark Public Health Act of 1848, "it was quite impossible to work out any smoke bill. ... The clause was ridiculous. In Lancashire no three men were found to agree upon any effectual plan for preventing smoke." Significantly, Manchester's nuisance regulation embodied the pragmatic cultural style of its science and technology by focusing on the hardware rather than its undesirable by-products or potential health hazards. In the same spirit, Bright's telling criticism would soon lead reformers to adopt new standards that simply prohibited the emission of visible "black smoke" for more than a few minutes at a time.[11]

This approach also reflected the fractures within the medical community at mid-century over the role coal smoke played in causing diseases of the lungs. Within the loose parameters of the prevailing miasmatic, or filth-based, theories of etiology, a respectable contingent of expert opinion posited that carbonous compounds either effected no harm to the body or acted positively as a prophylactic disinfectant of the organic agents of lung infections. Another group assumed a middle-ground position that the chemical emissions were in some tangential way injurious because they irritated the lungs or depleted the oxygen in the air. Only a minority took a stand that these particulates and gases actually engendered the onset of respiratory disorders. Although a consensus was equally lacking on the influence of other environmental factors in disease causation, the sanitary crusade led by Edwin Chadwick channeled the attention of policy makers and medical professionals alike into a public discourse on water management. In the midst of a series of truly terrifying cholera epidemics, the risks to human well-being from the ubiquitous exhaust rising from the city's countless chimneys were largely discounted as far less important.[12]

Instead of engendering mainstream protest against coal smoke, the battle against urban air pollution established a beachhead of scientific research on an extreme fringe of public health concerns, in the chemical industry. And even here, the link to lung disease was made indirectly as a deductive inference from the inescapable conclusion that the noxious fumes from alkali factories and other acid-spewing concerns were toxic to plant life in the immediate vicinity. In the 1850–1860s, Manchester became the center of this area of study for two reasons. The country's largest concentration of alkali manufacturing was located nearby in Merseyside towns like Widnes and St. Helens, and Robert Angus Smith, the preeminent student of this chemical process, happened to live in the city.

The hydrochloric acid raining down from the discharges thrown into the air by the booming factories had turned the surrounding countryside into an industrial wasteland void of vegetation. In 1863, landowners and manufacturers agreed to support legislation to impose national standards for the reduction of these damaging emissions. Practical methods for removing up to 95 percent of the escaping acid vapors were readily available, narrowing the question to one of uniform enforcement rather than technical know-how. Smith was appointed head inspector because he had already earned a national reputation in what he would soon be calling the science of chemical climatology.[13]

For over a decade, the scientist and his fellow members of the Literary and Philosophical Society—the Lit and Phil—had been conducting a groundbreaking series of experiments to identify the physical and biological composition of city air. In 1852, Smith had inaugurated the study with a report on levels of acidity and organic contamination at different distances from the center of the city. He had collected rain from the upwind edge of the suburbs at Greenheys fields on the southwest side and comparable samples about a mile and a half away, from a location close to the Exchange Building. He had discovered that "the rain was found to contain sulphuric acid (H_2SO_4) in proportion as it approached the town and with the increase of acid the increase also of organic matter." After measuring three times more acid rain in the center of the city than on the outskirts, Smith had restricted his conclusions to an economic explanation of the corrosive effects of the pollution on inert objects such as textile goods, metal parts, and building materials.[14]

Three years later, Peter Spence took up the investigation and pushed it forward toward the logical conclusion that the invisible gases of fossil fuels were harmful also to living organisms such as plants and animals. Few were better qualified to reach that conclusion: the chemical manufacturer had invented a process to recycle the waste by-products of coal mining and gas making to produce alum, a mordant substance used in dyeing and printing textiles. He had also been convicted of violating the air pollution regulations and had been forced to move his factory farther out of town.

Two million tons of coal were consumed annually within a two-mile radius of the Exchange. Spence conducted a careful analysis of the chemical composition of the resulting smoke. There was a "mass of atmospheric poisons," he declared, "slowly rising from our firegrate, and wending their way quite deliberately up the chimney, preparatory to pouring themselves down the throat of the first pedestrian they meet in the street." The amateur scientist was especially alarmed about calculations that demonstrated that "for every working day the diffusion of about 200 tons of sulphurous acid gas, which . . . being more than double the weight of air, will under almost any circumstances descend to the lower strata of the atmosphere, and surround us, destroying vegetation, and though in itself one of the best correctives of miasma, yet certainly a most insalubrious atmosphere to breathe constantly," surely presented a threat to human health.

Spence seemed equally upset by the complete absence of attention in the smoke abatement movement to the hidden dangers lurking in the black fumes. A keen appreciation of the paradox of reform amplified his distress. "But the invisible evil is completely ignored," Spence exclaimed. " 'Burn your smoke!' is the united cry of the Sanitary Association, the public and the law. . . . In this case not only does the cure of the visible not effect the cure of the invisible evil, but every effort to effect the cure of the one only increases the noxiousness of the other. Perfect freedom from smoke would, if accomplished, only increase the evil arising from the purely gaseous result of combustion."[15]

Further discussion of the subject was suspended in the Lit and Phil during an interval of relatively clean air that resulted from the Cotton Famine of the American Civil War, but a renewal of the investigation paralleled the factories' return to full-blast production. It was at this time that Spence delivered a paper to this intellectual oasis of the social elite that reinforced previous reports. He had combined Smith's geographic approach with his own work on acid rain by exposing litmus paper to the air for twelve-hour periods at various locations. Like Smith, he had found tremendous differences between results at his home in Smedley, two miles downwind of the central city, and at Gilda Brook, on the opposite side of town.

After his earlier study, Spence had also planted twenty camellias in his backyard to test the effects of high levels of sulphurous compounds in the air on living things. "I have full proof at Smedley," he stated in Darwinian terms, that "vegetable life on the whole of that side of town is a mere struggle for existence." Eight years later, he transplanted to the south side the four "miserable specimens" that had survived. Over the past season, they had recovered and had bloomed with beautiful flowers. The chair of the session at which Spence reported these findings was Robert Angus Smith, who appears by then to have been convinced that both the visible smoke and the acidic gases of smokestack emissions were harmful to organic life.[16]

In 1868, Dr. Leigh drew out these studies' implications for human health. The doctor made air pollution a keynote in his inaugural report as Manchester's first medical officer of health. The town council had promoted him from his job as chemical analyst for the municipal gasworks because he was willing to defend its decision to deny the working classes access to indoor plumbing. At the same time, this restrictive quid pro quo on water management appears to have freed him to become outspoken on the issue of air pollution. He asserted:

> The normal condition of the working man of middle age in Manchester is bronchitic, and all observation tends to establish the fact that an impure atmosphere increases enormously the tendency to consumption. Ozone is never found in the air in Manchester, whilst the solid particles constantly floating in the atmosphere from our factory chimneys and other sources, keep up a constant irritation in the air tubes, producing ultimately chronic bronchitis and emphysema of the lungs. ... The general deterioration of health from a polluted condition of the atmosphere, arising from faulty ashpits, deficient drainage and ventilation, gaseous emanations from sewers, over-crowding of persons in small apartments, want of cleanliness, and a variety of other causes, predisposes the inhabitants to take on diseases which in happier circumstances they would successfully resist.[17]

As Dr. Leigh's long and eclectic list indicates, miasmatic etiologies of disease causation contained large gray areas that obscured the links between environmental pollution and bodily disease. As historian Bruno Latour observes, miasmatic theories contained a systemic contradiction that tended to undermine the authority of science. "Since anything might cause illness," he reasons, "it was necessary to act against everything at once, but to act everywhere is to act nowhere. Sometimes the hygienists give a definition of their science that is coextensive with reality."[18] In comparison, Pasteur, Koch, and other "microscopists" would establish stronger connections between the laboratory and medicine, microbes and disease.

The inclusive notion of the myriad conditions that could potentially cause a disposition to illness made the job of mobilizing public opinion behind a single concern like clean air all the more difficult. By the late 1860s, Manchester's professional and amateur circles of science had both been able to show a relationship between factory emissions and the health of living organisms. Robert Angus Smith, Peter Spence, and others had also made a compelling case that the unseen gases released in the industrial city posed a health hazard that was at least equal to that posed by the black smoke from the incomplete combustion of coal. However, their earnest warnings of danger could easily have gotten swallowed up in the confusing cacophony of voices dispensing medical advice to the public.

By now, the microscope was beginning to reveal a previously imperceptible world of germs, adding yet another layer of scientific controversy over discussions of the cause of human disease. Even in the most favorable light of public opinion, microbes played a still mysterious role in the coming of sickness and death. Louis Pasteur in France and J. B. Dancer in Manchester helped to initiate a gradual change in the emphasis of medicine from chemistry to biology. The discovery of invisible toxic gases and dangerous microorganisms in the air ironically had the further effect of shifting sensory priorities from a centuries-old reliance on the nose to a dependence on the eye. From a commonsense reliance on bad smells to indicate the presence of miasma, science now relied on observations using a microscope to identify disease-causing agents. Closely related was the shift in authority from the bodily senses of the common person in the street to the official reports of the trained scientists in the municipal laboratory. During the transitional decade of the 1870s leading up to Koch's major advance, however, urban reformers had to continue to use traditional indicators, arguments, and tactics in their long-running battle to replace bad air with good.[19]

Vapors and Violators

Manchester's professionals in science, technology, and medicine laid the groundwork for the city's reformers to launch a new campaign against air pollution. Spearheaded by the Manchester and Salford Sanitary Association (MSSA), the efforts of the urban environmentalists turned from investigation of air quality to instigation of public prosecutions of violators of the smoke abatement laws. After deferring to Dr. Leigh's appointment, the association supported his leadership in calling attention to the role bad air played in the city's achievement of an unenviable reputation as the unhealthiest place in the nation.

In 1873, the MSSA set up the Subcommittee on Noxious Vapours from Chemical and Other Works, which was composed of two doctors and a scientist. Two years later, the members of the subcommittee admitted difficulty in establishing "reliable statistics as the effect of such vapours on human life."[20] Still, they had no doubt about the need for stronger enforcement of the "smoke clauses" in the case of blatant violators. To convince policy makers of the "continued prevalence of ordinary smoke nuisances," they hired a "practical man" to observe infringements of the current legal standards, which prohibited the emission of "dense black smoke" for more than three minutes in a half-hour period. While he recorded sixty-nine offenses in a week, the two official inspectors reported only four. To bolster their case that the inspectors were not doing an adequate job, the subcommittee hired a second observer, who found thirty-five breeches of the law in a week. His list of worst offenders included Smethurst's factory in the heart of the central business district, where "dense smoke" poured out "for eleven minutes. ... Standing in the street you were smothered in dirt from it."[21]

In addition to petitioning Town Hall for more forceful remedial action, the MSSA lobbied the medical societies to fill in the gaps in the study of the human toll paid for public acquiescence in the creation of an urban atmosphere of suffocating smoke and toxic gases. In the following year, 1876, the Northwest Association of Medical Officers of Health responded with a geographic comparison of mortality rates for respiratory diseases throughout the country. Compiling data for a five-year period, the statistical analysis showed an average annual range of deaths per thousand from 2.3 in the healthiest rural district to 7.7 in the inner city Township of Manchester, the very worst district.

The sheer number of victims of lung disease in 1876 was equally horrendous. For Manchester and Salford combined, just over one-quarter of total deaths, or 3,509, were attributable to this cause, while another 14,630 people out of a population of roughly 550,000 suffered from nonfatal cases of bronchitis, pneumonia, and so forth. This death rate was more than three times the rate in rural areas and twice the national average.

The cost of bad air in terms of lives lost and bodies diminished by chronic illness was indeed high. It was this disturbing realization that drove the small, underfunded group of moral suasionists that was the MSSA to undertake the Herculean task of moving the Smoke Abatement Exhibition from London to

Lancashire.[22] The Lancashire stay of the exhibition marked a historic cross-roads in the battle for clean air because it changed perceptions of the problem and turned urban environmentalists in new directions. Supplying a retrospective look at past efforts and a careful examination of current proposals, the event went far to dispel the mirage of the value of a quick technological fix. Several energy-generating devices held real promise of greater fuel efficiency and decreased air pollution, but often at a prohibitive price. Higher costs for the purchase of the equipment and the payment of fuel bills severely limited their practical appeal. Gas cooking stoves, for instance, represented high technology compared to their traditional coal-fired equivalents, but few beyond the well-to-do could afford to install and operate them because gas was more expensive than coal.

The exhibition also provided a forum for confessing that complete identification of the intricate relationship between well-being and sickness was problematic. Only a few medical experts were willing to take such a strident stand as Dr. Leigh by attributing extraordinary mortality rates in the cities to the single cause of coal smoke. And Leigh's position was seriously compromised by the political imperative of deflecting attention away from the massive contamination of working-class neighborhoods that had tons and tons of putrefying human wastes in their backyards. Most physicians were willing to go no farther than making a strong case that coal's particulates and gases were a contributing factor in the loss of human health and in the onset of disease.[23]

In affording the reform movement an opportunity to pause for reflection, the exposition also generated enthusiasm for launching new initiatives on the basis of a reordering of tactical priorities and long-term goals. In Manchester, a progressive industrialist, Herbert Philips, took the lead in turning the MSSA committee into a full-fledged organization in its own right, the Manchester and Salford Noxious Vapours Abatement Association (MSNVAA). It became the main vehicle of reform and infused civic discourse with a powerful array of fresh ideas about energy technologies, public health, town planning, and environmental justice. Most important, perhaps, its spokesmen played upon middle-class anxieties about the political power gained by the working classes with the achievement of universal manhood suffrage in 1884. A half-century of extreme spatial segregation between central-city slums and garden suburban enclaves now threatened to hand control of local government to organized labor and its mass of followers.

Bad air took on new political meaning as a potent source of class conflict by driving all who could afford it to move beyond municipal borders to less polluted havens at the city's edges. "The estrangement thus created between the cultured classes and those compelled to live in depressing surroundings," MSNVAA secretary Fred Scott feared, "has been frequently pointed out as productive of many evils." Chief among them, he believed, was the male intemperance caused by the futile efforts of the suffering housewife to transform dingy, sad surroundings into a bright, welcoming refuge for family life. Moreover, the blacks raining down on the neighborhood kept the woman from opening the windows, contributing further to a lack of wholesome ventilation inside the home. "All who can afford to escape from the polluted atmosphere of the town for their leisure hours naturally do so," Scott affirmed.[24]

While commonsense notions linking interior air circulation to good health were standard in miasmatic medicine, they were given added authority by the new discoveries of bacteriology. Germ theory tended to reinforce, not undercut, traditional concepts of disease causation. Scientific research demonstrating that sunlight killed infection-spreading microbes strengthened the position of smoke abatement advocates, who favored strict enforcement of air pollution standards.

Dark canopies of choking smog punctuated at times by eerie, blinding fogs created troublesome images of a civilization sinking underground into the depths of moral depravity and race degeneracy. For the most part, however, working-class political mobilization was heading in different directions. As we have seen, Charles Rowley helped channel central-city residents into an interrelated campaign for better housing, slum clearance, and indoor plumbing. At the same time, the group devoted to smoke abatement also strove to build class-bridging alliances by highlighting the novel conceptual links among the body, the city, and nature.[25]

Six years after the Smoke Abatement Exhibition, the MSNVAA had moved far enough ahead in this new knowledge to lay out a significantly different agenda for urban environmental reform. Announced in a series of published lectures, the agenda was characterized by a much tighter focus on the impacts of air pollution on human well-being and by a more militant, confrontational stand toward the town council. This shift to positive environmentalism marked the transition from Victorian to Progressive reform.

True enough, some of the old points of view against the emissions of coal combustion were carried over with little change. For example, arguments that the emissions caused economic damage to buildings and property remained a stock part of reform discourse. Yet an unmistakable change in emphasis and tactics was deeply embedded in the 1888 platform. Dr. Henry Simpson of the Manchester Royal Infirmary assumed a more aggressive posture toward the risks the city's bad air posed to the public health. On the one hand, the physician expressed a sophisticated understanding of the complicated nature of disease and fitness, including a long list of variables such as personal habits, housing conditions, food supplies, work load, recreational opportunities, and the resilience of the body's "original constitution." He also was aware that an important segment of the medical profession believed that elimination of overcrowding and malnutrition were much more important objectives than cleaning up the atmosphere.[26] On the other hand, he took a strong stand that good air needed to be number-one priority of reform.

Simpson exploited recent concerns about city fogs to assert that the harmful effects of the blacks and acid rain were no longer a subject of scientific doubt. He hammered home his point by repeating the findings of Robert Angus Smith that coal soot was not pure carbon but a spongy material impregnated with sulphurous acid. "It is disagreeable to breathe," he declared, "and in fog is often productive of pain and a feeling of tightness in the chest, very oppressive indeed. All chest affections are made worse by it. There is more cough, the phlegm is black from the particles of soot that have been carried into the air tubes and are got rid of by coughing." On the basis of his practice at the Manchester Hospital for Consumption and Diseases of the Throat, the doctor went further in drawing a scientific nexus between air pollution and public health. "It invariably happens as I have seen over and over again," he reported, "that in the Infirmary patients with chest diseases are worse when a fog prevails. They cough more, and their breathing is more laboured and difficult. Their lungs are not only incommoded by noxious vapour, but the supply of oxygen is diminished, and the various processes of which the life of the body consists are carried on with greater difficulty and less activity than they should be."[27]

Marshaling the authority of official experts, the reformers' platform also called upon City Analyst Charles Estcourt to identify the sources of Manchester's bad air. After pointing a finger at factory emissions, Estcourt reinforced Dr. Simpson's assertion that "we breathe in those particles of carbon, and the acid, now sulphuric, is also taken into our lungs, there to produce the evils to which attention is being repeatedly called by the medical profession of this city." His studies revealed that about one ton of soot was released into the atmosphere for each one hundred tons of coal consumed in the steam plants of local industry. Chemical tests of the fuel used in the plants established that it contained an average of 1.5 percent sulphur. In contrast, Estcourt discounted the contribution of domestic fires since they generally used better, low-sulphur coals, and most of their soot stuck to the chimneys. "It is patent to all observers," he concluded, "that although mechanical stokers and proper stoking and firing may keep back the black particles from the smoke as emitted from the chimneys, still that invisible demon, sulphurous acid gas, which becomes sulphuric, is emitted exactly as before."[28]

One additional position paper warrants careful consideration because of its contribution to a better understanding of the dilemma of reform. As Estcourt realized, progress in smoke abatement would tend to encourage greater energy consumption with the unintended consequence of producing more and more noxious, albeit invisible, gases. In this case, the MSNVAA drew upon the scientific expertise of plant biologist Robert Holland. Consultant to agricultural societies and private landlords, Holland spoke with special authority on acid rain because of his experience as the forester of a large estate outside of Swansea. This Welsh city was a center of copper smelting, which gave out enormous amounts of sulphurous gases as opposed to the hydrochloric acid emissions of the alkali plants.

Holland had fought a losing battle against acid rain. He had helplessly watched the destruction of five thousand trees during his first eight years on the job and another two thousand in what remained of the woodland during the last six years of his employment. Although soot arrested the growth of the plants by coating their leaves and blocking sunlight, it was the sulphurous gases that killed them. "Wherever the rain runs down the trunks of the trees it carries acid with it," Holland stated, "and leaves a line of decayed wood to mark its course. But even this is not all; for the very soil around the tree becomes poisoned with acid. All herbage disappears for several yards around their roots; and that the soil is poisoned I have proved by collecting it, and sowing mustard seeds in it, which would not germinate."

Holland warned that all vegetation in England was suffering the toxic effects of this insidious process. He outlined a bleak prognosis for nature by drawing attention to his work for the town council's park committee. Manchester's "fine open spaces," he complained, had been "rendered hideous by the blackness of everything within them—trees stunted, dying—flowers struggling to bloom, and sometimes their special scent [?] scarcely recognisable. It is no exaggeration; and as long as the surrounding chimneys send out volumes of sulphurous acid and of carbon, there can be no improvement."[29] Holland's testimony is especially important because he showed that nature's fate inside the city and its fate beyond the city's borders were tied together.

The new platform provided the MSNVAA with a foundation of scientific and medical authority upon which to mount a different kind of political movement. Between 1890 and 1892, the outlines of its new agenda of reform emerged. The smoke abatement crusaders were motivated to change course not only as a result of the intellectual ferment embodied in the lecture series, but also because their efforts to get municipal officials to enforce the existing regulations had largely met with defeat in the courtroom. This campaign had become a frustrating uphill struggle for several reasons. Uniformity of enforcement was lacking within the various local jurisdictions of the metropolitan area, most violators realized it would cost them less to pay small fines than to bring their factories into compliance, and technology had not provided air pollution control devices that worked.

Still, it would be a mistake to write off the nuisance abatement strategy as a complete failure. On the contrary, the effort was keenly felt by Manchester's manufacturers, which formed self-defense organizations such as the Society of the Chemical Industry. "It is ... clear that at the time of the society's foundation," contends business historian Sarah Wilmont, "the industry was under pressure from groups like the Manchester Noxious Vapours Abatement Society, and from Parliament in the shape of a new noxious gases regulation bill. ... The Manchester section of the society, formed in 1883, was singularly active in using both the branch organization and the national society as a platform for resisting pollution regulation." Under even more intense fire after the implementation of the new agenda, the chemical industry hired a top gun, Ivan Levinstein, to work virtually full-time coordinating its counterattack from behind the scenes of several local business associations.[30]

In response, the now-seasoned reformers not only turned up the heat on the innumerable industrial producers of smoke but also turned to regional and national solutions. To discourage polluters from escaping from Manchester to nearby localities known for not enforcing the law, the MSNVAA proposed to form an umbrella organization covering southeast Lancashire. It would coordinate the campaign to lobby Parliament for legislation broadening the alkali acts and bringing every type of coal-burning device under national inspection. Claiming that all such devices contributed to the injury of the public health, the association also argued that the standards for air quality should be raised. The problematic prohibition of "dense black smoke" should be replaced with a more encompassing intolerance of even "moderate" emissions. The call for enlarging the geographic scope of administrative remedies to a regional and national scale was a logical reflection of the reformers' greater appreciation of just how far acid rain spread over the environment.[31]

The centerpiece of the reformers' new agenda represented a more radical departure from previous political objectives. Initiating a Progressive-style class-bridging movement, the MSNVAA demanded that the town council cut the gas rates. The municipally owned utility had long been a source of such lucrative profits that gas customers were, in effect, giving property owners a subsidy in the form of lower tax bills. Shopkeepers had protested the inequity of this financial burden in the past, but now the reformers appealed to a much broader, more inclusive concept of social and environmental justice. They envisioned universal distribution of gas to every type of energy consumer from efficient central stations at prices competitive with coal.[32]

During the 1880s, rapid advances in the manufacture of relatively cheap "water gas" and the invention of the incandescent illuminating mantle had completely transformed gas from a light-bearing to a heat-generating fuel. Moreover, the introduction of penny-slot meters supplied a flexible, pay-as-you-go mechanism to bring gas lighting and cooking within reach of the mass of city residents. The reformers discussed several other resources that could be distributed from central stations, such as electricity, compressed air, and pressurized water, but these remained on the horizon in 1890 in contrast to the proven technology of gas distribution, which was already in place throughout the metropolitan area.[33]

The MSVNAA confronted Town Hall not only with the injustice of the price of gas, but also its delivery of an essential service below acceptable standards of quality. The association had the gas tested for sulphur content. The results found that it contained twice the maximum amount allowed by Parliament for London's utility companies and more than three times the actual amount they distributed to their customers. For the average middle-class Mancunian household with four burners lit between six and eleven o'clock in the evening, about one and a half teaspoons of sulphuric acid vapor was emitted into the air. Besides the economic damage to interior furnishings, the noxious gas was detrimental to health, according to the report.[34]

To further strengthen the case for a major change in the Corporation's energy and environmental policies as a matter of public health reform, the MSNVAA promoted additional research on the harm acid rain caused plant life. This strategy served the dual purpose of drawing stronger links between invisible gases and the well-being of human bodies and of forcing elected officials to take remedial action to restore nature in the public parks. Joining hands with the Manchester Field Naturalists Society, the reformers petitioned the Local Government Board to expand its jurisdiction under the Alkali Act of 1881 to include the inspection of all factories releasing effluents bad for the public health and welfare. The memorial declared that it was "scarcely possible" for the urban naturalists "to work to any purpose so long as the present excessive pollution of the air, especially acid vapours, is permitted."[35]

Fumes and Flowers

In 1891 and 1892, the town gardening section of the Manchester Field Naturalists Society undertook a series of air quality experiments that represented the climax of the Progressives' effort to prove the interdependence of the health of the body, the city, and the environment. Conducted by professional and amateur scientists, the research broke new ground in both methodology and findings. The goal was to demonstrate that the adoption of energy policies that promoted the best use of technology could result in a reduction both in the suffering of the town's human population and in the waste and degradation of the country's natural resources. The logical implications of the study pointed toward a greater reliance on central-station service and gave priority to urban public health over rural plant life. But these conscious choices do not mean that the members of the gardening society were unaware of the larger ecological ramifications of their proposals. A central focus of their experiments was the invisible toxic gases of coal combustion, the "invisible evil" that was the known enemy of both urban and rural horticulture. The naturalists were willing to make the practical trade-offs in bucolic scenery necessary to improve the quality of daily existence in city neighborhoods.[36]

The transformation of the members of the garden society into the shock troops for the battle for urban environmental reform began with an absolute rout in their first skirmish with bad air. Perhaps with naive expectations, these would-be botanists volunteered in 1891 to undertake the civic mission of giving the city a face-lift. The obvious choice for a makeover was the pride and joy of Manchester Liberalism, the Town Hall and its adjoining Albert Square. The amateur horticulturists were perfect candidates for the archetype of the affluent club man or woman with an interest of some kind in the city beautiful movement. The society normally sponsored events such as a slide lecture on the life cycle of the coral polyp or an exhibit of Chinese snuff bottles. By the time of their "Autumn Soirée," however, their experience in bedecking the spacious civic plaza with flowers had, according to society chair Charles Bailey, "given us a valuable object-lesson on the atmospheric conditions of Manchester. ... Those plants were seen to suffer, and had to be carted away as failures." No one, he hoped, "would forget that lesson."[37]

Disappointed but not disheartened, the society turned to a professional chemist, Dr. G. H. Bailey of Owens College (now the University of Manchester) for expert advice on devising a counterattack against the poisoning of the air. Lecturing his rapt audience in the language of popular science, the professor used the extreme, and hence convincing, case of winter fogs to illustrate his message on the public health crisis of atmospheric pollution. His preliminary measurements indicated that the number of potentially deadly bacteria had jumped tenfold during the fogs of the previous year. The same leap was registered in the quantity of sulphurous acid. "But still more striking was the effect of the fog on light," he declared. While smog in the city center normally cut the amount of disease-killing sunlight to twenty-five percent of the illumination levels in the southwest suburbs, fog drastically reduced that figure down to the virtual darkness of only three to five percent. To dramatize his thesis, the scientist projected onto a screen graphs charting the parallel lines of climatic and health conditions. "These showed," he explained, "that the mortality figures were exceptionally high during the prevalence of fog, and especially so in respect of diseases of the respiratory organs."[38]

Here, then, were the outlines for a frontal assault to defeat air pollution with science. Dr. Bailey proposed that a series of subdistrict experimental stations be set up throughout the metropolitan area to test for three indicators: microorganisms, acid rain, and natural sunlight. Manchester's medical officer of health Dr. John F. W. Tatham stood up to voice his approval for this strategy because "of the many factors which went to make the frightful death rate of the city, the fog plus smoke must be regarded as the most important element." He pledged the support of his office to help correlate the disease and mortality statistics of the subdistricts with the three air quality indicators.[39]

Dr. Bailey invented a scientifically verifiable apparatus for each test, and his recruits served at the thirteen monitoring outposts. Two of the professor's colleagues joined him and the medical officer of health to take command of this exercise in experimental science. To measure the organic materials and the sulphurous gases, the team used gas meters with cranks to collect air samples in flasks, then subjected the samples to a battery of chemical tests. To gauge light levels, Dr. Bailey cleverly concocted a special solution that liberated iodine to a degree that was in direct proportion to the intensity of exposure to the sun. The experts also instructed their troops in less formal methods, such as observing how far they could see under different meteorological conditions.

Altogether the experiments allowed the team to construct a series of scales comparing air quality in places from the congested central-city slum of Ancoats to the suburban haven of Didsbury, five miles away. For the most part, the resulting tables reinforced Professor Bailey's preliminary findings (see

Table 13.1 Comparison of mortality rates in Ancoats and suburban districts, 1891–1892

Locality	Zymotic diseases	Pulmonary diseases	All other diseases	Total
1891				
Suburbs	241	534	954	1,729
Ancoats	510	1,549	1,698	3,757
1892				
Suburbs	175	429	904	1,508
Ancoats	455	1,166	1,630	3,251

Source: Town Gardening Committee, "The Atmosphere of Manchester and Salford: Second Report of the Air Analysis Committee," *Reports and Proceedings of the Manchester Field Naturalists and Archaeologists' Society* (1893): 81, 91.
Note: Figures are number of deaths per 100,000 inhabitants.

Table 13.2 Comparison of sunlight levels in Ancoats and Didsbury, 1891–1892

	1891				1892							
Locality	Sep.	Oct.	Nov.	Dec.	Jan.	Feb.	Mar.	Apr.	May	June	July	Aug.
Weekdays												
Didsbury	39.6	24.7	10.4	9.5	7.2	15.4	25.9	38.7	51.0	55.3	44.2	36.8
Ancoats	25.4	12.8	4.7	3.2	2.3	12.1	13.6	24.3	32.7	25.5	26.3	21.3
Sundays												
Didsbury	32.0	30.0	11.0	11.0	15.6	11.1	22.6	55.0	52.6	60.5	32.6	39.0
Ancoats	19.8	17.6	6.0	3.4	4.7	10.0	20.8	38.5	34.8	36.0	20.6	23.2

Source: Town Gardening Committee, "The Atmosphere of Manchester and Salford: Second Report of the Air Analysis Committee," *Reports and Proceedings of the Manchester Field Naturalists and Archaeologists' Society* (1893): 81, 91.
Note: Figures are milligrams of iodine liberated per 100 cubic centimeters of liquid exposed.

tables 13.1 and 13.2). Important too, the study showed that rain samples did not provide a reliable indicator of the level of harmful fumes and that elevated levels of carbon dioxide were not, as Robert Angus Smith had hypothesized, a significant contributor to bad air. Relying on the authority of germ theory, the researchers now placed the greatest emphasis on the rays of the sun as a disinfectant that killed harmful bacteria. The bottom line, they reported, was that "pollution of the atmosphere by organic matter and by gaseous emanations must be regarded as one of the most fertile sources of disease and of the lowering of tone which are invariably associated with overcrowded districts."[40]

Despite the elite makeup of the garden club, its report underscored the environmental injustice of Manchester's sharp class divisions that resulted in rigid patterns of spatial segregation. The most politically potent expression of the need for municipal reform was a comparison of mortality rates in the suburbs and in Ancoats. The society's study made the jam-packed central-city district the centerpiece of the council's failed policies on energy and pollution control. The correlation of public health and air quality statistics hammered home with compelling authority the point that Mancunians forced by poverty to live in Ancoats were dying from pulmonary diseases at a rate "at least four-fold what it should be under anything like favourable conditions," at levels that "in times of continued fog... rise to double even this excessive rate."[41]

The science of the garden club seemed to strengthen the resolve of the leaders of the smoke abatement movement to press their agenda of reform with more forceful action. Over the remainder of the 1890s, small but significant advances were made toward the fulfillment of their goals. In 1895, for example, the town council finally conceded to insistent demands for lower gas rates by shaving three pence off the base price of two shillings, six pence per thousand cubic feet and by dropping rental charges for simple cooking burners. The subsequent increase in the amount of gas consumed more than offset the lost revenue, but elected officials stubbornly insisted on continuing to take the profits from the gasworks to pay for the general expenses of the city, thus keeping taxes low.

More important in setting the limits of urban reform, Town Hall adamantly refused to cut the rate down to two shillings per thousand cubic feet, the tipping point at which gas would become competitive with coal for heating purposes. In a similar way, the Corporation inaugurated central-station electric service in 1893, although the pressure to light up the business district came from entrepreneurs looking for franchise concessions, not from environmentalists in search of clean air. Eight years later, the first tram car powered by the new source of energy began running on the municipally owned traction system.[42]

The Field Naturalists Society research also persuaded urban reformers to move forward in adopting a regional perspective on the enforcement of smoke abatement regulations. The metropolitan scope of the study helped restart stalled proposals to consolidate the scattered local groups into a single organization. In 1894, the MSNVAA joined with its counterparts in Oldham, Rochdale, Middleton, and Bolton to form the Lancashire Smoke Abatement League. The group still faced an uphill battle to get the inspectors to issue citations and the magistrates to levy meaningful fines. Many of those supposed to enforce the laws were not only fellow manufacturers but also frequent offenders of the law themselves.

Although League members won isolated skirmishes here and there, their efforts were generally frustrated. Therefore, they shifted the main thrust of their attack to the national level, where they sought remedial legislation, arguing that jurisdiction over all violations of air quality standards should be placed in the hands of independent "civil scientists" like the administrators of the alkali acts. The culmination of this lobbying campaign came in 1899 when the League gained a meeting with the president of the Local Government Board. He was persuaded to take the reformers' brief to the Home Secretary, who rejected it outright. Without the evolution of air pollution control to a regional scale analogous to that of the control being established over river conservancy, the limits of environmental reform had been reached. As Dr. William Graham, the medical officer of health of Middleton observed, "It is surprising how action has lagged behind knowledge in dealing with smoke prevention, and especially in the face of the great sanitary sin and the injustice inflicted on the industrial population forced to live amongst it."[43]

Conclusion: Energy and Environment

In November 1911, Manchester held another smoke abatement exposition. Coming thirty years after the first, it gave environmental reformers an opportunity to take stock of the progress of their movement to replace bad air with good. Science, technology, and medicine had made impressive advances toward the goal of raising standards of living and reducing rates of mortality. Without question, bacteriology had achieved the biggest gains by appearing to bring some of the most deadly epidemic diseases under control. Central-station gas and electric service had also accomplished much in supplying energy more efficiently than previous methods. And fear of fog had retained its potency in mobilizing political support for more effective pollution controls.[44]

But paradoxically, reformers had very little to show for all of their hard work in terms of realizing the ideal of the smokeless city. At best they could claim that the dark canopies still enveloping urban England would have been much worse without their dedication to the cause of pure, clean air for both town and country. As Sarah Wilmont demonstrates, the chemical industry in Manchester bore the full brunt of the reformers' assault on bad air and poisoned water. Thrown on the defensive, they fought back by uniting together in various trade associations. "Although contemporary commentators castigated public opinion for its weak opposition to air pollution," she confirms, "my investigations suggest both that this opposition was well organized after 1870, and that the manufacturing sector did feel under pressure as a result. This pressure was felt not withstanding the lack of a truly 'popular' anti-pollution movement, and the extreme variation in the enforcement of pollution controls locally."[45] But the reformers faced an impossible task because whatever incremental improvements they scored in air quality were more than overwhelmed by exponential gains in the consumption of fossil fuels in the city.

The science of bacteriology in the hands of the medical profession had undoubtedly come to be seen as the single most important weapon in the battle to improve the quality of urban life. To be sure, the doctors were scoring their greatest victories in the conquest of waterborne diseases rather than respiratory diseases, which seemed to be caused by poor air quality. The science of microbiology was supplying powerful tools to sanitary engineers for purifying the water and disposing of human and other organic liquid wastes.

According to popular perception, the main beneficiaries of germ theories were children under five years old who contributed one-half of the annual death toll in the industrial city. Germ theories were also enlisted in the cause of reducing the spread of infectious diseases caused by bacteria in the air. Health policies were designed to isolate the sick in special sanatoriums beyond the reach of the city's suffocating smog. The local medical community was prudently cautious in sorting out the exact causes of the drop in the overall death rate in the central city from thirty to twenty-five per thousand inhabitants since the time of the first smoke abatement convention. "Manchester, however," according to the current medical officer of health, Dr. James Niven, "is still conspicuous for its high mortality, and it is especially conspicuous for its excessive death rate from phthisis [tuberculosis], from pneumonia, from bronchitis, and from heart disease." In this regard, little had changed in the cleaning up of the air, and there was no reason to dispute Dr. Tatham's estimation that black soot and noxious vapors cut ten years off the lives of members of the working class.[46]

Similarly the hope environmental reformers had placed in technology for a breakthrough in smoke-eating devices was only partially fulfilled. Gas and electric utility managers were making solid headway by installing equipment that reduced the emission of particulates, building chimneys higher to diffuse the invisible gases, and locating their central stations farther away from populated areas. In Manchester, for example, fifty-four thousand homes had gas cookers in 1911, which cut the amount of coal burnt in its residential neighborhoods by sixty thousand tons a year. In a similar way, the municipal electric works had 10,500 customers, who used the equivalent of over four hundred thousand gaslights. Its generators provided another fifty thousand horsepower that replaced steam engines. Five years earlier, in 1906, the first all-electric textile mill in the metropolitan area had been built. Though still powered by a self-contained on-site steam plant, the factory was a model, and it could easily become smokeless if it was plugged into the grid of remote networks of power.[47]

Nevertheless, this type of step-by-step advance was offset by an even faster acceleration in the rate of energy consumption. As the chair of the Smoke Abatement League of Great Britain, John W. Graham, rather awkwardly explained, "We are, even as it is, less the victims of Smoke and Fog than were a generation ago." If it were not for "the phenomenal increase of manufacturers and of population during this wonderful but ugly era of development, we should see more clearly the effect which gas and electricity, mechanical stokers, hot blasts, combustion chambers, artificial draught, and slow combustion grates have caused." The exposition made its own unwitting contribution to society's incessant demand for more and more energy. Its model homes were overstuffed with electric and gas appliances, fueling the desire for every up-to-date convenience of modern life. An emerging mass culture of consumption would keep idealized visions of the smokeless city in the realm of dreams, not reality.[48]

The most problematic aspect of expectations from the first exposition turned out to be the matter of sustaining the support of public opinion. In part, the antismoke crusaders had based their strategy for mobilizing political power into an irresistible force on something they inherently could not control, weather conditions that produced "pea-souper" fogs. Still, there probably were enough of these disorienting episodes to punctuate their constant cautionary refrains about the impending doom of the city. A more decisive restraint on their ability to build the popular pressure needed to change the course of urban environmental policy was the limited appeal of their message among the masses.[49]

At least in Manchester, working-class activism after 1880 remained pragmatically focused on the more physical, bricks and mortar types of municipal reform. The city's genteel reformers tried to use the gas rate issue to bridge the sociopolitical gap between the classes, but given the crying needs of the slum, each water closet hooked up, social-housing unit constructed, and substandard dwelling demolished represented a tangible reward for the neighborhood. In contrast, each victory in the battle against air pollution was difficult to discern, let alone measure in some concrete way. One does not have to accept Stephen Mosley's thesis that working people were convinced by their bosses to think of smoke in positive terms, equating it with jobs and prosperity, to agree with his conclusion that "protests and campaigns against the 'smoke nuisance' failed to attract widespread public support."[50]

A more plausible explanation of why the movement for clean air only partially reached its goals rests upon the paradox that literally made the reformers' achievements impossible to see. The reformers faced the "problem of the commons." This timeless dilemma gives people who fish a counterproductive disincentive against conserving remaining stocks. If one person doesn't catch what is left of the fish, then another will until there are none left. Each polluting company had to deal with an analogous quandary of paying extra to eliminate its own relatively small contribution of bad air to the atmosphere while all the others continued to add theirs without penalty or cost. In other words, there was no politically practical way to make smoke producers pay their fair share of the social costs of the degradation of the environment and the consequent deterioration of the public health and welfare.[51]

Furthermore, the reformers confronted the equally baffling enigma that every gain in reducing emissions of the visible particulates of smoke undercut their related efforts to reduce emissions of unseen poisonous gases. The problem can be restated as the old adage "out of sight, out of mind." For example, one of the primary responses of the manufacturers was to build higher smokestacks. Such technological strategies placated local critics while depriving reformers of specific targets to attack for the environmental harm acid rain caused entire regional ecologies. The electric dynamo became a key icon of the technological sublime in the Machine Age, a dazzling symbol of power and modernity, and the 1911 convention's scale model of the smokeless city of tomorrow was emblematic of this cultural definition of the engines of progress. Yet a fascination with energy technologies further obscured the long-term repercussions on the human body and the natural world of burning fossil fuels.

The utopian fantasy of the smokeless city offered comforting reassurances that engineers could design such an ultimate, high-tech community without cost to the public health or the environment. A quarter-century later, little had changed to shake faith in this ethos of technocracy. At the World's Fair of 1939 in New York City, the largest diorama ever built, constructed by Henry Dreyfus for Consolidated Edison, and the most popular display, Futurama, created by Norman Bell Geddes for General Motors, envisioned a pollution-free metropolis of giant generator stations, superhighway networks, and gasoline-powered automobiles. Instead, an increasing reliance on the technological fix would only engender the development of an ever more energy-intensive consumer society.[52]

The organizers of the smoke abatement exposition of 1911 thus deserve praise for making the ethical choice to save the town's people from smoke even at the cost of knowingly sacrificing the country's trees to acid rain. Given a restricted range of politically viable alternatives, these Progressives were justified in taking comfort in the belief that they were making a difference in reducing the suffering of Mancunians from bad air. In the fashionable language of social environmentalism, their final report concluded:

> Few will deny that a large proportion of the evils of slums, the dreariness of towns, and high death rates are evils fostered by the thick black pall of Smoke which hangs over practically all our Cities, shutting out the sunshine and corrupting a health-giving breeze into a wave swirling black soot, fog, and grime into the innermost recesses of the Home and the Office. Good health and a higher moral tone will follow as an inevitable result when the value of a Smokeless City has been properly realized.[53]

Reformers pursuing the same goals in Chicago also ran into stiff resistance. Businessmen objected to their crusade against smoke because dirty coal was the cheapest form of energy. The Chicago reform battle, led by middle-class women, took on the lynchpin of the industrial city, the railroad companies. Assuming a David-against-Goliath imagery, the homemakers confronted some of the most powerful corporate moguls in the nation. With seats in neither the city council nor the boardroom, these reformers could make their case only in the civic forum of public opinion. While a few businesspeople stood to gain from clean air, the vast majority simply wanted to keep their energy bills to a minimum. Paying for environmental amenities came at too high a price in the rush of progress toward a consumer society.

CHAPTER FOURTEEN

Visible Smoke

Pollution and Gender Politics in Chicago

Introduction: The Revolt of the Housewives

In September 1908, the women of Chicago declared war on smoke. Encouraged by a crusading newspaper and a new administration at city hall, Annie Myers Sergel, referred to publicly as Mrs. Charles H. Sergel, and her Anti-Smoke League turned a technical debate among policy experts into a mass political movement. The women, joined by their children on roller skates, took to the streets, signing up supporters by the thousands. And they promised to go on strike, vowing to halt domestic routines such as cleaning house, washing children, playing bridge, and shopping. "For the present," they declared, "we neglect our sweeping and dusting and devote our time and that of others employed by us to this work exclusively; that for a while we live in unmitigated dirt and walk on heaped-up cinders, forgetting and ignoring the discomfort of this course in the joy of banding together in so grand a cause."[1]

Although the women's threat of revolt was tongue-in-cheek, their crusade for clean air and sunlight was real enough. They had chosen the perfect enemy, the Illinois Central (IC) Railroad Company, which ran its belching locomotives alongside the lakefront neighborhoods of the well-to-do on the South Side. Unlike the pollution rising into the atmosphere from the city's seventeen-thousand factory chimneys, train smoke suffocated people and befouled their clothes at the street level. Chicagoans hated railroads because their emissions invaded the home, breaching the walls of this private sanctuary from the industrial city. As one angry resident along the IC line complained, "everything inside is permanently blackened and injured by the smoke and soot and the health of my family is impaired."[2] Like the public water supply, the bad air transgressed the spatial boundaries between city, house, and body. The high visibility of the locomotives' black trails of grit and dust making their way into residential areas made the corporate guilt of the railroad companies an obvious target for the muckraking Progressives.

Moreover, the IC line destroyed the peace and beauty of the lakefront, the one urban space in Chicago that had achieved virtually sacred status. Environmental protection of this area had inspired generations of reformers, including Daniel Burnham, who had overseen the transformation of Jackson Park into site of the World's Fair of 1893. Burnham had followed up that work by designing a parkway along the lakefront from the South Side community of Hyde Park to downtown. Now he was putting the finishing touches on the greatest of his blueprints for the city of tomorrow. The Plan of Chicago embodied an environmental ethic of nature conservation. Besides proposing the creation of forest preserves on a metropolitan scale, Burnham called for an unbroken string of shoreline parks and recreational islands along the entire lakefront.[3]

This combination of the particularly obnoxious railroad technology and the sentimental attachment to a special place created a potent political issue. The women deserve credit for their skill in turning a narrow, not-in-my-backyard complaint into a cause that inspired a broad popular front. In less than a month, the Anti-Smoke League gathered forty thousand signatures on its petition, as well as endorsements from a diverse coalition of women's clubs, neighborhood improvement associations, and professional groups. "Everybody wants to join the anti-smoke party," a daily newspaper proclaimed, "there is not a shadow of a doubt how the people feel."[4]

As Annie Sergel and nearly two hundred of her supporters jam-packed the council chambers on 20 October 1908 to present their demands, they knew they would receive a warm reception from the current administration. Since assuming office in 1907, Mayor Fred Busse had led Chicago's first effective assault on the smoke nuisance. The former coal dealer had surprised some Progressives by taking the lead in forming a partnership with building owners to implement practical programs to reduce emissions from coal burning equipment. Public opinion seemed to galvanize the administration to mount a frontal assault on bad air. Chief Smoke Inspector Paul S. Bird ordered a crackdown on offenders, and Municipal Judge Scovel enforced the new policy with a vengeance. The jurist took a strong stand, lecturing the convicted that "everyone has a right to pure air" and levying the maximum fines.

The health commissioner, Dr. W. A. Evans, lent additional authority to the phalanx of public officials adding their weight to the battle against smoke. Raising the warning flag of infection, the physician announced that "the diseases of bad air, such as consumption and pneumonia, cause 10,000 deaths annually in Chicago and the number of deaths is on the increase." He too drew direct links between the environment and the health of the body. One of the moral slogans of his clean-air campaign cautioned, "Foul air befouls the body—be dirty and you'll be sickly."[5]

The aldermen too seemed eager to enlist in what had grown into a popular crusade for environmental reform. After Mayor Busse gaveled the enthusiastic women into silence, the council got down to the business of translating popular sentiment into political pressure. The Anti-Smoke League petition termed the IC's pollution an "unbearable public nuisance" and called upon the city to force the railroad to abate it by converting its engines to electric power. The council took the offensive, revoking a right-of-way permit the company needed to build a new extension line. Thus holding the railroad franchise hostage, the aldermen also took steps to enact a long-term policy that would lead eventually to the electrification of all the steam railroads within the city.

In the face of this solid front, the railroad seemed to cave in to the women's demands. IC president John T. Harahan conceded that the company had already begun a full-scale investigation of conversion costs. Mayor Busse hinted that a deal was in the works. In the meantime, Harahan agreed to substitute cleaner-burning, albeit more expensive, fuels for the offensive soft coals. But this promise offered only short-term relief since the less smoky anthracite and semibituminous coals cost two and a half times as much as local "poor man's coal."[6]

The women's campaign of 1908 marked a major turning point in perceptions of the urban environment. Sergel's protest against the soot and noise in her backyard grew into something much bigger and more important. The historical significance of her antismoke crusade springs not so much from its originality as from its success in redefining the terms of the policy debate about the protection of the city and its inhabitants from the downside of industrialization. Historians have recently underscored the ways in which women entered the public sphere during this period as a more assertive and self-conscious force, creating a "maternal politics." In this case, feminist perspectives meant enlarging the concept of public welfare by establishing a natural, moral, and legal right to breathe clean air. Furthermore, railroad corridors from downtown terminals to suburban stations and more distant country sidings were graphic metaphors of the environmental reach of the industrial city.[7]

These Progressives redefined the city's air in legal terms analogous to those used to discuss its water supplies. They drew upon the reform experience of the previous generation in using state power to make steady improvements in the sanitary conditions of the city. Joining pure water as crucial to public health and welfare in the popular understanding, clean air now required similar governmental initiatives and legal remedies if the community was to be protected from offensive sources of pollution like the IC locomotives. Since the Civil War, the actions of municipal health departments had been sustained in the courts when the departments exercised police power in the name of protecting public water supplies from the epidemic spread of disease-causing germs. The reformers sought to bring the air that people breathed under the same umbrella of legal protection. In effect, they sought to socialize the costs of bad air by transforming its status from a private to a public nuisance, thus making it subject to government regulation.[8]

The story of Annie Sergel and her followers is important not only as a case study of the politics of gender during the Progressive Era, but also as a revealing episode in the concurrent effort of scientific and technological experts to play a more influential role in urban planning and policy formation. The women's campaign against smoke was closely intertwined with the related but independent reform movement to create a new approach to public health based on germ theories of disease. In this case, however, the absence of evidence of a direct biological link between smoke and disorders of the lungs caused many leading experts of the new public health to reject air pollution as a medical problem. They sought instead to distinguish themselves by narrowing their role to that of curing the ills of individuals infected with microorganisms. In the case of contagious diseases, this meant isolating the sick from the healthy. Reflecting the new approach, the *Journal of the American Medical Association* argued in 1905 that "the crusade against unnecessary city smoke is more social than medical, and yet has [not attained] a real interest for physicians. The direct harmfulness of smoke to the human organism is not wholly clear."[9]

In comparison to that of Great Britain, the medical profession in the United States was conservative; it was well behind leading opinion on urban air pollution and public health. In the early 1890s, the Manchester Field Naturalists Society had drawn strong links between the bad air of the central-city slums and their extraordinarily high rates of lung disease. Turn-of-the-century follow-up studies of air quality in London neighborhoods also drew causal relationships between amounts of particulates, gases, and sunlight, and the disease rates among the residents in the test zones. Moreover, the expert authority of Manchester's medical officers of health from Dr. John Leigh to Dr. James Niven had consistently attributed that city's extremely high death rates to lung disease. Another decade would pass before the American association would acknowledge a correlation between polluted air and respiratory distress.

In part, the effort to use germ theories to raise the medical profession to higher social status was built on putting women down, on calling them sentimental and moralistic—in a word, unscientific. The new public health questioned women's authority both as the primary guardians of health in the domestic realm and as the "municipal housekeepers" of society in the public sphere. It represented a serious challenge to maternal politics, the Anti-Smoke League, and similar campaigns for the promotion of the public welfare and moral order through environmental reform.

Of course, not all doctors, sanitarians, and municipal reformers joined in the attack on policy options to cleanse the urban environment as an essential part of the battle against the spread of disease. On the contrary, the same idiom of science strongly reinforced proposals for expanding the government's public works programs and regulatory efforts to improve the purity of the water supply, and germ theories of disease were enlisted also in the battle to bring air quality under the jurisdiction of state and local health departments. If nothing else, the demonstrated role of sunlight in killing germs established a scientific link between good air and good health.[10]

Unfortunately, historians have too readily accepted the self-serving claims of the advocates of the new public health without critical examination. As Nancy Tomes indicates, in giving voice to women reformers most scholars have simply reiterated the sharp dichotomies of contemporary rhetoric that pitted miasmatic theories against germ theories, and sentimental women against scientific men. By showing how domestic sanitarians of the Gilded Age focused attention on preventing disease, Tomes demonstrates how they could accept new ideas about the causes of disease without great conflict during the Progressive Era. "Although older sanitarians tended to be distrustful of what they felt to be the oversimplifications of bacteriology and of experimental methods," she concludes, "their hygienic formulations were easily expanded to incorporate germs into the schema of household dangers.... The ability of microorganisms to produce dangerous toxins or poisons could be easily assimilated into older notions of decay and putrefaction as sources of infection."[11]

The campaign mounted by Chicago's Anti-Smoke League helps to illuminate the links among gender, science, and the reformulation of environmental policy. Although it was not the first civic crusade devoted to cleansing the industrial city of dirty air, it represented a striking departure from the past. The largest difference was the interjection of gendered perceptions of the health hazards and environmental impact associated with coal smoke. Chicago's Progressives no longer viewed this problem as simply a question of faulty engineering and economic waste that called for technological solutions. On the contrary, they placed greater emphasis on recent chemical, biological, and medical research in demanding sunlight and clean air as a public right. "Excessive soft coal smoke," one of Sergel's allies now claimed in the idiom of science, "perceptibly reduces the proportion of oxygen in the air and . . . irritates the mucous surfaces creating conditions which make it less possible for the lungs to extract the oxygen from the air. Smoke is not merely the visible, black, sooty discharges of the chimney but embraces also noxious, unburned, invisible gases." For these Progressives, pure air became a limited natural resource that had to be conserved in order for the public health and welfare to be protected.[12]

Becoming Smoke City

The glut of coal in Chicago gave the city's heavy energy users a competitive edge in national markets. These food processing and manufacturing industries not only added to the city's magnetic appeal as a good place to get a job, they helped swell its voracious appetite for fossil fuels. After 1880, both the improvement of old technologies and the invention of new ones, such as mechanical streetcars and electric lighting, contributed to a meteoritic rise in coal consumption (see fig. 6.3). The sheer geographic size of the Eastern Interior Coal Basin inspired grandiose thoughts of unlimited supplies of cheap fuel in ways similar to Lake Michigan's appeal as a seeming fountain inexhaustible. "Chicago," a booster proclaimed in 1883, "stands without a rival. The broad prairies of Illinois and adjoining states not only yield rich harvests for our granaries and produce markets, but down below the soil there is a harvest of coal extending for miles and miles, stored away long ago, and this is inexhaustible."[13]

Just as important, as figure 14.1 shows, the increases in the city's coal usage outpaced even its extraordinary gains in population, giving rise to an energy-intensive society. By the time of the World's Fair of 1893, a smog like Manchester's "dark canopy" had enveloped Chicago. A resident's account of his escape from the city's dirty air provides revealing insight into Chicago's

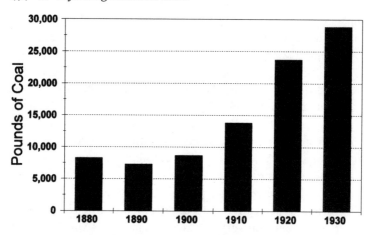

Figure 14.1. Per capita coal consumption in Chicago, 1880–1930
Source: Data from Chicago Board of Trade, *Annual Report* (1850–1931).

final transformation into an industrial ecology. S. E. Gross, one of the city's largest and most notorious house builders, kept his father informed about his trip to the mountains of Switzerland to restore his health. "Breathing pure air has become a luxury to me," he wrote on 13 October 1892, "and I do not relish the idea of again breathing the dust and smoke ladened [sic] atmosphere of the downtown business district of Chicago."[14]

This human-created pall contributed to the World's Fair visitors' sense of unreality and disorientation and made Chicago the latest version of a shock city. There "remains in the atmosphere," the smoke inspector explained in his annual report, "the finer particles, impalpable but all-pervading. These constitute the gray haze which hangs like a fog over the city, shutting out the sunlight, blurring the sky, and narrowing the firmament into a cramped, grimy arch." Advocates of a city beautiful were so embarrassed by the smog that they formed the Society for the Prevention of Smoke. Visitors to the exhibition could not help but notice the city's air pollution. H. G. Wells noted that "Chicago burns bituminous coal, it has a reek that outdoes London, and right and left of the [railroad] line rise vast chimneys, huge blackened grain-elevators, flamed crowned furnaces and gauntly ugly and filthy factory buildings." Frustrated by the seeming hopelessness of its cause, the Anti-Smoke League soon disbanded, leaving no legacy of reform for Sergel to draw upon in her battle for clean air.[15]

A closer look at the two decades from 1890 to 1910 reveals a dramatic jump in coal consumption; it was at the end of this period that Sergel sparked a mass movement. In a single generation, air quality had taken a significant turn for the worse. At the time of the World's Fair, the metropolitan area was burning about 5 million tons of coal a year. By the time of the Anti-Smoke League's protest, this figure had more than quadrupled, to over 21 million tons. In addition, the city's steam boilers were burning 175.5 million gallons of crude oil, with a heat value of 1.2 million tons of coal, from wells in Illinois and other Midwestern states. The petroleum boosted the Chicago area's annual fossil fuel consumption to the equivalent of nearly 22.5 million tons of coal. In comparison, the city of Manchester was consuming about 3 million tons a year. Of course, Manchester covered a much smaller territory and its industry had already dispersed throughout its regional conurbation. On average, each Mancunian burned four tons of coal a year, while each Chicagoan burned twice as much.[16]

A finer-grained snapshot of energy use and environmental pollution was recorded in the massive report on air quality released by the Chicago Association of Commerce (CAC). In an effort to minimize the railroads' share of city smoke, in 1912 it made an exhaustive study of fuel consumption in the metropolitan area. The railroads sponsored the study: no one was in a better position than the railroads to record precisely where the coal was coming from in the countryside and to whom it was going to in the city. The report covered the almost two hundred square miles within the city's borders and about an equal amount of space on the suburban fringe (see figs. 14.2 and 14.3). Annual use of the fuel reached an astonishing 387,000 tons per square mile in the central business district (A-5). Outside the densely packed commercial center, two industrial, working class zones accounted for the greatest concentration of energy use. The Packingtown area of the stockyards, central manufacturing district, and rail yards (A-9) was one; the South Chicago area of steel mills, heavy industries, and railroad shops (A-14) was the other. In Sergel's lakefront neighborhood, the amount of fuel consumed annually averaged about 150,000 tons per square mile (A-10).[17]

The report confirms the birth of a Machine Age of intense energy use in the period before the outbreak of World War I. The researchers calculated that three hundred thousand buildings were emitting coal smoke in Chicago. Although three-quarters of these were houses and apartments, which represented only about a fifth of total fuel use, factories and power plants, metallurgical furnaces, and railroads accounted for most of the demand. Like the brewery, these industries were using more and more energy to increase production with new methods of mechanization, heating, and cooling. Given the low price of coal compared to other costs, such as wages, the use of more machines made good economic sense. In addition, new technologies such as electric traction replaced an organic energy system of horses and hay with an

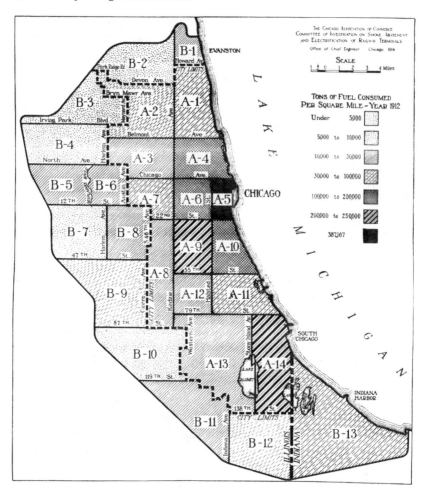

Figure 14.2. Coal use by district in Chicago, 1912
Source: Chicago Association of Commerce, *Smoke Abatement and Electrification of Railroad Terminals in Chicago* (Chicago: McNally, 1915), 126.

inorganic one of iron and coal. The automobile too was making a significant contribution to bad air. The city's twenty-four thousand horseless carriages consumed almost twenty-six million gallons of gasoline. Although their number was less than half that of horse-drawn vehicles, they represented about 60 percent of the traffic in the downtown area, where pollution levels were highest. Researchers conducting traffic counts were already observing a telltale "blue haze" created by exhaust lingering at street level during the rush hours.[18]

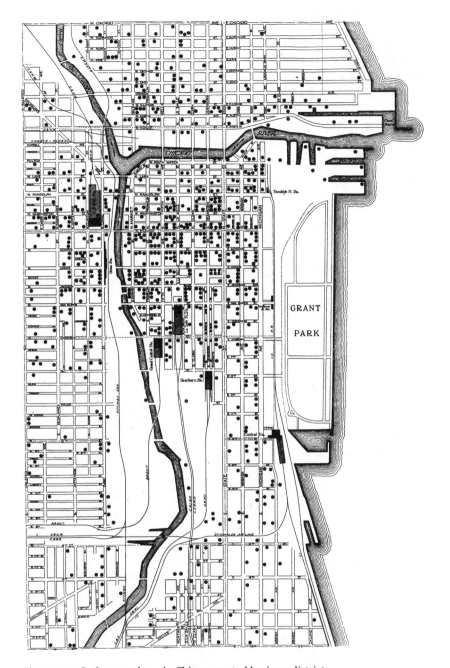

Figure 14.3. Coal steam plants in Chicago central business district
Source: Chicago Association of Commerce, *Smoke Abatement and Electrification of Railroad Terminals in Chicago* (Chicago: McNally, 1915), 286.

While the compilation detailing the full scale and scope of the consumption of fossil fuels in the industrial city was important in itself, the CAC report also provided an equally exhaustive study of the ways in which the fuels produced air pollution. It advanced understanding of the problem by showing that different types of use generated different mixes of smoke particulates, coal soot, and noxious gases. The picture was complicated by the different types of fuel used for various purposes. For example, residential heating plants used 13 percent of the coal, but produced only 4 percent of the smoke. Almost all of the high-quality hard coals were used for this purpose, which largely explains the residential figures. In contrast, railroad locomotives using local soft coals generated disproportionately high amounts of smoke and sulphur gases in relation to fuel consumption. The stop-and-go nature of train movement made control of emissions more difficult for the railroads than it was for stationary power plants, whose demand was more steady. Still, tests by the railroad companies demonstrated that employment of experienced firemen and of fireboxes insulated with brick arches could make a major difference in improving fuel efficiency and reducing air pollution.[19]

A final contribution of the CAC report was a comprehensive definition of air pollution that went beyond those in previous studies of fossil fuel emissions. Echoing Manchester's pioneering crusaders for clean air, it complained that the standard tests did not measure the invisible gases released in coal combustion. The report cited the work of the Manchester Field Naturalists Society with approval. Following in its footsteps, the Chicago researchers conducted extensive field tests to gather air samples for analysis in the laboratory. They found that two-thirds of the city's bad air was related the use of coal and oil, but they identified many other "allies of smoke" as well. Most important was the dirt and dust on the streets and in the alleys that was constantly being thrown back into the air by passing vehicles. Approximately 20 percent of city land, or forty square miles, was devoted to these arteries of transportation. One-half, or 2,633 miles of roadway, was still unpaved. An inescapable, if unintended, implication of this research was the pivotal role of City Hall in the health and welfare of the people. Taken together, the findings of the report strongly supported the position of not only Annie Sergel but also Jane Addams in demanding that the public sector take a much more active part in municipal housekeeping and environmental reform.[20]

Furthermore, the CAC report conclusively proves that Sergel and her followers were responding to a rapid and striking decline in air quality during the opening decade of the new century. The women's movement attracted widespread support in part because the decline of the urban environment was real, not just a matter of changing perceptions or some social construction built of rising intolerance of locomotive smoke. Returning from a national tour in 1908, the city's first smoke inspector, Frederick Adams, concluded that Chicago "was the dirtiest and filthiest city in the country—Pittsburgh alone excepted. ... A year ago it was impossible to see the Board of Trade Building from the City Hall," a short distance of five blocks. Early depictions of train and factory smoke as proud plumes of progress had turned into nightmare images of hell as the smoke cast a dark pall of gloom over the city. Industrialization had an undeniable downside, a visible deterioration of the quality of living in the city.[21]

Imagining the City Healthy

Although industrial technology caused serious environmental problems, contemporaries believed that it also promised the best hope of supplying the appropriate solutions. Early smoke abatement programs, such as the one mounted by the Citizens' Association in the early 1880s, aimed at educating factory and building owners on the proper use of their equipment. Chicago's second crusade to reduce air pollution illustrates that the problem was much more deep-seated and intractable than a simple case of faulty job training and negligent performance. The Society for the Prevention of Smoke tried to clean up the city's image by eliminating its most conspicuous environmental shortcoming. The Society did hire an engineer who pursued a traditional reform strategy that relied on technical education and equipment improvements, but the organization also gained official authority to arrest violators of environmental regulations and to prosecute the resulting cases in the courts.[22]

The campaign ran into a solid wall of opposition from the businessmen operating the city's soft-coal furnaces. Downtown real estate developers, steamboat owners, railroad executives, manufacturers, and other industrial and commercial energy consumers fought back, stressing the economic necessity of low-cost fuel. They found it cheaper to waste fuel than to install equipment of adequate size or to spend an amount adequate to attract and train workers who would be skilled enough to operate the furnaces properly. After initially assuming a defensive posture, the polluters mounted a successful counteroffensive in the law courts and in the political arena. Depriving Chicago of the cheapest coal from local mines, they warned, would deliver a crippling economic blow to the city and the state. The crisis atmosphere of the depression of 1893 served to hammer home their point.[23]

The Society disbanded the following year, but the search for ways to use technology to engineer the environment would continue. Driven by the rapid deterioration of its air quality, Chicago had little choice. Over the course of the next decade, a consensus emerged among a growing corps of experts, including coal suppliers and consumers, engineers and architects, and city bureaucrats and politicians. After the debacle of the Society's efforts, the advocates of a technological fix gave greater emphasis to equipment design and architecture, especially in new industrial and commercial structures. They also promoted the use of alternative technologies such as electricity for light and power, and gas for home cooking purposes.

To prod energy consumers to invest in technology, this loose alliance of businessmen and technical experts sponsored a series of "reasonable reforms." Beginning in 1903, it helped establish a Department for the Inspection of Steam Boilers and Steam Plants. By the time of the inauguration of the Busse administration four years later, Chicago had built this agency into an effective, professional bureaucracy for the enforcement of the smoke abatement laws. It mostly worked cooperatively with building owners to solve problems, reserving prosecution for the worst offenders.

Until the diffusion of mechanized stokers in the mid-1910s, however, the poorly paid and untrained sweating man with a coal shovel continued to serve as the most convenient scapegoat for opponents of the smoke evil. On the railroads, at least, violations of the smoke ordinances led companies to levy fines against the workers who operated the offending locomotives. Further investigation would demonstrate that maintaining the exact balance of fuel, oxygen, and heat was extremely difficult even under the best circumstances. Yet these tests by the railroads demonstrated that better training and equipment could make a significant difference in reducing smoke emissions.[24]

Urban planners such as Daniel Burnham also relied upon technology and the cult of efficiency to gain support from business leaders for city beautiful ideas. In helping to plan Washington, D.C., in the early 1900s, Burnham had been able to achieve the removal the railroad tracks crossing the National Mall by making personal appeals to company executives. This unexpected achievement encouraged him to incorporate into the Chicago plan a large-scale scheme for the removal of all of the freight yards from the central business district in addition to the consolidation of the passenger stations. Appropriately enough, this part of the great plan of 1909 used the metaphor of the machine to describe the workings of the city's transportation system. Burnham also supported Sergel's group's demand for electrification of the lakefront passenger lines.[25]

While the Progressives too believed in the technological fix, they were fundamentally different from previous municipal reformers. Their gendered construction of the public welfare embraced an inclusive, democratic vision of urban society. The recent articulation of germ theories of disease armed them with a powerful rhetorical weapon in the fight for social and environmental justice. Insurgents like Annie Sergel and the supporters of the Anti-Smoke League mounted a serious challenge to the authority of the male-dominated engineering profession, contesting the engineers' claim to leadership in the formation of environmental policy.

Use of the idiom of medical science opened a new style of civic discourse on the link between public health and air pollution. In this case, maternal politics blended new and old. It mixed germ and miasma paradigms by adopting modern ideas of the cause of disease and by establishing remedies for preventing its spread. In a similar way, it combined technological innovations, such as electric traction, and traditional values such as the concept of natural rights. Rooted in common law, it created moral and legal imperatives for political change.

The municipal sanitarians who maintained an environmental orientation forcefully advocated an alternative strategy to eliminate the air pollution caused by the industrial city's insatiable demand for more energy. Rather than viewing coal smoke as a regrettable but inevitable by-product of progress, they saw it as an intolerable source of death and human misery. This position set them apart from both the earlier mugwump reformers and the aspiring practitioners of a purely scientific medicine. Unlike the new-breed public health professionals, the sanitarians espoused a holistic social approach to the problem. Rather than narrowing the definition of disease to what could be seen in a microscope and limiting policy to the treatment or isolation of sick individuals, they called for a positive role for the State in eliminating the sources of air pollution. And rather than applying the engineers' approach of supplying incremental cost-saving improvements in technology to individual energy consumers, these champions of the environment demanded clean air as a public right. "Pure air," Health Commissioner Evans asserted in terms echoing Judge Scovel's, "is just as essential to a high level of public health as pure water."[26]

Sergel and her allies organized their protest against Chicago's dirty air in large part around health concerns, especially about pulmonary tuberculosis. Until the late nineteenth century, diagnosis with this frightening and hopeless disease was a virtual death sentence. Since physicians were unable to isolate a cause of the wasting illness—"consumption"—they attributed it to heredity. Yet, other predisposing causes, including environmental factors, also seemed to play a contributing role in the progress and ultimate outcome of the ailment. Moreover, it afflicted people in a baffling variety of ways, ranging from slow decline or rapid death in most cases to seeming recovery in a few others. In the absence of a cure, fresh air in a hygienic sanitarium was probably the most common remedy prescribed.

When the Prussian doctor Robert Koch identified a specific bacteriological agent of the disease in 1882, hope dawned that it could be prevented if not cured. In the early 1890s, the new science reached the United States, launching the tuberculosis movement in its crowded centers of population.[27] The reformers, especially the advocates of fresh-air treatments, took an aggressive stand on the interrelationship between promotion of the public health and improvement of the urban environment. Calling for an "ethics of the air," one doctor proclaimed that "no man has any more right to contaminate the air we breathe than he has to defile the water we drink. No man has any more moral right to throw soot into our parlors than he has to dump ashes into our bedroom. . . . Poison taken into the body through the lungs is just as much a poison as is some other poison swallowed into the stomach."[28]

From this point of view, the success of the postwar generation of sanitarians in cleaning up the city's water supply represented undeniable proof of the causal link between environmental control and reduction of epidemic disease. In Chicago, for example, the number of deaths from waterborne contagions dropped significantly for the first time during the decade following the turn of the century. The city's perennial number-one killer, diarrheal diseases, lost their top ranking while several others also declined, including diphtheria, meningitis, and typhoid fever, the last of which fell dramatically from seventh to twelfth place. The drop in mortality from diseases caused by bacteria spread in the water supply meant an increase in the relative danger of airborne diseases. Tuberculosis remained the third greatest killer, but pneumonia moved into first place, adding all the more urgency to the effort to clean up the atmosphere. To Progressives like Annie Sergel, the idiom of engineering and its incremental approach to reducing the city's smoke were clearly inadequate to such a great humanitarian crusade.[29]

In contrast, the community of acknowledged experts in sanitary engineering considered the achievements of the past generation as perfect justification for their continued leadership. From their point of view, the slow but accumulating progress in curbing waterborne epidemics vindicated their strategy of technological improvement and education. Railing against the champions of the city beautiful during the World's Fair, for instance, Health Commissioner Arthur Reynolds ridiculed the antismoke crusaders as a threat to Chicago's prosperity. The doctor defended industry's use of cheap bituminous coal, called for patience, and proposed that all firemen be licensed.

Dr. Reynolds was not alone among medical professionals in holding the line against the policy implications of turning the city's air into a public health issue comparable to the water supply. The new breed of physicians represented by American Medical Association cautioned against drawing connections between contaminated air and public health. But by 1905, even this group of self-proclaimed scientists was willing to admit that "smoke and other products of soft coal combustion vitiate the atmosphere and constitute an influence genuinely depressing to the organism." Still, the Association restricted its recommendations to a single meaningless remedy: take the children out to the countryside once in a while for a dose of fresh air.[30]

The stakes in the policy debate between the traditionalists and the insurgents were high. From the perspective of the businessman and like-minded professionals, an excessive emission of coal smoke was essentially a crime of negligence that caused property damage to building interiors and their furnishings. The appropriate punishment was a fine for each offense, levied on the individual furnace owner. At the time of the women's strike, the city calculated the economic loss from bad air at almost $18 million a year. Marshall Field estimated that smoke damage cost him $150,000 annually in soiled goods, cleaning bills, and the redecorating necessary to keep his department store up to the standards expected by his customers. For a few businessmen like him, clean air had pecuniary value.

From the perspective of maternal politics, on the other hand, polluting the air was an immoral act against society that should be dealt with in the most stringent terms. According to the president of the Women's Club, Mrs. John B. Sherwood, "Chicago's black pall of smoke ... is responsible for most of the low, sordid murders and other crimes within its limits. A dirty city is an immoral city, because dirt breeds immorality. Smoke and soot are therefore immoral." The proper legal remedy for such an intolerable public nuisance was an injunction that would permanently forbid any further offense. Polluters could write off fines as a necessary cost of doing business, but an injunction could completely shut them down.[31]

In this respect, the environmental reformers built upon the American legal tradition in drawing analogies between water and air. Under common, or judge-made, law, reasoning by analogy between established principles and novel situations was one of the most acceptable and effective methods of creating new legal precedents. The focus of the previous generation of sanitarians on purifying the water supply had generated a large and wide-ranging body of legislation and common law compared to the few governmental initiatives to curb air pollution. In the area of nuisance abatement law, the courts had generally assumed an expansive posture by extending their jurisdiction over a long list of the harmful impacts of industrialization on the environment.[32]

In effect, the courts asserted that a nuisance was whatever a judge declared it to be. In a landmark case testing Chicago's 1881 antismoke ordinance, for instance, the state high court announced in typical language that "anything that is detrimental to certain classes of property and business in a populous city, and is a personal annoyance to the public at large within the city, needs not to be defined by ordinance or by lexicographers to be known to the common mind as a public nuisance. It is so *per se.*" Water and air pollution cases gave the bench ample opportunity to take an equally open-ended approach to imposing not only penalties for damages but also injunctions, including absolute cease-and-desist orders, without regard to the cost to the offender.[33]

The policy implications of the contrasting perspectives on the smoke problem presented by the traditionalists and the environmentalists were by no means lost on contemporaries, including aspiring groups of experts. Their conflict goes a long way in explaining the impetus and direction of environmental reform in the wake of Chicago's second antismoke crusade. Beginning in 1894, the city's major mine operators and soft-coal dealers took the lead in sponsoring the remedial legislation that culminated nine years later in the creation of the separate steam boiler and smoke inspection department. On the surface, the act marked a welcomed step forward because it required the installation of proper equipment, but more subtle provisions significantly hamstrung the city's ability to reduce air pollution.

The hidden agenda of the coal suppliers' plan was a crucial shift in jurisdiction from the health department, with its virtually unlimited power to abate public nuisances, to the new agency, which had to staff its top office with a licensed engineer. This political initiative to keep reform contained within what the suppliers considered reasonable bounds also sheds light on the mayoral candidacy of a relatively obscure party boss, coal dealer Fred Busse, and his subsequent appointment of a blue-ribbon commission of businessmen to oversee the work of the new department. His administration's tough stand on the enforcement of the smoke ordinances was aimed at protecting the city's soft-coal interests as much as prosecuting the polluters. The CAC report embodied the same objectives. "The problem of smoke abatement in Chicago is difficult," it equivocated, "because among the conditions which have been effective in stimulating the growth of the city there must be included the proximity of the city to an abundant supply of fuel.... The Illinois-Indiana coal field ... extends almost to Chicago's threshold. This coal is Chicago's coal and she must use it."[34]

In contrast, the new perspectives on the environment opened by the idiom of medical science helps account for the unprecedented political mobilization of women behind the homemakers' revolt against smoke. During the

Progressive Era, women became much more vocal in promoting their own agenda of municipal reform, and they felt comfortable with the new mode of discourse, whose emphasis on health, beauty, and cleanliness echoed familiar themes of Victorian domesticity. In comparison, men felt more at ease expressing themselves in the idiom of technology and its popular ideological by-product, scientific management.[35]

As municipal housekeepers, women supported the Anti-Smoke League as a logical extension of the city beautiful movement. The crusade for clean air along the lakefront represented a perfect opportunity for women to play a more assertive role in the public arena as militant advocates of reform while maintaining their traditional functions as guardians of moral and physical well-being. The new public health further strengthened this drive for political legitimacy by linking the spread of tuberculosis in children to contaminated milk supplies and infected school classrooms. In 1908—the year of the Anti-Smoke League's protest—the women's lobby scored an important success by making Chicago the first large city to pass an ordinance making the pasteurization of milk compulsory.[36] This victory strengthened the resolve of women like Sergel to press their reform agenda for clean air.

Redefining Environmental Policy

The political momentum for environmental reform channeled through Chicago's network of women's organizations and reinforced by scientific research proved difficult but not impossible to blunt in the years leading up to World War I. The controversy over air quality triggered a series of well-publicized investigations that provided forums for the proponents of the two modes of thought about the urban environment to debate one another and to defend their respective professional status as experts. A review of this phase of the antismoke campaign reveals that the causes of public health and environmental protection were no match for the raw economic and political power of entrenched business interests. From the outset, the IC was strong enough to mount a cynical public relations campaign of false promises, which gave Mayor Busse enough maneuvering room to sidetrack the women's demands into the back rooms of the business leaders.[37]

The railroads' need to marshal a powerful army of consultants and lobbyists onto the political battlefield to defeat the women reflected the strength of the environmentalists' political, legal, moral, and scientific positions. The Anti-Smoke League clearly held the initiative during the early stages of the policy debate. The first inquiry, in 1908, stemmed from their petition to the city council for the electrification of the lakefront railroad. The aldermen justified focusing their hearings exclusively on the Illinois Central line because it "comes into the very best part of town. It occupies much of the lakefront. It is in the midst of a park and boulevard system which it at present greatly harms."[38]

A council committee heard testimony from several experts, including physicians and engineers. Health Commissioner Evans admitted that pinpointing causal links between smoke and disease was difficult. Nonetheless, there was no doubt in the doctor's mind that coal emissions were harmful to good health. He pointed to indirect evidence such as the stunted growth and death of Grant Park vegetation that was coated with soot and tar from passing IC trains. He also summarized several scientific studies conducted in English cities on the effects of coal smoke's invisible gases. "This accumulation of sulphurous and sulphuric acid poisons plants and men to some degree," he concluded.[39]

Assistant Smoke Inspector G. E. Ryder added weight to the health commissioner's opinions. He exposed the fallacy of the IC's efforts to mollify Chicago's women by using less smoky fuels. "The invisible gases which arise from these fuels," the engineer declared, "are as destructive to vegetation and as detrimental to public health as the visible smoke and invisible gases which are evolved from bituminous coals." Other experts laid a legal foundation for regulatory action by positing that "the right of control of the purity of the air by government is superior to the right of control of water in proportion as the purity thereof is more necessary for life and health than is that of water."[40]

The IC resorted to delaying tactics and finally responded a year later by announcing that electrification was prohibitively expensive at the current time.[41] But when the city's renamed Department of Smoke Inspection then began its own study of the city's smoke problem, the railroad's managers realized that they would have to take much more forceful steps to slow the political momentum for reform. Working through the Chicago Association of Commerce, they commissioned a group of seven experts to assess the technological feasibility of electrifying the city's rail terminals.

In September 1910, the consultants reported to the CAC executive committee, but their findings were suppressed. Only three years later, when the Alderman Theodore K. Lang exposed the cover-up, were the results of the study revealed. The railroad's demand that the report be buried was understandable because the consultants had recommended in favor of electrification on grounds of technological efficiency, cost savings, and environmental improvement. Confronted with expert opinion they did not want to hear, the railroad executives had decided to sponsor a much more comprehensive study, one that would take years to complete. Agreeing to pour up to a half-million dollars into the project, they had persuaded Mayor Busse to appoint four representatives to its seventeen-member governing board, thereby giving it official sanction. This time the staff of experts would be drawn almost exclusively from the railroad companies to ensure the right results.[42]

While the new CAC effort got underway, the railroads faced additional unfavorable reports from acknowledged sources of expert authority. In February 1911, the city's Department of Smoke Inspection issued the first comprehensive survey of coal use in Chicago. The report concluded that the railroads used less than 20 percent of the fuel consumed annually, but that "fully one half of the dirt caused by soft coal smoke comes from steam locomotives." The following year, Samuel Insull, the president of the Commonwealth Edison Company and one of the nation's foremost leaders in the utility business, offered to implement the women's demand for electrification. Speaking to the American Institute of Electrical Engineers, the English-born Chicagoan immediately distanced himself from their politics of environmental reform. Proclaiming his allegiance to the business leaders, he testified that "I am not in sympathy with an agitation to force the steam railroads in this country to electrify. That is a question ... of capital."[43]

Nonetheless, Insull then laid out plans in elaborate detail for the modernization and rationalization of the city's railroads. According to his plan, they would save tens of millions of dollars in operating expenses. In addition, his comprehensive economic calculations showed that electric traction consumed less than 40 percent of the coal used for comparable steam locomotion, representing an annual savings of about 1.3 million tons of fuel in the metropolitan area. By implication, energy conservation on this large a scale would represent a significant improvement in air quality.[44]

Conclusion: Sidetracking Environmental Reform

In spite of all of the accumulating evidence that smoke is harmful to health, the shift in decision making from the open arena of democratic politics to the closed circles of elite business and professional meetings derailed the movement for environmental reform. The momentum of a populist crusade inspired by women going door-to-door could not be sustained once the question was handed over to experts operating outside the civic sphere for resolution. Here the social construction of science and technology came under the domination of capital and the power of its controlling business interests. They would now determine not only the meaning of progress and efficiency but also the very definition of disease, at least in areas relating to an industrial economy and its environmental impacts.

By the time Alderman Lang exposed the CAC cover-up in June 1913, Sergel's Anti-Smoke League was moribund. Five years had already passed since her group had taken to the streets. Not even news of the scandalous duplicity of the CAC on behalf of the railroads could revive her campaign for clean air. Nonetheless, the CAC's betrayal of the public trust did not go unnoticed. Even the editors of the staunchly Republican, probusiness *Chicago Tribune* expressed shock. "A policy which was directed toward obtaining careful consideration of such a subject as electrification was wisely adopted," the editors reasoned, "but ill carried out when the consequence was an attempt at suppression and deceit."

A sneak preview of the CAC's new research project by one of the paper's reporters had strongly implied that it was working toward a foregone conclusion. "It is too early yet to draw many conclusions from the data in hand," the reporter had surmised, "but certain more or less startling tendencies are indicated.... There seems to be good authority for the statement that a certain amount of smoke, if not absolutely beneficial, has no deleterious effect on persons suffering from diseases of the respiratory organs. In this connection, a large and complicated chart has been prepared."[45] By the time the CAC finally released its long-delayed report, in December 1915, the entire question was moot because the nation was gearing up for war.

Ironically, this landmark study pointed toward a gradual convergence of opinion on the environmental impact of fossil fuels on the city and its inhabitants. Costing more than three hundred thousand dollars and culminating in a report that ran well over a thousand pages, the massive investigation was an impressive tour de force by the engineering and scientific communities. A steady stream of research on the invisible gases released by the burning of soft coal led inexorably to the judgment that its use was detrimental to human health in addition to the natural and built environment. The medical literature on the topic of lung disease was steadily moving toward this inescapable conclusion, and even the authors of the railroad-sponsored report had to admit that "there is a general agreement among sanitary authorities that polluted air is harmful to health." While refusing to draw any direct causal links between coal smoke and disease, the study conceded that emissions of "soot, dust, and gases" exacerbated cases of pneumonia and tuberculosis. By 1915, the American Medical Association had also completely reversed its position on the subject. "The purification of the atmosphere," its journal now trumpeted, "should ... receive the same attention as pure food and pure water are receiving, for it is just as important."[46]

The ironies of the policy debate on the smoke problem did not stop with the emerging consensus on the harmful effects of air pollution but extended to the proposed remedies. On the eve of America's entry into World War I, scientific research should have convinced the engineers to adopt a new point of view on the health impacts of industrial ecologies, and the perspectives of medical science should have resulted in plans for the protection of the environment. But the suppression of coal smoke as a public nuisance no longer received serious consideration. The logic of germ theories led away from the prevention of the social causes of ill health to the treatment of sick individuals. Early hopes of ameliorating the most egregious social conditions of the industrial city, such as child labor, inadequate housing, and dangerous work places now turned to frustration and defeat. "The main feature of the new public health," according to a recent account of the tuberculosis movement, "was a de-emphasis on the general environment and a concentration on the individual as a source of disease."[47]

Buried in the pages of the CAC report was confirmation that electrification would result in major reductions in fuel consumption and air pollution. The figures for energy savings computed by the railroads' experts closely resembled Insull's calculations of 1.3 million tons of coal a year. According to the report, if the railroads electrified, Chicago would have about 20 percent less smoke polluting its air. The engineers had no doubt about the technical feasibility of electrification within the city. To think otherwise in 1915 would have flown in the face of extensive experience and common sense. Perhaps no city in the world had such ample existing infrastructure, and Burnham's plans called for further expansion on a grand scale. Swapping electric for steam locomotives would have fit right in with his strategy of creating spacious new switching yards at the suburban fringes of the city.

But the businessmen were able to exploit the authority of experts to narrow the discourse on the formation of public policy to the one option they found acceptable, maximization of corporate profits. The bottom line of the massive report was a single economic figure. The cost of a complete conversion from steam to electric was nearly $275 million. The railroads therefore dismissed any modernization program as simply too expensive. The *Tribune* was outraged: the "report is as barren as Sahara," it charged. The CAC's straw man argument about all-or-nothing conversion was patently absurd. "Having set up a wholly unreasonable and impracticable proposal, and having exposed its unreasonableness and impracticability," the paper chided, "no alternative is discussed or proposed. . . . But what of gradual and progressive electrification?" On this telling question, the railroad leaders were conspicuous by their silence.[48]

The coming of the war put an end to the discussion of policy questions about energy and the environment. National defense production goals took priority, and Chicago's smoke abatement efforts were suspended. The results were obvious. In 1918, Health Commissioner John D. Robertson observed that "the air all too frequently was heavily laden not only with the black smoke but all the noxious gases which are produced" in the operation of steam boiler plants. The severe fuel and food shortages that brought American cities to a standstill had a pivotal effect in reorienting industrial policy makers from their focus on self-contained technologies to an emphasis on central-station electric service. Tragic outbreaks of infantile paralysis during 1916 and 1917, followed immediately by the great influenza pandemic, gave urgency to pleas for a compromise on environmental policy along the lines proposed by the engineering and business communities. The traumatic experiences of the war at home thus led to the creation in the 1920s of regional power grids, including the construction of huge generator stations far from city centers. With their fuel-efficient machinery and tall smokestacks, these huge utilities virtually eliminated visible smoke emissions while pumping ever greater amounts of invisible toxic gases into the atmosphere.[49]

The policy debate over air quality during the Progressive Era resulted in the triumph of a socially constructed vision of technological progress that did not include serious concern for the protection of the environment. The new reformers joined the old in the search for the holy grail of technological progress. From the beginning, the women of the Anti-Smoke League had looked to a technological solution, electrification. But they had also proposed a wide array of other moral, political, and legal remedies. Without all of those remedies, the public authority was powerless to force the polluters to choose between negotiating in good faith and facing intolerable penalties.

The idiom of medical science presented a fresh opportunity to look at the city's atmosphere in new ways. Under the banner of health, beauty, and morality, Chicago women took the lead in forcing decision makers to give consideration to the social costs of technology. The analogy between the water people drink and the air they breathe helped the women make a compelling case for a more inclusive concept of the public welfare, one that would bring the atmosphere, like the water supply, under the jurisdiction of government regulations. But unfortunately the new public health had the ironic effect of reorienting the attention of reformers away from the broad perspectives of social environmentalism and toward a narrow concern with individual treatment of disease. Given these crosscurrents of reform, the outcome should come as no surprise.

While more coal emissions posed a serious challenge to the engineering and business communities, the suburbanization of industry and power plants afforded an easy way for them to put both out of the sight and mind of the urban public. The war strongly reinforced this solution. In the 1920s, urban and regional planners would formulate public policy that called for technology to repair the environmental damage caused by an ever more energy-intensive society. As automobiles had once been held out as the solution to the pollution problems of the horse, now superhighways and giant power plants were touted as the best way to create the smokeless city of tomorrow. Perhaps the final irony of this story, then, is the electrification of the IC's lakefront suburban passenger trains in 1926, too late for Annie Sergel to enjoy.

CHAPTER FIFTEEN

Conclusion
Machine Age Cities

By the time of World War I, Manchester's and Chicago's moments as shock cities had long passed. Rather than objects of horror and wonder, they were now typical of large metropolitan areas in the Americas, Europe, and Asia. When the Duke of Bridgewater built his aqueduct to bring cheap coal to Manchester in the 1760s, London was the only city in the world with a million people. Now there were numerous second-rank industrial cities that exceeded this population mark. Each was different, of course, and they often were given monikers based on their own primary industries just has Cottonopolis and Porkopolis had been. But in other respects these other industrial cities shared important characteristics that made them all little Manchesters and Chicagos.

The interplay between technology and society helps account for similarities in the physical form of these industrial ecologies. The streetcar and the commuter train expanded the boundaries of the built environment, making possible the specialization of land use into distinct functional and residential districts. Giving birth to the Age of Energy, the duke's audacious aqueduct project brought the steam engine and the factory system to the city, which, in turn, engendered a novel type of urban topography. His artificial river also brought coal barges and thus unprecedented levels of dirty smoke and toxic wastes. The pollution spewing out of the factories combined with the workers' need to live in the factories' shadow to create the ecology of the industrial zones. These areas were marked by smokestacks and power plants, inadequate public amenities and commercial services, slum dwellings and unhealthy people. The rise of these working-class *quartiers* in the city center gave good reason for all who could afford it to seek safe haven in the suburbs. An emerging middle class then imposed a moral environmentalism on this bifurcated social geography to account for its inequality.

The spatial segregation of the industrial city fostered not only a historically unique physical form but also a new type of urban politics. Perhaps the main battle between labor and capital was played out inside the factories, on the shop floor. But it also overflowed into the streets, creating a divisive political geography of class and ethnicity/religion. When rich and poor, master and servant had lived in close proximity, they had benefited from mutual bonds of self-interest in maintaining good conditions in their parishes and boroughs. Infectious diseases, fires, tainted drinking supplies, noises, smells, and many other factors influencing the quality of daily life in a neighborhood were concerns that affected everyone in more or less the same way. In contrast, the geography of the industrial city often pitted one political subdivision against the next in a general struggle over how the local government would be funded and how its goods and services would be distributed.

As a result, the political formation of urban space took on much greater importance than it had in previous eras. Before the nineteenth century, the municipal corporation had little influence in shaping the built environment. It had only a limited role in regulating and operating markets and wharves, and it had no responsibility for the quality of daily life except during erratic episodes of plague and other states of emergency. But in the industrializing cities of the Victorian Age, the balance between the public and the private sectors began to shift in response to the new scale of environmental problems. The cholera epidemics of the 1830s that inspired Edwin Chadwick's Sanitary Idea marked a crossroads in the process of expanding governmental authority over the health and welfare of the community. The concurrent spatial segregation of urban society into separate spheres became embedded in the public sector as a powerful lens that bent the formation of policy through a filter of inequality. By explaining urban conditions in terms of the moral behavior of the individuals affected by those conditions, the Victorians could establish a regime of environmental injustice. Under a banner of low-cost government, moreover, local leaders could portray wide disparities in the distribution of municipal utilities and services as examples of good government.

Viewing Manchester and Chicago through the lens of political culture reveals sharp contrasts in the formation of environmental policy. In the 1840s,

Manchester's Dissenting Liberals adopted many of the traditions of its Anglican Tory opponents. Keeping tight reins on voting rights and property taxes, Town Hall remained a bastion of hierarchy and privilege. From the comfort of their suburban homes, the city's ruling elite practiced a politics of exclusion that reinforced patterns of spatial segregation by class and ethnicity/religion. The Liberals' original contribution was municipal capitalism, which facilitated private economic gain that was dressed in the utilitarian guise of profit for the Corporation.

The American Revolution's ideals of actual representation, universal manhood suffrage, and local self-government did make a difference for Chicago. The Midwestern city had to employ a set of public institutions and partisan dynamics unlike those in Manchester to cope with the problems of its industrial ecology. Chicago's explosive demographic and spatial growth in the mid-nineteenth century forced its highly privatized system of government to give way to more inclusive, citywide approaches to public health and environmental control. It did not take long for the value of the ballot box to be learned by the city's immigrant majority of Irish Catholics and German forty-eighters, who also helped to create the American Dream of home ownership. Sweeping away the segmented system with a ward-based regime of professional politicians, City Hall became a democratic, albeit anarchistic and corrupt, forum of opportunity. From the grass roots of their saloons, barbershops, and real estate offices, the party bosses promoted a politics of urban growth that offered public goods and services to all who could afford them. Restrained by the insistence on low-cost government on the part of property owners large and small, the politicians often ended up betraying the majority of their constituents for personal and partisan gain.

Political culture on both sides of the Atlantic encouraged urban imperialism at the expense of nature. In spite of pollution problems, the Victorians rarely questioned the expansion of the city's commercial markets and the industrial production that reduced the natural world into a mere set of commodities. Manchester's spinning mills created the first global-scale model of this ruthless exploitation. Soil exhaustion and an endless search for virgin land became the hallmarks of plantation society in the Americas, to say nothing of the far greater, human toll of racial slavery: the cotton trade linked Africa and the Americas to Manchester's textile industry. In the name of progress, Chicago too became an insatiable engine of consumption, stripping bare the forests of the Midwest, slaughtering the buffalo of the Great Plains, and uprooting prairies and planting coals towns in their place. The success of the two cities in transmuting nature into gold reinforced belief in this alchemy of industrialization among their entrepreneurs. Throughout the nineteenth century, they and their rivals in other cities engaged in a fierce competition to build bigger and faster machines of production, simultaneously accelerating the pace and extent of the degradation of the environment.

Toward the end of the century, the proliferation and the sheer magnitude of industrial ecologies had reached crisis proportions in the United States and Europe. Some scientists predicted the exhaustion of the coal supply; others foresaw racial degeneration among the masses living in these heavily polluted environments. The voices of doom took on urgency in the midst of real events such as typhoid fever epidemics, deadly fogs, catastrophic floods, and militant protests by organized labor against insufferable conditions in both the factories and the neighborhoods. Novel ideas also helped build conviction among the middle classes on behalf of urban reform. Germ theories of disease eroded confidence that spatial barriers alone were sufficient to keep families safe from deadly infections, but at the same time, the new knowledge offered hope. By applying the powerful tools of modern technology and scientific management, a rising generation of experts could use the new theories to solve old problems. Launching their project to reconstruct the city, the reformers promised that uplift in the conditions of the working classes would lead ultimately to a restoration of moral order.

In many respects, the urban Progressives made significant headway toward the fulfillment of their goals. Muckraking journalism was one of their most effective tactics as they mounted a battle against the "shame of the city."[1] The reformers adopted a new approach, social environmentalism, to attack specific problems of the industrial city, such as slum housing, contaminated water, and dirty air. They also used an innovative political style of coalition building in order to overcome opposition from special interests. The Progressives sought to shift the balance of power between the public and private sectors and to produce a more highly regulated capitalism. They put their faith in nonpartisan boards of experts to solve problems in the step-by-step fashion of bureaucracy. In both Manchester and Chicago, they campaigned for the enactment of stiffer health, building, and boiler-inspection codes and worked for the professionalization of inspectional services. In addition, they went beyond municipal borders to support the creation of regional agencies of environmental control such as the Mersey and Irwell Joint Committee and the Sanitary District of Chicago.

On a national level, the Progressives planted the seedbed of the modern preservation and conservation movements. Octavia Hill's involvement in the Thirlmere Defense Association led her to become one of the founders of

England's National Trust. In the United States a similar project, the Hetch Hetchy Dam in Yosemite, California, inspired the naturalist John Muir to start the Sierra Club. Although wilderness preservation remained the concern of only a small elite, the conservation of natural resources gained the support of Parliament and Congress. In the United States President Teddy Roosevelt became an outspoken champion of legislation designed to ensure the wise use of the nation's land and water. One of his top lieutenants, Chief Forester of the Agriculture Department Gifford Pinchot, attributed the origins of the "conservation idea" to a conference organized, ironically, by Lyman E. Cooley of the Lakes-to-the-Gulf Deep Waterway Association.[2] In spite of the limitations of the intent and enforcement of the new laws, the legislation was evidence that the movement for environmental reform was heading in the right direction.

By the 1920s, the cities were a far better place to live than they had been during Chicago's moment as a shock city. True enough, they were a far cry from the utopias envisioned by Edward Bellamy, Ebenezer Howard, and Daniel Burnham. Yet the overall quality of daily life had been enhanced by Progressivism. The significant, even dramatic, decline in mortality deserves first mention. In the four decades between 1880 and 1920, the rate fell from 26.2 deaths per 1,000 persons to 16.8 in Manchester, and from 20.8 to 14.2 in Chicago.[3] Although sorting out the exact causes of these declines is difficult, the result is nonetheless impressive. The more qualitative indicators of reform include better standards of housing construction; additional playgrounds and parks; less contamination of water, milk, and food; the removal of sewage from densely populated areas; and cleaner streets and alleyways as horses were replaced with cars and trucks. The growth of public welfare agencies and social settlement houses also enhanced the well-being of the community.

In contrast, air pollution got worse in geographic extent and probably in absolute intensity as well. Rapid-transit lines, interurban electric trains, and automobiles expanded the boundaries of the city to metropolitan proportions. The consumption of energy continued to grow at an exponential pace. Traditional sources of smokestack emissions were not reduced, and the 1920s became the heyday of regional grids, or "giant power," for the electric utility industry. The lightening bolt was one of the icons of the Machine Age; the other was the assembly line that produced the Model-T Ford. As early as 1915, investigators in Chicago observed that "during the morning and evening hours, the blue haze of automobile smoke is distinctly noticeable in important thoroughfares."[4] The term *Fordism* expressed not only a modern method of industrial production but also a popular culture of mass consumption. New layers of energy technology laid the foundation for that culture's ascendancy.

The legacy of Progressivism was thus mixed. Urban reformers made steady gains in some specific areas, such as fighting waterborne diseases, but lost ground in others, such as battling air pollution. Ultimately they were unable to answer the bigger questions embedded in Tocqueville's paradox of progress. In fact, very few of them paused to consider whether the holy grail of a higher standard of living needed redefinition in terms other than the quantitative measure of more stuff for more people. At best, the reformers sought to curb needless waste so rising levels of consumption could be sustained indefinitely into the future. The Progressives did not raise serious doubts about the spatial segregation of the city by class, ethnicity/religion, and race. Their plans for suburbia and garden cities retained the Victorians' social geography of separate spheres. The reintegration of society was not a part of their admirable efforts to ameliorate urban environmental problems and restore moral order. Given all the limits of reform, a house in the suburbs remained the sanctuary of safety for those who could afford it.

In the postwar decade, Los Angeles appropriately became the first shock city of the Machine Age. Diverting an entire river through a 240-mile aqueduct, city boosters turned a sun-baked desert into a virtual Garden of Eden. The gas-guzzling automobile then fueled the city's mushroomlike growth into a "fragmented metropolis" of highly segregated suburban enclaves. Touted as a wonder of environmental control, the city also showed signs that it would suffer the horror of suffocating in the fumes of the millions of vehicles that made possible the rampant sprawl. Seeking to escape the smog, some Angelinos would move farther out, compounding the problem of auto emissions and highway congestion still more. Others moved to newly built houses that were perched precariously on hilltops and seashore cliffs, setting the stage the next round of ecological disasters. And the next shock cities would continue to appear in due course as the forces of urban expansion and rising energy use and industrial production continued to gather momentum around the world.[5]

NOTES

Chapter One

1. Alexis de Tocqueville, *Democracy in America*, 2 vols. (1835; reprint, New York: Vintage, 1945); and see Abraham S. Eisenstadt, ed., *Reconsidering Tocqueville's Democracy in America* (New Brunswick, NJ: Rutgers University Press, 1988), for a recent appraisal. See Seymour Martin Lipset, *The First New Nation: The United States in Historical and Comparative Perspective* (New York: Basic Books, 1963), for the phrase "first new nation."

2. Alexis de Tocqueville, *Journeys to England and Ireland* (1836?; reprint, London: Faber and Faber, 1908), 94, for the quotation; and see Seymour Drescher, *Tocqueville and England* (Cambridge, MA: Harvard University Press, 1964).

3. Drescher, *Tocqueville and England*, 65, for the first quotation; Tocqueville, *Journeys to England and Ireland*, 104, for the remaining quotations.

4. Max Lerner, "Tocqueville and America," in Alexis de Tocqueville, *Democracy in America*, ed. J. P. Mayer and Max Lerner (New York: Harper and Row, 1966), xliii–iv, for the first quotation, and xxv–lxxxviii and 528–31 for the chapter (vol. 2, pt. 2, chap. 20), "How an Aristocracy May Be Created by Industry," that draws directly on Tocqueville's experience in Manchester. See Tocqueville, *Journeys to England and Ireland*, 108, for the second quotation. For an insightful analysis of the two volumes, see Seymour Drescher, "More than America: Comparison and Synthesis in *Democracy in America*," in Eisenstadt, ed., *Reconsidering Tocqueville's Democracy in America*, 77–93. On the process of class formation, see E. P. Thompson, *The Making of the English Working Class* (New York: Vintage, 1966).

5. Tocqueville, *Journeys to England and Ireland*, 106–7, for the quotations.

6. Ibid., 105–6, for the first two quotations; Tocqueville, *Democracy in America*, 2:529, for the last quotation. After explaining how the laws of economics were conspiring to divide the classes, the full passage states that "there is no resemblance between master and workman, and daily they become more different. There is no connection except that between the first and last links in a long chain. Each occupies a place made for him, from which he does not move. One is in a state of constant, narrow, and necessary dependence on the other and seems to have been born to obey, as the other was to command. What is this, if not an aristocracy?"

7. Tocqueville, *Democracy in America*, 2:528–31; Tocqueville, *Journeys to England and Ireland*, 108–10. On technology and gender in the textile industry, see Maxine Berg, *The Machinery Question and the Making of Political Economy, 1815–1848* (Cambridge: Cambridge University Press, 1980).

8. Tocqueville, *Democracy in America*, 2:530–31; Drescher, *Tocqueville and England*.

9. Tocqueville, *Journeys to England and Ireland*, 105–6.

10. For a useful introduction, see Merritt Smith and Leo Marx, eds., *Does Technology Drive History? The Dilemma of Technological Determinism* (Cambridge, MA: MIT Press, 1994).

11. Sam Bass Warner Jr., *Streetcar Suburbs: The Progress of Growth in Boston, 1870–1900* (Cambridge, MA: Harvard University Press, 1962); and Sam Bass Warner Jr., *The Urban Wilderness: A History of the American City* (New York: Harper and Row, 1972). For a case study of neighborhood secession, see Richard Sennett, *Families against the City: Middle Class Homes of Industrial Chicago, 1872–1890* (Cambridge, MA: Harvard University Press, 1970).

12. Paul Boyer, *Urban Masses and Moral Order in America, 1820–1920* (Cambridge, MA: Harvard University Press, 1978).

13. For a useful introduction, see Peter Coates, *Nature: Western Attitudes since Ancient Times* (Berkeley: University of California Press, 1998). Still useful is Lewis Mumford, *Technics and Civilization* (New York: Harcourt, Brace, and World, 1934).

14. C. J. Shearman, "On the Causes of Sickness and Mortality in the Manufacturing Towns of the North-West of England," *Literary and Philosophical Society of Manchester, Proceedings* 2 (1862): 186.

15. For a recent historiographical review of the field, consider William Cronon, "A Place for Stories: Nature, History, and Narrative," *Journal of American History* 78 (March 1992): 1347–76; Martin Melosi, "The Place of the City in Environmental History," *Environmental History Review* 17 (Spring 1993): 1–21; and Christine Meisner Rosen and Joel Arthur Tarr, "The Importance of an Urban Perspective in Environmental History," *Journal of Urban History* 20 (May 1994): 299–310. For a consideration of social theory, see Rick Halpern, "Respatializing Marxism and Remapping Urban Space," *Journal of Urban History* 23 (January 1997): 221–30; and David Goldblatt, *Social Theory and the Environment* (Boulder, CO: Westview, 1996). On the origins of the new environmentalism, see Samuel P. Hays, *Beauty, Health, and Permanence: Environmental Politics in the United States, 1955–1985* (New York: Cambridge University

Press, 1987); and Robert Gottlieb, *Forcing the Spring: The Transformation of the American Environmental Movement* (Washington, DC: Island, 1993).

16. For England, see Martin J. Weiner, *English Culture and the Decline of the Industrial Spirit, 1850–1980* (Cambridge: Cambridge University Press, 1981); for the United States, see John F. Kasson, *Civilizing the Machine: Technology and Republican Values in America, 1776–1900* (New York: Penguin, 1977).

17. Bill Luckin, "Sites, Cities, and Technologies," *Journal of Urban History* 17 (August 1991): 429.

18. For a provocative introduction to present-day urban environmentalism, see Mike Davis, *Ecology of Fear: Los Angeles and the Imagination of Disaster* (New York: Metropolitan Books/Henry Holt, 1998). For an overview of the twentieth century, see Gottlieb, *Forcing the Spring*. For environmental justice issues, consider Giovanna Di Chiro, "Nature as Community: The Convergence of Environment and Social Justice," in *Uncommon Ground: Toward Reinventing Nature*, ed. William Cronon (New York: Norton, 1995), 298–320; Jeffrey C. Ellis, "On the Search for a Root Cause: Essentialist Tendencies in Environmental Discourse," in Cronon, *Uncommon Ground*, 256–68; and Martin V. Melosi, "Equity, Eco-Racism and Environmental History," *Environmental History Review* 19 (Fall 1995): 1–16. Also see the model case study by Andrew Hurley, *Environmental Inequalities: Class, Race, and Industrial Pollution in Gary, Indiana, 1945–1980* (Chapel Hill: University of North Carolina Press, 1995).

19. Asa Briggs, *Victorian Cities* (London: Odhams, 1963), 56, 12, 55, respectively. For a careful consideration of this work, see its foreword, by Andrew Lees and Lynn Hollen Lees, i–xiv. Also see Thompson, *Making of the English Working Class*; and Harold J. Dyos, ed., *The Study of Urban History* (London: Arnold, 1968). For a definition of the new social history, see Alice Kessler-Harris, "Social History," in *The New American History*, ed. Eric Foner (Philadelphia: Temple University Press, 1990), 163–84; Eugene D. Genovese and Elizabeth Fox-Genovese, "The Political Crisis of Social History: A Marxian Perspective," *Journal of Social History* 10 (Winter 1976): 205–20; and Jon C. Teaford, "Finis for Tweed and Steffens: Rewriting the History of Urban Rule," *Reviews in American History* 10 (December 1982): 133–49. For an assessment of urban history, see Howard Gillette Jr. and Zane Miller, eds., *American Urbanism: A Historiographical Review* (Westport, CT: Greenwood, 1987). The observers of each city have received historical attention. For Manchester, see Steven Marcus, *Engels, Manchester, and the Working Class* (New York: Random House, 1974). For Chicago, see Arnold Lewis, *An Early Encounter with Tomorrow: Europeans, Chicago's Loop, and the World's Colombian Exposition* (Urbana: University of Illinois Press, 1997). For an analysis of the larger context of the city as idea during the nineteenth century, see Andrew Lees, *Cities Perceived: Urban Society in European and American Thought, 1820–1940* (New York: Columbia University Press, 1985).

20. J. P. Kay, *The Moral and Physical Condition of the Working Classes Employed in the Cotton Manufacture in Manchester* (1831; reprint, Shannon: Irish University Press, 1971); Léon M. Faucher, *Manchester in 1844: Its Present Condition and Future Prospects* (London: Simpkin, Marshall, 1844), 16.

21. Friedrich Engels, *The Condition of the Working Class in England* (1845; reprint, Stanford, CA: Stanford University Press, 1958), 61; Jane Addams, *Twenty Years at Hull-House* (1910; reprint, New York: Signet, 1961), 81; William T. Stead, *If Christ Came to Chicago* (Chicago: Laird and Lee, 1894), 187, for the respective quotations. Engels was aware of Kay's work and makes several references to it in his book *Condition of the Working Class* (passim). For different perspectives on Kay's importance, compare Graeme Davison, "The City as a Natural System: Theories of Urban Society in Early Nineteenth-Century Britain," in *The Pursuit of Urban History*, ed. Derek Fraser and Anthony Sutcliffe (London: Edward Arnold, 1983), 349–70; Mary Poovey, "Curing the 'Social Body' in 1832: James Phillips Kay and the Irish in Manchester," *Gender and History* 5 (1993): 196–211; and Christopher Hamlin, "The Industrial Revolution as a Physiological Problem," a paper presented to the Twentieth International Congress of History of Science (Liege, Belgium, July 1997). For additional sources on visitor descriptions of the industrial city, see the preface of William Cronon's *Nature's Metropolis: Chicago and the Great West* (New York: Norton, 1991), which has a wonderful compilation of descriptions of Chicago as a city of smoke. I thank Bill Luckin for raising questions about the city as a place for experiencing disorientation. But also see Karen Sawislak, *Smoldering City: Chicagoans and the Great Fire, 1871–1874* (Chicago: University of Chicago Press, 1996); and Carl Smith, *Urban Disorder and the Shape of Disbelief* (Chicago: University of Chicago Press, 1995).

22. Kay, *Moral and Physical Condition*, 6; Robert Fishman, *Bourgeois Utopias: The Rise and Fall of Suburbia* (New York: Basic Books, 1987), 74. Also see Briggs, *Victorian Cities*, 88–138, for a first-rate chapter on Manchester as a "Symbol of a New Age." While preindustrial cities had distinct social topographies, they were not marked by such stark segregation by class. In addition, the location of a large proportion of the poor in the suburbs meant much lower concentrations of poverty. See M. J. Power, "The Social Topography of Restoration London," in *London 1500–1700: The Making of the Metropolis*, ed. A. L. Beier and Roger Finlay (London: Longman, 1986), 199–223.

23. Engels, *Condition of the Working Class*, 55, 56. For insight on Engel's experience in Manchester, see Marcus, *Engels, Manchester, and the Working Class*. Also see John R. Stilgoe, *Metropolitan Corridor: Railroads and the American Scene* (New Haven, CT: Yale University Press, 1983); and Wolfgang Schivelbusch, *The Railway Journey: The Industrialization of Time and Space in the 19th Century* (Berkeley: University of California Press, 1977).

24. Briggs, *Victorian Cities*, 17.

25. See Christopher Hamlin, *Public Health and Social Justice in the Age of Chadwick: Britain, 1800–1854* (Cambridge: Cambridge University Press, 1998), for a valuable discussion of contemporary definitions of public health and welfare.

26. Engels, *Condition of the Working Class*, 56. Also see Hamlin, *Public Health and Social Justice*; and Anthony S. Wohl, *Endangered Lives: Public Health in Victorian Britain* (Cambridge, MA: Harvard University Press, 1983), for a graphic picture of the health effects of

the industrial city on its inhabitants. Of course, this approach does not diminish the importance of studies that consider the city's impacts on the larger environment. Cronon's *Nature's Metropolis* offers a model of this type of scholarship.

27. On the workplace environment, consider David Rosner and Gerald Markowitz, eds., *Dying for Work: Workers' Safety and Health in Twentieth-Century America* (Bloomington: Indiana University Press, 1989); and Christopher C. Sellers, *Hazards of the Job: From Industrial Disease to Environmental Health Science* (Chapel Hill: University of North Carolina Press, 1997). On mapping the public health of the city, see Marilyn E. Pooley and Colin G. Pooley, "Health, Society, and Environment in Nineteenth-Century Manchester," in *Urban Disease and Mortality in Nineteenth-Century England*, ed. R. Wood and John J. H. Woodward (London: Betsford, 1984), 148–75. This study is fairly basic, but a much more sophisticated effort is under way using death certificates in London. See Bill Luckin and Graham Mooney, "Urban History and Historical Epidemiology: The Case of London, 1860–1920," *Urban History* 24 (March 1997): 37–55.

28. David Sibley, *Geographies of Exclusion: Society and Difference in the West* (London: Routledge, 1995), ix, for the first quotation; Mary Douglas, *Purity and Danger: An Analysis of the Concepts of Pollution and Taboo* (London: Routledge, 1966), 2, for the second quotation.

29. City of Chicago, Department of Health, *Annual Report* (1892): 8–9, for the quotation. See Fishman, *Bourgeois Utopias*; and Michael H. Ebner, *Creating Chicago's North Shore: A Suburban History* (Chicago: University of Chicago Press, 1988), for a discussion of the suburban ethos. For a glimpse of the Irish in Manchester, see M. Busteed and R. Hodgson, "Irish Migration and Settlement in Nineteenth Century Manchester, with Special Reference to the Angel Meadow District," *Irish Geography* 27 (1994): 1–13. Also see James Gilbert, *Perfect Cities: Chicago's Utopias of 1893* (Chicago: University of Chicago Press, 1991), for insight on the ways in which the planners of the World's Fair used spatial segregation to embody their ideas of social and moral order; and Carl Smith, *Urban Disorder*, for a contribution to the understanding of Victorian concerns about the city as a place of disorder.

30. Briggs, *Victorian Cities*, 20, 16, respectively for the quotations; see also Genovese and Fox-Genovese, "Political Crisis." For works on women, see Suellen M. Hoy, "'Municipal Housekeeping': The Role of Women in Improving Urban Sanitation Practices, 1880–1917," in *Pollution and Reform in American Cities, 1870–1930*, ed. Martin V. Melosi (Austin: University of Texas Press, 1980), 173–98; Nancy Tomes, "The Private Side of Public Health: Sanitary Science, Domestic Hygiene, and the Germ Theory, 1870–1900," *Bulletin of the History of Medicine* 64 (Winter 1990): 509–39; Harold L. Platt, "'Invisible Gases': Smoke, Gender, and the Redefinition of Environmental Policy in Chicago, 1900–1920," *Planning Perspectives* 10 (January 1995): 67–97; Maureen A. Flanagan, *Seeing with Their Hearts: Chicago Women and the Vision of the Good City, 1871–1933* (Princeton, NJ: Princeton University Press, 2002); and Angela Gugliotta, "Class, Gender, and Coal Smoke: Gender Ideology and Environmental Injustice in Pittsburgh, 1868–1914," *Environmental History* 5 (April 2000): 165–93.

31. Terrence J. McDonald, "The Burdens of Urban History: The Theory of the State in Recent American Social History," *Studies in American Political Development* 3 (1989): 3–29, followed by Ira Katznelson's "The Burdens of Urban History: Comment," 30–51, and McDonald's "Reply," 51–55. Also see Terrence J. McDonald, "Introduction," in William L. Riordan, *Plunkitt of Tammany Hall*, ed. Terrence J. McDonald (Boston: Bedford/St. Martin's, 1994), 1–41. For early statements of the problem, see sources in note 19 above. For a critique similar to McDonald's from the point of view of a political scientist, see Kenneth Finegold, *Experts and Politicians: Reform Challenges to Machine Politics in New York, Cleveland, and Chicago* (Princeton, NJ: Princeton University Press, 1995), 3–32.

32. For definitions of working-class environmentalism, see sources in note 18 above.

33. In the case of Chicago, see Robin Einhorn, *Property Rules: Political Economy in Chicago, 1833–1872* (Chicago: University of Chicago Press, 1991), for the early period. Also see Clifton K. Yearly, *The Money Machines: The Breakdown and Reform of Governmental and Party Finance in the North, 1860–1920* (Albany: State University of New York Press, 1970). For insight on how local government works today, see the *Chicago Tribune*'s investigation of a day in the life of the City Council (2–4 November 1997).

34. Tocqueville, *Journeys to England and Ireland*, 105, 106.

Chapter Two

1. A. B. Reach, *Manchester and the Textile Districts in 1849*, ed. C. Aspin (Helmshore, U.K.: Helmshore Local History Society, 1972), vi for the quotation and v–vii for background. On the cholera epidemic in London, see Bill Luckin, *Pollution and Control: A Social History of the Thames in the Nineteenth Century* (Bristol: Hilger, 1986), 69–99; and see Anthony S. Wohl, *Endangered Lives: Public Health in Victorian Britain* (Cambridge, MA: Harvard University Press, 1983), 118–41, for insight on contemporary reactions to the epidemics. The 1848–1849 scourge would eventually take 62,000 lives. For the American phase of the epidemic, see Charles Rosenberg, *The Cholera Years: The United States in 1832, 1849, and 1866* (Chicago: University of Chicago Press, 1962).

2. Reach, *Manchester*, 1.

3. Mike Williams and D. A. Farnie, *Cotton Mills in Greater Manchester* (Preston, U.K.: Carnegie, 1992), 20, passim, for a similar, modern perspective on the development of the textile towns of Lancashire. In this context, an essential introduction to a vast literature on the Industrial Revolution includes Geoffrey Timmins, *The Last Shift: The Decline of Handloom Weaving in Nineteenth-Century Lancashire* (Manchester: Manchester University Press, 1993); Robin Lloyd-Jones and M. J. Lewis, *Manchester and the Age of the Factory* (London: Croom-Helm, 1988); E. P. Thompson, *The Making of the English Working Class* (New York: Vintage, 1966); Eric J. Hobsbawm, *Industry and Empire* (London: Weidenfeld and Nicolson, 1969); and Maxine Berg, *The Age of Manufactures: Industry, Innovation, and Work*, 2nd ed. (London: Routledge, 1994).

4. E. P. Thompson, as quoted in Reach, *Manchester*, v. For insight on the limits of middle-class penetration of working-class life in the industrial city, see Clive Behagg,

"Secrecy, Ritual, and Folk Violence: The Opacity of the Workplace in the First Half of the Nineteenth Century," in *Popular Culture and Custom in Nineteenth Century England*, ed. Robert D. Storch (London: Croom Helm, 1982), 154–79.

5. Christopher Hamlin, *Public Health and Social Justice in the Age of Chadwick: Britain, 1800–1854* (Cambridge: Cambridge University Press, 1998), for the single best introduction to the history of public health during the Victorian Era. Also see Hamlin's valuable and stimulating study *A Science of Impurity: Water Analysis in Nineteenth Century Britain* (Bristol: Hilger, 1990). For broad perspectives on the political origins of the market system in England, see Karl Polanyi, *The Great Transformation* (Boston: Beacon, 1944).

6. See James Wheeler, *Manchester: Political, Social, and Commercial History* (Manchester: Simms and Dinham, 1842), 245–51, for statistical data. The earliest use of a term to denote an interrelated system of cities that I could find was in the Manchester Statistical Society's *Report ... on the Condition of the Working Classes, in an Extensive Manufacturing District, in 1834, 1835, and 1836. Read at the Statistical Section of the British Association ... 1837* (London: Ridgway et al., 1838). This was followed four years later by William Cooke Taylor's *Notes of a Tour in the Manufacturing Districts of Lancashire*, 3rd ed., Reprints of Economic Classics (1842; reprint, New York: Kelly, 1968).

7. Hugh Malet, *Bridgewater: The Canal Duke, 1736–1803*, rev. ed. (1961; reprint, Manchester: Manchester University Press, 1977), 65 for the first quotation, 52–67 for an account of the construction of the canal. See J. Aikin, *A Description of the Country ... round Manchester* (London: Stockdale, 1795), 113–14, for the second quotation and for a contemporary account of the project.

8. For the development of canals and other means of improved transportation in the Manchester region, see Owen Ashmore, *The Industrial Archaeology of Lancashire* (Newton Abbot, U.K.: David and Charles, 1969). For national perspectives, see the contemporary compendium by Joseph Priestley, *Historical Account of the Navigable Rivers, Canals, and Railways throughout Great Britain*, 2nd ed., Reprints of Economic Classics (New York: Kelly, 1968); and the more recent surveys, Charles Hadfield, *British Canals: An Illustrated History* (London: Phoenix House, 1959); and J. Douglas Porteous, *Canal Ports: The Urban Achievement of the Canal Age* (London: Academic Press, 1977), 3–35.

9. Francis Egerton, Duke of Bridgewater, as quoted in Malet, *Bridgewater*, 80.

10. Ibid., 27–43. When it was by carried by packhorses and carts that held loads of 2,000–4,000 pounds when conditions permitted, Worsley coal delivered to the urban market commanded an average price of 5.5d per hundredweight (cwt). From 1761 to 1793, the duke charged 3.5d/cwt. He then raised the price to 4d/cwt, the maximum set in his parliamentary acts. For insight on coal mining in Lancashire before the Industrial Revolution, see John Langton, *Geographical Change and Industrial Revolution: Coalmining in South West Lancashire, 1590–1799*, Cambridge Geographical Studies, No. 11 (Cambridge: Cambridge University Press, 1979), which includes an explanation of measures of weight in the coal mining industry on pp. 243–47.

The first basic measurement was the basket, which was initially a measure of volume but gradually became a measure of weight, 120 pounds. Thus, a hundredweight, or cwt, also became a 120 pounds, and a ton was 20 cwt, or 2400 pounds.

11. See note 3, above; R. L. Hills, *Power in the Industrial Revolution* (New York: Kelly, 1970); R. P. Sieferele, "The Energy System: A Basic Concept of Environmental History," in *The Silent Countdown: Essays in European Environmental History*, eds P. Brimblecome and C. Pfister (Berlin: Springer-Verlag, 1990), 9–20; and Eric Clavering, "The Coal Mills of Northeast England: The Use of Waterwheels for Draining Coal Mines, 1600–1750," *Technology and Culture* 36 (April 1995): 211–41.

12. Clavering, "Coal Mills," 212–13, for the quotation; Richard G. Wilkinson, "The English Industrial Revolution," in *The Ends of the Earth: Perspectives on Modern Environmental History*, ed. Donald Worster (New York: Cambridge University Press, 1988), 80–99; and John Hatcher, *The History of the British Coal Industry*, vol. 1, *Before 1700: Towards the Age of Coal* (Oxford: Clarendon, 1993). While the transition from firewood to coal came too late to save London from burning down in 1666, it was well enough along to influence architectural standards and building codes for the city's reconstruction after the fire. Also consider the effects of the wood famine on the colonization of North America. See John U. Nef, "An Early Energy Crisis and Its Consequences," *Scientific American* 237 (November 1977): 140–57; and William H. Te Brake, "Air Pollution and Fuel Crisis in Pre-Industrial London, 1250–1650," *Technology and Culture* 16 (1975): 337–59. For Manchester coal statistics, see Malet, *Bridgewater*, 78–82.

13. See Malet, *Bridgewater*, 78–82; and Hills, *Power*, 89–115. For estimates of the number of engines in the eighteenth century, see Asa Briggs, *The Power of Steam: An Illustrated History of the World's Steam Age* (Chicago: University of Chicago Press, 1982), 50–54. A British hogshead is equal to 54 imperial gallons or 64.85 U.S. gallons. Newcomen's original engine, then, could pump a maximum of 7,782 U.S. gallons per hour, which is equivalent to 5.5 horsepower. In terms of efficiency, these machines reached only 5 percent, compared to 50–60 percent for waterwheels of the same period. See Clavering, "Coal Mills," 214–29.

14. Malet, *Bridgewater*, 84–92. Porteous, in *Canal Ports*, 20–22, also shows that the duke had a water mill that served several purposes at Worsley. The mill, which became the center of an integrated economic village, processed not only coal, but also stone, lime, sand, dirt, and manure. The mill ground food for the workers, sawed wood that would be used for mine timbers and boat making, and mixed sand and mortar for use as building materials.

15. Clavering, "Coal Mills," which provides a richly detailed analysis of the predominance of waterpower technologies in the area of Newcastle upon Tyne. For the cultural reception of the steam engine, see Donald S. L. Cardwell, *From Watt to Clausius: The Rise of Thermodynamics in the Early Industrial Age* (Ithaca, NY: Heinemann, 1971), 67–120; and Greg Myers, "Nineteenth-Century Popularizations of Thermodynamics

and the Rhetoric of Social Prophecy," in *Energy and Entropy: Science and Culture in Victorian Britain, Essays from Victorian Studies*, ed. Patrick Brantlinger (Bloomington: Indiana University Press, 1989), 307–38. See Porteous, *Canal Ports*, 16 for the number of canal acts; and Priestley, *Historical Account of the Navigable Rivers, Canals, and Railways*, for an inventory of them.

16. See below in the section titled "Hands and Feet, Hooves and Yokes."

17. Manchester cottons were fustian blends of either linen or woolen warps and cotton woofs. The cotton yarns produced by hand-spinning methods were not strong enough for the warp.

18. Aikin, *Description of the Country*, 154, for the quotation; Ashmore, *Industrial Archaeology*, 27–72; and see note 3, above. For a general introduction to Manchester's role, see Nicholas J. Frangopalo, ed., *Rich Inheritance: A Guide to the History of Manchester* (Manchester: Manchester Education Committee, 1962), 39–45; and Alan Kidd, *Manchester*, Town and City Histories, ed. Stephen Constantine (Keele, Staffordshire: Ryburn/Keele University Press, 1993), 11–37.

19. Thomas Baines and William Fairbairn, *Lancashire and Cheshire Past and Present*, 2 vols. (London: Mackenzie, 1867), 1:84 for the quotation and 1:1–140 for a finely detailed description of the region. For the best survey of the watershed as an industrial ecology, see "First Report of the Commissioners . . . The Pollution of Rivers (Mersey and Ribble Basins)," vol. 1: "Reports and Plans," *Parliamentary Papers* (1870), vol. 40. Also see J. F. Bateman, *History and Description of the Manchester Waterworks* (Manchester: Day, 1884), 39–55; and Hills, *Power*, 94–100.

20. Richard Wright Proctor, *Memories of Manchester Streets* (Manchester: Sutcliffe, 1874), 2–3, for the quotation. Proctor was referring to the 1820s, when he and friends would swim in the Irwell River and fish for eels with their hands. "Even the river Irwell," he lamented, "though now leaving the foot of Hunt's bank darkly and unlovably flowed on its ancient way, within our limited remembrance, a much cleaner, purer stream" (pp. 5–8). For additional testimony twenty years later on the river as a fading amenity for children (and adults), see Louis M. Hayes, *Reminiscences of Manchester* (Manchester: Sherratt and Hughes, 1905), 61–63. For an early reference to Hunt's Bank as a prominent landmark in Manchester, see the first act creating the Mersey and Irwell Navigation (1720, 7 George, c. 15), which refers in the preface to the path "from Liverpool . . . to a place called Hunts-bank in Manchester."

21. Joseph E. Inikori, "Slavery and the Revolution in Cotton Textile Production in England," in *The Atlantic Slave Trade: Effects on Economies, Societies, and Peoples in Africa, the Americas, and Europe*, eds. Joseph E. Inikori and Stanley L. Engerman (Durham: University of North Carolina Press, 1992), 145–82. Also see Hobsbawm, *Industry and Empire*, chaps. 1–2; Jane Jacobs, *Cities and the Wealth of Nations* (New York: Random/Vintage, 1984); Robert L. Heilbroner, *The Worldly Philosophers* (New York: Simon and Schuster, 1953). For insight on where the profits went from the first revolution in spinning, consider C. Knick Harley, "Cotton Textile Prices and the Industrial Revolution," *Economic History Review* 1 (1998): 49–83.

22. Aikin, *Description of the Country*, 167 for the quotation and 167–74 for a detailed account of the processes of spinning and weaving. Also see Andrew Ure, *The Cotton Manufacture of Great Britain*, Reprints in Social and Economic History, ed. S. B. Saul (1836; reprint, London: Johnson Reprint, 1970), 1:169–273, for a second detailed description of the machines' operations; Timmons, *Last Shift*, 40–41, for calculations of the time spent in preparing and spinning a pound of cotton; and Hills, *Power*, 91–115, on horse power on the farm. Also see Maxine Berg, "Women's Work, Mechanisation, and the Early Phases of Industrialisation in England," in *The Historical Meaning of Work*, ed. Patrick Joyce (Cambridge: Cambridge University Press, 1987), 69–76; and Jan de Vries, "The Industrial Revolution and the Industrious Revolution," *Journal of Economic History* 54 (June 1994): 249–70. The quality of the yarn was measured in the count of hanks per pound of cotton. A hank was 840 yards of yarn. For example, a fine cotton yarn of "100 count," i.e., 100 hanks, represented a pound of cotton spun into a length of yarn 84,000 yards long.

23. Timmins, *Last Shift*, 37–41; Frangopalo, *Rich Inheritance*, 39–45; Williams and Farnie, *Cotton Mills*, 13–47; Harley, "Cotton Textile Prices." Also see Seigfried Giedion, *Mechanization Takes Command* (New York: Oxford University Press, 1948); Gilbert J. French, *Life and Times of Samuel Crompton*, Documents in Social History, ed. Anthony Adams (1859; reprint, New York: Kelly); and W. English, *The Textile Industry* (London: Longman, 1969).

24. Aikin, *Description of the Country*, 154 for the quotation and 13–20, 157–69, 183–92. For land-use statistics, see Baines and Fairbairn, *Lancashire and Cheshire*, 1:30–31. The 28 percent of the land that was not under cultivation, or 317,000 acres, was wasteland of mountain and moor. Also see Baines and Fairbairn, *Lancashire and Cheshire*, 71–72, for the horses of Lancashire. For a good discussion of the symbiotic growth of these "natural" sources of power, see Hills, *Power*, 89–115. For a closely related approach to changes in energy use that posits a model of self-reinforcing symbiosis as opposed to a linear transition, see Francis T. Evans, "Roads, Railways, and Canals: Technical Choices in 19th-Century Britain," *Technology and Culture* 22 (1975): 1–34.

25. Aikin, *Description of the Country*, 157, for the quotation; see also pp. 178–81; Lloyd-Jones and Lewis, *Manchester and the Age of the Factory*, 21–37.

26. See the sources listed in note 24, above, for horses. In addition, see F. M. L. Thompson, "Nineteenth Century Horse Sense," in *The Industrial Revolutions*, vol. 3, *The Industrial Revolution in Britain*, eds. Julian Hoppit and R. A. Church (London: Blackwell, 1994), 264–87. For population figures, see Aikin, *Description of the Country*, 154–57; and the parliamentary census statistics listed in Baines and Fairbairn, *Lancashire and Cheshire*, 2:440; and Bateman, *History and Description of the Manchester Waterworks*, 81.

27. Williams and Farnie, *Cotton Mills*, 6–8, 58–50; Baines and Fairbairn, *Lancashire and Cheshire*, 1:86; Ashmore, *Industrial Archaeology*, 58–70.

28. Hills, *Power*, 134–64; Williams and Farnie, *Cotton Mills*, 51–73; Briggs, *Power of Steam*, 48–61.

29. Briggs, *Power of Steam*, 60, for the quotation; see also pp. 48–61.

30. Malet, *Bridgewater*, 67–77, 93–104.

31. Hadfield, *British Canals*, 27–32, 57–78. On Runcorn, see Porteous, *Canal Ports*.

32. Hadfield, *British Canals*, 33–150. The canals linking Manchester to its satellite towns and outside markets were completed as follows: the 15-mile Bury and Bolton in 1791; the 11-mile Ashton and Oldham in 1792; and the 31.5-mile Rochdale (and the Grand Trunk to London and south England) in 1804. The building of the canals resulted in a reduction in coal prices from traditional local sources such as Worsley, Oldham, Ashton, Hyde, Dukinfield, Newton, and Denton. Improved transportation also added to the supply by bringing in new competition from such areas as Bradford and Bolton. See Aikin, *Description of the Country*, 205; and Frangopalo *Rich Inheritance*, 39–45.

33. Hills, *Power*, 116–32; Williams and Farnie, *Cotton Mills*, 48–72; Lloyd-Jones and Lewis, *Manchester and the Age of the Factory*, 23–43.

34. Manchester, *Police Commissioners Report* (1800), 3, as reported in Daphne deJersey Gemmill, "Manchester in the Victorian Age: Factors Influencing the Design and Implementation of Smoke Abatement Policy" (M.A. essay, Department of Epidemiology and Public Health, Yale University, 1972), 3, for the quotation; Ashmore, *Industrial Archaeology*, 175–79. For insight on depictions of Irishtown, see Mary Poovey, "Curing the 'Social Body' in 1832: James Phillips Kay and the Irish in Manchester," *Gender and History* 5 (1993): 196–211; W. J. Lowe, *The Irish in Mid-Victorian Lancashire: The Shaping of a Working-Class Community* (New York: Lang, 1989); and Steven Fielding, "A Separate Culture? Irish Catholics in Working-Class Manchester and Salford, c. 1880–1939," in *Workers' Worlds: Cultures and Communities in Manchester and Salford, 1880–1939*, ed. Andrew Davies and Steven Fielding (Manchester: University of Manchester Press, 1992), 23–48.

35. For a useful bibliography on central place theory, see William Cronon, *Nature's Metropolis: Chicago and the Great West* (New York: Norton, 1991), 447–53. Also see Jacobs, *Cities and the Wealth of Nations*.

36. Lloyd-Jones and Lewis, *Manchester and the Age of the Factory*, 85–102, 160–65, passim. Also see Gary S. Messinger, *Manchester in the Victorian Age: The Half-Known City* (Manchester: Manchester University Press, 1985), 2–26.

37. Lloyd-Jones and Lewis, *Manchester and the Age of the Factory*.

38. Aikin, *Description of the Country*, 192, for the quotation; see also pp. 147–217. Also see Wheeler, *Manchester*, 255–65.

39. "Directions for Walking the Streets of Manchester and the Conduct of Carriages" (1809), as quoted in Messinger, *Manchester in the Victorian Age*, 12. Also see Ira Katznelson, *Marxism and the City*, Marxist Introductions, gen. ed. Steven Lukes (Oxford: Clarendon, 1992), 148, passim. See note 26, above, for a discussion of Manchester's population.

40. Richard Cobden, letter to Frederick Cobden (September 1832), as quoted in Lloyd-Jones and Lewis, *Manchester and the Age of the Factory*, 35.

41. Richard Holden, as quoted in ibid., 16. For a detailed analysis of the effects of the textile industry on water quality in the MIRB, see "First Report of the Commissioners." For the introduction of gas lighting, see Williams and Farnie, *Cotton Mills*, 59–60, 70–72; and A. Redford and I. S. Russell, *The History of Local Government in Manchester*, 3 vols. (London: Longman, 1939–1940), 1:263–71. The company's light bill went down from £2,000 to £600. In 1807, the city's public authority, the police commissioners, installed gas lighting in the town hall, but the installation of a municipal gasworks and street lighting took another ten years.

42. Robert Fishman, *Bourgeois Utopias: The Rise and Fall of Suburbia* (New York: Basic Books, 1987), 75, for the quotation; see also pp. 73–102. Also see Asa Briggs, *Victorian Cities* (London: Odhams, 1963), 11–58, 88–138; and Harold J. Dyos and D. A. Reeder, "Slums and Suburbs," in *The Victorian City: Images and Realities*, ed. Harold J. Dyos and Michael Wolff (London: Routledge and Kegan Paul, 1973), 1:359–88; and S. Martin Gaskell, *Slums* (Leicester, U.K.: Leicester University Press, 1990). On the origins of the modern suburb in England and the United States, also see Robert L. Fishman, "American Suburbs/English Suburbs: A Comparison," *Journal of Urban History* 13 (May 1987): 237–51; and the reply by Kenneth T. Jackson on pp. 302–6. On London's social geography, also see M. J. Power, "The Social Topography of Restoration London," in *London 1500–1700: The Making of the Metropolis*, ed. A. L. Beier and Roger Finlay (London: Longman, 1986), 199–223.

43. Aikin, *Description of the Country*, 206, for the quotation; Wheeler, *Manchester*, 255–65; and J. Everett, *Panorama of Manchester, and Railway Companion* (Manchester: Everett, 1834), 177–87. Frangopalo puts the beginning of licensed hackney service from St. Ann's Square in 1810, two years later. Frangopalo, *Rich Inheritance*, 60–73.

44. See Timmins, *Last Shift*, 35–70; and Reach, *Manchester and the Textile Districts*, 14–20, on the daily routines of the mill hands and their journeys between work and home.

45. William E. A. Axon, "The History of Ancoats," the inaugural lecture at Ancoats Hall Working Men's Social Club (11 May 1878), as reported in William E. A. Axon, *The Annals of Manchester* (London: Heywood, 1886), 41, for the quotation; Timmins, *Last Shift*, 64. Also see the autobiographical account of the district's native son, Charles Rowley, *Fifty Years of Work without Wages*, 2nd ed. (London: Hodder and Stoughton, 1911).

46. Williams and Farnie, *Cotton Mills*, 19–12, 159–67; Lloyd-Jones and Lewis, *Manchester and the Age of the Factory*, 23–43.

47. John C. Thresh, *An Inquiry into the Causes of Excessive Mortality in No. 1 District, Ancoats* (Manchester: Heywood, 1889), 11–12, for the quotation; see also p. 38. One of the best contemporary accounts of building techniques in Manchester is provided in Friedrich Engels, *The Condition of the Working Class in England* (1845; reprint, Stanford, CA: Stanford University Press, 1958), 64–71.

48. Aikin, *Description of the Country*, 192. For investigations of conditions in Ancoats, see "Report of the Medical Officer of Health," City of Manchester, *Proceedings of the*

Common Council (1884): 342–514; J. H. Crosfield, *The "Bitter Cry" of Ancoats and of Impoverished Manchester: Being a Series of Letters on Municipal Topics* (Manchester: Ireland, 1887); Thresh, *Inquiry*; and Manchester Corporation, Sanitary Committee, *Housing of the Working Classes* (Manchester: Blacklock, 1904). For a brilliant analysis of the economic logic of the jerry-built housing unit, see P. Rushton, "Housing Conditions and the Family Economy in the Victorian Slum: A Study of a Manchester District" (Ph.D. diss., University of Manchester, 1977).

49. Behagg, "Secrecy," 157, for the quotation; see also pp. 154–79, and Ira Katznelson, "Working Class Formation and the State: Nineteenth-Century England in American Perspective," in *Britain and America: Studies in Comparative History, 1760–1970*, ed. David Englander (New Haven, CT: Yale University Press, 1997), 171–95. For a fascinating look inside the workingman's pub, see Anne Secord, "Science in the Pub: Artisan Botanists in Early Nineteenth-Century Lancashire," *History of Science* 32 (September 1994): 269–315. Also see Brian Harrison, *Drink and the Victorians: The Temperance Question in England, 1815–1872*, 2nd ed. (1971; reprint, Staffordshire: Keele University Press, 1994).

50. Lloyd-Jones and Lewis, *Manchester and the Age of the Factory*, 36, for the quotation; see also pp. 23–43. A commercial directory for 1815 lists fifty-two different pubs that were used by approximately five hundred country weaver/manufacturers.

51. See Genevieve Massard-Guilbaud, "The Genesis of an Urban Identity: The Quartier de la Gare in Clemont-Ferrand, 1850–1914," *Journal of Urban History* 26 (September 1999): 779–808; G. F. Chadwick, "The Face of the Industrial City: Two Looks at Manchester," in Dyos and Wolff, eds., *The Victorian City*, 1:247–56; and Kevin Lynch, *The Image of the City* (Cambridge, MA: MIT Press, 1960).

52. Lloyd-Jones and Lewis, *Manchester and the Age of the Factory*, 103–30; Timmins, *Last Shift*, 91–106; and Kidd, *Manchester*, 103–19. See Wheeler, *Manchester*, 280–90, for a good account of the first railroad.

53. Wolfgang Schivelbusch, *The Railway Journey: The Industrialization of Time and Space in the 19th Century* (Berkeley: University of California Press, 1977).

54. Estimates on the horsepower in Manchester were made on the basis the following sources: James Murray and Richard Birley, "Amount and Employment of Steam and Water Power in the Undermentioned Townships," *Manchester Statistical Society, Transactions* 1 (24 January 1837), which covers Chorlton upon Hardy, Salford, Broughton, and Pendleton; James Meadows, "Quantity of Coal Brought into Manchester, in the Years 1834 and 1836," *Manchester Statistical Society, Transactions* 1 (November 1837); Bateman, *History and Description of the Manchester Waterworks*, 40; and Gemmill, "Manchester in the Victorian Age," 4–18.

55. Thompson, *Making of the English Working Class*, 191, for the quotation.

56. F. Munger, "Contentious Gatherings in Lancashire, England, 1750–1893," in *Class Conflict and Collective Action*, ed. Charles Tilly and Louise Tilly (Beverly Hills, CA: Sage, 1981), 73–110; and V. A. C. Gatrell, "Incorporation and the Pursuit of Liberal Hegemony in Manchester, 1790–1839," in *Municipal Reform and the Industrial City*, ed. Derek Fraser (Leicester: Leicester University Press, 1982), 15–60. For the formation

of urban middle-class politics, see Jurgen Habermas, *The Structural Transformation of the Public Sphere: An Inquiry into a Category of Bourgeois Society* (1962; reprint, Cambridge, MA: MIT Press, 1991).

57. Derek Fraser, *Urban Politics in Victorian England: The Structure of Politics in Victorian Cities* (Leicester: Leicester University Press, 1976), 14 and passim. Fraser's understanding of Manchester is based in large part on the Ph.D. work of V. A. C. Gatrell, "The Commercial Middle Class in Manchester, c. 1820–1857" (Ph.D. diss., Cambridge University, 1971). In a summary of this study, Fraser, like Gatrell, counts the working class out of public life. See, for example, Gatrell, "Incorporation." But cf. Munger, "Contentious Gatherings"; Behagg, "Secrecy"; and Brian R. Brown, "Industrial Capitalism, Conflict, and Working Class Contention in Lancashire, 1842," in Tilly and Tilly, *Class Conflict*, 111–42.

58. Redford and Russell, *History of Local Government in Manchester*, 1:198, for the quotation; see also pp. 1:191–240.

59. Gatrell, "Incorporation," provides the most detailed and compelling analysis of the origins of urban politics in Manchester. Also see Shena Simon, *A Century of City Government, Manchester, 1838–1938* (London: Allen and Unwin, 1938). See Munger, "Contentious Gatherings," 76, for the phrase "contention for power"; and Thompson, *Making of the English Working Class*, for a narrative of this struggle. The historiography of the condition-of-England question constitutes another small library. For recent perspectives that seem to point to what seems to be a declining standard of living during this period, see John C. Brown, "The Condition of England and the Standard of Living: Cotton Textiles in the Northwest, 1806–1850," *Journal of Economic History* 50 (1990): 591–614; Charles H. Feinstein, "Pessimism Perpetuated: Real Wages and the Standard of Living in Britain during and after the Industrial Revolution," *Journal of Economic History* 58 (September 1998): 625–58; and Graham Mooney and Simon Szreter, "Urbanization, Mortality, and the Standard of Living Debate: New Estimates of the Expectation of Life at Birth in Nineteenth-Century British Cities," *Economic History Review* 51 (1998): 84–112.

60. Redford and Russell, *History of Local Government in Manchester*, 1:241, for the quotation; see also pp. 1:191–275. Gatrell, in "Incorporation," 29, agrees that Fleming was "the undisputed autocrat of the town's local government between 1810 and 1819." Fleming, like many Tories, had made great profits from the cotton trade. In this case, the origins of the family's wealth came from Fleming's grandfather, who had invented a new dye process. The interlocking nature of his various official and unofficial positions was also typical of elite rule by a closed social circle. In addition to his office as the treasurer of the police commission, Fleming held posts as the treasurer of the Highway Surveyors, a member of the Gas Committee, a churchwarden, and the president of socially important local political clubs.

61. Kidd, *Manchester*, 94, for the quotation; see also pp. 81–102; Thompson, *Making of the English Working Class*, 631–711.

62. Gatrell, "Incorporation," 20; Fraser, *Urban Politics*, 25–111; Redford and Russell, *History of Local Government in Manchester*, 1:311–42. The Manchester Police and Gas

Act of 1829 (11 George IV, c. 47) contained extensive new land-use regulations, especially affecting private building owners. For example, the public authority could set construction standards for gates and doors, force property owners in built-up areas to pay for street improvements, and prohibit private sewer connections to public storm drains. Like the 1792 act, this reform measure redefined the political boundaries not only between the social classes but also between the public and private sectors. Also see Alan Wilson, "Technology and Municipal Decision-Making: Sanitary Systems in Manchester, 1868–1910" (Ph.D. diss., University of Manchester, 1990). On street lights as a symbol of class struggle, see Wolfgang Schivelbusch, *Disenchanted Night: The Industrialization of Light in the Nineteenth-Century*, trans. Angela Davies (Berkeley: University of California Press, 1988).

63. Bill Luckin, *Pollution and Control*, 69, 96; see also pp. 69–99; Axon, *Annals*, passim; Messinger, *Manchester in the Victorian Age*, 33–64.

64. Nicholas C. Edsall, "Varieties of Radicalism: Attwood, Cobden, and the Local Politics of Municipal Incorporation," *Historical Journal* 16 (1973): 93–107; see p. 103 for the first quotation and n. 26 for the table. Fraser, *Urban Politics*, 150, for the second quotation; see also pp. 115–53. Also see Wendy Hinde, *Richard Cobden: A Victorian Outsider* (New Haven, CT: Yale University Press, 1987). For a personal, albeit critical, evaluation of Sir Joseph Heron, see Hayes, *Reminiscences*, 195. For the climax of Chartism, the Plug Riots of 1842, see a rebuttal to the official version by a labor leader, and a rebuttal to *his* version by a shopkeeper, reprinted from the *Manchester City News*, in J. H. Nodal, ed., *City News, Notes, and Queries* (Manchester: Manchester City News, 1878), 1:524, 552, 583, 600 (21 September–19 October 1878). Also see Brown, "Industrial Capitalism."

65. Briggs, *Victorian Cities*, 88–138; Gary S. Messinger, *Manchester in the Victorian Age*, 89–112; Steven Marcus, *Engels, Manchester, and the Working Class* (New York: Random House, 1974); 28–66.

66. J. P. Kay, *The Moral and Physical Condition of the Working Classes Employed in the Cotton Manufacture in Manchester* (1831; reprint, Shannon: Irish University Press, 1971); and Paul Boyer, *Urban Masses and Moral Order in America, 1820–1920* (Cambridge, MA: Harvard University Press, 1978).

67. For background on Kay and his links to the Cross Street Chapel and Manchester Statistical Society, see T. S. Ashton, *Economic and Social Investigations in Manchester: A Centenary History of the Manchester Statistical Society* (London: King, 1934), 1–13; and Hamlin, *Public Health and Social Justice*, 52–83.

68. Kay, *Moral and Physical Condition*, 47 (original emphasis).

69. Ibid., 12. Kay would follow the logic of his convictions to move from medical to educational reform. Also see Graeme Davison, "The City as a Natural System: Theories of Urban Society in Early Nineteenth-Century Britain," in *The Pursuit of Urban History*, ed. Derek Fraser and Anthony Sutcliffe (London: Edward Arnold, 1983), 349–70; Poovey, "Curing the 'Social Body'"; and Hamlin, *Public Health and Social Justice*, 52–83.

70. Maurice Spiers, ed., *Victoria Park, Manchester: A Nineteenth-Century Suburb in Its Social and Administrative Context*, Remains, Historical and Literary, Connected with the Palatine Counties of Lancaster and Chester, 3rd ser., vol. 23 (Manchester: Chetham Society, 1976), 2, for the quoted phrase; see also pp. 1–12. Fishman, *Bourgeois Utopias*, 74–91.

71. *Manchester Courier*, 4 April 1836, as quoted in Spiers, *Victoria Park*, 13, n. 2; Fishman, *Bourgeois Utopias*, 91–102. When Victoria Park was reorganized in 1845 as a private park with Cobden's brother, Frederick, in charge, it had already attracted thirty-nine of the city's best families.

72. Fishman, *Bourgeois Utopias*, 92; Mary Douglas, *Purity and Danger: An Analysis of the Concepts of Pollution and Taboo* (London: Routledge, 1966). Also see David Sibley, *Geographies of Exclusion: Society and Difference in the West* (London: Routledge, 1995).

73. Kay, *Moral and Physical Condition*, 6; Léon M. Faucher, *Manchester in 1844: Its Present Condition and Future Prospects* (London: Simpkin, Marshall, 1844), 26–27.

74. Engels, *Condition of the Working Class*, 68, 70, for the quotations; see also pp. 61–71. For further insight on the influence of local and market forces on housing stocks and styles, see M. J. Daunton, *House and Home in the Victorian City: Working-Class Housing, 1850–1914* (London: E. Arnold, 1983).

75. Richard Baron Howard, "On the Prevalence of Diseases Arising from Contagion, Malaria, and Certain Other Physical Causes amongst the Labouring Classes in Manchester," in *Local Reports on the Sanitary Condition of the Labouring Population of England*, U.K. Poor Law Commissioners (London: Clowes and Sons, 1842), 324, for the quotation; see pp. 294–336 for the full report. See Hamlin, *Public Health and Social Justice*. Hamlin's point is well-taken that Chadwick represented a significant turning away from holistic notions of health to narrower concepts of disease and its causes. Hamlin also illuminates the links between medicine, science, and public health on one side, and politics, social justice, and environmental ethics on the other. He brilliantly shows how Chadwick's focus on engineering the physical city helped justify the turning of a blind eye to a range of related health issues, such as nutrition, clothing, and housing. Given all that, Chadwick's popular appeal still needs explaining. The very simplicity and unity of his plan, and its conceptual analogy to circulation in the human body might have been one source of its popularity. Although Chadwick appears to have been as ideologically rigid as Hamlin portrays him to be, the reformer still deserves credit for envisioning the city's relationship to water as a dynamic energy system that includes an "ultimate sink," or a method of duplicating nature's ability to turn waste into food. As Hamlin demonstrates, Chadwick's comprehensive approach was largely rejected by the engineering community in favor of piecemeal methods that better met the needs of the engineers' clients—city governments. A renewal of Chadwick's unified approach to water management would have to await the insights gained in the 1890s from advances in the germ theory of

disease causation. See Nancy Tomes, *The Gospel of Germs: Men, Women, and the Microbe in American Life* (Cambridge, MA: Harvard University Press, 1998); and Michael Worboys, *Spreading Germs: Disease Theories and Medical Practice in Britain, 1865–1900* (Cambridge: Cambridge University Press, 2000).

76. Alan Wilson, "Technology and Municipal Decision-Making," 13. I have drawn extensively on this excellent, albeit unpublished, piece of scholarship. Also see the older, more comprehensive study, Redford and Russell, *History of Local Government in Manchester*, and the informative meditation by a city insider, Simon, *Century of City Government*.

77. Fraser, *Urban Politics*, 214–33; Gatrell, "Incorporation." On the council's culture of secrecy and its self-contained committee system of power, see Charles Rowley, *Fifty Years of Work*, 55–58; and Sidney Webb and Beatrice Webb, *Methods of Social Study* (1932; reprint, New York: Kelley, 1968), 194–97.

78. Howard, "On the Prevalence of Diseases," 307, 310. In addition, see Lyon Playfair, "Report on the State of Large Towns in Lancashire," in *Second Report*, U.K. Commissioners for Inquiring into the Status of Large Towns and Populous Districts (London: Clowes and Sons, 1845), 345–486. See Redford and Russell, *History of Local Government in Manchester*, 2:130–70, for the local context of public health reform; and Hamlin, *Public Health and Social Justice*, 188–216, 245–74, for the national context. Chadwick's partners in the Town Improvement Company included R. A. Slaney, Neil Arnott, Nassau Senior, and Lord Francis Egerton, the most important aristocrat in the Manchester area.

79. See Redford and Russell, *History of Local Government in Manchester*, 2:130–70, for a detailed account. Also see Wilson, "Technology and Municipal Decision-Making," 24–85. Each cartload contained 1.5 tons of waste. The key legislation included the Manchester Police Act of 1844, 7 & 8 Victoria, c. 40, and the Sanitary Improvement Act of 1845, 8 & 9 Victoria, c. 141.

80. See Redford and Russell, *History of Local Government in Manchester*, 2:171–204, for a general description of the politics of the waterworks. Also see J. F. Bateman, *History and Description of the Manchester Waterworks*, for the most complete account of the project, by its chief engineer.

81. Bateman, *History and Description of the Manchester Waterworks*, 20–107; Town Clerk Joseph Heron's testimony presented in "First Report of the Commissioners," xxxiii, 454–64; Redford and Russell, *History of Local Government in Manchester*, 2:171–204; Simon, *Century of City Government*, 349–56.

82. City of Manchester, *Proceedings of the Common Council* (2 December 1868): 75. See chapter 5 for a fuller description of the debate between the council, Parliament's public health investigators, and local sanitary reformers.

83. Reach, *Manchester and the Textile Districts*, 2–3.

84. Ibid., 3, 8, 6. Also see Secord, "Science in the Pub."

85. Mooney and Szreter, "Urbanization," 98; Reach, *Manchester and the Textile Districts*, 22. For the statistical report, see H. P. Holland, "Chorlton-upon-Medlock: Report on

its Sanitary Condition," in *First Report*, U.K. Commissioners for Inquiring into the Status of Large Towns and Populous Districts (London: Clowes and Sons, 1844), 1:202–17; and insights into the report's meaning in Hamlin, *Public Health and Social Justice*, 188–216.

86. Reach, *Manchester and the Textile Districts*, 11.

Chapter Three

1. J. Seymour Currey, *Chicago: Its History and Builders*, 2 vols. (Chicago: Clarke, 1912), 1:365, for the quotation; see also pp. 363–66. This account draws heavily on Rufus Blanchard, *Discovery and Conquests of the North-West, with the History of Chicago* (Wheaton, IL: Blanchard, 1881), and newspaper accounts. The best contemporary coverage of the event is found in the *Chicago Daily Journal*, 13–17 March 1849; and the *Chicago Democrat*, 13–17 March 1849. For an illustration of the aftermath of the flood and additional details, see Joseph Kirkland, *The Story of Chicago*, 2 vols. (Chicago: Dibble, 1892–1894), 1:208. The city's monikers are quoted in Lloyd Lewis and Henry Justin Smith, *Chicago: The History of Its Reputation* (New York: Harcourt Brace, 1929), 39.

2. See William Cronon, *Nature's Metropolis: Chicago and the Great West* (New York: Norton, 1991), 23–96, for an extended analysis of the city's rise as a commercial entrepôt; and William Cronon, "To Be the Central City: Chicago, 1848–1857," *Chicago History* 10 (Fall 1981): 130–40, for a focused examination of 1848 as a turning point in the city's history. The basic reference work on the history of Chicago is A. T. Andreas, *History of Chicago*, 3 vols. (1884–1886; reprint, New York: Arno, 1975). Its modern counterpart is Bessie Louise Pierce, *A History of Chicago*, 3 vols. (New York: Knopf, 1957). Pierce also produced the most comprehensive collection of traveler accounts. See Bessie Louise Pierce, ed., *As Others See Chicago: Impressions of Visitors, 1673–1933* (Chicago: University of Chicago Press, 1933).

3. For the history of disease in Chicago during the antebellum period, see Constance B. Webb, *A History of Contagious Disease Care in Chicago before the Great Fire* (Chicago: University of Chicago Press, 1940), 31–92; John Rauch, "Sanitary History of Chicago," in Chicago Board of Health, *Report of the Board of Health of the City of Chicago for 1867, 1868, and 1869; and a Sanitary History of Chicago from 1833–1870* (Chicago: Lakeside, 1871); Isaac D. Rawlings et al., *The Rise and Fall of Disease in Illinois*, 2 vols. (Springfield, IL: Schepp and Barnes, 1927); John B. Hamilton, "The Epidemics of Chicago," *Bulletin of the Society of Medical History of Chicago* 1 (October 1911): 73–86; Thomas Neville Bonner, *Medicine in Chicago, 1850–1950: A Chapter in the Social and Scientific Development of a City*, 2nd ed. (Urbana: University of Illinois Press, 1991), 3–43; and William K. Beatty, "When Cholera Scourged Chicago," *Chicago History* 11 (Spring 1982): 2–13. For broader perspectives, see Charles Rosenberg, *The Cholera Years: The United States in 1832, 1849, and 1866* (Chicago: University of Chicago Press, 1962).

4. The storm caused widespread flooding throughout northern Illinois and southern

Wisconsin. See note 1, above. Also see Henry Cox and John H. Armington, *The Weather and Climate of Chicago* (Chicago: University of Chicago Press, 1914), for a historical overview of the record rainfalls.

5. Robin Einhorn, *Property Rules: Political Economy in Chicago, 1833–1872* (Chicago: University of Chicago Press, 1991).

6. Mayor James Woodward, "Inaugural Address," as reported in the *Chicago Daily Journal*, 16 March 1849. For the city's formative era of politics, see Einhorn, *Property Rules*. Also essential for an understanding of the role of government in the process of city building during this period is Ann Durkin Keating, *Building Chicago: Suburban Developers and the Creation of a Divided Metropolis* (Columbus: Ohio State University Press, 1988). The concept of privatism and its close identification with capitalism are drawn from the seminal works of Sam Bass Warner Jr., *The Private City: Philadelphia in Three Periods of Its Growth* (Philadelphia: University of Pennsylvania Press, 1968); and Sam Bass Warner Jr., *The Urban Wilderness: A History of the American City* (New York: Harper and Row, 1972).

7. For an introduction, see Cronon, *Nature's Metropolis*, 23–54. An alternative explanation for the city's motto is provided by a contemporary, John Lewis Peyton, in *Over the Alleghenies and across the Prairies*, 2nd ed. (1848; reprint, London: Simpkin, Marshall, 1870), as quoted in Pierce, *As Others See Chicago*, 105. According to this traveler's tale, Chicago was the "Garden City" because its "houses were very small and the gardens enormous. The gardens in the west division in fact having no enclosures, might be supposed to extend indefinitely westward." Many home owners maintained sizable vegetable plots, creating this impression of a city of gardens.

8. Friedrich von Raumer, *America and the American People* (New York: Langley, 1846), 451, as quoted in Pierce, *As Others See Chicago*, 11, for the quotation. Also see the accounts of the Chicago portage by the French explorers Jacques Marquette and John Francis Buisson de St. Cosme in Pierce's book, pp. 13–23. The initial route followed by Marquette and Joliet actually reached the Mississippi River via the Wisconsin River at Portage, Wisconsin, and returned up the Illinois and Des Plaines rivers to reach Chicago. For European explorers, see Samuel Eliot Morison, *The European Discovery of America*, vol. 1, *The Northern Voyages* (New York: Oxford University Press, 1971). For the system of river and lake cities taking shape in the Midwest, see Richard C. Wade, *The Urban Frontier: The Rise of Western Cities, 1790–1830* (Cambridge, MA: Harvard University Press, 1959); and Wyatt Winton Belcher, *The Economic Rivalry between St. Louis and Chicago, 1850–1880* (New York: Columbia University Press, 1947). For a recent examination of the meaning of the Erie Canal in American history, see Carol Sheriff, *The Artificial River: The Erie Canal and the Paradox of Progress, 1817–1862* (New York: Hill and Wang, 1996). For cotton as the engine of American economic growth, see Douglas C. North, *The Economic Growth of the United States, 1790–1860* (New York: Norton, 1961). For an ecological primer for the Chicago area, see the work of the geographers Irving Cutler, *Chicago: Metropolis of*

the Mid-Continent, 2nd ed. (Dubuque, IA: Kendall/Hunt, 1976), 5–14; and Harold M. Mayer, "The Launching of Chicago: The Situation and the Site," *Chicago History* 9 (Summer 1980): 68–79. According to Mayer, the Chicago portage was located where present-day Damen Avenue crosses the South Branch about two and a half miles west of the central business district. For perspectives on Chicago society as a frontier settlement, see Jacqueline Peterson, " 'Wild Chicago': The Formation and Destruction of a Multiracial Community on the Midwestern Frontier, 1816–1837," in *The Ethnic Frontier*, ed. Melvin Holli and Peter d'A. Jones (Grand Rapids, MI: Eerdmans, 1977), 25–71.

9. Cronon, *Nature's Metropolis*, xv. For a critical assessment of the book, see William Cronon and others, "William Cronon's *Nature's Metropolis*: A Symposium," *Antipode* 26 (April 1994): 113–76.

10. Cronon, "To Be the Central City," 130–32; Cronon, *Nature's Metropolis*, 55–96, 263–309. For additional insight on the withdrawal of capital from St. Louis by Eastern merchants in the wake of Kansas-Nebraska Act of 1854 and its reinvestment in Chicago, see Jeffery S. Adler, *Yankee Merchants and the Making of the Urban West* (Cambridge: Cambridge University Press, 1991). On urban rivalry in the Midwest, see Harry N. Scheiber, "Urban Rivalry and Internal Improvements in the Old Northwest, 1820–1860," *Ohio History* 71 (October 1962): 227–39, 290–92. For Chicago's rivalry with other cities of the Midwest, see Lawrence H. Larsen, "Chicago's Midwest Rivals: Cincinnati, St. Louis, and Milwaukee," *Chicago History* 5 (Fall 1976): 141–51. On Chicago's leading citizen, see William L. Downard, "William Butler Ogden and the Growth of Chicago," *Journal of the Illinois State Historical Society* 75 (Spring 1982): 47–60.

11. Mayer, "Launching of Chicago"; Glen Holt, "The Birth of Chicago: An Examination of Economic Parentage," *Journal of the Illinois State Historical Society* 76 (Summer 1983): 83–94; and John Dennis Haeger, *The Investment Frontier: New York Businessmen and the Development of the Old Northwest* (Albany: State University of New York Press, 1981). For sources on the canal, see Michael P. Conzen and K. J. Carr, eds., *The Illinois and Michigan Canal National Heritage Corridor: A Guide to Its History and Sources* (DeKalb: Northern Illinois University Press, 1988). The standard history is James William Putnam, *The Illinois and Michigan Canal: A Study in Economic History*, vol. 10 in Chicago Historical Society's Collection (Chicago: University of Chicago Press, 1918). Also see John M. Lamb, "Early Days on the Illinois and Michigan Canal," *Chicago History* 3 (Winter 1974–1975): 168–76. On the harbor, see Weston A. Goodspeed and Daniel D. Healy, eds., *History of Cook County*, 2 vols. (Chicago: Goodspeed Historical Association, 1909), 1:106–46; Currey, *Chicago*, 260–61; and John W. Larson, *Those Army Engineers: A History of the Chicago District, U.S. Army Corp of Engineers* (Washington, DC: Government Printing Office, 1980).

12. Perry R. Duis, *Challenging Chicago: Coping with Everyday Life, 1837–1920* (Chicago: University of Illinois Press, 1998), 5, for the quotation; see also pp. 3–17. John Kinzie was responsible for the drawing by New York City lithographers of the 1834 map, which included his North Side "addition." See *Chicago Democrat*, 18 June 1834.

13. *Chicago Democrat*, 18 February, 16 July, 13 August, and 1 October 1834; Goodspeed and Healy, *History of Cook County*; Currey, *Chicago*, 260–61; Blanchard, *Discovery and Conquests*, 1:581–86; Patrick E. McLear, "The Rise of the Port of Chicago to 1848" (Ph.D. diss., University of Missouri, Kansas City, 1967). For larger perspectives on the role of the engineers, see Todd Shallot, *Structures in the Stream: Water, Science, and the Rise of the U.S. Army Corps of Engineers* (Austin: University of Texas Press, 1994).

14. Robin Einhorn, "A Taxing Dilemma: Early Lake Shore Protection," *Chicago History* 18 (Fall 1989): 34–51. U.S. Environmental Protection Agency, Great Lakes National Program Office, *Great Lakes Atlas*, 3rd ed. (Washington, DC: U.S. Environmental Protection Agency, Great Lakes National Program Office, 1999), http://www.epa.gov/glnpo/atlas. Sandbars continued to form and block the entrance to the harbor into the 1850s. See, for example, Goodspeed and Healy, *History of Cook County*, 1:202, 209, 221, 252.

15. Peyton, *Over the Alleghenies*, as quoted in Pierce, *As Others See Chicago*, 100, 108 (original emphasis); see also pp. 99–112. On the extent of the wet prairies of the region, see Hugh Prince, *Wetland of the American Midwest: A Historical Geography of Changing Attitudes* (Chicago: University of Chicago Press, 1997).

16. Putnam, *Illinois and Michigan Canal*; Michael P. Conzen, "The Historical and Geographical Development of the Illinois and Michigan Canal National Heritage Corridor," in Conzen and Carr, *Illinois and Michigan Canal*, 1–17.

17. *Chicago American*, 10 April 1839, as quoted in Goodspeed and Healy, *History of Cook County*, 1:136. For a sampling of mud stories, see Lewis and Smith, *Chicago*, 40–43. The origins of these stories can be traced back to the accounts of pioneers that were recorded in the 1870s and 1880s. For example, see William Bross, *History of Chicago: Historical and Commercial Statistics . . . Republished from the Daily Democratic Press* (Chicago: Jansen, McClurg, 1876), 119; and Charles Cleaver, *Early Chicago Reminiscences* (Chicago: Fergus, 1882). The most detailed examination of Chicago real estate and settlement patterns is Homer Hoyt, *One Hundred Years of Land Values in Chicago* (Chicago: University of Chicago Press, 1933).

18. *Chicago Democrat*, 18 November and 2 December 1835; 24 February and 2 March 1836; *Chicago American*, 21 and 28 November 1835; Goodspeed and Healy, *History of Cook County*, 1:112–30; Currey, *Chicago*, 1:206–8; Kirkland, *Story of Chicago*, 1:238–40; Einhorn, *Property Rules*, 54–57.

19. *Chicago American*, 13 June 1835; Putnam, *Illinois and Michigan Canal*.

20. For a map depicting the stands of trees in Chicago in 1830, see Harold M. Mayer and Richard C. Wade, with the assistance of Glen E. Holt, *Chicago: Growth of a Metropolis* (Chicago: University of Chicago Press, 1969), 13. Also see the description of Chicago's trees in 1834 by an eyewitness, R. Goudy, as quoted in Blanchard, *Discovery and Conquests*, 1:612–13.

21. Currey, *Chicago*, 1:6, for the quoted phrases; Milo M. Quaife, *Chicago's Highways, Old and New, from Indian Trails to Motor Roads* (Chicago: Keller, 1923), for the information on overland modes of transportation.

22. For a good description of alternative building materials and costs of construction in

Chicago, see Christine Meisner Rosen, *The Limits of Power: Great Fires and the Process of City Growth in America* (New York: Cambridge University Press, 1988), 92–109. Also see Peterson, "Wild Chicago," 38, for evidence that Chicago's pioneers knew about the limestone in their immediate vicinity. She suggests the place called Hardscrapple, on the Southwest Side where the river meets Mud Lake, was given its name because of the rocky outcroppings there. Milo Quaife traces the origins of the plank road to Russia. He states that it was brought to Chicago by way of New York City in 1847–1848, but the story of the planking of Lake Street four years earlier seems to contradict this theory of technological lineage. See Quaife, *Chicago's Highways*, 129–30.

23. Blanchard, *Discovery and Conquests*, 1:583–84, 614; Lewis and Smith, *Chicago*, 62–63. For a pioneering study of the destruction of the northern forests, see James Willard Hurst, *Law and Economic Growth: The Legal History of the Lumber Industry in Wisconsin, 1836–1915* (Cambridge, MA: Harvard University Press, 1964). Also see Cronon, *Nature's Metropolis*, 148–206.

24. Blanchard, *Discovery and Conquests*, 1:584–85.

25. John Alexander Jameson, as quoted in Hoyt, *One Hundred Years of Land Values*, 62; see also p. 48. Goodspeed and Healy, *History of Cook County*, 1:167; Lewis and Smith, *Chicago*, 56; Pierce, *History of Chicago*, 2:318–19.

26. See Einhorn, *Property Rules*, for a sophisticated analysis of the political economy of funding public works with general property taxes as opposed to special assessments.

27. Chicago Department of Public Works, *The Movable Bridges of Chicago: A Brief History* (Chicago: City of Chicago, 1983), 1–5. Land values soared to set new records near the bridge. See Hoyt, *One Hundred Years of Land Values*, 37.

28. *Chicago Democrat*, 4 May 1849, for the quotation; Einhorn, *Property Rules*, 104–7, for the strained effort to make the bridge crisis conform to an overreaching thesis.

29. Bross, *History of Chicago*, 119, for the quotation; Pierce, *History of Chicago*, 2:316–17, for contemporary references to the rats. On the theory of path dependencies in historical context, see Martin V. Melosi, *The Sanitary City: Urban Infrastructure in America from Colonial Times to the Present* (Baltimore: Johns Hopkins University Press, 2000), 10–12.

30. Hoyt, *One Hundred Years of Land Values*, 45–74.

31. Ibid., 48; and Louis C. Hunter, *Steam Power*, vol. 2 of *A History of Industrial Power in the United States, 1780–1930* (Charlottesville: University Press of Virginia, 1985), 3–66; John F. Stover, "The Illinois Central and the Growth of Illinois and Chicago in the 1850s," *Railroad History*, Bulletin No. 159 (Autumn 1988): 39–50. Also see the most comprehensive general work on the subject, Sam Schurr and Bruce Netschert, *Energy in the American Economy, 1850–1975: An Economic Study of Its History and Prospects* (Baltimore: Resources for the Future/Johns Hopkins University Press, 1960). A cord of wood is a stack measuring four feet by four feet by eight feet, or 128 cubic feet. A cord of seasoned hardwood weighs 1.00–2.25 tons, and

has about half the heat value of an equivalent weight of soft coal. An acre of forest contains thirty to forty cords of wood. A skilled lumberjack could cut a cord a day; the task would take two to three times as long for an unskilled worker.

32. *Chicago Daily Journal*, 18 October 1849, as quoted in Hoyt, *One Hundred Years of Land Values*, 61.

33. Ibid.; *Chicago Democrat*, 7 August 1849; Goodspeed and Healy, *History of Cook County*, 1:210, 241. For statistics on the epidemic, see Webb, *History of Contagious Disease Care*, 1–31. The role of crisis in forcing communities to reconceptualize themselves and their sense of urban space is the subject of Michael H. Frisch, *Town into City: Springfield, Massachusetts, and the Meaning of Community, 1840–1880* (Cambridge, MA: Harvard University Press, 1972).

34. For references to Chicago as the New Venice of the West, see Goodspeed and Healy, *History of Cook County*, 1:144–45. Two basic sources for the history of the waterworks are Louis P. Cain, *Sanitation Strategy for a Lakefront Metropolis: The Case of Chicago* (DeKalb: Northern Illinois University Press, 1978); and James C. O'Connell, "Technology and Pollution: Chicago's Water Policy, 1833–1930" (Ph.D. diss., University of Chicago, 1980).

35. Edwin O. Gale, *Reminiscences of Early Chicago and Vicinity* (Chicago: Revell, 1902), 319–20. When the lake became inaccessible during the winter, the water bearers used the river.

36. Ibid., 321–22.

37. Currey, *Chicago*, 1:248, for the fire; and Goodspeed and Healy, *History of Cook County*, 1:209, for a report of an earlier fire on 30 July 1850 that burned twenty houses and the Chicago Theater due to a lack of water. On the waterworks, see Goodspeed and Healy, *History of Cook County*, 1:151, 161, 218, 223; and "Short History of the Public Water System of the City of Chicago," in City of Chicago, Department of Public Works, *Annual Report* (1890): 446–69, for the statistics. The company extended a fourteen-inch pipe 320 feet into the lake to obtain its supply.

38. See Currey, *Chicago*, 1:142–43, on Gurnee and his stand on municipal ownership; see Pierce, *History of Chicago*, 2:200, on John Wentworth and his *Chicago Democrat* as the head of the opposition.

39. *Chicago American*, ? June 1842, as quoted in Goodspeed and Healy, *History of Cook County*, 1:161, for the quoted phrase; Gale, *Reminiscences*, 321–26; Einhorn, *Property Rules*, 134–37; and Louis P. Cain, "Raising and Watering a City: Ellis Sylvester Chesbrough and Chicago's First Sanitation System," *Technology and Culture* 13 (1972): 353–71.

40. *Chicago Daily Democrat*, 14 March 1849, for the meeting; *Chicago Daily Journal*, 16 March 1849, for Mayor Woodward's call for an appropriation to buy lime. On the origins of the medical profession in Chicago, see Bonner, *Medicine in Chicago*, 3–18; and Webb, *History of Contagious Disease Care*, 1–31.

41. *Chicago Daily Democrat*, 14 March 1849. Notice of the meeting had appeared four days

earlier, before the flood. Although this catastrophe may have added urgency to the cause, the original impetus for the citizen's rally was the necessity of writing a petition on the day before the inauguration of the new municipal administration. The city did set up temporary quarantine hospitals of tents on the beach at various peak periods of the epidemic. See Hamilton, "Epidemics of Chicago," 80; and Beatty, "When Cholera Scourged Chicago," 5–10, for accounts of the city's response to the crisis.

42. Dr. Charles Dyer, as quoted in Kirkland, *Story of Chicago*, 1:235. For the larger context, see Rosenberg, *Cholera Years*; and Christopher Hamlin, *A Science of Impurity: Water Analysis in Nineteenth Century Britain* (Bristol: Hilger, 1990).

43. Nathan S. Davis, "On the Intimate Relation of Medical Science to the Whole Field of Natural Sciences," in Illinois State Medical Society, *Transactions* (1853): 22, as quoted in Bonner, *Medicine in Chicago*, 179.

44. City of Chicago, *A Century of Progress in Water Works, 1833–1933* (Chicago: Chicago Department of Public Works, Bureau of Engineering, 1933), 13–15, 34–35; Keating, *Building Chicago*, 39–40, 190, for the transformation of the municipal water supply from a necessity of public health to a private amenity after 1856, when an eight-year process of removing the free hydrants and fountains began. Also see Einhorn, *Property Rules*, 133–39. See Pierce, *History of Chicago*, 2:313–15, on the consequences of the fire; and *Chicago Tribune*, 28 February 1854, for clues on its causes. In this editorial, the paper defended the practice of putting the waterworks on standby status during the evening hours with a promise of a maximum ten-minute delay in firing up the pumps to full pressure after receiving an alarm. In two fires the previous week on the North Side, the hydrants had been dry and the houses had burned to the ground. For wood-frame buildings, a ten-to-fifteen-minute delay in getting water can mean the difference between repairable damage and total loss.

45. City of Chicago, *Century of Progress*, 13–15; "Report of the Department of Water," in City of Chicago, *Annual Report* (1935): 57b, for a consistent series of statistics from 1854 to the date of the report.

46. By the mid-1850s, advertisements proclaiming the virtues and the quantities of different "brands" of coal were common in the daily press. See for example, *Chicago Tribune*, 12 January 1856. For resort to the Calumet area for fuel wood during a temporary shortage, see *Chicago Democrat*, 29 October 1850.

47. Joseph Moses and John Kirkland, *History of Chicago*, 2 vols. (Chicago: Munsell, 1895), 1:410; Damian Grivetti, "The Rise and Fall of Coal Mining in the Illinois Valley, 1850–1950," in *The Industrial Revolution in the Upper Illinois Valley*, eds. Michael P. Conzen, Glenn M. Richard, and Carl A. Zimring, Studies on the Illinois and Michigan Canal Corridor, No. 6 (Chicago: Committee on Geographical Studies, University of Chicago, 1993), 151–68; and see above note 2, above.

48. Moses and Kirkland, *History of Chicago*, 1:410; Mayer and Wade, *Chicago*, 29; Goodspeed and Healy, *History of Cook County*, 1:280. On the importance of the Pennsylvania anthracite mines to the growth of the American economy, see Alfred Chandler Jr.,

"Anthracite Coal and the Beginnings of the Industrial Revolution in the United States," *Business History Review* 46 (Summer 1972): 141–81; and Howard Benjamin Powell, *Philadelphia's First Fuel Crisis: Jacob Cist and the Developing Market for Pennsylvania Anthracite* (University Park: Pennsylvania State University Press, 1978). For insight on the environmental and human costs of this enterprise, see Anthony F. C. Wallace, *St. Clair: A Nineteenth-Century Coal Town's Experience with a Disaster Prone Industry* (New York: Knopf, 1987); and Grace Pallandino, *Another Civil War: Labor, Capital, and the State in the Anthracite Regions of Pennsylvania, 1840–1868* (Urbana: University of Illinois Press, 1990).

49. Stover, "Illinois Central," 44.

50. J. W. Foster, *Report upon the Mineral Resources of the Illinois Central Railroad* (New York: Roe, 1856), 27. See also the commentary on La Salle coal and railroads, *Chicago Weekly Democrat*, 9 June 1855; and see State of Illinois, Department of Mines and Minerals, *A Compilation of the Reports of the Mining Industry of Illinois from the Earliest Records to the Close of the Year 1930* (Springfield: Illinois Department of Mines and Minerals, 1930), for a history of coal mining in the state, as well as Grivetti, "The Rise and Fall of Coal Mining." Cf. Andreas, *History of Chicago*, 2:673, which puts the 1852 figure at 44,800 tons. For 1860, the Chicago Board of Trade statistics show a local consumption of 150,000 tons. See the Chicago Board of Trade, *Annual Report* (1860): 51–52.

51. U.S. Bureau of the Census, *Eighth Census of the United States, Manuscript of Industry, Cook County, Illinois* (Washington, DC: U.S. Bureau of the Census, 1860). On the origins of the gas company, see W. G. C. Rice, *Seventy-Five Years of Gas Service in Chicago* (Chicago: Peoples Gas, Light, and Coke Company, 1925); Illinois Bureau of Labor Statistics, *Ninth Biennial Report, 1896*, pt. 3, *Franchises and Taxation: The Gas Companies of Chicago* (Springfield: Illinois Bureau of Labor Statistics, 1896), 239–320; Pierce, *History of Chicago*, 2:319–20.

52. U.S. Bureau of the Census, *Eighth Census ... Manuscript of Industry, Cook County*. The listing of steam engines but no fuel costs was particularly evident in the case of sawmills, furniture factories, and other firms using wood as a raw material.

53. Board of Trade, *Annual Report* (1858): 37, and (1859): 72, for the first and second quotations, respectively. See Cronon, *Nature's Metropolis*, 55–96, on the impact of the railroad on Chicago's markets and seasonal rhythms.

54. Peyton, as quoted in Pierce, *As Others See Chicago*, 105; and Hoyt, *One Hundred Years of Land Values*, 49–59, 65–74.

55. On early notices of river pollution from slaughterhouse wastes, see Goodspeed and Healy, *History of Cook County*, 1:215. In 1850, the city began paying the canal commission to use its pumps to help clean the river (Goodspeed and Healy, *History of Cook County*, 1:218). See U.S. Bureau of the Census, *Eighth Census ... Manuscript of Industry, Cook County*, Reel 60, 9th Ward, 1, for McCormick's fuel use. The sanitation of the city will be taken up in the next chapter.

56. Hoyt, *One Hundred Years of Land Values*, 49–59, 65–74; Goodspeed and Healy, *History of Cook County*, 1:277–78. In what would become an urban pattern, the closing down

of one vice district soon resulted in the rise of another somewhere else. In this case it moved to the Kilgubbin area at the fork, of the river. Two years later, the latter shantytown of about two thousand persons was also raided and burned down. See Goodspeed and Healy, *History of Cook County*, 1:290–99.

57. Dr. E. McArthur in *Northwestern Medical and Surgical Journal* 2 (1849): 278, as quoted in Webb, *History of Contagious Disease Care*, 10; and see Goodspeed and Healy, *History of Cook County*, 1:234, for injury to horses.

58. The classic essay on the urban horse is Joel A. Tarr, "Urban Pollution: Many Long Years Ago," *American Heritage*, October 1971, 65–69, 106. For more recent perspectives, see Clay McShane and Gijs Mom, "The Golden Age of the Horse and Its Substitution by Mechanization and Motorization: A Bibliographical Introduction" (unpublished manuscript, in author's possession 1999). For Chicago, see Duis, *Challenging Chicago*, 9–11. On the coming of car culture, see James J. Flink, *America Adopts the Automobile, 1895–1910* (Cambridge, MA: MIT Press, 1970).

59. James E. Herget, "Taming the Environment: The Drainage District in Illinois," *Journal of the Illinois State Historical Society* 71 (May 1978): 1–18; Prince, *Wetland*, 140–55; Kirkland, *Story of Chicago*, 1:230–32; Goodspeed and Healy, *History of Cook County*, 1:210–18; O'Connell, "Technology and Pollution," 18–35; and Keating, *Building Chicago*, 41–43.

60. Mayor Woodward as quoted in the *Chicago Daily Journal*, 16 March 1849, for the first several quotations; *Chicago Democratic Press*, 5 May 1853, as quoted in Goodspeed and Healy, *History of Cook County*, 1:246, for the last. Woodward's idea has become the centerpiece of a massive federal project of flood protection and pollution control, the Tunnel and Reservoir Plan (TARP), or Deep Tunnel. Although the complete history of this important public works project remains to be written, see Timothy B. Neary, "Chicago-Style Environmental Politics: Origins of the Deep Tunnel Project," *Journal of Illinois History* 4 (Summer 2001): 83–102.

61. Chicago Board of Sewerage Commissioners, *Report and Plan of Sewerage for the City of Chicago, Illinois, adopted by the Board of Sewerage Commissioners December 31, 1855* (Chicago: Charles Scott, 1855), 6. The original commissioners were William B. Ogden, Joseph D. Webster, and Sylvester Lind. See Goodspeed and Healy, *History of Cook County*, 1:257, for a report of the December 1854 mass meeting. Historians have long admired Chesbrough as "something of a hero ... a talented problem-solver," in the words of Robin Einhorn (*Property Rules*, 138), but he must be regarded as just the opposite from an environmental perspective. For the most part, scholars have too readily reflected the narrow economic viewpoints of the engineers and businesspeople who have dominated the decision-making process. Scholars' tendency to look at sanitation technology in isolation from the interrelated issues of water supply, medicine, and social policy has also helped to build Chesbrough's reputation. Recent studies have begun to criticize those in charge of the management of Chicago's water system as myopic penny-pinchers, but few have attempted to assess the costs to the environment and the resulting price

paid in terms of human misery, sickness, and death. A more holistic approach promises to put the urban infrastructure in a broader context, in addition to providing a more balanced judgment of the policy makers in charge of this crucial area of common concern.

62. Chicago Board of Sewer Commissioner, *Report*, 5–8 and passim (original emphasis). The commissioners put the final cost of their plan at $2.3 million for a district bounded by Division Street on the north, Rueben Street (now Sangamon Street) on the west, North Street (now Roosevelt Road) on the south, and the lake on the east.

63. Einhorn, *Property Rules*, 133–43, on political economy; Kirkland, *Story of Chicago*, 1:231–32, on the test case; and Currey, *Chicago*, 1:7, for other contemporary objections to the plan's cost burdens on property owners. But also see Chesbrough's later confession of cost compromises that made his sewers less than self-cleaning: E. S. Chesbrough, "The Drainage and Sewerage of Chicago," *Public Health Papers and Reports* 4 (1877): 18–26. On sewer technology also see Christopher Hamlin, "Edwin Chadwick and the Engineers, 1842–1854: Systems and Anti-Systems in the Pipe-and-Brick Sewers War," *Technology and Culture* 33 (October 1992): 680–88; and Joel Tarr, "The Separate vs. Combined Sewer Problem: A Case Study in Urban Technology Design Choice," *Journal of Urban History* 5 (May 1979): 308–39.

64. See John Stover, *The History of the Illinois Central Railroad* (New York: Macmillan, 1975), 40–45, 76–79; and Caillon J. Corliss, *Main Line of Mid-America* (New York: Creative Age, 1950), 56–69, for the building of the breakwater/terminal. See Goodspeed and Healy, *History of Cook County*, 1:257; and Lewis and Smith, *Chicago*, 67, for the city's project to raise the grade by dredging the river.

65. Currey, *Chicago*, 8, for the quotation and a description of the building technique; also see pp. 1:6–7. See Duis, *Challenging Chicago*, 7, for the pavement's origins in Chicago.

66. *Chicago Tribune*, 16 January 1855. Between July 1861 and January 1862, the U.S. Army purchased 8,332 of the 11,165 horses sold in the city, according to newspaper reports culled by Duis (*Challenging Chicago*, 9). Also see Graham Russell Hodges, *New York City Cartmen, 1667–1850* (New York: New York University Press, 1986), for insight on the teamsters and their animals in American urban life; and note 57, above, for broader perspectives.

67. Robert West Howard, *The Horse in America* (Chicago: Follett, 1965), 168–77. The Chicago Historical Society has a collection of the sales catalogs. See, for example, Woodlawn Stud Farm, *Catalogue of the Thoroughbred and Trotting Stock, at the Woodlawn Stud Farm* (Chicago: Jameson and Morse, 1871).

68. Elias Colbert, *Chicago: Historical and Statistical Sketch of the Garden City* (Chicago: Sherlock, 1868), 73–76; Pierce, *History of Chicago*, 2:324–29, on the street railways; U.S. Bureau of the Census, *Eighth Census of the United States, Manufacturing Industries* (Washington, DC: U.S. Bureau of the Census, 1860), 86; Isaac D. Guyer, *History of Chicago: Its Commercial and Manufacturing Interests and Industry* (Chicago: Church,

Goodman and Cushing, 1862), 167 and passim, on manufacturers of whips and other horse-related goods; and the city directories of the period for additional sources of information on this vast subject. Unfortunately, the very ubiquity of the horse in city life suggests that the city directories, especially in the antebellum period, are generally unreliable in capturing the full scope of businesses engaged in serving these animals and their masters.

69. Chicago Board of Sewer Commissioners, *Report*, 15; Mayer and Wade, *Chicago*, 94–98.

70. Lloyd Wendt and Herman Kogan, *Give the Lady What She Wants: The Story of Marshall Field and Company* (Chicago: Rand McNally, 1952), 13–51.

71. Alfred D. Chandler Jr., *The Visible Hand: The Managerial Revolution in American Business* (Cambridge, MA: Harvard University Press, 1977), 243. For a general introduction, see Stanley Baron, *Brewed in America: A History of Beer and Ale in the United States* (Boston: Little, Brown, 1962); Thomas C. Cochran, *The Pabst Brewing Company: The History of an American Business* (New York: New York University Press, 1948); Peter Mathias, *The Brewing Industry in England, 1700–1830* (Cambridge: Cambridge University Press, 1959); and W. J. Rorabaugh, *The Alcoholic Republic: An American Tradition* (New York: Oxford University Press, 1979). The leadership of the brewing industry in Chicago is confirmed by the 1890 census, which shows that it had the highest ratio of capital and machinery to labor among the city's ten leading manufacturers. U.S. Bureau of the Census, "Statistics of Cities," pt. 2 of *Eleventh Census of the United States, Manufacturing Industries* (Washington, DC: U.S. Bureau of the Census, 1890), 130–45.

72. On Lill and Diversey, see Guyer, *History of Chicago*, 37–43; Paul M. Angle, "Michael Diversey and Beer in Chicago," *Chicago History* 8 (March 1969): 321-26; *One Hundred Years of Brewing: A Supplement to the Western Brewer* (Chicago: Rich, 1903), 202; and Rudolf A. Hofmeister, *The Germans of Chicago* (Champaign, IL: Stipes, 1976), 133–35. For an excellent overview of the city's ethnic population that includes maps of its settlement patterns, see Chicago Department of Development and Planning, *Historic City: The Settlement of Chicago* (Chicago: Chicago Department of Development and Planning, 1976).

73. The most complete descriptions of beer making are found in *One Hundred Years of Brewing*, 58–104; and John P. Arnold and Frank Penman, *History of the Brewing Industry and Science in America: A Memorial to Dr. John E. Siebel and Anton Schwartz* (Chicago: n.p., 1933).

74. Oscar E. Anderson, *Refrigeration in America: A History of a New Technology and Its Impact* (Princeton, NJ: Princeton University Press, 1953), 7–28; A. L. Hunt, "Manufactured Ice," in U.S. Bureau of the Census, *Twelfth Census of the United States, Manufactures* (Washington, DC: U.S. Bureau of the Census, 1900), 9:675–97; Guyer, *History of Chicago*, 40–42; Andreas, *History of Chicago*, 3:337–38.

75. William B. Ogden, as quoted in Downard, "William Butler Ogden," 53. For Chicago, see *One Hundred Years of Brewing*, 232–33; Huck's original brewery stood on the "Ogden Block," bounded by Chicago Avenue and Superior, Rush, and Cass (now Huron) streets. In 1855, he moved to the corner of State and Banks streets, where he built

a much larger beer garden and brewery that included two miles of underground cellars. Also see the 1860 *Lakeside City Directory*, as reported in *One Hundred Years of Brewing*, 310. For the pivotal importance of lager beer, see *One Hundred Years of Brewing*, 98–104; and Arnold and Penman, *History of the Brewing Industry*, 57–61, including their assessment that "the introduction of lager beer revolutionized the American brewing industry" (p. 57).

76. *One Hundred Years of Brewing*, 78–79; see p. 332 for biographical information on Gottfried. Mathias, *Brewing Industry in England*, 81–98, for an account of the advent of steam power in London's breweries.

77. Mathias, *Brewing Industry in England*, 36.

78. *One Hundred Years of Brewing*, 76–86; and Arnold and Penman, *History of the Brewing Industry*, 88–95; for technological history; U.S. Bureau of the Census, *Eighth Census ... Manuscript of Industry, Cook County*, Reel 60, 9th Ward, 2, for notice of a twenty-horsepower steam engine. Cf. Guyer, *History of Chicago*, 37–43, for slightly higher figures. In 1839, Newberry and Dole installed the first grain elevator, which was horse-powered. In 1848, Chicago gained its first steam-powered elevator; by 1860, there were thirteen in operation. See Andreas, *History of Chicago*, 1:579–80; and Moses and Kirkland, *History of Chicago*, 1:123–26. For the phrase "organic machine," see Richard White, *The Organic Machine: The Remaking of the Columbia River* (New York: Hill and Wang, 1995).

79. See Chicago Board of Trade, *Annual Report* (1871): 36–37, for barley trade figures; (1900): 194 for reference to the legal weight of a bushel of barley.

80. City of Chicago, Board of Public Works, *Annual Report* (1898): 242, summarizes the amount of paving that was completed between 1855 and 1896; see Goodspeed and Healy, *History of Cook County*, 2:251, for the number of places selling alcohol in 1854.

81. See Joseph Charles, *Origins of the American Party System: Three Essays* (Williamsburg, VA: Institute of Early American History and Culture, 1956); Richard Hofstadter, *The Idea of the Party System: The Rise of Legitimate Opposition in the United States, 1780–1840* (Berkeley: University of California Press, 1969); and Eric Foner, *Free Soil, Free Labor, Free Men: The Ideology of the Republican Party before the Civil War* (New York: Oxford University Press 1970). On the local level, see Robin L. Einhorn, "The Lager Beer Riot and Segmented Government: Chicago, 1855," a paper presented to the Social Science History Association (Chicago, 1987).

82. Einhorn, "The Lager Beer Riot"; Pierce, *History of Chicago*, 2:190–245. An 1852 census of the city gives a slight edge of foreign-born over native-born: 19,419 versus 19,314. This slim majority would become larger over the course of the decade. See Goodspeed and Healy, *History of Cook County*, 2:238.

83. Einhorn, *Property Rules*, 188–230. For insight on the ways in which urban politics is composed of a diversity of power centers, see David C. Hammack, *Power and Society: Greater New York at the Turn of the Century* (New York: Russell Sage Foundation, 1982).

84. *Chicago Times*, 2 January 1865, 3.

Chapter Four

1. E. S. Chesbrough, as quoted in City of Chicago, Department of Public Works, *Annual Report* (1877): 6, for the title phrase, "fountain inexhaustible."

2. *Chicago Tribune*, 26 March 1867; *Chicago Times*, 26 March 1867. Chicago was awarded the engineering design award at the 1867 Paris Exposition. See James C. O'Connell, "Technology and Pollution: Chicago's Water Policy, 1833–1930" (Ph.D. diss., University of Chicago, 1980), 46.

3. *Chicago Times*, 26 March 1867. For insight on the sexual imagery of the mid-nineteenth century, see G. J. Barker-Benfield, *The Horrors of the Half-Known Life* (New York: Harpers, 1976).

4. See William Cronon, *Nature's Metropolis: Chicago and the Great West* (New York: Norton, 1991); and the earlier, but still relevant, James Willard Hurst, *Law and the Conditions of Freedom in the Nineteenth Century United States* (Madison: University of Wisconsin Press, 1956).

5. Robin Einhorn, *Property Rules: Political Economy in Chicago, 1833–1872* (Chicago: University of Chicago Press, 1991), 138, for the quotation. She does not necessarily share this view of Chesbrough. Also see David E. Nye, *American Technological Sublime* (Cambridge, MA: MIT Press, 1994). For a sophisticated historiographical essay on this topic, see Christopher Hamlin, *A Science of Impurity: Water Analysis in Nineteenth Century Britain* (Bristol: Hilger, 1990), 1–15. For further insight, consider Bill Luckin, *Pollution and Control: A Social History of the Thames in the Nineteenth Century* (Bristol: Hilger, 1986).

6. Chesbrough, as quoted in City of Chicago, Department of Public Works, *Annual Report* (1877): 6, for the first quoted phrase; E. S. Chesbrough, *Chicago Sewerage: Report of the Results of Examination Made in Relation to Sewerage in Several European Cities, in the Winter of 1856–1857* (Chicago: Board of Sewage Commissioners, 1858), 55, 92, for the second quotation. Cf. Luckin, *Pollution and Control*, for a perceptive evaluation of London's environmental history during this period; and Martin V. Melosi, "Sanitary Service and Decision Making in Houston, 1876–1945," *Journal of Urban History* 20 (May 1994): 365–406, for an analysis parallel to mine.

7. *Chicago Tribune*, 17 January 1865, for the first quotation; *Chicago Times*, 26 March 1867, for the second quotation.

8. B. T. W., "Cleansing the River," letter to the *Chicago Tribune*, 12 January 1865, for the names of the two parties; and Joel Tarr, *The Search for the Ultimate Sink: Urban Pollution in Historical Perspective* (Akron, OH: University of Akron Press, 1996), for the second, apt phrase. The initials on the letter may be for Bacon Wheeler, a member of the Committee of Thirty. For Chesbrough's preferred plan of wastewater removal, see his recommendations as a member of the Committee of Consulting Engineers, "Plan for Cleaning the Chicago River," as reported in the *Chicago Tribune*, 7 March 1865. The plans of both the reform group and the engineers will be examined below.

9. E. S. Chesbrough, "The Drainage and Sewerage of Chicago," *Public Health Papers and Reports* 4 (1877): 18, for the first quotation; see also pp. 18–26. Chesbrough, *Chicago Sewerage*.

10. See Louise Carroll Wade, *Chicago's Pride: The Stockyards, Packingtown, and Environs in the Nineteenth Century* (Urbana: University of Illinois Press, 1987), 25–46; Ann Durkin Keating, *Building Chicago: Suburban Developers and the Creation of a Divided Metropolis* (Columbus: Ohio State University Press, 1988), 33–51; and Einhorn, *Property Rules*, 204–15, for good accounts of the pollution problems created by the extraordinary growth of industry along the river during the Civil War period, as perceived by the business elite and daily press. What the three sources do not take fully into consideration is the impacts the river's overload of decaying organic wastes from the packing houses and distilleries had on the health of the people forced by poverty to live in close proximity to the riverfront. On business structures, see Alfred D. Chandler Jr., *The Visible Hand: The Managerial Revolution in American Business* (Cambridge, MA: Harvard University Press, 1977).

11. Chesbrough, "The Drainage and Sewerage," 24, for the quotation. Also see above, note 10, and Christine Meisner Rosen, "Differing Perceptions of the Value of Pollution Abatement across Time and Place: Balancing Doctrine in Pollution Nuisance Law, 1840–1906," *Law and History Review* 11 (January 1993): 303–81.

12. On the Bridgeport pumps, see G. P. Brown, *Drainage Channel and Waterway* (Chicago: Donnelly, 1894), 306–27. The pumps, according to Brown, had a capacity of 10,000 cubic feet per minute (cfm). They were installed in 1848, and they were dismantled in 1873 and sold for less than one-tenth of their purchase price, after the deep cut seemed to make them superfluous. This decision seems especially short-sighted since the river stink returned as soon as seasonal surface runoff neutralized or reversed the gravity-induced currents. New pumps would be needed within five years. Also see A. T. Andreas, *History of Chicago*, 3 vols. (1884–1886; reprint, New York: Arno, 1975), 1:55–74; and Constance B. Webb, *A History of Contagious Disease Care in Chicago before the Great Fire* (Chicago: University of Chicago Press, 1940), 93–119. The concluding section of this chapter will further discuss the dismantling and the reinstallation of the Bridgeport pumps.

13. See O'Connell, "Technology and Pollution," 36–48.

14. Dr. E. Andrews, as quoted in John Rauch, "Sanitary History of Chicago," in Chicago Board of Health, *Report of the Board of Health of the City of Chicago for 1867, 1868, and 1869; and a Sanitary History of Chicago from 1833–1870* (Chicago: Lakeside, 1871), 68–69. See the same for a reproduction of the map enhanced with a second overlay for the 1866 cholera epidemic. For insight on nineteenth-century theories of disease, see Hamlin, *Science of Impurity*; Luckin, *Pollution and Control*; and Carlo Cipolla, *Miasmas and Disease: Public Health and the Environment in the Pre-Industrial Era* (New Haven, CT: Yale University Press, 1992). For the history of medical mapping, see S. Jarcho, "Yellow Fever, Cholera and the Beginnings of Medical Cartography," *Journal of the History of Medicine* 25 (1970): 131–142; L. G. Stevenson, "Putting

Disease on the Map: The Early Use of Spot Maps in Yellow Fever," *Journal of the History of Medicine* 20 (1965): 226–61; and Richard Harrison Shryock, *The Development of Modern Medicine: An Interpretation of the Social and Scientific Factors Involved* (1936; reprint, Madison: University of Wisconsin Press, 1979). For evidence that big cities became reservoirs of disease, see A. D. Cliff, *Deciphering Global Epidemics: Analytical Approaches to the Disease Records of World Cities, 1888–1912*, Cambridge Studies in Historical Geography, No. 26; (Cambridge: Cambridge University Press, 1998).

15. E. C. Larned, as quoted in the *Chicago Tribune*, 18 December 1864. See Wade, *Chicago's Pride*, 34–41, for insight on the environmental impacts of the meatpacking industry. Wade also deserves credit for identifying Larned's devastating letter to the press. Also see Rauch, "Sanitary History"; Andreas, *History of Chicago*, 1:63–69; John B. Hamilton, "The Epidemics of Chicago," *Bulletin of the Society of Medical History of Chicago* 1 (October 1911): 73–86; and Webb, *History of Contagious Disease Care*, 93–119.

16. Dr. Nathan Davis, as quoted in City of Chicago, Board of Health, *Annual Report* (1867–1869): 97; see also pp. 60–66, 93–119.

17. Ibid.; O'Connell, "Technology and Pollution," 58–60, for the quotation.

18. Weston A. Goodspeed and Daniel D. Healy, eds., *History of Cook County*, 2 vols. (Chicago: Goodspeed Historical Association, 1909), 1:313–16.

19. Chesbrough, "Drainage and Sewerage," 24; Goodspeed and Healy, *History of Cook County*, 1:313–16. For the harbor, see Andreas, *History of Chicago*, 2:70–74, and John W. Larson, *Those Army Engineers: A History of the Chicago District, U.S. Army Corp of Engineers* (Washington: Government Printing Office, 1980), 81–130.

20. See Graeme Davison, "The City as a Natural System: Theories of Urban Society in Early Nineteenth-Century Britain," in *The Pursuit of Urban History*, ed. Derek Fraser and Anthony Sutcliffe (London: Edward Arnold, 1983), 349–70; and Christopher Hamlin, "Providence and Putrefaction: Victorian Sanitarians and the Natural Theology of Health and Disease," *Victorian Studies* 28 (Spring 1985): 381–411. Cf. John Duffy, *The Sanitarians: A History of American Public Health* (Urbana: University of Illinois Press, 1990).

21. See Keating, *Building Chicago*, for maps comparing the water and sewer systems over time. Also see Einhorn, *Property Rules*, 144–230.

22. For the text of Dr. Davis's proposals, see Committee of Physicians, "Report on the Means of Improving the Sanitary Condition of Chicago," *Chicago Medical Examiner* 6 (1865), as quoted in William K. Beatty, "When Cholera Scourged Chicago," *Chicago History* 11 (Spring 1982): 11–12. This report represents possibly the earliest call in Chicago for a building code to prevent overcrowding and to regulate boarding houses. The doctors had observed that bad and overcrowded housing for recent arrivals was ready-made for the spread of disease. Also see Webb, *History of Contagious Disease Care*, 51–119.

23. The group organized by the city's businessmen, the Committee of Thirty, included one physician, Dr. Daniel Brainard. See *Chicago Tribune*, 4 January 1865, for a complete

list of the membership. Brainard would be one of the victims of the 1866 cholera epidemic. See Beatty, "When Cholera Scourged Chicago," 13; and Cain, *Sanitation Strategy for a Lakefront Metropolis: The Case of Chicago* (DeKalb: Northern Illinois University Press, 1978).

24. See especially, *Chicago Tribune*, 6 January 1865; and Wade, *Chicago's Pride*; Keating, *Building Chicago*; and Einhorn, *Property Rules*, 204–15.

25. *Chicago Tribune*, 4 January 1865, for the quotation and for the full text of the manifesto. For the activities of the Committee of Thirty, also see *Chicago Tribune*, 6, 15, 18, and 21 January 1865; and *Chicago Times*, 10 and 16 January 1865, including the map of the Calumet Plan on the latter date. The committee had a concentration of members of the Board of Trade who also had an interest in civic affairs. See Andreas, *History of Chicago*, 2:335–58; and Wade, *Chicago's Pride*, 32–41.

26. See note 25, immediately above. For biographical sketches of Larned and Dexter, see Andreas, *History of Chicago*, 2:463, 472–73.

27. William B. Ogden, letter to E. H. Sheldon (29 December 1864), as quoted in the *Chicago Tribune*, 11 January 1865; for the endorsement of Gooding see *Chicago Tribune*, 6 January 1865. Also review the discussion at an open public meeting called by the Committee of Thirty, *Chicago Tribune*, 21 January 1865. For a portrait of the indefatigable city builder, see William L. Downard, "William Butler Ogden and the Growth of Chicago," *Journal of the Illinois State Historical Society* 75 (Spring 1982): 47–60.

28. For an introduction to the shifts in the balance of power set off by the war, see Harold M. Hyman, *A More Perfect Union: The Impact of the Civil War and Reconstruction on the Constitution* (New York: Knopf, 1973), 326–46; and Morton Keller, *Affairs of State: Public Life in Late Nineteenth Century America* (Cambridge, MA: Harvard University Press, 1977). For the local context, see Einhorn, *Property Rules*, 208–16. For Ogden's ownership of the Mud Lake area, see Brown, *Drainage Channel*, 318–27.

29. *Chicago Tribune*, 4 January 1865. Given the large number of proposed remedies, the final version of the bill sponsored by the Committee of Thirty dropped reference to any specific plan. Instead, it deferred the decision to the river commission. In a similar way the city council looked to the panel of consulting engineers to settle the question. See *Chicago Tribune*, 18 and 21 January 1865.

30. *Chicago Tribune*, 18 January 1865, for Hayes's quotation and report of the meeting; *Chicago Tribune*, 19 January 1865, for the editorial comment; and *Chicago Tribune*, 25 January 1865, for a reply to the editorial in the form of a letter from Hayes. Also see *Chicago Times*, 10 and 16 January 1865. Holden was a leader of the first political ring, or organization of local politicians. See Richard Schneirov, *Labor and Urban Politics: Class Conflict and the Origins of Modern Liberalism in Chicago, 1864–1897* (Urbana: University of Illinois Press, 1998), 49–50.

31. *Chicago Tribune*, 21 January 1865. Cf. the retort of the paper's editor against "a few soreheads" in the council, *Chicago Tribune*, 24 January 1865. Significantly, neither the newspaper nor the members of the Committee of Thirty attempted to answer directly the objections to the antidemocratic nature of their proposals.

32. State of Illinois, *General Laws* (1866), "I & M Canal Authorization Act of 16 February 1866."
33. Wade, *Chicago's Pride*, 40–41. In November 1865 the council belatedly followed up with a public nuisance and license ordinance to give effect to the state law.
34. *Chicago Tribune*, 7 March 1865, for a full transcript of the report by the Committee of Consulting Engineers. The other two members were John Van Nortwick and E. B. Talcott. The engineers dismissed the Calumet Plan on the basis of the inadequacy of the river's water supply to flush the Chicago River during the summer and fall when it was most needed. They surveyed Ogden's proposed route to find substantial evidence supporting his claim that the riverbed of the Des Plaines was deep enough to make a suitable alternative drainage channel. Although the cost of Ogden's scheme would be only $100,000, the panel ended up rejecting it because they believed the results would soon prove a "disappointment." As we will see below, Ogden would build the drainage ditch as a private project in 1871 with fateful consequences for the city's efforts to control the hydraulic environment. In comparison, the two auxiliary canals were estimated to cost about $500,000 each, the intercepting sewer system $1 million, and the deep-cut project at $2.1 million.
35. Ibid.
36. Ibid.
37. Ibid. for the panel's report; *Chicago Times*, 23 January 1865, for the wave-box proposal.
38. John B. Rice quoted in *Chicago Times*, 26 March 1867.
39. Ibid.
40. John H. Rauch, *A Report to the Board of Health of the City of Chicago on the Necessity of an Extension of the Sewerage of the City* (Chicago: Ottaway, Brown and Colbert, 1873), 18, for the quotation in the heading; Charles Rosenberg, *The Cholera Years: The United States in 1832, 1849, and 1866* (Chicago: University of Chicago Press, 1962), 193 for the quotation in the text and 192–212 for the impact of the New York reform; and Webb, *History of Contagious Disease Care*; and Rauch, "Sanitary History," 111. Also see Gert H. Brieger, "Sanitary Reform in New York City: Stephen Smith and the Passage of the Metropolitan Health Bill," in *Sickness and Health in America: Readings in the History of Medicine and Public Health*, ed. Judith Walzer Leavitt and Ronald L. Numbers (Madison: University of Wisconsin Press, 1997), 437–51. The parallels in the origins of the acts are striking. Both were sponsored by medical professionals and elite business groups and both had to overcome the opposition of local politicians. Local chronicler Andreas attributes the model legislation to attorney Anthony Elliot, who apparently made a tour of the cities to study public health policy and practice during the smallpox and cholera epidemics. Dr. Rauch and other physicians served on the local reform committee that lobbied for the bill in Springfield. See Andreas, *History of Chicago*, 2:551–53.
41. Rosenberg, *Cholera Years*, 175–225; Duffy, *Sanitarians*; George M. Fredrickson, *The Inner Civil War: Northern Intellectuals and the Crisis of the Union* (New York: Harper and Row, 1965); Letty Anderson, "Fire and Disease: The Development of Water Supply

Systems in New England, 1870–1900," in *Technology and the Rise of the Networked City in Europe and America*, ed. Joel A. Tarr and Gabriel DuPuy (Philadelphia: Temple University Press, 1988), 137–56; and Martin V. Melosi, *The Sanitary City: Urban Infrastructure in America from Colonial Times to the Present* (Baltimore: Johns Hopkins University Press, 2000). For Chicago women during the war, see J. Christopher Schnell, "Mary Livermore and the Great Northwestern Fair," *Chicago History* 5 (Spring 1975): 38–43; and Beverly Gordon, "A Furor of Benevolence," *Chicago History* 15 (Winter 1986–1987): 48–65. On professionalization, see Thomas L. Haskell, *The Emergence of Professional Social Science: The American Social Science Association and the Nineteenth-Century Crisis of Authority* (Urbana: University of Illinois Press, 1977); and Thomas L. Haskell, ed., *The Authority of Experts: Studies in History and Theory* (Bloomington: Indiana University Press, 1984).

42. See F. Garvin Davenport, "John Henry Rauch and Public Health in Illinois, 1877–1891," *Journal of the Illinois State Historical Society* 50 (Autumn 1957): 277–93; and Thomas Neville Bonner, *Medicine in Chicago, 1850–1950: A Chapter in the Social and Scientific Development of a City*, 2nd ed. (Urbana: University of Illinois Press, 1991), 179–86.

43. See Bruno Latour, *The Pasteurization of France* (Cambridge, MA: Harvard University Press, 1988), on the sociology of medicine and the search for a new paradigm; and Christopher Hamlin, *Science of Impurity*, for a comprehensive survey of the various avenues of the search for a substitute for miasmatic etiologies. The classic essay on separate spheres is Barbara Welter, "The Cult of the True Womanhood, 1820–1860," *American Quarterly* 18 (Summer 1966): 151–74. For Chicago, this cultural phenomenon is carefully examined in Richard Sennett, *Families against the City: Middle Class Homes of Industrial Chicago, 1872–1890* (Cambridge, MA: Harvard University Press, 1970).

44. John H. Rauch, "Intramural Interments in Populous Cities, and Their Influence upon Health and Epidemics" (Chicago: Rauch, 1866), as quoted in Andreas, *History of Chicago*, 2:550–51. Also see Webb, *History of Contagious Disease Care*, 93–119. The old City Cemetery was located on the current site of the Chicago Historical Society. A few graves remain nearby to this day. In addition to a registry of vital statistics, an official list of medical practitioners was also complied. In 1868, Chicago had 378 doctors and 44 midwives.

45. Rauch, "Sanitary History."

46. Ibid., 270, for the quotation. Rauch identifies the source of his quotation only as "Parks, the best authority on the subject." Most likely the reference is to Edmund A. Parkes, author of *A Manual of Practical Hygiene*, which went through several American editions. See Christopher Hamlin, *What Becomes of Pollution? Adversary Science and the Controversy on the Self-Purification of Rivers in Britain, 1850–1900* (New York: Garland, 1987), 600. On the role of social statistics, see Mary O. Furner, "The Republican Tradition and the New Liberalism: Social Investigation, State Building, and Social Learning in the Gilded Age," in *The State and Social Investigation in Britain and the United States*, ed. Michael J. Lacey and Mary O. Furner, Woodrow Wilson Center Series (Washington, DC, and Cambridge: Woodrow Wilson Center

Press and Cambridge University Press, 1993), 171–241. Also see Rauch, *Report to the Board of Health.*

47. Rauch, *Report to the Board of Health,* 8, 18.

48. See two recent provocative studies; Schneirov, *Labor and Urban Politics*; and Eric L. Hirsch, *Urban Revolt: Ethnic Politics in the Nineteenth-Century Chicago Labor Movement* (Berkeley: University of California Press, 1990). Also highly useful on the city's political culture is Richard C. Lindberg, *To Serve and Collect: Chicago Politics and Police Corruption from the Lager Beer Riot to the Summerdale Scandal* (New York: Praeger, 1991).

49. Roger D. Simon, "The City-Building Process: Housing and Services in New Milwaukee Neighborhoods, 1880–1910," *Transactions of the American Philosophical Society* 68 (July 1978): 1–64; and Terrence J. McDonald, *The Parameters of Urban Fiscal Policy: Socio-Economic Change and Political Culture in San Francisco, 1860–1906* (Berkeley: University of California Press, 1986). For the urge to own a home among the working classes, see Stephen Thernstrom, *Poverty and Progress: Social Mobility in a Nineteenth Century City* (Cambridge, MA: Harvard University Press, 1964); and John T. Mc-Greevy, *Parish Boundaries: The Catholic Encounter with Race in the Twentieth-Century North* (Chicago: University of Chicago Press, 1996). Although McGreevy's book is about the twentieth century, it contains important insights on the religious motives of Catholics to become home owners within their own parish.

50. Melosi, *Sanitary City,* 58–102, for a comprehensive survey of the postwar public health movement in urban America. On the financing of political parties, see Clifton K. Yearly, *The Money Machines: The Breakdown and Reform of Governmental and Party Finance in the North, 1860–1920* (Albany: State University of New York Press, 1970). On the financing of city government, see McDonald, *Parameters of Urban Fiscal Policy.* In 1885, Chicago was the third largest of the thirteen large urban centers in the United States, but last among them in per capita taxes. See Schneirov, *Labor and Urban Politics,* 46–53, 62. On the legal status of the city, see Harold L. Platt, "Creative Necessity: Municipal Reform in Gilded Age Chicago," in *The Constitution, Law, and American Life: Critical Aspects of the Nineteenth-Century Experience,* ed. Donald G. Nieman (Athens: University of Georgia Press, 1992), 162–90. The other piece of the quid pro quo between the professional politicians and the business elite was the use of the police force to break strikes by organized labor. See Lindberg, *To Serve and Collect,* 59–78.

51. Cronon, *Nature's Metropolis.*

52. Christine Meisner Rosen, *The Limits of Power: Great Fires and the Process of City Growth in America* (New York: Cambridge University Press, 1988), 89–176. Also essential for understanding the shifts in land use is Homer Hoyt, *One Hundred Years of Land Values in Chicago* (Chicago: University of Chicago Press, 1933), 87–127.

53. Rosen, *Limits of Power,* 156. River traffic on the Main Branch created a formidable barrier to residential development of the north division. In the incessant contest between keeping the swing bridges open for the boats and closing them for the pedestrians and horse-drawn vehicles, the shippers won most of the time.

In the 1860s, several private and public projects to tunnel under the river were proposed. The city opened a tunnel designed by Chesbrough to the West Side on Washington Street in 1869 and completed another tunnel to the North Side on LaSalle Street two years later. See Andreas, *History of Chicago*, 2:63–69; and Jack M. Wing, *The Tunnels and Water System of Chicago* (Chicago: Wing, 1874).

54. *Chicago Tribune*, 29 June 1864, as cited in Wade, *Chicago's Pride*, 49.

55. *Chicago Times*, 12 December 1865, as quoted in Wade, *Chicago's Pride*, 54; see also chaps. 4 and 9 of Wade's book. The classic study of the two communities is Charles Bushnell, "Some Social Aspects of the Chicago Stock Yards," *American Journal of Sociology* 7, nos. 3, 4, 5, and 6 (1901 1902).

56. Wade, *Chicago's Pride*, 36–41.

57. Rauch, *Report to the Board of Health*.

58. See Wade, *Chicago's Pride*, chapters 4, 9, and 12, on the early growth of Packingtown; Simon, "City-Building Process," for insight on special assessment taxes and working-class home ownership; and Robert A. Slayton, *Back of the Yards: The Making of a Local Democracy* (Chicago: University of Chicago Press, 1986), 36 for the map by Eugene Senn and 30–38 for the social geography of Packingtown. On the politics of special assessment taxation in Chicago, see Einhorn, *Property Rules*.

59. Goodspeed and Healy, *History of Cook County*, 2:308, for the first quotation; Keating, *Building Chicago*, 17, for the second quotation. Also see Samuel W. Block Jr., *Hyde Park Houses: An Informal History, 1856–1910* (Chicago: University of Chicago Press, 1963), chaps. 1–2; and *Chicago: Pictorial and Biographical: De Luxe Supplement* (Chicago: Clarke, 1912), 1:173–77.

60. *Chicago: Pictorial and Biographical*; Goodspeed and Healy, *History of Cook County*, 2:307–10; Keating, *Building Chicago*, chap. 5. In typical fashion, Cornell became the first supervisor of the new township. On the suburban ethos and middle-class reactions to the postwar city, see Michael H. Ebner, *Creating Chicago's North Shore: A Suburban History* (Chicago: University of Chicago Press, 1988); and Sennett, *Families against the City*.

61. See State of Illinois, *Special Laws of Illinois*, 4 vols. (Springfield: State of Illinois, 1969), 1:342–79; Andreas, *History of Chicago*, 3:167–72; Glen E. Holt, "Private Plans for Public Spaces: the Origins of Chicago's Park System, 1850–1875," *Chicago History* 8 (Fall 1979): 187–84; and Platt, "Creative Necessity," on the birth of Chicago's parks. The author of the parks bills was an attorney and reformer, Ezra B. McCagg, who had headed the North Western Sanitary Commission.

62. Although the South Park Commission embraced the townships of Hyde Park, Lake, and South Chicago, the residents of the lakefront suburbs north of 59th Street were clearly its primary beneficiaries. For insight on Washington Park as an ethnic buffer zone into the 1920s, see James T. Farrell, *Studs Lonigan: A Trilogy containing Young Lonigan, The Young Manhood of Studs Lonigan, Judgment Day* (New York, Modern Library, 1963); and Charles Fanning and Ellen Skerrett, "James T. Farrell and Washington Park: The Novel as Social History," *Chicago History* 8

(Summer 1979): 80–91. Significantly, the next generation of city planners would build the elevated structure for train travel down State Street that also functioned to mark the dividing line between the lakefront residential communities and their industrial counterparts. Still later generations would use expressways as racial Berlin walls. The most obvious of these is the Dan Ryan Expressway, which separated the Robert Taylor and Stateway Gardens high-rise housing projects from Mayor Richard J. Daley's white-only Bridgeport. Regarding State Street as a borderline, see the map supplied by Bushnell in "Some Social Aspects of the Chicago Stock Yards." On racial planning, see Roger Biles, *Richard J. Daley: Politics, Race, and the Governing of Chicago* (DeKalb: Northern Illinois University Press, 1995).

63. Wade, *Chicago's Pride*, 138–41. Also see the manuscript by Laura Willard, "History of Hyde Park: A Study of Local Government, 1896" (Chicago: Chicago Historical Society), 38–41.

64. Wade, *Chicago's Pride*, 136–41. The key case was *Chicago Packing Company v. Chicago* 85 Ill 221 (1878). The irony of the two battles against the packers was complete when Cornell was able to use this very ruling to beat them into submission while the city gained nothing tangible from the struggle in terms of the cleaning up of the environment. For the politics of ethnic division in the stockyards district, see Slayton, *Back of the Yards*, 151–71.

65. See Everett Chamberlin, *Chicago and Its Suburbs* (Chicago: T. A. Hungerford, 1874); Hoyt, *One Hundred Years of Land Values*; Keating, *Building Chicago*; and Ebner, *Creating Chicago's North Shore*.

66. For a general overview, see Keller, *Affairs of State*.

67. Slayton, *Back of the Yards*, 151–71; Sam Bass Warner Jr., *The Private City: Philadelphia in Three Periods of Its Growth* (Philadelphia: University of Pennsylvania Press, 1968); and Sam Bass Warner Jr., *The Urban Wilderness: A History of the American City* (New York: Harper and Row, 1972).

68. Schneirov, *Labor and Urban Politics*, chap. 2. Schneirov provides the most coherent and sophisticated interpretation of Chicago politics during the Gilded Age. Also see the important work of another labor historian, John B. Jentz, including "Artisan Culture and the Organization of Chicago's Workers in the Gilded Age, 1860 to 1890," in *German Workers' Culture in the United States, 1850 to 1920*, ed. Hartmut Keil (Washington, DC: Smithsonian Institution Press, 1988), 59–80; and "Class and Politics in an Emerging Industrial City: Chicago in the 1860s and 1870s," *Journal of Urban History* 17 (May 1991): 227–63. For insight on the radicals, see Bruce Nelson, *Beyond the Martyrs: A Social History of Chicago's Anarchists, 1870–1910* (New Brunswick, NJ: Rutgers University Press, 1988); and Hartmut Keil and John B. Jentz, eds., *German Workers in Industrial Chicago, 1850–1910: Comparative Perspectives* (DeKalb: Northern Illinois University Press, 1983). For a significant contribution regarding the ways in which gender shaped perceptions of the fire as well as reactions to it, see Karen Sawislak, *Smoldering City: Chicagoans and the Great Fire, 1871–1874* (Chicago: University of Chicago Press, 1996). Also important for understanding

the implications of the fire is Carl Smith, *Urban Disorder and the Shape of Disbelief* (Chicago: University of Chicago Press, 1995).

69. Rosen, *Limits of Power*, 95–109; Sawislak, *Smoldering City*, 136–62. On Germantown see Christiane Harzig, "Chicago's German North Side, 1880–1900: The Structure of a Gilded Age Ethnic Neighborhood," in Keil and Jentz, *German Workers*, 127–44.

70. Franklin MacVeagh, "Annual Report of the President," in the Chicago Citizens Association, *Annual Report* (1874): 13–18, for the insurance embargo quotation; and Harold L. Platt, "Creative Necessity." Also see Schneirov, *Labor and Urban Politics*, 51–64. For broader perspectives on the financing of urban political parties, see Yearly, *Money Machines*.

71. Schneirov, *Labor and Urban Politics*, 62. According to Schneirov, tax assessments did not reach 1873 levels until 1898, making Chicago in 1885 the city with the lowest per capita taxation among the thirteen largest urban centers in the country. Also see Goodspeed and Healy, *History of Cook County*, 2:567–84.

72. *Chicago Tribune*, 17 March 1875, for the quotation. See also *Chicago Tribune*, 5 March–15 April 1875; and see Goodspeed and Healy, *History of Cook County*, 2:541–675, for a chronicle of city, county, state, and national political history. Also see Schneirov, *Labor and Urban Politics*, 51, for home owner statistics. On average 22 percent of adult males owned real estate at the time of the great fire.

73. Schneirov, *Labor and Urban Politics*, 51.

74. See Stanley K. Schultz, *Constructing Urban Culture: American Cities and City Planning, 1800–1920* (Philadelphia: Temple University Press, 1989); and John F. Kasson, *Civilizing the Machine: Technology and Republican Values in America, 1776–1900* (New York: Penguin, 1977).

75. *Chicago Tribune*, 16, 18, and 21 July 1871, for the quotations, respectively. Also see *Chicago Tribune*, 28 July 1871 for the water-flow statistics and climatic report. The main natural factor creating unusually favorable conditions for a fast-flowing current is low barometric pressure, which can result in lake levels twelve to eighteen inches above normal.

76. *Chicago Tribune*, 21 July 1871, for the quotation; see also *Chicago Tribune*, 25 and 28 July 1871.

77. See *Chicago Tribune*, 26 July 1871, for a detailed account of the ceremonies, including the quotations included here.

78. Lindberg, *To Serve and Collect*, x. See Schneirov, *Labor and Urban Politics*, chap. 6, for Harrison's appointments.

79. Cain, *Sanitation Strategy*, tables 24–27, for financial statistics.

80. William Bross, *History of Chicago: Historical and Commercial Statistics ... Republished from the Daily Democratic Press* (Chicago: Jansen, McClurg, 1876), 43; J. F. Bateman, *History and Description of the Manchester Waterworks* (Manchester: Day, 1884), 181–85; U.S. Bureau of the Census, "Waterworks," in *Eleventh Census of the United States, Social Statistics of Cities* (Washington, DC: U.S. Bureau of the Census, 1890), 24.

81. Chicago Board of Public Works, "Report to the City Council," as reported in City of Chicago, *Proceedings of the Common Council* (29 March 1875): 109–10. For additional

contemporary evidence of an understanding of the cost benefits of a universal meter system, see the report written by two key city engineers, E. S. Chesbrough and D. C. Cregier, City of Chicago, Department of Public Works, *Annual Report* (1877): 11–13, 59.

82. City of Chicago, Department of Public Works, *Annual Report* (1877): 12, 59.

83. Ibid.; p. 12 for the quotation.

84. J. B. McClure, *Stories and Sketches of Chicago* (Chicago: Rhodes and McClure, 1880), 148–49.

85. City of Chicago, Department of Public Works, *Annual Report* (1935): 57b, for the statistics used in the text and figures; and City of Chicago, *A Century of Progress in Water Works 1833–1933* (Chicago: Department of Public Works, Bureau of Engineering, 1933), for a narrative of the expansion of the system. Between 1861 and 1886, the total average price of pumping one million gallons one foot high dropped from 8.64 to 5.43 cents. On the aldermanic pressure on coal contracts and their perversion, see the *Chicago Tribune*, 11 July 1876; and D. C. Cregier's later revelation of a corrupt scheme to use fraudulent tests on the quality of the coal to cover up sweetheart contracts for inferior fuel at inflated prices, as reported in F. W. Gerecke, *Report of Chief Engineer F. W. Gerecke, to the Commissioner of Public Works, Geo. B. Swift, on the Condition of the Water Works of the City of Chicago, February 25th and June 15, 1888* (Chicago: Chicago Department of Public Works, 1888), 21–24.

86. *Chicago Tribune*, 4 March 1875; Brown, *Drainage Channel*, 306–21.

87. *Chicago Tribune*, 18 July 1871.

88. Ibid., 7 March 1875.

89. Ibid., 15 March 1875, for the flood; Brown, *Drainage Channel*, 320–27.

90. Chesbrough, "Drainage and Sewerage"; City of Chicago, Department of Public Works, *Annual Report* (1877): 6–38.

91. Chesbrough, "Drainage and Sewerage," 25, 26, for the first and third quotations; Chesbrough, as quoted in City of Chicago, Department of Public Works, *Annual Report* (1877): 6–7, for the second quotation.

92. *Chicago Tribune*, 8 November 1879.

93. Ibid., 10 January 1880.

94. Ibid., 11 February 1881; Arthur Reynolds, "Three Chicago and Illinois Public Health Officers: John H. Rauch, Oscar C. DeWolf, and Frank W. Reilly," *Bulletin of the Society of Medical History of Chicago* 1 (August 1912); 87–134; Bonner, *Medicine in Chicago*, 179–86.

95. *Chicago Tribune*, 26 November 1882.

96. Ibid., 3 August 1884. Also see Bonner, *Medicine in Chicago*, 183–91.

97. *Chicago Tribune*, 5 August 1884. Also see Nancy Tomes, *The Gospel of Germs: Men, Women, and the Microbe in American Life* (Cambridge, MA: Harvard University Press, 1998).

98. Nelson, *Beyond the Martyrs*; Smith, *Urban Disorder*.

99. City of Chicago, Department of Public Works, *Annual Report* (1884): 1–66.

100. Ibid., 27.

Chapter Five

1. *Manchester Guardian*, 7 February 1852. The title phrase, "hardest worked river," is attributed to Sir John Kane by one of the central figures in this chapter, hydraulics engineer John Bateman. See John Bateman, "Report to the Irwell Flood Committee of the Manchester Corporation," City of Manchester, *Proceedings of the Common Council, 1868–1869* (19 October 1868): 20–32.

2. *Manchester Guardian*, 11 February 1852. In spite of the relatively small size of their community—less than 15 percent of the total population—the Irish Catholics of Manchester furnished the social elite a convenient and enduring "racial" and religious scapegoat for all the city's problems. See Mary Poovey, "Curing the 'Social Body' in 1832: James Phillips Kay and the Irish in Manchester," *Gender and History* 5 (1993): 196–211; M. Busteed and R. Hodgson, "Irish Migration and Settlement in Nineteenth Century Manchester with Special Reference to the Angel Meadow District," *Irish Geography* 27 (1994): 1–13; W. J. Lowe, *The Irish in Mid-Victorian Lancashire: the Shaping of a Working-Class Community* (New York: Lang, 1989); and Steven Fielding, "A Separate Culture? Irish Catholics in Working-Class Manchester and Salford, c. 1880–1939," in *Workers' Worlds: Cultures and Communities in Manchester and Salford, 1880–1939*, ed. Andrew Davies and Steven Fielding (Manchester: University of Manchester Press, 1992), 23–48.

3. *Manchester Guardian*, 7 February 1852, for initial reports on the Holmfirth disaster; *Manchester Guardian*, 11, 14, and 18 February 1852, for follow-up stories. Perhaps the most complete account is provided in the report of the testimony at the coroner's inquest in the *Manchester Guardian*, 21 February 1852. Also essential for understanding is Bateman's analysis of the event, John F. Bateman, "Some Account of the Floods which Occurred at the Manchester Waterworks in the Month of February 1852," *Literary and Philosophical Society of Manchester, Memoirs*, 2nd ser., 10 (1852): 137–54. Receiving less attention was the bursting of two half-completed reservoirs near Edenfield. The collapse of these dams caused no loss of life and only minor property damage, but the event was significant in the context of the craze for building reservoirs during a period when there were no established engineering standards of construction. In this case, the embankments were fatally built upon a bed of peat moss, which was also used to build up the walls. See *Manchester Guardian*, 18 February 1852. Bateman had already learned the lesson of the dangers of underestimating the amount of rain that could fall in short period. In October 1849 a storm surge had caused the collapse during a vulnerable stage of construction of one of the reservoirs he was in charge of. The American counterpart of the Holmfirth disaster was the Johnstown, Pennsylvania, flood of May 1889, which claimed 2,200 victims. See Willis Fletcher Johnson, *The History of the Johnstown Flood* (Philadelphia: Edgewood, 1889); and David G. McCullough, *The Johnstown Flood* (New York: Simon and Schuster, 1968).

4. *Manchester Guardian*, 21 February 1852.

5. Ibid.

6. Ibid., 7 February 1852, for the quotation; see also the issues of 11–21 February 1852.

7. Ibid., 11–21 February 1852.

8. Richard Wright Proctor, *Memories of Manchester Streets* (Manchester: Sutcliffe, 1874), 5–8. Cf. *Manchester Guardian*, 7 November 1852, which lists only one notable flood, on 8 October 1767, during the eighteenth century, but concurs with Proctor's list for the nineteenth century. Another good source for a list of floods during the nineteenth century is William E. A. Axon, *The Annals of Manchester* (London: Heywood, 1886).

9. Proctor, *Memories*, 7–8; and *Manchester Guardian*, ? August 1829; 7 September 1833; 21–24 December 1837; 25 January–1 February 1840; and 1–3 November 1843, for the floods. For the transformation of the city center's spatial features and dimensions under the early impacts of industrialization, the best description remains Leo H. Grindon, *Manchester Banks and Bankers*, 2nd ed. (Manchester: Palmer and Howe, 1878). Also see Robin Lloyd-Jones and M. J. Lewis, *Manchester and the Age of the Factory* (London: Croom-Helm, 1988); and Gary S. Messinger, *Manchester in the Victorian Age: The Half-Known City* (Manchester: Manchester University Press, 1985).

10. John Dalton, "Experiments and Observations to Determine Whether the Quantity of Rain and Dew Is Equal to the Quantity of Water Carried Off by Rivers, and Raised by Evaporation; with an Inquiry into the Origin of Springs," *Literary and Philosophical Society of Manchester, Memoirs* 5 (1799). On the origins of the group, see A. Thackray, "Natural Knowledge in a Cultural Context: The Manchester Model," *American Historical Review* 69 (1974): 672–709. Also see the study of its important sister group, T. S. Ashton, *Economic and Social Investigations in Manchester: A Centenary History of the Manchester Statistical Society* (London: King, 1934); and the general survey, R. H. Kargon, *Science in Victorian Manchester* (Manchester: University of Manchester Press, 1977).

11. John F. Bateman, "Observations on the Relation which the Fall of Rain Bears to the Water Flowing from the Ground," *Literary and Philosophical Society of Manchester, Memoirs*, 2nd ser., 10 (1846 [February 1844]): 157–90.

12. Ibid. For biographical information, see Peter Russell, "John Frederic La Trobe Bateman (1810–1899) Water Engineer," *Transactions of the Newcomen Society* 52 (1980–1981): 119–36; and Peter Russell, "John Frederic La Trobe Bateman," in *Dictionary of Business Biography: A Biographical Dictionary of Business Leaders Active in Britain in the Period 1860–1980*, ed. David Jeremy (London: Butterworths, 1984), 212–14. Bateman is also listed in the *Dictionary of National Biography* (London: Oxford University Press, 1953), 22-Supplement: 138–39. In 1841, Bateman married Fairbairn's only child, cementing his position within the elite inner circle of the local Nonconformist Liberals.

13. Bateman, "Observations," 163, for the first quotation; John F. Bateman, *History and Description of the Manchester Waterworks* (Manchester: Day, 1884), 27, for the second quotation.

14. Bateman, "Observations," 183.

15. Ibid.; and John F. Bateman, "Report of the Committee for Superintending the Placing of Rain Gauges ...," *Literary and Philosophical Society of Manchester, Memoirs*, 2nd

ser., 12 (1846 [March 1845]): 191–204, for the follow-up of the group's rainfall investigations; and Bateman, *History and Description of the Manchester Waterworks*, for the most complete account of this public utility. For the most detailed study of the city's sanitary history, see Alan Wilson, "Technology and Municipal Decision-Making: Sanitary Systems in Manchester 1868–1910" (Ph.D. diss., University of Manchester, 1990). My work has profited immeasurably from Wilson's pioneering research. Also see J. A. Hassan and E. R. Wilson, "The Longdendale Water Scheme 1848–1884," *Industrial Archaeology* 14 (1979): 102–19.

16. Bateman, *History and Description of the Manchester Waterworks*, 76, for the quotation. A. Redford and I. S. Russell, *The History of Local Government in Manchester*, 3 vols. (London: Longman, 1939–1940), 2:171–204. Also see chap. 2, above.

17. Redford and Russell, *History of Local Government in Manchester*, 2:172–73, for the first quotation. H. P. Holland, "Chorlton-upon-Medlock: Report on its Sanitary Condition," in *First Report*, U.K. Commissioners for Inquiring into the Status of Large Towns and Populous Districts (London: Clowes and Sons, 1844), 1:208, for the second quotation; see also pp. 1:202–17. Cf. Richard Baron Howard, "On the Prevalence of Diseases Arising from Contagion, Malaria, and Certain Other Physical Causes amongst the Labouring Classes in Manchester," in *Local Reports on the Sanitary Condition of the Labouring Population of England*, U.K. Poor Law Commissioners (London: Clowes and Sons, 1842), 294–336.

18. J. H. Nodal, ed., *City News, Notes, and Queries* (Manchester: Manchester City News, 1878), 1:524, 552, 583, 600 (21 September–19 October 1878).

19. Léon M. Faucher, *Manchester in 1844: Its Present Condition and Future Prospects* (London: Simpkin, Marshall, 1844), 16.

20. Bateman, *History and Description of the Manchester Waterworks*, 56–109; Redford and Russell, *History of Local Government in Manchester*, 2:171–204; Hassan and Wilson, "Longdendale."

21. Bateman, as quoted in "Water Supply to the Metropolis and Large Towns," *Parliamentary Papers, 1868–1869* [4169-I-II], xxxiii, 6, for the quotation; Bateman, *History and Description of the Manchester Waterworks*, 109–69, for the engineering of the project. See Hassan and Wilson, "Longdendale," for Bateman's rebuilding of the reservoir embankment in 1877 with a concrete base, and see the long interview of Bateman on the state of the waterworks in the *Manchester Guardian*, 11 February 1852.

22. *Manchester Guardian*, 11 February 1852.

23. "The Obstruction of Water-Courses," in *Manchester Guardian*, 14 February 1852. Also see the *Manchester Guardian* of 7 September 1833, which reports complaints against the Duke of Bridgewater for new obstructions on the Medlock, on which are blamed the unprecedented rise of river levels and consequent flooding.

24. See V. A. C. Gatrell, "Incorporation and the Pursuit of Liberal Hegemony in Manchester, 1790–1839," in *Municipal Reform and the Industrial City*, ed. Derek Fraser (Leicester: Leicester University Press, 1982), 15–60; and Derek Fraser, *Urban Politics in Victorian England: The Structure of Politics in Victorian Cities* (Leicester: Leicester University Press).

25. *Manchester Guardian*, 21 February 1852; and Conyers Morrell, "On the Pollution of Rivers and Water, and Its Prevention," *Manchester Statistical Society, Transactions* (1874–1875): 101–12, for the statistics on coal-waste by-products dumped into the MIRB. See Christopher Hamlin, *Public Health and Social Justice in the Age of Chadwick: Britain, 1800–1854* (Cambridge: Cambridge University Press, 1998). For overviews of Manchester during this era, see Alan Kidd, *Manchester*, Town and City Histories, ed. Stephen Constantine (Keele, Staffordshire: Ryburn/Keele University Press, 1993); and Redford and Russell, *History of Local Government in Manchester*.

26. Joseph Heron, as quoted in Wilson, "Technology and Municipal Decision-Making," 73. In making his case before a parliamentary committee in 1858, the city's expert lobbyist marshaled engineer Bateman into supporting the claim that the masses were incapable of operating indoor plumbing. See Wilson, "Technology and Municipal Decision-Making," 70–85. Unique among British municipal administrators in longevity and influence, Heron personified a regime of absolute Liberal hegemony that went uncontested by the Tories for fifty years. He was from an "ancient" Non-Conformist family, trained in the Moravian schools like Bateman, and handpicked by the first mayor, Thomas Potter, for town clerk, the top permanent post of the municipal corporation. When he was knighted in 1857, one of his contemporaries remembered that "his will was virtually considered law in all civic matters.... At the time it was, I think, a very common public belief that Sir Joseph Heron was not only Town Clerk, but Mayor and Corporation all in one" (Louis M. Hayes, *Reminiscences of Manchester* [Manchester: Sherratt and Hughes, 1905], 195).

27. Hamlin, *Public Health and Social Justice*, 220. Also see Hamlin's valuable and stimulating study, *A Science of Impurity: Water Analysis in Nineteenth Century Britain* (Bristol: Hilger, 1990).

28. A. T. H. Waters, "First Report of the MSSA Being a Letter Addressed to the Committee by A. T. H. Waters, Acting Secretary of the Association," in Manchester and Salford Sanitary Association (MSSA), *First Annual Report* (Manchester: Sowler, 1853), 29. See subsequent annual reports of the association (1853–1872) for events leading to the organization's acquiescence to the pail-closet system. For insight on this group, see Ashton, *Economic and Social Investigations*; and Michael Harrison, "Social Reform in Late Victorian and Edwardian Manchester, with Special Reference to T. C. Horsfall" (Ph.D. diss., University of Manchester, 1988).

29. On the influence of Robert Rawlinson in Manchester, see Shena Simon, *A Century of City Government, Manchester, 1838–1938* (London: Allen and Unwin, 1938), 165–80. For a biographical note on Rawlinson, See Christopher Hamlin, *What Becomes of Pollution? Adversary Science and the Controversy on the Self-Purification of Rivers in Britain, 1850–1900* (New York: Garland, 1987), 568.

30. Robert Rawlinson, *Public Health Act ... Report to the General Board of Health on a Preliminary Inquiry into the Sanitary Condition of ... the Township of Altrincham* (London: Clowes and Sons, 1850), as quoted in Simon, *Century of City Government*, 172–73; Wilson,

"Technology and Municipal Decision-Making," 64, for the statistics on scavenger removals; MSSA, *Annual Report* (1853–1855).

31. MSSA, *Annual Report* (1854): 2, for the quotation; Axon, *Annals*, xiv–xv, 252–79, for statistics on voting and population. In the 1851 election, 14,369 votes were cast in the parliamentary borough; the population was 316,215. As Alan Wilson and others point out, voting in municipal elections was much lower than that in other elections because of additional property and residency restrictions. See Wilson, "Technology and Municipal Decision-Making," 195–258. Both Wilson and Derek Fraser also underscore Manchester's uniquely uncontested local elections as another reason for very low voter turnouts. See Fraser, *Urban Politics*, 145–90.

32. Fraser, *Urban Politics*, 111–53, 178–213, for the splintering of Manchester Liberalism; and Clive Behagg, "Secrecy, Ritual, and Folk Violence: The Opacity of the Workplace in the First Half of the Nineteenth Century," in *Popular Culture and Custom in Nineteenth Century England*, ed. Robert D. Storch (London: Croom Helm, 1982), 154–79, for insight on the gendered dimensions of middle-class interaction with the working class. On water rates, see Bateman, *History and Description of the Manchester Waterworks*, 56–107; Redford and Russell, *History of Local Government in Manchester*, 2:171–204; and Simon, *Century of City Government*, 174–77.

33. *Manchester Guardian*, 11 August 1856. Also see *Manchester Guardian*, 8–13 August 1856, for coverage of the flood, including follow-up stories on the situation in Holmfirth and at the Manchester reservoirs.

34. *Manchester Guardian*, 15 August 1857, for the flood and coverage of the Bellhouse mill damage suit, and 15–20 August 1857, for full coverage of the flood; and Wilson, "Technology and Municipal Decision-Making," 195–258, for council politics and policy. On the important role of the Birley family on the Anglican Tory side of Manchester society, see Gatrell, "Incorporation," 25–60.

35. *Manchester Guardian*, 15–17 August 1857.

36. *Manchester Guardian*, 15 August 1857; MSSA, *Annual Report* (1857): 5. Also see George Greaves, "Our Sewer Rivers," *Manchester Statistical Society, Transactions* (1874–1875): 101–12.

37. Wilson, "Technology and Municipal Decision-Making," 195–258; Redford and Russell, *History of Local Government in Manchester*, 2:242–80; *Manchester Guardian*, 8 December 1860; Manchester Improvement Act, 28 Vict., c. 90.

38. *Manchester Courier*, 17 November 1866, for the first quotation; Hayes, *Reminiscences*, 201, for the second quotation; John Bateman, "Report to the Irwell Flood Committee," for the statistics on the flooded areas (Salford: 413 acres; Broughton: 437 acres; and Pendleton: 249 acres). In addition, 36 acres of Manchester were flooded. Also see *Manchester Guardian*, 17–19 November 1866; *Manchester City News*, 17 and 24 November 1866.

39. *Manchester City News*, 17 and 24 November 1866; *Manchester Guardian*, 17–24 November 1866.

40. *Manchester Guardian*, 24 November 1866; *Manchester City News*, 24 November 1866. Also see Hayes, *Reminiscences*, on the long-term water damage effects of the flood.

Hayes recalled later that "the damp got into the walls and foundations of the houses, and for years hardly a dry or healthy habitation could be found where the waters had full play. Sickness and a high death-rate were of course, only a natural sequence, and newcomers avoided Lower Broughton almost like a plague spot" (203). The Reverend Canon Richson was one of the key founders of the MSSA, and its chairman for several years.

41. "English Rivers," *London Daily News*, quoted in the *Manchester Guardian*, 20 June 1868. The Parliamentary River Pollution Commission was created in 1864 to study the Thames and three years later extended its work to include the MIRB. See Luckin, *Pollution and Control*, 69–99, for an account of cholera epidemics in London during the nineteenth century. Cf. Charles Rosenberg, *The Cholera Years: The United States in 1832, 1849, and 1866* (Chicago: University of Chicago Press, 1962).

42. For the local context, see Redford and Russell, *The History of Local Government in Manchester*, 2:242–80; and MSSA, *Annual Report* (1867), and *Annual Report* (1868). For the national intervention, see "First Report of the Commissioners … The Pollution of Rivers (Mersey and Ribble Basins)," vol. 1: "Reports and Plans," *Parliamentary Papers* (1870): vol. 40; and Hamlin, *Science of Impurity*. For a short biography of the first medical officer of health, see "Mr. John Leigh, M.R.C.S.," *Health Journal* 5 (July 1887): 17–19.

43. John Leigh, as quoted in City of Manchester, "Report of the Medical Officer of Health," *Proceedings of the Common Council* (April 1868): 1, for the quotation; *Manchester Guardian*, 18 June 1868. For the sources listed in the table, see "First Report of the Commissioners," 40, 454–64; and John Newton, "Water Closets versus Privies— Practically Considered with Reference to Manchester and Salford," a paper read to the Manchester and Salford Sanitary Association, as reported in the MSSA, *Annual Report* (1868). For Salford's 133,000 inhabitants, the comparable sanitary figures were 26,000 households, 22,000 privies, and 1,500 water closets. In both cases, the numbers do not add up because many households had to share the same privy, a notorious shortcoming of the city's dry conservancy system.

44. City of Manchester, "Report of the Medical Officer," 5, 1.

45. Joseph Heron, "Testimony before the Rivers Pollution Commission," as quoted in MSSA, *Annual Report* (1869): 7–8, for the second quotation. For the city's full response to the commission's questions, see City of Manchester, *Proceedings of the Common Council, 1868–1869* (2 December 1868): 69–102. On the Irish in Manchester, see note 2, above. Negligence on the part of working mothers was also commonly blamed for the high rate of infant mortality. See, for example, Mrs. Baines, "On the Prevention of Excessive Infant-Mortality," *Manchester Statistical Society, Transactions* (1868–1869): 1–20.

46. Edward Franklin, as quoted in "First Report of the Commissioners," 36–37. The report also includes the results of the various water-sample tests for sewage and industrial pollution. For insight on Franklin, see Hamlin, *Science of Impurity*.

47. Edward Franklin, as quoted in the *Manchester Guardian*, 18 June 1868; "First Report of the Commissioners," 40–54, passim.

48. "First Report of the Commissioners." For two follow-up studies of river pollution using chemical indicators, see Charles A. Burghardt, "The Pollution of the River Irwell and Its Tributaries," *Literary and Philosophical Society of Manchester, Proceedings* 25 (1886): 189–98; and George E. Davis and Alfred R. Davis, *River Irwell and Its Tributaries: A Monograph on River Pollution* (London: Heywood, 1890).

49. Bateman, "Report to the Irwell Flood Committee," 20. Also see note 1, above.

50. Bateman, "Report to the Irwell Flood Committee," 29. See *Manchester Guardian*, 18 June 1868, for the mayor's welcoming address to the parliamentary commission; and "First Report of the Commissioners."

51. City of Manchester, *Proceedings of the Common Council* (5 April 1876): 160.

52. City of Manchester, *Proceedings of the Common Council* (4 October 1876): 381–90; and Wilson, "Technology and Municipal Decision-Making," 86–133; Redford and Russell, *History of Local Government in Manchester*, 2:377–409. Also see MSSA, *Annual Report* (1876): 12, which concurs with Heron's judgment that "the usefulness of the Act is practically nullified." For a full debate on the merits and shortcomings of the two competing systems of sanitation, see MSSA, *Annual Report* (1868).

53. Wilson, "Technology and Municipal Decision-Making," 86–133, for the most comprehensive treatment of the sanitary reforms. The conversion process was fairly rapid, with the number of pail closets increasing from seven hundred in 1873 to sixty thousand by the end of the decade. By 1885, the process was virtually complete, with the number of pail closets reaching sixty-five thousand.

54. Simon, *Century of City Government*, 399; Wilson, "Technology and Municipal Decision-Making," 134–94.

55. Hassan and Wilson, "Longdendale," 102–19.

56. For statistics on the waterworks, see Bateman, *Manchester Waterworks*, 63; "First Report of the Commissioners," 120–350, 554–64. For insight on women's unequal environmental burdens, see Angela Gugliotta, "Class, Gender, and Coal Smoke: Gender Ideology and Environmental Injustice in Pittsburgh, 1868–1914," *Environmental History* 5 (April 2000): 165–93; and S. J. Kleinberg, *The Shadow of the Mills: Working-Class Families in Pittsburgh, 1870–1907* (Pittsburgh: University of Pittsburgh Press, 1989).

57. *Manchester Evening News*, 15 July 1872, for the quoted phrase. On the council's fears that it would have to compensate riparian owners, see the revealing responses of Mayor Neill to the parliamentary commission, *Manchester Guardian*, 16 June 1868.

58. *Manchester Guardian*, 13 and 15 July 1872, for the first and second quotations, respectively; John Bateman, quoted in "Report of the River Medlock Improvement Committee," City of Manchester, *Proceedings of the Common Council* (5 September 1877): 343, for third quotation; see pp. 343–62 for his full report.

59. "Report of the River Medlock Improvement Committee," City of Manchester, *Proceedings of the Common Council* (5 September 1877), 343–62. *Manchester Guardian*, 15–19 July 1872; *Manchester Evening News*, 15–20 July 1872.

60. *Manchester Evening News*, 15 and 18 July 1872, for the first and second quotations, respectively.

61. Ibid., 22 July 1872; *Manchester City News*, 22 July 1872.
62. *Manchester Guardian*, 15 July 1872; *Manchester City News*, 20 July 1872. See E. W. Binney
    and others, "Discussion of 'the Frightfully High Death-Rate of Manchester and
    Salford,'" *Literary and Philosophical Society of Manchester, Proceedings* 9 (1870): 112–
    15; and E. W. Binney, "The Quality of the Water Supplied to Manchester," *Literary
    and Philosophical Society of Manchester* 11 (1873): 81–83, for his research report. For
    two letters to the editor critical of the city's lack of action to sanitize the city
    and protect it against floods, see the *Manchester Guardian*, 19 July 1872. Also see
    Robert Martin, "Sanitary Progress, and Its Obstacles, in Manchester," *Manchester
    Statistical Society, Transactions* (1874–1875): 87–100; and Morrell, "On the Pollution
    of Rivers"; and E. W. Binney, "Quality of the Water."
63. *Manchester Guardian*, 16–17 July 1877, for an account of the flooding. Also see Bateman,
    History and Description of the Manchester Waterworks, 205–24, for a brief overview of
    the project.
64. City Council Resolution of 9 December 1874, as quoted in "Report of the River Medlock
    Committee," 340; Wilson, "Technology and Municipal Decision-Making," 195–
    258.
65. "Report of the River Medlock Committee," appendix A, pp. 343–51, for the Bateman-
    Lynde report, and appendix B, pp. 352–54, of the same publication for their list
    of communities within the metropolitan area that needed to be brought into the
    plan. This list included Rusholme, Withington, Bradford, Moss Side, Droylsden,
    Levenshulme, Newton Heath, Openshaw, Barton-upon-Irwell, Groton, Stretford,
    and Failsworth. Also see Wilson, "Technology and Municipal Decision-Making,"
    195–258, on a follow-up meeting a year later that also brought in Crumpsall,
    Blackley, Harpurhey, and Moston.
66. Wilson, "Technology and Municipal Decision-Making"; see City of Manchester, *Pro-
    ceedings of the Common Council* (30 October 1878): 454–57, for the terms of the
    agreement with Salford. Manchester insisted on a maximum payment of one-
    third of the estimated £180,000 cost of the project, which was based on the
    ratable property values of the land flooded in the 1866 disaster. Manchester ac-
    tually accounted for 16.6 percent of this value in 1866 and 17.3 percent under
    an 1878 reevaluation. Within each jurisdiction, two-thirds of the cost would be
    paid by special assessments levied upon the affected property owners. Under the
    formula, the Corporation would pay a maximum of £20,000 regardless of the
    final bill for the project.
67. See Graeme Davison, "The City as a Natural System: Theories of Urban Society in Early
    Nineteenth-Century Britain," in *The Pursuit of Urban History*, ed. Derek Fraser and
    Anthony Sutcliffe (London: Edward Arnold, 1983), 349–70; Thackray, "Natural
    Knowledge"; Hamlin, *Public Health and Social Justice*, 1–15; Kargon, *Science in Victo-
    rian Manchester*; Donald S. L. Cardwell, *From Watt to Clausius: The Rise of Thermody-
    namics in the Early Industrial Age* (Ithaca, NY: Heinemann, 1971); Patrick Brantlinger,
    ed., *Energy and Entropy: Science and Culture in Victorian Britain, Essays from Victorian
    Studies* (Bloomington: Indiana University Press, 1989); and Anson Rabinbach, *The*

Human Motor: Energy, Fatigue, and the Origins of Modernity (New York: Basic Books, 1990).

68. Two examples of this kind of apologia are Redford and Russell, *History of Local Government in Manchester*; and Wilson, "Technology and Municipal Decision-Making." While the former is easily explained as the official centennial history of the Corporation, the latter is more complex and ambiguous. Wilson seems to have been forced into an uncomfortable position by the weight of his thesis that dry conservancy was a superior alternative to a water-carriage system of sanitation. In the end, the burden of this argument is too much for the evidence to bear, especially that of the city's lack of progress in reducing its extraordinary rate of infant mortality for over a half-century. Moreover, Wilson either did not know or chose not to acknowledge the city's dark secret that it had been dumping a large proportion of the night soil it collected into the Medlock River ever since the opening of its processing plant in the 1870s: the Holt Town fertilizer factory, located just upstream from the city, regularly dumped its huge surplus of raw wastes into the river at night, contributing significantly to the river's pollution. See the exposure of this unconscionable practice in the *Manchester City News*, 17 November and 1 and 15 December 1888. For the political context of the ensuing scandal, see chap. 9, below. In many other respects, Wilson's dissertation represents exemplary research on urban infrastructure and public health policy.

69. Wilson, "Technology and Municipal Decision-Making," 255; see also pp. 195–258. I. Harford, *Manchester and Its Ship Canal Movement: Class, Work, and Politics in Late Victorian England* (Staffordshire: Ryburn, 1994), 21–31, 62–99; Redford and Russell, *History of Local Government in Manchester*, 2:305–402; Simon, *Century of City Government*, 395–423.

Chapter Six

1. Hermann Schluter, *The Brewing Industry and the Brewing Workers' Movement in America* (Cincinnati, OH: United Brewery Workmen of America, 1910), 63.

2. "Brew of the Year," *Western Brewer* 18 (5 July 1893): 1561–62 (figures for the period between July 1892 and July 1893); for the image, see *One Hundred Years of Brewing: A Supplement to the Western Brewer* (Chicago: Rich, 1903), 325; and American Brewing Academy, "History of the Brewing Industry," *Tenth Annual Report* (Chicago: Blakeley, 1901), 120, for the 1867 sales figure. In 1860, Schoenhofen and his partner, Matheus Gottfried, started their first brewery at Jefferson and Twelfth streets, making six hundred barrels during their first year. See *One Hundred Years of Brewing*, 323.

3. *One Hundred Years of Brewing*, 322–26. Also see "A Model Brewery," *Western Brewer* 10 (15 August 1885): 1557; "Brewing in Chicago," *Western Brewer* 17 (15 October 1892): 2251; and "Peter Schoenhofen, Deceased," *Western Brewer* 18 (15 January 1893): 83–84.

4. See Lewis Mumford, *The City in History: Its Origins, Its Transformations, and Its Prospects* (New York: Harcourt, Brace, and World, 1961); Joel A. Tarr and Gabriel DuPuy, eds.,

Technology and the Rise of the Networked City in Europe and America (Philadelphia: Temple University Press, 1988); Harold L. Platt, *The Electric City: Energy and the Growth of the Chicago Area, 1880–1930* (Chicago: University of Chicago Press, 1991); and David E. Nye, *Electrifying America: Social Meanings of a New Technology, 1880–1940* (Cambridge, MA: MIT Press, 1992).

5. U.S. Bureau of the Census, "Statistics of Cities," pt. 2 of *Eleventh Census of the United States, Manufacturing Industries* (Washington, DC: U.S. Bureau of the Census, 1890), 130–45. For an introduction to the American brewing industry, see Thomas C. Cochran, *The Pabst Brewing Company: The History of an American Business* (New York: New York University Press, 1948); Stanley Baron, *Brewed in America: A History of Beer and Ale in the United States* (Boston: Little, Brown, 1962); and Bob Skilnik, *The History of Beer and Brewing in Chicago, 1833–1978* (St. Paul, Minn.: Pogo Press, 1999). For firm size, see Philip Scranton, *Endless Novelty: Specialty Production and American Industrialization, 1865–1925* (Princeton, NJ: Princeton University Press, 1997). However, the brewing industry in Chicago fits his description of both large bulk producers and small specialty firms.

6. The two classic studies are Lewis Mumford, *Technics and Civilization* (New York: Harcourt, Brace, and World, 1934); and Seigfried Giedion, *Mechanization Takes Command* (New York: Oxford University Press, 1948). On the highly uneven nature of this process, see David A. Hounshell, *From the American System to Mass Production: The Development of Manufacturing Technology in the United States* (Baltimore: Johns Hopkins University Press, 1984).

7. *One Hundred Years of Brewing*, 105; John P. Arnold and Frank Penman, *History of the Brewing Industry and Science in America: A Memorial to Dr. John E. Siebel and Anton Schwartz* (Chicago: n.p., 1933), 56–57, 80, 98; Cochran, *Pabst*, 113–19. Also see Merritt Smith and Leo Marx, eds., *Does Technology Drive History? The Dilemma of Technological Determinism* (Cambridge, MA: MIT Press, 1994).

8. A. E. Dingle, "Drink and Working-Class Living Standards in Britain, 1870–1914," *Economic History Review* 25 (1972): 608–22; and Graham Mooney and Simon Szreter, "Urbanization, Mortality, and the Standard of Living Debate: New Estimates of the Expectation of Life at Birth in Nineteenth-Century British Cities," *Economic History Review* 51 (1998): 84–112. For the business culture in England, cf. Charles Graham, "Review of Pasteur," *Nature* 15 (11 and 18 January 1877): 213–16, 249–52; C. H. Bavington, "Presidential Address," *Journal of the Institute of Brewers* 11 (1905): 95–105; and the sources listed in note 9, below.

9. See W. J. Rorabaugh, *The Alcoholic Republic: An American Tradition* (New York: Oxford University Press, 1979); Joseph R. Gusfield, *Symbolic Crusade*, 2nd ed. (Urbana: University of Illinois Press, 1985); K. Austin Kerr, *Organized for Prohibition: A New History of the Anti-Saloon League* (New Haven, CT: Yale University Press, 1985). Cf. Brian Harrison, *Drink and the Victorians: The Temperance Question in England, 1815–1872*, 2nd ed. (1971; reprint, Staffordshire: Keele University Press, 1994); and D. M. Fahey, "Brewers, Publicans, and Working-Class Drinkers: Pressure Group Politics in Late Victorian and Edwardian England," *Histoire Sociale/Social History* 25 (May 1980): 85–103.

10. Skilnik, *History of Beer*, 31–32, passim, on the Schoenhofen Brewery; Susan K. Appel, "Brewery Architecture in America from the Civil War to Prohibition," in *The Midwest in American Architecture*, ed. John S. Garner (Urbana: University of Illinois Press, 1991), 185–214, on Chicago's leadership in brewery architecture and engineering.

11. For saloon/pub statistics, see House of Commons, *Sessional Papers, 1890–91*, vol. 77, par. 61; Brian Harrison, "Pubs," in *The Victorian City: Images and Realities*, ed. Harold J. Dyos and Michael Wolff (London: Routledge and Kegan Paul, 1973), 1:3–58; and Perry Duis, *The Saloon: Public Drinking in Chicago and Boston* (Urbana: University of Illinois Press, 1983). For an introduction to British brewing, see Alfred Barnard, *Noted Breweries of Great Britain and Ireland*, 4 vols. (London: Causton and Sons, 1889–1891); A. Gall, *Manchester Breweries of Times Gone By* (Manchester: n.p., 1978–1980); Peter Mathias, *The Brewing Industry in England, 1700–1830* (Cambridge: Cambridge University Press, 1959); and T. R. Gourvish and R. G. Wilson, *The British Brewing Industry, 1830–1980* (Cambridge: Cambridge University Press, 1994).

12. Clay McShane, "Transforming the Use of Urban Space: A Look at the Revolution in Street Pavements, 1880–1924," *Journal of Urban History* 5 (May 1979): 279–307. Also see Martin V. Melosi, *The Sanitary City: Urban Infrastructure in America from Colonial Times to the Present* (Baltimore: Johns Hopkins University Press, 2000).

13. See *One Hundred Years of Brewing*, 58–75, for a general history; and "Pneumatic Malting in Chicago," *Western Brewer* 17 (15 September 1992): 2013, which reports that "no manual labor will be required during the entire process of malting." For more general perspectives, see Nancy Tomes, *The Gospel of Germs: Men, Women, and the Microbe in American Life* (Cambridge, MA: Harvard University Press, 1998); Suellen Hoy, *Chasing Dirt: The American Pursuit of Cleanliness* (New York: Oxford University Press, 1995). Cf. Keith Vernon, "Pus, Sewage, Beer, and Milk: Microbiology in Britain, 1870–1940," *History of Science* 28 (September 1990): 289–325; and Michael Worboys, *Spreading Germs: Disease Theories and Medical Practice in Britain, 1865–1900* (Cambridge: Cambridge University Press, 2000).

14. Rorabaugh, *Alcoholic Republic*; Richard Wilson Renner, "In a Perfect Ferment: Chicago, the Know-Nothings, and the Riot for Lager Beer," *Chicago History* 5 (September 1976): 161–70; and Robin L. Einhorn, "The Lager Beer Riot and Segmented Government: Chicago, 1855," a paper presented to the Social Science History Association (Chicago, 1987). Cf. Paul E. Johnson, *A Shopkeeper's Millennium* (New York: Hill and Wang, 1978), and Anita Shafer Goodstein, *Nashville, 1780–1860: From Frontier to City* (Gainesville: University of Florida Press, 1989), on urban middle-class respectability.

15. On meatpacking, see William Cronon, *Nature's Metropolis: Chicago and the Great West* (New York: Norton, 1991), 207–62; and Louise Carroll Wade, *Chicago's Pride: The Stockyards, Packingtown, and Environs in the Nineteenth Century* (Urbana: University of Illinois Press, 1987).

16. Arnold and Penman, *History of the Brewing Industry*, 98. Also see Baron, *Brewed in America*, 60–62, 228.

17. U.S. Bureau of the Census, *Eighth Census of the United States, Manuscript for Industry*, Cook County, Illinois, Ward 9 (Washington, DC: U.S. Bureau of the Census, 1860), 2, which lists the brewery's output at 38,800 barrels. Cf. Isaac D. Guyer, *History of Chicago: Its Commercial and Manufacturing Interests and Industry* (Chicago: Church, Goodman and Cushing, 1862), 43, which puts the figure at 44,750 barrels and the brewery's underutilized capacity at 30 percent. For the 1870 figures, see U.S. Bureau of the Census, *Ninth Census of the United States, Manuscript for Industry*, Cook County, Illinois, Ward 9 (reel no. 60) (Washington, DC: U.S. Bureau of the Census, 1870), 3. For population statistics, see U.S. Bureau of the Census, *Ninth Census of the United States, Population* (Washington, DC: U.S. Bureau of the Census, 1870), 1:379–91. The number of foreign-born, 144,577, was slightly less than the number of native-born, 154,420. Yet, if the immigrants' children born in the United States were separated out from the native-born category, the foreign-born population would constitute a majority.

18. *One Hundred Years of Brewing*, 716–18, for a compilation of statistics on beer production and consumption from several nations. For German practice, see Mikael Hård, *Machines Are Frozen Spirit: The Scientification of Refrigeration and Brewing in the 19th Century: A Weberian Interpretation* (Boulder, CO: Westview, 1994); and James S. Roberts, *Drink, Temperance, and the Working Class in Nineteenth-Century Germany* (Boston: Allen and Unwin, 1984).

19. Louis Pasteur, *Studies on Fermentation: The Diseases of Beer, Their Causes, and the Means of Preventing Them* (London: Macmillan, 1879), vii. Also see Jacques Nicolle, *Louis Pasteur: A Master of Scientific Enquiry* (London: Hutchinson, 1961), 39–68, 109–19; and Bruno Latour, *The Pasteurization of France* (Cambridge, MA: Harvard University Press, 1988).

20. Pasteur, *Studies*, vii. For an introduction to the history of medicine, see John V. Pickstone, *Medical Innovations in Historical Perspective* (New York: St. Martin's, 1992); and Carlo Cipolla, *Miasmas and Disease: Public Health and the Environment in the Pre-Industrial Era* (New Haven, CT: Yale University Press, 1992).

21. Pasteur, *Studies*, 18, for the quotation; see also pp. 1–17. See Judith M. Bennett, *Ale, Beer, and Brewsters in England: Women's Work in a Changing World, 1300–1600* (New York: Oxford University Press, 1996); and Mathias, *Brewing Industry in England*, for a description of traditional practices of beer making into the early nineteenth century.

22. Pasteur, *Studies*, 10, 12.

23. Gourvish and Wilson, *British Brewing Industry*, 181–83, 196–200, 601; and George B. Wilson, *Alcohol and the Nation (A Contribution to the Study of the Liquor Problem in the United Kingdom from 1800 to 1935)* (London: Nickolson and Watson, 1940), for an extensive compilation of statistical data.

24. Cronon, *Nature's Metropolis*, 97–147; and *Western Brewer* 16 (15 June 1891): 1389–90, for beer production statistics.

25. For Manchester brewing statistics, see House of Commons, *Sessional Papers, 1831–32*,

vol. 34, 199; 1842, vol. 39, 507; 1851, vol. 53, 225; 1861, vol. 55, 607; 1872, vol. 54, 1; 1881, vol. 83, 25; 1890–91, vol. 77, 61; 1899, vol. 88, 185.

26. "Oil Fuel for Boilers," *Western Brewer* 15 (15 February 1890): 326–27. In 1889, oil came to Chicago via pipeline from Lima, Ohio. See Paul H. Giddens, *Standard Oil Company (Indiana): Oil Pioneer of the Middle West* (New York: Appleton-Century-Crofts, 1955), 1–33.

27. See Michael A. Tomlan, *Tinged with Gold: Hops Culture in the United States* (Athens: University of Georgia Press, 1992), for a first-rate account.

28. Ibid., 24, for the quotation; see also pp. 23–26; and "Chicago Hops Market for 1879," *Western Brewer* 5 (15 January 1880): 58.

29. Tomlan, *Tinged with Gold*, 45–81, 119–56; and Jno. E. Land, *Chicago: The Future Metropolis of the New World* . . . (Chicago: Land, 1883), 17–18. In 1960, three-quarters of the U.S. crop was grown in the Yakima Valley of the state of Washington.

30. J. MacFarlane, *The Coal-Regions of America: Their Topography, Geology, and Development* (New York: Appleton, 1873), 435, for the phrase "poor man's coal" and the quotation; see pp. 407–32 for a description of the Illinois coalfields. See Chicago Board of Trade, *Annual Report* (1850–1902), for coal use statistics. Also see S. O. Andros, *Coal Mining in Illinois* (Urbana: University of Illinois, 1915); A. T. Andreas, *History of Chicago*, 3 vols. (1884–1886; reprint, New York: Arno, 1975): 2:673–74; and A. A. Bishoff, *Coal Trade at Chicago: 5th Annual Review* (Chicago: Donohue, Henneberry, 1885), for the development of the Chicago coal trade. For a brief introduction to the history of coal in the United States, see Donald L. Miller and Richard E. Sharpless, *The Kingdom of Coal: Work, Enterprise, and Ethnic Communities in the Mine Fields* (Philadelphia: University of Pennsylannia Press, 1985); and Anthony F. C. Wallace, *St. Clair: A Nineteenth-Century Coal Town's Experience with a Disaster Prone Industry* (New York: Knopf, 1987).

31. Chicago Board of Trade, *Annual Report* (1860–1871), for coal statistics. On wartime fuel shortages, see Donald J. Pisani, "Forests and Conservation, 1865–1900," *Journal of American History* 72 (September 1985): 340–59; and Frederick Starr, *Report of the Commissioner of Agriculture for the Year 1865* (Washington, DC: Government Printing Office, 1866). On the clashes in the mine fields, see Grace Pallandino, *Another Civil War: Labor, Capital, and the State in the Anthracite Regions of Pennsylvania, 1840–1868* (Urbana: University of Illinois Press, 1990). On the larger national history of fuel use, see Sam Schurr and Bruce Netschert, *Energy in the American Economy, 1850–1975: An Economic Study of Its History and Prospects* (Baltimore: Resources for the Future/Johns Hopkins University Press, 1960).

32. MacFarlane, *Coal-Regions*, 434, for the quotation; Christine Meisner Rosen, "Businessmen against Pollution in Late Nineteenth Century Chicago," *Business History Review* (Autumn 1995): 351–97; and Harold L. Platt, "Creative Necessity: Municipal Reform in Gilded Age Chicago," in *The Constitution, Law, and American Life: Critical Aspects of the Nineteenth-Century Experience*, ed. Donald G. Nieman (Athens: University of Georgia Press, 1992), 162–90, for perspectives on environmental

reform during the Gilded Age. Also see City of Chicago, Department of Smoke Inspection, *Report of the Department of Smoke Inspection* (Chicago: City of Chicago, 1907–1911); and Chicago Association of Commerce, *Smoke Abatement and Electrification of Railroad Terminals in Chicago* (Chicago: McNally, 1915). For a general introduction, see R. Dale Grinder, "The Battle for Clean Air: The Smoke Problem in Post-Civil War America," in *Pollution and Reform in American Cities, 1870–1930*, ed. Martin V. Melosi (Austin: University of Texas Press, 1980), 83–104; and David Stradling, *Smokestacks and Progressives* (Baltimore: Johns Hopkins University Press, 1999).

33. MacFarlane, *Coal-Regions*, 416; see also pp. 214–35. Also see Andros, *Coal Mining*; and the definitive, A. H. Worthen, *Geological Survey of Illinois*, 8 vols. (Springfield, IL: State Journal Steam Press, 1866).

34. MacFarlane, *Coal-Regions*, 214–35; John H. M. Laslett, *Colliers across the Sea: A Comparative Study of Class Formation in Scotland and the American Midwest* (Urbana: University of Illinois Press, 2000), 77–100; Chicago Board of Trade, *Annual Report* (1858–1900), for coal prices; Orin Wainwright Rees, *Sulfur Retention in Bituminous Coal Ash* (Urbana: Illinois State Geological Survey, 1966); and Orin Wainwright Rees, *Composition of the Ash of Illinois Coals* (Urbana: Illinois State Geological Survey, 1964), for a chemical analysis of the coal.

35. George Woodruff et al., *The History of Will County, Illinois* (Chicago: Le Baron, 1878), 466, as quoted in Laslett, *Colliers across the Sea*, 77; see also pp. 77–100 on the growth of Braidwood and Streator. Also see Arthur Doerr, "Williamson and Franklin Counties: Coal Counties of Southern Illinois," *Journal of Geography* 49 (May 1950): 193–200, on some of the environmental impacts of soft-coal mining; and Miller and Sharpless, *Kingdom of Coal*, xxi–xx, passim, on the devastation of the environment in the anthracite districts of Pennsylvania.

36. Wallace, *St. Clair*, for the quoted phrase and for an analysis of the causes of mine disasters; Laslett, *Colliers across the Sea*, 77–100, for a careful look at the ethnic composition of Illinois mining towns. See Illinois Bureau of Labor Statistics, *Annual Coal Report* (Springfield, IL: Philips Brothers, 1903), 3, for pre-1882 statistics; and Illinois Department of Mines and Minerals, *A Compilation of the Reports of the Mining Industry of Illinois from the Earliest Records to 1954* (Springfield: State of Illinois, 1954), 106–253, for a compilation of coal mine legislation. For a graphic contemporary account of the power of the railroads over the lives of the miners in Illinois, see Henry Demerest Lloyd, *A Strike of Millionaires against Miners; or, The Story of Spring Valley*, 2nd ed. (Chicago: Belford-Clarke, 1890). Also see Paul M. Angle, *Bloody Williamson: A Chapter in American Lawlessness* (New York: Knopf, 1952); and Herbert Gutman, "Labor in the Land of Lincoln: Coal Miners on the Prairie," in *Power and Culture: Essays on the History of the American Working Class* (New York: New Press, 1987).

37. Laslett, *Colliers across the Sea*, 78, for Braidwood's trains; and the railroad-sponsored Chicago Association of Commerce, *Smoke Abatement*, for an examination of the technology of locomotive engines and their problems related to smoke emissions.

38. *Lakeside Annual City Directory of Chicago* (Chicago: Lakeside Press, 1880), 1294, for a list of coal dealers; Elmer Barton, *A Business Tour of Chicago, Depicting Fifty Years of Business* (Chicago: Barton, 1887), 63–64, for Barnett's business; and Bishoff, *Coal Trade*, 4, for statistics on coal sales in Chicago.

39. Bishoff, *Coal Trade*, 16. Also see Chicago Coal Exchange, *Constitution and By-Laws of the Chicago Coal Exchange* (Chicago: Bliss, Barnes, and Gritzner, 1874); and Chicago Coal Exchange, *Constitution and By-Laws of the Chicago Coal Exchange* (Chicago: Morris, 1886), for efforts to stabilize the price of anthracite coal.

40. For economic analysis of the coal industry, see notes 30–31, above; Reed Moyer, *Competition in the Midwestern Coal Industry* (Cambridge, MA: Harvard University Press, 1964); John G. Clark, *Energy and the Federal Government: Fossil Fuel Policies, 1900–1946* (Urbana: University of Illinois Press, 1978); and James P. Johnson, *The Politics of Soft Coal: The Bituminous Industry from World War I through the New Deal* (Urbana: University of Illinois Press, 1979).

41. See for example, J. Frank Duryea, "The Status of the Horse at the End of the Century," *Harpers Weekly* 43 (18 November 1899): 1172.

42. Joseph Moses and John Kirkland, *History of Chicago*, 2 vols. (Chicago: Munsell, 1895), 2:433. For other contemporary accounts, see Elias Colbert, *Chicago: Historical and Statistical Sketch of the Garden City* (Chicago: Sherlock, 1868), 73–74; and William Bross, *History of Chicago: Historical and Commercial Statistics . . . Republished from the Daily Democratic Press* (Chicago: Jansen, McClurg, 1876), 17–36. For a fascinating memoir of a Chicagoan who was a member of the elite, see Sterling Morton, "Horse and Carriage Days" (October 1956), a typescript originally published in *Townsfall*, available at the Chicago Historical Society. For more general perspectives, see Robert West Howard, *The Horse in America* (Chicago: Follett, 1965), 168–80; and Graham Russell Hodges, *New York City Cartmen, 1667–1850* (New York: New York University Press, 1986). For an ode to man's best friend, see Duryea, "Status of the Horse." On the transition from animals to machines, see James J. Flink, *America Adopts the Automobile, 1895–1910* (Cambridge, MA: MIT Press, 1970); and Clay McShane, *Down the Asphalt Path: The Automobile and the American City* (New York: Columbia University Press, 1994).

43. For statistics, see the 1863, 1870, and 1880 reports of the U.S. Commissioner of Agriculture, pp. 561, 47, and 200, respectively, in Starr, *Report of the Commissioner*. In 1888, Illinois became number two just behind Texas. See the 1887 report of the U.S. Commissioner of Agriculture, p. 566. For horse nutrition, Clay McShane to Harold Platt, personal communication, 14 November 2000.

44. Jessie M. Dillon, "Normal and the Horse Industry," *Journal of the Illinois State Historical Society* 29 (January 1937): 364–402. Also David Blanke, *Sowing the American Dream: How Consumer Culture Took Root in the Rural Midwest* (Athens: Ohio University Press, 2000).

45. See McShane, *Down the Asphalt Path*; Joel A. Tarr, "From City to Suburb: The 'Moral' Influence of Transportation Technology," in *American Urban History: An Interpretive Reader with Commentaries*, ed. Alexander B. Callow Jr. (New York: Oxford University

Press, 1973), 202–12; Charles W. Cheape, *Moving the Masses: Urban Public Transit in New York, Boston, and Philadelphia, 1880–1912* (Cambridge, MA: Harvard University Press, 1980); Paul Barrett, *The Automobile and Urban Transit: The Formation of Public Policy in Chicago, 1900–1930* (Philadelphia: Temple University Press, 1983); and John P. McKay, *Tramways and Trolleys: The Rise of Urban Mass Transportation in Europe* (Princeton, NJ: Princeton University Press, 1976).

46. Moses and Kirkland, *History of Chicago*, 2:434, for the quotation; and City of Chicago, Department of Public Works, *Annual Report* (1907): 407, for wheel tax figures. The population density estimate was calculated using 1890 census data, ward maps, and a mapping software program that computed the areas of the wards (nos. 20, 21, and 22).

47. City of Chicago, Department of Public Works, *Annual Report* (1883): 35 and 66, for the first and second quotations, respectively.

48. For insight on the hard work and long hours of a streetcar driver, see the letter to the editor from a Cottage Grove driver, "Cruelty to Men," *Chicago Tribune*, 11 July 1876. For a comprehensive survey of the street railway, see Bion Joseph Arnold, *Report on the Engineering and Operating Features of the Chicago Transportation Problem* (New York: McGraw, 1905). Also see Barrett, *Automobile and Urban Transit*.

49. Washington Park Jockey Club, *History of the American Derby* (Chicago: n.p., 1940). See also Washington Park Jockey Club 1885–1886 yearbook for the origins of the racetrack. Both of these are available at the Chicago Historical Society. On parks as horse spaces, see Roy Rosenzweig and Elizabeth Blackmar, *The Park and the People: A History of Central Park* (Ithaca, NY: Cornell University Press, 1998). On Chicago's parks and boulevard system, see Moses and Kirkland, *History of Chicago*, 2:510–21. At the end of the century, the city had 2,606 acres of parks and almost a hundred miles of paths for horses. For insight on the role of horses in male, upper-class society as well as the role of the Washington Park Jockey Club in elite society, consider the novels by Frank Norris, *The Pit* (1903; reprint, New York: Doubleday, 1928); and Theodore Dreiser, *Sister Carrie* (New York: Boni and Liveright, 1917). To compare with Boston, see William Dean Howells, *The Rise of Silas Lapham* (1885; reprint, New York: Signet, 1963).

50. Joel A. Tarr, "Urban Pollution: Many Long Years Ago," *American Heritage* (October 1971): 65–69, 106.

51. The classic account of the mechanization of food processing is Giedion, *Mechanization Takes Command*.

52. Mathias, *Brewing Industry in England*, xxiii, 25: Gourvish and Wilson, *British Brewing Industry*, 181–83, 196–200, 601.

53. Pasteur, *Studies*, 4, for the quotation. Pasteur's drawings indicate that he was using a microscope of 400–500 power. When he returned to the brewery eight weeks later, he found that its managers had purchased one of the instruments. Gourvish and Wilson, *British Brewing Industry*, 611, for the statistics; E. M. Sigsworth, "Science and the Brewing Industry, 1850–1900," *Economic History Review* 17 (1964–1965): 538, for the identity of the brewery where Pasteur conducted his research.

54. Pasteur, *Studies*, 24, for the quotation.

55. Ibid., 22, 57–58, 33, for the quotations; see also pp. 33–85, 143–234 for details on Pasteur's ingenious experiments on both barley worts and grapes.

56. Ibid., 6, for the quotation; see also pp. 143–234.

57. Ibid., 196, for the quotation; see also pp. 10–13, 172–219.

58. Ibid., 346, for the quotation; see also pp. 337–95; *One Hundred Years of Brewing*, 95–99; Nicolle, *Louis Pasteur*, 109–19.

59. Pasteur, *Studies*, 338.

60. Ibid., 233 for the quotations; see also pp. 327–95 for a full description of his methods.

61. Gourvish and Wilson, *British Brewing Industry*, 59.

62. *Western Brewer* 4 (15 July 1879): 579, for the quotation; and "The Microscope As Used in Brewing," *Western Brewer* 4 (15 August 1879): 684, for the follow-up story. Also consider the following sample of articles from the periodical: "Yeast and Turbid Beer," in vol. 4 (15 March 1879): 213–14; "Pure Air in Breweries," in vol. 5 (15 August 1880): 821; "Modern Brewing," in vol. 9 (15 August 1884): 1380; C. G. Matthews and W. Evershed, "Scientific Brewing," in vol. 9 (15 August 1884): 1382–83; M. Galland, "The Scientific Maltster," in vol. 9 (15 October 1884): 1734–35; "Fermentation," in vol. 10 (15 January 1885): 83–84; "Louis Pasteur, The Brewers' Chemist," in vol. 10 (15 March 1885): 482–83; "Dr. Hansen on Pure Yeast," in vol. 12 (15 September 1887): 1957–58; "Bottling and Pasteurizing of Beer," in vol. 14 (15 January 1889): 100. On the "school culture" of Germany, see Hård, *Machines Are Frozen Spirit*, 81–112, 210–19. On the German connection to the American brewing industry see, Dorothee Schneider, *Trade Unions and Community: The German Working Class in New York City, 1870–1900* (Urbana: University of Illinois Press, 1994), 130–76; and *One Hundred Years of Brewing*. On the American myth of technological progress, see John F. Kasson, *Civilizing the Machine: Technology and Republican Values in America, 1776–1900* (New York: Penguin, 1977).

63. *One Hundred Years of Brewing*, 76–94; Arnold and Penman, *History of the Brewing Industry*, 88–93. To produce a beer that was light in color and taste, brewers began during the 1870s to add corn and rice to the mash. They experimented with different recipes and ways to prepare these grains in order to remove undesirable elements such as the outer shell of the corn kernel. Eventually, they learned how to process the corn and rice in such a way that they could be added directly to the mash tub and their desirable elements extracted with great efficiency. Steam boiling and the use of grains other than barley was called the infusion method. This method of brewing, more than anything else, gave American beer its distinctive qualities. See Arnold and Penman, *History of the Brewing Industry*, 89; and Cochran, *Pabst*, 113–23, which describes in great detail the brewery's search for a new recipe to meet the public's taste preferences. See Cochran, *Pabst*, 107, for Pabst's recycling of brewers' grain, which reached a volume of one hundred tons of wet grain a day in the 1890s. Also see Robin Einhorn, *Property Rules: Political Economy in Chicago, 1833–1872* (Chicago: University of Chicago Press, 1991), 204, on brewery related animal-waste pollution of the North Branch of the Chicago River. In the 1860s,

a pig feed lot was located next to one brewery in order to take advantage of its cheap, albeit wet and heavy, grains.

64. One Hundred Years of Brewing, 131–34; Oscar E. Anderson, Refrigeration in America: A History of a New Technology and Its Impact (Princeton, NJ: Princeton University Press, 1953), 23–96; Arnold and Penman, History of the Brewing Industry, 92–95, on brewery refrigeration. Also see Harvey Levenstein, Revolution at the Table: The Transformation of the American Diet (New York: Oxford University Press, 1988), and Platt, Electric City, 201–34, on the impacts of World War I on Chicago's ice industry and its people's changing diets.

65. For a detailed comparison of the costs of ice and artificial refrigeration in the brewing industry (refrigeration was cheaper), see "Refrigeration Machines," Western Brewer 9 (15 May 1884): 833–36; for additional early reports on the adoption of this technology, see other Western Brewer articles: "The Ayers Rubber Refrigerator Car" (for Anheuser-Busch), in vol. 2 (15 March 1877): 77; "A New System of Refrigeration," in vol. 3 (15 April 1878): 222; "Brewery Refrigeration," in vol. 9 (15 July 1884): 1191–92; "David Boyle, Esq.," in vol. 9 (15 October 1884): 1731–32; "A Model Brewery" (Peter Schoenhofen, Chicago), in vol. 10 (15 August 1885): 1557; "An Immense Refrigerating Machine" (for Anheuser-Busch), in vol. 17 (15 April 1892): 805; "A St. Louis Refrigeration Plant" (Anheuser-Busch), in vol. 18 (15 January 1893): 88–89.

66. One Hundred Years of Brewing, 422; Schade's Brewers' Handbook (Chicago: Western Brewer, 1877), 26; and Wing's Brewer's Hand-Book of the United States and Canada: A Supplement to the Western Brewer (New York: Wing, 1880–1886), 43–45.

67. Arnold and Penman, History of the Brewing Industry, 90, for the first quotation; Schluter, Brewing Industry, 94, for the second; see pp. 89–188 of Schluter's book for a history of the brewery workers' struggle to organize. Also see Skilnik, History of Beer, 49–56, for local labor history; and Bruce Nelson, Beyond the Martyrs: A Social History of Chicago's Anarchists, 1870–1900 (New Brunswick, NJ: Rutgers University Press, 1988), for the larger context of worker culture in Chicago during the Gilded Age. Also see note 62, above.

68. "Malting in Chicago," Western Brewer 4 (15 September 1879): 771–72; "Pneumatic Malting," Western Brewer 12 (15 July 1887): 1472–74. Also see several other Western Brewer articles: "Pure Air in Breweries," in vol. 5 (15 August 1880): 821; M. Galland, "The Modern Maltster," in vol. 9 (15 October 1884): 1734–35; and "Malt House Improvements" (George Bullen's), in vol. 10 (15 January 1885): 73. For additional information on Louis Huck, see One Hundred Years of Brewing, 590; and Arnold and Penman, History of the Brewing Industry, 106–9.

69. Appel, "Brewery Architecture," 185–207; and One Hundred Years of Brewing, for many illustrations.

70. Appel, "Brewery Architecture," 201.

71. MacFarlane, Coal-Regions; Andros, Coal Mining; Worthen, Geological Survey of Illinois; chap. 14, below; and Maureen Flanagan, "The City Profitable, the City Livable: Environmental Policy, Gender, and Power in Chicago in the 1910s," Journal of Urban History 22 (January 1996): 163–90.

72. "Oil Fuel for Brewers," *Western Brewer* 15 (15 February 1890): 326–27. Others turned to crude oil as a cheap and clean-burning fuel, including the World's Fair and the cable car company on the South Side. In the 1900s, however, Standard Oil began to cancel fuel oil contracts as the demand for gasoline increased significantly.

73. *Lakeside Annual City Directory of Chicago* (Chicago: Lakeside Press, 1880) for locations. On water supplies see, for example, "The Lion Brewery," *Western Brewer* 2 (15 September 1877): 344, for details on Michael Brand's new plant on the banks of the Chicago River on the North Side. The artesian well was 1,600 feet deep and produced enough water to supply not only the brewery but also an extensive ice harvesting operation. Also see "Brewing in Chicago," *Western Brewer* 10 (15 September 1885): 1764–65, on the M. Gottfried Brewing Company. The journal was published in Chicago, which means that coverage of local breweries was more extensive than that of breweries in other places. The quarto-sized publication was exceptionally well illustrated with large engravings and photographs. Over the period, they show how the railroad was literally integrated into the design of the brewery.

74. The census of 1890 included a unique report on the housing conditions, health statistics, and ethnic composition of the city's wards. See U.S. Bureau of the Census, "Vital and Social Statistics," pt. 2 of *Eleventh Census of the United States*, vol. 7 (Washington, DC: U.S. Bureau of the Census, 1890), 161–81. While the percent foreign-born had the highest correlation with mortality rates among the available ward-level variables, the census report reveals important exceptions, particularly in wards where Germans had long been settled. By 1890, these neighborhoods had a mix of first-generation immigrants and their middle-class children. See Christiane Harzig, "Chicago's German North Side, 1880–1900: The Structure of a Gilded Age Ethnic Neighborhood," in *German Workers in Industrial Chicago, 1850–1910: Comparative Perspectives*, ed. Hartmut Keil and John B. Jentz (DeKalb: Northern Illinois University Press, 1983), 127–44. In 1890, the city was divided into thirty-four wards. In 1910, there were thirty-five wards.

75. This area, Germantown, near the southern edge of Lincoln Park at North Avenue and Clark Street is now called Old Town. See Rascher Map Publishing Company, *Fire Insurance Maps Of Chicago* (Chicago: Rascher Map Publishing Company, 1892), vol. 2, plates 112–226; *Hull House Maps and Papers* (New York: Crowell, 1895); Harzig, "Chicago's German North Side"; *One Hundred Years of Brewing*, 316; U.S. Bureau of the Census, "Vital and Social Statistics" (1890), 161–81; *Lakeside Annual City Directory of Chicago* (Chicago: Lakeside Press, 1889), 2001–2.

76. U.S. Bureau of the Census, *Thirteenth Census of the United States*, vol. 2, *Population* (Washington, DC: U.S. Bureau of the Census, 1910), 512–13; *Lakeside Annual City Directory of Chicago* (Chicago: Lakeside Press, 1910), 1487–88.

77. Although the case at hand does not point toward a conscious strategy of discrimination by the manufacturers, it does not exclude the possibility that this type of practice existed during the period under investigation. Racism was clearly evident in the policy decisions during the 1900s that led to the relocation of the

riverfront Levee, or vice district, from the central business district to the edge of the emerging ghetto on the Near South Side. Individual factory owners may have used similar calculations in planning where to put their facilities. Further research is needed before we can begin to discuss the origins of this type of discriminatory practice with any degree of confidence. We also need more historical studies of NIMBY (not in my backyard) politics that parallel Mike Davis's examination of Los Angeles. See Mike Davis, *The City of Quartz* (New York: Vintage, 1990), on present-day environmental injustice; Allan H. Spear, *Black Chicago: The Making of a Negro Ghetto, 1880–1920* (Chicago: University of Chicago Press, 1967), on racial segregation; Craig E. Colten, "Creating a Toxic Landscape: Chemical Waste Disposal Policy and Practice, 1900–1960," *Environmental History Review* 18 (Spring 1994): 85–116, on locational strategies to remove toxic industrial activities to remote sites; and Giddens, *Standard Oil*, on the location of the area's first oil refinery in the Calumet District. In this fragile environment, migratory birds continue to flock to the small remaining patches of wetland despite a century of toxic dumping. Efforts are under way to reclaim this district for the birds. See Emily Gaul, "Industrial Safety: Herons Find Sanctuary," *Reader* 24 (20 January 1995): 37–39; and "State Gives Cook County $400,000 to Buy Prairie," *Chicago Sun-Times* (1 February 1995).

78. See Platt, *Electric City*.

Chapter Seven

1. Horace T. Brown, "Reminiscences of Fifty Years Experience of the Application of Scientific Method to Brewing Practice," *Journal of the Institute of Brewing* 22 (1916): 295; see also pp. 267–348; and Louis Pasteur, *Studies on Fermentation: The Diseases of Beer, Their Causes, and the Means of Preventing Them* (London: Macmillan, 1879). On Brown, see Alfred Barnard, *The Noted Breweries of Great Britain and Ireland*, 4 vols. (London: Causton and Sons, 1889–1991), 3:428; E. M. Sigsworth, "Science and the Brewing Industry, 1850–1900," *Economic History Review* 17 (1964–1965): 536–54; and see Keith Vernon, "Pus, Sewage, Beer, and Milk: Microbiology in Britain, 1870–1940," *History of Science* 28 (September 1990): 289–325. In "Reminiscences," Brown names the following as the regular members of the Bacterium Club: Cornelius O'Sullivan, a Mr. Griess, P. B. Mason, H. E. Bridgman, and Adrian J. Brown.

2. Brown, "Reminiscences," 270, for the quotation; see also pp. 268–84 for further detail on the power of tradition within the brewing industry.

3. For an introduction, see Merritt Smith and Leo Marx, eds., *Does Technology Drive History? The Dilemma of Technological Determinism* (Cambridge, MA: MIT Press, 1994); and Wiebe Bijker et al., *The Social Construction of Technological Systems: New Directions in the Sociology and History of Technology* (Cambridge, MA: MIT Press, 1987). Also see Bruno Latour, *The Pasteurization of France* (Cambridge, MA: Harvard University Press, 1988).

4. Sigsworth, "Science," 536–54; Martin J. Weiner, *English Culture and the Decline of the Industrial Spirit, 1850–1980* (Cambridge: Cambridge University Press, 1981); and see note 7, below.

5. R. G. Wilson, "The British Brewing Industry since 1750," in *The Brewing Industry: A Guide to Historical Records*, eds. Lesly M. Richmond and Alison Turtow (Manchester: University of Manchester Press, 1990), 12–13, for the first quotation; Brown, "Reminiscences," 271, for the second. Also see the leading work on the industry, T. R. Gourvish and R. G. Wilson, *The British Brewing Industry, 1830–1980* (Cambridge: Cambridge University Press, 1994), 75; and Sigsworth, "Science."

6. On working-class culture and drink in England, see A. E. Dingle, "Drink and Working-Class Living Standards in Britain, 1870–1914," *Economic History Review* 25 (1972): 608–22; Brian Harrison, *Drink and the Victorians: The Temperance Question in England, 1815 1872*, 2nd ed. (1971; reprint, Staffordshire: Keele University Press, 1994); Brian Harrison, "Pubs," in *The Victorian City: Images and Realities*, ed. Harold J. Dyos and Michael Wolff, 2 vols. (London: Routledge and Kegan Paul, 1973), 1:3–58. For studies that focus on Manchester, see Robert D. Storch, "The Problem of Working-Class Leisure: Some Roots of Middle-Class Moral Reform in the Industrial North, 1825–1850," in *Social Control in Nineteenth Century Britain*, ed. A. P. Donajgrodzki (London: Rowman and Littlefield, 1977), 138–62; D. M Fahey, "Brewers, Publicans, and Working-Class Drinkers: Pressure Group Politics in Late Victorian and Edwardian England," *Histoire Sociale/Social History* 25 (May 1980): 85–103; and Anne Secord, "Science in the Pub: Artisan Botanists in Early Nineteenth-Century Lancashire," *History of Science* 32 (September 1994): 269–315.

7. Unfortunately, this exercise means entering into a historical controversy heavily weighted with the current ideological baggage of British industrial decline. With the rise of Margaret Thatcher in the 1970s, the country became engaged in a debate over whether it did enough to support research and development, and about who was to blame for any failures to maintain the nation's position of world leadership after the 1860s. For two leading declinists' interpretations, see Weiner, *English Culture*; and Correlli Barnett, *The Audit War: The Illusion and Reality of Britain as a Great Nation* (London: Macmillan, 1986). For the other side of the debate, see D. E. H. Edgerton and S. M. Horrocks, "British Industrial Research and Development before 1945," *Economic History Review* 47 (1994): 213–38; and Sidney Pollard, "Reflections on Entrepreneurship and Culture in European Societies," *Transactions of the Royal Historical Society*, 5th ser., 40 (1990): 153–73. For insight on biochemistry that lends some support to the declinist position, see Vernon, "Pus." For a valuable comparative case study, see Harm G. Schroter and Anthony S. Travis, "An Issue of Different Mentalities: National Approaches to the Development of the Chemical Industry in Britain and Germany before 1914," in *The Chemical Industry in Europe, 1850–1914: Industrial Growth, Pollution, and Professionalization*, ed. Ernst Homburg, Anthony S. Travis, and Harm G. Schroter, Chemists and Chemistry, no. 17 (Dordrecht, Netherlands: Kluwer Academic Publishers, 1998), 95–118. Also see Alfred D. Chandler Jr., *Scale and Scope: The Dynamics of Industrial Capitalism* (Cambridge, MA: Harvard University Press, 1990).

8. Cf. Peter Mathias, *The Brewing Industry in England, 1700–1830* (Cambridge: Cambridge University Press, 1959), 63–98, on technological innovation during the second

half of the eighteenth century; and Gourvish and Wilson, *British Brewing Industry*, 98–103.

9. Gourvish and Wilson, *British Brewing Industry*, 75–89. At the same time, the makers of Burton's pale ales and Dublin's dark stout were eating away at both ends of the beer market. Too uncritically, perhaps, these same scholars have also accepted the self-serving excuses put forward by contemporaries. The capital's brewers protested that there was little they could do to meet the competition because the secret ingredient of Burton's pale ales was the local water, which was as hard as London's was soft. However, this apologia simply begs the question of adaptivity since these same breweries would, in the 1880s, belatedly begin to make "running ales," a lighter, milder alternative to the increasingly unpopular porter. In addition, the premiere supplier of stout, Dublin's Guinness, would achieve a success similar to that of the Burton brewers by capturing a growing proportion of the drinkers who continued to prefer a darker brew. See Sigsworth, "Science," 543–45, for example.

10. Pasteur, *Studies*, 12, 14, for the first two quotations; and Gourvish and Wilson, *British Brewing Industry*, 179–266, for a detailed analysis of the economics of the brewing industry during this period. See Fahey, "Brewers, Publicans, and Working-Class Drinkers," 88, for statistics on tied houses.

11. Gourvish and Wilson, *British Brewing Industry*, 79, 62, for the quotations. Also see Sigsworth, "Science"; and Chandler, *Scale and Scope*, 266–68.

12. Gourvish and Wilson, *British Brewing Industry*, 169; see also pp. 24–63, 267–313; Dingle, "Drink and Working-Class Living Standards."

13. Wilson, "British Brewing Industry since 1750," 5.

14. Gourvish and Wilson, *British Brewing Industry*, 89–103. Guinness also became an outpost of scientific brewing and, like the Burton brewers, became a tremendous success. For the purposes here, however, I will focus exclusively on the makers of pale ales.

15. Brown, "Reminiscences," 285, for the quotation; see also pp. 344–48. Also see Gourvish and Wilson, *British Brewing Industry*, 58–63.

16. In general, see Barnard, *Noted Breweries*; and Lesly M. Richmond and Alison Turtow, eds., *The Brewing Industry: A Guide to Historical Records* (Manchester: University of Manchester Press, 1990). For Manchester, see A. Gall, *Manchester Breweries of Times Gone By* (Manchester: n.p., 1978–80); Christopher Grayling, *Manchester Ales and Porter: The History of Holt's Brewery* (Manchester: n.p., 1985); M. Jackson, *Two Hundred Years of Beer: The Story of Boddingtons Strangeways Brewery, 1778–1978* (Manchester: n.p., 1978). And for Dublin, see Patrick Lynch and John Vaizey, *Guinness's Brewery in the Irish Economy, 1759–1876* (Cambridge: Cambridge University Press, 1960).

17. Pasteur, *Studies*, 222. See Sigsworth, "Science," for a description of the rules of cleanliness practiced in the craft-based brewery; and Dingle, "Drink and Working-Class Living Standards," on domestic expenditures.

18. Wilson, "British Brewing Industry since 1750," 6, for the quotation; Gourvish and Wilson, *British Brewing Industry*, 205–9, on prices.

19. A. T. Andreas, *History of Chicago*, 3 vols. (1884–1886; reprint, New York: Arno, 1975), 3:574, states that five of twelve breweries were destroyed. Cf. *Chicago Tribune* (1 January 1876), 12, which reports that seventeen of thirty-four breweries burned. The truth lies somewhere in between since the U.S. census of 1870 lists twenty three breweries in Cook County. See Department of Interior, Census Office, *Ninth Census of the United States, Manufactures* (Washington, DC: U.S. Bureau of the Census, 1870), 3:649. The proximity of Milwaukee to Chicago represents a strange and interesting case of central place theory working in reverse. Given the perishable nature of beer during this era, its producers reaped benefits, not disadvantages, by being located close to the fastest-growing urban center of the region. See Thomas C. Cochran, *The Pabst Brewing Company: The History of an American Business* (New York: New York University Press, 1948), 30–35, for the antebellum marketing activities of Milwaukee brewers in Chicago. Their shipments began in 1852 but they remained a minor, secondary supplier until after the fire. The three largest shippers were Valentin Blatz, Charles T. Melms, and Phillip Best (of Pabst). Also see William L. Downard, *The Cincinnati Brewing Industry* (Columbus: Ohio University Press, 1973).

20. For an overview of the syndicates in Chicago, see Bob Skilnik, *The History of Beer and Brewing in Chicago, 1833–1978* (St. Paul, Minn.: Pogo Press, 1999), 57–68; and Perry Duis, *The Saloon: Public Drinking in Chicago and Boston* (Urbana: University of Illinois Press, 1983), 15–45. On the British managerial style, see Chandler, *Scale and Scope*, 266–67.

21. "Brewing Trade Statistics," *Western Brewer* 20 (15 November 1895): 2373. See also other *Western Brewer* articles: "The Lion Brewery," in vol. 2 (15 September 1877): 344; and "A New System of Refrigeration," in vol. 3 (15 April 1877): 222. And see *One Hundred Years of Brewing: A Supplement to the Western Brewer* (Chicago: Rich, 1903), 310–12, 422; S. Schoff, *The Glory of Chicago: Her Manufactories* (Chicago: Knight and Leonard, 1873), 121; *The Brewing and Malting Industry of Chicago* (Chicago: Reed, 1882), 29–30; and Josiah Currey, *Manufacturing and Wholesale Industries of Chicago*, 3 vols. (Chicago: Poole, 1918), 3:143–46. The original brewery was located on the lakefront at Cedar Street, not far from the ruins of Lill and Diversey. The rebuilt brewery was converted into a malt house after the Lion Brewery opened for business. The riverfront facility was located on Elston Avenue at Snow Street, just north of Fullerton Avenue. In 1877, Chicagoan David Boyle installed a compression ammonia type of refrigeration machine in the Bemis and McAvoy brewery. See *One Hundred Years of Brewing*, 126–28, 322.

22. "Brewing in Chicago," *Western Brewer* 25 (15 February 1900): 61–65, for details on the new facilities of the Brand Brewing Company. Also see Josiah Currey, *Manufacturing and Wholesale Industries of Chicago*, 3 vols. (Chicago: Poole, 1918), 3:143–46.

23. In 1868, the twenty-five-year-old German immigrant had arrived in Chicago without skills or money. Junk secured a job driving a beer wagon for Peter Schoenhofen's brewery, then after six years he started his own trucking business hauling barley

and malt, especially for the fast-growing firm of Louis Huck. See *One Hundred Years of Brewing*, 492. On the ice bus in 1880s, see Henry Hall, "The Ice Industry of the United States," in U.S. Bureau of the Census, *Tenth Census of the United States* (Washington, DC: U.S. Bureau of the Census, 1880), 21:4–41; and Richard O. Cummings, *The American Ice Harvests: A Historical Study in Technology, 1800–1918* (Berkeley: University of California Press, 1949). On the production of beer in Chicago, see *Wing's Brewer's Hand-Book of the United States and Canada: A Supplement to the Western Brewer* (New York: Wing, 1880–1886), 43–45.

24. Cochran, *Pabst*, 98–99, on cost savings and losses. Between 1887 and 1893, for example, worker productivity improved 34 percent. Yet Cochran cautions that the overall savings from scale economies was only 10–15 percent, not enough to knock out the small, local breweries of Chicago. After 1893, the advantage shifted back to these local enterprises. For a history of the industry's professionalization and Chicago's central role in its development, see John P. Arnold and Frank Penman, *History of the Brewing Industry and Science in America: A Memorial to Dr. John E. Siebel and Anton Schwartz* (Chicago: n.p., 1933). On Chicago as a center of brewery architecture, see Susan K. Appel, "Brewery Architecture in America from the Civil War to Prohibition," in *The Midwest in American Architecture*, ed. John S. Garner (Urbana: University of Illinois Press, 1991), 185–214.

25. Duis, *Saloon*, 274–304; Stanley Baron, *Brewed in America: A History of Beer and Ale in the United States* (Boston: Little, Brown, 1962), 286–307; and Maureen A. Flanagan, "Charter Reform in Chicago: Political Culture and Urban Progressive Reform," *Journal of Urban History* 12 (February 1986): 109–30.

26. For an introduction, see Robert H. Wiebe, *The Search for Order, 1877–1920* (New York: Hill and Wang, 1967); John Higham, "The Reorientation of American Culture in the 1890s," in *Writing American History: Essays on Modern Scholarship* (Bloomington: Indiana University Press, 1970), 73–102; Margaret Marsh, "From Separation to Togetherness: The Social Construction of Domestic Space in American Suburbs, 1840–1915," *Journal of American History* 76 (September 1989): 506–27; Louis Erenberg, "Ain't We Got Fun?" *Chicago History* 14 (Winter 1985–1986): 4–21; and Duis, *Saloon*, 86–113.

27. Duis, *Saloon*, 286–98; Cochran, *Pabst*, 180–88. The beer garden, of course, was the site of an important exception to the exclusion of women from public drinking. Yet even in this more cosmopolitan setting, only women who came escorted in a family group were welcome. Chicago's German community supported its fair share of these ethnic institutions. See Duis, *Saloon*, 154–57; Bruce Nelson, *Beyond the Martyrs: A Social History of Chicago's Anarchist, 1870–1910* (New Brunswick, NJ: Rutgers University Press, 1988), 127–52; and Paul Kruty, "Pleasure Garden on the Midway," *Chicago History* 16 (Fall/Winter 1987–1988): 4–27.

28. *One Hundred Years of Brewing*, 105–7, 310; Arnold and Penman, *History of the Brewing Industry*, 211.

29. Duis, *Saloon*, 204–29, on home deliveries. See Homer Hoyt, *One Hundred Years of Land Values in Chicago* (Chicago: University of Chicago Press, 1933), 153–59; and

Michael P. McCarthy, "Chicago, The Annexation Movement and Progressive Reform," in *The Age of Urban Reform*, ed. Michael H. Ebner and Eugene M. Tobin (Port Washington, NY: Kennikat, 1977): 43–54, on annexation. See Marsh, "From Separation to Togetherness," and Mary Corbin Sies, "The City Transformed: Nature, Technology, and the Suburban Ideal, 1877–1917," *Journal of Urban History* 14 (November 1987): 81–111, on changing gender roles in domestic life.

30. Potosi Brewing Company (of Wisconsin) advertisement (1908) and Rheingold Bottle Beer advertisement (1911), from Baron, *Brewed in America*, gallery between pp. 304 and 305. Also see Kruty, "Pleasure Garden."

31. Oscar E. Anderson, *Refrigeration in America: A History of a New Technology and Its Impact* (Princeton, NJ: Princeton University Press, 1953), 90, for the quotation; see also pp. 90–96 for additional details on how the natural ice famine "led to a new era in mechanical refrigeration" (p. 96). On the change in federal law and Pabst's bottling operations, see Cochran, *Pabst*, 123–28. On Pabst's response to the beer wars, see Cochran, *Pabst*, 148–59.

32. Between 1879 and 1888, the savings made possible by artificial refrigeration led Fred Pabst to abandon the use of natural ice. He realized substantial savings in the cost of operations while enjoying big gains in the quality of his products. See Cochran, *Pabst*, 107–10; and the commentary on cellar architecture in *One Hundred Years of Brewing*, 145–47. "The fermenting cellar of to-day," the centennial issue of the *Western Brewer* explained, "with its system of refrigeration by pipes running along the walls, kept to a temperature of 2 to 4 [Centigrade], cannot be compared with the damp, dark, moldy, ill-smelling chamber of former years, with the water dripping from the ceiling, and with wet and decaying wooden floors" (*One Hundred Years of Brewing*, 146).

33. *One Hundred Years of Brewing*, 114, for the first quotation; Philip Dreesbach, *Beer Bottlers' Handy Book* (Chicago: Wahl-Henius Institute, 1906), 182, for the second; see also pp. 22–122 of the *Handy Book* for a detailed description of bottling techniques. Also see *One Hundred Years of Brewing*, 105–14, for a general history; and Zymotechnic Alumni Association, *Chicago Brewery Equipment Directory* (Chicago: Zymotechnic Alumni Association, 1911), 200, for the bottling machine. The Zymotechnic publication also includes a firm-by-firm list of equipment in Chicago's breweries.

34. Duis, *Saloons*, 204–73; Robert C. Twombly, "Saving the Family: Middle Class Attraction to Wright's Prairie House, 1901–1909," *American Quarterly* 27 (March 1975): 57–72; Helen Lefkowitz Horowitz, "Hull-House as Women's Space," *Chicago History* 12 (Winter 1983–1984): 40–55; and Michael H. Ebner, *Creating Chicago's North Shore: A Suburban History* (Chicago: University of Chicago Press, 1988).

35. United States Brewers' Association, *Yearbook, 1910* (New York: United States Brewers' Association, 1910), 275–76. Natural ice would hold its own against machine-made products until World War I, when shortages of men and horses would combine with exorbitant freight rates to kill off this seasonal rural activity. See A. L. Hunt, "Manufactured Ice," in U.S. Bureau of the Census, *Twelfth Census of the United States, Manufactures* (Washington, DC: U.S. Bureau of the Census,

1900), 9:675–97; and Anderson, *Refrigeration*, 103–13, 207–11. On the eve of the war, natural ice supplied 67 percent of the Chicago ice market. For the death of this industry in Chicago, see Harold L. Platt, *The Electric City: Energy and the Growth of the Chicago Area, 1880–1930* (Chicago: University of Chicago Press, 1991), 201–34.

36. Arnold and Penman, *History of the Brewing Industry*, 74–75; David A. Hounshell, *From the American System to Mass Production: The Development of Manufacturing Technology in the United States* (Baltimore: Johns Hopkins University Press, 1984).

37. See Gourvish and Wilson, *British Brewing Industry*, 58–63, for an overview. For efforts within the Institute to establish a professional, college-based educational program, see several articles in the *Journal of the Institute of Brewing*: "Annual Banquet 1894," in vol. 1 (1895): 2–23; Frank E. Lott, "Training of a Brewer," in vol. 1 (1895): 177–96; C. H. Bavington, "Annual Presidential Address," in vol. 11 (1905): 95–105; and Arthur R. Ling, "The Relation of Our Institute to the Brewing Industry," in vol. 18 (1912): 350–66. For an outline of the Institute's proposal, see *Journal of the Institute of Brewing* 21 (1915): 278–91, 476–81.

38. On the history of the Institute, see Brown, "Reminiscences"; "Annual Banquet 1894"; William Frew, "A Modern School of Brewing, Its Curriculum and Equipment," *Journal of the Institute of Brewing* 4 (1898): 597–615; Ling, "Relation of Our Institute"; and Sigsworth, "Science." On the economic challenges of the 1900s, see Bavington, "Annual Presidential Address"; T. A. Glendinnings, "The Popular Type of Beer," *Journal of the Institute of Brewing* 11 (1905): 618–33; and W. Duncan, "Some Remarks on the Ales of the Present Day," *Journal of the Institute of Brewing* 12 (1906): 669–86. For modern statistical evidence of the decline in sales, see Dingle, "Drink and Working-Class Living Standards"; and George B. Wilson, *Alcohol and the Nation (A Contribution to the Study of the Liquor Problem in the United Kingdom from 1800 to 1935)* (London: Nickolson and Watson, 1940), 331–33, 369–70.

39. For the quotations, see C. H. Field, "The Chilling Process as Applied to Draught and Bottle Beer," *Journal of the Institute of Brewing* 11 (1905): 122 (transcript of discussion) and 114–15, respectively.

40. Glendinnings, "Popular Type of Beer." Also see Lott, "Training of a Brewer"; Horace T. Brown, "Recent Advances in the U.S.," *Journal of the Institute of Brewing* 3 (1897): 467–80; Frew, "Modern School of Brewing"; and Arthur Hadley, "Chilled Bottled Beers," *Journal of the Institute of Brewing* 20 (1914): 504–33.

41. Brown, "Recent Advances," 474; and Hugh Abbot, "Some Points in the Design and Management of a Modern Bottling Store," *Journal of the Institute of Brewing* 18 (1912): 523, for the first and second quotations, respectively. Also see the following articles from the *Journal of the Institute of Brewing*: Frew, "Modern School of Brewing"; Field, "Chilling Process"; Glendinnings, "Popular Type of Beer"; Percy K. Le May, "Non-Deposit Ales and Stout in Cask and Bottle, with Improved Keeping Qualities," in vol. 13 (1907): 2–25; Thomas Hyde, "Practical Notes on a Visit Through American and Canadian Ale Breweries," in vol. 13 (1907): 357–70; Emil Westergaard, "A Comparison between British and Continental Brewing Methods," in

vol. 13 (1907): 706–18; Leuig Chew, "Mechanical Refrigeration as Applied to the Brewing Industry," in vol. 18 (1912): 274–312. See note 38, above, on parallel efforts to advance professional education.

42. For a perceptive analysis, see Arnold Lewis, *An Early Encounter with Tomorrow: Europeans, Chicago's Loop, and the World's Columbian Exposition* (Urbana: University of Illinois Press, 1997). For a collection of firsthand accounts, see Bessie Louise Pierce, ed., *As Others See Chicago: Impressions of Visitors, 1673–1933* (Chicago: University of Chicago Press, 1933). On the stockyards, see the classical expose by Upton Sinclair, *The Jungle* (1905; reprint, New York: New American Library, 1960).

43. Louis M. Hayes, *Reminiscences of Manchester* (Manchester: Sherratt and Hughes, 1905), 203.

44. On the Romantics, see Peter Coates, *Nature: Western Attitudes since Ancient Times* (Berkeley: University of California Press, 1998); and Weiner, *English Culture.* On the Progressives, see Paul Boyer, *Urban Masses and Moral Order in America, 1820–1920* (Cambridge, MA: Harvard University Press, 1978); and Daniel T. Rodgers, *Atlantic Crossings: Social Politics in the Progressive Age* (Cambridge, MA: Harvard University Press, 1998); and note 26, above.

Chapter Eight

1. Lewis Mumford, *The City in History: Its Origins, Its Transformations, and Its Prospects* (New York: Harcourt, Brace, and World, 1961), 478; James H. Cassedy, "Hygeia: A Mid-Victorian Dream of a City of Health," *Journal of the History of Medicine and Allied Sciences* 17 (1962): 217–28; Christopher C. Sellers, "Thoreau's Body: Toward an Embodied Environmental History," *Environmental History* 4 (October 1999): 486–514; Nancy Tomes, "The Private Side of Public Health: Sanitary Science, Domestic Hygiene, and the Germ Theory, 1870–1900," *Bulletin of the History of Medicine* 64 (Winter 1990): 509–39; Nancy Tomes, *The Gospel of Germs: Men, Women, and the Microbe in American Life* (Cambridge, MA: Harvard University Press, 1998); Suellen Hoy, *Chasing Dirt: The American Pursuit of Cleanliness* (New York: Oxford University Press, 1995); and Annmarie Adams, *Architecture in the Family Way: Doctors, Houses, and Women, 1870–1900* (Montreal: McGill-Queen's University Press, 1996). Dolores Hayden discusses "material feminists," who had alternative designs for domestic and urban space. See Dolores Hayden, *The Grand Domestic Revolution: A History of Feminist Designs for American Homes, Neighborhoods, and Cities* (Cambridge, MA: MIT Press, 1981).

2. Robert Fishman, *Urban Utopias in the Twentieth Century: Ebenezer Howard, Frank Lloyd Wright, Le Corbusier* (New York: Basic, 1977); Robert C. Twombly, "Saving the Family: Middle Class Attraction to Wright's Prairie House, 1901–1909," *American Quarterly* 27 (March 1975): 57–72; Mary Corbin Sies, "The City Transformed: Nature, Technology, and the Suburban Ideal, 1877–1917," *Journal of Urban History* 14 (November 1987): 81–111; Michael H. Ebner, *Creating Chicago's North Shore: A Suburban History* (Chicago: University of Chicago Press, 1988); and Mel Scott, *American City Planning since 1890* (Berkeley: University of California Press, 1969).

3. Elizabeth Wilson, "Issue Paper: Culture and Gender Concerns in Spatial Development," in *Women in the City: Housing, Services, and the Urban Environment*, Organization for Economic Co-operation and Development (Paris: Organization for Economic Co-operation and Development, 1995), 43; H. Blake, "Women, the City, and the Design of Utopia," a paper presented to the Council of Europe Colloquy, the Challenges Facing European Society with the Approach of the Year 2000: Role and Representation of Women in Urban and Regional Planning Aimed at Sustainable Development (Ornskoldsvik, Sweden, 1994). Also see Jo Little, Linda Peake, and Pat Richardson, eds., *Women in Cities: Gender and the Urban Environment* (New York: New York University Press, 1998); and Maureen A. Flanagan, "Gender and Urban Political Reform: The City Club and the Women's City Club of Chicago in the Progressive Era," *American Historical Review* 95 (October 1990): 1032–50. Other scholars give emphasis to women's alternative designs for the city as paths not taken. See Dolores Hayden, *Grand Domestic Revolution*; Sies, "City Transformed"; and Gwendolyn Wright, *Moralism and the Model Home: Domestic Architecture and Cultural Conflict in Chicago, 1873–1913* (Chicago: University of Chicago Press, 1980).

4. Adams, *Architecture in the Family Way*, 5; John Sanders, as quoted in the *Manchester Guardian*, Oct. 1889?; Tomes, "Private Side." Also see Maureen Ogle, *All the Modern Conveniences: American Household Plumbing, 1840–1890* (Baltimore: Johns Hopkins University Press, 1996); and Michael Worboys, *Spreading Germs: Disease Theories and Medical Practice in Britain, 1865–1900* (Cambridge: Cambridge University Press, 2000).

5. See Tomes, "Private Side," 536n4. On the timing of the new wave of housing reform, see Anthony S. Wohl, *The Eternal Slum: Housing and Social Policy in Victorian London* (Montreal: McGill-Queen's University Press, 1977); and Anthony S. Wohl, "Introduction," in Andrew Mearns, *The Bitter Cry of Outcast London* (1883, reprint, New York: Leicester University Press, 1970). Although the former is vague on timing, the latter ties the rise of reform to the publication of Mearns's 1883 tract.

6. Daniel T. Rodgers, *Atlantic Crossings: Social Politics in the Progressive Age* (Cambridge, MA: Harvard University Press, 1998); Allen F. Davis, *Spearheads for Reform: The Social Settlements and the Progressive Movement, 1890–1914* (New York: Oxford University Press, 1967).

7. Robert H. Wiebe, *The Search for Order, 1877–1920* (New York: Hill and Wang, 1967); Thomas L. Haskell, *The Emergence of Professional Social Science: The American Social Science Association and the Nineteenth-Century Crisis of Authority* (Urbana: University of Illinois Press, 1977); Thomas L. Haskell, ed., *The Authority of Experts: Studies in History and Theory* (Bloomington: Indiana University Press, 1984).

8. Peter Baldwin, *Domesticating the Street: The Reform of Public Space in Hartford, 1850–1930* (Columbus: Ohio State University Press, 1999), 26; Paul Boyer, *Urban Masses and Moral Order in America, 1820–1920* (Cambridge, MA: Harvard University Press, 1978); Graeme Davison, "The City as a Natural System: Theories of Urban Society in Early Nineteenth-Century Britain," in *The Pursuit of Urban History*, eds. Derek Fraser

and Anthony Sutcliffe (London: Edward Arnold, 1983), 349–70; and Christopher Hamlin, *Public Health and Social Justice in the Age of Chadwick: Britain, 1800–1854* (Cambridge: Cambridge University Press, 1998).

9. See note 1, above. Given the health risks, flight to the suburbs made perfectly good sense.

10. Boyer, *Urban Masses*; Martin Hewitt, "The Travails of Domestic Visiting: Manchester, 1830–1870," *Historical Research* 71 (June 1998): 196–227; and Peter Shapely, "Charity, Status, and Parliamentary Candidates in Manchester: A Consideration of the Electoral and the Social Basis of Power, 1832–1910," *International Review of Social History* 44 (1999): 1–21.

11. Boyer, *Urban Masses*, 235; Wiebe, *Search for Order*; and Richard Hofstadter, *The Age of Reform: From Bryan to F. D. R.* (New York: Vintage Books, 1955).

12. Elizabeth Israels Perry, "Men Are from the Gilded Age, Women Are from the Progressive Era," *Journal of the Gilded Age and Progressive Era* 1 (January 2002): 25–48; and Maureen A. Flanagan, *Seeing with Their Hearts: Chicago Women and the Vision of the Good City, 1871–1933* (Princeton, NJ: Princeton University Press, 2002).

13. Margaret Marsh, "From Separation to Togetherness: The Social Construction of Domestic Space in American Suburbs, 1840–1915," *Journal of American History* 76 (September 1989): 507, for the quotation; see also pp. 506–27. Also see Robert Fishman, *Bourgeois Utopias: The Rise and Fall of Suburbia* (New York: Basic Books, 1987), 145–54; and Philip J. Ethington, "Recasting Urban Political History: Gender, the Public, the Household, and Political Participation in Boston and San Francisco during the Progressive Era," *Social Science History* 18 (Summer 1992): 301–33. Writing from an avowedly feminist point of view, Ann Hughes and Karen Hunt point out that better housing made women's work easier. In the social housing project they studied, moreover, women played a significant role in designing the houses and neighborhoods. To Hughes and Hunt, the full effect of suburban "garden city" ideals on gender is ambiguous. See Ann Hughes and Karen Hunt, "A Culture Transformed? Women's Lives in Wythenshawe in the 1930s," in *Workers' Worlds: Cultures and Communities in Manchester and Salford, 1880–1939*, ed. Andrew Davies and Steven Fielding (Manchester: University of Manchester Press, 1992), 74–101. Despite their focus on the United States, also see Richard Sennett, *Families against the City: Middle Class Homes of Industrial Chicago, 1872–1890* (Cambridge, MA: Harvard University Press, 1970); Twombly, "Saving the Family"; and Ann Douglas, *Feminization of American Culture* (New York: Knopf, 1997).

14. Samuel P. Hays, *Conservation and the Gospel of Efficiency: The Progressive Conservation Movement, 1890–1920* (Cambridge, MA: Harvard University Press, 1959).

15. On tram statistics, see Roy Frost, *Electricity in Manchester* (Manchester: Richardson, 1993), 27–30. The average commuter paid six-tenths of penny, meaning that most paid a half-pence fare. On health statistics, see the City of Manchester, "Annual Report of the Medical Officer of Health," *Proceedings of the Common Council* (1890–1920). On the complexity of the "condition of England" question, see Graham Mooney and Simon Szreter, "Urbanization, Mortality, and the Standard of Living Debate:

New Estimates of the Expectation of Life at Birth in Nineteenth-Century British Cities," *Economic History Review* 51 (1998): 84–112.

16. Lord Woolton, *Ancoats: A Study of a Clearance Area: Report of a Survey Made in 1937–1938* (Manchester: Manchester University Settlement, 1945), 11, for the quotation; see pp. 13–14 of the study for the demographic statistics. For additional insight on life in the new social estates, see Hughes and Hunt, "A Culture Transformed?" For similar reactions of alienation in the case of suburban social housing in Dublin, see Judith Walden, "Constructing Identity: Public Housing in Dublin, Ireland, 1939–1969" (Ph.D. diss., Northwestern University, Department of History, 1999). On housing reform during this period, also see Ernest Darwin Simon and J. Inman, *Rebuilding Manchester* (London: Longmans, Green, 1935).

17. Woolton, *Ancoats*, 11, 14, respectively for the quotations.

18. Richard Sennett, *Flesh and Stone: The Body and the City in Western Civilization* (New York: Norton, 1994). Also see Boyer, *Urban Masses*, 220–51.

19. Frederic C. Howe, *European Cities at Work* (New York: Charles Scribner's Sons, 1913), 361, as quoted in, Rodgers, *Atlantic Crossings*, 164. Also see Sies, "City Transformed"; Kenneth T. Jackson, *Crabgrass Frontier: The Suburbanization of the United States* (New York: Oxford University Press, 1985); and Adam W. Rome, *The Bulldozer in the Countryside: Suburban Sprawl and the Rise of American Environmentalism* (New York: Cambridge University Press, 2001).

Chapter Nine

1. Anthony S. Wohl, *The Eternal Slum: Housing and Social Policy in Victorian London* (Montreal: McGill-Queen's University Press, 1977).

2. Mike Williams and D. A. Farnie, *Cotton Mills in Greater Manchester* (Preston, U.K.: Carnegie, 1992), 90–119; Alan Kidd, *Manchester*, Town and City Histories, ed. Stephen Constantine (Keele, Staffordshire: Ryburn/Keele University Press, 1993), 103–19; and Henry Baker, "On the Growth of Manchester Population, Extension of the Commercial Centre of the City and Provision for Habitation: Census Period, 1871–81," *Manchester Statistical Society, Transactions* (November 1881): 1–27.

3. I. Harford, *Manchester and Its Ship Canal Movement: Class, Work, and Politics in Late Victorian England* (Staffordshire: Ryburn, 1994), is the best single source on this period's local political history. The semiofficial account of the ship canal by its leading proponent is B. T. Leech, *History of the Manchester Ship Canal*, 2 vols. (Manchester: Sherratt and Hughes, 1907). On perceptions of larger, national decline, see Martin J. Weiner, *English Culture and the Decline of the Industrial Spirit, 1850–1980* (Cambridge: Cambridge University Press, 1981).

4. Alan Wilson, "Technology and Municipal Decision-Making: Sanitary Systems in Manchester, 1868–1910" (Ph.D. diss., University of Manchester, 1990), 195–258; Harford, *Manchester and Its Ship Canal Movement*, 21–31, 62–99; A. Redford and I. S. Russell, *The History of Local Government in Manchester*, 3 vol. (London: Longman, 1939–1940), 2:395–423; Maurice Spiers, ed., *Victoria Park, Manchester: A Nineteenth-Century Suburb in Its Social and Administrative Context*, Remains, Historical and

Literary, Connected with the Palatine Counties of Lancaster and Chester, 3rd
ser., vol. 23 (Manchester: Cheetham Society, 1976), 33–50; and Robert Fishman,
Bourgeois Utopias: The Rise and Fall of Suburbia (New York: Basic Books, 1987), 73–102.

5. City of Manchester, "Report of the Medical Officer of Health," *Proceedings of the Common
Council* (1884): 342, for the quotation; see pp. 342–514, for the full report. This
account reinforces the charge Friedrich Engels had made forty years earlier that
the working classes were more or less imprisoned in their residential districts.
See Friedrich Engels, *The Condition of the Working Class in England* (1845; reprint,
Stanford, CA: Stanford University Press, 1958), 55–56.

6. John I. Rushton, "Charles Rowley and the Ancoats Recreation Movement" (Master's thesis, University of Manchester, 1959), 1–32; and Charles Rowley, *Fifty Years of Work
without Wages*, 2nd ed. (London: Hodder and Stoughton, 1911). Rowley's portrait
appears in Ford Madox Brown's painting, *Expulsion of the Danes*. Rowley, with his
distinctive red beard, is one of the Danes in the foreground. See Teresa Newman
and Ray Watkinson, *Ford Madox Brown and the Pre-Raphaelite Circle* (London: Chatto
and Windus, 1991); and Kenneth Bendiner, *The Art of Ford Madox Brown* (University
Park: Pennsylvania State University Press, 1998). On the social and religious composition of Manchester's Liberals, see V. A. C. Gatrell, "Incorporation and the Pursuit of Liberal Hegemony in Manchester, 1790–1839," in *Municipal Reform and the
Industrial City*, ed. Derek Fraser (Leicester: Leicester University Press, 1982), 15–60.

7. Rowley, *Fifty Years of Work*, 49–50, for the quotation. During this term in office, Rowley
was instrumental in getting a commission for Ford Madox Brown to paint a series
of murals in the Town Hall. See Bendiner, *Art of Ford Madox Brown*, 113, passim.

8. Bendiner, *Art of Ford Madox Brown*, 55, for the first quotation; Rowley, as quoted in Rushton, "Charles Rowley," 31, for the final quotation. On public baths in Manchester,
see E. T. Bellhouse, "On Baths and Wash-Houses for the People in Manchester,"
Manchester Statistical Society, Transactions (1877–1878): 241–51. On the council's cul-
ture of secrecy and self-contained committee system of power, also see Sidney
Webb and Beatrice Webb, *Methods of Social Study* (1932; reprint, New York: Kelley,
1968), 194–97; Redford and Russell, *History of Local Government in Manchester*; and
Derek Fraser, *Urban Politics in Victorian England: The Structure of Politics in Victorian
Cities* (Leicester: Leicester University Press, 1976); Rowley, *Fifty Years of Work*; and
William E. A. Axon, as quoted in J. H. Nodal, ed., *City News, Notes, and Queries*
(Manchester: Manchester City News, 1878).

9. Rowley, *Fifty Years of Work*, 198, for the quoted phrases; see also pp. 195–226.

10. Rushton, "Charles Rowley," 33, 41, for the two quotations; Rushton also discusses the
roots of the "recreation movement" idea. For an introduction to the social set-
tlement house on the American side, see Allen F. Davis, *Spearheads for Reform: The
Social Settlements and the Progressive Movement, 1890–1914* (New York: Oxford Univer-
sity Press, 1967). On the British side, see Asa Briggs, *Toynbee Hall: The First Hundred
Years* (London: Routledge and Kegan Paul, 1984); and Standish Meacham, *Toynbee
Hall and Social Reform, 1880–1914: The Search for Community* (New Haven, CT: Yale
University Press, 1987).

11. Rowley, *Fifty Years of Work*, 214, for the quotation; see also pp. 196–214. The most complete statement of his political beliefs can be found in Charles Rowley, *Social Politics* (Manchester: Heywood, 1885), which will be discussed below. On the formation of the HHS, see *Manchester Evening News*, 11 July 1889, in the first volume of the Healthy Homes Society's two-volume scrapbook, at the Local History Section of the Manchester Central Library.

12. Rowley, *Fifty Years of Work*, 33, 196, for the first and third quotations; William E. A. Axon, as quoted in Nodal, ed., *City News*, 41, for the second quotation.

13. Rowley, *Fifty Years of Work*, 196. See, for example, the childhood memories of Salford's Robert Roberts, *A Ragged Schooling* (Manchester: Manchester University Press, 1976); and Robert Roberts, *The Classic Slum: Salford Life in the First Quarter of the Century* (Manchester: Manchester University Press, 1971). More recently published, Frank McCourt's *Angela's Ashes: A Memoir* (New York: Simon and Schuster, 1996) captures a child's perceptions of normalcy in the midst of unrelenting hunger, deprivation, sickness, and death.

14. Joseph Heron, as quoted in Manchester and Salford Sanitary Association (MSSA), *Annual Report* (1869): 7–8. For a broader, parliamentary view of charity and politics, see Peter Shapely, "Charity, Status, and Parliamentary Candidates in Manchester: A Consideration of the Electoral and the Social Basis of Power, 1832–1910," *International Review of Social History* 44 (1999): 1–21. Also see Michael Worboys, *Spreading Germs: Disease Theories and Medical Practice in Britain, 1865–1900* (Cambridge: Cambridge University Press, 2000). He makes the important point that multiple germ theories based on a seed-and-soil metaphor existed before the 1880s and that England was slow in accepting modern, laboratory-based medical science during the following two decades.

15. Rowley, *Social Politics*, 6, 11–12, for the first and last quotation respectively; passim for the other quoted phrases.

16. Ibid., 17.

17. [Walter Tomlinson], "Bye-Ways of Manchester Life, No. 4: Among the So-Called Roughs" (1887): 1:7–9, in the Miscellaneous (Unknown) Clippings files in the Local History section of the Manchester Central Library.

18. MSSA, *Annual Report* (1886): 32, for the quotation. An additional irony of the soap sales was the source of the soap's manufacture, the Corporation's Holt Town facility for converting human and animal manure into fertilizer and other marketable by-products. See Wilson, "Technology and Municipal Decision-Making," 148–51. For the evolution of personal visitations as a tactic of charity work, see Martin Hewitt, "The Travails of Domestic Visiting: Manchester, 1830–1870," *Historical Research* 71 (June 1998): 196–227.

19. See the MSSA, *Annual Report* (1893): 32.

20. J. H. Crosfield, *The "Bitter Cry" of Ancoats and of Impoverished Manchester: Being a Series of Letters on Municipal Topics* (Manchester: Ireland, 1887), 14–15, for the quotations. The title is a play on another successful piece of muckraking, Andrew Mearns, *The Bitter Cry of Outcast London* (1883; reprint, New York: Leicester University Press,

1970). On the horrors of sickness and disability, see Wohl, *Endangered Lives*; and James C. Riley, *Sick, Not Dead: The Health of British Workingmen during the Mortality Decline* (Baltimore: Johns Hopkins University Press, 1997).

21. Anthony S. Wohl, "Introduction," in Mearns, *Bitter Cry of Outcast London*, 17, for the quotation; see also pp. 9–50 of Wohl's introduction for an analysis of the tract's impacts.

22. John C. Thresh, *An Inquiry into the Causes of Excessive Mortality in No. 1 District, Ancoats* (Manchester: Heywood, 1889), 38.

23. Ibid., 40–41.

24. S. Norbury Williams, "The Health Inquiry and Its Results …," a letter to the *Manchester City News*, 17 November 1888, for the quotation. Williams was the chair of the Manchester Ratepayers Association. Also see *Manchester City News*, 1 and 15 December 1888.

25. "Memorial," as reported in City of Manchester, *Proceedings of the City Council* (3 April 1889): 158, for the quotation; and *Manchester City News*, 1 December 1888, for a story on a meeting on the death rate in Ancoats, which was led by several workers and trade union officers as well as Rowley and members of the medical profession. Also see a similar appeal for the abatement of air pollution sent to Manchester's member of Parliament: "Memorial," as reported in the MSSA, *Annual Report* (1889): 78–79. Significantly, the petition was sponsored by a coalition of the MSSA, the Ancoats Healthy Homes Society, the Salford Working Men's Sanitary Association, the St. Mark's (Ancoats) Sanitary Association, and the Manchester Field Naturalists Society, which included working-class members.

26. John Sanders as quoted in *The National Advance*, 3 May 1890, in the HHS scrapbooks, 1:9–24 and passim. On the political mobilization of reform candidates, also see *Manchester Guardian*, 20 September 1890, and 29 April 1891. The large turnouts continued for several years. In 1894, for example, 21,560 people attended thirty-one meetings. The HHS-sponsored lectures continued for another decade. See *Manchester City News*, 15 September 1894 and HHS scrapbooks.

27. MSSA, *Annual Report* (1890): 11, for the quotation.

28. See the MSSA, *Annual Report* (1891–1896), and the HSS scrapbooks. In 1900, the rate cut was rescinded. See chap. 13, below. I suspect that the annexations of 1885 and especially 1890 that brought middle-class suburbs within municipal borders had a major effect on the MSSA's quick retreat from political activism among the working classes of the central city. Now that the association's members were voters in municipal elections, they might have seen a truly working-class political agenda as being in conflict with their own self-interest.

29. Dr. Thresh, as quoted in the *Manchester Guardian*, 12 February 1889. This meeting was sponsored by the Sanitary Reform Association of St. Mark's Church.

30. Ibid., 1 January 1894; *Manchester City News*, 3 March 1894; Redford and Russell, *History of Local Government in Manchester*, 2:418.

31. "Report of the Unhealthy Dwellings Committee," City of Manchester, *Proceedings of the Common Council* (1 May 1889): 278–88. Wohl shows that in the wake of the

publication of Mearns's *Bitter Cry* in 1883, the Tories became identified with housing reform in London and in Parliament. See Wohl, "Introduction." For the revival of the Conservatives in Manchester, see Kidd, *Manchester*, 158–59.

32. On housing, see City of Manchester, *Proceedings of the Common Council* (2 September 1896): 1321–33, (17 February 1897): 345–56, and (17 March 1897): 409–12; T. R. Marr, *Housing Conditions in Manchester and Salford* (Manchester: Sherratt and Hughes, 1904); and Ernest Darwin Simon and J. Inman, *Rebuilding Manchester* (London: Longmans, Green, 1935). For the influence of German social housing ideas, see Michael Harrison, "Social Reform in Late Victorian and Edwardian Manchester, with Special Reference to T. C. Horsfall" (Ph.D. diss., University of Manchester, 1988). In 1890, the Conservative majority in the city council reorganized jurisdiction over housing reform by abolishing the Unhealthy Dwellings Committee and placing it under the jurisdiction of the existing Sanitary Committee.

33. On sanitation, see Shena Simon, *A Century of City Government, Manchester, 1838–1938* (London: Allen and Unwin, 1938), 178–90; Wilson, "Technology and Municipal Decision-Making," 134–94; and the reminiscences of the period's medical officer of health, James Niven, *Observations on the History of the Public Health Effort in Manchester* (Manchester: Heywood, 1923).

34. See John Sanders, as quoted in the *Manchester Guardian*, October 1889? for the quotation in the section title; George Orwell, *The Road to Wigan Pier* (London: Harcourt Brace, 1937). Also see chap. 12, below. A bathhouse was opened in Ancoats in 1902, after nearly a decade of agitation. See MSSA, *Annual Report* (1902): 1–18.

35. Manchester Corporation, *Manchester Hydraulic Power System* (Manchester: Manchester Corporation, 1926); Manchester Corporation, *Waterworks Chronology, 1847–1974* (Manchester: Manchester Corporation, 1975); and P. F. Clarke, *Lancashire and the New Liberalism* (Cambridge: Cambridge University Press, 1971). In a similar way, the council refused to lower gas prices to levels that would yield a more normal rate of return, even though this would reduce the city's horrendous air pollution by encouraging the substitution of gas for coal for home heating purposes. See documentation of the long-running but frustrated campaign of reform in the MSSA, *Annual Report* (1892–1905). Yet another parallel case of policy continuity is that of the inequitable and discriminatory rules governing the use of the city parks. See Theresa Wyborn, "Parks for the People: The Development of Public Parks in Victorian Manchester," *Manchester Regional History Review* 9 (1995): 3–14.

36. Simon, *Century of City Government*; Spiers, *Victoria Park*, 33–50. Cf. Sam Bass Warner Jr., *Streetcar Suburbs: The Progress of Growth in Boston, 1870–1900* (Cambridge, MA: Harvard University Press, 1962).

37. *Manchester City News*, 9 June 1894. Also see Simon and Inman, *Rebuilding Manchester*, 1–25. Forty years later, the project had the same image. "In appearance," Simon and Inman lamented, "they are gaunt, gloomy, barrack-like" (Simon and Inman, *Rebuilding Manchester*, 21). Between 1900 and 1903, the electrification of the trams extended their range and made possible the lowering of fares, which were based

on the distance of the ride from the city center. See Roy Frost, *Electricity in Manchester* (Manchester: Richardson, 1993), 27–30.

38. Frost, *Electricity*; City of Manchester, *Proceedings of the Common Council* (6 May 1908): 367–434. A careful reading of the code, however, reveals that outdoor privies and indoor earth closets were still permitted under certain circumstances.

Chapter Ten

1. William T. Stead, *If Christ Came to Chicago* (Chicago: Laird and Lee, 1894). For insight on Stead's trip to the United States, see Paul Boyer, *Urban Masses and Moral Order in America, 1820–1920* (Cambridge, MA: Harvard University Press, 1978), 175–87.

2. Stead, *If Christ Came*, 410, for the quotations; see also pp. 407–19.

3. Ibid., 422, for the quotation; see also pp. 421–42. Also see Robert L. Fishman, *Urban Utopias in the Twentieth Century: Ebenezer Howard, Frank Lloyd Wright, Le Corbusier* (New York: Basic Books, 1977).

4. Stead, *If Christ Came*, 423. Also see Arnold Lewis, *An Early Encounter with Tomorrow: Europeans, Chicago's Loop, and the World's Columbian Exposition* (Urbana: University of Illinois Press, 1997).

5. Stead, *If Christ Came*, 421–42. On the World's Fair as inspiration, see Henry Adams, *The Education of Henry Adams: An Autobiography* (1918; reprint, Cambridge, MA: Houghton Mifflin, 1961), 331–45, 379–90. For the women's role at the World's Fair, including the leadership of Bertha Palmer, see Madeline Weimann, *The Fair Women: The Story of the Woman's Building, World's Columbian Exposition, Chicago, 1893* (Chicago: Academy Chicago, 1981). On the cultural significance of the fair, also see James Gilbert, *Perfect Cities: Chicago's Utopias of 1893* (Chicago: University of Chicago Press, 1991); and William Cronon, *Nature's Metropolis: Chicago and the Great West* (New York: Norton, 1991), 341–70.

6. Anne Firor Scott, "Saint Jane and the Ward Boss," *American Heritage* (December 1960): 98, for the quotation; see also pp. 12–17, 94–99. Of course, representations of the classic duel between Addams and Powers date back to contemporary times. See Ray S. Baker, "Hull House and the Ward Boss," *Outlook* 58 (28 March 1898): 256–57. For a useful bibliographical essay on Addams, see Eleanor J. Stebner, *The Women of Hull House: A Study in Spirituality, Vocation, and Friendship* (Albany: State University of New York Press, 1997), 11–26. On John Powers, who would serve from 1888 to 1927, see Humbert S. Nelli, *Italians in Chicago, 1880–1930* (New York: Oxford University Press, 1970), 88–124; Stead, *If Christ Came*, 171–86; and Lloyd Wendt and Herman Kogan, *Bosses in Lusty Chicago* (1943; reprint, Bloomington: Indiana University Press, 1971).

7. Jane Addams, *Chicago Tribune*, 20 February 1900, as quoted in Scott, "Saint Jane."

8. Jane Addams, *Twenty Years at Hull-House* (1910; reprint, New York: Signet, 1961).

9. Kathryn Kish Sklar, *Florence Kelley and the Nation's Work* (New Haven, CT: Yale University Press, 1995), 140–285, for background on Kelley's contributions to Hull-House. She served not only as a state official, but also as an agent for the U.S. Bureau of Labor in its pioneering survey of American cities. See Illinois Bureau of Labor Statistics,

Annual Reports of the Factory Inspectors of Illinois (Springfield: Illinois Bureau of Labor Statistics, 1892–1897); U.S. Commissioner of Labor [Carroll D. Wright], *Seventh Special Report of the Commissioner of Labor. The Slums of Baltimore, Chicago, New York, and Philadelphia* (Washington, DC: Government Printing Office, 1894); and Residents of Hull-House, *Hull-House Maps and Papers* (Boston: Thomas Y. Crowell, 1895). The ring around the central business district was also a choice site for the city's livery stables. (Photographic evidence from the Near North Side supports this analysis.) Addams observed at first hand the disproportionate number of horses quartered in the area and reported that the area also served as a central collection point for the city's rags. See Maud Gernon, Gertrude Howe, and Alice Hamilton, *An Inquiry into the Causes of the Recent Epidemic of Typhoid Fever in Chicago, Made by the Residents of Hull-House* (Chicago: City Homes Association, 1903), 19–20.

10. Jane Addams, "Why the Ward Boss Rules," in William L. Riordan, *Plunkitt of Tammany Hall*, ed. Terrence J. McDonald (Boston: Bedford/St. Martin's, 1994), 117–22; and Nelli, *Italians*, 95. Nelli estimates that only nine thousand of the ward's fifty thousand eligible voters, or less than 20 percent, were registered.

11. Thomas M. Guterbock, *Machine Politics in Transition: Party and Community in Chicago* (Chicago: University of Chicago Press, 1980), 3, for the quotation; M. Craig Brown and Charles N. Halaby, "Machine Politics in America, 1870–1945," *Journal of Interdisciplinary History* 17 (Winter 1987): 587–612; Kenneth Finegold, *Experts and Politicians: Reform Challenges to Machine Politics in New York, Cleveland, and Chicago* (Princeton, NJ: Princeton University Press, 1995). For payroller figures for the Nineteenth Ward, see Jane Addams, "Why the Ward Boss Rules," 117–22. For an overview of Chicago's political history, see Paul M. Green and Melvin G. Holli, eds., *The Mayors: The Chicago Political Tradition* (Carbondale: Southern Illinois University Press, 1987). On Harrison's close ties to the bosses and the underworld, see Edward R. Kantowicz, "Carter H. Harrison II: the Politics of Balance," in Green and Holli, *Mayors*, 16–32; Richard C. Lindberg, *To Serve and Collect: Chicago Politics and Police Corruption from the Lager Beer Riot to the Summerdale Scandal* (New York: Praeger, 1991); and Carter Harrison II, *The Stormy Years* (Indianapolis: Bobbs-Merrill, 1935).

12. Sklar, *Florence Kelley*, 221–22; see also pp. xi–xvi, 206–36, 300–302. On the independent role Chicago's middle-class women played in the public sphere, see Maureen A. Flanagan, *Seeing with Their Hearts: Chicago Women and the Vision of the Good City, 1871–1933* (Princeton, NJ: Princeton University Press, 2002). For additional insight on women settlement house workers as political activists, see Kathleen D. McCarthy, *Noblesse Oblige: Charity and Cultural Philanthropy in Chicago* (Chicago: University of Chicago Press, 1982), 99–109; and Karen M. Mason, "Mary McDowell and Municipal Housekeeping: Women's Political Activism in Chicago, 1890–1920," in *Midwestern Women: Work, Community, and Leadership at the Crossroads*, ed. Lucy Eldersveld Murphy and Wendy Hamand Venet (Bloomington: Indiana University Press, 1997), 60–75.

13. Addams, "Why the Ward Boss Rules," 121. To be sure, Addams makes ethnic references, but she seems to make them in a rhetorical, tongue-in-cheek manner in order

to disarm the prejudices of her audience. For example, she begins by calling the mostly Italian residents of the ward "peasants," and "primitive people," then quickly shifts from an ethnic to a class-based mode of analysis. See Addams, "Why the Ward Boss Rules," 117–22; and Allen F. Davis, *Spearheads for Reform: The Social Settlements and the Progressive Movement, 1890–1914* (New York: Oxford University Press, 1967), 148–62.

14. Addams, *Twenty Years,* 200–205.

15. Robert Hunter, *Tenement Conditions in Chicago: Report by the Investigating Committee of the City Homes Association* (Chicago: City Homes Association, 1901), preface; Edith Abbott, *The Tenements of Chicago, 1880–1935* (Chicago: University of Chicago Press, 1936), 50–61; and Thomas Lee Philpott, *The Slum and the Ghetto: Neighborhood Deterioration and Middle-Class Reform, Chicago, 1880–1930* (New York: Oxford University Press, 1978), 26–41, for a good, brief description of the report. For insight on the women's innovative use of maps, see Mary Jo Deegan, *Jane Addams and the Men of the Chicago School, 1892–1918* (New Brunswick, NJ: Transaction Books, 1988), 55–70.

16. Hunter, *Tenement Conditions.*

17. Abbott, *Tenements of Chicago.*

18. See Robert H. Wiebe, *The Search for Order, 1877–1920* (New York: Hill and Wang, 1967); John C. Sproat, *"The Best Men": Liberal Reformers in the Gilded Age* (New York: Oxford University Press, 1968); Herbert G. Gutman, *Work, Culture, and Society in Industrializing America* (New York: Vintage, 1977); George M. Fredrickson, *The Black Image in the White Mind* (New York: Harper and Row, 1971); John E. Bodnar, *The Transplanted: A History of Immigrants in Urban America* (Bloomington: Indiana University Press, 1885); and John Roche, *The Quest of the Dream: The Development of Civil Rights and Human Relations in Modern America* (New York: Macmillan, 1963). For a good case study of the politics of ethnic division, see Robert A. Slayton, *Back of the Yards: The Making of a Local Democracy* (Chicago: University of Chicago Press, 1986), 151–72.

19. Hunter, *Tenement Conditions,* 17, for the quotation; see also pp. 11–20, 104–5; Philpott, *Slum,* 41. I want to thank John Jentz for highlighting the importance of communications in the analysis of politics. For Chicago, see David Paul Nord, *Newspapers and New Politics: Midwestern Municipal Reform, 1890–1900* (Ann Arbor, MI: UMI Research, 1981).

20. Hunter, *Tenement Conditions,* 101–4; City of Chicago, *Proceedings of the City Council* (1902–1903): 174–86; *Chicago Tribune,* 29 April 1902; Jane Addams, "The Housing Problem in Chicago," *American Association of Political and Social Sciences, Annals* 20 (July–December 1902): 99–107.

21. For a sophisticated analysis of evolving theories of disease causation, see Christopher Hamlin, *A Science of Impurity: Water Analysis in Nineteenth Century Britain* (Bristol: Hilger, 1990). For an American context, see John Duffy, *The Sanitarians: A History of American Public Health* (Urbana: University of Illinois Press, 1990); for Chicago, see Thomas Neville Bonner, *Medicine in Chicago, 1850–1950: A Chapter in the Social and Scientific Development of a City,* 2nd ed. (Urbana: University of Illinois Press,

1991); and Fred O. Tonney, "The Introduction of Bacteriology into the Service of Public Health in Chicago," *Bulletin of the Society of Medical History of Chicago* 5 (January 1937): 22–23. For gendered perspectives, see Nancy Tomes, "The Private Side of Public Health: Sanitary Science, Domestic Hygiene, and the Germ Theory, 1870–1900," *Bulletin of the History of Medicine* 64 (Winter 1990): 509–39; and Suellen Hoy, *Chasing Dirt: The American Pursuit of Cleanliness* (New York: Oxford University Press, 1995). Although contemporary attention to typhoid fever may have been out of proportion to the prevalence of the disease, this social construction does not detract from the excellent scholarship on the subject. See in particular Joel Tarr, *The Search for the Ultimate Sink: Urban Pollution in Historical Perspective* (Akron, OH: University of Akron Press, 1996); Howard Markel, *Quarantine! East European Jewish Immigrants and the New York City Epidemics of 1892* (Baltimore: Johns Hopkins University Press, 1997); and Richard J. Evans, *Death in Hamburg: Society and Politics in the Cholera Years, 1830–1910* (Oxford: Clarendon, 1987).

22. Gernon, Howe, and Hamilton, *Inquiry*, 5; Nelson Algren, *Chicago: City on the Make* (Garden City, NY: Doubleday, 1951).

23. Tomes, "Private Side," Deegan, *Jane Addams and the Men*, 143–66.

24. *Chicago Tribune*, 18 January 1900, and 3 and 10 August 1902.

25. See *Chicago Tribune*, 23 and 28 August; 2, 6, 8, and 25 September 1902, for school-related stories. The Board of Education had ordered the water shut off in response to reports that an alarming number of people had been stricken by a disease. Further testing confirmed that the germs were being pumped through the distribution system and were reaching the drinking fountains in the schools. Also see *Chicago Tribune*, 22 August 1902, for the health department's official bulletin on the epidemic; and *Chicago Tribune*, 9 September 1902, for the report of the minister's sermon.

26. Alice Hamilton, *Exploring the Dangerous Trades: The Autobiography of Alice Hamilton, M.D.* (Boston: Little, Brown, 1943), 98–99; and see note 34, below. Also see Gernon, Howe, and Hamilton, *Inquiry*, 9–12, for a full account of Hamilton's experiments; and Addams, *Twenty Years*, 210–11, for Addams's observations not only on the epidemic of 1902, but also on the corruption-riddled system of sanitation services. For important insights on Hamilton's social activism, see Christopher Sellers, *Hazards of the Job: From Industrial Disease to Environmental Health Science* (Chapel Hill: University of North Carolina Press, 1997), 70–77.

27. *Chicago Tribune*, 22 August 1902, for the quotation. See *Chicago Tribune*, 13, 20, 22, and 28 August; and 3 and 30 September 1902, for the city's campaign in the Maxwell Street area.

28. *Chicago Tribune*, 18 December 1902, for the quotation. For the passage of the ordinance, see Chicago, *Proceedings of the City Council* (1902–1903): 1634–47. For Hamilton's scientific work, see Alice Hamilton, "The Fly as a Carrier of Typhoid," *Journal of the American Medical Association* 40 (28 February 1903): 576–83; and Naomi Rogers, "Germs with Legs: Flies, Disease, and the New Public Health," *Bulletin of the History of Medicine* 63 (1989): 606–8.

29. Philpott, *Slum*, 102, for the first quotation; see pp. 101–3 for additional details, including a list of thirty-four exemptions granted during the first three months of the law's operation. Abbott, *Tenements of Chicago*, 63, for second quotation; see also p. 64, on Ball. Also see *Chicago Tribune*, 26 March 1904, for additional biographical details on Ball. Trained as a civil engineer at Yale University, he had worked in the patent office on sanitary technologies and had served as an engineer in Washington's sewer department before becoming the chief inspector in New York.

30. Gernon, Howe, and Hamilton, *Inquiry*, 15, 12–13; see also pp. 12–20 for accounts and analysis of tenants' fruitless efforts to get the health department to enforce the law. See Nelli, *Italians*, 98–100, for evidence of middle-class immigrant Italian opposition to Powers. Also see the story of a spontaneous mass protest against intolerable environmental conditions, "Dirty Streets Cause Protest," *Chicago Tribune*, 26 July 1902. It is difficult to measure how common these kinds of householder uprisings to put pressure on aldermen for infrastructure improvements and public services were or how often they were recorded by the press. Nevertheless, the fact that at least one such story was covered by the newspaper suggests that people were concerned about the quality of their home and neighborhood environments.

31. Gernon, Howe, and Hamilton, *Inquiry*, 19, 20. See *Chicago Tribune*, 15–18 April 1903, for the press's initial response to the publication of the inquiry. Also see *Chicago Tribune*, 17 April 1903, for a full list of the properties determined by the report to be in violation of the law.

32. Gernon, Howe, and Hamilton, *Inquiry*, 16 for the quotation; see also pp. 15–19. See *Chicago Tribune*, 17 April 1903, for the reference to the health department defense.

33. *Chicago Tribune*, 10 October 1903, for a list of graft investigations. For perceptions of the riverfront and lakefront zones as defining the city's social geography, see "The Social Geography of Chicago," *Charities* 2, no. 4 (1903): 3–4; Addams, "Housing Problem"; and Charles Bushnell, "Some Social Aspects of the Chicago Stock Yards," *American Journal of Sociology* 7 (1901–1902).

34. *Chicago Tribune*, 16 April 1903, for the quotation; *Chicago Tribune*, 17–18 April 1903, for Dr. Reynolds's response. On Dr. Reynolds's history in the health department, see chap. 11, below, and Reynolds's own account of the department, Arthur Reynolds, "Three Chicago and Illinois Public Health Officers: John H. Rauch, Oscar C. DeWolf, and Frank W. Reilly," *Bulletin of the Society of Medical History of Chicago* 1 (August 1912): 87–134. Doctors and health providers rallied to his support during the crisis. See *Chicago Tribune*, 21–22 April 1903. For the damning admissions of the university's property manager, see *Chicago Tribune*, 13 June 1903. The well-respected city engineer, John Ericson, reacted with disbelief to Reynolds's accusation about the waterworks, but ordered an immediate investigation to remove any possible doubt. True to his word, he found a worker at the Harrison Street pumping station who admitted two days later that he had seen a backup of raw sewage flowing toward the water supply well. See *Chicago Tribune*, 22 April

1903. Also see Hamilton's *Exploring the Dangerous Trades*, 99–100, for her confession about the true cause of the 1902 typhoid fever outbreak.

35. *Chicago Tribune*, 18–22 April 1903. Also see "The Social Geography of Chicago."

36. *Chicago Tribune*, 22–27 April 1903, 3 June 1903; "Sanitary Ills Disclosed by Hull-House Workers," *Charities* 10 (13 June 1903): 587–88.

37. For the final sessions of the CSC and Dr. Reynolds's statement, respectively, see *Chicago Tribune*, 1, 4 and 10 July 1903. For charges of intimidation, see *Chicago Tribune*, 17 and 24 June 1903, and 15 November 1903.

38. *Chicago Tribune*, 9 June 1903, for the quotations; 31 July 1903 for the statistics.

39. *Chicago Tribune*, 3, 6, 13 and 17 June 1903. The craftspeople charged that Young and Kelly were taking bribes from the contractors building Wendell Phillips High School. The plumbers had called a work stoppage when asked to do a substandard job and appealed for support from Kelly, a former president of the local union. Instead, the city official came to the building site on behalf of the contractors and reportedly advised the men to "let this go on; you won't loose [sic] anything by it." Having blatantly disregarded the health risks posed for the school children and their families, the chief engineer of the board of education and the sanitary inspector of the local area admitted to going along with this fraudulent scheme to cut costs for the contractor. See *Chicago Tribune*, 20–31 July 1903; 13 and 23 August 1903; and 1, 15, and 20 September 1903; "Lax Methods of the Chicago Sanitary Bureau," *Charities* 11 (1 August 1903): 100.

40. City of Chicago Civil Service Commission, as quoted in *Chicago Tribune*, 23 July 1903.

41. On the Citizens' Association, see Harold L. Platt, "Creative Necessity: Municipal Reform in Gilded Age Chicago," in *The Constitution, Law, and American Life: Critical Aspects of the Nineteenth-Century Experience*, ed. Donald G. Nieman (Athens: University of Georgia Press, 1992), 162–90.

42. *Chicago Tribune*, 18, 23, and 29 August 1903; and 1 and 27–28 September 1903; "Chicago's Absurd Sanitary Bureau," *Charities* 11 (17 October 1903): 353–54.

43. Edwin Oakes Jordan, "Typhoid Fever and Water Supply in Chicago," *Journal of the American Medical Association* 39 (20 December 1902): 1561–66; *Chicago Tribune*, 6 August 1903, for the report of typhoid cases in Wilmette. For additional detail, see chap. 12, below.

44. *Chicago Tribune*, 22 September 1903, for the quotation; 25–29 September 1903 for full details on the story. The mayor's directive to give city business to favored insiders on a no-bid basis was not limited to Sullivan's plumbing work, according to Gildea. All steam fitting work, for example, was supposed to be given to Ed McDonald, the brother of the city's infamous underground lord of gambling and vice, Mike McDonald. In the case of the illegal water taps, the whistle-blower was company manager J. J. Bowen. His willingness to testify probably stems from the fact that Sullivan had recently filed criminal charges against him for embezzling funds from the company. For the water-theft stories, see *Chicago Tribune*, 6 and 8 August and 12 September 1903.

45. *Chicago Tribune*, 29 September 1903, for the mayor's quotation; see also *Chicago Tribune*, 1–4, 8, 10, 19–20, and 27 October 1903; and 15 and 18 November 1903. The new plumbing code was enacted in 1905. See Abbott, *Tenements of Chicago*, 64–65.

46. Clarke as quoted in the *Chicago Tribune*, 12 March 1904; see also *Chicago Tribune*, 9 March–4 April 1904, 21 April 1904, and 23 February 1905; Chicago, *Proceedings of the City Council* (1903–1904): 1137–38, 1302–3; Abbott *Tenements of Chicago*, 64–65; Philpott, *Slum*, 104–9.

47. See Ball's report on the Nineteenth Ward in City of Chicago, Department of Health, *Annual Report* (1906): 164–68, passim; and Charles Ball, "Report of Bureau of Sanitation, 1911 1919," in City of Chicago, Department of Health, *Annual Report* (1911–1918): 601–91.

48. Terrence J. McDonald, "The Burdens of Urban History: The Theory of the State in Recent American Social History," *Studies in American Political Development* 3 (1989): 12; see also pp. 3–29; Terrence J. McDonald, "Introduction," in Riordan, *Plunkitt of Tammany Hall*, 1–41; Jon C. Teaford, *The Unheralded Triumph: City Government in America, 1870–1900* (Baltimore: Johns Hopkins University Press, 1984); and Davis, *Spearheads for Reform*, chaps. 8–9. Also see Ira Katznelson, "The Burdens of Urban History: Comment," *Studies in American Political Development* 3 (1989): 30–51, and Terrence McDonald's "Reply," 51–55; and Finegold, *Experts and Politicians*, 3–32. For early statements of the problem, see Eugene D. Genovese and Elizabeth Fox-Genovese, "The Political Crisis of Social History: A Marxian Perspective," *Journal of Social History* 10 (Winter 1976): 205–20; and Jon C. Teaford, "Finis for Tweed and Steffens: Rewriting the History of Urban Rule," *Reviews in American History* 10 (December 1982): 133–49. On the tendency of consensus historians to cast the radicalism of the progressives in psychological terms, cf. Staughton Lynd, "Jane Addams and the Radical Impulse," *Commentary* 32 (July 1961): 54–59; and Christopher Lasch, *The New Radicalism in America, 1889–1963: The Intellectual as a Social Type* (New York: Knopf, 1965).

49. Addams, *Twenty Years*, 201.

50. On the limits of civil service reform and Harrison's attack on the independence of the Civil Service Commission, see Lindberg, *To Serve and Collect*, 35–57; on the related corruption of the health department, see Philpott, *Slum*, 105–9; and on the continuation of the machine and its base of support in the river wards, see Harold F. Gosnell, *Machine Politics, Chicago Model*, 2nd ed. (1937; reprint, Chicago: University of Chicago Press, 1968).

Chapter Eleven

1. *Chicago Daily News*, 3 August 1885, for the quotation; Also see *Chicago Times*, 4 August 1885, which reported a final, record-breaking total of 6.33 inches for the storm. The previous record was 4.14 inches, but the statistics only extended back to 1872. Perhaps more telling was the testimony of the city's sailors: "Old river men and vessel-owners who have sailed the lakes for thirty years or more state that

nothing like the present storm has ever been known at this season of the year" (*Chicago Times*, 3 August 1885).

2. *Chicago Daily News*, 3 August 1885, for the first quotation; 4 August 1885 for the characterization of DeWolf's mood. *Chicago Daily News*, 4 August 1885, and *Chicago Tribune*, 3 August 1885, for statements by Cregier and DeWolf; *Chicago Tribune*, 7 August 1885, for notice of Cregier's thirty-third anniversary in the service of the city.

3. *Chicago Tribune*, 6 August 1885, for the mortality statistics; 4–7 August 1885 for news of the cholera epidemic in Europe. See also Charles Rosenberg, *The Cholera Years: The United States in 1832, 1849, and 1866* (Chicago: University of Chicago Press, 1962).

4. *Chicago Times*, 31 July 1885. The real impact of the story came after the storm when the *Chicago Tribune*, on 16 August 1885, published the results of the investigation in its Sunday edition. The two-and-a-half columns of coverage included a humorous series of drawings mocking the mayor and the entire enterprise. The challenge of the satirical copy was equal to that of the images. More serious editorial comment in this Republican daily and the city's other major newspapers kept the story before the public.

5. See chap. 12, below. Also see Harold L. Platt, "Chicago, the Great Lakes, and the Origins of Federal Urban Environmental Policy," *Journal of the Gilded Age and Progressive Era* 1 (April 2002): 122–53; and Thomas Neville Bonner, *Medicine in Chicago 1850–1950: A Chapter in the Social and Scientific Development of a City*, 2nd ed. (Urbana: University of Illinois Press, 1991).

6. For an introduction to the historiography of the urban environment, see Joel Tarr, *The Search for the Ultimate Sink: Urban Pollution in Historical Perspective* (Akron, OH: University of Akron Press, 1996); and Martin V. Melosi, "Urban Pollution: Historical Perspectives Needed," *Environmental Review* 3 (Fall 1979): 37–45. On urban bosses and reform, see Terrence J. McDonald, "Introduction," in William L. Riordan, *Plunkitt of Tammany Hall*, ed. Terrence J. McDonald (Boston: Bedford/St. Martin's, 1994), 1–41; Maureen Flanagan, "The City Profitable, the City Livable: Environmental Policy, Gender, and Power in Chicago in the 1910s," *Journal of Urban History* 22 (January 1996): 163–90; and Harold L. Platt, "Creative Necessity: Municipal Reform in Gilded Age Chicago," in *The Constitution, Law, and American Life: Critical Aspects of the Nineteenth-Century Experience*, ed. Donald G. Nieman (Athens: University of Georgia Press, 1992), 162–90. For recent discussion on political culture, see Jurgen Habermas, *The Structural Transformation of the Public Sphere: An Inquiry into a Category of Bourgeois Society* (1962; reprint, Cambridge, MA: MIT Press, 1991); and Philip J. Ethington, *The Public City: The Political Construction of Urban Life in San Francisco, 1850–1900* (Cambridge: Cambridge University Press, 1994). For the organizational synthesis, see Robert H. Wiebe, *The Search for Order, 1877–1920* (New York: Hill and Wang, 1967); Jerry Israel, ed., *Building the Organizational Society: Essays on Associational Activities in Modern America* (New York: Free Press, 1972); and Thomas L. Haskell, ed., *The Authority of Experts: Studies in History and Theory* (Bloomington: Indiana University Press, 1984). On the social history of medicine, some of the

best work has been about England. See Anthony S. Wohl, *Endangered Lives: Public Health in Victorian Britain* (Cambridge, MA: Harvard University Press, 1983); and Bill Luckin, *Pollution and Control: A Social History of the Thames in the Nineteenth Century* (Bristol: Hilger, 1986). For the United States, see John Duffy, *The Sanitarians: A History of American Public Health* (Urbana: University of Illinois Press, 1990); Paul Starr, *The Social Transformation of American Medicine* (New York: Basic Books, 1982); and Christopher C. Sellers, "Factory as Environment: Professional Collaboration, Industrial Hygiene, and the Modern Sciences of Pollution," *Environmental History Review* 18 (Spring 1994): 55–83.

7. See Platt, "Creative Necessity," for perspectives on the Citizens' Association; and Richard Schneirov, "Class Conflict, Municipal Politics, and Governmental Reform in Gilded Age Chicago, 1871–1875," in *German Workers in Industrial Chicago, 1850–1910: A Comparative Perspective*, ed. Hartmut Keil and John B. Jentz (DeKalb: Northern Illinois University Press, 1983), 183–205, for the politics of the post–Civil War decade.

8. *Chicago Times*, 7 August 1885, for the quotation; also see *Chicago Tribune*, 7 August 1885. Evidence that contaminated river water was reaching the crib had begun surfacing a few years earlier. One of the crib attendants, Captain Peter Falcon, for example, testified that "I have seen on more than one occasion river water entering the crib." See *Chicago Tribune*, 8 November 1879. Also see chap. 4, above.

9. *Chicago Times*, 7 August 1885, and *Chicago Tribune*, 7 August 1885.

10. *Chicago Times*, 22 June 1880, as quoted in Donald David Marks, "Polishing the Gem of the Prairie: The Evolution of Civic Reform Consciousness in Chicago, 1874–1900" (Ph.D. diss., University of Wisconsin, 1974), 71; see also pp. 71–84. See also the Citizens' Association of Chicago, *Annual Reports* (1879–1881): passim; Chicago Citizens' Association, *Report of the Main Drainage Committee, 1880* (Chicago: Hazlitt and Reed, 1880).

11. Chicago Citizens' Association, *Report of the Committee on the Main Drainage and Water Supply of Chicago* (Chicago: Hazlitt, 1885). See *Chicago Tribune*, 28 August 1885, for a complete transcript of the report.

12. See chap. 7, above.

13. M. Delafontaine, "Chemical Examination of the Chicago Water Supply," in Chicago Citizens' Association, *Report of the Committee on the Main Drainage* (1885), 24, for the quotation; see also pp. 23–24. Bacteriological tests were also included in the array of studies of the quality and safety of the water supply sponsored by the Citizens' Association. See B. W. Thomas, "Microscopical Examination of the Chicago Water Supply," *Report of the Committee on the Main Drainage* (1885), 21–23. Throughout the pre-1885 period, water quality investigators found the Fullerton Avenue conduit the most egregious case of engineering failure. Part of Chesbrough's original 1850s plan, the conduit had a reversible pump that could either supply the North Branch with lake water to flush it out or dump its heavily polluted water into the lake. The prevailing lake currents near the shore flowed from north to south, and the conduit outfall was only four miles away from the Two-Mile Crib.

14. For reports on the reform group's activities and political demands, see *Chicago Tribune*, 31 July–29 August 1885. Also see the Chicago Citizens' Association, *Annual Report* (1885): 29. Reilly was one of the most effective critics of the administration. For his biting commentary, see *Chicago Morning News*, 2–29 August 1885. For biographical information on Reilly, see the account of one of his contemporaries, Arthur Reynolds, "Three Chicago and Illinois Public Health Officers: John H. Rauch, Oscar C. DeWolf, and Frank W. Reilly," *Bulletin of the Society of Medical History of Chicago* 1 (August 1912): 87–134. On the new journalism, see David Paul Nord, *Newspapers and New Politics: Midwestern Municipal Reform, 1890–1900* (Ann Arbor, MI: UMI Research, 1981).

15. *Chicago Daily News*, 8 August 1885, for the quotation; see also *Chicago Tribune*, 1–2 September 1892. On the importance of newspapers during the Progressive Era of reform, see Nord, *Newspapers and New Politics*. For the report, see Chicago Citizens' Association, *Report of the Committee on the Main Drainage* (1885). Also see the Chicago Citizens' Association, *Annual Report* (1885): 29.

16. *Chicago Tribune*, 29 August 1885, for the quotation.

17. *Chicago Daily News*, 22 August 1885, for the quotation. Also see *Chicago Daily News*, 14 August 1885. For contemporary understandings, see G. P. Brown, *Drainage Channel and Waterway* (Chicago: Donnelly, 1894), 15–25, 37–48; John H. Rauch, *Preliminary Report to the Illinois State Board of Health: Water Supplies of Illinois and the Pollution of Its Streams* (Springfield, IL: Rokker, 1889); J. H. Long, "Chemical Investigations of the Water Supplies of Illinois," in Rauch, *Preliminary Report*; and F. W. Reilly, "Relation of the Medical Profession to the Water Supply of Chicago: With Especial Reference to the Sanitary Waterway and Main Drainage Channel," an address made to the Chicago Physicians Club (11 November 1896), as reported in Chicago, Department of Health, *Annual Report* (1895): 259–72. For insight on experts' confusion about water quality and how to measure it, see Christopher Hamlin, *A Science of Impurity: Water Analysis in Nineteenth Century Britain* (Bristol: Hilger, 1990); Michael Worboys, *Spreading Germs: Disease Theories and Medical Practice in Britain, 1865–1900* (Cambridge: Cambridge University Press, 2000); and Nancy Tomes, *The Gospel of Germs: Men, Women, and the Microbe in American Life* (Cambridge, MA: Harvard University Press, 1998). For progress in working out standardized methods of testing water quality, see Patricia Peck Gossel, "A Need for Standard Method: The Case of American Bacteriology," in *The Right Tools for the Job: At Work in Twentieth-Century Life Sciences*, ed. Adele E. Clarke and John H. Fujimura (Princeton, NJ: Princeton University Press, 1992), 287–311.

18. Chicago Drainage and Water Supply Commission, as quoted in Brown, *Drainage Channel*, 358, for the quotation; see also *Chicago Tribune*, 29 August 1885. See Brown, *Drainage Channel*, 336–73, for a copy of the report; and *Chicago Tribune*, 16 October 1886, for a report on the work of the commission that already outlines the policy options. Also see Chicago Citizens' Association, *Report of the Committee on the Main Drainage* (1885).

19. "Preliminary Report of the Drainage and Water Supply Commission," as reported in International Waterways Commission, "Reports of the International Waterways Commission, 1906," in Report of the Minister of Public Works (Canada), *Sessional Paper No. 19a. A., 1907* (Ottawa: Dawson, 1907), 2:186–201. A complete copy of the report can also be found in Brown, *Drainage Channel*, 336–73. The idea of a deep-water highway had originated during the Civil War as a military innovation, but congressional support for such an expensive internal improvement had faded fast after the conflict ended. See James C. O'Connell, "Technology and Pollution: Chicago's Water Policy, 1833–1930" (Ph.D. diss., University of Chicago, 1980), 82–111, on the background of the Citizens' Association investigation.

20. Rauch, *Preliminary Report*.

21. Brown, *Drainage Channel*, 374–404.

22. Lyman Cooley, as quoted in Marks, "Polishing the Gem," 38.

23. *Chicago Tribune*, 5–30 May 1889, for an account of the legislative history of the bill in the statehouse. Also see Brown, *Drainage Channel*, 374–404, which includes a copy of the enabling act. For Cooley's involvement, see "Lyman Edgar Cooley," in *Dictionary of American Biography*, ed. Allen Johnson and Dumas Malone (New York: Scribner's Sons, 1929) vol. 2, pt. 2, 391–92; and Robert A. Waller, "Illinois Waterway from Conception to Completion, 1908–1933," *Journal of the Illinois State Historical Society* 65 (Summer 1972): 125–41. On Manchester's "invention" of the industrial park, see Robert Nicholls, *Trafford Park: The First Hundred Years* (Chichester, U.K.: Phillimore, 1996); and I. Harford, *Manchester and Its Ship Canal Movement: Class, Work, and Politics in Late Victorian England* (Staffordshire: Ryburn, 1994). On the influence of the ship canal and industrial park in Chicago, see Elmer Corthell, "The Manchester Ship Canal," *Journal of the Western Society of Engineers* 4 (February 1899): 1–11.

24. *Chicago Tribune*, 25 May 1889 for the quotation, 11 November 1889 for the second quotation, and 5–30 May 1889. Brown, *Drainage Channel*, 374–404; O'Connell, "Technology and Pollution," 82–111; and Waller, "Illinois Waterway," 125–41.

25. *Chicago Tribune*, 11 November 1889, for the quotations; see also 3–14 December 1889 for the campaign and election returns.

26. *Chicago Tribune*, 13 December 1890, for the quotations; see also 11–12 December 1890 for related stories.

27. Lyman E. Cooley, *The Lakes and Gulf Waterway as Related to the Chicago Sanitary Problem* (Chicago: Weston, 1890); vii, 10, respectively for the quotations; see p. 17 for statistics on the riverboats. Also see Lyman E. Cooley, *The Diversion of the Waters of the Great Lakes by Way of the Sanitary and Ship Canal of Chicago* (Chicago: Clohesey, 1913). After Cooley's death, the booster genre lived on. For example, see the booster tract prepared by a sanitary district lawyer, George F. Barrett, *The Waterway from the Great Lakes to the Gulf of Mexico* (Chicago: Sanitary District of Chicago, 1926).

28. For the maneuvers in the legislature, see *Chicago Tribune*, 4, 17–18, and 25 April 1891; and 2 November 1891. For editorial support for Cooley, see the city's main

Democratic daily, *Chicago Times*, 15 and 17 April 1891; and the *Chicago Inter-Ocean*, 29 April 1891.

29. *Chicago Tribune*, 4 November 1891, for the quotation. For the election, cf. *Chicago Tribune*, 1–4 November 1891, and *Chicago Times*, 1–4 November 1891. For the battle for control of the board, see *Chicago Times*, 9 December 1891; *Chicago Tribune*, 6, 9, 14, 16, and 30 December 1891; and 2, 10, and 16–18 January 1892. Also see the proceedings of the Sanitary District for 8, 15, and 18 December 1891; and 1, 9, and 15–18 January 1892.

30. *Chicago Tribune*, 18 January 1900. The best account of the creation of the sanitary district is Brown, *Drainage Channel*, 374–404. Also see O'Connell, "Technology and Pollution," 82–111.

31. For Major Handbury's report to the convention, see *Morning News*, 12 October 1887; and *Chicago Tribune*, 12 October 1887. In 1895, the Army Corps had filed a report that predicted a lowering of lake levels in just this range. For the repercussions, see International Waterways Commission, "Joint Report on the Chicago Drainage Canal, 1907," as reported in Report of the Minister of Public Works (Canada), *Sessional Paper*, 2:174–86; Western Society of Engineers, *The Levels of the Lakes as Affected by the Proposed Lakes and Gulf Waterway* (Chicago: Citizens' Association, 1889); and especially, George Y. M. Wisner et al., "Levels of the Lakes as Affected by the Proposed Lake Michigan and Mississippi Waterway," *Journal of the Association of Engineering Societies* 8 (March 1889): 123–54.

32. Max Richard White, *Water Supply Organization in the Chicago Region* (Chicago: University of Chicago Press, 1935).

33. For an introduction to the huge literature on the world's fair, see James Gilbert, *Perfect Cities: Chicago's Utopias of 1893* (Chicago: University of Chicago Press, 1991).

34. See O'Connell, "Technology and Pollution," 102, for the accusation of a cover-up.

35. John D. Ware, as quoted in City of Chicago, Department of Health, *Annual Report* (1891): 7, for the quotation.

36. "Preliminary Report of the Drainage and Water Supply Commission," 196–201.

37. Stanley K. Schultz, *Constructing Urban Culture: American Cities and City Planning, 1800–1920* (Philadelphia: Temple University Press, 1989). On party finance, see Clifton K. Yearly, *The Money Machines: The Breakdown and Reform of Governmental and Party Finance in the North, 1860–1920* (Albany: State University of New York Press, 1970). On Cregier, see *Testimonial and Banquet to DeWitt C. Cregier, 1885–1886* (Chicago: Jeffery, 1886); and William Sooy Smith et al., "DeWitt C. Creigier: Memorial," *Journal of the Western Society of Engineers* 4 (February 1899): 122–24.

38. *Chicago Tribune*, 25 August 1892.

39. Health Commissioner Ware as quoted in *Chicago Tribune*, 30 August 1892.

40. City of Chicago, Department of Health, *Annual Report* (1893): 9, for the statistic of forty thousand privy vaults. Cf. *Chicago Tribune*, 11 September 1892, for a discussion of this problem and a higher estimate of fifty thousand.

41. *Chicago Tribune*, 26 August 1892.

42. *Chicago Tribune*, 2 September 1892, for coverage of the meeting at city hall. Also see the politically related story, "Talk of Fair Delay," from the day before the meeting, in *Chicago Tribune*, 1 September 1892. Also see issues of the paper from September to December 1892 for the progress of the cleanup campaign.

43. *Chicago Tribune*, 11 September 1892, for coverage of the meeting. See Phyllis Allen, "Americans and the Germ Theory of Disease" (Ph.D. diss., University of Pennsylvania, 1949), which, though dated, is still useful. She points out, for example, that Dr. Nathan Davis was among the host of American physicians who rejected germ theory during its early testing days in the 1870s and 1880s. Also see Constance B. Webb, *A History of Contagious Disease Care in Chicago before the Great Fire* (Chicago: University of Chicago Press, 1940), 1–61. See Suellen Hoy, *Chasing Dirt: The American Pursuit of Cleanliness* (New York: Oxford University Press, 1995), 76–78, for the role of the Municipal Order League and its leader, Ada Sweet, in the cleanup campaign.

44. Reynolds, "Three Chicago and Illinois Public Health Officers," 113–21; O'Connell, "Technology and Pollution," 101–3.

45. Editor of the *British Medical Journal*, quoted in Ernest Hart, "Health Conditions of Chicago," *Chicago Medical Recorder* 5 (July 1893): 10, as quoted in Bonner, *Medicine in Chicago*, 187. On the Hygeia Water Company deal, see *Chicago Tribune*, 25 August, 1902; and O'Connell, "Technology and Pollution," 101–4. As the editor points out, the lessons of the fair in terms of advanced technologies of water purification and sewage treatment and disposal were lost on city officials. The equipment built for the fair was dismantled. On Chicago's image as smoke city, see William Cronon, *Nature's Metropolis: Chicago and the Great West* (New York: Norton, 1991), prologue; and chap. 14, below. For other visitors' views of the city see, Bessie Louise Pierce, ed., *As Others See Chicago: Impressions of Visitors, 1673–1933* (Chicago: University of Chicago Press, 1933).

46. Reynolds, "Three Chicago and Illinois Public Health Officers," 127, for the quotation; see also pp. 126–28. Also see City of Chicago, Department of Health, *Annual Report* (1894), for the best testament to Reilly's efforts to professionalize the department.

47. See City of Chicago, Department of Health, *Annual Report* (1894): 156–81, for the department's analysis of the quality of the city's drinking water. On the introduction of a bacteriological laboratory, see Fred O. Tonney, "The Introduction of Bacteriology into the Service of Public Health in Chicago," *Bulletin of the Society of Medical History of Chicago* 5 (January 1937): 22–23.

48. City of Chicago, Department of Health, *Annual Report* (1894): xiv, for the quotation.

49. For the quotations, see City of Chicago, Department of Health, *Annual Report* (1895): 15, and (1896): 178, respectively. See City of Chicago, Department of Heath, *Annual Report* (1896): 187 for the report on water quality, and (1894): 157 for definitions of the four categories of water quality.

50. F. W. Reilly, "Relation of the Medical Profession to the Water Supply of Chicago." On the sanitary revolution in England and Europe, see note 6, above; and Richard A.

Lewis, *Edwin Chadwick and the Public Health Movement, 1832–1854* (London: Longmans, Green, 1952); Bruno Latour, *The Pasteurization of France* (Cambridge, MA: Harvard University Press, 1988); and John V. Pickstone, "Ways of Knowing: Toward a Historical Sociology of Science, Technology, and Medicine," *British Journal for the History of Science* 26 (December 1993): 433–58.

51. Reilly, "Relation of the Medical Profession"; City of Chicago, Department of Health, *Annual Report* (1894); and O'Connell, "Technology and Pollution," 112–27.

52. On the new public health, see note 6, above. Also see Joel Tarr, "Disputes over Water-Quality Policy: Professional Cultures in Conflict, 1900–1917," in Tarr, *Search for the Ultimate Sink*, 159–78.

53. See Merlin Waterson, *The National Trust: The First Hundred Years* (London: BBC Books, 1994), 14–38; and B. W. Clapp, *An Environmental History of Britain since the Industrial Revolution* (London: Longman, 1994), 134–37.

54. John Bateman, as reported in "Water Supply to the Metropolis and Large Towns: Report of the Commissioners on Water Supply," *Parliamentary Papers* 1868–69 [4169-I-II] xxxiii, pt. 1, 6; see also pp. xxv, 2–26, 464–70; and City of Manchester City Council, *The Thirlmere Water Supply Scheme: Speeches of Mr. Alderman King and Mr. Alderman Curtis* (London: Roworth, 1878). Also see J. F. Bateman, *History and Description of the Manchester Waterworks* (Manchester: Day, 1884).

55. Bateman, *History and Description of the Manchester Waterworks*, 206, for the quotation; see also pp. 205–24. Bateman in "Water Supply to the Metropolis"; and John F. Bateman and J. J. Revy, "Description of a Proposed Cast Iron Tube for Carrying a Railway across the Channel between the Coasts of England and France," *British Association Reports, Transactions of the Sections* (1869): 206–9.

56. Sir John James Harwood, *History and Description of the Thirlmere Water Scheme* (Manchester: Blacklock, 1895), for the semiofficial account by one of its main promoters. In addition to this account, see J. Wilson, *Thirlmere to Manchester: A Compendious History of the Promotion, Progress, and Construction of the Great Thirlmere Waterworks Scheme* (Ambleside, U.K.: Middleton, 1894). For the economy-minded position of the lone vocal dissenter to the project, see ? King, *Manchester and Its Waterworks: Where Are We? A Letter on the Present Position of the Question, and Especially on Its Financial Aspects, to His Fellow-Members of the Manchester City Council* (Manchester: Sever, n.d. [1883?]).

57. King, *Manchester and Its Waterworks*.

58. Editorial in *The Standard* (2 November 1877), as quoted in Thirlmere Defence Association, *Extracts from the Leading Journals on the Manchester Water Scheme* (Windermere: Garnett, 1878), 6–7. For additional quotations and testimony by leading actors in the debate, cf. the aldermanic debate between supporter Harwood, *History and Description of the Thirlmere Water Scheme*; and King, *Manchester and Its Waterworks*.

59. Thirlmere Defence Association, *Manchester and Thirlmere Water Scheme: The Case of the Thirlmere Defence Association with Plan and Views of the Lake* (Windermere: Garnett, n.d. [1877?]), 11.

60. John Grave, Letter to the *Times*, 15 December 1877, as quoted in Harwood, *History and Description of the Thirlmere Water Scheme*, 247–55.

61. Octavia Hill, Letter to the *Times*, 18 December 1877, as quoted in Harwood, *History and Description of the Thirlmere Water Scheme*, 255–57. Hill's letter was a direct response to Grave's letter.

62. See Wilson, *Thirlmere to Manchester*, 3–37, for a detailed history of the politics of the bill in Parliament; and Harwood, *History and Description of the Thirlmere Water Scheme*, 37–116, for the legislative debate. The final act was the Manchester Corporation Waterworks Act, 42 Vic., c. xxxvi, 23 May 1879.

63. Harwood, *History and Description of the Thirlmere Water Scheme*, 138, 137, for the phrase and quotation, respectively.

64. Ibid.; Harford, *Manchester and Its Ship Canal Movement*, 85, passim, for his concept of "producer ideology"; see also pp. 79–99, for an account of worker political mobilization. Also see Alan Kidd, *Manchester*, Town and City Histories, ed. Stephen Constantine (Keele, Staffordshire: Ryburn/Keele University Press, 1993), 171–79. Cf. Richard Schneirov, *Labor and Urban Politics: Class Conflict and the Origins of Modern Liberalism in Chicago, 1864–1897* (Urbana: University of Illinois Press, 1998).

65. Harford, *Manchester and Its Ship Canal Movement*, 127. Harford makes a convincing argument that its promoters cooked the books to shrink the projected cost down to £4.5 million, which makes its true cost of over £15 million all the more impressive. On Thirlmere, see Wilson, *Thirlmere to Manchester*, 13–37; Harwood, *History and Description of the Thirlmere Water Scheme*, 137–65. In 1902–1904, the second pipeline was built; in 1901–1914, the third was built; and in 1922–1925, a fourth, double-sized, fifty-four inch pipe was built to complete the project. See Manchester Corporation, *Waterworks Chronology, 1847–1974* (Manchester: Manchester Corporation, 1975).

66. Manchester Corporation, *Waterworks Chronology*.

67. See Kidd, *Manchester*, 166–84, for a discussion of the term "Tory democracy."

68. Alan Wilson, "Technology and Municipal Decision-Making: Sanitary Systems in Manchester, 1868–1910" (Ph.D. diss., University of Manchester, 1990), 127.

69. See Harford, *Manchester and Its Ship Canal Movement*, 79–99; Kidd, *Manchester*, 171–79.

70. Wilson, "Technology and Municipal Decision-Making," 134–94.

71. Charles A. Burghardt, "The Pollution of the River Irwell and Its Tributaries," *Literary and Philosophical Society of Manchester, Proceedings* 25 (1886): 191, 193.

72. Wilson, "Technology and Municipal Decision-Making," 195–258.

73. James Niven, *Observations on the History of Public Health Effort in Manchester* (Manchester: John Heywood, 1923), 4, for the quotation; see also pp. 2–14. Niven names William Stanfield as his ally in the Sanitary Department.

74. A. Redford and I. S. Russell, *The History of Local Government in Manchester*, 3 vols. (London: Longman, 1939–1940), 2:379–401; Wilson, "Technology and Municipal Decision-Making," 134–258; Shena Simon, *A Century of City Government, Manchester, 1838–1938* (London: Allen and Unwin, 1938), 178–87.

75. Redford and Russell, *History of Local Government in Manchester*, 2:333–52; Harford, *Manchester and Its Ship Canal Movement*; Kidd, *Manchester*, 115–19.

76. Wilson, "Technology and Municipal Decision-Making," 151–94.

77. Simon, *Century of City Government*, 181–83.

78. Ibid., 181–82.

79. Ibid., 259–356. Also see chap. 12, below.

80. For Manchester, see Bateman, *History and Description of the Manchester Waterworks*, 182–85; Harwood, *History and Description of the Thirlmere Water Scheme*, 45, 121; Simon, *Century of City Government*, 351–56. For Chicago, see City of Chicago, Department of Public Works, *Annual Report* (1935): 57b.

81. Niven, *Observations*, 5, for the quotation; Simon, *Century of City Government*, 350–56.

82. City of Chicago, Board of Public Works, *Annual Report* (1874): 14.

83. City of Chicago, Board of Public Works, *Annual Report* (1875): 11–13, (1877): 11–13, and (1884): 25–27. See City of Chicago, *Revised Municipal Code of Chicago* (Chicago: City of Chicago, 1905), 662–78, for the schedule of rates.

84. City of Chicago, Department of Public Works, *Annual Report* (1935): 57b, for the waterworks statistics.

85. Samuel Haber, *Efficiency and Uplift: Scientific Management in the Progressive Era, 1890–1920* (Chicago: University of Chicago Press, 1964); Samuel P. Hays, *Conservation and the Gospel of Efficiency: The Progressive Conservation Movement, 1890–1920* (Cambridge, MA: Harvard University Press, 1959); and Martin Schiesl, *The Politics of Efficiency* (Berkeley: University of California Press, 1977). For Ericson's travail, see John Ericson, "The Water Works System of Chicago," a paper read at a meeting of the Western Society of Engineers in Chicago, 15 May 1901; John Ericson, "Chicago Water Works," *Journal of the Western Society of Engineers* 18 (October 1913): 763–96; John Ericson, "An Improved Water Supply for Chicago and the Relation of Metering to Service," *Journal of the Western Society of Engineers* 14 (October 1924): 1–8; and John Ericson, "The Water Supply Problem in Relation to the Future Chicago," *Journal of the Western Society of Engineers* 30 (April 1925): 125–41. For biographical information, see Albert Nelson Marquis, ed., *The Book of Chicagoans: 1911* (Chicago: Marquis, 1911), 218.

86. City of Chicago, Department of Public Works, *Annual Report* (1902–1911), for water fund figures, and (1910): xvi–xvii for Mayor Busse's calculation of the surplus.

87. Ericson, "Chicago Water Works," 3, for the quotation. Also see Edward W. Bemis, Ray Palmer, and Henry. W. Clausen, *Report of Committee on Water Waste to the Water Committee of the Chicago City Club* (Chicago: n.p., 19 January 1914); George A. Soper, John D. Watson, and Arthur J. Martin, *A Report to the Chicago Real Estate Board on the Disposal of the Sewage and Protection of the Water Supply of Chicago, Illinois* (Chicago: Chicago Real Estate Board, 1915); and Chicago Bureau of Public Efficiency, *The Water Works System of the City of Chicago* (Chicago: Chicago Bureau of Public Efficiency, 1916); and City of Chicago, Department of Public Works, *Annual Report* (1905): 48.

88. See Yearly, *The Money Machines*.

Chapter Twelve

1. N. Bradley as quoted in *Manchester Guardian*, 10 September 1896. Also see ibid., 3–29 September 1896. For the best overview of the subject, see Alan Wilson, "Technology and Municipal Decision-Making: Sanitary Systems in Manchester 1868–1910" (Ph.D. diss., University of Manchester, 1990). The expression "clever microbes" can be attributed to testimony by Balfour Browe, MP and leader of the City of Manchester's team of representatives, in Local Government Board, *Inquiry: Application to the Local Government Board for Sanction to Borrow Money for Purposes of Sewerage and Sewage Disposal before Major-General H. D. Crozier, R. E., and Theodore Thompson, M.D., Inspectors, Jan 12–13, 1899* (Manchester: Local Government Board, 1899), 9.

2. See Harold L. Platt, "Chicago, the Great Lakes, and the Origins of Federal Urban Environmental Policy," *Journal of the Gilded Age and Progressive Era* 1 (April 2002): 122–53, for a more chronologically extended version of this chapter. Also see John W. Larson, *Those Army Engineers: A History of the Chicago District, U.S. Army Corp of Engineers* (Washington, DC: Government Printing Office, 1980); and an older work that has both significant value and serious mistakes, Louis P. Cain, *Sanitation Strategy for a Lakefront Metropolis: The Case of Chicago* (DeKalb: Northern Illinois University Press, 1978). See Joel Tarr, *The Search for the Ultimate Sink: Urban Pollution in Historical Perspective* (Akron, OH: University of Akron Press, 1996), for more general perspectives.

3. See I. Harford, *Manchester and Its Ship Canal Movement: Class, Work, and Politics in Late Victorian England* (Staffordshire: Ryburn, 1994); and B. T. Leech, *History of the Manchester Ship Canal*, 2 vols. (Manchester: Sherratt and Hughes, 1907): 2:177–79.

4. See Elmer Corthell, "The Manchester Ship Canal," *Journal of the Western Society of Engineers* 4 (February 1899): 1–11; and Platt, "Chicago, the Great Lakes."

5. For an introduction, cf. Nancy Tomes, *The Gospel of Germs: Men, Women, and the Microbe in American Life* (Cambridge, MA: Harvard University Press, 1998); and Michael Worboys, *Spreading Germs: Disease Theories and Medical Practice in Britain, 1865–1900* (Cambridge: Cambridge University Press, 2000).

6. Daniel T. Rodgers, *Atlantic Crossings: Social Politics in the Progressive Age* (Cambridge, MA: Harvard University Press, 1998); and Fred O. Tonney, "The Introduction of Bacteriology into the Service of Public Health in Chicago," *Bulletin of the Society of Medical History of Chicago* 5 (January 1937): 22–23. Also see for example, John V. Pickstone, "Ways of Knowing: Toward a Historical Sociology of Science, Technology, and Medicine," *British Journal for the History of Science* 26 (December 1993): 433–58; Bruno Latour, *The Pasteurization of France* (Cambridge, MA: Harvard University Press, 1988); Nancy Tomes, *Gospel of Germs*; Christopher Hamlin, *Public Health and Social Justice in the Age of Chadwick: Britain, 1800–1854* (Cambridge: Cambridge University Press, 1998); and John T. Cumbler, *Reasonable Use: The People, the Environment, and the State: New England, 1790–1930* (New York: Oxford University Press, 2001).

7. Christopher Hamlin, "William Dibdin and the Idea of Biological Sewage Treatment," *Technology and Culture* 29 (April 1988): 218, for the quotation; see also pp. 192–218.

8. W. D. Farnham, "The Weakened Spring of Government: A Study in 19th Century History," *American Historical Review* 68 (1965): 662–80, for the quoted phrase. For comparative perspectives, see Daniel M. Fox, *Health Policies, Health Politics: The British and American Experience* (Princeton, NJ: Princeton University Press, 1986).

9. Bradley was no friend of science. In fact, his tirade against bacteriology must stand as one of the most demagogic and emotional outbursts of the entire debate. In particular, see Nathaniel Bradley, "Manchester Sewage Problem, with Suggestions for Its Solution and Suggested Amendment of the Rivers Pollution Prevention Act," *Manchester Statistical Society, Transactions* (1896–1897): 135–57.

10. See Martin J. Weiner, *English Culture and the Decline of the Industrial Spirit, 1850–1980* (Cambridge: Cambridge University Press, 1981), 14–15.

11. Stanley K. Schultz, *Constructing Urban Culture: American Cities and City Planning, 1800–1920* (Philadelphia: Temple University Press, 1989). Also see Barbara Gutmann Rosenkrantz, "Cart before the Horse: Theory, Practice and Professional Image in American Public Health, 1870–1920," *Journal of the History of Medicine and Allied Sciences* 29 (January 1974): 55–73; Rima D. Apple, "Constructing Mothers: Scientific Motherhood in the Nineteenth and Twentieth Centuries," *Society for the Social History of Medicine* (August 1995): 161–78; Thomas L. Haskell, ed., *The Authority of Experts: Studies in History and Theory* (Bloomington: Indiana University Press, 1984); and Martin V. Melosi, *The Sanitary City: Urban Infrastructure in America from Colonial Times to the Present* (Baltimore: Johns Hopkins University Press, 2000).

12. *Manchester Guardian*, 3 September 1896; and see 5 October 1897, for the reply of the MIJC to Alderman Thompson's position and for the most complete account of Sir Roscoe's definition of the "limits of impurity." For biographical information on Roscoe, see Charles Coulston Gillispie, ed., *Dictionary of Scientific Biography* (New York: Scribner's Sons, 1970–1976), 2:536–39.

13. *Manchester Guardian*, 10 September 1896.

14. See the memoirs of the city's officer of health, James Niven, *Observations on the History of the Public Health Effort in Manchester* (Manchester: Heywood, 1923), on public health policy; Derek Fraser, *Urban Politics in Victorian England: The Structure of Politics in Victorian Cities* (Leicester: Leicester University Press, 1979), for the political culture of Manchester.

15. Sidney Webb and Beatrice Webb, *Methods of Social Study* (1932; reprint, New York: Kelley, 1968), 198, 195, for the quotations; Harford, *Manchester and Its Ship Canal Movement*, 62–98, 147–66, Appendix B.

16. *Manchester Guardian*, 3 September 1896. On the Thirlmere aqueduct, see chap. 11, above.

17. *Manchester Guardian*, 10 September 1896. For an early examination of the relationship between the science of bacteriology and the technology of sewage disposal, see F. J. Faraday, "On Some Recent Observations in Micro-Biology and Their Bearing on the Evolution of Disease and the Sewage Question," *Literary and Philosophical Society of Manchester, Proceedings* 25 (1885): 46–55.

18. City of Manchester, *Proceedings of the City Council* (9 September 1896): 1342, 1360, for the quotations; see also pp. 1337–89 for the city surveyor's full report.

19. *Manchester Guardian*, 10 September–11 December 1896.

20. Ibid., 18 September 1897.

21. R. M. Parkhurst, letters the editors, *Manchester Guardian*, 8 and 14 September 1897; "Technologist," letter to the editors, *Manchester Guardian*, 15 September 1897.

22. R. M. Parkhurst, as quoted in *Manchester Guardian*, 25 September 1897.

23. "The Scientific Aspects of Sewage Purification," *Manchester Guardian*, 26 October 1897; see 14, 15, 16, 20, and 27 September 1897; and 2, 5, 6, and 25 October 1897, for additional commentary with science-related aspects.

24. *Manchester Guardian*, 2 September 1897, for Saxon's quotation, and 7 October 1897, for a similar statement by Thompson.

25. *Manchester Guardian*, 25 September–31 October 1897; see 1 November 1897, for the vote.

26. *Manchester Guardian*, 7 April 1898, for Leech's assumption of leadership, and 26 March 1898 for the proceedings in the courts. For the scientific work at Davyhulme as reported by Fowler, see *Manchester Guardian*, 21 March and 5 April 1898.

27. LGB, *Inquiry: Application*, 6–7, for the quotation; see also the full application. For biographical information on Fowler, see "Gilbert John Fowler," *Chemical Society Journal* (December 1953): 4191–92.

28. Manchester Corporation, Rivers Department, *Experts' Report on Treatment of Manchester Sewage, October 30 1899* (Manchester: Blackrock, 1899); *Manchester Guardian*, 15 October 1901; Wilson, "Technology and Municipal Decision-Making," 259–329.

29. Wilson, "Technology and Municipal Decision-Making," 259–329.

30. *Chicago Tribune*, 17–19 January 1900; *Missouri v. Illinois* 200 U.S. 496 (1906). Missouri had filed a similar suit in the U.S. Circuit Court in case its bid for original jurisdiction before the high court was denied. See *Chicago Tribune*, 18 January 1900. The other two key cases considered in this chapter are *Sanitary District of Chicago v. United States* 266 U.S. 405 (1925), and *Wisconsin v. Illinois*, 278 U.S. 367 (1929).

31. *Chicago Tribune*, 18 January 1900, for the quotation and for a range of contemporary opinions.

32. Sanitary District of Chicago, *Memorial Presented by the Trustees of the Sanitary District of Chicago to the Congress of the United States: Deep Waterway from Lake Michigan to the Mississippi River* (Chicago: Sanitary District of Chicago, 1900), 13, 19, respectively for the quotations. Also see *Chicago Tribune*, 19 January 1900, for the trustees' inflated hopes to get the federal government to take over the canal as part of an Atlantic-to-the-Gulf deep-sea waterway. Cf. House Committee on Rivers and Harbors, "Report upon ... a Navigable Waterway 14 Feet Deep from Lockport, Ill., ... to the Mouth of the Illinois River ... by the Mississippi River Commission and by a Board of Officers of the Corps of Engineers, U.S. Army," 59th Cong., 1st sess., 1905, HR 263. For the problems suffered by ship captains trying to navigate the swift currents, see *Chicago Tribune*, 17 February 1900.

33. See Rudolph Hering, *Report to Hon. Robert R. McCormick, President, on the Calumet Subdivision of the Sanitary District of Chicago* (Chicago: n.p., 15 October 1907).

34. For the SDC's promotional efforts, see Sanitary District of Chicago, *Industrial Development along Chicago Sanitary and Ship Canal* (Chicago: Sanitary District of Chicago,

1906); and Sanitary District of Chicago, Real Estate Development Committee, *The Manufacturing Site Possibilities of the Land along the Chicago Sanitary and Ship Canal* (Chicago: Sanitary District of Chicago, 1916).

35. See chap. 10, above.

36. Edwin Oakes Jordan, "Typhoid Fever and Water Supply in Chicago," *Journal of the American Medical Association* 39 (20 December 1902): 1563–65, for the quotations; see also pp. 1561–66. For biographical information and an account of Jordan's role in the *Illinois v. Missouri* case, see Carolyn G. Shapiro-Shapin, " 'A Really Excellent Scientific Contribution': Scientific Creativity, Scientific Professionalism, and the Chicago Drainage Case," *Bulletin of the History of Medicine* 71 (1997): 385–411.

37. Shapiro-Shapin, " 'Really Excellent Scientific Contribution' "; Lyman E. Cooley, *The Diversion of the Waters of the Great Lakes by Way of the Sanitary and Ship Canal of Chicago* (Chicago: Clohesey, 1913); and Rudolph Hering, *Report to Hon. Robert R. McCormick.*

38. Jordan, "Typhoid Fever," 1564–5, 1566.

39. *Missouri v. Illinois*, 518, 522, for the quotations.

40. Ibid., 523, 525–26, for the quotations.

41. Ibid., 521, 522, 518, for the quotations.

42. For Major Handbury's report to the convention, see the *Morning News*, 12 October 1887; and *Chicago Tribune*, 12 October 1887. For the repercussions, see International Waterways Commission, "Reports of the International Waterways Commission, 1906," in Report of the Minister of Public Works (Canada), *Sessional Paper No. 19a. A., 1907* (Ottawa: Dawson, 1907), 2:174–86; Western Society of Engineers, *The Levels of the Lakes as Affected by the Proposed Lakes and Gulf Waterway* (Chicago: Citizens' Association, 1889); and especially, George Y. M. Wisner et al., "Levels of the Lakes as Affected by the Proposed Lake Michigan and Mississippi Waterway," *Journal of the Association of Engineering Societies* 8 (March 1889): 123–54. Also see chap. 11, above.

43. Inland Waterways Commission, "Reports of the International Waterways Commission, 1906," 185, for the quotation. The IWC also hired Rudolph Hering and George W. Fuller as consulting engineers to report on alternative methods of ending the contamination of Chicago's water supply by the industrial and human wastes of the burgeoning Calumet district. The engineers reported that rapid advances in sewage treatment technology now made it a cost-effective option to additional diversions of lake water. The treaty is found in Don Courtney Piper, *The International Law of the Great Lakes: A Study of Canadian–United States Co-operation* (Durham, NC: Duke University Press, 1967), 124–30. On the origins of the treaty, see L. M. Bloomfield and Gerald F. Fitzgerald, *Boundary Waters Problems of Canada and the United States (The International Joint Commission, 1912–1958)* (Toronto: Carswell, 1958); and Alan O. Gibbons, "Sir George Gibbons and the Boundary Waters Treaty of 1909," *Canadian Historical Review* 34 (June 1953): 124–38. For the role of Chicago's withdrawal in the negotiations, see Piper, *International Law*, 71–103; Cornelius Lynde, "The Controversy concerning the Diversion of Water from Lake Michigan by the Sanitary District of Chicago," *Illinois Law Review* 25 (1930): 243–60; Hildegard

Willmann, "The Chicago Diversions from Lake Michigan," *Canadian Bar Review* 10 (1932): 575–83; and William L. Griffin, "A History of the Canadian–United States Boundary Waters Treaty of 1909," *University of Detroit Law Journal* 37 (1959–1960): 76–95.

44. Sanitary District of Chicago, *Industrial Development*, 10. For other, similar statements, Robert R. McCormick, "Future Value of the Drainage Canal," in *Chicago Record-Herald*, 18 December 1909; and Sanitary District of Chicago, Real Estate Development Committee, *Manufacturing Site Possibilities*.

45. Hering, *Report to Hon. Robert R. McCormick*, 33–34. Cf. George A. Soper, John D. Watson, and Arthur J. Martin, *A Report to the Chicago Real Estate Board on the Disposal of the Sewage and Protection of the Water Supply of Chicago, Illinois* (Chicago: Chicago Real Estate Board, 1915), for a telling critique of the engineering flaws of the Cal-Sag canal plan.

46. Sanitary District of Chicago, *Proceedings*, 27 March 1907, contains a copy of Taft's report, as well as the district's response, a call to mount a lobbying campaign for the needed legislation.

47. *Sanitary District of Chicago v. United States* supplies a basic chronology of events in the case. Also see Sanitary District of Chicago, *Proceedings*, 16 January 1913, for Cooley's report on his efforts in Washington and a copy of Secretary of War Henry L. Stimson's rejection of the district's petition; and Cooley, *The Diversion of the Waters*; and Lyman E. Cooley, *Supplement to the Brief on "The Diversion of the Waters of the Great Lakes by Way of the Sanitary and Ship Canal of Chicago"* (New York: Clohesey, 1913). For the SDC's position in the case, see C. Arch Williams, *The Sanitary District of Chicago: History of Its Growth and Development* (Chicago: Sanitary District of Chicago, 1919); and George M. Wisner, *Report on Sewage Disposal: The Sanitary District of Chicago* (Chicago: Klein, 12 October 1911). For an account of the Canadians' stream of protests against Chicago's withdrawal of water, see J. Q. Dealey, "The Chicago Drainage Canal and the St. Lawrence Development," *American Journal of International Law* 23 (1929): 307–28. *Sanitary District of Chicago v. United States* became further complicated in the early 1920s by the intervention of Wisconsin and several other Great Lakes states. They argued that Chicago's withdrawal violated their riparian rights by lowering the lake levels. In response, several states in the Mississippi River Valley lined up behind the city in supporting its claims that the use of the water was within the national interest because it improved inland navigation. In 1925, the Supreme Court would confirm the decision of the lower bench. See *Sanitary District of Chicago v. United States* and *Wisconsin v. Illinois*, which became the lead case in the controversy four years later.

48. For the concerns about lake dumping and the passage of the Mann Act, which set an eight-mile limit on the dumping of dredgings into Lake Michigan, finally giving health department officers partial relief, see *Chicago Record-Herald*, 21 April, 12–14 May, and 20 June 1910. For early scientific investigations of the bacteriology of the bottom of lake in the Calumet area, see *Chicago Record-Herald*, 27 November 1906; 13 October 1908; 27 January 1909, and 10 and 27 February 1909.

49. *Chicago Record-Herald*, 10 April 1908, for the quotation; see 25 October 1907 for a related story on the mismanagement of the bureau.

50. Ibid., 10 February 1910, for the quotation; see 27 November 1906; 15 October 1907; 13 October 1908; and 27–29 January and 27 February 1909 for related stories. On the "annual water famine," see *Chicago Record-Herald*, 9 August 1909, which details the extent of the problem in the Back of the Yards and other working-class areas of the Southwest Side of the city.

51. G. B. Young, "The Result of the Experimental Employment of Hypochlorite Treatment to a Portion of the Chicago City Water Supply," *American Journal of Public Health* 4 (April 1914): 310, for the quotation; and City of Chicago, Department of Health, *Annual Report* (1911–1918): 450–82, 1432.

52. Young, "Result of the Experimental Employment," 313, for the quotations.

53. George M. Wisner, *Report on Sewage Disposal*, 17.

54. George A. Johnson, "The Purification of Public Water Supplies," in *Water Supply Papers*, U.S. Department of the Interior, United States Geological Survey (Washington, DC: Government Printing Office, 1913), 65, for the quotation; and George A. Johnson, "Description of Methods of Operation of the Sterilization Plant of the Jersey City Water Supply Company . . . ," in *Proceedings of the Annual Convention of the American Water Works Association* (Baltimore: American Water Works Association, 1909), 134–45, for the single best source on the origins of the chlorination of public water supplies. Also see J. L. Leal, "The Sterilization Plant of the Jersey City Water Supply Company at Boonton, N. J.," in *Proceedings of the Annual Convention of the American Water Works Association*, 100–109; and George W. Fuller, "Description of the Process and Plant of the Jersey City Water Supply Company . . . ," in *Proceedings of the Annual Convention of the American Water Works Association*, 110–33.

55. J. J. Flather and Judge William A. Magie, as quoted in Johnson, "Purification," 165 and 66, respectively.

56. *Proceedings of American Water Works Association* (1909).

57. Flather, as quoted in Johnson, "Purification," 153; Wisner, *Report on Sewage Disposal*, 69.

58. Young, "Result of the Experimental Employment," 313. Also see City of Chicago, Department of Health, *Annual Report* (1911–1918): 450–82, 1432.

59. Johnson, "Purification," 71.

60. Wisner, *Report on Sewage Disposal*, 69.

61. Cornelius Lynde, "Controversy concerning the Diversion," 250, for the first quotation; *Wisconsin v. Illinois* for the second quotation. For the role of district court judges as protectors of local interests, see Charles L. Zelden, *Justice Lies in the District: The U.S. District Court, Southern District of Texas, 1902–1960* (College Station: Texas A&M University Press, 1993). For biographical information on Landis, see "Kenesaw Mountain Landis," in *The Book of Chicagoans: 1917*, ed. Albert Nelson Marquis (Chicago: Marquis, 1917), 400.

62. See for example, Arthur N. Talbot, "Recent Progress in Sewage Purification," *Journal of the Western Society of Engineers* 5 (December 1900): 543–60.

63. Wilson, "Technology and Municipal Decision-Making," 259–329.

64. See Edward Ardern and W. T. Lockett, "Experiments on the Oxidation of Sewage without the Aid of Filters," *Journal of the Society of the Chemical Industry* 33 (May 1914): 523–39; and A. Redford and I. S. Russell, *The History of Local Government in Manchester*, 3 vols. (London: Longman, 1939–1940), 3:112–20.

65. For the earliest American reports, see Leslie C. Frank, "English Experiments on Sewage Aeration Reviewed as Preliminary to Baltimore Tests," *Engineering Record* 71 (6 March 1915): 288–89; Edward Bartow and F. W. Mohlman, "Sewage-Treatment Experiments with Aeration and Activated Sludge," *Engineering News* 73 (1 April 1915): 647–48; T. Chalkley Hatton, "Activated-Sludge Experiments at Milwaukee, Wis.," *Engineering News* 74 (15 July 1915): 134–37; M. N. Baker, "Activated Sludge in America: An Editorial Survey," *Engineering News* 74 (22 July 1915): 164–71; George W. Fuller, "Current Tendencies in Sewage Disposal Practice," *Journal of the Western Society of Engineers* 26 (August 1921): 273–88; and T. Chalkley Hatton, "Modern Sewage Treatment," *Journal of the Western Society of Engineers* 22 (February 1917): 87–100. For the triumph of the activated sludge method, see T. Chalkley Hatton, "Activated-Sludge Process Has Come to Stay," *Engineering News-Record* 93 (2 October 1924): 538–39; and Edward Bartow, "The Development of Sewage Treatment by the Activated Sludge Process," *American City* 32 (March 1925): 296–99.

66. For details, see Platt, "Chicago, the Great Lakes." Chicago's water management policy remains under the supervision of the court today. For a recent controversy involving excessive taking of water from Lake Michigan, see the *Chicago Tribune*, 4–12 May 1997; and the *Chicago Sun-Times*, 4–12 May 1997. The city also promised once again to implement universal metering, to include 350,000 residential buildings whose owners now pay flat fees. As in the past, however, the project lacks a timetable. See *Chicago Tribune*, 9 April 2003. The problem of waste water being diverted into the lake also remains unsolved. Despite billions of dollars being poured into the deep-tunnel project to prevent sewage from contaminating Lake Michigan, such contamination occurs two to three times a year during heavy rains. See Timothy B. Neary, "Chicago-Style Environmental Politics: Origins of the Deep Tunnel Project," *Journal of Illinois History* 4 (Summer 2001): 83–102. As I was writing this chapter in 2001, a sudden severe storm hit Chicago on the very day, 2 August, as the great 1885 flood. The result was essentially the same: over a billion gallons of polluted water were released into the lake, closing the beaches for the next several days. Unlike in 1885, heavy doses of chlorine were then added to the water supply. See *Chicago Tribune*, 3–8 August 2001.

67. See Schultz, *Constructing Urban Culture*.

Chapter Thirteen

1. See Smoke Abatement Committee, *Report of the Smoke Abatement Committee, 1882* (London: Smith Elder, 1883). For biographical information, see "Octavia Hill," *The Dictionary of National Biography, 1912–1921*, ed. H. W. C. Davis and J. R. H. Weaver (London: Oxford University Press, 1927), 257–59; E. Moberly Bell, *Octavia Hill: A Biography*

(London: Constable, 1942); and "Ernest Hart," *The Oxford Companion to Medicine*, ed. John Walton et al. (Oxford: Oxford University Press, 1986), 1:521.

2. For technological innovation, see Smoke Abatement Committee, *Report*; Harold L. Platt, *The Electric City: Energy and the Growth of the Chicago Area, 1880–1930* (Chicago: University of Chicago Press, 1991); and Thomas P. Hughes, *Networks of Power: Electrification in Western Society, 1880–1930* (Baltimore: Johns Hopkins University Press, 1983). For consideration of the politics of technology in England, see Bill Luckin, *Questions of Power: Electricity and Environment in Inter-War Britain* (Manchester: Manchester University Press, 1990). For medical science, see Christopher Hamlin, *A Science of Impurity: Water Analysis in Nineteenth Century Britain* (Bristol: Hilger, 1990); Francis Barrymore Smith, *The Retreat of Tuberculosis, 1850–1950* (London: Croom, Helm, 1988); and Michael Worboys, *Spreading Germs: Disease Theories and Medical Practice in Britain, 1865–1900* (Cambridge: Cambridge University Press, 2000). On the reception of germ theory, see Bruno Latour, *The Pasteurization of France* (Cambridge, MA: Harvard University Press, 1988). For the London fogs, see Bill Luckin, "The Social and Cultural Repercussions of Environmental Crisis: The Great London Smoke Fogs of the Late Nineteenth and Early Twentieth Centuries," in *The Modern Demon: Pollution in Urban and Industrial European Societies*, ed. C. Bernhardt and G. Massard-Guilbaud (Clermont-Ferrand, France: Presses Universitaires Blaise Pascal, 2002), 212–38.

3. E. Schramm, "Experts in the Smelter Smoke Debate," in *The Silent Countdown: Essays in European Environmental History*, ed. P. Brimblecome and C. Pfister (Berlin: Springer-Verlag, 1990), 207; see also pp. 196–209. Also F. J. Bruggemeier, "Waldsterben: the Construction and Deconstruction of an Environmental Problem," in Bernhardt and Massard-Guilbaud, eds., *Modern Demon*, for further insight on German forestry as well as a cautionary tale on the historical interpretation of science.

4. See Bill Luckin, "'The Doom of a Great City': London and the 'Killer Fog,' 1870–1914," a paper presented at the annual meeting of the Society for the History of Technology (London, August 1996); and Anthony S. Wohl, *Endangered Lives: Public Health in Victorian Britain* (Cambridge, MA: Harvard University Press, 1983).

5. Shena Simon, *A Century of City Government, Manchester, 1838–1938* (London: Allen and Unwin, 1938), 207–8. In the 1990s, a national report on air quality still showed Manchester dead last in the nation. See Stephen Mosley, "The 'Smoke Nuisance' and Environmental Reformers in Late Victorian Manchester," *Manchester Regional History Review* 10 (1996): 40–47.

6. Manchester has a long tradition of both professional and amateur science. For an introduction, see R. H. Kargon, *Science in Victorian Manchester* (Manchester: Manchester University Press, 1977); T. S. Ashton, *Economic and Social Investigations in Manchester: A Centenary History of the Manchester Statistical Society* (London: King, 1934); and Anne Secord, "Science in the Pub: Artisan Botanists in Early Nineteenth-Century Lancashire," *History of Science* 32 (September 1994): 269–315. For a preliminary overview of smoke abatement reform in England, see B. W. Clapp, *An Environmental History of Britain since the Industrial Revolution* (London: Longman, 1994), 11–42.

7. John Leigh, *Coal-Smoke: Its Nature, and Suggestions for Its Abatement* (London: Heywood, 1883), 4–5. On politics of water management and sanitation policy, see chaps. 5, 12, above.

8. A. B. Reach, *Manchester and the Textile Districts in 1849*, ed. C. Aspin (Helmshore, U.K.: Helmshore Local History Society, 1972), 1; *London Daily News*, 25 October 1877. Also see Leigh, *Coal-Smoke*, 4–5, for an additional, detailed description of the "blacks."

9. Manchester, *Police Commissioners' Report* (1800), as quoted in Daphne deJersey Gemmill, "Manchester in the Victorian Age: Factors Influencing the Design and Implementation of Smoke Abatement Policy" (M.A. essay, Department of Epidemiology and Public Health, Yale University, 1972), 3, for the quotation. For contemporary sources of statistics, see James Murray and Richard Birley, "Amount and Employment of Steam and Water Power in the Undermentioned Townships [Chorlton-upon-Hardy, Salford, Broughton, and Pendleton]," *Manchester Statistical Society, Transactions* 1 (24 January 1837); Henry Ashworth, "An Account of the Number of Steam Engines ... in Bolton ... in March, 1837," *Manchester Statistical Society, Transactions* 1 (23 May 1837); Smoke Abatement Committee, *Report*, 1–10; Thomas Baines and William Fairbairn, *Lancashire and Cheshire Past and Present*, 2 vols. (London: Mackenzie, 1867); and J. F. Bateman, *History and Description of the Manchester Waterworks* (Manchester: Day, 1884), 40. For more recent scholarship, see R. L. Hills, *Power in the Industrial Revolution* (New York: Kelly, 1970); and Mike Williams and D. A. Farnie, *Cotton Mills in Greater Manchester* (Preston, U.K.: Carnegie, 1992). The private sector in England made considerable progress in engine efficiency, reducing the amount of coal burned from fifteen pounds per horsepower hour in 1799 to six pounds in 1852. See Louis C. Hunter, *Steam Power*, vol. 2 of *A History of Industrial Power in the United States, 1780–1930* (Charlottesville: University Press of Virginia, 1985). In 1854, the private sector also took the initiative in promoting boiler safety by forming an association for self-policing and inspection services. See the annual reports for 1861–1890 of the Association for the Prevention of Steam Boiler Explosions, and for the Attainment of Economy in the Use of Steam, available in the Local History Section, Manchester Central Library.

10. See William Graham, *Smoke Abatement in Lancashire: A Paper Read before the Public Medicine Section of the British Medical Association, London, 2 August 1895* (Manchester: Cornish, 1896), for the most complete account of early reform efforts in Manchester. For an exhaustive study of the problem, also see Chicago Association of Commerce, *Smoke Abatement and Electrification of Railroad Terminals in Chicago* (Chicago: McNally, 1915). And see note 6, above, for references to Manchester's unique approach to science and technology. For Manchester's special moment and the concept of shock cities, see Asa Briggs, *Victorian Cities* (London: Odhams, 1963); and chapter 1, above. For the ascendancy of Manchester liberalism, see V. A. C. Gatrell, "Incorporation and the Pursuit of Liberal Hegemony in Manchester, 1790–1839," in *Municipal Reform and the Industrial City*, ed. Derek Fraser (Leicester: Leicester University Press, 1982), 15–60.

11. Simon, *Century of City Government*, 202, 203, for the first and second quotation, respectively; Graham, *Smoke Abatement*, 7–10; and Gemmill, "Manchester in the Victorian Age," 19–63. Additional insight is provided by Ann Beck, "Some Aspects of the History of Anti-Pollution Legislation in England, 1819–1954," *Journal of the History of Medicine* 14 (October 1959): 475–89. See also the important insights provided by Sarah Wilmont in "Pollution and Public Concern: The Response of the Chemical Industry in Britain to Emerging Environmental Issues, 1860–1901," in *The Chemical Industry in Europe, 1850–1914: Industrial Growth, Pollution, and Professionalization*, ed. Ernst Homburg, Anthony S. Travis, and Harm G. Schroter, Chemists and Chemistry, No. 17 (Dordrecht, Netherlands: Kluwer Academic Publishers, 1998), 121–48.

12. For a useful review of contemporary opinion on the medical significance of air pollution, see Peter Thorsheim, "Miasma, Smoke, and Germs: Air Pollution and Health in Nineteenth-Century Britain," a paper presented to a meeting of the American Society for Environmental History (Baltimore, March 1997). The essential source on the Sanitary Idea is Christopher Hamlin, *Public Health and Social Justice in the Age of Chadwick: Britain, 1800–1854* (Cambridge: Cambridge University Press, 1998). For an exceptional departure from a primary focus of the sanitary movement during the 1850s, see Peter Spence, *Coal, Smoke, and Sewage: Scientifically and Practically Considered; with Suggestions for the Sanitary Improvement of Towns, and the Beneficial Application of the Sewage: A Paper Read before the Literary and Philosophical Society of Manchester* (Manchester: Cave and Sever, 1857).

13. See Roy M. MacLeod, "The Alkali Acts Administration, 1863–84: The Emergence of the Civil Scientist," *Victorian Studies* 9 (December 1965): 81–112; John M. Eyler, "The Conversion of Angus Smith: The Changing Role of Chemistry and Biology in Sanitary Science, 1850–1880," *Bulletin of the History of Medicine* 54 (Summer 1980): 216–34; and Peter Reed, "Robert Angus Smith and the Alkali Inspectorate," in Homburg, Travis, and Schroter, eds., *The Chemical Industry in Europe*, 149–63. The industry trade name for hydrochloric acid was muriatic acid. The process of making alkali also generated significant amounts of sulphur.

14. Robert Angus Smith, "On the Air and Rain of Manchester," *Literary and Philosophical Society of Manchester, Memoirs*, 2nd ser., 10 (1852): 207–17.

15. Spence, *Coal, Smoke, and Sewage*, 21, 14, 4, for the quotations. Spence proposed a solution unique in the annals of urban sanitary reform. He called for the adoption of the infrastructure of sewer pipes to carry the city's exhaust fumes to a gigantic chimney at least six hundred feet high. The draft created would cause a vacuum which would suck these emissions and sewer gases away to where they would not be harmful to people in buildings and on the streets. Also see "Peter Spence," in *The Dictionary of National Biography*; C. S. Nicholls, ed., *"Missing Persons"* (Oxford: Oxford University Press, 1993), 627.

16. Peter Spence, "On Sulphurous Acid in the Air of Manchester," *Literary and Philosophical Society of Manchester, Proceedings* 8 (1869): 137–39; and Robert Angus Smith, as reported in the same article, p. 139; and J. B. Dancer, "Microscopical Examination

of the Solid Particles from the Air of Manchester," *Literary and Philosophical Society of Manchester, Proceedings* 7 (1868): 157–61. Also see Eyler, "Conversion of Angus Smith," for insight on his changing positions on the relationships among the natural environment, industrial pollution, and human health.

17. John Leigh, in City of Manchester, "Report of the Medical Officer of Health," *Proceedings of the Common Council* (1868): 1, for the quotation. Also see City of Manchester, "Report of the Medical Officer of Health," *Proceedings of the Common Council* (1872): 35–36; Alan Wilson, "Technology and Municipal Decision-Making: Sanitary Systems in Manchester, 1868–1910" (Ph.D. diss., University of Manchester, 1990); and John V. Pickstone, *Medicine and Industrial Society: A History of Hospital Development in Manchester and Its Region, 1752–1946* (Manchester: University of Manchester, 1985).

18. Latour, *Pasteurization of France*, 20–21; see also pp. 1–58.

19. Ibid., 59–150; Carlo Cipolla, *Miasmas and Disease: Public Health and the Environment in the Pre-Industrial Era* (New Haven, CT: Yale University Press, 1992); Jacques Nicolle, *Louis Pasteur: A Master of Scientific Enquiry* (London: Hutchinson, 1961); Hamlin, *Science of Impurity*; and John V. Pickstone, "Ways of Knowing: Toward a Historical Sociology of Science, Technology, and Medicine," *British Journal for the History of Science* 26 (December 1993): 433–58.

20. Manchester and Salford Sanitary Association (MSSA), *Annual Report* (1875): 7.

21. Ibid., appendix A, pp. 19, 20, for the quotations; see also MSSA *Annual Report* (1873–1875). They referred to the Public Health Act of 1866 as the legislative foundation for prosecutions. Also see Gemmill, "Manchester in the Victorian Age," 64–78; and Mosley, "'Smoke Nuisance.'" The pressure was clearly felt by the chemical industry in Manchester. See Wilmont, "Pollution and Public Concern," 121–48.

22. MSSA, *Annual Report* (1876), for the health statistics; Thomas A. Welton, "On the Published Results of the Census of 1881," *Manchester Statistical Society, Transactions* (1882–1883): 121–39, for the population statistics. On the human toll of chronic sickness, see Wohl, *Endangered Lives*; James C. Riley, *Sick, Not Dead: The Health of British Workingmen during the Mortality Decline* (Baltimore: Johns Hopkins University Press, 1997); and Graham Mooney and Simon Szreter, "Urbanization, Mortality, and the Standard of Living Debate: New Estimates of the Expectation of Life at Birth in Nineteenth-Century British Cities," *Economic History Review* 51, no. 1 (1998): 84–112.

23. On technology, see Smoke Abatement Committee, *Report*. On medical science, compare Leigh, *Coal Smoke*, and Henry Simpson, "The Pollution of Air, as Affecting Health," in *Lectures on Air Pollution*, ed. Manchester and Salford Noxious Vapours Abatement Association (Manchester: Manchester and Salford Noxious Vapours Abatement Association, 1888), 8:97–107. Dr. Simpson was a physician who practiced in the Manchester Royal Infirmary and the Manchester Hospital for Consumption and Diseases of the Throat.

24. Fred Scott, "The Need for Better Organization of Benevolent Effort in Manchester and Salford," *Manchester Statistical Society, Transactions* (1884–1885): 143, as quoted in Mosley, "'Smoke Nuisance,'" 41; also see the Mosley article for background on

the leaders of the MSNVAA, and see MSAA, *Annual Report* (1882–1892), for the history of the organization's activities.

25. Thorsheim, "Miasma, Smoke, and Germs"; Luckin, "'Doom of a Great City'"; Rosilyn Williams, *Notes on the Underground: An Essay on Technology, Society, and Imagination* (Cambridge, MA: MIT Press, 1990); I. Harford, *Manchester and Its Ship Canal Movement: Class, Work, and Politics in Late Victorian England* (Staffordshire: Ryburn, 1994); and P. F. Clarke, *Lancashire and the New Liberalism* (Cambridge: Cambridge University Press, 1971). Also see Michael Harrison, "Social Reform in Late Victorian and Edwardian Manchester, with Special Reference to T. C. Horsfall" (Ph.D. diss., University of Manchester, 1988). Harrison shows a close interconnection among the memberships of the various urban reform movements and associations. Horsfall, for example, was not only a maker of race degeneracy jeremiads, but also a leader in housing reform, a supporter of the smoke abatement crusade, a member of the Field Naturalist Society, and a devotee of several other, similar causes.

26. Simpson, "Pollution of Air"; and for the economic costs of pollution, see John Holden, "The Pollution of Air, as Affecting the Architect and His Work," in Manchester and Salford Noxious Vapours Abatement Association, ed., *Lectures on Air Pollution*, 7:87–96.

27. Simpson, "Pollution of Air," 103–4, 105.

28. Charles Estcourt, "Why the Air of Manchester Is So Impure," in Manchester and Salford Noxious Vapours Abatement Association, ed., *Lectures on Air Pollution*, 4:42, 44, for the quotations; see also pp. 39–51.

29. Robert Holland, "Air Pollution as Affecting Plant Life," in Manchester and Salford Noxious Vapours Abatement Association, ed., *Lectures on Air Pollution*, 9:122, 121, for the quotations; see also 110–25. On the dilemma of reform, Holland expressed his conclusions in terms similar to those employed by Estcourt. "The burning of carbon, so as to render the smoke invisible," he stated, "does not in the slightest degree lessen the quantity of the invisible sulphurous acid" (p. 125). Cf. Schramm, "Experts in the Smelter Smoke Debate." Also see Theresa Wyborn, "Parks for the People: The Development of Public Parks in Victorian Manchester," *Manchester Regional History Review* 9 (1995): 3–14. Wyborn highlights the ways in which class distinctions were made by the park-gate guards, who filtered out all but members of the most refined classes.

30. Wilmont, "Pollution and Public Concern," 141–42, for the quotation; see also pp. 141–48 for industry responses with a focus on Manchester.

31. MSNVAA, *Annual Report* (1890), as reported in MSSA, *Annual Report* (1890): 70–79.

32. MSNVAA, *Annual Report* (1888–1895).

33. On working-class adoption of gas lighting, see Luckin, *Questions of Power*.

34. MSNVAA, *Annual Report* (1892): 60–62; and Harry Grimshaw, "Note on the Presence of Sulphur in Illuminating Gas," *Literary and Philosophical Society of Manchester, Proceedings* 20 (1880): 51–54. See Estcourt, "Why the Air of Manchester Is So Impure" for a discussion of alternative, central-station technologies; Roy Frost, *Electricity in Manchester* (Manchester: Richardson, 1993), for the coming of a municipal power

station in 1893; and A. Redford and I. S. Russell, *The History of Local Government in Manchester*, 3 vols. (London: Longman, 1939–1940), 1:311–42; and Derek Fraser, *Urban Politics in Victorian England: The Structure of Politics in Victorian Cities* (Leicester: Leicester University Press, 1976).

35. MSNVAA, *Annual Report* (1890), as reported in MSSA, *Annual Report* (1890): 79, for the quotation; see also MSNVAA, *Annual Report* (1892): 66–70. On the parks, see Wyborn, "Parks for the People."

36. The work of the Manchester Field Naturalists Society is contained in three reports of the Town Gardening Committee published in the *Reports and Proceedings of the Manchester Field Naturalists and Archaeologists' Society*: "The Atmosphere of Manchester: Preliminary Report of the Air Analysis Committee" (1891), 1–10; "The Work of the Air Analysis Committee" (1891), 66–72; and "The Atmosphere of Manchester and Salford: Second Report of the Air Analysis Committee" (1893), 73–98. Also see G. H. Bailey, "Some Aspects of Town Air as Contrasted with That of the Country," *Literary and Philosophical Society of Manchester, Memoirs*, 4th ser., 8 (1893): 11–17. For an ideal example of the history of science "from the bottom up," see Secord, "Science in the Pub."

37. Town Gardening Committee, "The Autumn Soirée: Air Pollution and Fog in Manchester," in *Reports and Proceedings of the Manchester Field Naturalists and Archaeologists' Society* (1891): 41, for the quotation; and "The Owens College Museum: Corals and Their Allies," in *Reports and Proceedings of the Manchester Field Naturalists and Archaeologists' Society* (1891): 40–41, for a previous, more typical meeting. For the American counterpart, see William H. Wilson, *The City Beautiful Movement* (Baltimore: Johns Hopkins University Press, 1989); Maureen A. Flanagan, "Gender and Urban Political Reform: The City Club and the Women's City Club of Chicago in the Progressive Era," *American Historical Review* 95 (October 1990): 1032–50; and Daniel T. Rodgers, *Atlantic Crossings: Social Politics in the Progressive Age* (Cambridge, MA: Harvard University Press, 1998).

38. Town Gardening Committee, "Autumn Soirée," 42, for the quotations.

39. Ibid., 41–43.

40. Town Gardening Committee, "Atmosphere of Manchester and Salford: Second Report," 80, for the quotation; see also pp. 73–98 for the full details of the study.

41. Ibid., 81, for the quotation. For reform in Ancoats, see J. H. Crosfield, *The "Bitter Cry" of Ancoats and of Impoverished Manchester: Being a Series of Letters on Municipal Topics* (Manchester: Ireland, 1887); Charles Rowley, *Fifty Years of Work without Wages*, 2nd ed. (London: Hodder and Stoughton, 1911), and chap. 9, above.

42. MSSA, *Annual Report* (1893–1901); Roy Frost, *Electricity*.

43. Graham, *Smoke Abatement*, 11, for the quotation; MSSA, *Annual Report* (1893–1899); and Wilson, "Technology and Municipal Decision-Making" on the Local Government Board's exertion of authority over Manchester's sewage disposal policy.

44. Manchester and District Smoke Abatement Society, *The Manchester and Salford Smoke Abatement Exhibition, November 10–25, 1911, City Exhibition Hall, Manchester* (Manchester: Manchester and District Smoke Abatement Society, 1912). See Latour,

Pasteurization of France. Thanks to Angela Gugliotta for reminding me that the exact reasons for the decline in mortality at the end of the nineteenth century remain undefined. See, for example, Nancy Tomes, "The Private Side of Public Health: Sanitary Science, Domestic Hygiene, and the Germ Theory, 1870–1900," *Bulletin of the History of Medicine* 64 (Winter 1990): 509–39; Joel D. Howell, *Technology in the Hospital: Transforming Patient Care in the Early Twentieth Century* (Baltimore: Johns Hopkins University Press, 1995); and Mooney and Szreter, "Urbanization."

45. Wilmont, "Pollution and Public Concern," 146.

46. James Niven, "The Relation of Smoke and Health," in Manchester and District Smoke Abatement Society, *The Manchester and Salford Smoke Abatement Exhibition*, 116, for the quotation; see pp. 115–24 for his full paper, including mortality statistics, and the volume's introduction, p. 9, for reference to the statement of Niven's predecessor. Cf. Mooney and Szreter, "Urbanization."

47. Manchester and District Smoke Abatement Society, *Manchester and Salford Smoke Abatement Exhibition*, 25–30 for utility statistics; and Williams and Farnie, *Cotton Mills*, 134, for the electrification of the Acme Mill in Pendleton. Also see Hughes, *Networks of Power*. For a brief description of the municipal hydraulic power system, see Redford and Russell, *History of Local Government in Manchester*, 2:333–52.

48. Manchester and District Smoke Abatement Society, *Manchester and Salford Smoke Abatement Exhibition*, 19, for the quotation.

49. See Niven, "Relation of Smoke and Health," 120–21, for statistics on fog in Manchester; and Luckin, "'The Doom of a Great City.'"

50. Mosley, "'Smoke Nuisance,'" 46, for the quotation; and Stephen Mosley, "Public Perceptions of Smoke Pollution in Victorian Manchester," in *Technologies of Landscape: From Reaping to Recycling*, ed. David E. Nye (Amherst: University of Massachusetts Press, 1999), 161–86. Mosley fails to present any evidence to support his claim that Manchester's working class adopted the position of the chemical industry in regard to air pollution.

51. For the term, see Joel Tarr, *The Search for the Ultimate Sink: Urban Pollution in Historical Perspective* (Akron, OH: University of Akron Press, 1996). For additional insight, also see Arthur F. McEvoy, *The Fisherman's Problem: Ecology and Law in the California Fisheries, 1850–1980* (Cambridge: Cambridge University Press, 1986); and Theodore Steinberg, *Nature Incorporated: Industrialization and the Waters of New England* (New York: Cambridge University Press, 1991).

52. David E. Nye, *American Technological Sublime* (Cambridge, MA: MIT Press, 1994); and Helen A. Harrison, ed., *Dawn of a New Day: The New York World's Fair, 1939/40* (New York: New York University Press for the Queens Museum, 1980).

53. Manchester and District Smoke Abatement Society, *Manchester and Salford Smoke Abatement Exhibition*, 113, for the quotation.

Chapter Fourteen

1. *Chicago Record-Herald*, 19 September 1908, for the quotation; see also *Chicago Record-Herald*, 24 September and 20 October 1908; and *Chicago Tribune*, 2–3 and

8 October 1908. For a general overview of antismoke reform during this period, see R. Dale Grinder, "The Battle for Clean Air: The Smoke Problem in Post–Civil War America," in *Pollution and Reform in American Cities, 1870–1930*, ed. Martin V. Melosi (Austin: University of Texas Press, 1980), 83–104; David Stradling, *Smokestacks and Progressives* (Baltimore: Johns Hopkins University Press, 1999); and Angela Gugliotta, "Class, Gender, and Coal Smoke: Gender Ideology and Environmental Injustice in Pittsburgh, 1868–1914," *Environmental History* 5 (April 2000): 165–93. Biographical information on Annie Myers Sergel is sketchy and mostly comes by way of her husband, Charles Hubbard Sergel. See A. N. Marquis, ed., *The Book of Chicagoans: 1911* (Chicago: Marquis, 1911), 608; and Charles's obituary in *Chicago Tribune*, 8 January 1926.

2. *Chicago Record-Herald*, 2 October 1908, for the quotation; and *Chicago Tribune*, 17 October 1908, for additional, personal accounts of conditions along the IC route. According to air sample studies, Chicago had three times the amount of particulates from air pollution as London. See *Chicago Tribune*, 12 October 1908. For insight on family life during the Gilded Age, see Richard Sennett, *Families against the City: Middle Class Homes of Industrial Chicago, 1872–1890* (Cambridge, MA: Harvard University Press, 1970). Cf. Gwendolyn Wright, *Moralism and the Model Home: Domestic Architecture and Cultural Conflict in Chicago, 1873–1913* (Chicago: University of Chicago Press, 1980).

3. For an introduction to the 1909 Plan of Chicago, see Thomas S. Hines, *Burnham of Chicago: Architect and Planner* (New York: Oxford University Press, 1974).

4. *Chicago Tribune*, 2 October 1908, for the quotation; see also *Chicago Tribune*, 3 October 1908; *Chicago Record-Herald*, 19 September and 6 October 1908. For the origins of Chicago's attachment to its lakefront, see Robin Einhorn, "A Taxing Dilemma: Early Lake Shore Protection," *Chicago History* 18 (Fall 1989): 34–51. For perspectives on the city beautiful movement, see William H. Wilson, *The City Beautiful Movement* (Baltimore: Johns Hopkins University Press, 1989).

5. *Chicago Record-Herald*, 31 July 1908, for the first quotation; *Chicago Record-Herald*, 17 April 1908, for the second quotation; City of Chicago, Department of Health, *Annual Report* (1907–1910): 25, for the third quotation. For a brief introduction to the history of Chicago's antismoke campaigns and local legislation, see the February 1911 report in Chicago Department of Smoke Inspection, *Report of the Department of Smoke Inspection* (Chicago: City of Chicago, 1907–1911); and Chicago Association of Commerce (CAC), *Smoke Abatement and Electrification of Railroad Terminals in Chicago* (Chicago: McNally, 1915), 18–26, 82–96. For an overview of the Busse administration, see Maureen A. Flanagan, "Fred A. Busse: A Silent Mayor in Turbulent Times," in *The Mayors: The Chicago Political Tradition*, ed. Paul M. Green and Melvin G. Holli (Carbondale: Southern Illinois University Press, 1987), 50–60. For Busse's antismoke program, see *Chicago Record-Herald*, 18 April–2 October 1907.

6. *Chicago Record-Herald*, 17 September 1908 and 8, 10, and 20 October 1908.

7. For the role of women reformers, see Maureen A. Flanagan, *Seeing with Their Hearts: Chicago Women and the Vision of the Good City, 1871–1933* (Princeton, NJ: Princeton

University Press, 2002); Gugliotta, "Class"; Linda Kerber, "Separate Spheres, Female Worlds, Women's Place: The Rhetoric of Women's History," *Journal of American History* 75 (June 1988): 9–39; and Suellen Hoy, "'Municipal Housekeeping': The Role of Women in Improving Urban Sanitation Practices, 1880–1917," in Melosi, ed., *Pollution and Reform*, 173–98. Also see Suellen Hoy, *Chasing Dirt: The American Pursuit of Cleanliness* (New York: Oxford University Press, 1995). On "maternal politics," see S. Koven and S. Michel, "Womanly Duties: Maternalist Politics and the Origins of Welfare States in France, Germany, Great Britain and the United States, 1880–1920," *American Historical Review* 95 (October 1990): 1076–1108; and Philip J. Ethington, "Recasting Urban Political History: Gender, the Public, the Household, and Political Participation in Boston and San Francisco during the Progressive Era," *Social Science History* 18 (Summer 1992): 301–33.

8. Adam W. Rome, "Coming to Terms with Pollution: The Language of Environmental Reform, 1865–1915," *Environmental History* 1 (July 1996): 6–28; Theodore Steinberg, *Nature Incorporated: Industrialization and the Waters of New England* (New York: Cambridge University Press, 1991); and John T. Cumbler, *Reasonable Use: The People, the Environment, and the State: New England, 1790–1930* (New York: Oxford University Press, 2001).

9. "Smoke," *Journal of the American Medical Association* 44 (1905): 1619–20. For historical perspectives, see Carlo Cipolla, *Miasmas and Disease: Public Health and the Environment in the Pre-Industrial Era* (New Haven, CT: Yale University Press, 1992); and Michael E. Teller, *The Tuberculosis Movement: A Public Health Campaign in the Progressive Era* (Westport, CT: Greenwood, 1988). For debate among experts in the area of water quality, see J. Tarr, J. McCurley and T. Yosie, "The Development and Impact of Urban Wastewater Technology: Changing Concepts of Water Quality Control, 1850–1930," in Melosi, ed., *Pollution and Reform*, 59–82.

10. For example, see A. Jacobi, "Smoke in Relation to Health," *Journal of the American Medical Association* 49 (1907): 813–15; T. W. Schaifer, "The Contamination of the Air of Our Cities with Sulfur Dioxide, the Cause of Respiratory Disease," *Boston Medical and Surgical Journal* 157 (1907): 106–10; and O. Klotz, "Pulmonary Anthracosis: A Community Disease," *American Journal of Public Health* 7, no. 4 (1914): 887–916. As early as 1882, Chicago's Department of Health had hired a chemist with a Ph.D. as its chief smoke inspector. See City of Chicago, Department of Health, *Annual Report* (1881–1882): 34–44. On governmental involvement in the interrelated areas of water supply and public health, see Louis P. Cain, *Sanitation Strategy for a Lakefront Metropolis: The Case of Chicago* (DeKalb: Northern Illinois University Press, 1978).

11. Nancy Tomes, "The Private Side of Public Health: Sanitary Science, Domestic Hygiene, and the Germ Theory, 1870–1900," *Bulletin of the History of Medicine* 64 (Winter 1990): 529, for the quotation; see also pp. 509–39; Nancy Tomes, *The Gospel of Germs: Men, Women, and the Microbe in American Life* (Cambridge, MA: Harvard University Press, 1998). For insight on the antebellum roots of women's involvement in public health, see Regina Morantz, "Making Women Modern: Middle-Class

Women and Health Reform in Nineteenth-Century America," *Journal of Social History* 10 (June 1977): 490–507. Also see note 7, above.

12. *Chicago Record-Herald*, 21 October 1908.

13. *Chicago's First Half Century: The City as It Was Fifty Years Ago and as It Is Today* (Chicago: Inter-Ocean Publishing Company, 1883), 98.

14. Letter from S. E. Gross to his father, 13 October 1892, Gross papers, Chicago Historical Society. For visitors to Chicago in the 1890s, see Arnold Lewis, *An Early Encounter with Tomorrow: Europeans, Chicago's Loop, and the World's Columbian Exposition* (Urbana: University of Illinois Press, 1997).

15. Chief Smoke Inspector F. U. Adams as quoted in City of Chicago, Department of Health, *Annual Report* (1894): 196–197a; H. G. Wells, *The Future in America* (1906; reprint, New York: Arno, 1974), 59–60, as quoted in James Gilbert, *Perfect Cities* (Chicago: University of Chicago Press, 1991), 209. For the reform effort of the 1890s, see Christine Meisner Rosen, "Businessmen against Pollution in Late Nineteenth Century Chicago," *Business History Review* (Autumn 1995): 351–97.

16. Board of Trade, *Annual Report* (1880–1902); and CAC, *Smoke*, 40, 110. Of the 21.2 million tons of coal in the metropolitan area, 17.6 million tons were consumed in Chicago. For perspectives on the emergence of an energy-intensive society, see Harold L. Platt, *The Electric City: Energy and the Growth of the Chicago Area, 1880–1930* (Chicago: University of Chicago Press, 1991); and David Nye, *Electrifying America: Social Meanings of a New Technology, 1880–1940* (Cambridge, MA: MIT Press, 1992). On the deconcentration of the textile industry in the Manchester area, see Mike Williams and D. A. Farnie, *Cotton Mills in Greater Manchester* (Preston, U.K.: Carnegie, 1992).

17. CAC, *Smoke*, 111–27.

18. Ibid., 48–51, 156, 191, 200–201.

19. Ibid., 103–10, 156–57, 173–74, 210–78, 1123–44.

20. Ibid., 194, for the quoted phrase; see also pp. 40–41, 194–278.

21. F. U. Adams, as quoted in *Chicago Record-Herald*, 27 May 1908. In the 1900–1910 decade, the air quality of other major cities also suffered striking deterioration. In the case of New York City and Philadelphia, the anthracite coal strike of 1902 led to the introduction of cheap soft coal, which remained the fuel of choice for all but home-heating purposes after the strike. In the case of Pittsburgh, the exhaustion of natural gas from nearby wells led to a similar result. See Robert Wiebe, "The Anthracite Strike of 1902: A Record of Confusion," *Mississippi Valley Historical Review* 48 (September 1961): 229–51; and Gugliotta, "Class." For two relevant and highly revealing studies on the social construction of disease, see Barbara E. Smith, *Digging Our Own Graves: Coal Miners and The Struggle Over Black Lung Disease* (Philadelphia: Temple University Press, 1987); and Linda Bryder, *Below the Magic Mountain: A Social History of Tuberculosis in Twentieth-Century Britain* (New York: Oxford University Press, 1988). Bryder points out that "it has never been determined precisely who was the most likely to contract the disease [of tuberculosis]. ... The historian investigating epidemiology often discovers more about

the assumptions and prejudices of the inquirers than about disease patterns themselves" (p. 4).

22. For the early reform effort, See Harold L. Platt, "Creative Necessity: Municipal Reform in Gilded Age Chicago," in *The Constitution, Law, and American Life: Critical Aspects of the Nineteenth-Century Experience*, ed. Donald G. Nieman (Athens: University of Georgia Press, 1992), 162–90; and note 5, above. For the reform effort of the 1890s, see Rosen, "Businessmen Against Pollution."

23. Ibid.; Carl Smith, *Urban Disorder and the Shape of Disbelief* (Chicago: University of Chicago Press, 1995); and Bruce Nelson, *Beyond the Martyrs: A Social History of Chicago's Anarchists, 1870–1910* (New Brunswick, NJ: Rutgers University Press, 1988).

24. For the period from 1894 to 1903, see the smoke inspector reports in City of Chicago, Department of Health, *Annual Report* (1894–1903); for the subsequent period, see note 5, above; City of Chicago, Department of Smoke Inspection, *Report of February 1911*; City of Chicago, Department of Smoke Inspection, *Annual Report* (1912); and the extensive coverage of the department reported in the *Chicago Record-Herald*, 26 September, 2 October, 12 November, and 1 and 11 December 1907; 13 March, 17 and 24–29 April, 5 and 10 May, 31 July, 19 and 23 August, and 1, 18, and 26 September 1908; 26 January, 17 and 30 April, 25 May, 16 September, and 21 October 1909. CAC, *Smoke*, 1123–24, 1145, on experiments with trained versus untrained firemen. In one test using inexperienced workers, boiler efficiency dropped from 73.2 to 59.7 percent, and smoke density doubled from 18 to 36 percent. The tests suggest that a nontechnological solution to the visible smoke problem was available in form of a better-trained labor force. However, this solution could be viable as public policy only to the degree that enforcement of the smoke abatement laws was effective enough that pecuniary penalties would prompt building owners to create a more skilled (and better-paid) workforce.

25. See Kristen S. Schaffer, "Daniel H. Burnham: Urban Ideals and the 'Plan of Chicago,'" (Ph.D. diss., Cornell University, 1993), 342–46, 381–90. This fascinating and important study provides an ingenious analysis of the plan by comparing earlier drafts and the final report. Schaffer shows that many issues concerning social and environmental reform were eliminated from the published version. On Burnham's support of electrification, see *Chicago Record-Herald*, 20 February 1907.

26. Dr. Evans, as quoted in the *Chicago Record-Herald*, 25 November 1908. Also see W. A. Evans, "The Harm of Smoke," in the Committee on Local Transportation's report of 1908, for a fuller discussion of the new public health perspectives on air pollution. On changing perspectives in public health, John Duffy, *The Sanitarians: A History of American Public Health* (Urbana: University of Illinois Press, 1990); Jon A. Peterson, "The Impact of Sanitary Reform upon American Urban Planning," *Journal of Social History* 13 (1979): 84–89; and F. Garvin Davenport, "The Sanitation Revolution in Illinois," *Journal of the Illinois State Historical Society* 66 (1973): 306–26. For an extensive bibliography of contemporary medical literature in the United States and Europe on diseases of the lungs, see CAC, *Smoke*, 1147–59. For the role of the city engineer in policy formation, see Stanley K. Schultz, *Constructing Urban*

Culture: American Cities and City Planning, 1800–1920 (Philadelphia: Temple University Press, 1989); and Eric H. Monkkonen, *America Becomes Urban: The Development of U.S. Cities and Towns, 1780–1980* (Berkeley: University of California Press, 1988).

27. The classic account of this medical history is R. Dubos and J. Dubos, *The White Plague* (Boston: Little, Brown, 1952). For a much better analysis of the American case that incorporates a concept of the social construction of disease, see Teller, *Tuberculosis Movement*, 1–54. A wonderful parallel study of England's public health policy is Bryder, *Below the Magic Mountain*. Another, less valuable history of the English experience is Francis Barrymore Smith, *The Retreat of Tuberculosis, 1850–1950* (London: Croom, Helm, 1988).

28. Charles A. L. Reed, "The Smoke Question Viewed from a National Standpoint," *American Medicine* (29 April 1905): 703.

29. City of Chicago, Department of Health, *Annual Report* (1893): 22–24; and City of Chicago, Department of Health, *Annual Report* (1907–1910): 376, for a statistical summary of deaths in Chicago.

30. "Smoke," *Journal of the American Medical Association*, 1619, for the quotation.

31. See the Department of Smoke Inspections' report of February 1911, p. 27, for the estimate of smoke related damages; *Chicago Record-Herald*, 27 May 1908, for figures on Marshall Field's losses; and Mrs. John B. Sherwood, as quoted in Grinder, "Battle for Clean Air," 86.

32. Rome, "Coming to Terms"; Christine Meisner Rosen, "Differing Perceptions of the Value of Pollution Abatement across Time and Place: Balancing Doctrine in Pollution Nuisance Law, 1840–1906," *Law and History Review* 11 (January 1993): 303–81.

33. *Harmon v. City of Chicago* 110 Ill 406 (1884), for the quotation. For a general overview of the common law, see H. G. Wood, *A Practical Treatise on the Law of Nuisances* (Albany, NY: Parsons, 1875), 470–535. In Illinois, the leading cases involving the use of injunctions to abate an environmental nuisance include, *Ottawa Gas-Light Company v. Thompson* 39 Ill 598 (1864); *Cooper v. Randall* 53 Ill 24 (1869); and *Oehler v. Levy* 234 Ill 595 (1908). In a local case at the time of the women's crusade, the Department of Health closed a malting plant on the South Side as a nuisance because it emitted unbearable foul odors. The malting operation was kept closed until it installed devices to neutralize the sour smells rising from the roof. See City of Chicago, Department of Health, *Annual Report* (1906): 190–92.

34. CAC, *Smoke*, 284. For insight on the politics of Chicago's antismoke legislation, see Mayor J. P. Hopkins, City of Chicago, Office of the Mayor, *Annual Report* (1894): xi–xii; Frederick Adams, Smoke Inspector, *Annual Report* (1894), 201–14, which contains a summary of the proceedings of the coal suppliers' conference; and the Department of Smoke Inspections' report of February 1911, pp. 14–16.

35. See note 7, above.

36. Teller, *Tuberculosis Movement*; William H. Wilson, *The City Beautiful Movement* (Baltimore: Johns Hopkins University Press, 1989); Isaac D. Rawlings et al., *The Rise and Fall of Disease in Illinois*, 2 vols. (Springfield, IL: Schepp and Barnes, 1927), 1:364–95. Also see Samuel Haber, *Efficiency and Uplift: Scientific Management in the Progressive*

Era 1880–1920 (Chicago: University of Chicago Press, 1964); and Samuel P. Hays, *Conservation and the Gospel of Efficiency: The Progressive Conservation Movement 1890–1920* (Cambridge, MA: Harvard University Press, 1959).

37. The women cannot be faulted for giving up or for being lulled into believing that their demands were being met. Sergel, Sherwood, and other representatives of women's organizations continued to confront Mayor Busse and IC officials, demanding that they to translate pledges into action. However, as these promises wore thin over a year's time, the women were treated with condescension, were patronized, and were eventually locked out. See *Chicago Record-Herald*, 24 November 1908; and 6 and 7 January, 5 February, 15 and 17 April, 9 June, 8 July, and 1, 21, and 29 October 1909.

38. Committee on Local Transportation's report of 1908, p. 7.

39. Ibid., 20.

40. Ibid., 37, for the first quotation; *Chicago Tribune*, 20 October 1908, for the second quotation. Engineering and economic experts also made an extensive report on the feasibility of electrification of the IC lines. See *Chicago Tribune*, 20 October 1908. Dr. Evans took issue with the American Medical Association editorial (see notes 9 and 10, above). Refuting its position, Evans cited several contrary scientific studies and declared that air pollution was indeed a medical as well as a social problem. See Evans, "Harm of Smoke," 22–27.

41. For extensive coverage of the IC decision and local reaction, see *Chicago Record-Herald*, 21–29 October 1909.

42. *Chicago Tribune*, 3 and 12 June 1913; CAC, *Smoke*. At least ten of the thirteen staff members were employed by the railroad companies. Twelve were engineers; one was a statistician.

43. See the Department of Smoke Inspection's report of February 1911, p. 39, for the first quotation; Samuel Insull, "The Relation of Central-Station Generation to Railroad Electrification," in *Central-Station Electric Service*, ed. W. E. Keily (Chicago: privately printed, 1915), 255, for the second quotation, and 255–307 for Insull's full report.

44. Insull, "Relation of Central-Station Generation." The estimates of coal savings were based on calculations of a steam-to-electric ratio of 2.55 to 1. See Insull, "Relation of Central-Station Generation," 299.

45. *Chicago Tribune*, 4 June 1913, for the first quotation, and 9 April 1913, for the second quotation. Although the railroads were caught off guard by Lang's revelations, they soon recovered and struck back with an ultimatum of their own. Unless the city dropped its insistence upon participating in the planning of a new terminal for the Near West Side and approved the railroad's proposal, the companies would refuse to build any additional facilities. The ultimatum was clearly tied to an attempt to force the city to reverse Lang's victory in gaining approval for an electrification ordinance. In the end, the railroads prevailed. See *Chicago Record-Herald*, 10–13 June 1913; *Chicago Tribune*, 3–5 November 1915.

46. Evans, "Harm of Smoke," 20–21, for the first quotation; CAC, *Smoke*, 75–76, for the second quotation; and "The Smoke Nuisance," *Journal of the American Medical*

Association 65 (30 October 1915): 1575, for the third quotation. Important in the establishment of a link between coal smoke and disease was the work of European doctors and scientists, especially in London. See the bibliography of contemporary sources listed in CAC, *Smoke*, 1147–59; and Bill Luckin, *Questions of Power: Electricity and Environment in Inter-War Britain* (Manchester: Manchester University Press, 1990).

47. Teller, *Tuberculosis Movement*, 67. As Teller points out, the change in epidemiology from a social to an individual focus also brought a shift from cleaning up the environment to treating sick persons in isolation wards.

48. *Chicago Tribune*, 4 November, 3 and 9 December 1915. The city's smoke abatement officials also issued a scathing rebuttal that highlights many of the CAC report's dubious assumptions. See City of Chicago, Department of Smoke Inspection, "General Review of the Report of the Chicago Association of Commerce on Electricity and Smoke Abatement" (typescript, Municipal Reference Library, 1915). For additional insight on the railroad companies, see David Stradling and Joel A. Tarr, "Environmental Activism, Locomotive Smoke and the Corporate Response: The Case of the Pennsylvania Railroad and Chicago Smoke Control," *Business History Review* 73 (Winter 1999): 677–704.

49. City of Chicago, Department of Health, *Annual Report* (1911–1918): xvii, for the quotation. Air quality deteriorated rapidly with the approach of the war, possibly putting Chicago behind Pittsburgh in the battle against pollution. See *Chicago Tribune*, 8–10 March 1917. For perspectives on World War I, see Platt, *Electric City*; and Harold L. Platt, "World War I and the Birth of American Regionalism," *Journal of Policy History* 5 (1993): 128–52.

Chapter Fifteen

1. Lincoln Steffens, *The Shame of the Cities* (New York: McClure, Philips, 1904).

2. Gifford Pinchot, *Breaking New Ground* (New York: Harcourt, Brace, Jovanovich, 1947), 320–36, in *American Environmentalism: Readings in Conservation History*, 3rd edition, ed. Roderick Frazier Nash (New York: McGraw-Hill, 1990), 73–79, 80.

3. City of Manchester, Medical Officer of Health *Annual Report* (1921), 23; and City of Chicago, Department of Health *Annual Report* (1911–1918), 1425.

4. Chicago Association of Commerce, *Smoke Abatement and Electrification of Railroad Terminals in Chicago* (Chicago: McNally, 1915), 193.

5. Robert M. Fogelson, *The Fragmented Metropolis: Los Angeles, 1850–1930* (Cambridge, MA: Harvard University Press, 1967); and Mike Davis, *The City of Quartz* (New York: Vintage, 1990). Also see Mike Davis, *Ecology of Fear: Los Angeles and the Imagination of Disaster* (New York: Metropolitan Books/Henry Holt, 1998); and Adam Rome, *The Bulldozer in the Countryside: Suburban Sprawl and the Rise of American Environmentalism* (New York: Cambridge University Press, 2001).

INDEX

Abbot, Hugh, 293
Abbott, Edith, 341, 349
Adams, Annmarie, 303-4
Adams, Francis, 176-77
Adams, Frederick, 479
Addams, Jane, 16, 22, 305, 307, 331,
    333-61, 383, 396, 423, 478
Age of Energy, 231, 493
Age of Industry, 201
Age of Steam, 9, 231
Aiken, J., 31, 35-37, 46, 52-53
air pollution: in Chicago, 117, 168-69, 247,
    295-96, 468-91; and industrial cities,
    230-31, 250-51, 266-68, 302, 310-11,
    497-98; in Manchester, 44, 48, 203-4,
    442-67; in rural areas, 236, 245, 248.
    See also coal; nuisance abatement
Alison, William, 64
Alkali Act of 1881, 458. See also air
    pollution
Allen, Rev. G. S., 215-16
Allison, John, 398

Allsopp brewery, 273, 279
Altrincham, England, 209
American Institute of Electrical
    Engineers, 487
American Medical Association, 483, 488.
    See also Journal of the American Medical
    Association
American Public Health Association, 158
American Water Works Association, 435
Ancoats Brotherhood. See Ancoats
    Recreation Movement
Ancoats district (Manchester), 51-55,
    69-70, 75-76, 164, 212, 222, 225, 267,
    311-12, 313-32, 394, 460-62. See also
    Holt Town; Rowley, Charles; slums;
    urban space
Ancoats Healthy Homes Society. See
    Healthy Homes Society
Ancoats Recreation Movement, 305,
    318-19, 331. See also Rowley,
    Charles
Andrews, E., 142-44

Anheuser-Busch Brewing Company, 239, 282–83, 287–88

Anti–Corn Law League, 68

antismoke laws. *See* nuisance abatement

Anti-Smoke League, 468–73, 480–88. *See also* air pollution, in Chicago; nuisance abatement; Sergel, Annie Myers

Appel, Susan, 266

Ardern, Edward, 438

Ardwick and Ancoats Dispensary, 64, 70–71

Ardwick Green (Manchester), 49

Arkwright, Richard, 38

Army Corps of Engineers, 87–92, 146, 373, 376, 409, 423, 430–32

Arts and Crafts Movement, 305. *See also* Romanticism

Back of the Yards (Chicago). *See* Packingtown

back-to-backs. *See* housing

bacteriology. *See* environmental science; medical science

Bacterium Club, 273–76, 279, 291–92. *See also* brewing industry; Brown, Horace T.

Bailey, Charles, 459

Bailey, G. H., 459–62

Baldwin, Peter, 306

Ball, Charles, 357–58, 360

balloon frame. *See* wood, as building material

Ban River (Ireland), 201

Bartlett, Rev. W. A., 347

Barton Aqueduct, 27–28

Barton Moss (Manchester), 27

Bass brewery, 273, 279

Bateman, John Frederic, 201, 213; and meteorology, 201–3, 224; and water management, 220–21, 227–29; and water standards, 180; and water supply, 205–6, 227, 389–93. *See also* Lake Thirlmere reservoir plan;

Longdendale Valley reservoirs; water management

Bateman-Lynde plan, 228, 230, 398, 399

Belfield, W. T., 193

Bellamy, Edward, 297, 302, 307, 334, 497

Bellhouse, J. & W., 212

Bennett Street Sunday School (St. Paul's), 317

Berlin, Germany, 85

Biehn, Joseph F., 431–32

Binney, E. W., 227

biology. *See* environmental science; medical science

Bird, Paul S., 469–70

Birley family, 211–12

Birmingham, England, 4, 198, 292

Bixby, W. H., 432

Blackley Estate, 331. *See also* housing

Black Monday riot of 8 February 1886, 394

Blaine, Anita McCormick, 341

Blake, H., 302, 308–9

Board of Consulting Physicians, 148

Board of Public Works (BPW) (Chicago), 133, 140, 149, 152–54

Board of Sewerage Commissioners (Chicago), 121–22

Board of Trade. *See* Chicago Board of Trade

Bolton, England, 39, 55, 384, 463

Boone, Levi, 110, 132

Booth (Mayor), 226

Borough Funds Act, 418

Bosdin, Sir Leech T., 419–20

Boulton, Matthew, 40

Boulton and Watts engines. *See* steam engines

Boundary Water Treaty of 1909, 429

Boyer, Paul, 307–8

Bradley, Nathaniel, 408, 410

Braidwood, Illinois, 246, 248–50

Brainard, Daniel, 110

Brand, Michael, 283–85

Brand, Rudolph, 284. *See also* Brand breweries

Brand breweries, 283–85. *See also* Brand, Michael; Brand, Rudolph; Lion Brewery

brewing industry: and agricultural production, 243–45; and bottled beer, 286–91; and the British syndicates in Chicago, 280–86; in Chicago, 118, 126–31, 232–33, 268–71, 282–86; in England/UK, 242–43, 258–59, 273–80, 282, 291–94; mechanization of, 262–66, 284–86, 289–91, 293; and prohibition, 235–36, 238, 288, 290–91, 292; and quality control, 239–40, 258, 260–61, 276, 281, 293; and science, 240, 258–62, 273–80; and "scientific brewing," 235, 240–41, 262, 265–66, 273–75, 277–78, 282, 284–86; in the United States, 232–33, 290, 292. *See also* horses; Pasteur, Louis; public houses; saloons; *and individual breweries*

Bridgewater Canal. *See* transportation, and canals in Manchester

Briggs, Asa, 15, 21, 23

Bright, John, 210, 447

Bross, William, 180

Brotherhood of Ancoats. *See* Ancoats Recreation Movement

Broughton Bridge, 226

Broughton district (Manchester), 196–97, 207–8, 209, 214–15, 296

Brown, Ford Madox, 317

Brown, Horace T., 273–75, 279–80, 291, 293. *See also* Bacterium Club; brewing industry; Institute of Brewing

Browne, Balfour, 419–20

Bubbly Creek, 435. *See also* Packingtown

Budweiser. *See* Anheuser-Busch Brewing Company

Burghardt, Charles A., 397–98

Burnham, Daniel, 297, 334, 469, 480, 497. *See also* Plan of Chicago; World's Columbian Exposition of 1893

Burton-upon-Trent, England, 273–74, 278–81

Busch, Adolphus, 287. *See also* Anheuser-Busch Brewing Company

Bushnell, Horace, 306

Busse, Fred, 432, 469–70, 484, 486–87

Cal-Sag canal. *See* Sanitary District of Chicago

Calumet District (Chicago), 387, 424–27, 432. *See also* Sanitary District of Chicago

Calumet Plan, 149–50, 154

Canada, 428–31

canals. *See* Illinois and Michigan Canal; Manchester Ship Canal; Sanitary District of Chicago; transportation

Carlsberg brewery, 261

Carrington Moss district (Manchester), 400, 412

Carter, William, 176–77

central-station technology. *See* electricity; gas lighting

Chadwick, Edwin, 26, 70, 72, 122, 138, 146, 306, 447–48. *See also* Sanitary Idea

Chandler, Alfred, Jr., 126

Chartist, 204

chemistry. *See* environmental science; medical science

Chesbrough, Ellis S.: and sewerage/drainage, 149, 153; and water management, 121–23, 135–36, 139, 142, 152, 156, 184, 188–89, 367; and water supply, 141–42, 145–46

Chicago: bridges in, 78, 101–3; as entrepôt, 85–92, 95–97, 122–23; environmental setting of, 8–9, 78–81, 85–95, 106–7, 139; fires in, 108, 112, 163–64, 172, 178; Germans in, 104, 127–29, 172–74, 236–37, 252, 262, 266; great annexation of 1889, 287; harbor of, 90–92, 95–97, 122–23, 146; population of, 96, 104, 132, 237, 240, 295; as shock

Chicago (cont.)
city, 295. *See also* air pollution; brewing industry; Civil Service Commission; class formation; environmental justice; environmental science; epidemics; floods; gas lighting; horses; housing; Irish Catholics; medical science; political culture; public health; sanitation; slums; streets and sidewalks; transportation; water management; water pollution
Chicago Academy of Homeopathic Physicians and Surgeons, 190
Chicago and Alton Railroad Company, 253
Chicago Association of Commerce (CAC), 475–79, 484, 486–89
Chicago Board of Trade, 86, 117, 144, 154, 157, 243. *See also* Committee of Thirty
Chicago Brewers, Limited, 282
Chicago College of Pharmacy, 158
Chicago Department of Health, 145, 157–61, 191–92, 336–38, 381, 386–87
Chicago Department of Public Works, 176–79, 183–84, 186, 189, 194, 381. *See also* Chesbrough, Ellis S.; Cregier, DeWitt Clinton; sanitation; surplus fund; water management
Chicago harbor. *See under* Chicago
Chicago Hydraulic Company, 107–9, 110, 121
Chicago Medical College, 367
Chicago Medical Society, 145, 157, 193, 348, 384. *See also* epidemics; medical science, in Chicago; public health
Chicago River, 78–80, 85, 91–92, 117–18, 144–45, 149, 154–56, 166, 186–89, 191, 284, 346–47, 362, 366–67, 373–76, 378, 385, 409, 422–23, 431. *See also* Great Lakes; Illinois and Michigan Canal; Lake Michigan; water management; water pollution
Chicago River Commission, 150
Chorlton-upon-Medlock district (Manchester), 76, 225, 327

Cincinnati, Ohio, 282
Citizens' Association of Chicago, 173–75, 247, 354, 359, 365–72, 385, 479
City Homes Society, 335, 341–43, 357–58. *See also* Addams, Jane; housing, in Chicago; Hull-House; slums, in Chicago
city planning, 301–4, 306, 310, 331, 334–35, 480. *See also* urban space
Civic Federation, 333
Civil Service Commission (CSC), 350–51, 352–55
Clarke, Charles, 357–58
class formation: in Chicago, 162–63, 171–75, 246, 252–54, 256–57, 286–88, 290; and industrial cities, 10, 238; in Manchester, 53–54, 56–67, 204, 208, 223, 311–12, 314–16; in rural areas, 250
Clavering, Eric, 30
Cleansing Department, 397. *See also* sanitation, in Manchester
coal: and coal dealers, 114, 251, 484; and coal miners, 250; and coal mining, 28–30, 246–50; as fuel, 12, 27–30, 39, 55–56, 113–17, 185–86, 245–46, 268, 446–47, 470, 473–80. *See also* air pollution; class formation, in rural areas; energy systems, cities as
coal mining. *See under* coal
Cobden, Richard, 47, 62–63, 68, 210
Commission of Health (Chicago), 435
Committee of One Hundred. *See* Citizens' Association of Chicago
Committee of Thirty, 149–54
Conrad Seipp Brewery, 270, 283
conurbation. *See under* Manchester
Cook County, Illinois, 97–98, 120
Cook County Drainage Commission, 120
Cooley, Lyman E., 370–76, 409, 422–23, 431, 497
Cornell, Paul, 167–69. *See also* Hyde Park
Corporation (in Manchester). *See* Manchester Corporation

cotton. *See* textile industry

Cotton Famine, 215, 222–23, 449. *See also* textile industry

Cottonopolis. *See* Manchester

Cregier, DeWitt Clinton, 136, 156, 184, 189, 194, 363, 372, 380–81, 404

Crescent district (Salford), 196, 207–8, 215, 221, 226

Crompton, Samuel, 36, 42–44, 46

Cronon, William, 79, 85–86, 163, 243

Crosfield, J. H., 316, 318, 323–24

Cross Street Chapel (Manchester), 57, 62, 64, 68

Dalton, John, 31, 201

Dancer, J. B., 451

Danforth, I. N., 193

Davis, Allen, 359

Davis, Nathan, 110–11, 145, 147–48, 159, 193

Davyhulme sewerage treatment facility, 402, 409, 412–14, 418–21, 437–38. *See also* environmental science; sanitation; water management; water pollution

Deansgate district (Manchester), 74

Dearborn Street bridge. *See* Chicago, bridges in

deep-cut canal. *See under* Illinois and Michigan Canal

Delafontaine, M., 367

Denton, J. Bailey, 398

Department for the Inspection of Steam Boilers and Steam Plants, 480, 484. *See also* Department of Smoke Inspection

Department of Health. *See* Chicago Department of Health

Department of Public Works. *See* Chicago Department of Public Works

Department of Smoke Inspection, 486–87. *See also* Department for the Inspection of Steam Boilers and Steam Plants

Des Plaines Plan, 150–52

Des Plaines River, 80, 85, 141, 150–51, 187

DeWolf, Oscar C., 191–92, 363–64

Dexter, Wirt, 150

Dibdin, William, 410, 414–16

Dickens, Charles, 64

Didsbury. *See* suburbs, and Manchester

Dillon, Isaiah, 124

Dillon family horse farm, 252–53

Disraeli, Benjamin, 64

District No. 1 in Ancoats. *See* Ancoats district

Diversey, Michael, 127

Dore, John C., 177

Douglas, Mary, 20, 68

Douglas, Stephen, 92–93, 132

Drainage and Water Supply Commission, 367–68, 370, 424. *See also* Sanitary District of Chicago; water management

drainage channel (Chicago). *See* Sanitary District of Chicago

Drescher, Seymour, 4

dressed beef industry, 154, 164–69, 238–39. *See also* Packingtown

Dreyfus, Henry, 466–67

Drinkwater, Peter, 39, 446

Ducat, Arthur C., 136

Duis, Perry, 87

Duke of Bridgewater. *See* Egerton, Francis

Dyer, Charles, 109–11

E. Anheuser Brewing Company. *See* Anheuser-Busch Brewing Company

Eastern Interior Coal Basin, 484

Edison, Thomas A., 443

Egerton, Francis (Duke of Bridgewater), 27–30, 40–41, 44, 225, 493

Einhorn, Robin, 81, 103

Eldred, Fred, 352

electricity, 237, 256, 271, 289, 330, 334–35, 443, 464–65, 487. *See also* hydroelectric power systems

Ellsworth Zouaves, 136

energy systems, cities as, 12–15, 27–30, 104–5, 113–17, 126–27, 156, 230–37, 245–49, 266–68, 272–72, 291, 294–97, 463–67, 473–80, 487–91, 493–98. *See also* air pollution; coal; electricity; horses; industrial cities; petroleum; sanitation; steam engines; technology; transportation; water pollution; waterpower; wood

Engels, Friedrich, 16–17, 20, 69, 203, 296

environmental justice: in Chicago, 111, 125, 160–61, 173–75, 267–71, 333–61, 379–83, 385–86, 388, 469–73, 498; and industrial cities, 17–23, 24, 199–200; in Manchester, 68–74, 208–11, 213, 217–19, 222–23, 296–97, 321–28, 398–99, 402–3, 440, 444–45, 498. *See also* Manchester, and municipal capitalism; political culture; Progressivism; social environmentalism; surplus fund; urban space

environmental science, 200–203, 216, 220, 229, 376, 443, 454–56, 473, 482, 488–91; and biology/bacteriology, 366–67, 388–89, 405, 409–10, 412–17, 418–21, 437–40; and chemistry, 141, 190, 370, 397–98. *See also* air pollution; Davyhulme sewerage treatment facility; medical science; sanitation; water pollution

epidemics: cholera epidemic of 1832, 53, 61–62, 63–67, 494; cholera epidemic of 1849–1855, 80, 105–6, 108–11; cholera (and erysipelas) epidemic of 1863–1866, 142–44, 147–48, 157, 216; cholera epidemic of 1885, 363; cholera epidemic of 1890, 381, 383; typhoid fever epidemic of 1890–1893, 377–79, 381–87; great influenza pandemic of 1919, 490; infantile paralysis epidemic of 1916–1917, 490; typhoid fever epidemic of 1902, 343–50, 409, 423; typhoid fever epidemic of 1911, 432–33. *See also* medical science; public health; sanitation; water pollution

Ericson, John E., 405–6

Erie Canal–Great Lakes route, 85–87

Estcourt, Charles, 455–56

Etherow River. *See* Longdendale Valley reservoirs; Mersey-Irwell Rivers Basin

Ethical Culture Society, 340

Études sur la bière (Pasteur), 241, 273

Evans, W. A., 432, 481, 486

Exchange Building, 25, 47, 51, 58, 448–50

factory. *See* brewing industry; dressed beef industry; textile industry

Fairbairn, William, 201–2, 446

Faraday, Michael, 263

Faucher, Léon, 16, 69, 203, 204

Fetter, Frank A., 341

Field, Marshall, 372, 483

Field Naturalists Society. *See* Manchester Field Naturalists Society

Fishman, Robert, 17, 49, 68

Flanagan, Maureen, 359

Flather, J. J., 434–35

Fleming, Thomas, 59–60

floods: in Chicago, 78–81, 93–94, 151, 187–88, 362–64; in Manchester/Salford, 34, 196–98, 200, 202, 205–7, 211–15, 223–25, 227, 296. *See also* water management

Ford, Henry, 291. *See also* Model T

Foster, J. W., 115–16

Fowler, Gilbert John, 420, 438

France, 241–43

Frankland, Edward, 216–17, 219–20

Frankland, Percy, 420

Fullerton Avenue Conduit, 188–90, 192–93. *See also* Lake Michigan; public health; water management

Gage, George W., 153

Gage, Lyman, 372

Gale, Edwin, 107–8

garden cities, 301–2, 311–12, 331.
See also city planning

Gaskell, Elizabeth, 64

gas lighting: in Chicago, 116; and
industrial cities, 271–72, 443, 453; in
Manchester, 48, 60–61, 71, 327, 458–59,
462, 464–65

Gatrell, V. A. C., 61

Geddes, Norman Bell, 466–67

Gehrmann, Adolph, 387

Gem of the Prairies. See Chicago

Germantown. See Chicago, Germans in

Germany, 85, 240–42, 259, 273, 282

germ theories. See medical science

Ghetto district (Chicago), 342, 348

Gildea, John W., 10, 356

Gilmore (Dr.), 383–84

Gindele, John G., 149–51, 153

Glasgow, 75

Gooding, William, 150–51, 153–54,
177

Gottfried, Matheus, 129

Gourvish, T. R., 276–78, 280

Graham, John W., 465

Graham, William, 463

Grave, John, 390–93

Greater Manchester, 399–400. See also
Manchester, as conurbation

Great Lakes, 85–86, 364, 376, 428–31,
437–39. See also Army Corps of
Engineers; Lake Michigan; water
management

Gross, S. E., 474

Grosvenor Square (Manchester), 49

Gruenhut, Joseph, 178

Grundy (Alderman), 215–16, 318

Guinness brewery, 281

Gurnee, Walter, 108

Guthrie, Ossian E., 366–67, 374

Haas, William, 127

Hamilton, Alice, 345–48

Hamlin, Christopher, 64, 208, 410, 439

Hanbury, J. M., 277–78

Handbury, Thomas, 376. See also Army
Corps of Engineers

Hansen, Emil Christian, 261

Harahan, John T., 470

Hargreaves, James, 35

Harper, William Rainey, 351–52

Harrison I, Carter H., 175, 184, 189–90,
194, 339

Harrison II, Carter H., 339, 349, 351–52,
356–57

Hart, Ernest, 442

Harwood, Sir John, 394–95, 414–15, 419–20

Hayes, S. S., 152

Health Department. See Chicago
Department of Health

Healthy Homes Society, 305, 319–20,
326–27. See also Rowley, Charles

Herget, James, 120

Hering, Rudolph, 368–70, 376, 378,
429–30

Hering Commission. See Drainage and
Water Supply Commission

Heron, Sir Joseph, 63, 208, 217–18, 222,
226–27, 321

Herrmann, Ernst F., 357

Hesing, Anton, 173

Heywood, Abel, 317

Heywood, John, 317

Hill, Octavia, 391–93, 442, 496–97

Holden, C., 152–53

Holland, H. P., 76, 203–4

Holland, Robert, 456

Holmes, Oliver Wendell, 427–28. See also
United States Supreme Court

Holmfirth, England, 197–99, 206, 214–15

Holt Town (Manchester), 212, 222, 325,
397, 400

Home Secretary, 463

Hopkins, John, 386
hops. *See* brewing industry, and
  agricultural production
horses: and power, 30, 38; and
  transportation, 28, 38, 40–41, 46, 49,
  95, 98–101, 118, 119, 123–24, 126–27,
  176, 251–57, 286–87, 475–76. *See also*
  streets and sidewalks
housing: in Chicago, 98–99, 118, 162,
  166–71, 169–70, 173–74, 382–83; and
  health, 301–4, 306; in Manchester,
  69–74, 215, 311–12; and reform, 301–9,
  313; and reform in Chicago, 340–44;
  and reform in Manchester, 313–32,
  401–2. *See also* Addams, Jane; Rowley,
  Charles; slums; suburbs; urban space
Housing Code Ordinance of 1890
  (Manchester), 396
Howard, Ebenezer, 301–3, 307, 311, 331,
  497
Howard, Richard Baron, 70, 71, 203
Howe, Frederic C., 312
Hubbard, Gurdon, 97
Huck, John A., 129
Huck, Louis C., 265–66, 283
Hull-House, 333–34, 336–40, 342, 350–53.
  See also Addams, Jane
Hulme (Manchester), 75–76, 327
Humphrey Booth Charities, 208
Hunter, Robert, 341
Hyde (Manchester), 76
Hyde Park (Chicago), 164, 167–69, 267,
  295, 362, 424, 427, 432–33, 435–36
hydraulic power systems, 400
hydroelectric power systems, 425, 428, 430
Hygeia, 301–2. *See also* Richardson,
  Benjamin Ward

ice, 128–30, 260, 284, 287, 289. *See also*
  brewing industry, mechanization of
Illinois, state government of, 120, 150,
  153–54, 168, 250, 370–72, 373–74.
  See also Illinois State Board of Health

Illinois and Michigan Canal (I&M Canal),
  86, 87, 141–42, 144–45, 151, 187; and
  the deep-cut plan, 139, 153–57, 175–77,
  186–88, 422–23. *See also* water
  management
Illinois Central Railroad, 92, 114–17,
  122–23, 149, 167, 253, 468–69, 485–91
Illinois River, 85, 93, 370–71, 373–76, 409,
  421–22, 425, 439. *See also* Chicago
  River; Sanitary District of Chicago;
  water management
Illinois River Valley. *See* Illinois and
  Michigan Canal; Illinois River;
  Sanitary District of Chicago; water
  management
Illinois State Board of Health, 158, 187,
  370, 385. *See also* Rauch, John H.; Reilly,
  Frank W.
industrial cities, 7–11, 13–14, 196–99,
  230–31, 232–37, 257–58, 266–72,
  294–97, 328. *See also* brewing industry;
  Chicago; dressed beef industry; energy
  systems, cities as; Manchester; shock
  cities; textile industry
industrial revolution, 28, 30, 34–44.
  See also textile industry
Inikori, Joseph E., 35
Inland Waterways Commission, 428–29
Institute of Brewing, 291–94. *See also*
  brewing industry
Insull, Samuel, 487, 489
Interstate Canal and River Convention of
  1887, 376. *See also* Sanitary District of
  Chicago
Irish Catholics: in Chicago, 104, 173, 175,
  237, 252, 384; in Manchester, 65–66,
  74, 197, 211–12, 219, 225–26, 407
Irk River. *See* Mersey-Irwell Rivers Basin
Irwell Flood Committee, 220
Irwell River. *See* Mersey-Irwell Rivers Basin

Jersey City, New Jersey, 434–35
Jewish Ghetto. *See* Ghetto district

Johnson, George A., 434–36
Joint Rivers Authority. *See* Mersey and
    Irwell Joint Committee
Joliet, Illinois, 176, 187
Joliet, Louis, 85
Jordan, Edwin Oakes, 423–27
Journal of the American Medical Association,
    424. *See also* American Medical
    Association
Junk, Joseph, 284–85
Junk, Magdalena, 284–85, 289
Junk's brewery, 284–85

Kay[-Shuttleworth], James P., 16–17, 64–67,
    71–72, 209
Keating, Ann, 167
Kelly, Florence, 336, 339, 341
Kelly, John S., 352–54
Kilgubbin district (Chicago), 118
Kinder Printing Company, 220
Kinzie, John, 96–97
Koch, Robert, 369, 443, 451, 482.
    See also medical science

Ladies' Branch of the MSSA. *See* women, in
    Manchester
lager beer riot of 21 April 1855, 132
lager-style beer. *See* brewing industry
Lake Calumet, 93. *See also* Calumet District
Lake District, England. *See* Lake Thirlmere
    reservoir plan
Lake Michigan, 80, 87–93, 137–39, 155,
    296, 334, 346–47, 365–67, 370, 376,
    387–89, 405, 424–27, 431–33, 437.
    See also Chicago River; environmental
    science; Great Lakes; water
    management; water pollution
Lake Michigan Water Association, 432
Lake Plan. *See* Calumet Plan
Lakes-to-the-Gulf Deep Waterway
    Association, 497
Lake Thirlmere reservoir plan, 227,
    329–30, 389–95, 402–3, 414, 418

Lancashire Smoke Abatement League,
    463
Landis, Kenesaw Mountain, 436–37
Lang, Theodore K., 486–88
Larned, Edwin C., 144, 149–50.
    See also Committee of Thirty
LaSalle, Illinois, 115–17, 248
Lathrop, Julia, 341
Latour, Bruno, 450–51
Lederer, John, 432
Leech, Sir Bosdin T., 419–20
Lehle, Louis, 284
Leigh, John, 216–17, 220, 222, 316, 323–24,
    329, 398–99, 444–45, 450–53, 472
Lerner, Max, 4
Letchworth, England, 311. *See also* garden
    cities
Levinstein, Ivan, 457
Lewis, M. J., 45, 54
Liberals. *See* political culture, of
    Manchester
Lib-Lab alliance, 394–95. *See also* political
    culture, of Manchester
Lieb, Herman, 178
Lill, William, 127
Lill and Diversey brewery, 127–30, 239–40
Lindberg, Richard C., 178
Linde, Carl, 241, 263
Lion Brewery, 284. *See also* Brand breweries
Lit and Phil. *See* Manchester Literary and
    Philosophical Society
Little Ireland district (Manchester), 197,
    211–12
Liverpool, England, 34, 230, 314, 328, 390,
    398, 408
Lloyd (mayor of Manchester), 414
Lloyd-Jones, Robin, 45, 54
Local Government Act. *See* Parliament
Local Government Board, 399, 402–3, 408,
    412–13, 418–20, 458–59, 463
Lockett, W. T., 438
Lock Katrine, 390
Lockport, Illinois, 421

London, 49, 75, 138, 167, 198, 230, 258–62, 276–81, 292, 324, 341, 390, 443, 458, 474, 493

Long, John Henry, 192–93, 367

Longdendale Valley reservoirs, 203, 205–7, 211, 214, 390, 394–95. *See also* Bateman, John Frederic; floods; Manchester; water management

Looking Backward (Bellamy), 297, 307

Lord Bishop of Carlyle, 391–93

Los Angeles, California, 498

Luckin, Bill, 62

Lynde, James G., 213, 228, 412

MacFarlane, James, 246–48

Machine Age, 252, 286, 297, 466, 475, 498. *See also* Progressivism

Mackenzie, A., 430–32

Main Branch (of the Chicago River). *See* Chicago River

malt liquor industry. *See* brewing industry

Manchester: and brewing industry, 292; as conurbation, 25–27, 44–45, 55, 216, 313–14, 398, 462–63; environmental setting of, 6, 31–34, 201, 206–9, 444–45; and municipal capitalism, 71–74, 325, 327, 330–31, 390, 396, 400–401, 406–7, 458–59; police commission of, 58–63; population of, 26, 46, 54–55, 313–14, 330; and public baths, 318. *See also* air pollution; class formation; Davyhulme sewerage treatment facility; environmental justice; environmental science; epidemics; floods; gas lighting; horses; housing; Irish Catholics; political culture; public health; sanitation; slums; streets and sidewalks; suburbs; textile industry; transportation; water management; water pollution

Manchester and Salford Noxious Vapours Abatement Association (MSNVAA), 453–59

Manchester and Salford Sanitary Association (MSSA), 209–10, 212, 216, 222, 322–27, 331, 401, 451–53

Manchester Corporation, 204–5, 211, 222, 224, 226, 415

Manchester Cottons, 31. *See also* textile industry

Manchester Field Naturalists Society, 458–63, 478

Manchester Hospital for Consumption and Diseases of the Throat, 455

Manchester Liberals. *See* political culture, of Manchester

Manchester Literary and Philosophical Society, 200–203, 227, 397–98, 448–50

Manchester Police Act of 1844, 58–63

Manchester Royal Infirmary, 454–55

Manchester Ship Canal, 314, 394–95, 398, 400, 402–3, 409, 417

Manchester Statistical Society, 64–65, 68

Manchester University Settlement, 312

Marquette, Jacques, 85

Marsh, Margaret, 309

Marshall, W. L., 373. *See also* Army Corps of Engineers

Mason, Roswell B., 149, 153–54, 176

Massachusetts Experimental Station, 410, 423, 438–39. *See also* environmental science

Mathias, Peter, 130

Mavor, William, 343, 348

McAlpine, William J., 109, 111–13

McArthur, E., 119

McConnel and Kennedy (spinning factory), 42, 51, 57

McCormick, Robert R., 429

McCormick Reaper Company, 117, 118, 164

McDonald, Terrence J., 21, 359

McNally, Andrew, 372

McShane, Clay, 252

McVickar, Brockholst, 109–11

Meade, T. de Courcy, 412–15

meatpacking. *See* dressed beef industry; Packingtown

medical officer of health, 216–17. *See also* medical science; public health; *and individual medical officers of health*

medical science: in Chicago, 144–48, 157–58, 366–67, 368–69, 381–84, 387, 471–73, 480–85, 488–91; and etiology of disease, 241, 267, 301–4, 306–10, 344–48, 364, 409–10, 423–28, 437, 443, 447–48, 454; in Manchester, 450–56, 471–73. *See also* Chicago Department of Health; environmental science; epidemics; public health; Rauch, John H.; Reilly, Frank W.

Medlock River. *See* Mersey-Irwell Rivers Basin

Medlock Vale, 224

Mercantile Association (Chicago), 157

Mersey and Irwell Joint Committee, 399–400, 402–3, 407, 408–9, 411–12, 415–16, 418–19. *See also* Local Government Board; Mersey-Irwell Rivers Basin

Mersey-Irwell Rivers Basin (MIRB), 31–34, 46, 47, 196–97, 200, 204–5, 207–8, 211–16, 219–25, 228–30, 310, 314, 397–403, 411–12. *See also* floods; Mersey and Irwell Joint Committee

Mersey River. *See* Mersey-Irwell Rivers Basin

miasma theories. *See* medical science

middle class. *See* class formation

Middleton, England, 463

Midway Gardens, 288

Milliken, Isaac, 132

Millowners Committee, 219–20, 222, 224

Miltemore, Ira, 107, 113

Milwaukee, Wisconsin, 86, 282

Mississippi River, 85, 93, 421–22

Mississippi River Plan. *See* Des Plaines Plan

Model T, 252, 254, 497

moral environmentalism, 10–11, 20–21, 70–71, 296, 301–4, 308–9. *See also* environmental justice; social environmentalism

Morris, William, 296, 317, 394

Mosley, Sir Oswald, 57

Mosley, Stephen, 466

Mud Lake (Chicago), 80, 85, 93, 151

Muir, John, 497

Mumford, Lewis, 302, 312

municipal capitalism. *See under* Manchester

municipal housekeeping. *See under* women

Municipal Order League, 384

Murray, A. and G. (spinning factory), 41–42, 51, 57

Nagel, John, 350–52

Naperville, Illinois, 99

National Health Society, 442

National Trust, 390, 497

Neill, Robert, 215, 221

Newberry, Walter, 109

Newberry and Dole, 114

Newcomen engine. *See* steam engines

New Islington Hall, 318–19. *See also* Ancoats district

New York City, 157, 162, 341, 377

Niagara Falls, 428

Nicholson pavement, 123–24. *See also* streets and sidewalks

Nineteenth Ward (Chicago). *See* Hull-House

Niven, Dr. James, 398–99, 403, 464, 472

Nonconformists. *See* political culture, of Manchester

North Branch (of the Chicago River). *See* Chicago River

North Shore (Chicago). *See* suburbs, and Chicago

Northwest Association of Medical Officers of Health, 452

Northwestern Fertilizer Company, 168–69

Northwestern University, 370

nuisance abatement, 141–42, 154–56, 160, 168–69, 247, 447, 457, 470–73, 479, 483–84. *See also* air pollution; sanitation; urban space; water pollution

Nye, David, 137

O'Connell, James, 142

Ogden, William B., 86, 92, 102, 122, 127, 129, 150–51, 153–54, 187

"Ogden-Wentworth Ditch," 187. *See also* Des Plaines Plan

O'Hara, Daniel, 173

oil. *See* petroleum

Oldham, England, 463

"Old Sally" engine, 185. *See also* steam engines

Olmsted and Vaux (park designers), 168

Orwell, George, 330

Owens College. *See* University of Manchester

Pabst, Fred, 288–89. *See also* Pabst brewery

Pabst brewery, 239, 287, 288–89

Packingtown (Chicago), 164–67, 169–70, 267, 295, 336, 341, 434–35, 475. *See also* dressed beef industry; slums, of Chicago

pail-closet system. *See* sanitation, in Manchester

Palmer, Bertha, 335

Palmer, Potter, 163

Panama Canal, 375. *See also* Sanitary District of Chicago

Paris, 259, 261

Parkhurst, R. M., 416–17

parks. *See under* urban space

Parliament, 4, 26, 60–61, 204–5, 211, 213, 216, 222, 313–14, 393–94, 399, 406, 418–19, 457–58

Parliamentary Rivers Pollution Commissions. *See* Rivers Pollution Commissions

Pasteur, Louis, 240–43, 258–62, 273–77, 451. *See also* brewing industry; medical science

Pearse, Langdon W., 438

Peel Park (Salford), 196, 208, 332. *See also* urban space, and parks

Pendleton (Manchester), 214

Percherons. *See* horses

Percival, Thomas, 201

Perkins, W. H., 420

Peterloo Massacre of 16 August 1819, 59–60, 204, 394

petroleum, 268, 476

Pettenkofer, Max, 119, 160

Peyton, John Lewis, 92–93

Philips, Herbert, 453

Philips Park Cemetery (Manchester), 225–26

Philpott, Thomas, 349

Phoenix distillery, 268

Pinchot, Gifford, 497

pipeline act of 1890, 288–89

Pittsburgh, Pennsylvania, 115–16, 287, 479

Plan of Chicago, 469, 489. *See also* Burnham, Daniel

Playfield, Sir Lyon, 204

Plug Plot of 1842, 63, 394

Pochin, H. D., 216

political culture: of Chicago, 80–83, 125–26, 132–34, 135–36, 145, 151–53, 156–57, 161–63, 171–75, 189–91, 193–95, 335–42, 344, 348–49, 351–61, 362–89, 404–7, 409–11, 421, 437–41, 485–90, 494–96; of Manchester, 56–63, 214, 217–19, 221–22, 225–27, 229–30, 313–18, 320–21, 323–26, 330–32, 391–407, 409–11, 413–14, 437–41, 494–96. *See also* environmental justice; urban space pollution. *See* air pollution; sanitation; water pollution

Porkopolis. *See* Chicago

positive environmentalism. *See* social environmentalism

Potter, John, 210

Powers, John, 335–36, 339–41, 352

Prendergast, Richard, 372–74

Proctor, Richard, 200

Progressivism, 297, 301–13, 320–22, 362–65, 367–68, 395–96, 409–11, 413–14, 428, 439–41, 454, 457–58, 467, 470–73, 496–98

prohibition. *See under* brewing industry

public health: in Chicago, 108–11, 118–19, 137–38, 146–48, 157–61, 190–93, 257, 346–47, 356, 358, 363–64, 367, 377–89, 431–36, 469–70, 480–85, 488–91; in industrial cities, 301–4, 306–7, 389, 427–28, 440–41; in Manchester, 207–11, 217–19, 323–26, 396–404. *See also* air pollution; Chicago Department of Health; environmental science; epidemics; floods; medical science; sanitation, water management; water pollution; *and individual public health acts*

Public Health Act of 1848 (England), 26, 209, 216, 447

Public Health Act of 1875 (England), 228, 443

public houses, 53–54, 236, 274, 276–77, 280–82, 292, 294. *See also* brewing industry; saloons

pubs. *See* public houses

Pure Water Commission, 388, 424. *See also* water management, and Chicago water supply

railroads. *See under* transportation; *and individual railroad enterprises*

Randle's Sluices, 413

Rauch, John H., 158–61, 166, 187, 193, 384

Rawlinson, Robert, 209–10, 216–22

Reach, Angus, 24–26, 46, 74–76, 445

Reform Act of 1832. *See* Parliament

Reform Act of 1884. *See* Parliament

refrigeration machines. *See* brewing industry, mechanization of

regional planning. *See* city planning

Reilly, Frank W., 368, 384–88

Rensselaer Polytechnic Institute, 370

Reynolds, Arthur, 348, 351–53, 355, 386, 405, 482–83

Rheingold beer, 288

Rhodes Wood Reservoir. *See* Longdendale Valley reservoirs

Rice, John B., 156

Richardson, Benjamin Ward, 301–3, 334

Richson, Rev. Canon, 215–16

Riis, Jacob, 341

River Medlock Improvement Committee, 227. *See also* sanitation; water management

Rivers Pollution Act of 1879 (England), 222, 227–28, 399

Rivers Pollution Commissions, 216–22

Robertson, John D., 489–90

Rochdale, England, 463

Rochdale Canal. *See* transportation, and canals in Manchester

Rock Island Railroad, 116

Rodgers, Daniel, 304–5, 307, 439

Romanesque Revival style (*Rundbogenstil*), 236, 266. *See also* Chicago, Germans in

Romanticism, 296, 305, 317

Roscoe, Sir Henry E., 319, 412–16

Rosen, Christine M., 163–64

Rosenberg, Charles, 157

Rowley, Charles, 305, 307, 313, 317–20, 394, 454

Royal Exchange Building. *See* Exchange Building

Runcorn, England, 40, 413

Rush Medical College, 110, 158
Ruskin, John, 296, 303, 317, 391
Ryder, G. E., 486

St. Ann's Square riots of 1792, 57–59
St. George's district (Manchester), 74
St. Helens, England, 448
St. Joseph, Michigan, 99
St. Louis, Missouri, 85, 248, 282, 421–22, 427–28
St. Mark's Church, 9
St. Paul's Church, 317. *See also* Rowley, Charles
Saladin pneumatic malting machine, 265–66. *See also* brewing industry
Salford, England, 196–97, 207–8, 214–16, 226–28, 394, 400, 410. *See also* Manchester; Mersey-Irwell Rivers Basin
Salford Twist Mill, 48
saloons, 236, 283, 286, 290–91. *See also* brewing industry; public houses
Samuel Whitbread brewery, 258–59, 277
Sanders, John, 326
sand-filtration. *See* water management
Sands district (Chicago), 118
Sanitary Congress of 1897, 416
Sanitary District of Chicago, 366–77, 399, 407, 409, 421–39. *See also* Cooley, Lyman E.; water management; water pollution
Sanitary Idea, 21, 70–74, 122, 138, 146, 207–10, 222, 230, 301–4, 310, 329–30, 398, 494. *See also* Chadwick, Edwin
sanitation: in Chicago, 119–23, 158–60, 166, 175–77, 191–92, 257, 340, 342, 353–54, 357–58, 421–37; in Manchester, 70–74, 210, 217–19, 219, 329–30, 381–83, 396–403. *See also* Chicago Department of Public Works; Davyhulme sewerage treatment facility; Holt Town; nuisance

abatement; public health; Sanitary Idea; water management; water pollution
Sauk County, Wisconsin, 245
Saxon (Alderman), 417–18
Schlitz, Joseph, 282
Schluter, Hermann, 232–33, 236, 265, 271
Schneider, George, 108
Schneirov, Richard, 174
Schoenhofen, Peter, 233, 285
Schoenhofen brewery, 232–33, 236, 283, 285
Schramm, E., 443–45
science. *See* brewing industry, and "scientific brewing"; environmental science; medical science; Pasteur, Louis
Scott, Anne Firor, 335, 359
Scott, Fred, 454
Scovel (Judge), 469–70, 481
Second Industrial Revolution, 294
Sennett, Richard, 312
Sergel, Annie Myers, 468–75, 478, 480–85, 491. *See also* Anti-Smoke League; women
sewerage. *See under* water management
Shaw, George Bernard, 319
Sherman, F. C., 145
Sherwood, Mrs. John B., 483
shock cities, 11–12, 493–98; Chicago as, 15, 295; Manchester as, 4–7, 15, 24–25, 203–4
Shuttleworth, James P. Kay. *See* Kay[-Shuttleworth], James P.
Siemens, Charles W., 443
Sigsworth, E. M., 275
Simon, Shena, 444
Simpson, Henry, 454–55
Sklar, Kathryn Kish, 339–40, 359
slums: in Chicago, 191–92, 297, 336–39, 341–42, 349–50, 353–54; in industrial cities, 301–2, 306–7, 313, 360–61; in

Manchester, 41–56, 65–71, 75–76, 203–4, 225, 296, 311–12, 317–18, 320–22, 328–30. *See also* Ancoats district; housing; Hull-House; Little Ireland district; Packingtown; suburbs; urban space

slush fund. *See* surplus fund

Smith, Robert Angus, 205, 448–50, 461

smoke. *See* air pollution; nuisance abatement

Smoke Abatement Exhibition, 1881–1882, 442–43, 452–53

Smoke Abatement League of Great Britain, 465

Social Democratic Federation, 394–95. *See also* political culture, of Manchester

social environmentalism, 296, 301–4, 307–11, 320–26, 329–30, 334–35, 396–97, 467, 496–98. *See also* environmental justice; moral environmentalism; Progressivism; urban space

Social Science Association (England), 301

Society for the Prevention of Smoke, 446–47, 474, 479

Society of the Chemical Industry, 457

solid waste. *See* sanitation

South Branch (of the Chicago River). *See* Chicago River

South Fork (of the South Branch of the Chicago River). *See* Chicago River

South Park Commission, 168. *See also* urban space, and parks

Spence, Peter, 449–50

State of Illinois. *See* Illinois, state government of

Stead, William T., 16, 290, 324, 333–35, 385

steam engines, 39–40, 86, 107–8, 113, 130, 184–86, 240, 256, 446–47, 476–81

Stephenson, George, 55

Stockport, England, 39, 203

stockyards. *See* dressed beef industry; Packingtown

Storey, Wilbur F., 136–37

Strangeways district (Manchester), 215

street railways. *See under* transportation

streets and sidewalks, 14; in Chicago, 95, 97–101, 119–20, 123–24, 255–56, 478; in Manchester, 46–47. *See also* gas lighting; horses; sanitation; transportation

suburbs: and Chicago, 124, 170–71, 286, 288, 356, 427; and industrial cities, 301–2, 308, 330–32; and Manchester, 41–56, 65–71, 209, 228, 317–18, 399–401, 453–54, 460–62. *See also* Calumet district; housing; Hyde Park; Manchester, as conurbation; slums; urban space; Victoria Park

Sullivan, John H., 356–57

Sulzer, Andrew, 127

surplus fund (of Chicago waterworks), 148, 175, 178–80, 194, 378–81, 405–6

Swampland Act of 1850, 120

Swansea, Wales, 456

Taft, William Howard, 430, 437

Talcott, E. B., 177

Tallman, W. L., 383–84

Tatham, John F. W., 398, 460, 464

Tazewill County, Illinois, 252–53

Teaford, Jon, 359

technology, 137, 234–36, 443. *See also* brewing industry; electricity; energy systems, cities as; gas lighting; hydraulic power system; hydroelectric power systems; industrial revolution; steam engines; textile industry; transportation

Temple Estate, 331

Tenement Conditions in Chicago (Hunter), 341

textile industry, 6–7, 30–31, 34–45, 49–52, 55–56, 197–99, 219–21, 235, 313–14, 446–47

Thirlmere Defence Association, 391–93

Thirlmere reservoir. *See* Lake Thirlmere reservoir plan

Thomas, B. W., 366

Thompson, E. P., 21, 26

Thompson, Joseph, 412–14, 418–19

Thresh, Dr. John C., 324–28

tied houses. *See* public houses

Timmins, Geoffrey, 51

Tocqueville, Alexis de, 3–7, 22–23, 31, 296, 498

Tomes, Nancy, 301–4, 306, 472

Tomlinson, Walter, 322

Tories. *See* political culture, of Manchester

Torside Reservoir. *See* Longdendale Valley reservoirs

Tourtel brewery, 261

Town Improvement Company, 72

Toynbee Hall, 334

Trafford district (Manchester), 398, 400

Trafford Park Industrial Estate, 400

transportation: and automobiles, 476; and canals in England, 279; and canals in Manchester, 27–28, 40–43, 47–48, 51, 234; in Chicago, 86, 104, 124, 130–31, 140, 297; and lake shipping in Chicago, 104, 113–14, 247; and railroads in Chicago, 104, 117, 171, 247, 250–51, 468–69, 487–91; and railroads in England, 279, 281; and railroads in Manchester, 55; and street railways in Chicago, 253–56, 297, 475–76; and trams (street railways) in Manchester, 311, 330. *See also* horses; Illinois and Michigan Canal; Manchester Ship Canal; Sanitary District of Chicago; streets and sidewalks; *and individual transportation enterprises*

Two-Mile Crib. *See* water management, and water supply in Chicago

Unhealthy Dwellings Committee (Manchester). *See* housing, and reform in Manchester

Union Stock Yard and Transit Company. *See* dressed beef industry

United States Army Corps of Engineers. *See* Army Corps of Engineers

United States Brewing Company, 284

United States Congress, 87, 120, 171, 288–89, 377, 422–23, 430–31

United States Supreme Court, 421–22, 427–28, 437–39

University of Chicago, 350–53

University of Manchester, 410, 412

urban space: and parks, 158, 168, 306, 322, 456, 469, 486; and political formation of, 18–23, 92, 95–97, 118, 161–63, 171–76, 316–32, 350–55, 381–83, 494–98; and spatial segregation of, 5–6, 10, 20–21, 63–74, 163–72, 208–11, 217–19, 229–30, 295–97, 302–4, 337–40, 365, 395–96, 402–3. *See also* environmental justice; housing; nuisance abatement; streets and sidewalks; *and individual urban and suburban districts*

Victoria Park (Manchester), 67–68, 73, 267, 314, 316, 330. *See also* suburbs, and Manchester

von Liebig, Justus, 259

Wade, Louise, 169

Ware, John D., 21, 377–78, 381–82, 385

Washington, D.C., 480

Washington Park Jockey Club, 257. *See also* horses

wastewater. *See* water pollution

water management: and Chicago, 106–13, 138–39, 147–52, 160–61, 175–77,

193–94, 355–56, 363–77, 376, 404–7, 421–37; and chlorination, 433–37; and industrial cities, 14, 309–10; and Manchester, 404–7; and sewerage/drainage in Chicago, 118–23, 188–89, 382–83; and sewerage/drainage in Manchester, 216–22, 226–30, 325, 397–403, 408–21; and water meters, 183, 194, 207–13, 404–6, 436–39; and water supply in Chicago, 178–86, 346–47, 377–82, 388–89, 403; and water supply in Manchester, 72–74, 200, 203–6, 219–20, 222–23, 389–93, 395, 403–4. *See also* Bateman, John F.; Chesbrough, Ellis S.; Chicago River; Davyhulme sewage treatment facility; epidemics; Ericson, John E.; floods; Fullerton Avenue Conduit; Illinois and Michigan Canal; Lake Michigan; Longdendale Valley reservoirs; Mersey-Irwell Rivers Basins; public health; Sanitary District of Chicago; Sanitary Idea; sanitation; surplus fund; water pollution

water pollution: in Chicago, 107, 139–46, 149, 154–56, 166, 186–89, 192–93, 296; in Manchester, 44, 48, 203–4, 207–10, 216, 219–21; in rural areas, 248–49, 325. *See also* Chicago River; Lake Michigan; Mersey-Irwell Rivers Basin; nuisance abatement; water management

waterpower, 29–30, 38–39, 205, 335

water supply. *See* water management

Water Tower (Chicago landmark), 127, 136, 156, 157, 175, 179, 185, 239

waterworks. *See* water management

Watt, James, 39

Webb, Sidney and Beatrice, 413–14

Wells, H. G., 474

Wentworth, John, 187–88

Western Brewer (trade journal), 262

Western Society of Engineers, 438

Whiley, Henry, 397

Whitbread, Samuel. *See* Samuel Whitbread brewery

White City. *See* World's Columbian Exposition of 1893

Wickersham (Dr.), 364

Widnes, England, 448

Will-Grundy-Livingston District. *See* Braidwood, Illinois

Williams, Eli B., 99–101

Williams, T. W., 190

Wilmont, Sarah, 457, 463–64

Wilson, Alan, 70, 421

Wilson, Elizabeth, 302, 308–9

Wilson, R. G., 276–78, 280–81

Winthrop, John, 95

Wisner, George M., 434–36

Wohl, Anthony, 313

working class. *See* class formation

Woman's Christian Temperance Union, 288. *See also* brewing industry, and prohibition

women: in Chicago, 245, 286–88, 290, 339–40, 348, 351, 359–60, 468–73; in Manchester, 210, 326–27; and municipal housekeeping, 304, 472, 484–85, 490; and reform, 302–4, 308–9, 322–23, 470–73. *See also individual names*

wood: as fuel, 29, 104–5, 116, 244–45; as building material, 99–101

Woodhead, Sims, 416

Woodhead Reservoir. *See* Longdendale Valley reservoirs

Woodward, James, 81–83, 103, 120–21

Woolton (Lord), 312

Wordworth, William, 296

World's Columbian Exposition of 1893, 283, 295, 297, 302, 334–35, 377–78, 381, 384–85, 469, 473–74

World's Fair. *See* World's Columbian Exposition of 1893

World's Fair of 1939, 466–67

World War I, 236, 290, 331, 489–91
Worsley mine, 28. *See also* coal
Worthington brewery, 273–74, 278. *See also* Brown, Horace T.
Wright, Frank Lloyd, 288, 302

Yakima Valley, Washington, 245
Yellowstone National Park, 389
Young, Andrew, 352–53, 357
Young, G. B., 432–33